HUMAN HERITAGE

A WORLD HISTORY

HUMAN HERITAGE

CHARLES E. MERRILL PUBLISHING CO.
A Bell & Howell Company
Columbus, Ohio
Toronto • London • Sydney

A WORLD HISTORY

F. Kenneth Cox
Miriam Greenblatt
Stanley S. Seaberg

Staff

EDITORIAL

Project Director	Myra Immell
Project Editors	Robert Kohan, Brenda Smith
Contributing Editors	Rosemarie Trenjan, Mary Nye Fetters, John Lawyer
Project Assistants	Ruth Solt, Sharon McKinnon, Carol Fitzmier, Annette Hoffman
Art Director	Lester Shumaker
Designer-Illustrator	Larry Koons
Project Artists	Barbara White, Paul Helenthal
Photo Editors	Susan Marquart, Marty Pardo
Researcher	Marcia Earnest

PRODUCTION

Cartographers	Robert Forget, Kathie Kelleher
Illustrators	Brian Cody, Ken Graning, Margaret Hathaway, Jim Jackson, Dick Kranz, Dave Mankins, Charles Platt, Hellen Tullen
Indexers	Mary Jo Baumeister, Vera L. Cyre

ISBN 0–675–02890–6

Published by

CHARLES E. MERRILL PUBLISHING CO.

A Bell & Howell Company

Columbus, Ohio 43216

PREFACE

*Not to know what happened before one was born
is to remain a child.*

CICERO

Cicero, the Roman orator who spoke the words you have just read, lived many years before the birth of Christ. But his words are just as true today as then. What happened before you were born is history, just as what happens today is history.

Most people know what they are and have what they have because of a belief that was followed, an action that was taken, or an event that happened long before they were born. How would people communicate if the Phoenicians had not refined and spread the alphabet? Where would many people be now if Queen Isabella had not given Columbus the funds and ships he needed to make his voyages?

Questions of a different type also come to mind. Why does England have a royal family while the United States does not? Why don't all western Europeans speak the same language? The answers to these questions can be found in *Human Heritage*, which explores the past and discusses it in an easy-to-read style complimented by colorful maps, charts, and illustrations.

Each of the 13 units opens with a two-page time chart and closes with a two-page review. The time chart highlights the important events of the time period covered in the unit. The review summarizes the main points of the unit and provides exercises that focus on those points and develop social studies skills. Overview questions alert you to the unit theme. One-page unit introductions give you the broad picture of the topics covered. Two-page Cultural Close-Ups that focus on a person, culture, or event allow you an in-depth look at history in the making.

The text's 40 chapters are divided into sections and subsections, each of which is followed by a question or group of questions. Unfamiliar terms are boldfaced and are defined. Many are redefined in the glossary, which also offers a pronunciation key. A review section at the end of each chapter provides a summary of main points and exercises designed to review, clarify, and reinforce understanding.

Human Heritage uses art, photographs, and the written word to acquaint you with the distant and not-so-distant past. An ancient Greek named Dionysus once said "History is philosophy teaching by examples." *Human Heritage* records those examples.

CONTENTS

CHARTS, DIAGRAMS, AND ILLUSTRATIONS

MAPS
CONTENT MAPS

CULTURAL CLOSE-UP MAPS

COVER PHOTOS

(left to rt.; top to bot.) Smithsonian Institution (1) 78-8736; (2) 78-8733; (3) 78-8723; (4) 78-8727; (5) Eugene Gilliom; (6) Smithsonian Institution 78-8759; (7) Freer Gallery; (8) Hirshhorn Gallery; (9) Smithsonian Institution; (10) ARAMCO; (11) Courtesy of British Museum; (12) Vladimir Bibic; (13) Reproduced from the collection of the Library of Congress; (14) NASA.

PHOTO CREDITS

UNIT OPENINGS

(left to rt.; top to bot.) **UNIT 1** Courtesy of the American Museum of Natural History; Smithsonian Institution; Michael Collier; Australian Information Service; American Museum of Natural History. **UNIT 2** Smithsonian Institution; The Bettmann Archive; James Jennings, Research Mediagraphics; Kojo Photo; R. Scott Krupkin; the Metropolitan Museum of Art, Fletcher Fund. **UNIT 3** Turkish Tourism and Information Office; Vladimir Bibic; Smithsonian Institution; Courtesy of British Museum; Vladimir Bibic; Vladimir Bibic. **UNIT 4** The Bettmann Archive; Aileen Soskis for Tom Stack & Assoc.; Eugene Gilliom; Reproduced from the collection of the Library of Congress; The Bettmann Archive. **UNIT 5** Smithsonian Institution; Courtesy of British Museum; Photo by the Vatican Museums; Courtesy of British Museum; Courtesy of British Museum. **UNIT 6** The Bettmann Archive; Photo by the Vatican Museums; M. Gilson for Tom Stack & Assoc.; Courtesy of British Museum; Trinity College Library, Ireland; Bibliotheque Nationale, Paris. **UNIT 7** Smithsonian Institution, Freer Gallery; Vladimir Bibic; Dumbarton Oaks, Wash. D. C. ; Smithsonian Institution, Freer Gallery; Historical Pictures Service; Bibliotheque Nationale, Paris. **UNIT 8** Northern Ireland Tourist Board; National Museum of Ireland; Historical Pictures Service; Courtesy of British Museum; Vladimir Bibic; Courtesy of Parke, Davis and Co. © 1980. **UNIT 9** National Museum of Ireland; Courtesy of Parke, Davis and Co. © 1980; Bob Kohan; Bibliotheque Nationale, Paris. **UNIT 10** Photo by the Vatican Museums; Bibliotheque Nationale, Paris; Bibliotheque Nationale, Paris; Bibliotheque Nationale, Paris; National Gallery of Art, Wash. D. C. **UNIT 11** Courtesy of Parke, Davis and Co. © 1980; Reproduced from the collection of the Library of Congress; Library of Congress; John Freeman Group. **UNIT 12** The Prado, Madrid; The National Gallery of Art, Wash. D. C.; The Sheffield City Museum; Whitney Museum of American Art; Collection, The Museum of Modern Art, N. Y. **UNIT 13** Reproduced from the collection of the Library of Congress; Courtesy of Parke, Davis and Co. © 1980; Harry T. Peters Collection, Museum of the City of N. Y.; Smithsonian Institution, National Collection of Fine Arts; Smithsonian Institution; NASA; Steve Lissau.

PHOTOS

American Museum of Natural History, courtesy of: 12, 18, 23 (1. and r.). **American Numismatic Society:** 327. **ARAMCO:** 314 (1. and r.), 613 (bot. r.), 634. **Art Institute of Chicago, collection of:** 556 (bot. r.) (detail) Manet, "The Races at Longchamp", 557 (top 1.) Seurat, "Sunday Afternoon on the Island of La Grande Jatte." **Australian Information Service:** 5, 37 (1.). **City of Bayeau, France:** 415. **Trustees of the Chester Beatty Library:** 311 (1.). **Bettmann Archive:** 9, 90, 100, 103, 113, 129, 131, 134, 138, 140, 142, 144, 145, 154, 165, 170, 194, 201, 213, 215, 217, 557 (bot. 1.), 557 (bot. r.). **Vladimir Bibic:** 54, 64, 108, 116, 221, 278, 643. **Bibliotheque Nationale, Paris:** 563. **Bildarchiv Preussischer Kulturbesitz:** 570, 598. **Bernice P. Bishop Museum, Honolulu:** 582. **Fred Ward for Black Star:** 613 (bot. 1.). **Bodleian Library:** 350 Ms. Bodley 264, fol. 72v.; 353 Ms. Bodley 264, fol. 112; 360 Ms. Douce 93, fol. 28; 411 Ms. Bodley 264, fol. 220; 492 (1.) Ms. Arch. Seld. A. 1. **Boston Public Library;** 322. **Pierre Boulat, collection of:** 613 (top. r.). **Norma Brenneman:** 352. **British Library, reproduced by permission:** 101 Miscellany, fol. 117v. **British Museum, courtesy of:** 45, 185, 309 Ms. Or. 6810, sheet 5v., 358, 483. **British Travel Association:** 447 (1.). **Chase Manhattan Bank:** 204. **Chicago Historical Society, courtesy of:** 473. **The Cleveland Museum of Art:** 438 (detail) Toscani, "The Race of the Palio in the Streets of Florence", Holden Collection. **Colchester Museum, England:** 218. **Colonial Williamsburg Foundation:** 446. **Dumbarton Oaks, Wash. D. C.:** 228, 295, 299, 300 A. Weyl-Carr, 303, 304. **Biblioteca Estense, Italy:** 397. **The Folger Shakespeare Library:**

459. French Government Tourist Office: 24. **Copyright The Frick Collection, N. Y.:** 372. **German Information Center:** 256, 422, 566. **Eugene Gilliom:** 127, 132, 146, 171 (r.), 183, 281, 329, 332 (1. and r.), 367, 619. **Giraudon:** 254, 413, 441, 450 Lauros, 462, 506 Lauros. **Larry Hamill:** 125, 156, 235. **Harringa Collection print courtesy of Life Magazine:** 581. **The John Woodman Higgins Armory, Worcester, Mass.:** 354 (1. and r.), 355, 385. **Historical Pictures Service:** 78, 175, 181, 189, 193 (1. and r.), 195, 202, 210, 225 (1. and r.), 241, 242, 244 (1. and r.), 247, 252, 260, 272, 297, 298 (1. and r.), 305, 311 (r.), 319, 328, 335, 349, 370, 371, 375, 378, 382, 387, 389, 407, 453, 457, 458, 467, 468, 471, 557 (top r.), 575, 576 (1. and r.), 579, 612 (bot. r.). **Imperial War Museum, Trustees:** 595. **India Information Service:** 635, 636. **Library of Congress, reproduced from the collection of:** 15, 109, 182, 243, 245, 283, 284, 419, 421, 446 (1.), 452, 454, 472, 492, 507, 508, 518, 520 (1. and r.), 530, 533, 541, 548, 558, 567, 569 (1. and r.), 573, 584, 601, 624. **National Museum of Ireland:** 266, 267, 273. **Joey Jacques:** 633. **Japan National Tourist Organization:** 589. **James E. Jennings, Research Mediagraphics:** 71. **Bob Kellar Collection:** 556 (top r.). **Larry Koons:** 347. **The Louvre:** 436 (r.). **The Mansell Collection:** 529. **Steve Marquart:** 383. **George Matchneer:** 400. **The Metropolitan Museum of Art:** 57 Museum excavations, 158 Wolfe Fund, 198 Rogers Fund, 368 Gift of J. Pierpont Morgan, 403 Rogers Fund, 406, 444 H. Brisbane Dick Fund, 495 (r.) Gift of J. Pierpont Morgan, 227 (r.) Rogers Fund. **Museum of Modern Art, Film Stills Archive, N. Y.:** 612 (top 1.). **National Archives:** 351, 401. **National Gallery, Wash. D. C.:** 97, 211, 230, 223 Samuel H. Kress Collection, 365 Widener Collection, 384 Widener Collection, 390 Widener Collection, 435 (detail) Kress Collection, 439 Kress Collection, 443 Kress Collection, 499, 512 (detail) Andrew W. Mellon Collection. **National Gallery, London:** 364. **The National Maritime Museum, London:** 461, 505, 509 (detail). **The National Museum, Denmark:** 286. **National Portrait Gallery, London:** 445, 447 (r.). **William Rockhill Nelson Gallery:** 107 (both.). **New School for Social Research, courtesy of:** 612 (top r.) (detail) Benton, "The Changing West". **Don Nieman:** 231, 366, 414, 418. **Norwegian Information Service:** 279. **The Oriental Institute, The University of Chicago:** 11, 30, 55, 110. **Embassy of Pakistan:** 75. **Parke, Davis and Co. © 1980, courtesy of:** 20, 50, 67. **The Prado, Madrid:** 412 Cranach, "Hunting Party in Honor of Charles V at the Castle of Torgau", 556 (bot. 1.) Velasquez, "Las Ninas". **Biblioteca Riccardiana, Florence:** 359. **Museo della Civilta Romana:** 155, 199. **Museo Nazionale Romana:** 161. **Romisch Germanisches Zentralmuseum:** 261. **Franklin D. Roosevelt Library:** 617. **San Antonio Chamber of Commerce:** 552. **San Francisco Museum of Modern Art:** 613 (mid. r.) (detail). **Stanley Seaberg:** 128, 200, 317, 363. **City of Sheffield England:** 532. **Singer Sewing Machine Co.:** 531. **Smithsonian Institution:** 9, 21, 22, 27, 31, 32, 33, 43, 44, 51, 65, 66, 72, 77, 80, 81, 82 Freer Gallery, 89, 92 (1. and r.), 99, 114 Freer Gallery, 126, 133, 137, 139, 141, 145 (r.), 150, 168, 171 (1.), 172, 196, 277, 313, 321 Freer Gallery, 323, 477, 491, 494, 526, 528, 534, 543, 545 National Collection of Fine Arts, 556 (top 1.), 599 National Collection of Fine Arts. **Sovfoto:** 339. **Tom Stack and Associates:** 60 Clare Small, 61 Clare Small, 192 M. J. Gilson, 440 Michael Blake, 37 (r.) Warren Garst, 625 (r.) Gary Stallings, 626 Gary Stallings. **Trinity College Library, Ireland:** 265 Book of Kells, fol. 27 v. **Biblioteca Trivulziana, Milan:** 423. **Uffizi Gallery, Florence:** 469 (r.). **United Nations:** ii, iii, 115, 608, 638. **UNESCO:** 639 Paul Almasy. **UPI:** 612 (bot. 1.), 613 (top 1.). **U. S. Army Photograph:** 607. **U. S. Olympic Committee, Photo Archives:** 154. **The University Museum, University of Pennsylvania:** 10, 47. **Vatican Museums Photo:** 98, 160, 187, 188, 209, 455 (detail). **The Virginia Museum, courtesy of:** 495, 515. **The Walker Art Gallery, Liverpool:** 523. **Thomas L. Williams:** 497.

AUTHORS

F. Kenneth Cox is a teacher of Ancient History in the Bethel Park School District of Bethel Park, Pennsylvania, where has taught for more than 12 years. A graduate of Clarion State College and West Virginia University, Cox has taught special classes for the gifted and has been instrumental in the development of a seventh grade social studies curriculum and a Minimal Skills Competency Test.

Miriam Greenblatt is a free-lance writer, editor, and educational consultant. During the past 17 years she has contributed to more than 20 elementary, junior high, and high school social studies texts, workbooks, testing programs, and teacher's guides. A graduate of Hunter College of the City of New York and the University of Chicago and an ex-teacher, Greenblatt is a member of the Illinois Council for Social Studies, the National Council for Social Studies, the Asia Society, and the Chicago Reading Round Table. She is also treasurer of the American Historical Association's Committee on History in the Classroom.

Stanley S. Seaberg is a teacher of social studies and humanities at Henry M. Gunn Senior High School in Palo Alto, California, where he has taught since 1966. Seaberg was the recipient of a General Electric Fellow in Economics, Claremont Graduate School, 1962; John Hay Fellow, Yale University, 1963–1964; NDEA Fellow, University of Washington, 1966, and San Francisco State, 1968; and a Fulbright grant, 1972. He has authored several social studies texts and has been a consultant for the California State Framework for the Social Studies.

PROLOGUE

The world is not the same today as it was when Wilbur and Orville Wright flew their first airplane at Kitty Hawk. Nations have won their independence, rulers and heroes have come and gone, wars have been won and lost, and scientists and inventors have brought twentieth-century people into the Space Age. But what led to life as people know it today? From where and from whom did such people as Fleming and Doty get their inspiration? This way of life so taken for granted by people today did not just come about overnight. It is a result of the past — of many, many years of history. This text provides views of that history.

SCIENCE AND TECHNOLOGY IN THE TWENTIETH CENTURY

Date	Event	Date	Event
1903	first successful airplane flight made by Wright Brothers	1969	first lunar landing made by Neil Armstrong and Edwin Aldrin, Jr.
1905	theory of relativity, advanced by Albert Einstein	1977	first manned flight of new space transportation system made by U.S. space shuttle Enterprise
1926	television successfully demonstrated by John Baird	1977	laser beam used to remove destroyed body tissue of burn patients
1926	first liquid-fuel rocket successfully launched by Robert Goddard	1979	U.S. surgeons use microsurgery to perform first successful reattachment of major limb to body
1928	first antibiotic drug, penicillin, discovered by Sir Alexander Fleming		
1940	use of blood plasma for transfusions introduced by Dr. Charles Drew		
1942	first nuclear chain reaction produced by Enrico Fermi		
1944	first automatic digital computer completed at Harvard University		
1957	first artificial earth satellite, Sputnik I, launched by Russia		

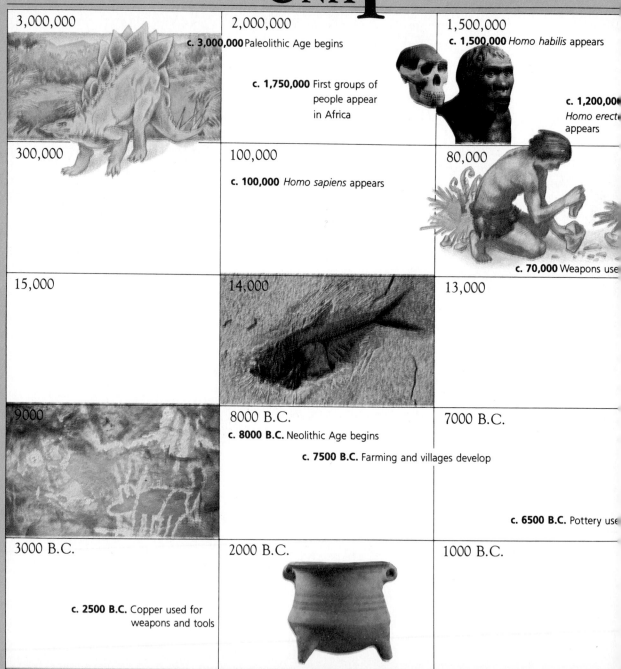

3,000,000	2,000,000	1,500,000
	c. 3,000,000 Paleolithic Age begins	**c. 1,500,000** *Homo habilis* appears
	c. 1,750,000 First groups of people appear in Africa	**c. 1,200,000** *Homo erectus* appears
300,000	**100,000**	**80,000**
	c. 100,000 *Homo sapiens* appears	
		c. 70,000 Weapons use
15,000	**14,000**	**13,000**
9000	**8000 B.C.**	**7000 B.C.**
	c. 8000 B.C. Neolithic Age begins	
	c. 7500 B.C. Farming and villages develop	
		c. 6500 B.C. Pottery use
3000 B.C.	**2000 B.C.**	**1000 B.C.**
c. 2500 B.C. Copper used for weapons and tools		

PREHISTORIC TIMES

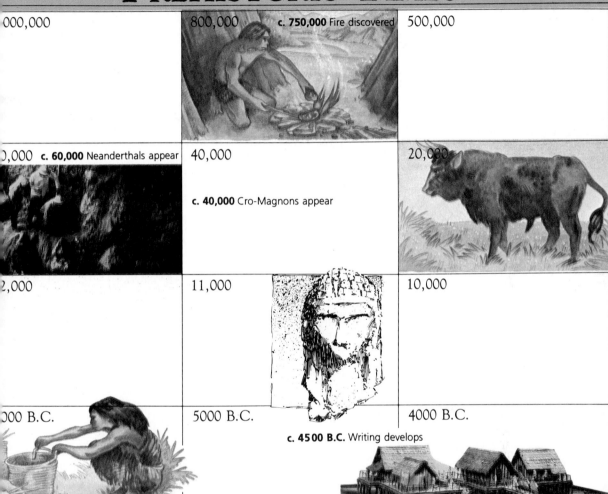

000,000	800,000 **c. 750,000** Fire discovered	500,000
0,000 **c. 60,000** Neanderthals appear	40,000 **c. 40,000** Cro-Magnons appear	20,000
2,000	11,000	10,000
000 B.C.	5000 B.C. **c. 4500 B.C.** Writing develops	4000 B.C.

1.   HOW IS HISTORY DETERMINED?
2.   HOW DID PEOPLE LIVE DURING PREHISTORIC TIMES?

Most experts believe that there have been people on earth for more than 1,750,000 years. During most of those years there was no written history because people did not develop the skill of writing until about 5000 years ago. The period of time beginning with the appearance of people on earth and ending with the first written records of history is called the **prehistoric period**. After that time people began to advance culturally and to live in cities. This was the beginning of **civilization**.

Before the rise of cities, people went through several stages of development. At first, they wandered from place to place in search of food. Experts call this period the **hunting-and-food-gathering period**. During this period people made several important discoveries. These included tools, speech, fire, clothing, art, and religion.

About 10,000 years ago people invented farming and became food producers instead of hunters and food-gatherers. Once they began to farm, they settled in one place and developed such skills as making pottery and working metals. They also developed trade and created formal ideas about government. Over time, villages grew up, and the people learned more and more skills.

Almost all of what is known about the prehistoric period has been learned in the last few hundred years. Each year scientists discover something new about the distant past. Each discovery brings them closer to piecing together the mystery of how civilization was formed.

CHAPTER 1

CLUES TO THE PAST

$\mathbf{G}$eologists, or scientists who study the earth, say that the earth is more than 4 billion years old. **Archaeologists**, or scientists who study ancient peoples and civilizations, say that there have been people on earth for more than 1 million years. But people did not learn to write until about 5000 years ago. How then has so much been learned about the people who lived on this earth in the far distant past?

LEGENDS

Every group of people on earth has **legends**, or folktales, that explain the past. The Chinese, for example, have a legend

about the beginnings of China. It says that the universe was a huge egg. When the egg split open, the upper half became the sky, and the lower half became the earth. Out of the split egg came P'an Ku, the first man. Each day for 18,000 years P'an Ku grew taller, the sky grew higher, and the earth grew thicker. Then P'an Ku died. His head split and became the sun and the moon. His blood filled the rivers and the seas. His hair became the forests and the meadows. His perspiration became the rain. His breath became the wind and his voice the thunder. His fleas became the ancestors of the Chinese.

The Africans have a legend about why the sun shines more brightly than the moon. It says that God created the Moon and then the Sun. The Moon was bigger and brighter than the Sun. The Sun became jealous and attacked the Moon. They fought and wrestled until the Sun begged for mercy. Then they wrestled again. This time the Sun threw the Moon into the mud. Dirt splashed all over the Moon, and it was no longer as bright as before. To stop the fighting, God stepped in. He told the Sun that from then on it would be brighter and shine during the day for kings and workers. He told the Moon that from then on it would only shine at night for thieves and witches.

Like the Chinese and the Africans, the Rumanians have their own legends. One is about the creation of mountains and valleys. It says that when God finished making the heavens He measured them with a little ball of thread. Then He started to create the earth to fit under them. A mole came along and offered to help. So God let the mole hold the ball of thread.

While God was weaving and shaping the earth, the mole let out the thread little by little. God was too busy to notice that at times the mole let out more thread than it should have. When God was finished, He was amazed to find that the earth was too big to fit under the heavens.

The mole, seeing what it had done, was afraid. So it ran off and buried itself in the earth. God sent the bee to find the mole and ask it what should be done. When the bee found the mole, it would not answer the question.

The bee hid in a flower, hoping the mole would think it was alone and start talking to itself. The mole thought out loud, saying that it would squeeze the earth so that the mountains would stick up, the valleys would sink down, and the earth would be smaller. Upon hearing this, the bee buzzed off. The mole heard the buzzing and became angry. It put a curse on the bee, saying "Henceforth, feed on yourself."

The bee told God what the mole had said. God squeezed the flat earth so the mountains rose up, the valleys sank down, and the earth fit under the heavens. God then made the mole's curse a blessing. Since then the bee makes its own honey. The mole lives underground and is afraid to come out.

The Chinese, African, and Rumanian legends are all concerned with creation and the heavens. This is not true of all legends. Many are about the deeds of godlike men and women or strange and wonderful lands.

Many of these legends were later written down. Some of them came to be thought of as historical fact. In time archaeologists and **anthropologists**, or scientists who study the origin and development of humans, became curious about how much of certain legends was fiction and how much was fact. That curiosity led them to search out the truth of some of the legends.

1. How have legends helped the study of history?

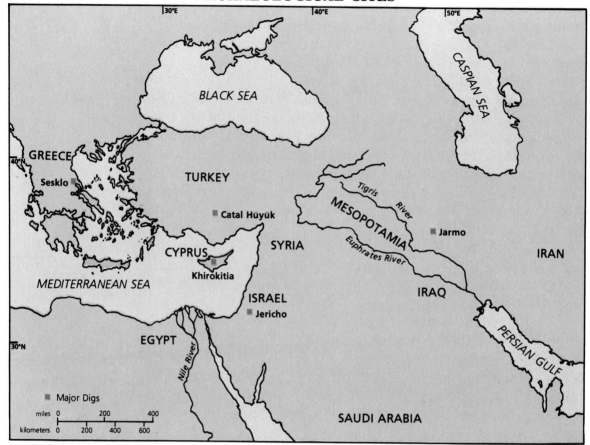

ARCHAEOLOGY

Archaeology began about 500 years ago. At that time many people found they could dig up old marble statues and ornaments made by the ancient Greeks and Romans and sell them for a great deal of money. People began to study these **artifacts,** or things made by early people. They found they could learn from them about the ways of life of people who had lived long ago. Artifacts do not have to be works of art. They can be any item made by people rather than by nature. The earliest artifacts were pieces of hard rock that had been chipped into the form of cutting or digging tools or weapons such as arrowheads.

Around 1700 some Italian farmers discovered they were living on top of an ancient Roman city named Herculaneum that had been buried for more than 1000 years. In 1719 archaeologists began to uncover the ancient city. After more than 50 years they uncovered not only Herculaneum but another Roman city called Pompeii. The archaeologists found that the cities had, among other things, fine houses, theaters, streets, and temples. More important, from what they unearthed they learned exactly how ancient Romans lived.

The discovery of the two Roman cities was followed in 1799 by what some people consider one of the greatest of all archaeological discoveries. This was the finding in Egypt of the Rosetta Stone, a slab of stone on which was carved ancient Egyptian picture-writing and its Greek translation. Although

---

EGYPTIAN ARTIFACTS

Archaeologists have uncovered many artifacts in Egypt. This spearhead (left), from about 15,000 B. C., is one of the oldest objects found in the region. The Rosetta Stone (right), from around 200 B. C., is one of the most famous archaeological finds. On it is carved a decree issued by Egyptian priests to honor a leader.
What kind of artifacts have archaeologists uncovered?

scholars knew the Greek language well, they had not been able to **decipher**, or decode, the ancient Egyptian language. The Rosetta Stone gave them the key to the meaning of Egyptian picture-writing. Now they could learn much more about the history of Egypt and its people.

A great many archaeological finds have been uncovered since the discovery of the Rosetta Stone. Between 1850 and 1950 archaeologists uncovered five lost civilizations in different parts of the world. During approximately the same time period, they also unearthed prehistoric artifacts from every part of Europe. Since then, archaeologists have discovered several ancient Indian and Chinese civilizations. These were just the beginning. Finds are still being made today in every part of the world.

1. What do archaeologists learn from artifacts?
2. Why is the discovery of the Rosetta Stone considered so important?

TELLS AND KITCHEN MIDDEN   In Iraq, in the valley of the Tigris and Euphrates Rivers, when ancient mud houses collapsed, other houses were built on top of them. Over thousands of years they formed **tells**, or great mounds which rise high above ground level. Some of the tells have 20 or more levels, each representing a time period of at least 100 years. From these tells archaeologists have dug out tools, pottery, and other household items.

Archaeologists call the remains of ancient households **kitchen midden**. They first began to study kitchen midden in Denmark in 1848. Since then they have been able to learn a great deal from the kitchen midden they have uncovered. Their location, size, and depth allow scientists to estimate the size of the population at the time. The utensils tell how advanced the people were. Often the archaeologists find bones or animal remains that tell them about climate, seasons, tools, hunting patterns, and eating habits.

1. What caused tells to form?
2. Of what value to archaeologists are kitchen midden?

Placing the Past in History

Over thousands of years whole cities of past civilizations were covered over with mud, dust, and rubbish. This packed

Pitcher

down into hard soil or clay or hardened into stone. New civilizations came along, and new buildings were constructed on top of the old ones. Archaeologists **excavated**, or dug deep into the earth, to find the remains of these lost civilizations. Once they were unearthed, the finds still had to be dated.

1. Why do archaeologists excavate?

DATING ARCHAEOLOGICAL REMAINS   In 1832 C. J. Thomsen, a Danish archaeologist, divided the stages of historic progress into three **ages**, or periods, based on the materials used

---

TELLS

Tells have revealed much about life in the ancient Middle East. Archaeologists have dug out a step trench in the side of this Turkish tell that shows 14 levels. The lowest level dates from about 4000 B.C.; the highest level from 700 A. D. Arrows point to the artifacts (right) found at each level.
How were tells formed?

for tools and weapons. They were the stone age, the bronze age, and the iron age. Later, scientists divided the stone age into three periods—old, middle, and new. Then they discovered that the ages appeared at different times in different parts of the world.

Still later, archaeologists discovered that the kinds of materials used in tools were not as important as the changes in the ways early people got their food. So they began to consider the ages in terms other than materials used for tools and weapons. Instead, they began to think of them in terms of food production and the development of cities.

To determine the date of an archaeological site, scientists first used trees. Each year trees form a new growth ring. By counting the number of rings in a cross-section taken from the tree trunk, scientists could determine age. They took the core and matched its pattern with those of trees whose age they knew. In this way they could carry dating back as far as 3000 years.

Then in 1946 an American chemist named Willard Frank Libby discovered that all living matter contains a radioactive element called carbon-14. He developed a method for determining age by measuring the amount of carbon-14 in objects. In 1960 Libby won the Nobel Prize in chemistry for his work with carbon-14. Because of Libby's efforts, scientists now can tell almost exactly how old an object is back as far as 20,000 years. This means that they can fix reasonably exact dates for ancient civilizations. They also can identify and compare distant civilizations within set time periods. The result has been more careful and exact conclusions about human history.

Axe

1. Into what three ages did Thomsen divide the stages of historic progress?
2. In what terms did later scientists consider the ages?
3. How did archaeologists determine the date of archaeological sites before carbon-14 was developed?
4. What did Willard Libby contribute to the study of history?

THE CHALLENGE OF MODERN HISTORY

The major challenge for historians in the past was the lack of information. Historians today face a different problem—too much information. Historians using computers can collect and file in seconds more **data**, or information organized for analysis, than their ancestors could in a lifetime. Some people call this the "Information Revolution."

Modern historians must know how to select the information they need from a huge amount of published facts. This need for selection has led them to become **specialists**, or people devoted to one branch of study or research. Most concentrate on a smaller time period than they did in the past. For example, a historian may be an expert in fifteenth-century military life or in the religion of one specific country.

Archaeologists, for example, have to do more than just excavate a site. They need to interpret and record what they have uncovered. They will want to preserve whatever they find, and at times they will have to restore certain objects. This means help from a lot of different specialists, including historians, anthropologists, geologists, chemists, linguists, architects, engineers, and photographers. By working together these people can increase human knowledge about the past.

1. What was the major challenge for historians in the past?
2. What is the major challenge for historians today?

CHAPTER REVIEW

SUMMARY

1. Most experts believe that people have been on earth for more than 1,750,000 years.

2. People developed the skill of writing only about 5000 years ago.

3. One way experts have learned about how people lived before writing developed is through legends.

4. Every group of people on earth has legends that explain its past.

5. Artifacts are another way by which experts have learned how people lived in prehistoric times.

6. Archaeologists have unearthed several lost civilizations in different parts of the world.

7. After archaeologists unearth remains of former civilizations, they have to date their finds.

8. At first, scientists used trees to determine the dates of archaeological sites.

9. Since 1946 scientists have used the carbon-14 method of dating, which was developed by Willard Libby.

10. In the past historians lacked information, but today so much information is available that many historians have to specialize.

11. Historians work together with archaeologists, anthropologists, and many other scientists to increase human knowledge about the past.

BUILDING VOCABULARY

1. *Identify the following:*
   P'an-Ku   Pompeii   Rosetta Stone   Willard Libby
   Herculaneum

2. *Define the following:*

prehistoric period	geologists	artifacts	excavated
civilization	archaeologists	decipher	ages
hunting- and food-	anthropologists	tells	data
gathering period	legends	kitchen midden	specialists

REVIEWING THE FACTS

1. When did people develop the skill of writing?
2. What is the relationship between cities and civilization?
3. How did the first people obtain food?
4. About how long ago did people become farmers?
5. With what are legends concerned?
6. How did archaeology begin?
7. Why are excavations important?
8. What do archaeologists do with the artifacts they unearth?
9. In what ways is carbon-14 a better dating tool than trees?
10. Why have so many historians become specialists?

DISCUSSING IMPORTANT IDEAS

1. Do you think it is important to try to date archaeological sites as exactly as possible? Why or why not?
2. What legends do you know? Do you think they are fact or fiction? Why or why not?
3. How do peoples' ideas about the past change as more knowledge becomes available?
4. Do you think it is important for people to work together in order to learn about the past? Why or why not?

USING MAPS

Refer to the map on page 8, and answer the following questions:
1. What is the main subject of the map?
2. How many major digs are shown?
3. Where are the digs located?
4. Which dig is on an island?

CHAPTER

FOOD GATHERERS

Experts believe that people first lived in the lands known today as South Africa and East Africa. Originally these lands contained many small lakes bordered by low trees and bushes. Beyond the lakes were great stretches of tall grasses where many kinds of animals lived. There were large animals which were the ancestors of modern deer, sheep, pigs, jaguars, and baboons. There were small animals such as snakes, lizards, turtles, mice, ground squirrels, and porcupines. Here and there the grasslands were broken up by groups of trees. Birds of many sizes and colors filled the skies, and fish of all kinds swam in the clear lake waters.

The people who lived in these lands stood about four and a half feet, or about 1.4 meters, tall. They had large jaws and teeth, and their noses were more or less flat. Because of their short foreheads, their hair started just above their eyebrows. They probably had dark skin and thick patches of hair on their backs, arms, and legs.

GATHERING FOOD

The people lived in small **bands**, or groups, of about 20 members. When the food supply was good, the bands grew as large as 40 or 50. Almost none of the band members were more than 30 years old. More than half of the children born into a band died from illnesses or were killed by animals before their first birthday.

The people within a band felt very close to one another. They lived and worked together and shared their food. They fed and cared for band members who became injured or sick.

Each band gathered its food within an area known as its **home territory**, which might cover ten miles, or 16 kilometers. When times were hard, it could be as much as 50 miles, or 80

kilometers. There were campsites at various places throughout the home territory. Sometimes they were on the mud flats of lakes. Other times they were in dry riverbeds where the people were protected from the wind. The band stayed at a campsite until they used up the nearby food supply. Then they would move to the next campsite.

Women and children gathered most of the food. They collected berries, nuts, and fruit. They took eggs out of bird and turtle nests. They poked sticks into bee nests to get honey. They also used the sticks to dig roots from the ground.

Men of the band did the hunting. Since their only weapons were sticks and stones, they usually hunted only small animals. Once in a while, though, they were able to kill a larger animal that was too old or too badly hurt to run away. A good kill meant that the band would have enough food for several days.

The men also fished for food. Sometimes they fished from a flat rock. They lay on the rock and dangled their hands in the water. When a fish came close, they reached out and grabbed it.

1. How were early people organized?
2. Where were the campsites of early people?
3. How did early people get their food?

MAKING TOOLS   At first the only tools people had were sticks and stones which they found on the ground. After a time they learned to shape stones to make them more useful. At first they knocked **chips**, or small pieces, from a stone by hitting it with another stone. They kept knocking chips off until the stone had the shape they wanted. Later they learned to knock off **flakes**, or long, sharp-edged chips, and used them as tools.

The earliest well-shaped tool was the **fist-hatchet**, or hand-ax. One end had a cutting edge, and the other end was shaped to fit a person's hand. The fist-hatchet was an **all-purpose tool**, or one that can be used to do many different things. People used it to cut the meat off dead animals and to split animal bones. They also used it to scrape animal skins, cut down trees, and chop up plants and vegetables. Later, people developed special tools for such different purposes as scraping, chopping, and polishing.

EARLY TOOLS

For more than 2 million years prehistoric people lived by hunting animals and gathering plants. They also used tools made of wood and stone. The wooden tools have decayed. But archaeologists have found many stone tools.
For what purposes did prehistoric people use stone tools?

The people usually made their tools of **flint**, a stone found on the surface of the earth throughout much of Europe, Africa, and western Asia. In eastern Asia where there was not much flint, the people made their tools of quartz instead.

1. In what two ways did people make stone tools?
2. What was the earliest well-shaped stone tool made ?

LEARNING TO TALK   Early people did not always know how to talk. At first they simply made different kinds of noises. Each noise meant something different. A certain kind of grunt meant the person was happy. A **hoot**, or loud cry, may have meant that a dangerous animal was nearby. A soft cry may have meant that a child was lost. A whimper meant a person was cold, lonely, or scared. A yell probably meant a person was angry.

Early people also had other ways to express meaning. They pointed at objects. They tugged at elbows or pulled at shoulders to get attention. They probably used different kinds of hand signs for such important things as water, food, animals, and weapons.

Gradually people developed language. Experts have no way of knowing for certain when or how this happened. But they think it came about when people began to hunt large animals with spears and bows and arrows. Since they had to hunt in a group, they had to be able to give one another instructions. Noises and hand gestures were not enough.

1. How did early people communicate with one another before they learned how to talk?
2. Why do experts think people developed language?

DISCOVERING FIRE   The food-gatherers and hunters cut up the animals and fish they caught with stone knives. They ate the meat raw because they did not know it could be cooked.

Although people knew about fire, they did not know how to make it. The fires they knew about were made by nature. They saw the fires that came after bolts of lightning struck trees and after volcanoes sent burning coals across the land. They saw piles of dry leaves and brush suddenly burst into flame.

After hundreds of thousands of years, people discovered they could make fire themselves. To do this, they either rubbed one stick back and forth against another stick, or rapidly turned a stick in a hole in a dry log.

GROUP LIFE
    Experts believe that most food gatherers lived in groups made up of several families. In order to survive, the people within each group learned to help each other. Here a group of hunters provide aid to a wounded companion.
What kinds of discoveries were shared by food gatherers?

Once the people learned to make fire, their lives began to change. They could cook their food instead of eating it raw. They discovered that cooked food was easier to chew and digest, especially for older people with few teeth. They also found they had to spend less time eating. This gave them more time to do other things.

By about 750,000 years ago, people were using fire to keep themselves warm. They also used it as a weapon. They threw burning sticks of wood at animals to drive them away. By about 80,000 years ago, people were using fire to harden the points of their wooden weapons. The fire-hardened points were strong enough to go through horse, leopard, and rhinoceros skin. Now hunters were able to get more food.

1. How did early people know about fire?
2. How did early people make fire?
3. How did the use of fire change people's lives?

SHELTER AND CLOTHING   Early people did not live in houses. They usually camped out in the open. They protected themselves from the wind by digging pits in the ground or by using such natural spots as the dry bed of a river. They took shelter under an overhanging rock or piled up brush to build **windbreaks**, or protection from the wind.

Early people used caves only for such emergencies as escaping from a sudden storm or a large animal. Caves were too cold and damp to live in all the time. When people heated the caves by fire, the smoke got in their lungs and hurt their eyes.

After hunters began killing large animals, they found that the animal skins could be used to protect their bodies and keep them warm. They learned to cut off the skin and scrape it to remove any remaining meat. The women then took the skin and laid it out in the sun to dry. Even though the dried skin was stiff and hard, the fur was soft and warm. Later, people discovered that rubbing and pounding fat into the skin while it was drying would make it softer and less stiff.

At first people just wrapped the skins around themselves. Later they learned how to fasten several skins together. They used a sharp stone or bone to punch holes in the skins. Then they drew **thongs**, or long thin strips of animal skin, through the holes to join one skin to another. Before long they learned to shape a piece of bone until it was smooth and thin and pointed at one end. They made a hole in the thicker end and drew a thong through it. Thus, they had the first needle and thread.

Clothing made a big difference in the way people lived. It protected them from the cold and the rain. With clothing, people could move from a warm, dry area into a cooler, wetter area.

1. Where did early people usually live?
2. What did early people use for clothing?

EARLY PEOPLE

The first people on earth are known as *Homo habilis*, or "man with ability." Next came *Homo erectus*, or "man who

Grind Stone

MAMMOTH SKELETON
Prehistoric people hunted animals such as the mammoth for food. By 8000 B. C., mammoths and other large animals started to die out, and people began to hunt smaller animals such as deer. Today the remains of mammoths have been found in many parts of the world and are displayed in museums.
How did prehistoric people hunt for food?

walks upright." Then, about 100,000 years ago, *Homo sapiens*, or "man who thinks," came along.

There are two types of Homo sapiens. The first is the Neanderthal, named after the Neander River in western Germany where their remains were first discovered in 1857. Since then experts have found Neanderthal remains throughout Europe and in parts of Asia and Africa.

Neanderthal people were excellent hunters. They used traps to catch birds and small, fast-running animals. They used **pitfalls** to catch big animals like the rhinoceros and the elephant. A pitfall was a large hole that was covered over by branches, leaves, and dirt. As an animal ran across the pitfall, it would crash through the covering and fall into the pit. There it was speared over and over until it bled to death. The Neanderthals also caught big animals by driving them into swampy mudholes. The heavy animals would sink deeper and deeper into the mud until they could no longer move their feet. Then the Neanderthals would kill them with spears and stones.

The second type of Homo sapiens is the Cro-Magnon, named after the rock shelter in France where their remains were first discovered. Cro-Magnon people arrived about 40,000 years ago. After a while they drove out the Neanderthals.

Cro-Magnon people looked very much the way people look today. Men were about 5 feet 8 inches, or about 1.8 meters, tall. Women were about 5 feet 3 inches, or about 1.6 meters, tall. Both men and women had high foreheads, curving noses, large jaws, and small teeth. Their skin color depended on where they lived. People who lived in cool areas had lighter-colored skin than those who lived in warm areas.

Cro-Magnons were very skillful tool makers. They were the first to make flake tools. They made a tool called a **burin** which they used only to make other tools. They also made great use of such materials as bone, antler, and ivory, which were more workable than wood or stone. As a result the Cro-Magnons were able to make needles, beads, jewelry, and fishing hooks. They also invented weapons which helped them to increase their food supply, such as the bow and arrow and the **spear thrower**, or a device that throws a spear farther than an arm can.

PREHISTORIC PEOPLE

These drawings show the facial features of a Neanderthal (left) and a Cro-Magnon (right).

What were the lives of prehistoric people like?

Many Cro-Magnons, especially those who lived in cold areas, built huts in which they lived for part of the year. The walls and roof of the huts were made of animal skins held up by wooden posts. Stones and heavy bones piled on the bottom of the skins kept them on the ground.

1. What kind of hunting techniques did Neanderthals use?
2. What did the Cro-Magnons invent?

ART AND RELIGION   Neanderthal and Cro-Magnon people were artists as well as hunters and food-gatherers. They collected shells and stones with interesting shapes. Cro-Magnons made necklaces and bracelets which they decorated with designs or pictures of animals. They carved statues out of ivory and bone or molded them out of clay.

CAVE PAINTING

Prehistoric artists painted scenes of animals and people on the walls of caves. Experts believe the artists either rubbed the paint onto the rock or blew it onto the surface through a hollow bone.

Why did prehistoric artists make cave paintings?

Cro-Magnons covered the walls of certain caves with pictures painted in vivid reds, browns, yellows, and blacks. The pictures showed hunters and such animals as bisons, horses, reindeer, and **mammoths**, or hairy elephants.

Many anthropologists think these paintings were linked to religion. The people believed that everything was alive and filled with spirits. They thought that creating an animal in paint gave them a kind of magic power over that animal's spirit. They felt this would help them find the animal and kill it in the hunt.

Neanderthal and Cro-Magnon people also believed in a life after death. Archaeologists have found a number of skeletons buried in caves. Near the skeletons were tools and weapons, and around them was a rough circle of stones.

1. What was the main art form of the Cro-Magnons?
2. What were some religious beliefs of Neanderthal and Cro-Magnon people?

CHAPTER REVIEW

SUMMARY

1. People first lived in the lands which today are known as South Africa and East Africa.
2. Early people lived in small hunting and food gathering bands that moved from place to place in search of food and a place for shelter.
3. After a while people learned to shape stones into tools.
4. As time went on, people developed language, discovered how to make fire, and began making clothing.
5. About 100,000 years ago Homo sapiens appeared.
6. The first type of Homo sapiens is the Neanderthal.
7. The Neanderthal people were excellent hunters.
8. The second type of Homo sapiens is the Cro-Magnon, who appeared about 40,000 years ago and drove out the Neanderthal.
9. The Cro-Magnon were skillful toolmakers and artists.

BUILDING VOCABULARY

1. *Identify the following:*

South Africa	Homo habilis	Homo sapiens	Cro-Magnon
East Africa	Homo erectus	Neanderthal	

2. *Define the following:*

bands	fist-hatchet	hoot	pitfalls
home territory	all-purpose tool	windbreaks	burin
chips	flint	thongs	spear thrower
flakes			mammoths

REVIEWING THE FACTS

1. What did early people look like?
2. Why did more than one half the children born into a band fail to reach their first birthday?
3. Why did prehistoric bands move from one campsite to another?
4. How did early men and women divide up the work of getting food?
5. In what ways did early people use the fist-hatchet?
6. How did the discovery of fire affect peoples' lives?
7. Why did early people usually camp out in the open instead of living in caves?
8. What difference did clothing make in the way people lived?
9. When do experts believe Homo sapiens appeared on earth?
10. What did the Cro-Magnons do to improve their success in the hunt?

DISCUSSING IMPORTANT IDEAS

1. Why did the people within a prehistoric band feel very close to one another?
2. Do you think the development of language is important? Explain.
3. Was daily life easier or harder after the discovery of fire? Explain.
4. Do you think Cro-Magnons would find it difficult to get along today? Explain.

CHAPTER

FOOD PRODUCERS

3

Around 8000 B.C. a new age began that came to be called the Neolithic, or new stone, Age. The age before the Neolithic Age is called the Paleolithic, or old stone, Age.

At one time experts believed that the main difference between the Neolithic and Paleolithic Ages was the way in which people worked with stone. During the Paleolithic Age they shaped stone by chipping. During the Neolithic Age they shaped it by grinding.

Today experts know much more about prehistoric people. They now believe that the main difference between the two Ages centers around how people got their food. Paleolithic people obtained their food by hunting and gathering. Neolithic people obtained most of their food from farming.

FARMERS AND HERDERS

Two important discoveries changed people from food gatherers to food producers. First, people learned they could grow their own food. Second, they learned they could herd animals.

People probably learned they could grow their own food when a woman of a hunting-and-food-gathering band spilled some wild grain she was taking back to the campsite to be cooked. About a month later she noticed tiny green shoots coming up through the ground. She did not think much about it because the band moved away to other campsites. Seven months later the band returned to the first campsite. This time the woman saw something even stranger. Tall stalks were growing, and each stalk carried grain just like the grain she had spilled on the ground months before. The woman decided to spill some more grain in the same place. A month later, tiny green shoots came up through the ground. Seven months later, the world's first farmer harvested her first crop.

People probably learned they could herd animals when a hunting band built fences to close in a herd of wild animals it had chased into a ravine. The hunters killed one animal at a time,

saving the rest for later. After a while, the captured animals began to lose their fear of people and became **domesticated**, or tamed. Thus, the hunters became herders. They still wandered from place to place with the animals. But they were able to kill an animal whenever they wanted. After a while they began to breed animals for certain qualities. They bred more timid cattle, fatter pigs, and sheep with thicker coats of wool.

The results of the change from food gathering to food producing were so immense that experts call the beginning of farming the Neolithic Revolution.

1. How did people probably learn to farm?
2. What happened when hunters learned to control the movement of animal herds?

EARLY VILLAGES   The most important result of the Neolithic Revolution was that people no longer had to move from one area to another. They could settle in a place that had good soil and a water supply. There they could build permanent shelters and develop villages of about 150 to 200 persons.

The earliest known villages in the world have been found in the Middle East. Oldest of all is Jericho in Israel, which archaeologists think dates back to 8000 B.C. Another early

village is Çatal Hüyük in southern Turkey. People lived there from about 6500 to 5700 B.C. Archaeologists know a great deal about Çatal Hüyük because it was once burned down by a fire, which blackened rather than destroyed wooden and cloth objects. The blackening helped preserve the objects.

The houses in Çatal Hüyük were made of sun-dried mud brick. They had flat roofs made of reeds plastered over with mud. The walls and roofs were supported by a **post-and-lintel**, or a horizontal length of wood or stone placed across two upright posts. The post-and-lintel was an important contribution to architecture. It enabled builders to support a weight above an open space.

As protection against attack, the houses had no doors. People went in and out by ladder from a hole in the roof. The houses were crowded one against the other. But since the village was built on the side of a hill, some houses stood higher than others. This permitted them to have windows in one wall. Here and there among the houses were open courtyards which contained large ovens used to bake bread.

Each house had two or three rather dark rooms. The floors were covered with carpets of **rush**, or grasslike plants. The

---

ÇATAL HÜJÜK
The people of Çatal Hüjük grew wheat, hunted animals, and made weapons and jewelry. This picture shows the remains of homes in Çatal Hüjük recently found by archaeologists.
How were homes built in Çatal Hüjük?

LAKE DWELLERS

Around 5000 B. C. groups of farmers settled along the marshy banks of lakes in central Europe. There they built wooden homes over the water on wooden piles. In time, they enlarged the size of their farmlands.
How did most early villages begin?

sleeping platforms were covered with mats. Heat came from wood burning in a **hearth**, or fireplace.

Beyond the houses stood vegetable gardens, apple orchards, and fields of wheat and barley. Still farther out were pastures where sheep and cattle grazed. Surrounding everything was open plain.

1. What was the main result of the Neolithic Revolution?
2. What were some features of Neolithic villages?
3. What were some features of Neolithic houses?

INVENTIONS   During the Neolithic Age people learned to make pottery by baking clay. First they mixed the clay with straw and **dung**, or animal wastes. The straw kept the clay from cracking when it was heated. The dung made the clay stronger. Then the people pounded the mixture to remove any moisture. Next they wound coils of rope-shaped clay in a circle until they built up a pot. They smoothed the sides of the pot and placed it in a trench dug into the ground. After covering the pot with a thick bed of branches, straw, and dung, they set fire to the trench. The sides of the trench and the surface layers of straw and wood kept in the heat. As a result, the clay baked at a high temperature. After the fire died down and the trench cooled off, the hardened pot was lifted out ready for use.

People used pottery for dishes and for carrying and storing food. They also used it for cooking. This enabled them to add such things as bread, soup, and stews to their diet.

INVENTIONS
Farmers invented many objects to make their work easier. One invention was the mortar and pestle (right) for grinding grain.
For what purposes were inventions used?

Another Neolithic invention was the **loom**, or a machine used to weave cloth. People took wool from their sheep, spun it into thread, and wove the thread into cloth. They dyed the cloth bright colors. Sometimes they made patterns of circles and squares. The people used the cloth for clothing. They also wrapped it around the bodies of their dead.

During the Neolithic Age people began to use metal. They picked up lumps of copper, lead, gold, and silver which they found lying on the ground. They hammered the cold metal to make beads and jewelry. After a while they learned how to shape the metal into weapons. However, since metals found on the ground were scarce, people continued to use mostly stone, bone, and wood.

1. What were some inventions of the Neolithic Age?
2. How did Neolithic people make pottery?

POPULATION   Another important result of the Neolithic Revolution was an increase in the food supply. With more food available, the **population**, or number of people, began to grow.

Experts think there were about 5 million people in the world when the Neolithic Revolution began. Within 4000 years the population had jumped to about 90 million.

During the Paleolithic Age everyone except infants and sick people spent most of their time obtaining food. With the increase in the food supply, some people could work at **occupations**, or jobs, that had nothing to do with food. They could become potters, metal workers, carpenters, weavers, or jewelry makers. They could exchange the products they made for grain, fruit, and meat. The longer the people worked at their crafts, the more skilled they became. Both the amount and the quality of their products increased, and villages gradually became wealthy.

Metal Worker

Sometimes craftspeople in one village exchanged their products with craftspeople in another village. Gradually people began to trade over longer and longer distances.

1. What effect did farming have on population?
2. What effect did farming have on people's occupations?

GOVERNMENT People in Neolithic villages owned more than people before them. They had a fairly steady food supply. They had permanent houses to shelter them and utensils in which to prepare, serve, and store their food. They had **textiles**, or woven cloth. They had toys, jewelry, and such cosmetics as rouge and lipstick. They also had mirrors made from polished **obsidian**, or hardened lava from a volcano.

Everything the people owned depended on their use of a given piece of land. As a result, they wanted to protect what they had. They began to think about setting and maintaining boundaries and about passing their land on to their children.

Gradually the people within the villages developed a government which was different from what people had known in Paleolithic times. Then members of a band usually followed the ideas of two or three leaders. Everyone had a chance to talk and argue before coming to some kind of agreement. Neolithic village government was in the hands of a single **chief**, or leader. The chief spent all his time planning and directing village activities. He was helped by a small group of people who also spent all their time doing government work.

1. What new ideas did Neolithic people have about land?
2. How did government change from Paleolithic times?

RELIGION   Experts believe that the chiefs of most Neolithic villages were priests as well as rulers. They handled certain religious duties for the entire village. These duties included offering prayers for things the people needed, such as fertile soil, sunshine and water for crops, and healthy animals. It also included prayers to keep away mice and insects that might damage grain.

At first Neolithic people prayed to the forces of nature which they saw around them. Thunderbolts and rainstorms were male, and fields were female. The bull was a symbol of power and strength.

Before long the people created gods and goddesses to represent the forces they feared. The most important was the Earth Mother, the goddess of fertility. Many of the houses of Catal Hüyük contained **shrines**, or altars, on which stood the stone statue of a goddess.

1.   For what did Neolithic people pray?
2.   What goddess was the most important in Neolithic villages?

CHAPTER REVIEW

SUMMARY

1.   The Neolithic Age began about 8000 B.C.

2.   The main difference between the Neolithic and Paleolithic Ages was that Neolithic people obtained most of their food from farming rather than hunting and gathering.

3.   People became food producers instead of food gatherers by learning to grow food and to herd animals.

4.   The shift from food gathering to food producing brought about so many changes in the way people lived that it is known as the Neolithic Revolution.

5.   The most important result of the Neolithic Revolution was that people were able to settle in one place and develop villages.

6.   The earliest villages developed in the Middle East.

7.   Neolithic villagers learned to make pottery, invented the loom, and began to use metal.

8.   Another important result of the Neolithic Revolution was an increase in the food supply.

9.   The increase in the food supply led to an increase in population and the development of occupations that had nothing to do with obtaining food.

10.   Neolithic villagers developed many new ideas about land and government.

11.   The chiefs of most Neolithic villages were both rulers and priests.

12.   Religion was important to Neolithic people.

BUILDING VOCABULARY

1. *Identify the following:*
   Neolithic Age   Jericho   Çatal Hüyük   Earth Mother
   Paleolithic Age

2. *Define the following:*
   domesticated   hearth   population   obsidian
   post-and-lintel   dung   occupations   chief
   rush   loom   textiles   shrines

REVIEWING THE FACTS

1. What did experts in the past believe was the main difference between the Neolithic and Paleolithic Ages?

2. What do experts today believe was the main difference between the Neolithic and Paleolithic Ages?

3. What did people do with their animals once they lost their fear of humans and became domesticated?

4. What is the oldest known village in the world, and why is knowledge of this village so important?

5. Why do archaeologists know a great deal about Çatal Hüyük?

6. Why is the post-and-lintel an important contribution to architecture?

7. How did the people of Çatal Hüyük protect themselves from attack?

8. How did the invention of pottery affect people's diet?

9. Why did Neolithic people continue using mostly stone, bone, and wood rather than metal?

10. What effect did farming have on trade?

DISCUSSING IMPORTANT IDEAS

1. Do you think you would have enjoyed living in Çatal Hüyük? Give reasons for your opinion.

2. Why was religion important to Neolithic people?

3. Do you think the development of food producing deserves to be called a revolution? Give reasons for your opinion.

4. How would you have organized village activities if you were a Neolithic chief?

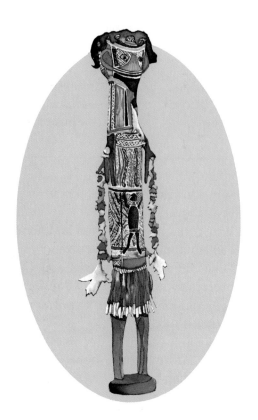

contact with other areas of the world. Since the arrival of the British, aborigine life has been greatly changed.

The aborigines lived in groups all over Australia. They used tools and weapons of wood and stone. Those who lived along the coasts fished for food. Those who lived in the desert areas hunted animals and gathered wild foods. Men hunted large animals like the kangaroo or an ostrich-like bird called an **emu**. Women and children gathered seeds, berries, and roots and trapped small animals.

Myths, or legends, were important to the aborigines and were passed from the old to the young. The myths told where the first aborigines came from, how the land was formed, and how people should act. They taught the difference between right and wrong. They kept the aborigines united and also helped to keep peace and order.

THE ABORIGINES

The first people to live in Australia are called aborigines, which means "first inhabitants." Archaeologists have discovered sites which indicate that the aborigines have lived in Australia for at least 20,000 years. Before British settlers arrived in 1788, the aborigines had little or no

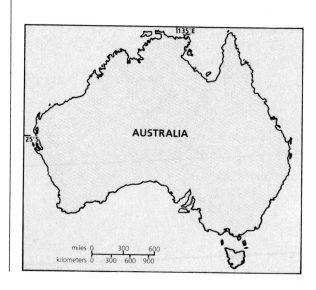

When British settlers came, they arrived in large numbers. Soon they outnumbered the aborigines. The settlers took aborigine land. Without their land, the aborigines could not live as they had in the past. Although few British settlers went to desert areas, ranchers and traders set up outposts there. Aborigines came to the outposts to trade. Some stayed on and took jobs, mostly as ranch helpers. Church missionaries set up posts to teach them Christianity.

Around 1930 the Australian government decided to try to bring aborigines into mainstream society. But the values of the aborigines were different from those of most other Australians. Many aborigines could not understand the need for money. They did not place any importance on owning things. As their groups were broken up, they felt alone and helpless.

Since the 1960's the government has set land aside for the aborigines and has tried to let them decide their own way of life. However, much of the land is too poor to support many people. The aborigines want to keep their old beliefs. But it is almost certain that the more contact they have with other Australians, the more they will have to change.

1. How did the aborgines live before British settlers came to Australia?
2. Why were myths important to the aborigines?
3. How did the arrival of the British affect the aborigines?
4. What has been the government's policy toward aborgines since 1960?

UNIT REVIEW

SUMMARY

1. Much of what is known about prehistoric times comes from legends and artifacts.
2. In the Paleolithic Age people lived in small bands that moved from one campsite to another and got food by hunting, fishing, and gathering.
3. During the Paleolithic Age people discovered how to use fire, developed a spoken language, and made tools.
4. Civilization began in the Neolithic Age, when people learned how to grow food and herd animals and then began building permanent shelters and settling down in one place.
5. During the Neolithic Age people learned how to make pottery and weave cloth, and developed new ideas about government and religion.

REVIEWING THE MAIN IDEAS

1. Explain why prehistoric people had to learn how to farm before the growth of villages was possible.
2. Explain how farming and living in villages changed daily tasks, religion, and government.

DEVELOPING SKILLS

Reading a history textbook is one of the most common ways in which people learn about the past. But in order to get the most out of reading, there are certain skills a person has to have. One skill is being able to identify the main idea of a paragraph.

Sometimes the main idea is stated in the first sentence of the paragraph. This sentence is called a **topic sentence** because it contains the main **topic,** or idea, of the paragraph. Sometimes the main idea is stated in the last sentence of the paragraph. This sentence is called a **summary sentence** because it **summarizes,** or sums up, what the paragraph is all about. Sometimes the main idea is not stated directly. Then the paragraph contains information about the main idea, but the reader must decide what the idea actually is.

This exercise is designed to provide practice in identifying the main idea of a paragraph. Listed are references to paragraphs in the textbook. Below each are three possible main ideas. Reread each paragraph, and then choose the correct main idea.

1. Chapter 1: paragraph at the bottom of page 8 and the top of page 9.
a. The city of Herculaneum had been buried for more than 1000 years.
b. Archaeologists uncovered Pompeii after they uncovered Herculaneum.
c. Uncovering Herculaneum and Pompeii helped archaeologists learn exactly how ancient Romans lived.
2. Chapter 2: first paragraph under "Learning to Talk" on page 19.
a. Early people did not always know how to talk.
b. Before people knew how to talk, they used different kinds of noises to express meaning.
c. A yell probably meant a person was angry.

3. Chapter 3: second paragraph on page 28.

a. People probably learned how to grow food by accident.

b. The world's first farmer was a woman.

c. Grain was the first food people learned how to grow.

SUGGESTED UNIT PROJECTS

1. Working in groups of four or five, without speaking, act out a story about tracking down and killing an animal.

2. Draw a picture showing one of the earliest uses of fire.

3. Make a chart comparing life in the Paleolithic Age with life in the Neolithic Age. Be sure to include information about how people obtained food, where people lived, what kind of government people had, and what inventions people made.

4. In 1971 a hunting-and-food-gathering people called the Tasaday were discovered on an island in the Philippines. Prepare a report on the Tasaday.

SUGGESTED READING

Batterberry, Michael and Ariane Ruskin. *Primitive Art*. New York: McGraw-Hill, 1973. An illustrated account of the art of prehistoric people.

Collier, James Lincoln. *The Making of Man: The Story of Our Ancient Ancestors*. New York: Scholastic Book Services, 1974. A description of the way of life of prehistoric people.

Millstead, Thomas. *Cave of the Moving Shadows*. New York: Dial Press, 1979. Tells the story of a 12-year-old Cro-Magnon boy who must choose between his training as a magician and his wish to be a hunter.

Simak, Clifford. *Prehistoric Man*. New York: St. Martin's Press, Inc., 1971. Traces the development of tools, fire, permanent shelter, religion, art, and farming.

Steele, William O. *The Magic Amulet*. New York: Harcourt Brace Jovanovich, 1979. Tells the story of a young wounded hunter left behind by his band who must find a new band to join in order to survive.

Unit 2

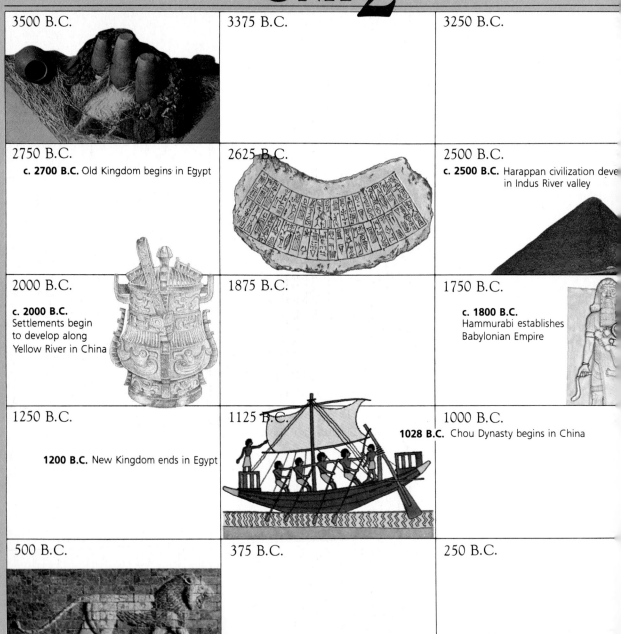

3500 B.C.	3375 B.C.	3250 B.C.
2750 B.C. **c. 2700 B.C.** Old Kingdom begins in Egypt	2625 B.C.	**2500 B.C.** **c. 2500 B.C.** Harappan civilization develops in Indus River valley
2000 B.C. **c. 2000 B.C.** Settlements begin to develop along Yellow River in China	1875 B.C.	**1750 B.C.** **c. 1800 B.C.** Hammurabi establishes Babylonian Empire
1250 B.C. **1200 B.C.** New Kingdom ends in Egypt	1125 B.C.	**1000 B.C.** **1028 B.C.** Chou Dynasty begins in China
500 B.C.	375 B.C.	250 B.C.

THE RIVER VALLEY CIVILIZATIONS

...B.C.	3000 B.C.	
	**3000 B.C.** Ur is a major Sumerian city	
...C.	2250 B.C.	2125 B.C.
	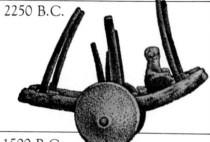	**2060 B.C.** Middle Kingdom begins in Egypt
	c. 2300 B.C. Sargon I creates world's first empire	
...C.	1500 B.C.	1375 B.C.
...0 B.C. New Kingdom begins in Egypt	**1523 B.C.** Shang Dynasty begins in China	**c. 1370 B.C.** Amenhotep IV becomes pharaoh of Egypt
	1500 B.C. Mohenjo-daro and Harappa begin to decline	
	c. 1480 B.C. Thutmose III expands Egyptian control into Syria and Palestine	
	750 B.C.	625 B.C.
	672 B.C. Assyrians conquer Egypt	

1. HOW DID ENVIRONMENT INFLUENCE THE WAYS IN WHICH THE PEOPLE OF THE RIVER VALLEYS LIVED?

2. IN WHAT WAYS WERE THE RIVER VALLEY CIVILIZATIONS ALIKE? IN WHAT WAYS WERE THEY DIFFERENT?

Around 4000 B.C. civilizations began to develop. Two of these, Mesopotamia and Egypt, were in an area now called the Middle East. A third, the Indus River valley, was in Pakistan and India. A fourth, the Yellow River valley, was in China. Each civilization developed separately. Yet all started as villages along the banks of a river.

The people of these civilizations depended on the rivers for food. The rivers flooded and left behind rich soil good for raising crops. The people learned to control the floodwaters and to store the water to use on their fields in the dry season. This took much planning. People had to learn to work together. They set up governments to make laws so they would know what was expected of them. They became more organized. The population grew. The people began to build cities.

In each civilization farmers were able to produce more food than needed. In time, fewer farmers were needed to produce food. Thus, many people became free to do other things. Certain kinds of work came to be considered more important. Some people had more land or lived better. People no longer were equal.

People could not produce everything they wanted. So they began to trade their **surplus**, or extra, products for the goods they did not have. As trade grew, there was a need for records. This led to writing.

Trade and conquest helped spread customs and ideas. Soon ideas and customs of one civilization were being borrowed and changed by others.

CHAPTER 4

MESOPOTAMIA

The Tigris and Euphrates are twin rivers that begin in the mountains of eastern Turkey. They flow more than 1000 miles, or 1600 kilometers, southeast across a great plain. Then the waters join and empty into the Persian Gulf. Today the land between the two rivers is called Iraq. In ancient times it was called Mesopotamia, "the land between the rivers." Around 5000 B.C. the people who lived in this area began to move south in search of more farmland. The land in the southeast was rich and fertile. It also had a lot of fish and waterfowl which could be used for food.

THE RISE OF SUMER

The people who settled in southern Mesopotamia around 3500 B.C. were called Sumerians. Their area of Mesopotamia was called Sumer. The Sumerians were a short, stocky, black-haired people. Sumerian civilization is the earliest known on earth. For the first time a people began to control their physical environment.

The Sumerians knew they had to control the twin rivers. The rivers flooded each spring. When the waters went down, natural **levees**, or raised areas of earth, remained behind. The Sumerians built these even higher and used them to keep back the floodwaters. When the land was dry, they poked holes in the levees. The river water that ran through the holes watered the fields where they had planted crops. The main crop of the Sumerians was barley. Other crops included wheat, sesame, and flax. The Sumerians also grew fruit trees, date palms, and many kinds of vegetables.

The water that flowed through the holes in the levees made channels in the soil. Eventually the Sumerians enlarged the channels until they became canals. They used the canals to **irrigate**, or water, their crops. They also built rafts so they could travel up and down the canals.

There was no building stone and little timber in Sumer. The Sumerians had to find other materials to use for their houses and public buildings. They mixed mud from the river with crushed reeds to make bricks. They left the bricks out in the sun to bake. They used the bricks to build their cities. One of the great cities of Sumer was Ur. The Sumerians were the first city-builders in this area of the world.

1. Who were the Sumerians?
2. How did they control the twin rivers?
3. What was their main building material?

CITY-STATES   Each Sumerian city was considered a state in itself, with its own god and government. Each **city-state** was made up of the city plus the farmland around it. Each city was surrounded by a wall of sun-dried brick. The wall had bronze gates that were opened during the day and closed at night to keep out lions and bandits.

Sumerian Figurine

STANDARD OF UR

This design shows a victory feast in the city-state of Ur. In the upper row, the king and his officers are entertained by musicians. The second and third rows show servants bringing animals and war prizes to the banquet.

What does the standard show about relations among the Mesopotamian city-states?

Narrow, winding streets led from the gates to the center of the city. Near the center were the houses of the upper class—priests and merchants. These houses were two stories high with wooden balconies. The balconies overlooked courtyards around which the living quarters were built. The courtyards provided light and air for rooms. Outside walls were windowless to keep out the hot sun and the smells of the streets.

Behind the houses of the rich were houses of the middle class—government officials, shopkeepers, and craftspeople. These houses also were built around open courtyards. But they were only one story high. Further out were the houses of the lower class—farmers, sailors, unskilled workers, and people who made their living by fishing.

The Sumerians were very proud of their cities. Often one city-state would go to war with another city-state. They fought over boundary lines. They also fought to prove which city-state was stronger.

1. What were some physical features of a city-state?
2. What were Sumer's social classes? Who belonged to each?

RELIGIOUS AND FAMILY LIFE   At the center of each Sumerian city was a temple, called a **ziggurat**. The word "ziggurat" means "mountain of god" or "hill of heaven." The ziggurat was made up of a series of square terraces. Each terrace was smaller than the one below it. Great stairways led to the top of the ziggurat, which was the home of the city's chief god. Only priests could enter the home of the god.

Around the ziggurat were courts. The courts and the temple were the center of Sumerian life. Craftspeople worked there. Children went to school there. Farmers, craftspeople, and traders stored their goods there. The poor were fed there. All great events were celebrated in this area.

The Sumerians believed that all the forces of nature, such as wind, rain, and flood, were alive. Because they could not control these forces, the Sumerians viewed them as gods. In all, there were more than 3000 gods.

The Sumerians believed that at first there were only male gods. Then female gods appeared. The male gods found they had to work very hard to please the female gods. The male gods decided that they needed servants to do the work for them. So, from the mud of the river, they made humans who would be

---

ZIGGURAT

This sketch shows the ziggurat of Ur. Many workers helped in the building of the ziggurat. Ziggurats were made of sun-dried brick. The outer walls were covered with tile.
Where were ziggurats located in a Mesopotamian city-state?

their servants. The Sumerians believed that they were on earth only to serve the gods. If the gods were unhappy with them, their crops would not grow, and they would not live a happy life. Therefore, the main goal of each Sumerian was to please the gods.

Only priests, however, could know the will of the gods. This made Sumerian priests very powerful. For example, all the land was owned by the city's god. But the priests controlled and administered the land in the god's name. The priests also ran the schools.

The schools in Sumer were only for the sons of the rich. Poorer boys worked in the fields or learned a trade. The schools were called **edubbas**, or tablet-houses, because their main purpose was to teach students how to write. Classes were held in rooms off the temple courtyards. Students sat in rows on brick benches. They wrote with wedge-shaped instruments on clay tablets about the size of a postcard. Sumerian writing was called **cuneiform**. It was made up of hundreds of word signs.

When a student graduated from school, he became a **scribe**, or writer. He worked for the temple, the palace, the government, or the army. Some scribes went to work for a merchant or set up their own business as public writers.

Although only Sumerian males went to school, females did have rights. They could buy and sell property. They could run businesses, including taverns. They were allowed to own and sell slaves.

Although a woman could handle her husband's affairs when he was away, the husband was the head of the household. He could divorce his wife by saying, "You're not my wife." If he needed money, he had the right to sell or rent his wife and children as slaves for up to three years. He also arranged the marriages of his children.

Children were expected to support their parents when their parents became too old to support themselves. Children were also expected to obey any family member, including brothers or sisters. All family members were expected to obey the gods and the priests.

1. What served as the center of Sumerian life?
2. Why did the Sumerians believe they should please the gods?
3. What was school like in Sumer?
4. What rights did Sumerian women have?

Sumerian Woman

PRIESTS AND KINGS   At first Sumerian priests were also kings of city-states. One of the most famous **priest-kings** was Gilgamesh of Uruk. Tales told about Gilgamesh made him seem more like a god than a person. One tale written about 1700 B.C. is the oldest known story in the world.

In the story Gilgamesh and his friend Enkidu travel the world performing great acts of courage. When Enkidu dies, Gilgamesh searches for a way to live forever. He learns that only the gods can live forever and that all people must die someday. He also learns that people can and should take pride in what they do. Part of the Gilgamesh story tells of a great flood that covered the entire world. The account of the flood is very much like the biblical story of Noah and the ark.

The Sumerian priest-king received advice from an **assembly**. The assembly was made up of free men. When war broke out with another city-state, the assembly would choose one of its members to serve as military leader until the war was over. As time went on, these military leaders stayed in charge even after peace had returned. They gained more and more power. By about 3000 B.C. they replaced the priests as permanent kings. At the same time kingship became **hereditary**, or passed down from father to son.

1. What did Gilgamesh do?
2. How did Sumerians who were not priests become kings?

LATER MESOPOTAMIAN CIVILIZATIONS

About 2400 B.C. the power of Sumer started to fade. New civilizations would soon develop in Mesopotamia as conquerors moved in from nearby areas.

SARGON I   Sargon I was a ruler from an area in northern Mesopotamia known as Akkad. About 2300 B.C. he moved his armies south and began to conquer the city-states of Sumer one by one. He united the conquered city-states with Akkad and became known as king of Sumer and Akkad. Thus, Sargon I created the world's first **empire**, or group of states or countries under one ruler. He later extended this empire to include all of Mesopotamia.

Under Sargon I, Akkadian became the language of the people. Sumerian was used only for religious purposes. The

Akkadians, however, worshipped the Sumerian gods. They also wrote their language in Sumerian cuneiform. Sargon I ruled his empire for more than 50 years. Shortly after his death, the empire fell.

1. Where did Sargon I come from?
2. What happened to Sumer under Sargon I's rule?

HAMMURABI OF BABYLON   Following the death of Sargon I, the separate city-states again rose to power. Then, about 1800 B.C., a new group of people called Amorites entered the Tigris-Euphrates valley and built cities of their own. One of these cities was Babylon. The king of Babylon, Hammurabi, conquered Akkad and Sumer. He became the ruler of a great new empire.

The people of Babylon took as their own much of the culture of the people they had conquered. For example, the Babylonians took over the language of the city-states. They worshipped the same Sumerian gods that the Akkadians had worshipped, but they gave the gods Babylonian names.

MESOPOTAMIA

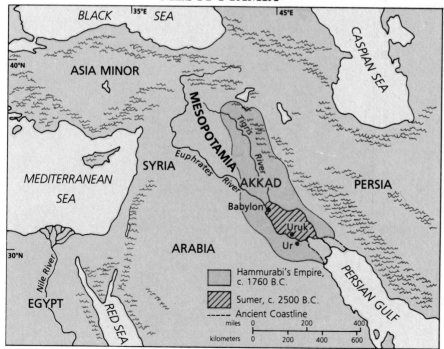

Hammurabi was a great conqueror. He extended his rule to the Mediterranean Sea. As a ruler, he carried out many **reforms**, or improvements. He improved the irrigation system by building and repairing canals. He reformed religion by raising the god of Babylon above all other gods. The people began to worship this god as well as their own local god. By worshipping a common god, they became more united. Hammurabi also reorganized the tax system and began a government housing program.

The reform for which Hammurabi became most famous, however, was his code of law. Each city-state had had its own code. Hammurabi took what he felt were the best laws from each code. He put these together and then issued one code by which the entire empire was to live. Hammurabi wanted to make sure that his code was carried out fairly and justly. To do this, he appointed royal judges. Judges who were not honest, and witnesses who did not tell the truth, were punished.

CODE OF HAMMURABI

The code of Hammurabi defended the rights of the individual. Here a Babylonian citizen pleads for justice before Hammurabi and his court.
Why was the code of Hammurabi important?

Hammurabi's code covered almost everything in daily life. A person was believed innocent until proven guilty. Once proven guilty, a person was punished. The punishments ranged from fines to death. There were no prison sentences. Members of the upper class usually were punished more severely than members of the middle or lower classes.

During Hammurabi's rule Babylon became an important trade center. The Babylonians brought their goods to city markets by carrying them overland on the backs of wild asses or by floating them down the twin rivers on rafts. People from far-away parts of the world came to trade. Some experts think they came from as far away as India and China. These traders paid gold and silver for the grain and cloth the Babylonians produced.

Hammurabi ruled for more than 40 years. The time he reigned is known as the Golden Age of Babylon.

1. What happened to Sumerian culture under Hammurabi's rule?
2. What were some reforms Hammurabi made?

CONTRIBUTIONS OF MESOPOTAMIA

From the beginnings of Sumer until the death of Hammurabi, the influence of Mesopotamia on other civilizations was felt in many ways. The "inventions," customs, and ideas of the Sumerian and Babylonian cultures were copied and, in some cases, improved upon by other peoples. Some are still in use today in a slightly different form.

The Sumerians developed the earliest known civilization in the world. For this reason, Mesopotamia has been called "the cradle of civilization." The oldest written records known are Sumerian. The Sumerians were the first people to write down their laws. Sumerian cuneiform became the model for the writing of other civilizations.

Cuneiform Clay Cones

The Sumerians also invented many things that helped to improve their well-being. They invented the wheel, which helped them to transport people and goods. They invented the plow, which enabled farmers to grow more food with less effort. And they invented the sailboat, which replaced muscle power with wind power.

By mapping the night sky, the people of Mesopotamia developed a 12-month calendar based on the cycles of the moon. The calendar marked the times for religious festivals. It also told farmers when to plant their crops.

From Mesopotamia also came contributions to the field of mathematics. The people developed a number system based on 60. From that system came the 60-minute hour, the 60-second minute, and the 360-degree circle. The people of Mesopotamia also used a clock that was operated by controlled drops of water.

1. Why Mesopotamia called "the cradle of civilization?"
2. What did the people of Mesopotamia contribute to other cultures?

CHAPTER REVIEW

SUMMARY

1. Civilization began in an area known as Mesopotamia, located between the Tigris and Euphrates rivers.

2. Sumer was the first known civilization in the world.

3. The chief occupation of the Sumerians was farming.

4. The Sumerians developed an irrigation system for growing crops.

5. Sumerian civilization consisted of a series of city-states, the most important of which was Ur.

6. Life in each Sumerian city-state centered around the temple and its courts.

7. The Sumerians believed that all forces of nature were alive and were gods.

8. Each Sumerian city-state had its own chief god and government.

9. Eventually kingship developed in Sumer, becoming permanent and hereditary about 3000 B.C.

10. The oldest known story in the world was written about a Sumerian priest-king called Gilgamesh.

11. Sargon I of Akkad created the world's first empire by conquering the Sumerians in 2300 B.C.

12. About 1800 B.C. Hammurabi conquered Akkad and Sumer and established the Babylonian empire.

13. Hammurabi unified the Babylonian Empire by setting up a single code of law and by raising the god of Babylon above all others.

14. Hammurabi's rule, which lasted over 40 years, was known as the Golden Age of Babylon.

15. Major contributions of the Mesopotamian civilizations to later civilizations include a model for writing, the wheel, the plow, the sailboat, and a number system based on 60.

BUILDING VOCABULARY

1. *Identify the following:*

Tigris and Euphrates	Ur	Sargon I	Babylon
Mesopotamia	Gilgamesh	Akkad	Hammurabi
Sumer			

2. *Define the following:*

surplus	ziggurat	scribe	hereditary
levees	edubbas	priest-king	empire
irrigate	cuneiform	assembly	reforms
city-state			

REVIEWING THE FACTS

1. Where did civilization first begin?
2. Why did the Sumerians build levees?
3. Why were sun-dried bricks the main building material of the Sumerians?
4. What was a Sumerian city like?
5. Why was the ziggurat and its courts important to the Sumerians?
6. Who went to school in Sumer?
7. What was expected of children in Sumer?
8. According to the story of Gilgamesh, what did he learn about life?
9. What did Sargon I accomplish?
10. How did Hammurabi unite the Babylonian Empire?

DISCUSSING IMPORTANT IDEAS

1. Why were the twin rivers important to the Sumerians?
2. Why was religion an important part of Sumerian life?
3. What personal qualities does the story of the priest-king Gilgamesh of Uruk teach? Do you think these qualities are important? Explain.
4. Why did Hammurabi believe it was important to have a single code of law for the Babylonian Empire? Do you agree? Why or why not?

USING MAPS

Refer to the map on page 49, and answer the following questions:

1. Describe the general location of Mesopotamia.
2. Which was larger in area—Sumer or Hammurabi's empire?
3. Does the Tigris lie to the east or the west of the Euphrates?
4. Which city—Babylon or Ur—is further east? How can you tell?

CHAPTER 5

EGYPT

A people called Egyptians settled in the Nile River valley of northeast Africa. They probably borrowed from the Sumerians the idea of farming, seeds for wheat and barley, and the idea of writing. The Egyptian civilization lasted longer than those of Mesopotamia. While the city-states of Mesopotamia fought among themselves, Egypt became a rich, powerful, and united nation. The Egyptians built a civilization that lasted for more than 2000 years.

THE NILE

The Nile River flows north 4000 miles, or 6400 kilometers, from the mountains of central Africa to the Mediterranean Sea. The last 600 miles, or 960 kilometers, is in Egypt. There the river cuts a narrow, green valley through the desert. Shortly before the Nile reaches the sea, it branches to form a fan-shaped area of fertile land called a **delta**. Most ancient Egyptians lived in this delta area. For a long time they were protected from foreign invasions by the desert, the sea, and waterfalls called **cataracts**.

The Egyptians had an advantage over the people of the other river valley civilizations. They knew that every year, about the middle of July, the Nile would overflow its banks. By November the floodwaters would go down. But the waters left behind large amounts of rich soil good for growing crops.

The Egyptians learned to control the flood waters. To do this, they built a system of dams and ditches to drain the extra water from the land. They also dug out **basins**, or bowl-shaped holes. They used these to hold and store the extra water. A machine called a **shadoof** lifted the water from the river to the basins. To bring the water to the fields during the dry season, the Egyptians dug irrigation canals.

LIFE ALONG THE NILE

The Nile River valley is only 3 percent of Egypt's land area. Yet most Egyptians lived and worked in this area. In this wall painting farmers harvest grapes to make wine.

Why was the Nile River important to the Egyptians?

While cattle and goats grazed nearby, the Egyptians raised flax, wheat, barley, and grapes along the banks of the river. Poor Egyptians ate mostly bread, vegetables, and fish. Rich Egyptians also ate meat.

1. Where did the Egyptians live?
2. What advantage did they have over the people of other river valley civilizations?
3. How did the Egyptians control the Nile River?

THE OLD KINGDOM

At first Egypt consisted of two **kingdoms**, or states having kings as rulers. One was Upper Egypt. It lay in the south in the river valley. The other was Lower Egypt. It lay in the north in the delta.

Around 3100 B.C. Narmer, a king of Upper Egypt, led his armies from the valley north into the delta. He conquered Lower Egypt and married one of its princesses. Narmer united the two kingdoms into a single nation. He wore a double crown, the high white one of the south plus the shallow red one of the north. Narmer had many titles. He was called "Lord of Upper and Lower Egypt," "Wearer of Both Crowns," and "Lord of the Two Lands." Narmer set up a new capital at Memphis, a city on the border between Upper and Lower Egypt.

Around 2700 B.C. a period known as the Old Kingdom started in Egypt. It lasted for about 650 years. During the Old Kingdom Egyptian cities became centers of religion and government. There lived kings, priests, government officials, and craftspeople who worked for the temples or the government.

Most Egyptians, however, did not live in the cities. They lived on large estates along the banks of the Nile. The rich Egyptians who owned the estates lived in wood and brick houses with beautiful gardens and pools. The walls were decorated with brightly colored paintings that showed scenes of daily life. The household included the owner's family, servants, and craftspeople. The craftspeople were hired to build boats, weave linen, and make tools and pottery.

Most Egyptians were farmers who lived in villages on the estates. At first their houses were made of reeds and mud, later of sun-baked mud-brick. The houses usually had only one room

Narmer's Palette

EGYPTIAN LIFE STYLES

The wealth of many Egyptians came from owning land and cattle. This wall painting shows aspects of life on the estate of an Egyptian noble. Nobles had their workers keep careful records of produce and animals.

How did the life of the rich differ from that of the poor in Egypt?

and a roof made of palm leaves. They were built on high ground so that they and the people would be safe from the yearly flood. The farmers worked in the fields and the vineyards and took care of the cattle. During the dry season they built monuments, dug ditches, and repaired roads.

1. What did Narmer do?
2. In what kinds of homes did rich Egyptians live during the Old Kingdom?
3. Why did Egyptian farmers build houses on high ground?

THE PHARAOH The Egyptians believed that the strength and unity of their nation came from having a strong ruler. At first Egyptian rulers were called kings. Later they were called **pharaoh**, meaning "great house." To the Egyptians the pharaoh was a ruler, a priest, and a god. The pharaoh was the center of Egyptian life and ruled on earth the way the other gods ruled in heaven.

The pharaoh owned all the land in Egypt. However, the pharaoh gave gifts of land to rich Egyptians and priests. To make sure that the land produced well, the pharaoh saw to it that dams and irrigation canals were built and repaired. The pharaoh also ordered the building of brick **granaries**, or storage buildings for grain. The granaries were used to store the grain from good harvests so that the people would not starve in times of bad harvests.

The pharaoh also chose all the government officials. The officials made certain that taxes were collected and building permits were issued. Trade with foreign lands was in the pharaoh's hands. The word of a pharaoh was law.

The Egyptians believed that what happened to Egypt depended on the pharaoh's actions. As chief priest, the pharaoh performed certain rituals. For example, the pharaoh made the first break in the irrigation dikes each year to open the land to the water. When the water went down, the pharaoh drove a sacred bull around the capital city. The Egyptians believed that this ritual would make the soil fertile. Then they could grow good crops. The pharaoh was the first to cut the ripe grain. The Egyptians believed this ritual would guarantee a good harvest.

Pharaohs were treated with great respect. Whenever they appeared in public, the people played special music on flutes and

cymbals. They also bowed and "smelled the earth," or touched their heads to the ground.

1. What did the pharaoh do?
2. How did the people show their respect for the pharaoh?

THE PYRAMIDS   Another way the people of the Old Kingdom showed their feeling for the pharaohs was by building them great tombs called **pyramids**. Because the sun sank in the west, these "Houses of Eternity" were built on the west bank of the Nile. They were designed to protect the pharaohs' bodies from floods, wild animals, and robbers after they died. The Egyptians believed that the pharaohs would be happy after death if they had their personal belongings. Therefore, they placed the pharaohs' clothing, weapons, furniture, and jewelry in the pyramids.

The Egyptians tried to protect the pharaoh's body because they believed that the soul could not survive without the body. It was important for a pharaoh's soul to live after death. In that way, the pharaoh would continue to take care of Egypt and its people.

It took a great number of people and a lot of work to build the pyramids. Farmers worked on them during the three summer months that their fields were flooded. They used copper tools to cut huge granite and limestone bricks from quarries across the Nile valley or in Upper Egypt. The blocks were tied with ropes on wooden sleds, pulled to the Nile, placed on barges filled with sand, and floated across the river. Another group of workers then unloaded the stone blocks and pulled them to the place where the pyramids were being built. Huge mud and brick ramps were built alongside each pyramid. The workers dragged the blocks up the ramps to each new layer of the pyramid. They built 80 pyramids in this way.

1. Why were the pyramids built?
2. Who built the pyramids? How were they built?

RELIGIOUS BELIEFS   The Egyptians believed in many gods. Most Egyptian gods had the bodies of humans and the heads of animals. Two of the most important gods were the river

---

THE GODDESS ISIS

Each Egyptian village had its own gods and goddesses. Some were worshipped throughout the land. Isis was the most famous goddess. Here she stretches out her winged arms as a sign of her motherly care.

How did Egyptians regard their gods and goddesses?

THE UNDERWORLD

Egyptians believed that after a person died Osiris judged how well the person obeyed the commands of the gods. In this drawing, the heart of a dead scribe is weighed on a scale. Since Osiris has made a favorable decision, the scales are shown in balance.

How did Egyptians prepare for life after death?

god Hapi and the sun god Re. They were important because the Egyptians depended on the river and the sun. The river brought them water and fertile soil. The sun helped their crops to grow.

Another important god was Osiris, the god of the harvest and of eternal life. According to Egyptian legend, Osiris was an early pharaoh who gave his people laws and taught them farming. He and his wife Isis ruled over the dead. The Egyptians believed that the souls of the dead went to the underworld. There they were weighed on a scale. If a person had led a good life and knew certain magic spells, the scales balanced. Then Osiris would grant the person life after death. To learn the correct magic spells, the Egyptians studied a special book called the *Book of the Dead.*

The Egyptians also used a process called **embalming** to preserve the bodies of the dead. At first they used the process to preserve the body of the pharaoh. Later the custom of embalming became more widespread. To embalm a body, the Egyptians placed it in a wooden box and covered it with a chemical called natron. Natron dried up the water in the body, causing the body to shrink. After the shrunken body had dried, it was wrapped with long strips of linen. The wrapped body was known as a **mummy**. The mummy of a poor person was usually buried in a cave or in the sand. The mummy of a rich person was placed inside a special case or coffin, on which an artist had painted the person's portrait. The coffin was then placed in a tomb.

1. Who were some Egyptian gods? What did they do?
2. What did the Egyptians believe happened to a person after death?
3. How did the Egyptians preserve a person's body after death?

THE MIDDLE KINGDOM

Around 2300 B.C. government officials, jealous of the pharaoh's power, took control of Egypt. Almost 200 years of confusion followed. Finally a new line of pharaohs took over and again brought unity. Out of this unity came a new period called the Middle Kingdom.

A main difference between the Middle Kingdom and the Old Kingdom was that the pharaoh had less power. After death pharaohs were no longer buried in pyramids. Instead, they were

ANCIENT EGYPT

buried in tombs cut into cliffs. Another difference was that the Egyptians began to trade with countries beyond the Nile Valley.

The Middle Kingdom lasted over 300 years. It came to an end in 1750 B.C. when Egypt was invaded by the Hyksos, a people from western Asia. The Hyksos crossed the desert in horse-drawn chariots and used weapons made of bronze and iron. The Egyptians had always fought on foot with weapons made of copper and stone. They were not used to the Hyksos' weapons or style of fighting and were defeated.

The Hyksos ruled Egypt for about 150 years. They copied some Egyptian customs and tried to get the support of the Egyptian people. But the Egyptians hated them and worked to gain their freedom. Around 1600 B.C. an Egyptian prince named Ahmose, using Hyksos weapons and style of fighting, led an uprising and drove the Hyksos out of Egypt.

1. How did the Middle Kingdom come about?
2. Who were the Hyksos? How did they defeat the Egyptians?
3. What ended Hyksos rule?

THE NEW KINGDOM

Ahmose founded another line of pharaohs and began the period known as the New Kingdom. During this time Egypt changed in many ways. It became richer, and its cities grew larger.

Ramses II

During the New Kingdom most pharaohs were interested mainly in war and conquest. They were no longer content to remain within the Nile Valley but marched their armies into lands to the east. It was during this period that the Egyptian empire was established. One warrior-pharaoh, Thutmose III, with an army of 20,000 archers, spear throwers, and charioteers, expanded Egyptian control into Syria and Palestine.

One of the few pharaohs who was not interested in conquest was Hatshepsut, Thutmose III's stepmother. Her main interests were trade and the building of temples. During her rule Egyptian traders sailed along the coast of east Africa and brought new wealth into Egypt.

1. What were some of the changes that took place in Egypt during the New Kingdom?
2. How was Hatshepsut different from the other pharaohs of the New Kingdom?

KARNAK TEMPLE
Warring pharaohs of the New Kingdom built large temples. Ramses II, who ruled the Egyptian Empire at its height, built this temple at Karnak to honor the god Amen. The temple has many statues and monuments.
What do temples reveal about the way the pharaohs ruled?

RELIGION The Egyptians of the New Kingdom began to worship a new god. As the god of the city of Thebes, his name had been Amen. When Thebes became the capital of Egypt, the Egyptians combined the god Amen with their sun god Re. They called the new god Amen-Re. He became the most powerful god of all, and people built many temples in his honor. These temples were built in part by slaves who had been captured by the warring pharaohs.

The temples were more than houses of worship. They were industrial centers, treasuries, and schools. As industrial centers, they provided work for the sculptors and craftspeople who carved statues, built furniture, and made clothes for the priests. As treasuries, their warehouses flowed over with copper, gold jewelry, glass bottles, bundles of grain, dried fish, and sweet-smelling oils. As schools, the temples were places where young boys were trained to be scribes. The right to be a scribe was hereditary.

The scribes wrote religious works which included spells, charms, and prayers. They kept records of the pharaohs' laws and lists of the grain and animals paid as taxes. They copied fairy tales and adventure stories. The scribes also wrote down medical prescriptions.

There were several kinds of Egyptian writing. One was the **hieroglyphic system**, or a writing system based on pictures. The Egyptians carved and painted **hieroglyphs**, or picture symbols, on their monuments. However, the scribes needed an easier form of writing to keep records. So they developed two other kinds of writing in which hieroglyphs were rounded off and connected.

1. For what purposes were Amen-Re's temples used?
2. What did scribes do?

DECLINE OF EGYPT   Over time the priests of Amen-Re gained much power and wealth. They owned one-third of Egypt's land and began to influence government decisions. As time passed, the pharaoh's power declined.

HIEROGLYPHS

Ancient Egyptians viewed hieroglyphs as a gift from the gods. The pictures were first used as a way of keeping records. Later they represented the sounds of spoken language. Here hieroglyphs are painted on a coffin lid.
How did hieroglyphs differ from cuneiform?

Cat Mummy

Then, about 1370 B.C., a new pharaoh named Amenhotep IV came to the throne. He did not like the priests. He did not agree with them on what was good for the country. He wanted Egyptians to look to the pharaoh for both religious and political leadership. Amenhotep IV closed the temples of Amen-Re and fired all the temple workers. He set up his own religion and god, Aton. He changed his name to Akhnaton, which means "Spirit of Aton." But only his family and close advisors accepted the new religion. After Amenhotep IV's death the priests forced the new pharaoh to return to the older religion.

Little by little Egypt lost its power. Several things helped to make Egypt weak. One was the struggle between the priests and the pharaohs. Another was the pharaohs' attempts to keep neighboring countries under Egyptian control. Too much energy and money was spent on war. Then, too, other peoples of the eastern Mediterranean were beginning to use iron weapons. Since Egypt had no iron ore, a great deal of money was spent to bring in small amounts to make weapons.

By 1150 B.C. Egypt's empire was gone. Over the next several **centuries**, or periods of 100 years, Egyptian civilization continued to decline until Egypt was conquered by a people called Assyrians in 672 B.C.

1. What did Amenhotep IV do?
2. Why did Egypt become weak?

CONTRIBUTIONS OF THE EGYPTIANS

The Egyptians made many contributions to other civilizations. One was a type of paper called **papyrus**. It was made from a reed also called papyrus. To make paper, the Egyptians cut the stems of the reed into thin strips which were pressed together to make a sheet. Then they pasted the sheets together to make a roll. Some rolls were as long as 100 feet, or 30 meters. In order to write on papyrus, the Egyptians invented ink. The dry climate of Egypt preserved some writings so well that they can still be read today.

Papyrus had other uses, too. It was made into baskets and sandals. It was tied in bundles to make columns for houses. Even rafts and riverboats were made of papyrus.

The Egyptians were excellent mathematicians. They used a number system based on 10. They also used fractions and whole numbers. They used geometry to **survey**, or measure, land. When floodwaters washed away the boundary markers that separated one field from the next, the Egyptians surveyed the fields to see where one began and the other ended.

The Egyptians knew the Nile flooded about the same time every year. They used this knowledge to develop a calendar. The calendar contained three seasons of 120 days each, plus five special feast days for the gods.

The Egyptians also made contributions in the field of medicine. As dentists, eye doctors, veterinarians, and surgeons,

---

MEDICAL PRACTICE IN ANCIENT EGYPT

An Egyptian doctor gives medicine to a patient. The doctor's assistant holds a scroll listing directions for treating the illness. Egyptian skill in medicine was highly valued in the Mediterranean area for 2500 years.

What kind of medical help did Egyptian doctors give their patients?

Egyptian doctors were the first medical specialists. The Egyptians were the first to use splints, bandages, and compresses. They were experts at sewing up cuts and at setting and splinting broken bones. They treated less serious problems, too, such as indigestion and baldness. For indigestion they used castor oil. For baldness they used a mixture of dog toes, dates, and a donkey hoof.

1. What were some contributions the Egyptians made to other civilizations?

CHAPTER REVIEW

SUMMARY

1. Egyptian civilization began in the Nile River valley over 5000 years ago.

2. About 3100 B.C. Narmer united Upper and Lower Egypt into one nation.

3. The Old Kingdom began around 2700 B.C. and lasted for about 650 years.

4. The kings of Egypt became known as pharaohs and were viewed by the Egyptians as rulers, priests, and gods.

5. During the Old Kingdom pyramids were built as tombs for the pharaohs.

6. The Egyptians worshiped many gods.

7. The Egyptians placed great importance on life after death and created a process to preserve bodies as mummies.

8. The Middle Kingdom began about 2100 B.C. and lasted until the Hyksos' invasion of Egypt in 1750 B.C.

9. The New Kingdom began after Ahmose, an Egyptian prince, drove the Hyksos out of Egypt around 1600 B.C.

10. During the New Kingdom most of the pharaohs were interested mainly in war and conquest.

11. During the New Kingdom the priests of Amen-Re became very powerful.

12. The pharaoh Amenhotep IV, or Aknaton, tried to establish a new religion in Egypt around 1370 B.C. but did not succeed.

13. Toward the end of the New Kingdom, Egypt began to decline.

14. The Egyptians made several contributions to later civilizations, including surveying, certain medical treatments, and a paper called papyrus.

BUILDING VOCABULARY

1. *Identify the following:*

Egypt	Re	Middle Kingdom	Thutmose III
Nile	Hapi	Hyksos	Hatshepsut
Old Kingdom	Osiris	Ahmose	Amen-Re
Narmer	*Book of the Dead*	New Kingdom	Amenhotep IV

2. *Define the following:*

delta	kingdoms	embalming	centuries
cataracts	pharaoh	mummy	papyrus
basins	granaries	hieroglyphic system	survey
shadoof	pyramids	hieroglyphs	

REVIEWING THE FACTS

1. What did the Egyptians borrow from the Sumerians?

2. What did the Nile give to the Egyptian people?

3. What did Egyptian farmers do when they were not working in the fields?

4. Why did the Egyptians show such great respect for the pharaoh?

5. How did the Middle Kingdom differ from the Old Kingdom?

6. What role did the Hyksos play in the development of Egyptian civilization?

7. How did the New Kingdom differ from the Middle Kingdom?

8. What kinds of writing did the Egyptians have and what were they used for?

9. Why did Akhnaton oppose the priests of Amen-Re?

10. How did the Egyptians use the papyrus reed?

DISCUSSING IMPORTANT IDEAS

1. Why do you think some experts call Egypt "the gift of the Nile?" Do you think that is a good name? Explain.

2. Why was religion an important part of Egyptian life?

3. Why were scribes important to Egyptian government?

4. Do you think Akhnaton was wise to oppose the priests of Amen-Re? Give reasons for your opinion.

USING MAPS

Refer to the map on page 62, and answer the following questions:

1. What is the time period of the map of ancient Egypt?

2. How many kingdoms are shown?

3. During which kingdom did ancient Egypt occupy the largest area?

4. Which river is longer—the Nile or the Euphrates? How can you tell?

5. Which city—Memphis or Thebes—is further south? How can you tell?

6. How far is Memphis from Thebes?

EBLA

In the 1970's archaeologists working in northwest Syria uncovered the ruins of an ancient city. By studying and translating some of the clay tablets they found in the ruins, they learned of a great civilization called Ebla.

Ebla existed between 2700 B.C. and 2200 B.C. The archaeologists discovered that Ebla had been as great a power in the ancient Near East as Egypt or Mesopotamia. Ebla was an important trading center. It grew wealthy through trade agreements with neighboring states. Ebla's wealth helped it become a large and powerful city-state.

Approximately 30,000 people lived inside the walls that surrounded Ebla.

Another 230,000 people lived in the suburbs and in the nearby city-states that Ebla controlled. These city-states paid **tribute**, or taxes, to Ebla in grain and livestock.

The people of Ebla were called Eblaites. They were closely related to the Phoenicians, a people from the plains north of Mesopotamia, and to the Hebrews, a people from the deserts south of Mesopotamia. The Eblaites spoke a language much like ancient Hebrew. Most earned their living by making metal and wood products, textiles, and pottery.

People entered and left Ebla through four gates, each of which was dedicated to a different god. Streets led from the gates to the center of the city where the temples and the king's palace stood. The walls of the palace were 50 feet, or about 15 meters, high. Inside was a large **archive**, or place to store records. There, more than 15,000 clay tablets were kept on wooden shelves. A great stairway with steps inlaid with shell led to the audience court of the palace. There the king met with people who wanted his help.

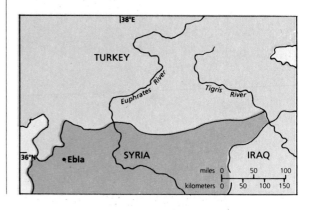

The kings of Ebla were elected by the people for seven years. They were responsible for the welfare of widows, orphans, and the poor. The kings had to account to the people for their actions. A king who did not do his duty could be removed.

The king had close to 12,000 government officials helping him. Most of the kings could not read or write. As a result, scribes carried out the royal decrees and handled the daily activities of the government. They wrote peace agreements, kept trading records, and described events. They also collected prayers and hymns. The scribes kept their records on clay tablets, which they covered on both sides with columns of Sumerian cuneiform.

The kings of Ebla were powerful and prosperous until about 2400 B.C. Then they went to war with Sargon I of Akkad over the Euphrates River. Whoever controlled the river gained the trade in metals from Asia Minor and in wood from Syrian forests near the Mediterranean. Around 2300 B.C. Sargon I defeated the Eblaites.

Later, Sargon I's grandson Naram-Sin captured and burned Ebla. Although the city rose again, it did not survive for long. In 2000 B.C. it was destroyed by the Amorites, who rebuilt it and introduced a new culture. After 1800 B.C., however, the city once again declined. Within 200 years it had disappeared completely.

1. How did archaeologists find out about Ebla?
2. How was Ebla ruled?
3. What led to the fall of Ebla?

CHAPTER 6
EASTERN RIVER VALLEYS

In 3500 B.C. civilization began in Sumer. Some 400 years later it began in Egypt. Several hundred years after that, river valley civilizations began to appear in the East. By 2500 B.C. cities started to develop in the Indus River valley of South Asia. By 1500 B.C. they were being established in the Yellow River valley of China.

The people of these eastern civilizations were more isolated than the people of Mesopotamia or Egypt. They were cut off from other parts of the world by high mountains, broad deserts, and large bodies of water. As a result, they became **self-sufficient**, or able to take care of all of their needs. Compared to the Sumerians and the Egyptians, they did little trading.

Less is known about life in the eastern civilizations than is known about Sumerian or Egyptian life. Very few remains have been found of the ancient eastern civilizations. Much of what is known about them comes from legend. Until more records are found, the early life of these eastern peoples will remain in part a mystery.

The Indus River Valley

The Indus River flows through the countries known today as Pakistan and India. About 2500 B.C. a group of people called Harappans settled in the valley of the Indus. Although others had lived there before, the Harappans were the first to create a civilization. Harappan civilization extended about 1000 miles, or 1600 kilometers, from the foothills of the Himalayas to the Indian Ocean. This was more than twice the size of either Mesopotamia or Egypt.

The lives of the people were shaped by the Indus River. The river fertilized the land and made its soil rich. But when the river flooded, it swept away everything in its path. The people had to control the Indus in order to settle near it. To do this, they built dikes and dams. They cleared the land for farming. They built irrigation systems to bring the water to their dry land. They grew crops of barley, wheat, peas, melons, and dates. They also fished in the river.

The Harappans were the earliest known people to grow cotton. They spun the cotton, wove it into cloth, and dyed it bright colors. They produced cotton cloth hundreds of years before anyone else.

The river influenced the way Harappans built their cities. To protect the cities from floods, the Harappans built them on raised mounds. They used the soft river mud to make bricks, which they baked in the sun. Then they went one step further. They **fired**, or baked, some bricks in **kilns**, or ovens. They used these kiln-dried bricks as a covering over the mud bricks. These fired bricks were stronger and lasted much longer than the

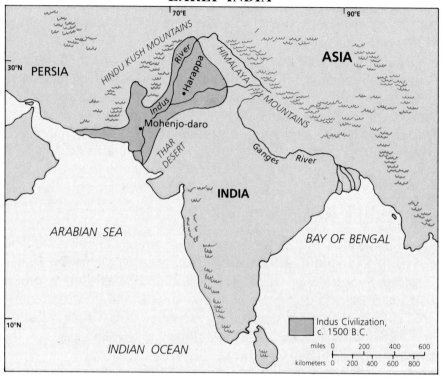

sun-dried ones. The Harappans used the fired bricks for their houses and public buildings.

1. Who were the Harappans?
2. In what ways did the Indus River influence the Harappans?
3. How did the Harappans make bricks?

HARAPPA AND MOHENJO-DARO   Harappan civilization centered around two major cities, Harappa and Mohenjo-daro. These cities were about 400 miles, or 640 kilometers, apart. Many experts believe they were twin capitals.

Harappa and Mohenjo-daro are the oldest examples yet found of **planned communities**, or cities built to a definite plan. Both cities contained hundreds of small buildings. Some of the buildings served as homes, while others served as shops. The buildings were laid out on a planned street **grid**, or uniform network. The streets crossed each other at almost perfect right angles. The buildings that lined the streets were arranged in blocks of about the same size.

Most of the buildings were two stories high and were built around a courtyard. The courtyard opened into several rooms. The outer walls of the buildings had no windows, and the walls fronted on narrow lanes in such a way as to break the force of the wind. Almost every building had its own well, a bathroom, and drains. The drains carried waste away from the houses and emptied it into drain holes lined with brick. These drains were cleaned often. This sanitation system helped protect the health of the Harappan people.

The more important buildings of Harappa and Mohenjo-daro were built high above the houses and shops so as to be safe from neighboring peoples and floods. In each city a **citadel**, or fortress, stood on a mound at least 40 feet, or 12 meters, high. It was surrounded by a thick brick wall. Inside the citadel at

---

THE GREAT BATH AT MOHENJO-DARO

The people of Mohenjo-daro may have washed themselves at the Great Bath. To make the Bath watertight, they used cement, tar, and four layers of brick.
What was the purpose of the Great Bath?

Mohenjo-daro was a huge watertight tank called the "Great Bath." Some experts believe it was used for religious ceremonies or baths. Next to the Great Bath stood a huge granary. Traders from other regions who stopped at Mohenjo-daro probably left their goods there.

Harappa also contained a series of huge granaries. The floor of each granary was supported on low walls. In the walls were air holes that allowed the air to move around in the granary. This kept the grain dry and prevented it from spoiling. Nearby were circular brick platforms. Each had a scooped out area in the center where grain could be pounded. The platforms were placed so that workers pounding grain could be watched over from the citadel.

1. In what ways were Harappa and Mohenjo-daro alike?
2. What were some of the outstanding features of Harappa and Mohenjo-daro?

DECLINE OF THE HARAPPANS   No one knows for certain how Harappan civilization came to an end. One reason may have been that the people used up their **natural resources**, or materials supplied by nature. For example, farmers may have tried to raise more and more crops on the same plots. This would have robbed the soil of chemicals needed to make it fertile enough to produce well. Without good harvests there would not have been enough food to feed everyone, especially if the Harappan population was increasing.

Another reason may have been that the Harappans cut down too many trees to fuel their ovens. Without tree cover, the floods became heavier and forced the people to leave their cities and farming villages and move on. It is known that parts of Mohenjo-daro had to be rebuilt several times because of floods. At first the city was rebuilt carefully. But as time went on, the new buildings were not made as well, and the older ones were patched up. Then, too, the people may just have gotten tired of rebuilding and decided to move somewhere else.

A third reason may have been that the Indus valley was invaded. The Harappans could not defend themselves, and all were killed. Unburied skeletons of groups of men, women, and children were found in the streets of the ruins of Mohenjo-daro. Every skeleton showed some kind of injury.

All that is certain is Harappan civilization began to change about 1500 B.C. Homes were no longer built as well. Pottery was no longer made as carefully. By 1200 B.C. a group of people called Aryans had taken over the Indus valley, and Harappan civilization ceased to be.

1. What are three possible reasons why Harappan civilization came to an end?

EVIDENCE OF A LOST CIVILIZATION   Very little is known about the Harappan people and their civilization. As yet, no one has been able to read Harappan writing. There is no record of the civilization's political history. No royal tombs have been discovered. All that is known about Harappan religion is that the people had more than one god and most were female.

Much of what is known comes from the ruins of Harappa and Mohenjo-daro. There scientists have found jewelry made of gold and a blue stone called lapis lazuli, as well as weapons of stone, copper, and bronze. Scientists have also found clay models of animals, rattles, dice, and toy carts with movable wheels. The carts are very much like those many farmers of Pakistan and India use today to transport goods.

One of the most important finds was a series of tiny seals made of soapstone. An animal and a line of writing were carved

---

HARAPPAN SEAL
    This Harappan seal is 1 inch, or 6.5 centimeters, square. It shows a bull facing an incense burner. In eastern civilizations the bull was a symbol of strength. The seal also shows the mysterious Harappan writing.
How did Harappans use seals?

---

on each seal. Most of the seals had a small hole in them and could be worn as necklaces or bracelets. The seals may have stated the names, titles, or trades of a person, family, or business. Experts believe the seals were used to stamp the wet clay that sealed packages of goods. Some Harappan seals have been found as far away as Sumer.

1. Why is so little known about the Harappans?
2. What examples of Harappan civilization have experts found?

THE YELLOW RIVER VALLEY

About 2000 B.C., or 500 years after the Harappans settled in the Indus River valley, a civilization developed in the Yellow River valley of northern China. There are no records of its beginnings, and no remains have been found. For this reason, much of what happened comes from legend.

According to Chinese legend, a man-god named Yü the Great drove out the serpents and dragons that lived along the

---

THE WISE MAN FU HSI

The Chinese used legends of man-gods to explain the beginnings of their civilization. One legend was about Yü. Another was about Fu Hsi. In this drawing, Fu Hsi points to eight geometric designs used to tell the future. He discovered them by studying the marks on the back of a turtle.

Why do modern historians study legends?

SHANG CHINA

Yellow River. He drained the land so that people could live there and grow crops. He also made the rivers flow to the east. Yü founded a kingdom called Hsia. He is believed to have united most of northern China under his rule.

Many experts believe that the early settlers of China chose the Yellow River valley for their home because it was fertile. The river flooded every year, bringing rich soil with it. But since the flood could also wipe out everything in its path, the Chinese call the river "the great sorrow."

The valley was cut off from other civilizations. The people who lived there developed their way of life without borrowing from other civilizations. By 1800 B.C. there were villages and farms all along the river. The people farmed the land and used the river for travel and some trade. They made clay ovens, cupboards, benches, and pottery, and built small round clay houses with thatched roofs.

CITIES OF THE SHANG   The first records of Chinese civilization come from a **dynasty**, or ruling family, called Shang. The Shang came to power in 1523 B.C. They built the first

Chinese cities. Most were designed in the same way. At the center stood a palace and a temple. Public buildings and the homes of high government officials were built around the palace. An outer district surrounded the city's center. Within this district were workshops, burial grounds, and the homes of the poor.

Most of the Shang people, however, did not live in the city. The city was the home of the rich, the learned, and the skilled. The poorer people lived in the countryside. They were farmers who grew such grains as millet, wheat, and rice. They also raised cattle, sheep, and hens. They produced the silk used to make the clothes of the very rich.

1. Who were the Shang?
2. What were Shang cities like? Who lived in them?
3. Where and how did the poorer Shang people live?

Shang Vessel

SPIRITS, ANCESTORS, AND KINGS   The Shang worshipped **spirits**, or supernatural beings, which they believed lived in the mountains, rivers, and seas. The people believed they had to please the spirits. If the spirits became angry or unhappy, the people might suffer a poor harvest or lose a battle.

The Shang believed that **ancestors**, or those from whom one is descended, also influenced people's fortunes. So they offered their ancestors food, wine, and special prayers. They hoped that their ancestors would help them in time of need and bring them good fortune. Because of this respect for ancestors, family ties were very important to the Shang. They had rules about how family members should act toward one another. The young were taught to obey their parents and to respect older people. Wives were trained to obey their husbands.

The Shang believed that their kings received their power from the spirits of nature and their wisdom from their ancestors. For this reason, religion and government were closely linked. An important duty of the king was to contact the nature spirits to make sure that they provided enough water for farming.

Kings also asked the advice of their ancestors before making important decisions. They had messages scratched on a flat, polished piece of bone. The bone had a hole drilled in it. A hot bar was put in the hole. The heat from the bar produced a pattern of cracks on the bone. The cracks were believed to be the ancestors' replies to a king's question. A special interpreter gave the king the meaning of the ancestors' replies. These bones are known as **oracle bones**. The writing on them is the oldest known form of Chinese writing.

Under the kings was a large class of **nobles,** or people of high rank in a kingdom. They spent much of their time hunting for pleasure and as a preparation for war. The nobles often fought with each other about land. They united only when they had to fight other people who refused to accept Shang rule.

The nobles rode into battle in horse-drawn bronze chariots. They wore bronze helmets and armor made of buffalo or rhinoceros hide. They were skilled in the use of the bow and arrow. Their arrows had sharp points of bone or bronze. Soldiers marched on foot behind the nobles' chariots. These soldiers usually were poor peasants whom the nobles had forced to leave their farms and join the army.

1. How did the Shang people feel about the nature spirits? About their ancestors?
2. What was the role of Shang kings?
3. How did the nobles spend much of their time?

SHANG ELEPHANT

This richly decorated bronze elephant is 9 inches, or 22.5 centimeters, in height. It is an example of the high quality of Shang art. The Shang made bronzes of real and imaginary animals.

For what purpose did the Shang use items of bronze?

Shang Dagger

DECLINE OF THE SHANG   There was a large gap between the rich and the poor during the rule of the Shang. The rich lived in cities in wooden houses. They owned bronze weapons and ornaments, and wore linen, wool, fur, and silk clothes. The poor lived in the countryside and worked with wooden or stone tools. Their houses were thatched or mud huts or caves scooped out of the ground. Neither group felt any loyalty toward the other.

Many experts believe that this gap between rich and poor weakened the Shang civilization. In 1028 B.C. a people known as Chou invaded the Shang kingdom. The Shang nobles and peasants were not united enough to resist the invaders. Shang civilization came to an end.

The Shang left behind a great gift to the world in their works of bronze. These included sculptures, cups, vases, fancy vessels, and other items used for religious purposes. Art experts consider these objects the finest works of bronze ever made.

1. What may have been one reason for the decline of Shang civilization?
2. What did the Shang give to the world?

CHAPTER REVIEW

SUMMARY

1. Eastern river valley civilizations began to develop in the Indus River valley about 2500 B.C. and the Yellow River valley about 2000 B.C.

2. The first known people to establish a civilization in the Indus River valley were the Harappans.

3. Like other river valley peoples, the Harappans learned to control the river.

4. The Harappans are believed to have been the first people to produce cotton cloth, to bake bricks in ovens, and to construct sanitation systems.

5. The Harappan cities of Harappa and Mohenjo-daro are the oldest known planned communities.

6. No one knows for certain how Harappan civilization came to an end, but about 1200 B.C. Aryans moved into and took over the Indus River valley.

7. The earliest dynasty in China, the Hsia, probably started about 2000 B.C.

8. The first recorded Chinese dynasty, the Shang, came to power in 1523 B.C.

9. The Shang believed that their lives were influenced by spirits and ancestors.

10. The oldest known form of Chinese writing is found on Shang oracle bones.

11. The Shang produced many fine works of art made from bronze.

12. Shang civilization ended with the Chou invasion about 1028 B.C.

BUILDING VOCABULARY

1. *Identify the following:*

Indus River	Harappa	Aryans	Shang
Yellow River	Mohenjo-daro	Yü the Great	Chou
Harappans	Great Bath	Hsia	

2. *Define the following:*

self-sufficient	planned communities	natural resources	ancestors
fired	grid	dynasty	oracle bones
kilns	citadel	spirits	nobles

REVIEWING THE FACTS

1. How did the Harappans protect their cities from floods?

2. Why were oven-fired bricks more useful than sun-baked ones?

3. Why were Harappa and Mohenjo-daro healthy places in which to live?

4. Who took over the Indus valley from the Harappans?

5. What evidence suggests the possibility of trade between Harappa and Sumer?

6. What is the Chinese legend of Yü the Great?

7. Why do the Chinese call the Yellow River "the great sorrow?"

8. Why were family ties important to the Shang people?

9. What did the Shang kings use oracle bones for?

10. Why was the gap between rich and poor a disadvantage to the Shang?

DISCUSSING IMPORTANT IDEAS

1. Why is so little known about the early life of people in the Indus River and Yellow River valleys?

2. Why did the peoples of eastern river valleys develop their ways of life without borrowing from other civilizations?

3. What do you think may happen to a civilization if it uses up its natural resources? Why?

4. What may happen to a civilization if different classes are not loyal to each other?

USING MAPS

Compare the maps on pages 74 and 79, and answer the following questions:

1. Which civilization—early Indian or Shang China—occupied a larger area?

2. Which civilization—early Indian or Shang China—is further east? Further south? How can you tell?

3. Which river—the Indus or the Yellow—is the longer?

4. Which civilization—early Indian or Shang China—appears to lie in a more mountainous region?

UNIT REVIEW

SUMMARY

1. Around 4000 B.C. civilization began developing along river banks in different parts of the world.
2. People learned how to control the rivers, depended mostly on farming for a living, and built cities and developed writing.
3. Each of the four earliest civilizations developed separately.
4. Each of the earliest civilizations contributed many things to later civilizations, including the wheel, plow, surveying, sanitation, and medical treatments.

REVIEWING THE MAIN IDEAS

1. For each of the four civilizations in the unit, explain how the environment influenced the way the people lived.
2. Explain in what ways the four civilizations described in the unit were alike and in what ways they were different. Include the following:
   a. how the people earned their living
   b. how the people controlled the river
   c. materials used for building
   d. form of government
   e. religious beliefs
   f. importance of trade
   g. ways of traveling
   h. influence of other civilizations
   i. contributions to other civilizations
   j. reasons why the civilization came to an end

DEVELOPING SKILLS

In studying history, it is important to be able to read maps. A person can learn many things about a civilization from maps. They tell where a civilization is located and what natural features, such as rivers, are found there. They tell where people built their cities. They tell about the distances between places and in what direction one place is from another.

Some maps tell other things, too. They tell whether the land is flat or hilly. They tell whether there is enough rainfall for farming or if the land is a desert where few crops will grow. They tell something about the climate—whether it is mostly hot or cold or has four seasons in the year. They tell about the natural resources.

Without maps, it would be difficult to know as much about how people lived in the past.

This exercise is designed to give you practice in reading a map. Look at the map of the river valley civilizations on page 85, and answer the following questions.

1. On what **continent,** or large mass of land, were three of the four river valley civilizations located?
2. Into what body of water does the Nile River flow?
3. What two river valley civilizations could be reached directly by ships sailing on the Indian Ocean?
4. In what direction does the Yellow River flow?

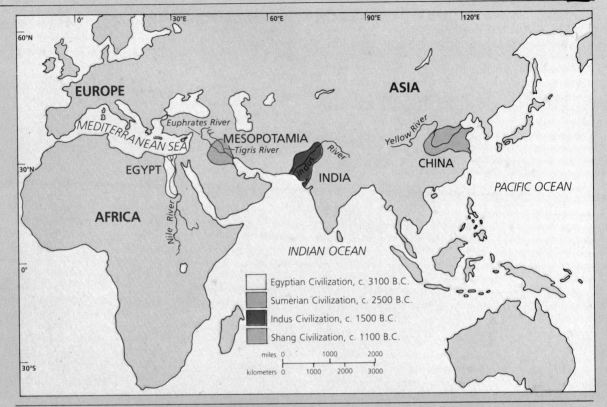

Egyptian Civilization, c. 3100 B.C.
Sumerian Civilization, c. 2500 B.C.
Indus Civilization, c. 1500 B.C.
Shang Civilization, c. 1100 B.C.

SUGGESTED UNIT PROJECTS

1. Write a letter that an Egyptian farmer working on a pyramid might send home.

2. Make a tablet out of clay, and put a line of cuneiform writing on it.

3. Prepare an advertisement for a Sumerian school. Include the courses offered and the jobs graduates can fill.

4. Describe the sights a Harappan farmer in Mohenjo-daro would find impressive.

5. Take the role of a Shang ruler, and have three classmates take the roles of a noble, a farmer, and a married woman. Discuss the similarities and differences in the way each person views life.

SUGGESTED READING

Hodges, Elizabeth Jamison. *A Song for Gilgamesh.* New York: Atheneum Publishers, 1971. Weaves the story of a Sumerian potter with Gilgamesh's journey to the Land of the Living.

Macauley, David. *Pyramid.* Boston: Houghton Mifflin Company, 1975. An illustrated account of the building of a pyramid combined with many facts about Egyptian culture.

Westwood, Jennifer. *Gilgamesh, and Other Babylonian Tales.* New York: Coward, McCann & Geoghegan, 1970. A retelling of ancient tales that captures the style and flavor of the originals.

UNIT 3

2025 B.C. **c. 2000 B.C.** Persians settle in Iran	1950 B.C. **c. 1900 B.C.** Abraham leads Hebrews into Canaan	1875 B.C. 

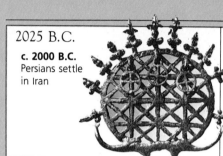

1575 B.C.	1500 B.C.	1425 B.C. **c. 1400 B.C.** Hittites refine iron or

1125 B.C. **c. 1100 B.C.** Assyrian Kingdom expands	1050 B.C.	975 B.C. **1000 B.C.** David rules Hebrews **c. 969 B.C.** Phoenician trade increases **922 B.C.** Hebrews establish two kingdoms

675 B.C.	600 B.C. **612 B.C.** Ninevah falls to Chaldeans **c. 600 B.C.** Medes defeat Persians **550 B.C.** Cyrus founds Persian Empire	525 B.C. **515 B.C.** Hebrews rebuild Jerusalem **521 B.C.** Darius's reign begins in Persia **539 B.C.** Persians capture Babylon

225 B.C. 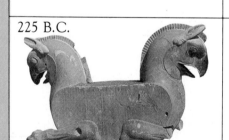	150 B.C.	75 B.C. 

IDEAS AND ARMIES

300 B.C.	1725 B.C.	1650 B.C.
c. 1830 B.C. Phoenicians settle in northern Canaan **1800 B.C.** Hebrews migrate to Egypt		
350 B.C.	1275 B.C.	1200 B.C. **c. 1200 B.C.** Phoenicians develop alphabet
	c. 1240 B.C. Moses leads Hebrews out of Egypt	
00 B.C.	825 B.C. **814 B.C.** Phoenicians found Carthage **800 B.C.** Assyrians conquer Mesopotamia	750 B.C. **722 B.C.** Assyrians conquer Israel
50	375 B.C.	300 B.C.
	**c. 300's B.C.** Civil war occurs in Persian Empire	

1. WHAT WERE THE IMPORTANT CULTURAL AND RELIGIOUS CONTRIBUTIONS OF THE PHOENICIANS AND HEBREWS?

2. HOW DID THE RISE OF EMPIRES AFFECT THE ANCIENT PEOPLES OF THE MIDDLE EAST?

From 1200 to 900 B.C. the Middle East went through a time of confusion. Egypt and Mesopotamia had lost much of their power and wealth. Many peoples of the Middle East were on the move, wandering here and there. Some of these wanderers came from the plains north of Mesopotamia. Others came from the desert areas to the south. Bad harvests or the need for grazing land forced them to find new places to live.

As time passed, the wanderers founded permanent settlements and began to develop new civilizations. Small groups, such as the Phoenicians and Hebrews, settled near the eastern end of the Mediterranean Sea. There they set up small kingdoms and learned to live in peace. They developed new ideas, like the alphabet and belief in one god, and became interested in trade. Others, such as the Assyrians, Chaldeans, and Persians, formed powerful nations. The Assyrians and Chaldeans established themselves in southern Mesopotamia. The Persians settled in the mountains between Mesopotamia and India.

The kings of the new nations were interested in war as well as in trade and ideas. They raised strong armies to protect their kingdoms. At the same time, they looked beyond their borders. They fought each other for control of trade routes, ports, and mountain passes.

Some of the kings were very successful. They created and ruled over empires which rose and fell. Kings had problems defending such large areas. They also found it hard to control the peoples they conquered. In spite of these weaknesses, however, each empire contributed to the development of the Middle East.

CHAPTER 7

PHOENICIANS AND HEBREWS

At the eastern end of the Mediterranean Sea lies a piece of land shared by Lebanon and Israel. In ancient times it was the bridge that connected Egypt and Mesopotamia, and it was known as Canaan. Soldiers, shepherds, and merchants who passed through Canaan carried new ideas and goods between Egypt and Mesopotamia.

Two groups—the Phoenicians and the Hebrews—settled in Canaan and formed small kingdoms. The Phoenicians and the Hebrews were interested in trade and in learning. Through these peaceful activities, they made important contributions to later civilizations.

THE PHOENICIANS

The Phoenicians lived in the northern part of Canaan. Most of what is known about them comes from the Bible, the writings of other ancient peoples, and the ruins of their cities and ships.

Two different groups formed the Phoenician people. One was the Canaanites, who came from the desert south and east of Canaan. The Canaanites were herders who wandered from pasture to pasture. The second group was the Aegeans, who came from the eastern Mediterranean near Greece. The Aegeans were traders and shipbuilders.

1. Who were the Phoenicians? From where did they come?

THE GROWTH OF TRADE   By 1200 B.C. the Phoenicians had built cities and towns along a narrow strip of land between the mountains and the sea. Though the land was fertile, there was not enough to grow food for all the people. Therefore, many Phoenicians turned to the sea to make a living.

PHOENICIAN TRADE

From the beginning of their history, the Phoenicians were sea-going traders. They opened up the entire Mediterranean to their horse-headed ships. Here Phoenician sailors unload cedar timber at a distant port.

Why was Phoenician trade important to the Mediterranean area?

The mountains that overlooked Phoenicia were covered with cedar forests. The forests provided timber which the Phoenicians used to build strong, fast ships. The Phoenicians also provided timber to the people of other lands. They started out as coastal traders. In time they became widely traveled merchant shippers who controlled the trade of the Mediterranean. They exchanged cedar logs, cloth, glass trinkets, and perfume for gold and other metals. Many Phoenician ships were traveling workshops. Sailors who were craftspeople carried their tools with them and worked on board the ships.

Phoenician sailors and explorers plotted their courses by the sun and the stars. They traveled to places where no one else dared to go. They brought the culture of the Middle East to unexplored areas of the western Mediterranean. Some experts believe that the Phoenicians actually sailed around the west coast of Africa to India. They may even have sailed across the Atlantic to the Americas 2000 years before Columbus.

From their business dealings, the Phoenicians learned the value of making agreements. They used the same idea to keep peace with their larger, more powerful neighbors. They signed peace **treaties**, or agreements between states or countries. Under the treaties the Phoenicians promised to supply free shipments of goods. In exchange, the other countries agreed to guarantee Phoenician independence.

1. Why did the Phoenicians turn to trade to make a living?
2. Where did the Phoenicians trade?
3. How did the Phoenicians keep peace with their powerful neighbors?

THE CITIES OF PHOENICIA   Phoenicia never became a united country. Mountains separated one group of Phoenicians from another. The only contact was through narrow mountain passes or by sea. As a result, Phoenicia remained a collection of independent city-states. The largest of these were Tyre, Byblos, Beirut, and Sidon.

Though the people of all the city-states spoke the same language and practiced the same religion, they did not always get along. The search for more profit from trade led to quarrels and jealousy. Phoenicians called themselves by the name of their city-state. Only outsiders called them Phoenicians.

PHOENICIAN CRAFTS
Many Phoenicians learned the craft skills of other lands and became artisans. The products of their workshops were known for their high quality. The amphora, or two-handled vase (left) held water, oil, and wine. Colorful glass beads (right) were exchanged in trade for such metals as gold.
What kinds of crafts were made in Phoenician cities?

At first each city-state was ruled by a king who also served as high priest. In time, rich merchant families forced the kings to share their power with councils of merchants. Soon the councils were telling the kings what to do.

Most Phoenician cities had stone walls around them for protection. Behind the walls stood the family-owned shops of merchants and craftspeople. Shopkeepers displayed and sold their goods outside the shops. Since timber was plentiful, many Phoenicians were excellent carpenters and cabinetmakers. They also excelled at metalwork, a skill learned from the Egyptians and Mesopotamians.

Phoenician cities were very crowded. The streets were narrow and the buildings close together. Most buildings were made of stone or brick and had high narrow doors, windows, columns, and tiled roofs. Some houses had roof gardens.

Outside the walls of the city stood the port. It was the center of activity. Ships docked to load and unload goods. Phoenician merchants kept records of shipments of papyrus, gold, and linen from Egypt, pottery from Mesopotamia, and copper and hides from Cyprus. The goods were stored in great warehouses near the docks until they went to market in Phoenicia or were shipped overseas.

The cities were important cloth-dyeing centers. The Phoenicians made an expensive purple dye that was in great demand. The name "Phoenician," in fact, means "the purple people." According to legend, a Phoenician god named Melqart was walking along the seashore with his girlfriend Tyrus and a dog. When the dog picked up a shellfish called a murex and bit into it, the dog's mouth turned purple. Tyrus liked the color so much that she said she would not marry Melqart unless he gave her a gown of that color. Melqart gave her the gown and started the dye-making trade in Phoenicia.

1. Why did Phoenicia remain a collection of city-states rather than becoming a united nation?
2. What were some of the features of a Phoenician city-state?
3. What is the legend of Melqart and Tyrus?

GODS AND GODDESSES   The Phoenicians believed in many gods who were closely linked to nature. Since they thought the gods met humans only on hills and under trees, they worshipped only in these places at first. Later they built temples. Each temple contained a **foyer**, or lobby; a main hall; and a **holy of holies**, where the image or sacred stone of a god was kept. Priests offered sacrifices of wine, perfume, animals, and humans at a nearby stone altar. Only priests could offer the sacrifices that strengthened the power of the gods and kept them friendly toward the people.

The Phoenicians believed in a life after death. At first they buried their dead in clay urns. Later, under Egyptian influence, they embalmed bodies, wrapped them in linen, and placed them in stone coffins in hillside cemeteries.

1. How did the Phoenicians view their gods?
2. Where did the Phoenicians worship before they built temples? Why did they worship there?
3. What were some features of Phoenician temples?

CARTHAGE   Some Phoenician sailors and traders set up trading posts all along the coast of North Africa. Other Phoenicians built **colonies**, or permanent settlements, in these areas. The settlements soon turned into cities.

The most famous of these cities was Carthage, founded in 814 B.C. in what is now Tunisia. Legend states that the city was founded by a Phoenician princess named Dido. Dido was the ruler of the city of Tyre. Her brother thought that he should rule instead. So he murdered Dido's husband and overthrew Dido. She fled to North Africa where she and her followers built Carthage.

Carthage soon became a Mediterranean power. It was a great trading city. Ships from Carthage may have traveled to the British Isles in search of tin, a metal highly valued by merchants.

1. Why did Phoenicians develop colonies along the coast of North Africa?
2. Who was Dido? What did she do?
3. Why was Carthage important?

THE ALPHABET   Through trade, Phoenicians spread ideas as well as goods. Their most important gift was the idea of an **alphabet**, or a series of symbols that stand for sounds. They did not invent the alphabet. They did, however, pass it on to others.

At first the Phoenicians used a system of picture writing. However, it was difficult to keep trade records this way. So the Phoenicians looked for an easier writing system. They borrowed from the people of the Canaanite towns that lay to the south a simple version of Egyptian hieroglyphs. By the time the Canaanite system of writing reached Phoenicia, it had become an alphabet.

The Canaanite system of writing had 22 symbols, or letters, from which any number of words could be formed. Since it was easy to use, the Canaanite system provided the writing system Phoenician traders needed for keeping records.

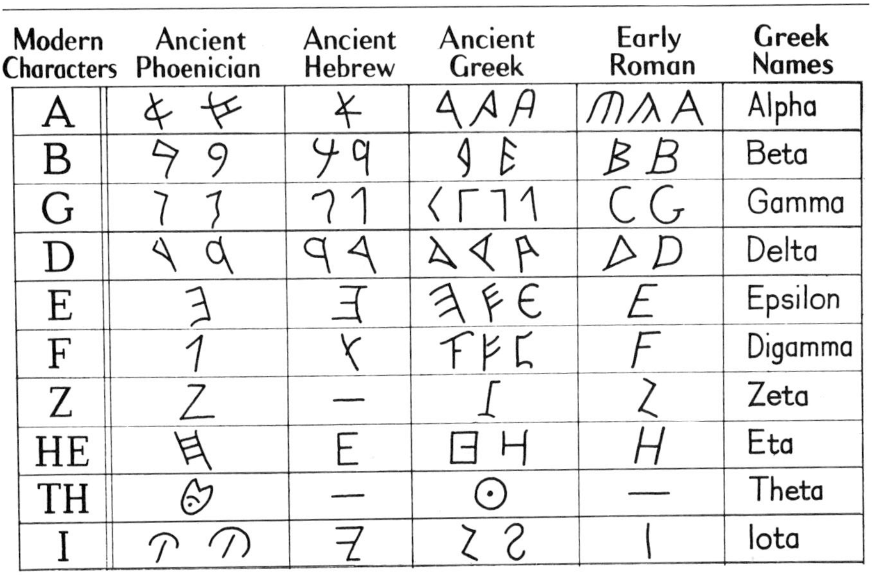

Modern Characters	Ancient Phoenician	Ancient Hebrew	Ancient Greek	Early Roman	Greek Names
A					Alpha
B					Beta
G					Gamma
D					Delta
E					Epsilon
F					Digamma
Z		—			Zeta
HE					Eta
TH		—		—	Theta
I					Iota

ALPHABETS

This chart shows how different alphabets developed from the Phoenician alphabet. The alphabets closely resemble each other in the shapes and names of the characters. How did the idea of an alphabet develop in the Mediterranean area?

The Phoenicians made the Canaanite alphabet their own. They carried it to Europe where the Greeks borrowed it and made a few changes. Later the Romans borrowed it from the Greeks. Most western alphabets, including the English, are based on the Roman alphabet.

1. Who created the alphabet?
2. Why were the Phoenicians interested in the alphabet?

THE HEBREWS

Like the Phoenicians, the Hebrews were a small group among the peoples of the ancient Middle East. Yet because of their religion, they have had a great influence on the world. Their religion still exists today. It is called Judaism.

The early Hebrews were traveling merchants. Leading long trains of donkeys loaded with goods, they walked from one trading post to the next. This habit of walking gave them their name. As they walked, their leather sandals and their donkeys' hooves kicked up much dust that settled on them. Other people began to call them *Abiru*, or "dusty ones." Later, Abiru became "Hebrew."

The Hebrews followed a route that started from the city of Ur on the Euphrates River. There Hebrew craftspeople made goods from gold, copper, and ivory. Hebrew merchants then stuffed the goods into bags, loaded them on donkeys, and started up the valley of the Tigris and Euphrates. At Harran, a city near the Turkish mountains, they exchanged the goods for silver. Sometimes the merchants continued westward and then south along the Mediterranean coast to trade with Egyptian, Phoenician, and Cretan merchants.

1. Who were the Hebrews? How did they get their name?
2. Where did the Hebrews trade? What did they trade?

THE GOD OF ABRAHAM   The story of the Hebrews and their god is written in the Bible. It states that Yahweh, or God,

PHOENICIA AND THE HEBREW KINGDOMS

ABRAHAM

Abraham taught the Hebrews to worship and obey Yahweh as the one true God. In this seventeenth-century painting, Abraham greets a friendly ruler who welcomes him to Canaan.

What kind of leader was Abraham?

made an agreement with Abraham, leader of the Hebrews. Abraham and his followers were to leave Ur and go to Canaan. There they were to worship and obey Yahweh as the one true god. In exchange, Yahweh promised that they and their descendants could always live in Canaan.

During ancient times most people believed in many gods. The gods behaved like humans but were more powerful. The Hebrews, however, believed that Yahweh was different from humans. Their god did not get hungry or thirsty, marry, or have children. Although Yahweh was powerful and could do whatever he wanted, he did only what was just and right.

Abraham led the Hebrews to Canaan around 1900 B.C. In Canaan, instead of trading, they raised flocks of sheep and grew wheat, figs, and olives. They stayed in Canaan for about 100 years. While there, the Hebrews organized themselves into 12

MOSES AT MOUNT SINAI
At Mount Sinai, God gave Moses the Ten Commandments on two stone tablets. This fifteenth-century European painting shows Moses receiving the Commandments and bringing them to the Hebrews. He throws down the tablets in anger when he sees the people worshipping a golden calf.
Why did Moses protest the worship of the golden calf?

tribes. Then a drought came, and they went to Egypt where they could get food.

1. Who was Abraham?
2. What agreement did God make with Abraham?
3. Why did the Hebrews leave their homes in Canaan? Where did they go?

MOSES AND THE TEN COMMANDMENTS   About 600 years after the Hebrews settled in Egypt, they were forced into slavery. Years later Moses, the Hebrew leader at the time, appeared before the pharaoh of Egypt. Moses told the pharaoh that Yahweh wanted the pharaoh to end Hebrew slavery and let the Hebrews leave Egypt. The pharaoh at first refused, but later agreed. Moses then led the Hebrews out of Egypt. The pharaoh once again changed his mind, and he led his army in pursuit. But the Hebrews crossed the Red Sea and escaped into the Sinai Desert. They believed that Yahweh helped them in their **exodus**, or escape.

Hebrew Ring and Seal

Life in the desert was hard, but Moses told the Hebrews not to give up. Moses led them to Mount Sinai. There he climbed to the top of the mountain to receive a message from God. Yahweh told Moses that He would protect the Hebrews and lead them back to Canaan. In return, the Hebrews were to make a **covenant**, or agreement, with Him. They were to promise to remain true to Him and obey certain laws, the most important of which became known as the Ten Commandments.

The Ten Commandments stated that the Hebrews were to give their loyalty only to Yahweh. They were not to worship other gods or idols. The Ten Commandments also taught that it is wrong to lie, steal, or kill, and that people should honor their parents and respect other people's property.

The Hebrews believed that God was just and that they, too, should be just. They did not try to influence the way God behaved by performing ceremonies or offering gifts. Instead, they used laws to try to influence the way people behaved. Their laws affected not only individuals but the whole community. The Hebrews believed in **social justice**. Everyone—male or female, rich or poor, neighbor or stranger—had a right to be treated fairly.

1. Who was Moses? What did he do for the Hebrews?
2. What are the Ten Commandments?
3. What did the Hebrews believe? How did they try to influence the way people behaved?

THE PROMISED LAND   Moses died shortly before the Hebrews reached Canaan. The Hebrews were afraid that without a strong leader, they would not be able to enter Canaan. The people who already lived there had built many walled cities on hilltops. Soldiers in lookout towers guarded the cities against enemy attack. But Joshua, a new leader, brought the Hebrews safely into the promised land.

Once they had settled in Canaan, the Hebrews became farmers and shepherds. They copied the Canaanites' tools and borrowed their alphabet. Canaan was rocky and dry. There was

HARVEST IN ANCIENT ISRAEL

Hebrew writers called Canaan "a land flowing with milk and honey." This area, however, had a dry climate and little water. The Hebrews had to work hard to farm the land. Here Hebrew farmers and their workers gather in the harvest.
Why was Canaan known as the Promised Land?

little water. So during the two months of the rainy season, the farmers collected and stored water in **cisterns**, or small caves or underground basins. During the dry season they used what they had stored to irrigate their crops of olives, flax, barley, wheat, and grapes.

Most of the Hebrews lived in one-room houses. The room was divided in two, with one section slightly higher than the other. During the day the Hebrews cooked and did other household chores in the lower level. At night donkeys and goats bedded down there, while the family slept in the upper level. The walls of the houses were made of mud-brick or stone plastered with mud and whitewashed. The floors were made of beaten clay. Wooden beams supported a flat thatched roof that was covered with clay.

1. What did the Hebrews do after they settled in Canaan?
2. In what kind of houses did most Hebrews live?

KINGS   After Joshua died, the 12 Hebrew tribes split apart. Each tribe had its own leader, called a **judge**. The judges settled disputes and led troops into battle.

In time, the Hebrews decided they needed a king to unite them. A warrior-farmer named Saul became their first king. He ruled well for several years. Toward the end of his reign, however, he lost the people's support. When Saul died in battle, David became the new king.

David reunited the Hebrews and defeated the Canaanites. He captured a Canaanite fortress and established on this site Jerusalem, the capital of the Hebrew kingdom. A fine musician, David wrote many of the **psalms**, or songs, found in the Bible.

After David died, his son Solomon became king. Through trade and treaties with other lands, Solomon brought peace and made the Hebrew kingdom more powerful. He obtained timber from Phoenicia to build a huge temple in Jerusalem. Solomon's wealth and wisdom became known all through the Middle East.

Many Hebrews, however, were not happy with Solomon. They resented the harshness of his rule. They did not like paying high taxes or working on his building projects. After Solomon died, the Hebrews in the northern part of the country set up their own separate kingdom, called Israel. The southern kingdom, which was ruled from Jerusalem, became known as Judah. For nearly 200 years the two kingdoms fought each other off and on. Gradually Israel and Judah became weak enough for others to conquer.

David Playing Harp

1. What happened to the Hebrews after Joshua died?
2. Why did the Hebrews want a king? Who was their first king?
3. What did David do for the Hebrews? What did Solomon do?
4. Into what two kingdoms did the Hebrew nation split following Solomon's death?

THE PROPHETS   **Prophets**, or persons claiming to have messages from God, appeared in the Hebrew kingdoms. They came from the cities and the villages. They were teachers,

HEBREW PROPHETS

Name	Teachings
Elijah c. 850 B.C.	Everyone should behave in a moral way.
Amos c. 755 B.C.	Prayers and sacrifices do not make up for bad deeds. Behaving justly is much more important than ritual.
Hosea 745–730 B.C.	God is a god of love and compassion who loves His people the way a father loves his children. God suffers when people turn from Him and do not follow His commandments.
Isaiah of Jerusalem 740–701 B.C.	People can have peace and prosperity only if they carry out God's will. The future depends on how justly one behaves in the present.
Micah 714–700 B.C.	Both rich and poor have to obey God's laws. It is important to "do justly, love mercy, and walk humbly with thy God."
Jeremiah 626–587 B.C.	Suffering is the result of wickedness. God will make a new covenant with the Jews in the future.
Ezekiel 593–571 B.C.	People are responsible for their own behavior.
Isaiah of Babylon c. 545 B.C.	God is the god of all people. God will free Israel and lead it back to the promised land.

farmers, and shepherds. The prophets criticized the way the Hebrews were living. The rich were mistreating the poor, and government officials were accepting bribes. The prophets reminded the Hebrews of their duty to God and to one another. They warned the Hebrews that Yahweh would punish them if they did not return to His ways.

Some of the prophets added a new meaning to the laws of Moses. They taught that the idea of social justice was for everyone. They explained that Yahweh was not just the god of the Hebrews but God of all peoples.

The people refused to listen to the prophets' warnings. Then it was too late. Powerful neighbors took over the Hebrew kingdoms. After 722 B.C. the Israelites, the people of the northern kingdom, disappeared. Though the people of Judah survived, most of them were forced to move to Babylon in 586 B.C.

While in Babylon, the people of Judah, who were then known as Jews, made changes in their religion. Having lost the great temple at Jerusalem, they had to find some other way to worship God. They began meeting in small groups on the **sabbath**, or day of rest, to pray and to talk about their religion and their history. From these meetings came the idea of a **synagogue**, or a community of Jews who gather together to practice their religion. The Jews wrote down their laws, sayings, and stories of the past on **scrolls**, or long rolls of parchment. The study of these sacred writings led the Jews to value learning. Their **rabbis**, or teachers, became important leaders.

Hebrew Priest

The Jews spent 70 years in Babylon before they were allowed to return to their homeland. Not all of them wanted to go. Those who did return rebuilt Jerusalem and the temple. Under a scribe named Ezra, they wrote down the laws of Moses in five books called the **Torah**, or the Law. Other writings were added later to make the Old Testament of the Bible.

1. Who were the prophets? What did they tell the Hebrew people?
2. What happened to the Hebrews who did not heed the prophets' warnings?
3. What changes did the Jews make in their religion while they were in Babylon?

MAJOR CONTRIBUTIONS   The Hebrews were the first people to believe in one god. At first they believed that God was concerned only about them. They expected other people to worship many gods. Later some of the prophets claimed that God cared about all peoples and all nations.

The Hebrews were the first to believe in a just god. As a result, they believed that individuals and society should likewise be just. Their laws were designed to teach people to treat one another fairly.

1. What major new ideas did the Hebrews contribute to later civilizations?

CHAPTER REVIEW

SUMMARY

1. Phoenician civilization began to develop about 1830 B.C.

2. Since Phoenicia's farmland was limited, many Phoenicians turned to the sea to make a living.

3. Phoenicia became well known for its cedar and an expensive purple dye.

4. The Phoenicians worshipped many gods.

5. One of the most important Phoenician contributions to later civilizations is the alphabet, which they borrowed about 1200 B.C. and then passed along.

6. The Phoenicians established many colonies along the North African coast, the most important of which was Carthage, founded in 814 B.C.

7. Around 1900 B.C. Abraham led the Hebrews from the city of Ur into the land of Canaan.

8. According to the Bible, God made an agreement with Abraham whereby the Hebrews could always live in Canaan if they would worship Him alone as the one true God.

9. After a drought hit Canaan around 1800 B.C., the Hebrews moved to Egypt.

10. Approximately 1200 B.C. the Hebrews, who had been enslaved by the Egyptians, escaped into the Sinai Desert, where they made a new covenant with God under Moses' leadership promising to obey the Ten Commandments and other laws.

11. The Hebrews settled once again in Canaan and after a while chose a king to rule over them.

12. In 922 B.C. the Hebrew kingdom split into the kingdoms of Israel and Judah, both of which were eventually conquered by powerful neighbors.

13. The Hebrews' major contribution to later civilizations was the belief in one just god rather than many gods.

BUILDING VOCABULARY

1. *Identify the following:*

Canaan	Judaism	Ten Commandments	Solomon
Tyre	Abiru	Joshua	Israel
Melqart	Yahweh	Saul	Judah
Tyrus	Abraham	David	Ezra
Carthage	Moses	Jerusalem	Torah
Dido			

2. *Define the following:*

treaties	alphabet	cisterns	sabbath
foyer	exodus	judge	synagogue
holy of holies	covenant	psalms	scrolls
colonies	social justice	prophets	rabbis

REVIEWING THE FACTS

1. Why were the Phoenicians successful long-distance sailors?

2. What two things did the Phoenicians get from their business dealings?

3. Why were many Phoenicians good carpenters and cabinetmakers?

4. Why were the Phoenicians called "the purple people?"

5. What did the Phoenicians learn from the Egyptians?

6. Why did God promise the land of Canaan to the Hebrews?

7. Why did the Hebrews believe in social justice?

8. Why were many Hebrews unhappy with King Solomon?

9. Why did the Jews make changes in their religion while they were in Babylon?

10. What led the Jews to place high value on learning?

DISCUSSING IMPORTANT IDEAS

1. How can those people who have very limited natural resources still manage to earn a living?

2. Why is the alphabet a major contribution to civilization?

3. How does the idea that God is just affect the way in which people behave?

4. Do you think it is all right for people to make changes in their religious beliefs and practices? Why or why not?

USING MAPS

Refer to the map on page 96, and answer the following questions:

1. How many kingdoms are shown? What are they?

2. Which kingdom is furthest south?

3. What kingdom is the largest?

4. How far north is the city of Tyre from the city of Jerusalem?

5. Which Phoenician city is directly west of Damascus?

6. Between what bodies of water does the Jordan River lie?

7. Which kingdom appears to be most mountainous? How can you tell?

The caste system divided people into four main groups. The highest caste was made up of priests and teachers. Next came rulers and warriors, then merchants, artisans, and unskilled workers.

Lowest of all people were the **outcasts**, or those who existed outside the caste system. They were also called **untouchables**. The untouchables had to work at the dirtiest jobs, such as handling dead animals and sweeping the streets. Because they worked with dirt and blood, they were thought to be impure. They were forbidden to touch caste members or drink from the same well.

The caste system included strict rules about every part of daily life. Each per-

HINDUISM

Hinduism is the major religion of India. It developed over thousands of years from the beliefs and practices of many different peoples.

Hinduism teaches that each person is born into a **caste**, or social group. The idea of caste began about 1500 B.C. At that time a dark-skinned people called Dravidians, who were living in northern India, were conquered by Aryans. The Aryans set up a caste system to limit contact between themselves and the Dravidians.

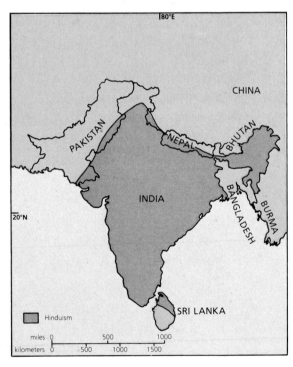

son's job was determined by his or her caste. Members of one caste could not marry, eat with, or work with members of another caste.

Hindus were willing to follow the rules of caste because of their belief in **reincarnation**, or rebirth of the soul into a new body. They believed that each person would be reborn again and again until that person reached spiritual perfection. The Hindus thought that a person's caste was a reward or punishment for the way he or she lived in a past life. Those who led a good, dutiful life might be reborn into a higher caste. Those who lived a bad life might be reborn into a lower caste, or even into the body of an animal.

The Hindus worshipped many gods. The three main gods were Brahma, the

Creator; Vishnu, the Preserver; and Shiva, the Destroyer. Together the three gods could be thought of as one god, called Brahman.

The Hindus made beautiful statues of their gods to worship at home and in temples. Brahma is shown with four heads to represent his great wisdom and the four quarters of the earth. Shiva is often shown as Lord of the Dance or with his wife Uma and his divine bull Nandi. Vishnu is usually seen as the hero of Indian epics.

1. How did the caste system begin?
2. How did the caste system influence the daily life of Hindus?
3. How did the belief in reincarnation support the caste system?

CHAPTER

MILITARY EMPIRES

While the Phoenicians and Hebrews were developing their civilizations, empires rose and fell in Mesopotamia. These empires were created by the Assyrians, Chaldeans, and Persians. None of these peoples were content to stay where their civilizations began. They raised powerful armies and expanded into neighboring lands. They developed new ways of ruling and increased trade. Thus, they spread their ideas and customs among many other peoples.

THE ASSYRIANS

About 1000 years after Hammurabi ruled, a people called Assyrians rose to power in Mesopotamia. Their country,

Assyria, lay in the upper part of the Tigris River valley. The Assyrians spoke the same language and used the same writing system as the Babylonians.

The Assyrians were warriors. Experts believe their liking for war was influenced by geography. Assyria's rolling hills and rain-watered valleys did not provide protection against invaders. Assyrian shepherds and farmers had to learn to fight to survive. In time, fighting became a way of life.

The Assyrians built up a powerful army. By 1100 B.C. they defeated their neighboring enemies. By 800 B.C. they were strong enough to take over cities, trading routes, and fortresses throughout Mesopotamia.

1. Where did the Assyrians live?
2. How did geography influence the Assyrian way of life?

THE ASSYRIAN ARMY   The Assyrian army was well organized. It was divided into **infantries**, or groups of foot soldiers, armed with shields, helmets, spears, and daggers. The army also had units of charioteers, cavalry, and archers.

At first the Assyrians fought only during the summer months when they did not have to be concerned about planting or harvesting crops. Later, as they took over more land, soldiering became a year-round job. When the Assyrians needed

ASSYRIAN WARFARE
Assyrian kings had descriptions of their conquests carved in stone. They also celebrated their victories by decorating palaces and temples with scenes of warfare. This palace relief shows units of the Assyrian army in a fierce battle. What kind of fighters were the Assyrians?

Assyrian Official

more soldiers, they hired them from other places or forced the people they had conquered to serve.

Assyrian power was due partly to Assyrian weapons. The weapons, which were made of iron, were harder and stronger than weapons made of copper or tin. Iron had been used in the Middle East for many centuries. But until about 1400 B.C. it was too soft to be made into weapons. Then a people called Hittites developed the process of **smelting**. They heated the iron ore, hammered out its impurities, and rapidly cooled it. This made the iron stronger and harder. The Assyrians borrowed the skill of smelting from the Hittites.

The Assyrians were cruel warriors. For several hundred years their armies spread death and destruction throughout the Middle East. They were especially skilled in attacking cities. They tunneled under the walls or climbed over them on ladders. They used beams mounted on movable platforms to ram holes through city gates. Once they captured a city, they set fire to its buildings and carried away its citizens and goods.

Anyone who resisted Assyrian rule was punished. Those who did not resist had to pay heavy taxes. The Assyrians also found a way to conquer people without fighting. They spread stories about their own cruelty. Their neighbors got scared and surrendered.

1. What were the strengths of the Assyrian army?
2. Why were the Assyrians feared?

KINGS AND GOVERNMENT   Assyria's kings were strong leaders. They had to be to rule an empire that extended from the Persian Gulf in the east to the valley of the Nile in the west. Assyrian kings spent much of their time fighting battles and punishing enemies. But they were also involved in such peaceful activities as building cities and palaces. A great Assyrian king, Ashurbanipal, created one of the world's first libraries. It contained 25,000 tablets of hymns, stories, and biographies.

The Assyrian kings had to control many peoples spread over a large area. To do this, they divided the empire into provinces. They then chose officials to govern the provinces. The officials collected taxes and made certain the king's laws were obeyed.

The provinces were linked by a system of roads. Although only the roads near major cities were paved, all were level enough for carts and chariots to travel on. Over the roads moved the trade of the empire. Government soldiers were posted at stations along the roads to protect traders from bandits. Messengers on government business used the stations to rest and change horses.

In time the empire became too large to govern. After Ashurbanipal died, various conquered peoples worked to end Assyrian rule. One group was the Chaldeans. In 612 B.C. they captured Nineveh, the Assyrian capital. The Assyrian Empire crumbled shortly after.

1. What was the role of the Assyrian kings?
2. Why were roads important to the Assyrians?
3. Why did the Assyrian Empire fall?

THE CHALDEANS

Like the Assyrians, the Chaldeans were warriors who conquered many different peoples. Under their king Nebuchad-

THE ASSYRIAN AND CHALDEAN EMPIRES

Assyrian Empire, c. 665 B.C.
Chaldean Empire, c. 570 B.C.

nezzar they extended their empire's boundaries as far west as Syria and Palestine.

Chaldean astronomers believed that changes in the heavens revealed the plans of the gods. So they studied the stars, the planets, and the moon. They recorded what they learned. Once they understood the movement of heavenly bodies, they made maps that showed the position of the planets and the phases of the moon. They developed one of the first sundials, and they were the first to have a seven-day week.

1. Where was the Chaldeans' empire?
2. Why were the Chaldeans interested in astronomy?
3. What did the Chaldeans contribute to later civilizations?

BABYLON   The Chaldeans called themselves Babylonians. They built a new capital at Babylon in which nearly 1 million people lived.

Babylon was the world's richest city up to that time. It had its own police force and postal system. The huge brick walls

---

BABYLON'S HANGING GARDENS

The city of Babylon had beautiful walls, buildings, and parks. Its "hanging gardens" were known as one of the Seven Wonders of the Ancient World.
What do the "hanging gardens" reveal about life in Babylon?

---

which encircled the city were so wide that two chariots could pass on the road on top of them. Archers guarded the approaches to the city from towers built into the walls.

In the center of the city stood palaces and temples. A huge ziggurat reached more than 300 feet, or over 90 meters, into the sky. Its gold roof could be seen for miles when the sun shone.

The richness of the ziggurat was equaled by that of the king's palace. The palace had "hanging gardens." The gardens consisted of a series of terraces planted with large trees and masses of flowering vines and shrubs, all of which seemed to hang in mid-air. Nebuchadnezzar built the gardens to please his wife.

To please the people, Nebuchadnezzar built a special street near the palace. It was paved with limestone and marble, and lined by walls of blue glazed tile. Each spring thousands of pilgrims crowded into Babylon to watch the gold statue of the god Marduk being wheeled along the street. The people believed that the procession would make their crops grow and help keep peace in the empire.

Outside the center of Babylon were houses and market-places. There craftspeople made pottery, cloth, and baskets which they sold to passing **caravans**, or groups of traveling merchants. Traders came to the marketplace from as far away as India and Egypt. Trade helped make Babylon rich.

Babylon was the center of a great civilization for many years. But as time passed, the Chaldeans began to lose their power. They found it hard to control the peoples they had conquered. Some years crops were poor and trade was slow. Then, in 539 B.C., Persians from the mountains to the northeast captured Babylon. Mesopotamia became just another part of the Persian Empire.

Babylonian Queen

1. What were some of the features of Babylon?
2. Why was Babylon such an important city?
3. What led to the fall of the Chaldeans?

THE PERSIANS

Originally the Persians were part of a people known as Aryans, who were cattle herders from the grasslands of central Asia. About 2000 B.C., however, the Persians began to separate from other Aryans. The Persians may have been searching for new pastures for their cattle. More likely they were drawn further west by reports of the rich civilizations in Mesopotamia and Egypt. They finally settled on a high plain between the Persian Gulf and the Caspian Sea where they established Persia. Today this region is called Iran, or "the land of the Aryans." Modern Persians are Iranians.

The Persians lived peacefully in the highlands for over 1000 years. They divided most of the country into large farms owned by nobles. The nobles spent most of their time riding horses and practicing archery. Their farms were worked by laborers.

There was little water on the hot plain. Farmers depended on springs that came down from the mountains. The farmers dug underground tunnels from the springs to the fields. The tunnels kept the water from evaporating in the hot sun. With the water the farmers were able to grow wheat and barley and to pasture flocks of fat-tailed sheep.

1. Where did the Persians come from? Where did they settle?
2. How did Persian farmers water the land?

Persian Metalwork

ARMY AND EMPIRE   About 600 B.C. the Persians were conquered by the Medes, a neighboring people. But the Medes were soon overthrown by the Persians under King Cyrus. Cyrus then organized an army to conquer new territory. The army grew until it numbered in the hundreds of thousands. Its officers were Persians, while its soldiers were either Persians or conquered peoples.

The best fighters in the Persian army were the Immortals. They earned this name because their number never fell below 10,000. When an Immortal became sick, was wounded, or died, another soldier took his place. The Immortals had the honor of leading the army into battle.

Within a short time the Persians ruled an empire that stretched from Egypt to India. The Persians were mild rulers who allowed their subjects to keep their own language, religion, and laws. The Persians believed that loyalty could be won more easily with fairness than with fear or force. They wanted their subjects to pay taxes and to produce goods for trade. They felt these things would not be done if those under their rule were treated badly.

DECREE OF CYRUS

Cyrus was a wise and generous ruler who treated conquered peoples kindly. So that the people would know his wishes, Cyrus had his decrees carved on stone and sent throughout the Persian Empire.

How was the Persian Empire governed?

One of the strongest Persian kings was Darius. He wanted a monument to honor his military victories. So he brought craftspeople from many lands to build a grand palace-fortress-treasury in the capital city of Persepolis. Buildings with many columns were constructed on giant stone terraces. In the gateways, workers carved figures which were half-human and half-beast. Persepolis became the most magnificent city in the empire.

The king did not govern the empire alone. There were many officials to carry out his orders. They all spoke Aramaic, the language used by Middle Eastern merchants.

The king chose a governor, a secretary, and a general for each of the 20 **satrapies**, or provinces, of the empire. In each

Persian Tomb

province the three officials collected taxes of gold, silver, sheep, horses, wheat, and spices and sent them to the royal treasury in Persepolis. The officials also settled local quarrels and protected the people against bandits. Each reported separately to the king. This forced them to be honest. If one official was keeping taxes or behaving badly, the others were sure to tell. The king would then remove the dishonest official from office.

Another group of officials was the inspectors. Called "The Eyes and Ears of the King," they traveled all over the empire. They decided if people could afford to pay their taxes. They also checked on rumors of possible rebellion. The inspectors never warned any provincial official they were coming. This made officials careful about doing a good job.

The last group of officials was the judges. They made sure that the king's laws were carried out properly.

1. How did the Immortals earn their name?
2. How did the Persians treat the peoples they conquered?

FAMILY LIFE   Persians lived in houses with pointed roofs and porches that faced the sun. Poor families had one-room houses. Noble families had houses with one set of rooms for men and another for women and children.

Persian families were large. Fathers ruled their families in much the same way the king ruled the empire. A father's word was law. Poor children worked with their parents. The children of nobles were cared for by their mothers until they were five years old. Then they were raised by slaves. Often they did not see their fathers until they reached adulthood. Boys were trained to ride horses, to draw a bow, and to speak the truth. Girls were not trained in any skills.

Rich women lived very sheltered lives. They spent most of their time at home apart from the men. If they had to leave the house, they stepped into a closed **litter**, or a carriage without wheels that was carried by servants. Poor women had more freedom, but they had to work hard.

1. What was life like in Persian families?
2. What were Persian boys taught? What were Persian girls taught?

RELIGION   At first the Persians worshipped many gods. About 570 B.C. a religious leader named Zoroaster told the

Persians about two gods. One god, Ahura Mazda, was wise and truthful. He created all good things in the world. The other god, Ahriman, made all evil things in the world. Ahura Mazda and Ahriman were at war with each other all of the time.

Zoroaster said that human beings had to decide which god they would support. Zoroaster then listed the good and bad deeds a person had performed. Good deeds were keeping one's word, giving to the poor, working the land, obeying the king, and treating others well. Bad deeds included being lazy, proud, or greedy. Zoroaster could tell from the list which god a person had chosen. He believed that in the end Ahura Mazda would defeat Ahriman. People who supported Ahura Mazda would enjoy happiness after death. Those who supported Ahriman would be punished.

1. What did Zoroaster teach?

TRADE   The Persians thought they should be warriors, farmers, or shepherds. They refused to become traders. They

THE PERSIAN EMPIRE

Persian Empire, c. 500 B.C.
Royal Road

believed that trade forced people to lie, cheat, and be greedy. They did, however, encourage trade among the peoples they conquered.

The Persians improved and expanded the system of roads begun by the Assyrians. One road, the Royal Road, ran more than 1600 miles, or over 2500 kilometers. A journey that took three months before the Royal Road was built took only 15 days after it was built. The Persians also opened a caravan route to China. Silk was first brought to the West along this route.

The Persians spread the idea of using coins for money. The first known coins had been made in Lydia, a tiny kingdom in Asia Minor bordering on the Aegean Sea. After conquering Lydia, the Persian king decided to use gold coins in his empire. This helped to increase trade. It also changed the nature of trade. Merchants who had sold only costly goods began to sell everyday, cheaper things as well. They sold chickens, dried fish, furniture, clothing, and pots and pans. Since people could get more goods, they began to live better than they had before.

1. What was the Persian attitude toward trade?
2. In what ways did the Persians contribute to the growth of trade within their empire?

CHAPTER REVIEW

SUMMARY

1. Around 800 B.C. the Assyrians established an empire in Mesopotamia.

2. The Assyrians developed a well-organized, full-time army.

3. The Assyrians borrowed smelting from the Hittites.

4. The Assyrian Empire was divided into provinces, linked by a system of roads.

5. In 612 B.C. the Chaldeans captured the Assyrian capital of Nineveh.

6. The Chaldeans, who called themselves Babylonians, were skilled astronomers.

7. Nebuchadnezzar built a new capital at Babylon that contained many wonders.

8. Babylon was the center of a great civilization for many years.

9. In 539 B.C. Babylon was captured by the Persians, who created an empire.

10. The Persians divided their empire into provinces and governed it well through various groups of officials.

11. Approximately 570 B.C. Zoroaster taught a new religion in which the forces of good and of evil were constantly fighting one another.

12. Though the Persians did not become traders themselves, they encouraged trade within their empire.

BUILDING VOCABULARY

1. *Identify the following:*

Hittites	Babylon	Cyrus	Persepolis
Ashurbanipal	Aryans	Immortals	Zoroaster
Nineveh	Medes	Darius	Lydia
Nebuchadnezzar			

2. *Define the following:*

infantries	caravans	satrapies	litter
smelting			

REVIEWING THE FACTS

1. What do experts believe influenced the Assyrians to become warriors?
2. What did the Assyrians learn from the Hittites?
3. How were the Assyrians able to conquer people without fighting?
4. What did Ashurbanipal do?
5. Why did the Babylonians wheel a statue of Marduk through the streets?
6. Who were "The Eyes and Ears of the King" and what did they do?
7. What good deeds were Persians expected to perform?
8. Why did the Persians refuse to become traders?
9. What did the Persians get from China?
10. What did the Persians learn from the Lydians?

DISCUSSING IMPORTANT IDEAS

1. What things helped the Assyrians to conquer their neighbors?
2. Why is a good system of transportation important?
3. Do you think the Persians were good rulers? Why or why not?
4. Would you support the Persian attitude toward trade? Why or why not?

USING MAPS

Compare the maps on pages 111 and 117, and answer the following questions:

1. What is the oldest empire shown?
2. In which empire was Nineveh?
3. Of the empires shown, which was the largest? How can you tell?
4. Which of the empires extended the furthest west?
5. About how far was it from Sardis to Susa along the Royal Road?

UNIT REVIEW

SUMMARY

1. From 1200 to 500 B.C. new civilizations rose and fell in the Middle East.
2. Phoenicians and Hebrews were peaceful people interested in trade and learning.
3. One of the major contributions of the Phoenicians was the alphabet.
4. The Hebrews contributed the belief in one god and the idea of social justice to later civilizations.
5. The Assyrians, Chaldeans, and Persians were empire builders who developed new methods of war and government.

REVIEWING THE MAIN IDEAS

1. Explain what influence trade had on the use of peace treaties, quarrels among city-states, the development of writing, the way people lived, and the spread of ideas and customs.
2. Compare and contrast the ways of life and accomplishments of peaceful groups such as the Phoenicians and the Hebrews and military groups such as the Assyrians, Chaldeans, and Persians.

DEVELOPING SKILLS

A most important element of history is time. It is not possible to study history without understanding time relationships. Historians, as well as students, must concern themselves with **chronology,** or the order or sequence in which events occur.

Often one event is a cause of a later event or a result of an earlier. Knowing the order in which events have occurred allows historians to arrive at certain conclusions.

History textbooks present chronology in various ways. Facts or events often are presented in a visual form. For example, look at the time chart on pages 86 and 87. It shows the important events discussed in this unit in the order in which they occurred. There is a time chart at the beginning of each unit. Each time chart provides a chronology of the important events in the unit.

Mastering chronology is an important social studies skill. This exercise is designed to provide practice in ordering events. Listed below are a number of events. Arrange them in proper order. Then, on a separate sheet of paper, draw a bar 8 inches, or 20 centimeters, long. Each 2 inches, or 5 centimeters, represents about 500 years. Label the events which follow in their proper order in relation to the four time spans on the bar. You have just created a *time line*.

a. Moses receives the Ten Commandments.
b. The Phoenicians build cities in Canaan.
c. Zoroaster preaches a new religion.
d. The Assyrians take over Mesopotamian cities, trading routes, and fortresses.
e. The Phoenicians found Carthage.
f. Solomon builds a temple in Jerusalem.
g. Cyrus expands the Persian Empire.
h. Abraham leads the Hebrews to Canaan.
i. Nebuchadnezzar builds a new capital at Babylon.
j. The Jews begin 70 years of exile in Babylon.
k. The Hittites develop smelting.

SUGGESTED UNIT PROJECTS

1. Write your name using the letters of the Phoenician alphabet.
2. Form two teams for debate. One will tell why the Hebrews at the time of Moses should be allowed to leave Egypt. The other will give reasons why they should not be allowed to leave.
3. Write a message that might have been delivered by a Hebrew prophet.
4. Prepare an editorial that might have appeared in a local Mesopotamian newspaper around 800 B.C., urging the people of Mesopotamia to surrender to the Assyrians. Include the benefits the Assyrians can offer, if any.
5. Write a report that one of "The Eyes and Ears of the King" might have sent to the Persian ruler.

SUGGESTED READING

Asimov, Isaac. *The Land of Canaan*. Boston: Houghton Mifflin Company, 1971. An account of the Hebrews, Phoenicians, Assyrians, Babylonians, and others who lived and fought over Canaan beginning in Neolithic times.

Collins, Robert. *The Medes and Persians: Conquerors and Diplomats*. New York: McGraw-Hill, 1975. An account of the daily lives, beliefs, and government of the ancient Persians.

Glubok, Shirley. *Digging In Assyria*. New York: Macmillan, 1970. An adaptation of archaeologist Sir Henry Layard's account of his excavation of Nineveh.

Levin, Meyer. *Beginnings in Jewish Philosophy*. New York: Behrman House, 1971. A discussion of the beliefs of Judaism and how they apply to life in today's world.

Seeger, Elizabeth. *Eastern Religions*. New York: Crowell, 1973. An introduction to the history, philosophy, and rituals of five Eastern religions.

Synge, Ursula. *The People and the Promise*. New York: S. G. Phillips, 1974. The exodus of the Hebrews from Egypt as viewed through the eyes of Leah as she experiences it from childhood to old age.

UNIT 4

2800 B.C.	2650 B.C.	2545 B.C.
c. 2800 B.C. Minoan civilization begins		
2125 B.C.	2020 B.C.	1915 B.C.
	c. 2000 B.C. Minoans control Mediterranean trade Myceneans move into Balkan peninsula	
1495 B.C.	1390 B.C.	1285 B.C.
	c. 1400 B.C. Myceneans capture Crete	
865 B.C.	760 B.C.	655 B.C.
	776 B.C. First Olympic games **c. 750 B.C.** Homer writes *Iliad* and *Odyssey*	**c. 580 B.C.** Philosophy a science begi
235 B.C.	130 B.C.	25 B.C.
	197 B.C. Romans defeat Greeks	

THE GREEKS

40 B.C.	2335 B.C.	2230 B.C.
10 B.C.	1705 B.C.	1600 B.C.
30 B.C.	1075 B.C.	970 B.C.
200 B.C. Dorians invade Greece **1185 B.C.** Trojan War		
0 B.C.	445 B.C.	340 B.C.
00 B.C. Sparta becomes military power **490 B.C.** Persian Wars begin **c. 462 B.C.** Golden Age of Athens		**338 B.C.** Philip of Macedonia conquers Greece **336 B.C.** Alexander the Great begins rule **431 B.C.** Peloponnesian Wars begin

1. HOW DID GREEK CULTURE DEVELOP?
2. WHAT DID THE GREEKS CONTRIBUTE TO WESTERN CIVILIZATION?

Western civilization owes a great debt to the Greeks. Much of what has been accomplished since ancient times is based on Greek thought and culture.

The list of Greek contributions is long. The following are just a few. In politics the Greeks gave the western world rule by the people and the first democratic constitution. They also provided the first study of written government.

In science the Greeks contributed the scientific method and many of the basic rules of geometry. In philosophy they contributed new ways of thinking.

In the arts the Greeks contributed the play, both tragedy and comedy. They also created new styles of architecture and magnificent sculpture. From the Greeks came the Olympic Games and athletic competition in such events as wrestling, boxing, discus throwing, and running.

The most important Greek contribution, however, cannot be seen or touched. It is a belief. The Greeks were the first to believe in the freedom and worth of the individual. They did not view people as the instruments of powerful gods. Instead, they saw people as intelligent beings who were capable of great achievements. The Greeks believed that they could best please the gods by developing their political and physical powers to the fullest. Thus, they gave people a sense of achievement and self-respect that has endured to the present.

CHAPTER   9

BEGINNINGS

Greek civilization developed out of a combination of two earlier civilizations, Minoan and Mycenean. The Minoans, who were also known as Cretans, were a seafaring people. Their civilization arose around 2800 B.C. on Crete, an island in the Mediterranean Sea.

THE MINOANS

At first the people of Crete grew wheat, barley, grapes, and olives. When the olive groves and vineyards produced more than they needed, the Minoans traded the surplus for goods they could not produce.

Since there were many forests on Crete, the Minoans learned to work with wood and became good carpenters. They also learned to work with metal. They put their metalworking and carpentry skills to use building ships and began to earn a living from sea trade instead of farming.

When pirates threatened them, the Minoans changed the design of their ships. They made the ships slimmer, with two or three masts instead of one. Thus, the ships could go faster. The Minoans also put a deck over the heads of rowers to protect them. And they placed a large wooden beam in the **prow**, or front part of the ship. The beam was used to smash a hole in enemy ships and sink them.

Over time the Minoans succeeded in driving off the pirates. By about 2000 B.C. Crete was the world's first important seafaring civilization. Minoan merchant ships traveled far to trade pottery, leather and bronze armor, and metal jewelry.

1. How did Minoans earn a living?
2. Why did Minoans change the design of their ships?
3. What were the new ships like?

Clay Figurine

THE PEOPLE   The Minoans were a small people with bronzed skin and long dark hair. The men wore striped loincloths, long robes embroidered with flowers, or trousers that bagged at the knees. The women wore full skirts and short-sleeved jackets that laced in the front. The Minoans were proud of their small waists and wore tight belts to show them off. They also wore lots of jewelry, such as gold and silver earrings, necklaces, bracelets, and rings.

The men farmed and fished. They raised cattle, long-horned sheep, and goats. They also served in the navy and the royal guard. The women performed household duties, attended sporting events, and went hunting in chariots.

The people of Crete loved sports. They built what was probably the world's first arena. It stood in the open air. Stone steps formed grandstands where about 500 people could sit and watch the action. The king and the royal party had their own special box seats.

Boxing matches were held in the arena. Another favorite sport held there was **bull leaping**, a form of bullfighting. A young man and woman "fought" the bull together. The man would grab the bull's horns. As the bull raised its head to toss him, the

BULL LEAPING

This painting from the palace of Knossos shows Minoans performing bull leaping. In the center, a woman leaps over the bull's back. Another woman puts her arm around the bull's horns so that it will lift its head and toss her. The woman behind the bull prepares to catch the leapers.

What was the purpose of bull leaping?

man would do a somersault, landing on his feet on the bull's back. He would then do a back flip. Standing behind the bull, the woman would catch her partner as he landed. Many experts believe bull leaping was a religious ceremony as well as a sport.

1. How did Minoans dress?
2. What were Minoan interests?

CITIES AND PALACES The Minoans built many cities, which were different from those of other ancient civilizations in two ways. At the heart of each Minoan city stood a palace rather than a temple. Also, Minoan cities did not have walls around them. Instead, the people depended for protection on the sea and on their navy.

One of the largest cities of Crete was Knossos. It covered about 28 acres, or 11.2 hectares. About one-fifth was taken up by a five-story palace that served as a government building, temple, factory, and warehouse. Its walls were built of stone and sun-dried brick framed with wooden beams. The Minoans plastered the inside walls and decorated them with brightly colored paintings called **frescoes**. The palace had bathrooms, complete with bathtubs and flush toilets. It also had hot and cold running water and portable fireboxes to heat the rooms.

The palace had several entrances. Passageways and rooms twisted and turned in all directions to form a **labyrinth**, or maze. Because labyrinth means "double ax," the palace was called the "House of the Double Ax." The palace was also called by that name because throughout it were pictures, carvings, and bronze models of a double ax.

Sea captains, merchants, and shipbuilders lived in houses around the palace. Beyond their houses stood those of the artisans who did not live and work in the palace. They made beautiful cups and vases, and designed delicate jewelry.

The houses were built side by side around courtyards. Most were two stories high. The lower walls were made of stone, the upper walls of sun-dried brick. Some houses were painted bright colors. On the inside walls were painted scenes of daily life. Each house also had its own well and drains.

Many early Minoan houses had no entrance from the street. To go in or out, a person lowered a ladder over the side of the house. Later, wooden doors and windows made of oiled and tinted **parchment**, or thin animal skin, were added.

1. What made the cities of Crete different from those of other ancient civilizations?
2. What was the "House of the Double Ax"?
3. What were some features of Minoan houses?

RULERS AND RELIGION   The kings of Crete were priest-kings. They made the laws and represented the gods on earth. They would climb to the top of Mount Juktas to look for a sign from heaven that would tell them the will of the gods. Then the kings would tell their people what the gods wanted them to do.

The Minoans had many gods. The main one was the Great Goddess, Mother Earth. She made plants grow and brought

Minoan Man

MINOAN RELIGION
This fresco shows a Minoan religious ceremony. As a musician plays the harp, two women and a man carry offerings to a shrine. Two pillars (left) support double axes with birds sitting on them. These objects stood for the power of the Great Goddess. What was Minoan religion like?

children into the world. To honor her, the Minoans built shrines. The shrines were built in palaces, on housetops, on hilltops, and in caves. The people believed that the hilltops led to heaven and the caves led to the underworld.

Sacred horns made of clay and covered with stucco rested against the back wall of each shrine. A hole between the horns held a bronze double ax. Around the horns were clay models of animals. The people left offerings of human hair, fruit, flowers, jewels, and gold at the shrines.

The Minoans believed that certain things were sacred. The lily was their sacred flower. The king wore a plumed crown of lilies and a lily necklace. The double ax was sacred. It stood for the power of Mother Earth and the authority of the king. The dove was sacred because it flew to the heavens. Snakes were sacred and were kept in most houses. They were thought to be spirits of the underworld who would protect the house.

1.   What was the role of the Cretan king?
2.   Why was Mother Earth an important goddess?
3.   What were some of the things the people of Crete considered sacred?

THE FALL OF THE MINOANS   No one is certain why Minoan civilization came to an end. Legend explains it with the story of Theseus and the Minotaur. A young Greek prince named Theseus was brought to Knossos. He was to be sacrificed to the Minotaur, a huge monster the king kept in the palace labyrinth. The Minotaur had the body of a man and the head of a bull, and lived on human flesh.

Theseus was put into the labyrinth. When he met the Minotaur, he did not try to run away. He fought the monster with a magical sword and killed it. When the Minotaur died, the power of the Minoans died too. And Theseus became the ruler of Crete.

THE EARLY AEGEAN WORLD

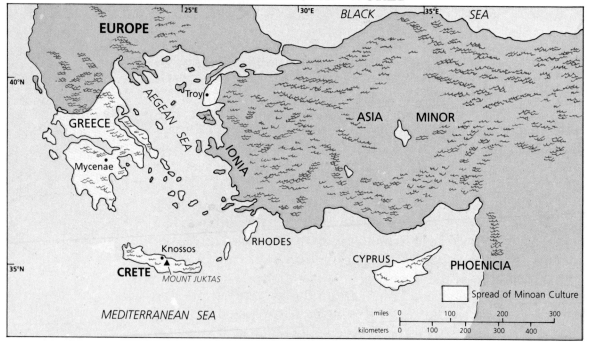

All that experts know for certain is that about 1400 B.C. control of the sea and of Crete passed into the hands of the Myceneans.

1. How does legend explain the fall of Minoan civilization?
2. What do experts know for certain about the fall of Minoan civilization?

THE MYCENEANS

The Myceneans came from the grasslands of southern Russia. Around 2000 B.C. they made their way west into Europe and then south through the Balkan **peninsula**, or piece of land that extends into the water. Finally they settled in the lowlands of mainland Greece.

The Myceneans did not build cities like the Sumerians or the Egyptians. Instead, their kings built fortress-palaces on hilltops. In time of danger or attack, the people in the villages outside the palace walls took shelter within the palace. The main feature of the palace was the **megaron**, or a squarish room with a hearth in its center. The hearth was surrounded by four pillars that supported the roof. The king held council meetings and entertained in the megaron. Meals were cooked and eaten there.

The land was divided into estates that were farmed either by slaves or by **tenants**, people who live on and work another person's property. The landowners gave the king horses, chariots, weapons, wheat, livestock, honey, and hides in exchange for protection. Tenants supplied many of these items.

Although they kept large herds of cattle, the Myceneans relied on hunting to provide more meat. They hunted rabbit, deer, boar, wild bulls, and game birds. Women rode with the men in chariots during the hunt. When the hunters were after big game, they used greyhounds. The game was captured with nets or killed with spears, slings, or bows and arrows.

Mycenean Gold Cup

1. From where did the Myceneans come? Where did they finally settle?
2. What did the Myceneans build instead of cities?
3. What did the Myceneans give their kings? What did the Myceneans receive in return?
4. Why did the Myceneans hunt? How did they hunt?

TRADERS AND PIRATES   Shortly after the Myceneans settled in the lowlands of Greece, they were visited by Minoan

MYCENEAN SEASCAPE
The Myceneans were great seafarers, who controlled Mediterranean trade for 200 years. This view shows the coastline of one of the Greek islands in the Aegean Sea. In this area, the Myceneans built many settlements.
How did geography affect the growth of Mycenean civilization?

traders from Crete. The Myceneans began to imitate Minoan gold and bronze work. They adapted Cretan script to their own language. They copied Minoan fashions. Most important of all, they learned how to build ships and how to navigate.

The Myceneans began to grow olives. They made presses to squeeze the oil from the olives. They used the oil for cooking, as fuel for lamps, and to rub on their bodies. They sold plain oil in large clay jars and perfumed oil in painted vases. The sale of the oil made the Myceneans rich. It also led to the establishment of Mycenean trading stations and settlements on nearby islands.

Despite their success in trade, the Myceneans were warriors at heart. In battle they wore fancy bronze armor, used small metal shields, and fought with spears and swords. At first they fought one another. After they learned about shipbuilding and navigation, they outfitted pirate fleets and began to raid nearby lands. By about 1400 B.C. they had replaced the Minoans as the main power of the Aegean world.

The Myceneans remained strong for nearly 300 years. Then a people called Dorians conquered them. Thousands of Myceneans fled the Greek mainland and settled in the Aegean islands and on the western shore of Asia Minor, the western peninsula of Asia between the Black and Mediterranean Seas. These settlements later became known as Ionia.

1. In what ways were the Myceneans influenced by the Minoans?
2. How did the Myceneans become rich and powerful?
3. What happened to the Myceneans around 1100 B.C.?

THE TROJAN WAR   The Myceneans are famous for their attack on Troy, a major trading city of Asia Minor. The Trojans controlled the trade routes to the Black Sea. They made money by taxing the ships that carried grain and gold from southern Russia to Greece.

Several hundred years after the Myceneans attacked Troy, a blind Greek poet named Homer wrote about the event in an epic poem called the *Iliad*. Homer also wrote a poem called the *Odyssey*, which tells about the wanderings of Odysseus, a Mycenean hero of the Trojan War. Homer drew his material for the two poems from songs and legends that had been handed down by word of mouth. He then added his own descriptions of everyday life.

According to Homer's account in the *Iliad*, the Trojan War was fought over a woman. The king of Troy had a son named Paris, who fell in love with Helen, the wife of a Mycenean king. When Paris took Helen to Troy, her husband became angry. He formed an army and sailed after them. But the walls of Troy were so tall, thick, and strong that the Myceneans could not get into the city. They had to camp on the plain outside.

After nine years of fighting, the Myceneans still had not taken Troy. Then Odysseus suggested a way they could capture the city. He had the Myceneans build a huge, hollow wooden horse. The best soldiers hid inside the horse, while the rest boarded their ships and sailed away.

Trojan Pots

THE TROJAN HORSE
The first Greek myths came from the Myceneans. Later the poet Homer gathered these legends and used them to write his works. This painting shows the Trojan horse from Homer's *Iliad*.
What historical event does Homer's *Iliad* describe?

The Trojans saw the ships leave and thought they had won the war. They did not know that the Mycenean ships would return after dark. The Trojans tied ropes to the wooden horse and pulled it into the city as a victory prize. When the Trojans fell asleep, the Mycenean soldiers hidden inside the horse came out. They opened the city gates and let in the rest of the Mycenean army. The Myceneans killed the king of Troy and burned the city. Then, with Helen, they returned to their homes.

1. Why was the city of Troy important?
2. How does the *Iliad* describe the Trojan War?

A "DARK AGE" The Dorians conquered the Myceneans about 1100 B.C. Their iron swords were not as well made as the Mycenean bronze swords. Nevertheless, the Dorian swords were stronger.

The Dorians were not interested in furthering civilization. As a result, the Aegean world entered a "Dark Age" that lasted for more than 300 years.

The "Dark Age" was a time of wandering and killing. Overseas trade stopped. The people of the Aegean forgot how to write and keep records. The skills of fresco painting and working with ivory and gold disappeared. The Dorian invasion cut the Aegean region off from the Middle East. The people had to create a new civilization on their own.

The people started over. Once again herding and farming became the main ways of life. Local leaders ruled small areas. These leaders called themselves kings, but they were little more than chiefs. At first the borders of the areas they ruled kept changing. But in time the borders became fixed, and each area became an independent community. The people of these communities began calling themselves Hellenes, or Greeks.

1. What happened in the Aegean world during the "Dark Age"?
2. How did the people of the Aegean world begin to create a new civilization?

CHAPTER REVIEW
SUMMARY

1. Minoan civilization began to develop on the Mediterranean island of Crete around 2800 B.C.

2. At first the Minoans were farmers, but eventually most turned to sea trade to earn a living.

3. Minoans were very fond of sports, especially bull leaping.

4. Since the Minoans depended on the sea and their ships for protection, their cities were not walled.

5. Minoans worshipped many gods, the most important of which was Mother Earth.

6. About 1400 B.C. control of the Mediterranean passed to the Myceneans, who came to Greece from southern Russia.

7. Instead of cities, the Myceneans built fortress-palaces on hilltops.

8. The Myceneans learned many things from the Minoans, including a writing script and the skills of shipbuilding and navigation.

9. The Myceneans fought a ten-year war against Troy.

10. The Trojan War and its results are described in two epic poems, the *Iliad* and the *Odyssey*, written by the blind Greek poet Homer.

11. About 1100 B.C. the Myceneans were conquered by the Dorians.

12. During the 300 years in which the Dorians were in power, the people of the Aegean area lost many skills and had to create a new civilization.

BUILDING VOCABULARY

1. *Identify the following:*

   Minoan   Mother Earth   Asia Minor   *Iliad*
   Mycenean   Theseus   Ionia   *Odyssey*
   Crete   Minotaur   Troy   Hellenes
   House of the Double Ax   Dorians   Homer

2. *Define the following:*

   prow   frescoes   parchment   megaron
   bull leaping   labyrinth   peninsula   tenants

REVIEWING THE FACTS

1. What civilizations combined to form Greek civilization?
2. How were the Minoans able to gain control of the Mediterranean Sea?
3. How do experts view bull leaping?
4. Why did Minoan cities have no walls around them?
5. What were some features of the palace at Knossos?
6. How did the Minoans honor Mother Earth?
7. What is the legend of Theseus and the Minotaur?
8. What uses did the Myceneans have for olive oil?
9. What is the legend of the Trojan Horse?
10. Why did the people of Greece have to create a new civilization?

DISCUSSING IMPORTANT IDEAS

1. Did the Minoans use their natural resources wisely? Why or why not?
2. Why was religion an important part of Minoan life?
3. What type of person do you think Odysseus was? Explain.
4. What may happen when a civilization is cut off from other civilizations?

USING MAPS

Refer to the map on page 130, and answer the following questions:

1. Where were the major Minoan settlements located?
2. What does the triangle symbol on the island of Crete represent?
3. To what areas of the world did Minoan civilization spread?
4. What Minoan settlement was located in Asia Minor?

THE CITY-STATES

The Hellenes of different communities shared a common language and many customs and beliefs. But they did not have much contact with one another. Their communities were separated by mountains and the sea. Thus, no single community controlled the others. Rather, each controlled its own affairs. Nevertheless a sense of unity began to develop among the people within each community. So by 750 B.C. the basic guidelines for Greek civilization were formed.

The Polis

Greek Woman

The **polis**, or city-state, was the geographic and political center of Greek life. At first each polis consisted of farming villages, fields, and orchards grouped around a fortified hill called an **acropolis**. Atop the acropolis stood the temple of the local god. At the foot was the **agora**, an open area used as a marketplace. Gradually artisans, traders, and members of the upper class settled near the agora. By 700 B.C. this inner section of the polis had become a city. Together with the villages and farmland around it, it formed a city-state.

Each city-state had its own government and laws. The average city-state contained between 5000 and 10,000 citizens. Workers born outside Greece, as well as women, children, and slaves, were not citizens. Citizens had certain rights that others did not have. They could vote, own property, hold public office, and speak for themselves in court. In return, they were expected to take part in government and to defend their polis in time of war.

For Greek citizens in ancient times, civic and personal honor were one and the same. The polis gave them a sense of belonging. They felt they had some say in what happened to them. They put the good of the polis above everything else.

Two of the greatest Greek city-states were Sparta and Athens. Sparta had the strongest army in Greece, while Athens had the strongest navy. Yet each developed differently with a different kind of government and a different way of life.

1. What was the polis? How did it develop?
2. Who were the citizens of the Greek city-states? What rights did they have? What duties did they have?
3. What were the two greatest Greek city-states?

Sparta

Sparta was in the southcentral region of Greece, in an area known as the Peloponnesus. By 500 B.C. it had become the greatest military power in Greece.

At first Sparta was ruled by a king. About 800 B.C. the **aristocrats**, or nobles, took over the government. From that time on Sparta had two kings who ruled jointly. Although they kept the title of king, they had little power. Their only tasks were to lead the army and conduct religious services.

Only aristocrats could be Spartan citizens. All citizens over the age of 20 were members of the Assembly, which passed laws and decided questions of war and peace. Each year it chose five overseers to manage public affairs and guide the education of young Spartans. The Council of Elders assisted the overseers. The Council was made up of men over 60 who were chosen for life. It suggested laws to the Assembly and served as a supreme court.

1. Where was Sparta?
2. What was the role of Spartan kings after 700 B.C.?
3. How was the government of Sparta organized?

ARISTOCRATS, HELOTS, AND PERIOECI   The Spartans had little interest in farming. The land was worked by **helots**, or slaves owned by the city-state. The helots had to turn over half of their crops to the aristocrats who owned the land but lived in the center of the polis.

The Spartans were not interested in industry or trade either. They left those to the **perioeci**, or merchants and artisans who lived in the villages. The perioeci were neither slaves nor citizens. The helots and perioeci worked, while the aristocrats trained for the army and war.

By about 750 B.C. there were 20 times as many helots and perioeci as there were aristocrats. The aristocrats were faced with a decision. They could make life better for their workers by letting them share in the government. Or they could keep things the way they were. To do that meant keeping the workers down by force. Since the aristocrats were afraid that any change would destroy their way of life, they decided to keep things the way they were.

1. What did the helots contribute to Sparta?
2. What did the perioeci contribute to Sparta?
3. Why did the aristocrats decide against letting workers share in the government?

Greek Roof Ornament

THE SPARTAN WAY OF LIFE   Spartans tried to become the strongest people in Greece. New-born babies were examined to see if they were healthy. If they were, they were allowed to live. If they were not, they were left on a hillside to die.

When Spartan boys turned seven, they were sent to live in military camps. There they were trained in groups under teenage

THE SPARTAN WAY OF LIFE
Spartan men spent most of their time serving in the army. In the photograph a group of young warriors perform exercises on a Spartan racecourse as part of their training. Why was the army so important in Sparta?

leaders. They learned to read, write, and use weapons. The boys received only small amounts of food. They had to go barefoot and were given only one cloak to wear. They walked in silence, with their eyes to the ground, and spoke only when necessary. They slept outdoors without a cover. Every ten days they were lined up and examined to make sure they were not getting fat.

Spartan men were expected to marry at age 20. But they could not have a household of their own. They had to live and eat in military barracks, where they shared expenses with other soldiers. They could retire from the army when they reached age 60.

Spartan women had more freedom than the women of other Greek city-states. In the other city-states women spent most of their time at home performing household duties. They did not go out without a chaperone, and then only to visit other women or attend religious festivals. They never spoke to men on the street or entertained their husbands' friends.

Spartan women mixed freely with their husbands' friends. They wrestled, boxed, and raced with men. Spartan women had to be healthy so they could produce healthy male warriors. When Spartan women sent their men into battle, they told the men to come home with their shields or on them. If the men brought their shields with them, it meant they had won the battle. Dead warriors were carried home on their shields.

The Spartans believed new ideas would weaken their way of life. So they tried to prevent change. When the people of other Greek city-states began to use coins as money, Spartans continued to use iron rods. Other city-states developed literature and sculpture. Spartans spent their time and energy only on the arts of war. Other city-states developed industry and trade and improved their standard of living. Sparta remained a poor farming society that depended on the labor of slaves.

From its beginnings until its downfall in 371 B.C., Sparta had only one goal—to be militarily strong.

Greek Vase

1. What was life like for a Spartan male?
2. How was the life style of Spartan women different from that of most other Greek women?
3. How was Sparta different from other Greek city-states?

ATHENS

Like all other Greek city-states, Athens started out as a monarchy. However, about 750 B.C. some Athenian nobles, merchants, and manufacturers took over the government. After a time, fights broke out between them and the farmers and artisans over land ownership and debt. Since the upperclass Athenians did not want the fights to turn into a revolution, they agreed to make reforms. To do this, they had to reorganize the government.

The first attempt to reorganize the government was made by Draco, a noble. But Draco failed in his efforts. So in 594 B.C. a rich merchant named Solon was chosen to undertake the task.

Solon developed a **constitution**, or a set of principles and rules for governing a community, that broke the political power of the rich. Solon set a limit on how much land a person could own and gave all landowners the right to vote in the Assembly.

THE ATHENIAN WAY OF LIFE
The people of Athens gathered in the agora to trade and to discuss important issues. Here a public speaker (center) addresses the crowd from the speaker's box. Many Athenians enjoyed taking part in debates.
How did life in Athens differ from life in Sparta?

The Assembly was given the power to pass laws. Solon cancelled all debts. He freed the people who had been forced into slavery because of debt. He also did away with the law that had allowed this. He offered citizenship to artisans who were not Athenians, and he ordered every father to teach his son a trade.

Under Solon, more Athenians began to take part in government. Trade also increased. Still, people were not happy. The rich thought Solon had gone too far, while the poor thought he had not gone far enough.

Around 560 B.C. the government was taken over by another Athenian named Peisistratus. Peisistratus was supported by the lower classes. He divided the large estates among the landless farmers. He decreed that a person no longer had to own land to be a citizen. He also encouraged sculpture and other arts.

1. Why did Athenian aristocrats agree to reform the government?
2. What were some of the reforms Solon made?
3. What changes did Peisistratus make?

A DEMOCRATIC CONSTITUTION   When Peisistratus died, his sons took over as leaders of the Athenian government. Not long after, their government was overthrown by the Spartans, who defeated the Athenians in a battle.

In 508 B.C. the Spartans were themselves overthrown by a noble named Cleisthenes. A year later Cleisthenes put into effect the world's first generally democratic constitution. It gave to Athenians such rights as freedom of speech and equality before the law. The political reforms made by Cleisthenes lasted until the fall of Greece almost 200 years later.

Cleisthenes opened the Assembly to all males over the age of 20. Each year the Assembly elected ten generals to run the army and navy and to serve as chief **magistrates**, or judges. One of the generals was named commander-in-chief.

The Council of Five Hundred handled the daily business of Athens. Members were chosen each year by lot. The names of 500 citizens were drawn from a large pot. Since no one could serve on the Council for more than two terms, every citizen had a chance to be a Council member.

Under Cleisthenes, citizens were required to educate their sons. Since there were no public schools, boys had a tutor or attended a private school. Starting at age seven, they studied writing, mathematics, and music. They also practiced sports and memorized the works of Homer and other noted Greek poets.

When they turned 18, Athenian males became citizens. They went to the temple of the god Zeus and took an oath of citizenship in front of their family and friends. In the oath they promised to help make Athens a better place in which to live. They also promised to be honorable in battle, preserve the constitution, and respect their religion.

1. What changes did Cleisthenes make in the laws of Athens?
2. What did Athenian boys do at school?
3. What did Athenians promise when they took their oath of citizenship?

THE PERSIAN WARS   At the time Athens was going through government changes, the Persians ruled the largest and most powerful empire in the western world. In 520 B.C. the Persians conquered Ionia—the Greek city-states in Asia Minor and on the Aegean islands. About 20 years later, the Ionians revolted and asked the city-states on the Greek mainland for

Greek Coin

help. Athens and another polis sent a few warships. After five years of fighting, the Persians put down the revolt. But Darius, the Persian king, was not satisfied. He wanted to punish the mainland Greeks for helping the Ionians.

In 490 B.C. Darius sent a fleet of 600 ships and a well-equipped army to Greece. The Persians landed on the plain of Marathon about 24 miles, or 38.4 kilometers, north of Athens. After several days the Persians decided to sail directly to Athens and attack it by sea. They began loading their ships. The cavalry, the strongest unit of the Persian army, boarded first. As soon as the cavalry was aboard, Greek soldiers ran down in close order from the hills around Marathon. The remaining Persians were not prepared to meet this kind of attack and were defeated. Winning the Battle of Marathon gave the Greeks a great sense of confidence.

Shortly after the Battle of Marathon, rich silver mines were found near Athens. The Athenians spent their new wealth on warships called **triremes**. Soon Athens had the largest navy in Greece. The Athenians planned to be prepared if the Persians returned.

The Persians did return. In 480 B.C. Darius' son Xerxes sent 250,000 soldiers across the Aegean. Within a few weeks the Persians conquered northern Greece. In order to stop them, 20 Greek city-states banded together. The Spartans led the army, while the Athenians led the navy.

First, 7000 Greek soldiers headed for the narrow pass of Thermopylae, about 100 miles, or 160 kilometers, from Athens. There they held off the Persian army for three days. This gave the Athenians time to flee to the island of Salamis. Meanwhile, all but 300 Spartans withdrew from Thermopylae. The Persians then killed the 300 Spartans and marched on Athens. Finding the city deserted, they set it on fire.

Then, the Greeks tricked the Persian fleet into sailing into the **strait**, or narrow strip of water, between Athens and Salamis. Since the strait was too narrow for all the Persian ships to enter at once, the Greeks could take them on a few at a time. Also, once the Persian ships were in the strait, their large size made them difficult to handle. With their lighter, faster ships, the Greeks defeated the Persian fleet.

Following the defeat, Xerxes returned to Asia. However, he left some troops behind. In 479 B.C. they were defeated by the

Marathon Runner

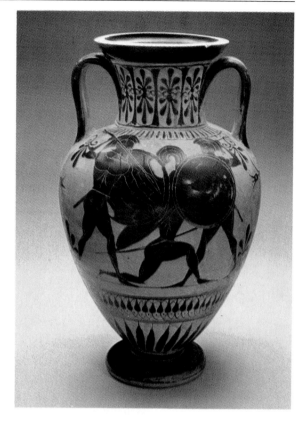

BATTLE OF SALAMIS
The Greek fleet, led by the Athenians, defeated the Persian navy in the Bay of Salamis (left). The Greeks won because of their knowledge of ships and of the sea. The urn (right) shows Greek soldiers in battle.
How did the victory at Salamis affect the outcome of the Persian Wars?

Greeks in the Battle of Plataea. A few days later Greek ships destroyed what was left of the Persian navy. The Persian Wars were over.

1. What started the Persian Wars?
2. What happened at the Battle of Marathon?
3. How did the Greeks stop Xerxes in 480 B.C.?
4. How did the Persian Wars finally come to an end?

THE DELIAN LEAGUE AND THE ATHENIAN EMPIRE
The Persians had been driven from Greece, but they still ruled Ionia. So the Athenians suggested that the Greek city-states form a **defensive league**, or protective group. Since the league

Pericles

had its headquarters on the island of Delos, it was called the Delian League. Sparta was one of the few Greek city-states that did not join the League.

Once a city-state became a League member, it could not withdraw unless all the other members agreed. The League had a common navy. Its ships were built and crewed by Athenians, but the other city-states paid the costs.

The League worked well for a while. But as time passed, Athens gained more and more power. Other city-states had to ask Athens for permission to sail or to trade. Criminal cases were brought to Athens for trial. Athenian coins replaced other Greek money. Athenian soldiers interfered in the politics of other Greek city-states. In short, the Delian League had turned into the Athenian Empire.

The main leader of Athens at the time was a general named Pericles. Pericles was known as the "first citizen" of Athens. He had a vision of Athens as the most beautiful and perfect city of the period. Therefore, he rebuilt the palaces and temples on the acropolis. It took 11 years to build the Parthenon, the temple of the goddess Athena. Much of this building was done with money that belonged to the Delian League.

Pericles also built the Long Walls. They were two parallel, fortified walls with tile roofs that connected Athens with its seaport of Piraeus some 5 miles, or 8 kilometers, away. Having the Long Walls meant Athens could get supplies even in wartime.

Pericles led the Athenians for almost 30 years. During this period art, philosophy, and literature reached new heights. Many people who came to Athens from other city-states settled there and became citizens.

1. Why was the Delian League formed?
2. Why did League members begin to resent Athens?
3. What did Pericles do?

DECLINE OF ATHENS   The more powerful Athens became, the more resentful other Greek city-states grew. Anti-Athenian feelings soon spread throughout Greece. When Athenians attacked one of Sparta's allies, a group of city-states led by Sparta declared war on Athens. The war, which was called the Peloponnesian War, lasted almost 30 years. It ended in 404 B.C.

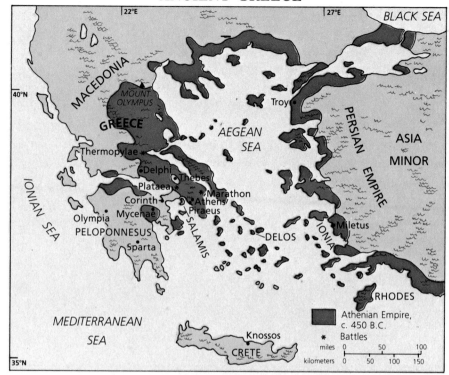

when Athens surrendered to Sparta. The Athenians lost their fleet, their power, and their confidence.

Between the war and a plague which struck during the war, Athens also lost more than one quarter of its population. Since much of its land was ruined, thousands of young Athenian men had to leave home. They hired out as soldiers in the Persian army.

When the Spartans took control of Athens in 404 B.C., they chose 30 Athenian men to rule Athens. Not long after, Athenians successfully revolted and once more set up a democracy. But Athens was never again as powerful as it had been before the Peloponnesian War.

1. Why did Sparta declare war on Athens?
2. What happened to Athens as a result of the Peloponnesian War?

DECLINE OF THE CITY-STATES

After the Peloponnesian War most Greeks began to lose their sense of community. The war had lasted a long time and had cost a great deal of money. People were discouraged. They began to lose interest in what was good for their city-state. Instead, they became more interested in making money and having a good time. Soon bitterness developed between the upper and lower classes within each polis.

After the war Sparta ruled Greece. But the Spartans were harsh rulers who angered other Greeks. In 371 B.C. a group of city-states led by Thebes overthrew Spartan rule. The rule of Thebes, however, was no better than that of Sparta. It weakened the city-states even more. The Greeks were no longer strong or united enough to fight off an invader. In 338 B.C. Philip II of Macedonia conquered Greece.

1. How did the Peloponnesian War help destroy the unity of each Greek city-state?
2. What were some other reasons for the decline of the Greek city-states?
3. Who conquered Greece in 338 B.C.?

CHAPTER REVIEW

SUMMARY

1. The geographic and political center of Greek life was the polis, or city-state, which developed around 700 B.C.

2. The two greatest Greek city-states were Sparta and Athens.

3. Since Sparta's main goal was to be militarily strong, much time and energy were spent training its citizens for war.

4. Spartan women had more freedom than the women of other Greek city-states.

5. Since they believed new ideas would weaken their way of life, Spartans tried to prevent change.

6. Between 750 and 507 B.C. Athens went through a series of government reorganizations and reforms, which changed the rules of Greek citizenship.

7. In 507 B.C. Cleisthenes put into effect the world's first generally democratic constitution.

8. Between 490 and 479 B.C. the Greek city-states fought several wars with the Persian Empire.

9. After the defeat of the Persians, Athens became, under Pericles, Greece's leading polis.

10. Sparta defeated Athens in the Peloponnesian War, which was fought between 431 and 404 B.C.

11. As a result of the Peloponnesian War, Greek city-states lost their sense of community.

12. Greece was conquered by Philip II of Macedonia in 338 B.C.

BUILDING VOCABULARY

1. *Identify the following:*

   Sparta   Cleisthenes   Thermopylae   Pericles
   Athens   Marathon   Salamis   Long Walls
   Solon   Xerxes   Delian League   Peloponnesian War
   Peisistratus

2. *Define the following:*

   polis   aristocrats   constitution   strait
   acropolis   helots   magistrates   defensive league
   agora   perioeci   triremes

REVIEWING THE FACTS

1. Why did Greek communities have little contact with one another?

2. About how many citizens did the average polis contain?

3. What did the citizens of a polis consider most important?

4. What was the main goal of Sparta's aristocrats?

5. Why was it important for Spartan women to be healthy?

6. Why did Sparta remain a poor farming society?

7. How did the Athenians choose members of the Council of Five Hundred?

8. Why was the Battle of Marathon important for the Greeks?

9. How did the Athenians use the silver they found in mines near Athens?

10. How did the Delian League become the Athenian Empire?

DISCUSSING IMPORTANT IDEAS

1. Do you think the Athenian nobles were wise to reform their government?

2. Do you approve of the Athenian method of choosing members of the Council of Five Hundred by lot? Why or why not?

3. Do you think Pericles deserved the title of "first citizen" of Athens? Why or why not?

4. What may happen to a community as a result of a long war?

USING MAPS

Refer to the map on page 147, and answer the following questions:

1. Which was further south—Athens or Sparta?

2. What symbol is used to show the location of Mount Olympus?

3. How many battles are shown?

4. Which battle is furthest north?

5. What is the name of the settlement located in Ionia?

6. Approximately how far was Athens from Sparta?

CHAPTER 11

CULTURAL CONTRIBUTIONS

The Greeks made many contributions to western civilization in the arts and sciences. Much of what they contributed came about because of their attitude toward their gods. They saw their gods as the source of all power.

The Greeks felt they could honor their gods by imitating them. This meant trying to be the best they could in everything they did. The greater the skill the Greeks showed in thinking, athletic games, or the arts, the more the gods were honored. The result was "the Golden Age" of Greek culture, also known as "the Classical Age of Greece."

RELIGIOUS BELIEFS AND PRACTICES

Although most Greeks held similar religious beliefs, there was no single Greek religion. Each city-state worshipped its own gods. Officials within each polis took charge of feasts and sacrifices. Heads of families could pray and offer sacrifices to the gods in their own households.

Greek priests often served as **oracles**, or persons who could communicate with the gods. Greeks went to the oracles for advice, which was given in the form of a **prophesy**, or a statement of what might happen in the future. Often the prophesy could be interpreted in more than one way. The person seeking advice had to decide what the prophesy really meant.

1. What religious practices did the Greek city-states have in common?
2. What did oracles do?

THE DELPHIC ORACLE

The most popular oracle was a priestess in the city of Delphi. Kings and common people came to seek her advice on many questions. She answered them in strange messages which priests alone could interpret.

Why were oracles important in ancient Greece?

THE GODS OF MOUNT OLYMPUS

During the Golden Age Greeks worshipped the gods of Mount Olympus. The most important gods are named in the chart below.

Most ancient peoples feared their gods. They believed that people were only instruments put on earth to obey and serve the gods. The Greeks were the first people to feel differently. They placed importance on the worth of the individual. Because they

OLYMPIAN GODS

Name	Realm
Zeus	ruler of Mount Olympus, king of the gods, god of the weather
Aphrodite	goddess of love and beauty
Apollo	god of the sun; patron of truth, archery, music, medicine, and prophecy
Ares	god of war
Artemis	goddess of the moon; mighty huntress and "rainer of arrows;" guardian of cities, young animals, and women; twin sister of Apollo
Athena	goddess of wisdom; city god of Athens; patron of household crafts; protectress in war of those who worshipped her; daughter of Zeus
Demeter	goddess of crops, giver of grain and fruit
Dionysus	god of fertility, of joyous life and hospitality, and of wild things
Hephaestus	god of fire and artisans; maker of Pandora, the first mortal woman; husband of Aphrodite
Hera	protectress of marriage, children, and the home; wife of Zeus
Hermes	god of orators, writers, and commerce; protector of thieves, and mischief-makers; guardian of wayfarers; messenger to mortals; son of Zeus
Poseidon	god of the sea and earthquakes, giver of horses to mortals

believed in their own value, the Greeks had a great deal of self-respect and approached their gods with dignity.

The Greeks built temples to honor their gods. Each temple, which had no roof, contained a statue of a god. In front of the statue was an altar. Because the Greeks considered the temple to be the god's home, they did not enter it. They worshipped outside at the entrance as a sign of respect.

Another way the Greeks honored their gods was with different kinds of festivals. Each festival reflected the power of the god in whose honor it was given. Out of the festivals came two important contributions to western culture—the Olympic Games and the theater.

1. Who were four important Greek gods?
2. How did the Greeks honor their gods?

THE OLYMPIC GAMES   Every four years, in the middle of summer, a festival was held in Olympia to honor Zeus. Olympia was not really a town. It was a group of temples and arenas built in fields. A 40-foot, or 12-meter, gold and ivory statue of Zeus stood in one of the temples.

The festival was known as the Olympic Games and was the most important sporting event in Greece. While the games were going on, the Greeks would stop fighting any war in which they were involved. When the Spartans refused to call a truce during the Peloponnesian War to compete in the games, they had to pay a fine.

Athletes came from all over Greece and from the Greek colonies in Africa, Italy, and Asia Minor to take part in the games. Individuals, rather than teams, competed. Only male athletes were allowed to take part. Women were not even allowed to watch. Each athlete had to swear on the sacred boar of Zeus that he would observe the rules of the games. Those who broke the rules were fined.

The Olympics consisted of many events. One of the most exciting was the chariot race, which was held in the Hippodrome, an oval track surrounded by grandstands. The chariots had small wheels and were open in the back. At first the chariots were pulled by four horses. In later Olympics only two horses were used. About 40 chariots started the race, but only a few were able to finish the nine miles, or 14.4 kilometers. The owner of the winning chariot received a crown made from olive leaves.

Zeus

Another major event was boxing. Boxers did not use their fists. They wrapped their hands with ox-hide thongs and slapped one another with the flat of the hand. There were no set rounds or points. A match between two boxers went on until one raised a finger in the air as a sign of defeat.

Another fighting event was the **pancratium**. It was a combination of boxing and wrestling in which no holds were barred between the two fighters. The only thing a fighter could not do was bite or gouge an opponent's eyes.

OLYMPIC GAMES

The modern Olympic Games are based on the original Olympics held in ancient Greece. Today's Olympic athletes come from many countries and compete in a variety of sports. One sport practiced in both the ancient and modern Olympic Games is the discus throw.

Why did the ancient Greeks hold the Olympic Games?

The winner of the **pentathlon** was considered the best all-round athlete. The pentathlon itself was five events in one. Athletes who took part had to run, do the long jump, throw the discus, hurl the javelin, and wrestle. Like winners of other events, the pentathlon winner was crowned with an olive-leaf wreath.

Olympic winners were considered heroes. Poets wrote about them. City-states held parades for them. Some city-states even gave them free meals for a year.

Between the various events at the games poets recited their verses. Herodotus, the "Father of History," first read his account of the Peloponnesian Wars at the Olympics. Greek historians even dated events by **Olympiads**, or the four-year periods between the games. The first recorded date in Greek history is 776 B.C., the date of the first Olympic Games.

1. Who took part in the Olympics?
2. What were three events in the Olympics?
3. How were Olympic winners treated?

Harp

THE THEATER The theater grew out of festivals given in honor of the god Dionysus. About 600 B.C. the Ionians began telling stories about Dionysus at festivals. A chorus chanted and danced each story to the music of a flute. At certain points the chorus fell silent. The chorus leader then delivered a **soliloquy**, or talk in which personal thoughts and feelings are expressed to the audience.

In time the chorus became shorter and the soliloquies longer. Stories were then told about other gods and heroes. About the time of the Peloponnesian Wars, a Greek poet named Aeschylus added an additional character to each story. Instead of singing or telling the story, it was acted out. Thus, Aeschylus created what came to be known as a play.

The first Greek plays were **tragedies**, or stories about suffering. All dealt with the past and with the relationship between people and gods. Not all of them had unhappy endings. However, all did point out that though people suffered, most individuals managed to carry on despite suffering.

Three of the greatest writers of tragedy were Aeschylus, Sophocles, and Euripedes. All three lived in Athens during its Golden Age. Aeschylus wrote about power and its effect on people. Sophocles showed that people suffered because of their sins and mistakes, and that suffering could make someone a better person. Euripedes tried to show that people suffered because they did bad things. Many of his plays dealt with people who broke the laws of their city-states rather than those of the gods.

Soon after the development of tragedy, a second type of play came into being. It was **comedy**, or a play with humor. Unlike tragedies, Greek comedies dealt with the present. Early comedies poked fun at individual politicians and other polis leaders, who often were in the audience. Later comedies did away with the chorus. They also changed from poking fun at an individual politician to poking fun at a certain type of person, such as a son who wastes money or a slave who plots against a master. One of the greatest writers of Greek comedy was Aristophanes. He found something humorous about almost everyone.

Greek plays were performed only at community festivals. Performances began at sunrise and went on all day. Tragedies were presented in the morning and comedies in the afternoon. All performers were men. Women were allowed to watch the plays but could not act in them.

GREEK OPEN-AIR THEATER
The Greeks performed many plays in open-air theaters. The stage was in the center and the seats were built in raised rows around it.
Why was the theater important in ancient Greece?

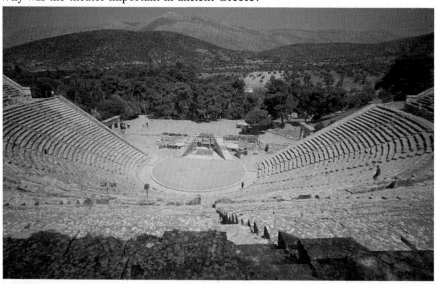

Each actor wore a huge canvas and plaster mask that showed the sex, age, and mood of the character. The mouth of the mask was shaped like a funnel. This helped carry the sound of the actor's voice to the entire audience. Actors also wore heavy padding under their robes and boots with thick soles. This made them seem larger than they really were.

The plays were given in open-air theaters. Some theaters were large enough to hold all of the people in the community. Anyone who could not afford to buy a ticket was admitted free. The audience sat on rows of stone seats and benches set on the slope of a hill. The seats were arranged in a semicircle around a stage that was level with the ground.

The Greeks considered support of the theater to be a public responsibility. An official of each polis chose the plays to be performed. The official then assigned each play to a wealthy citizen to stage. A panel of citizens judged the plays at each festival, and the author of the winning play was awarded an ivy crown.

1. How did the Greek theater start? How did it change over the years?
2. In what ways were tragedies and comedies different from one another?
3. How did the Greeks feel about the theater?

SCIENCE

Among the things on which the Greeks placed great importance was **intellect**, or the ability to learn and reason. The Greeks thought intellect should be used to its fullest. So they asked questions about the scheme of things and studied the laws of nature. They came to love wisdom. To the Greeks, studying the laws of nature and loving wisdom was the same thing. They called it *philosophia.* Today the people who search for such knowledge and wisdom are known as scientists and **philosophers,** or people who think about the meaning of life. Much of what they know is based on the studies and theories of the Greeks.

1. Why did the Greeks study the laws of nature?

SOCRATES   In 399 B.C. a trial was held in Athens. The person on trial was Socrates, a 70-year-old Athenian philosopher who was interested in the thinking process. Socrates gave up private business so he could spend his time searching for truth. He believed people could discover truth if they knew how to think.

In his search for truth, Socrates walked all over Athens trying to teach people how to think. He did this by asking questions. Each question was designed to make a person arrive step-by-step at a final conclusion, or truth. This form of questioning is known as the **Socratic method**.

All Athenians did not react in the same way to Socrates' teachings. Some were pleased that they had learned how to examine their own beliefs and to think things out. Others saw Socrates' ideas as dangerous. They did not like self-examination, particularly when it pointed up their own mistakes. In time, they considered Socrates a threat to Athens. Finally, they accused him of denying the gods, corrupting the young, and trying to overthrow the government, and they brought him to trial.

DEATH OF SOCRATES
Socrates faced death with self-control and dignity. In this eighteenth-century painting, he is surrounded by his sorrowing friends as he prepares to drink hemlock poison.
What influence did Socrates have on the Greeks?

Socrates was tried before a jury of some 500 citizens. He defended himself by speaking about truth and goodness. In his speech he said, "Wealth does not bring goodness. But goodness brings wealth and every blessing, both to the citizen and to the polis." He also said he would not change his beliefs even to save his life.

The jury found Socrates guilty and sentenced him to death. The sentence was carried out by making Socrates drink poisonous hemlock juice. Later the Athenians were sorry for having executed Socrates and put up a bronze statue in his honor.

1. What did Socrates try to teach? How did he do this?
2. How did the Athenians react to Socrates' teachings?
3. Why was Socrates tried?

PLATO Socrates left no writings. All that is known about him comes from one of his pupils, an Athenian aristocrat named Plato. Plato recorded the speeches Socrates made at his trial and just before his death.

Plato was 30 years old when Socrates died. Till then, Plato had wanted to become a politician. But in 399 B.C. he changed his mind. He left Greece, and for the next 12 years traveled in Egypt and Italy. When he returned home, he set up a school outside Athens in the sacred grove of the hero Academus. The school, where Plato hoped to train government leaders, became known as the Academy. Plato taught at the Academy for almost 40 years. The Academy itself lasted for almost 900 years after Plato's death.

Plato's beliefs were contrary to the ideas that had made Athens great. Plato believed in order. He thought that political liberty was disorder and did not approve of it. He thought only the wise and the good should rule.

Plato set down his ideas about an ideal state in a book called *The Republic*. It is the first book ever written on **political science**, or the study of government. In it Plato examined different types of government and explained how to avoid political mistakes.

Like Socrates, Plato believed in truth. He thought it could be found only after a long, hard search. He showed how difficult it is to discover truth in a work called *The Dialogues. The Dialogues* consists of a series of discussions in which different people talk about such things as truth and loyalty. Socrates is the

Plato

leading speaker in many discussions. Through these discussions Plato brings out the self-questioning that goes on within a person troubled by basic issues.

1. Why did Plato set up the Academy?
2. What were some of Plato's beliefs?

ARISTOTLE   One of Plato's brightest pupils was Aristotle. Aristotle came to the Academy when he was 17 years old and stayed for 20 years. Before he died in 322 B.C., he founded his own school in Athens and wrote more than 200 books.

Aristotle was known as "the master of them that know." He believed in using one's senses to discover the laws that govern

---

GREEK PHILOSOPHERS

The ideas of Greek thinkers influenced the development of western civilization. In this sixteenth-century European painting, Plato and Aristotle discuss the meaning of human achievement with their pupils.

What were the interests of the Greek philosophers?

---

the physical world. He was the first to **classify**, or group together, plants and animals that resemble each other. His system of classification, with few changes, is still used today. Over centuries it has helped scientists to handle a great amount of information in an orderly way.

Aristotle made another contribution to modern science when he added to the ideas of an earlier Greek scientist named Thales of Miletus. Thales developed the first two steps of what is known today as the **scientific method**. First, Thales collected information. Then, based on what he observed, he formed a **hypothesis**, or possible explanation. Aristotle provided the third step of the scientific method when he tested the hypothesis to see if it was correct.

Aristotle

Another important contribution Aristotle made was in **logic**, or the science of reasoning. He developed the **syllogism**, which consists of three related statements. The third statement is a conclusion based on the information given in the first two statements. For example:

> Athenians are Greeks.
> Socrates is an Athenian.
> Therefore, Socrates is Greek.

1.   What contributions did Aristotle make to science?

DISCOVERIES AND INVENTIONS   Greek scientists were not looking for ways to make life easier or better. They were trying to increase their store of knowledge. They had none of the equipment scientists have today, such as telescopes, micro-scopes, or scales that weigh small amounts. Still, they managed to make important discoveries.

Their curiosity about nature led Greek scientists to discover that natural events are not the result of the behavior of gods. They also learned that the world is governed by natural laws that humans can discover and understand.

There were many Greek scientists. The first was Thales of Miletus, who came from Ionia. Thales not only developed the first two steps of the scientific method, but he also predicted correctly an eclipse of the sun in 585 B.C. The contributions made by Thales and some other Greek scientists are listed in the chart on the following page.

GREEK SCIENTISTS

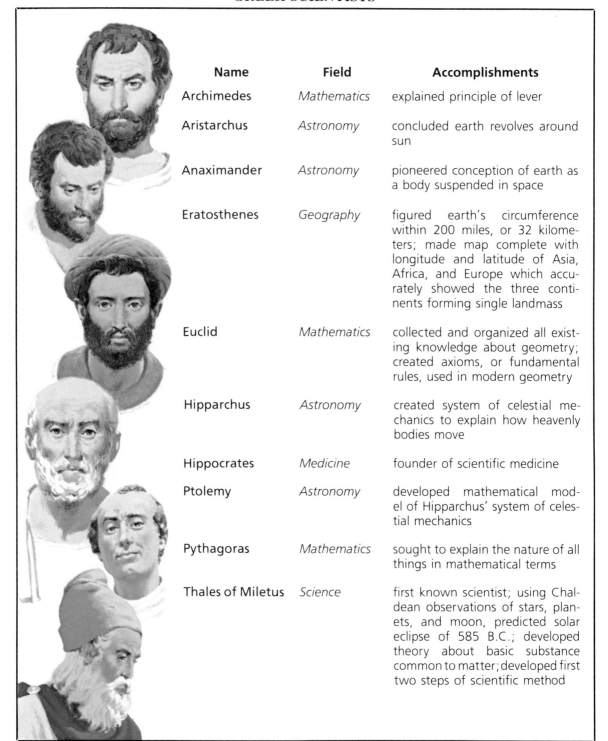

Name	Field	Accomplishments
Archimedes	*Mathematics*	explained principle of lever
Aristarchus	*Astronomy*	concluded earth revolves around sun
Anaximander	*Astronomy*	pioneered conception of earth as a body suspended in space
Eratosthenes	*Geography*	figured earth's circumference within 200 miles, or 32 kilometers; made map complete with longitude and latitude of Asia, Africa, and Europe which accurately showed the three continents forming single landmass
Euclid	*Mathematics*	collected and organized all existing knowledge about geometry; created axioms, or fundamental rules, used in modern geometry
Hipparchus	*Astronomy*	created system of celestial mechanics to explain how heavenly bodies move
Hippocrates	*Medicine*	founder of scientific medicine
Ptolemy	*Astronomy*	developed mathematical model of Hipparchus' system of celestial mechanics
Pythagoras	*Mathematics*	sought to explain the nature of all things in mathematical terms
Thales of Miletus	*Science*	first known scientist; using Chaldean observations of stars, planets, and moon, predicted solar eclipse of 585 B.C.; developed theory about basic substance common to matter; developed first two steps of scientific method

Greek scientists also contributed to the field of medicine. The "Father of Scientific Medicine" was Hippocrates, who was considered the perfect physician. He traveled all over Greece diagnosing illnesses and curing sick people. Hippocrates believed diseases came from natural causes. At the time, most other doctors thought diseases were caused by evil spirits entering the body.

Hippocrates drew up a list of rules about how doctors should use their skills only to help their patients. His rules are known as the **Hippocratic oath**. It binds doctors to honor their teachers, do their best for the sick, never give poisons, and keep the secrets of their patients. Doctors all over the world still promise to honor Hippocrates' oath.

1. What two major discoveries did Greek scientists make?
2. Who were three important Greek scientists? Why were they important?
3. What did Hippocrates do?

CHAPTER REVIEW

SUMMARY

1. Ancient Greeks believed individuals should honor their gods by doing the best they could in everything they did and said.

2. During the "Golden Age" the Greeks made many contributions in thinking, athletics, and the arts.

3. The Olympic Games, which were held every four years in honor of Zeus, were the most important sporting event in Greece.

4. The play developed out of a festival in honor of Dionysius.

5. Socrates was an Athenian philosopher who developed a form of questioning known as the Socratic method.

6. The Socratic method used questions to help a person arrive at a conclusion.

7. Socrates was tried and sentenced to death in 399 B.C. because many people were afraid of what he was teaching to the Greeks.

8. Plato, who was one of Socrates' pupils, founded a school and wrote the first book on political science.

9. Aristotle, who was one of Plato's pupils, helped modern science by developing a system of classification and by providing the third step in the scientific method.

10. Greek scientists learned that the world is governed by natural laws which humans can discover and understand.

11. Hippocrates believed diseases came from natural causes rather than from the behavior of the gods.

BUILDING VOCABULARY

1. *Identify the following:*
Golden Age	Herodotus	Euripedes	*The Republic*
Mount Olympus	Dionysus	Aristophanes	Aristotle
Zeus	Aeschylus	Socrates	Thales of Miletus
Olympic Games	Sophocles	Plato	Hippocrates

2. *Define the following:*
oracles	soliloquy	philosophers	scientific method
prophesy	tragedies	Socratic method	hypothesis
pancratium	comedy	political science	logic
pentathlon	intellect	classify	syllogism
Olympiads			Hippocratic oath

REVIEWING THE FACTS

1. How did the Greeks believe they could best honor their gods?
2. Why did the Greeks worship outside their temples?
3. What effect did the Olympic Games have on Greek warfare?
4. What role did women play in the Olympic Games?
5. What relationship was there between historians and the Olympic Games?
6. What did Greek actors wear on the stage to help their audience hear and see them better?
7. How did the Greeks view intellect?
8. How do people know what Socrates taught?
9. What are the three steps in the scientific method?
10. In what were Greek scientists most interested?

DISCUSSING IMPORTANT IDEAS

1. How important was religion in ancient Greek civilization? Explain.
2. Do you think that support of the theater should be a public responsibility? Explain.
3. Do you think the Athenians were right to put Socrates on trial? Why or why not?
4. Why is the scientific method important to modern science?

CHAPTER

THE HELLENISTIC PERIOD

12

After the Greek city-states lost their independence, many changes took place. The new rulers of Greece built empires and increased trade. At the same time, they spread Greek culture and customs. Before long, Greek ideas and achievements were influencing people from Gibraltar to India.

The Greek language came to be spoken by many people. Greek architecture was copied for new buildings. Children studied Greek literature in schools. People used Greek furniture in their homes. Greek plays became a popular form of entertainment. Business people adopted Greek methods of banking. Greek influence could be found in almost every part of daily life.

The period in which all of this took place has come to be called the "Hellenistic Age."

PHILIP II OF MACEDONIA

By 338 B.C. Greece had a new ruler, Philip II of Macedonia. Macedonia was a small, mountainous country north of Greece. Most Macedonians were farmers who tended the land. They cared little for the Greeks and had fought against them in the Persian Wars. Macedonian kings, however, were of Greek descent and admired Greek culture.

Philip became the ruler of Macedonia in 359 B.C. During his youth he was held hostage for three years in Thebes. In those years he learned to love Greek culture. At the same time that Philip came to respect Greek culture, he learned to hate the weaknesses of the Greek form of government.

Philip believed it was his destiny to unify the Greek city-states and spread Greek culture. As soon as he became ruler of Macedonia, he sought to fulfill that destiny. It took him a little over 20 years.

Philip went about reaching his goal in many ways. For example, until his time, the Macedonian army consisted of volunteers who fought only in summer. Philip turned this part-time volunteer army into a year-round, well-organized, professional one.

Philip developed a special infantry formation called a **phalanx** to be used in battle. Foot soldiers formed a solid body some 16 rows deep. Those in each line stayed so close together that their shields overlapped. This gave them added protection. The phalanx charged as a group, which meant it had more striking power than its enemies.

Philip also armed the soldiers with spears which were 14 feet, or over 4 meters, long. This was twice as long as ordinary spears. In addition, he added soldiers skilled in the use of slingshots and bows and arrows. These soldiers could fight in hilly areas where the phalanx was unable to go.

Philip flattered local Greek officials and gave them gold. He found ways to cause disagreements among Greek city-states. Then, when city-states were weak from fighting each other, his army invaded and took them over.

Philip made treaties with Greek leaders only to break them when the Greeks relaxed their guard. He saw marriage as a way of forming political **alliances**, or partnerships. He married six or seven times for this reason.

Teacher and Student

DEMOSTHENES

Demosthenes worked for the freedom of the Greek city-states. He was known for his ability as a public speaker. It is said he trained himself by shouting above the roar of the ocean waves with his mouth full of pebbles.

What did Demosthenes tell the Greeks about Philip of Macedonia?

Demosthenes, an Athenian **orator**, or public speaker, tried to warn the Greeks that Philip was dangerous. But most would not listen. They were unhappy with their local governments and tired of the bickering that constantly went on. They thought Philip might bring efficiency and discipline.

When Philip led his troops into central Greece in 338 B.C., Thebes and Athens raised a small army to stop the invasion. But the Greek army was not strong enough and was defeated. Having gained control of Greece, Philip began preparing for a campaign against the Persians. But in 336 B.C., in the middle of his preparations, Philip was killed. His son Alexander took over.

1. What did Philip II believe his destiny to be?
2. How did Philip II go about fulfilling his destiny?
3. Why was Philip II able to conquer the Greek city-states?

ALEXANDER THE GREAT

Alexander took over Philip's throne at the age of 20. He had been a commander in the army since he was 16. One of the first things he did upon becoming a commander was to cut his shoulder-length hair. At the same time, he ordered his soldiers to shave their beards. This, he said, would prevent enemy soldiers from grabbing them in close combat.

Alexander was physically strong and goodlooking. He had a lot of energy and a quick mind. Aristotle tutored him for three years in such subjects as literature, political science, geography, and biology. Because of this, Alexander included philosophers and scientists in his army. The philosophers advised him on political matters. The scientists collected plant and animal specimens from newly conquered lands. The specimens were sent back to Aristotle so he could examine and comment on them.

Alexander was a great general who feared nothing. He crushed the Persian Empire and then marched as far east as Pakistan. He would have gone farther, but his troops refused. In the course of his conquests, Alexander covered more than 22,000 miles, or over 35,000 kilometers, from the Nile to the Indus. And through all that territory, he never lost a battle.

1. What kind of person was Alexander?
2. What conquests did Alexander make?

ALEXANDER'S EMPIRE   Alexander had a vision of a worldwide state in which all people would live together in peace. He wanted to bring unity and justice to his empire.

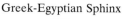
Greek-Egyptian Sphinx

Alexander believed there was only one way to achieve his goal. That was to unite Macedonians, Greeks, and Persians. He began by taking Persian soldiers into his army. Next he married a Persian woman and had 80 of his leading army officers marry Persian women, too. Then he began to dress in the Persian fashion and to follow some Persian customs.

One custom was for rulers to claim they were gods. So Alexander claimed he was a god and insisted that people treat him that way. The Macedonians and Greeks, however, refused to do so. The Greeks also objected to equal treatment for the Persians, whom they considered inferior. In fact, they looked down on all people who did not speak Greek or follow Greek

THE EMPIRE OF ALEXANDER THE GREAT

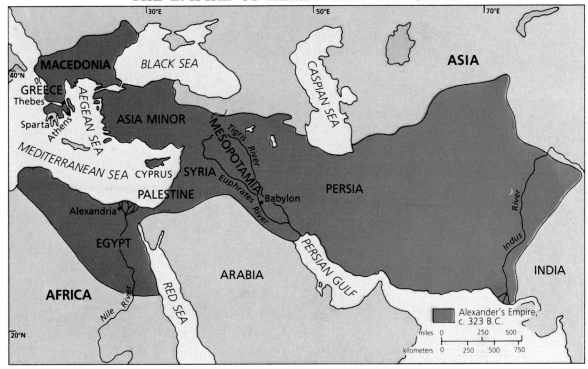

customs. They called such people **barbaroi**, from which the word "barbarians" comes.

As a result of such feelings, Alexander's attempt to achieve unity among his people was not successful.

1. What was Alexander's goal? Why did he hope to accomplish it?
2. How did Alexander treat his Persian subjects? How did the Greeks and Macedonians feel about this?

ALEXANDRIA   Alexander ruled for 13 years. During that time he founded about 70 cities, of which 16 were named Alexandria after him. He encouraged Greeks and Macedonians to settle in the new cities, which were scattered all over the empire.

The most famous Alexandria was in Egypt. Within 70 years after its founding, it had become a great center of trade and learning. Greeks from all over the eastern Mediterranean came there. They wanted to take advantage of its economic opportunities and be part of its intellectual and social life.

LIGHTHOUSE OF ALEXANDRIA
The lighthouse of Alexandria was one of the Seven Wonders of the Ancient World. A fire on top provided light to guide the ships into port.
What was life like in Alexandria?

Alexandria had two great harbors. They were protected by **breakwaters,** or barriers that break the force of waves. A lighthouse 400 feet, or about 130 meters, tall dominated the scene. Overlooking the main harbor was a palace containing a museum and a library staffed by famous philosophers and scientists. The library had the greatest collection of books of ancient times. There Euclid wrote his book on geometry. There Erotosthenes reasoned that a ship could reach India by sailing west from Spain.

1. What were some features of Alexandria, Egypt?

END OF THE EMPIRE

In 323 B.C., when Alexander was in Babylon, he caught a fever and died. He was 33 years old. His body was wrapped in gold and placed in a glass coffin in the Royal Tombs of Alexandria, Egypt. After his death, Alexander became a romantic legend. More than 80 versions of his life have been written in more than 20 languages.

After Alexander's death, fights broke out over who was to rule the empire. The areas Alexander had conquered in India returned to their original rulers. Three of Alexander's generals divided the rest of the empire among themselves. Antigonus became king of Macedonia. Ptolemy established the dynasty of the Ptolemies in Egypt. Seleucus formed the Seleucid Empire in Persia. Athens and Sparta again became independent city-states. Most other Greek city-states banded together into one of two leagues. But neither league had much power or importance.

1. What happened to Alexander's empire after he died?

THE GREEK INFLUENCE   Greek cultural influence, however, became stronger than ever after Alexander's death. The rulers who took Alexander's place adopted Greek as their language and used Alexander's titles. They even stamped his picture on their coins.

Trade grew. From Africa and Asia came spices, ivory, incense, pearls, and rare woods. From Syria and Egypt came

HELLENISTIC ART
Hellenistic artists showed action and feeling in their works. The portrait of a Greek-Egyptian (left) and the statue of the goddess of victory (right) reflect these qualities.
What aspects of life were influenced by the spread of Greek culture?

Hellenistic Coins

glass, metals, and linen. From Greece came olive oil, wine, and pottery. From Sicily and Egypt came wheat.

The cities that had been a part of Alexander's empire now existed mainly for trade. They grew along with trade. They kept Greek culture alive. City officials made their law, language, calendar, and coins Greek. Teachers brought Greek customs and ideas into the schools. Merchants and bankers used Greek methods to run their businesses.

The Greek city-states, however, were never the same again. Although they kept their political independence, they could not regain the power of the past. In time economic conditions worsened. Great factories had been built in the new Hellenistic cities. Greek manufacturers now found they could not compete with these factories. As a result, more and more young Greeks left their homes to earn a living in other countries. Population in the Greek city-states fell. There were not enough people to work the land, and many farms once again became wilderness. In 197 B.C., when Roman armies came, the Greeks were too few and too weak to resist.

1. How did Greek influence continue to grow and spread after Alexander's death?
2. What happened in Greece during the Hellenistic Age?

CHAPTER REVIEW
SUMMARY

1. Philip II, ruler of Macedonia, believed it was his destiny to unify the Greek city-states and spread Greek culture.

2. Philip conquered Greece in 338 B.C.

3. When Philip II died in 336 B.C., his son Alexander took over the throne.

4. Alexander was a great general who never lost a battle and whose conquests stretched from the Nile to the Indus Rivers.

5. Alexander tried without success to achieve unity among the Macedonians, Greeks, and Persians within his empire.

6. The most famous city founded by Alexander was Alexandria, Egypt, which contained a famous library.

7. After Alexander died in 323 B.C., his empire was broken up.

8. After Alexander's death, Greek cultural influence became stronger than ever.

9. Although the Greek city-states again became independent following Alexander's death, economic conditions in Greece grew worse.

10. The Greeks were conquered by the Romans in 197 B.C.

BUILDING VOCABULARY

1. *Identify the following:*

Hellenistic Age	Demosthenes	Alexandria	Ptolemy
Philip II	Alexander	Antigonus	Seleucus
Macedonia			

2. *Define the following:*

phalanx	orator	breakwaters	barbaroi
alliances			

REVIEWING THE FACTS

1. How did Philip II learn to love Greek culture?
2. What changes did Philip II make in his army?
3. How did Philip II view marriage?
4. Why did Demosthenes try to prove that Philip II was dangerous?
5. Why did Alexander order his soldiers to shave their beards?
6. What did Alexander learn from his tutor Aristotle?
7. How did Alexander help Aristotle?
8. Why was Alexander unable to achieve unity among his people?
9. Why did many Greeks go to Alexandria, Egypt?
10. Why were the Greeks unable to resist the Romans?

DISCUSSING IMPORTANT IDEAS

1. Would you have listened to Demosthenes? Why or why not?
2. Was Alexander wise in trying to achieve unity among his people? Explain.
3. Do you think Alexander deserved to be called "the Great"? Why or why not?
4. Can cultural influence spread without conquest? Explain.

USING MAPS

Refer to the map on page 169, and answer the following questions:

1. How far did Alexander's empire extend east to west? North to south?
2. What sea is located 40° north and 50° east?
3. What city is located approximately 30° north and 29° east?
4. Which Greek city-state was not part of Alexander's empire?

CONFUCIUS

During Confucius' lifetime, China had many problems. Powerful leaders fought each other for control of the land. Poor farmers worked hard. But they received little reward and were forced to pay heavy taxes.

Confucius thought that if people were taught to behave correctly, it would help to end China's troubles. He said that there were **Five Relationships** which were most important—ruler and ruled, father and son, husband and wife, older brother and younger brother, and friend and friend. He believed each person owed respect to those above him or her. For instance, sons owed respect and honor to their fathers. Those above were bound to set a good example for those below.

Confucius hoped to reform the government of China. Most rulers of the time

Confucius was a Chinese teacher and **scholar**, or student of knowledge, who was born in 551 B.C. His Chinese name was K'ung Fu-tzu, but in Latin he was called Confucius. Confucius developed a philosophy about how people should act and treat each other. It helped to shape Chinese society for over 2000 years.

Confucius was born to an upper-class family that had no money. He was a bright student who studied endlessly. He wanted to be a politician, but he was never very successful at politics. As a teacher, however, he was deeply respected.

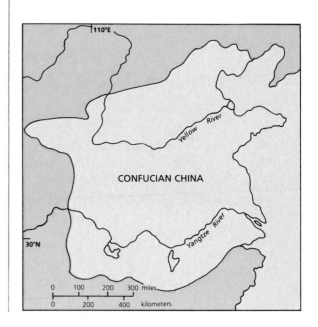

governed by military force. Confucius advised rulers to govern instead by being wise because the people would obey a wise ruler. He believed that "If one leads the people by goodness, the people will feel their duty and correct themselves."

Most government officials at the time were members of the upper class. They received their jobs because of family connections rather than ability. Confucius believed that only officials with education and ability should be appointed to government jobs.

Beginning around 200 B.C., Confucius' teachings were used in **civil service tests**, or tests for government jobs. At first only members of the upper class were allowed to take the tests. Later the system grew to include people from other classes.

Confucius' teachings were very demanding. To follow them people had to live ideal lives. For this reason, not everyone wanted to accept the teachings. Still, Confucius had many students who later became government officials. Within time, Confucius' ideas became the basis of both Chinese society and government and remained so until the early 1900's.

1. What was life like in China during Confucius' early years?

2. What did Confucius believe would help solve China's problems?

3. Who did Confucius believe should have government jobs?

UNIT REVIEW

SUMMARY

1. Greek civilization developed out of the Minoan and Mycenaean civilizations.
2. The polis was the geographic and political center of Greek life.
3. The Greeks developed government by the people and the first generally democratic constitution and made major contributions in the arts and sciences.
4. Even after the decline of the city-states Greek influence spread through military conquests and trade.
5. One of the most important Greek contributions to later civilizations was a belief in the worth of the individual.
6. Greek thought and culture is the basis of modern western civilization.

REVIEWING THE MAIN IDEAS

1. Explain what parts of the Minoan culture and the Mycenaean culture were carried over to the culture of the Greek city-states.
2. Compare the reasons for the decline of the Athenian empire to the reasons for the decline of Greece after the Peloponnesian wars.

DEVELOPING SKILLS

In learning about history, it is important to be able to tell the difference between fact and opinion. It is a fact, for example, that Christopher Columbus sailed westward from Europe in 1492 and discovered the New World. But whether or not he was a great explorer is a matter of opinion.

Some people feel Columbus was a great explorer. He persuaded his sailors to continue sailing in spite of unknown dangers. Also, his voyage led the way for large numbers of Europeans to come to the New World. If Columbus had not made his voyage, history probably would have been very different.

Other people, however, feel Columbus was not a great explorer. They point out that when Columbus landed in the New World, he thought he had reached Asia. They ask how Columbus could be great if he did not even know where he was.

Opinions depend on both facts and values, or what a person considers important. In order to think clearly, a person has to be able to tell the difference between fact and opinion.

This exercise is designed to give you practice in this skill. Read each of the following statements, and then tell whether it is fact or opinion.

1. Greek civilization developed out of a combination of two earlier civilizations, Minoan and Mycenean.
2. The Minoans contributed more important things to Greek civilization than the Myceneans did.
3. The Minoans depended on their ships for protection from attack.
4. The Myceneans depended on fortresses for protection from attack.

5. Mycenean communities generally were better protected than Minoan communities.

6. The polis was the geographic and political center of Greek life.

7. The Athenians developed the world's first generally democratic constitution which gave them certain rights.

8. Athens was a better place than Sparta in which to live.

9. If Athens had not lost the Peloponnesian War, Philip II of Macedonia would not have been able to conquer Greece.

10. One contribution the Greeks made to western civilization was the theater.

11. The most important contribution the Greeks made to western civilization was the idea of democracy.

12. Alexandria, Egypt was the most famous city founded by Alexander the Great.

SUGGESTED UNIT PROJECTS

1. Make a clay or papier-mache model of the Trojan Horse.

2. Make a chart with one column headed Athens and another headed Sparta. Under each, list the following information.
   a. Form of government
   b. Religious beliefs
   c. Type of education
   d. Main occupations
   e. Role of women
   f. Contributions to Greek culture

3. Compare the Athenian oath of allegiance with the oath of allegiance to the United States.

4. Write a speech that Demosthenes might have given about Philip of Macedonia.

5. Write seven newspaper headings about events in the life of Alexander the Great.

SUGGESTED READING

Cottrell, Leonard. *The Mystery of Minoan Civilization.* New York and Cleveland: The World Publishing Company, 1971. An account of Minoan civilization.

Edmonds, I. G. *The Mysteries of Troy.* New York: Thomas Nelson, Inc., 1977. A discussion of the history, literature, legends, archaeology, and art of ancient Troy.

Evslin, Bernard. *Greeks Bearing Gifts: The Epics of Achilles and Ulysses.* New York: Four Winds Press, 1976. A retelling of the *Iliad* and the *Odyssey*.

Fagg, Christopher. *Ancient Greece.* New York: Warwick Press, 1978. A discussion of the civilization of the ancient Greeks who first developed a democratic way of life.

Serraillier, Ian. *Heracles the Strong.* New York: Henry Z. Walck, Inc., 1970. A retelling of the legend of Heracles.

Van Duyn, Janet. *The Greeks: Their Legacy.* New York: McGraw-Hill, 1972. A description of the contributions the Greeks made to western civilization.

Walsh, Jill Paton. *Children of the Fox.* New York: Farrar, Straus and Giroux, 1977. Three stories set during the Persian Wars.

UNIT 5

1200 B.C.	1125 B.C.	1050 B.C.
1200 B.C. Latins settle on Palatine Hill		

650 B.C.	575 B.C.	400 B.C.
600 B.C. Etruscans rule central Italian peninsula	**509 B.C.** Romans set up republic **450 B.C.** Twelve Bronze Tablets become basis of Roman law	

100 B.C.	25 B.C.	100 A.D.
81 B.C. Lucius Sulla becomes dictator of Rome	**31 A.D.** Jesus is crucified **46 B.C.** Julius Caesar appointed dictator of Rome **27 B.C.** Octavian takes title of Augustus *Pax Romana* begins	

400 A.D.	575 A.D.	**600 A.D.** Archbishop of Rome takes title of Pope	650 A.D.
410 A.D. Alaric conquers Rome **476 A.D.** Roman Empire ends in West **529 A.D.** Benedictine Rule			

1050 A.D.	1125 A.D.	1200 A.D.
1054 A.D. Latin and Greek Churches separate		

THE ROMANS

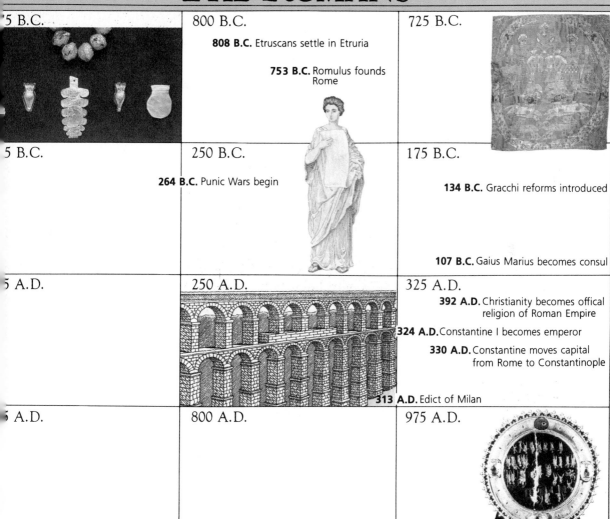

5 B.C.	800 B.C.	725 B.C.
	808 B.C. Etruscans settle in Etruria	
	753 B.C. Romulus founds Rome	
5 B.C.	250 B.C.	175 B.C.
	264 B.C. Punic Wars begin	**134 B.C.** Gracchi reforms introduced
		107 B.C. Gaius Marius becomes consul
5 A.D.	250 A.D.	325 A.D.
		392 A.D. Christianity becomes offical religion of Roman Empire
		324 A.D. Constantine I becomes emperor
		330 A.D. Constantine moves capital from Rome to Constantinople
		313 A.D. Edict of Milan
5 A.D.	800 A.D.	975 A.D.

1.   WHAT WAS ROMAN CIVILIZATION LIKE?
2.   HOW DID THE ROMANS INFLUENCE THE GROWTH AND DEVELOPMENT OF WESTERN CULTURE?

Rome began as a small settlement on a hill in central Italy. Before its fall hundreds of years later, it ruled most of the western world. At its peak the Roman Empire had a population of nearly 100 million. The empire was made up of many different peoples, including Egyptians, Spaniards, Syrians, Greeks, and Jews.

The Romans left a great legacy to western civilization. Rome itself became a model for many European cities. Roman architecture was copied in the United States and elsewhere. Some works of Roman literature are still treasured today. Many English, Spanish, French, and Italian words come from Latin, the language of the Romans. The English word "justice," for example, comes from the Latin word *jus*, meaning "law."

A famous Roman named Cicero once wrote, "What sort of thing is the civil law? It is of a sort that cannot be bent by influence or broken by power or spoiled by money." The Roman system of law was developed on the basis of the same justice for all. This idea helped shape the legal tradition of the western world.

After a slow start, Christianity grew and ripened in Rome. It helped to shape the Roman Empire, just as the empire helped to shape the Church. The Archbishop of Rome became the **Pope**, or head of the Roman Catholic Church.

The memory of Rome's greatness inspired western leaders for many centuries. The Roman heritage is a major ingredient of western civilization as it is known today.

CHAPTER 13
BEGINNINGS

Italy is a bootshaped peninsula that extends south from Europe into the Mediterranean Sea. On the west coast of the peninsula is the mouth of the Tiber River. Fifteen miles, or 24 kilometers, upstream, the river is shallow. There stands a group of seven hills. On the hill known as the Palatine a settlement was founded that came to be known as Rome.

FOUNDING OF ROME

Romans have a legend about the founding of their city. After the fall of Troy the gods ordered a Trojan prince called Aeneas to lead his people to a promised land in the West. When Aeneas' group reached Italy, they joined forces with a people known as Latins.

About 800 B.C. a Latin princess gave birth to twin sons fathered by the god Mars. The princess had taken an oath never to have children. Because she broke her word, she was punished. Her sons, Romulus and Remus, were taken from her and left to die on the bank of the flooding Tiber.

Romulus and Remus were found by a she-wolf, which fed and cared for them. One day a shepherd killed the she-wolf and discovered the babies. He took them to his home. There the shepherd and his wife raised them as their sons.

THE TRIUMPH OF ROMULUS

After defeating Remus in battle, Romulus gained the support of the people of Rome. Under his rule, Rome expanded until it became the most important city in the Tiber region. After his death, Romulus was worshipped as a Roman god. What is the legend of Romulus and Remus?

When the boys grew older, they decided to build a city on the Tiber. Romulus traced the city's boundaries with his plow. But the brothers could not agree on which one should rule the city. They decided to let the gods choose between them.

Each brother climbed to the top of a different hill to watch for a sign from the gods. When 12 vultures flew over the Palatine, the brothers took it to be the sign they sought. Since Romulus stood atop the Palatine, he claimed to be king. He and Remus then fought, and Remus was killed. Romulus became king of the city, which he named Rome.

Romulus and Remus

Over the years many experts have tried to discover the truth about the founding of Rome. All they have learned is that around 1200 B.C. groups of people with iron weapons began invading the lands around the Mediterranean. One group invaded Egypt and brought down the New Kingdom. Another group, the Dorians, moved into the Balkan peninsula. A third group settled on the Palatine. This group, called Latins, was the one to which the Romans belonged.

The area where the Latins settled had a pleasant climate and fertile soil. Nearby were swamps and dense forests which supplied the Latins with timber. The Latins built gravel roads to bring salt and other items from the coast.

By 776 B.C. the settlement on the Palatine had become a village of about 1000 people. Most of the people were farmers who lived in wooden huts and worked the land. Their main crops were wheat and barley.

1. According to legend, how was Rome founded?
2. From where did the Latins come? Where did they settle? How did they live?

THE ETRUSCANS

Around 800 B.C. a people called Etruscans settled in Etruria, the rolling hill country north of the Latin village on the Palatine. The Etruscans wrote in an alphabet borrowed from the Greeks. They spoke a language different from any other in the ancient world. To this day, no one knows for certain from where they came.

The Etruscans dug tunnels and built dams to drain their marshy fields. High on hilltops they built a number of cities, each

ETRUSCAN ITALY

surrounded by a thick wall. From these hilltop cities they could see all the surrounding land, including the plains over which enemies might attack.

The Etruscans were Italy's first highly civilized people. They were known as a "people of the sea." As pirates, they were feared and envied throughout the Mediterranean. As traders, they were admired and respected.

Etruscan farmers used mostly iron tools to grow barley, millet, wheat, grapes, and other fruits. They raised pigs, goats, sheep, ducks, chickens, and cattle. They used the cattle for food and to pull plows and wagons. They made different kinds of cheese from ewe's milk.

Etruscan miners dug copper, lead, iron, and tin. Etruscan metalworkers and sculptors turned these minerals into weapons, utensils, and jewelry. Etruscan merchants exchanged both minerals and finished goods for luxury items of gold, silver, and ivory from Syria, Cyprus, Greece, and other eastern Mediterranean countries.

The Etruscans had a strong army which marched into battle to the sound of bronze trumpets. The soldiers learned much about weapons and battle techniques from the Greeks. Their infantry formed a phalanx much like the one used by the Greeks. The Etruscans had one "weapon" no one else had—their shoes. They wore heavy leather shoes which laced firmly around the ankle. This gave them better footing than their enemies on rough or hilly ground.

Over time, the Etruscan cities grew in size and power. The Etruscans became rich. By 600 B.C. they dominated all of northern Italy, including the Latin village on the Palatine.

1. From where did the Etruscans come? Where did they settle?
2. How did Etruscans earn their livings?
3. What were some features of the Etruscan army?

DAILY LIFE   The Etruscans enjoyed bright colors, luxury, and a good time. They amused themselves by gambling with ivory dice, or by playing games similar to chess and backgammon. Frequently they attended or took part in such sports as wrestling, running, boxing, and horse racing.

Most of all, the Etruscans loved music and dancing. Sounds from a double flute or a stringed lyre accompanied most of their activities. Much of their dancing was linked to religion. The dances were intended to gain favor from the gods.

Etruscan Woman

Both Etruscan men and women danced. Dancing was just one of the freedoms enjoyed by Etruscan women. Unlike Greek or Latin women, Etruscan women were encouraged to take part in public celebrations. It was not unusual for an Etruscan woman to be seen eating and drinking with her husband. Etruscan women also could own property.

The Etruscans had a strong sense of **social order**, or the way groups of people are classed. At first there were no great class differences among them. Only acrobats and slaves, who were captives of war, were thought to be inferior. In later years, however, the people were divided into three classes. The upper

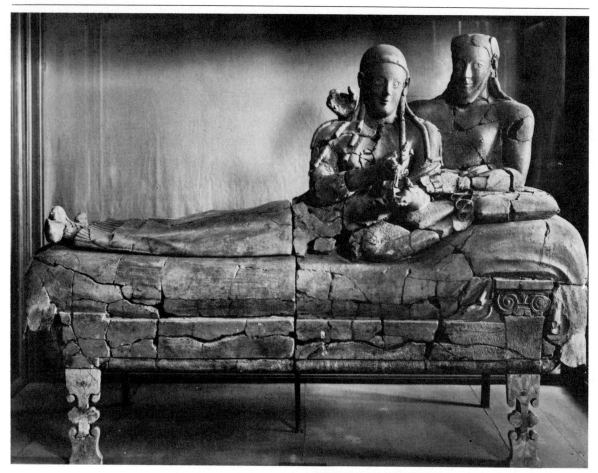

ETRUSCAN COUPLE
The Etruscans were known for their love of food, music, and sports. This tomb sculpture shows an Etruscan noble and his wife enjoying a meal. The Etruscans rested on couches while eating or listening to music.
Why were many Etruscans able to enjoy a pleasurable life?

class consisted of a small group of wealthy landowners, nobles, and priests. The middle class was made up of farmers and city workers, while the lower class was slaves.

A few wealthy families owned most of the land. They also owned most of the slaves who tended the land and did other work. The rich lived in rectangular one-story homes made of sun-dried brick on a frame of heavy timbers. A pitched roof covered with clay tiles extended beyond the house to protect the bricks and timber from rain. Most homes also had broad, walled courtyards open to the sky. A roofed hall led from the courtyard to three rooms that were lined up side-by-side across the width of the house. During the day the center room was usually used to conduct business. At night it was the scene of banquets and other entertainments enjoyed by wealthy Etruscans. Stone-lined drains led from each house into the main drains which ran along the pebble-paved streets.

1. What did Etruscans do for entertainment?
2. What was the role of Etruscan women?
3. How was Etruscan society divided?
4. What were some features of the homes of wealthy Etruscans?

RELIGIOUS BELIEFS   The Etruscans had many gods, most of whom were modeled after those of the Greeks. At first the Etruscans worshipped their gods outdoors on platforms of stone or earth. Later they built temples of wood, mud-brick, and clay on stone foundations. The temples had peaked tiled roofs adorned with sculptures.

The Etruscans believed that the universe was divided into provinces. Each province was ruled by different gods. Humans lived in the center of the universe, facing south toward the gods of nature and of earth. To the right lay the west, which was ruled by the gods of death and of the underworld. To the left lay the east, which was ruled by the gods of the heavens. The Etruscans believed that the west and the right were unlucky, while the east and the left were lucky. Thus, they planned their cities and built their temples to face the east and the left.

The Etruscans also believed that humans were powerless before the gods. More than anything else, Etruscans wanted to please the gods. But first they had to discover what the gods willed. They did this through a priestly group of aristocrats called **soothsayers**.

Etruscan Horse

The soothsayers read certain **omens**, or signs. One group of soothsayers read omens in the livers of sacrificed animals. The parts of the liver corresponded to the provinces ruled by different gods. Another group of soothsayers interpreted the will of the gods by studying the direction and sounds of thunder and lightning and the flight of birds.

1. How did Etruscans worship their gods?
2. What was the Etruscan view of the universe?
3. What did soothsayers do?

THE TOMBS OF GOLD   When an Etruscan noble died, a great banquet was held. At the banquet two of the noble's slaves fought one another to the death. The spirit of the slave who lost accompanied the noble's spirit to the underworld.

The dead were buried in underground tombs called **catacombs**. Much of what is known about Etruscan life comes from such tombs, whose inside walls were brightly painted with scenes of daily life. The tombs contained chairs and beds. The bodies of the dead rested on the beds.

Etruscans believed that life after death lasted longer and was more important than life on earth. So they carved their tombs out of natural rock, a material that would last for a long time. They filled the tombs with works of art and treasures of gold, silver, bronze, and ivory. Because of this, the Etruscan tombs are known as "tombs of gold."

Outside of each Etruscan city was a **necropolis**, or cemetery, made up of acres of these tombs. The necropolis outside the city of Caere is one of the largest Etruscan cemeteries. There, great mounds of earth are piled in the shape of a dome on top of foundations. Some of the mounds measure 100 feet, or about 30 meters, across. The foundations, which cover the tombs, are built on a grid of wide boulevards, each opening onto small plazas.

1. How did the Etruscans view life after death?
2. What were Etruscan tombs like?

CONTRIBUTIONS TO ROMAN CIVILIZATION

Etruscan Gold Clasp

In 616 B.C. Lucius Tarquinius became the first Etruscan ruler of Rome. No one is certain whether Tarquinius took the throne from the Latin king by force or by cleverness. Nevertheless, he founded a dynasty which ruled Rome for more than 100 years.

The Etruscans were more culturally advanced than the Latins. They made many contributions to Roman civilization. For example, the Etruscans taught the Latins how to use the arch in building bridges. They laid the foundations of Rome's first sewer system. They drained the swamp at the foot of the Palatine. This later became the place where the Roman Forum, an area much like the Greek agora, was built. The Forum housed a palace, government buildings, and law courts.

ETRUSCAN TOMB CHAMBER

The Etruscans looked forward to life after death and built many underground tombs. They believed the souls of the dead lived on in these chambers. To keep the departed soul happy, the Etruscans covered the walls of the tomb with colorful paintings.

What was Etruscan religion like?

The Etruscans borrowed the Greek alphabet and made some changes in it. The Romans, in turn, borrowed the alphabet from them.

The Romans also borrowed some Etruscan customs and symbols of authority. The slave fights held at Etruscan funerals were the model for **gladiatorial games** with which the Romans amused themselves. The gladiatorial games were fights between armed men, between men and animals, between women and dwarfs, and between animals.

The **triumph**, or the parade-like welcome given a Roman hero returning from battle, was an Etruscan custom before it became a Roman one. Also borrowed from the Etruscans was the **fasces**, or a bundle of rods bound around a central ax. It became the symbol of a Roman ruler's power to flog or execute.

The Etruscans also introduced the Romans to soothsayers and to gods with human forms. They built the first temple on Capitoline hill. The Capitoline later became the religious and political heart of Rome. Today it is the center of Rome's **municipal**, or city, government.

The Romans founded their cities according to a ritual borrowed from the Etruscans. Soothsayers read omens that told where the city's boundaries should be. A furrow was dug to mark the boundaries. The plow used to dig the furrow had a bronze blade, and was pulled by a white bull and cow yoked together. Workers then dug a trench at the center of the city. After each of the city's founders had tossed a handful of dirt into the trench, the priests took over. The priests laid out the main street and determined the principal cross street. The place where the two streets met was marked by a stone.

The Etruscans believed that the stone covered a shaft leading to the underworld. Three times a year an Etruscan priest lifted the stone to allow the souls of the dead to return to earth. The Romans believed the place where the two streets met was the **mundus**, or the meeting point for the worlds of the living and the dead. They opened the shaft to offer fruit and other gifts to the spirits of the underworld.

The Etruscans were not the first to develop or use many of the ideas and practices the Romans borrowed from them. They were, however, the people who brought these ideas to the notice of the Romans. Thus, they played an important role in the development of Roman civilization.

1. What were some of the contributions the Etruscans made to Roman civilization?
2. How did the Etruscans and the Romans found their cities?

CHAPTER REVIEW

SUMMARY

1. Rome was founded about 800 B.C. as a small settlement on the Palatine.
2. Rome's first settlers were Latins who invaded the Mediterranean region.
3. The main occupation of the Latins was farming.
4. North of the Latins lived the Etruscans, who conquered Rome in 616 B.C.
5. The Etruscans were noted throughout the Mediterranean world as traders and pirates.
6. The Etruscans enjoyed living and had a strong sense of social order.
7. The Etruscans worshipped many gods and used soothsayers to learn what the gods wanted.
8. The Etruscans placed importance on life after death and built elaborate tombs.
9. The Etruscans taught the Romans many things, including the use of the arch in building, an alphabet, and a ritual for establishing cities.

BUILDING VOCABULARY

1. *Identify the following:*

   Tiber River   Aeneas   Romulus and Remus   Lucius Tarquinius
   Palatine   Latins   Etruscans

2. *Define the following:*

   Pope   omens   gladiatorial games   municipal
   social order   catacombs   triumph   mundus
   soothsayers   necropolis   fasces

REVIEWING THE FACTS

1. Why did Romulus fight with his brother Remus?

2. How did the kind of shoes the Etruscans wore help them in battle?

3. Who were the first highly civilized people of the Italian peninsula?

4. Who owned most of the land in Etruria?

5. Why did Etruscan temples face the east and the left?

6. What was the purpose of the slave fights held at Etruscan funerals?

7. How have experts learned much of what they know about Etruscan life?

8. Who was the first Etruscan ruler of Rome?

9. What Etruscan custom did the Romans borrow to welcome home heroes?

10. How did the Etruscans and the Romans decide the boundaries of a city?

DISCUSSING IMPORTANT IDEAS

1. Why was religion an important part of Etruscan life?

2. Do you think the Etruscans used their natural resources wisely? Explain.

3. Do you think you would have enjoyed living in Etruria? Why or why not?

4. Do you think the Etruscan conquest of Rome was a good thing for the Romans?

USING MAPS

Refer to the map on page 184, and answer the following questions:

1. Where did the Etruscans settle in Italy?

2. What area of Italy did the Greeks settle?

3. What is the most northern river shown on the map?

4. Into what body of water does it flow?

5. What is the approximate latitude and longitude of Rome?

6. What is the northern border of Italy?

CHAPTER 14

THE ROMAN REPUBLIC

I n 509 B.C. Roman farmer-soldiers overthrew Tarquin the Proud, their Etruscan king. They abolished the monarchy and set up a **republic**, or a form of government in which the people choose their rulers.

Roman society was divided into two classes, **patricians** and **plebians**. Patricians were members of the oldest and wealthiest families. Plebians were poorer people, such as farmers and artisans.

Patricians made up about 10 percent of the population. They had the real say in the government because they were the only people allowed to perform the religious rituals required to hold public office.

Plebians were citizens. They paid taxes and served in the army. But they could not marry patricians or serve in the government. If they fell into debt, they could be sold as slaves.

THE GOVERNMENT

At the head of the Roman Republic were two **consuls** who were elected each year. The consuls were administrators and military leaders. Each could **veto**, or say no to, the actions of the other. Both had to agree before any policy could be made.

ROMAN GOVERNMENT OFFICIALS
Consuls and senators played an important part in the government of Rome. They came from Rome's wealthiest and most powerful families. Senators (left) enter a hall in the forum for a meeting. A consul (right) issues a decree. What did consuls and senators do?

Next in importance to the consuls was the Senate. It was made up of 300 men called senators who were chosen for life. The Senate handled the daily problems of government. It advised the consuls. It debated foreign policy, proposed laws, and approved public contracts for building roads and temples.

The government also included judges, assemblies, and **tribunes**. All Roman citizens belonged to assemblies, which could declare war or agree to peace terms. The office of tribune was not added to the government until 494 B.C. From then on, 10 tribunes were elected each year to protect the rights of the plebians.

Until about 450 B.C. Roman laws were not written down. Patricians told plebians what the laws were. The plebians, however, did not trust the patricians and resented having them explain the laws. So about 450 B.C. Roman laws were carved on 12 bronze tablets known as "Twelve Tables." The tablets were placed in the Forum so that everyone might see them and know their rights and duties. The laws dealt mainly with such things as wills, property rights, court actions, and the behavior of citizens in public. The laws carved on the Twelve Tables became the foundation for all future Roman law.

The election of tribunes and writing down of laws were the first steps to a more democratic government. Later, more plebian demands were met, which made the government even more democratic. By about 250 B.C., no one could be sold into slavery for debt. In addition, plebians were permitted to marry patricians and to hold public office.

1. What was the role of the consuls in the government of the Roman Republic?
2. What was the role of the Senate?
3. What were some of the changes made in Rome's government and laws by around 250 B.C.?

Roman Official

ROMAN EXPANSION

Once the Romans had established a republic, they set out to protect it. They were afraid that the Etruscans would try to regain control of Rome. To prevent this, the Romans crossed the Tiber River and conquered several Etruscan cities. Roman territory now bordered that of other Italian people. To protect their new boundaries, the Romans either conquered their neighbors or made alliances with them. By 290 B.C. Rome was the leading power in central Italy. By 275 B.C. it ruled the entire peninsula. Two centuries later Rome ruled most of the Mediterranean region.

The Romans were able to expand their territory because they had a strong army which was organized into **legions**. Each legion contained some 5000 soldiers called **legionaries** and was divided into groups of 60 to 120 soldiers.

The legion had several advantages over the phalanx. It was smaller and could move faster. Soldiers in a phalanx were used to fighting as a group and attacking only from one direction. Each legionary depended on his own fighting ability. The groups within a legion could split off from the main body and attack from the sides and the rear as well as the front.

Legionaries were well trained. They spent hours practicing with their double-edged iron swords. They went on long marches

---

ROMAN LEGION

The legions provided the military strength that made Rome great. They conquered new territories and guarded the frontiers. Here a Roman legion led by its general celebrates a military triumph.

What contributions did the legions make to the spread of Roman civilization?

every day. Before going to sleep, they had to build complete fortified camps, even when the legion would stay in the area only one night. They built roads out of lava blocks so troops and supplies could move forward more rapidly.

The Romans were mild rulers. At first they did not tax people they conquered. They let the conquered people keep their own governments and manage their own affairs. Some were even allowed to become Roman citizens. In return, the conquered were expected to serve in the Roman army and to support Rome's foreign policy. As a result, many enemies of Rome became loyal Roman allies.

1. Why did the Romans conquer Etruscan cities?
2. How did the Romans protect their new boundaries?
3. What were some features of the Roman legion?
4. What kind of rulers were the Romans?

The Punic Wars

By 264 B.C. the Romans had conquered some Greek city-states in southern Italy. This brought them into contact with the Phoenician city of Carthage. Carthage controlled all of North Africa, most of what is now Spain, and some islands off the coast of Italy. It also ruled the western half of Sicily, a large island at the toe of the Italian "boot." The Romans felt threatened by the Carthaginians. They also wanted the granaries which were on Sicily.

1. What territory did Carthage control?

THE FIRST PUNIC WAR   In 264 B.C. the Romans and Carthaginians clashed. A war broke out that lasted for 23 years. It was the first of three wars that came to be known as the Punic Wars.

The military strength of Carthage lay in its navy. Rome had no navy. The Romans built their first fleet to fight the Carthaginians. They modeled their ships after a Carthaginian warship they found abandoned on a beach. The Romans made one improvement on the Carthaginian model. They added a **corvus**, or type of movable bridge, to the prow. The Romans knew they could not outsail the Carthaginians, but they believed they could outfight them. The corvus allowed soldiers to board an enemy

Bronze Lamp

ship and fight hand-to-hand on its decks. In a sense, it changed a sea war into a land war.

The Romans lost many ships and men in storms during the first Punic War. Yet in the end they defeated the Carthaginians. In 241 B.C. the Carthaginians agreed to make peace and leave Sicily.

1. What was the military strength of the Carthaginians? Of the Romans?
2. Who won the First Punic War?

Hannibal

HANNIBAL AND THE SECOND PUNIC WAR   In 218 B.C. the Carthaginians, led by General Hannibal Barca, attacked the Romans by land from the north. Hannibal and his troops surprised the Romans by crossing the Alps into Italy. They came by way of Spain through southern Gaul, or present-day France. They brought elephants with them across the mountains to help break through the Roman lines. Hannibal's attack was the start of the Second Punic War.

Hannibal's army fought its way to the very gates of Rome, winning victory after victory. But when it got to the city, it did not have the heavy equipment needed to batter down the city's walls. It was short on supplies and soldiers, and could not get more because the Roman navy controlled the sea.

Unable to capture Rome, Hannibal and his troops roamed the countryside of southern Italy for 15 years. They raided and burned towns and villages and destroyed crops. Then, the Romans attacked Carthage, and Hannibal was called home to defend it. Hannibal lost his first battle—and the war—at a town south of Carthage. The power of Carthage was broken.

In 201 B.C. Carthage agreed to pay Rome a huge sum of money and to give up all its territories including Spain. The Spanish resources of copper, gold, lead, and iron now belonged to the Romans.

1. What role did Hannibal play in the Second Punic War?
2. What did the Romans gain from the Second Punic War?

THE THIRD PUNIC WAR   Following the Second Punic War there was peace for about 50 years. Then Carthage began to show signs of regaining power. To prevent this, the Romans attacked in 149 B.C. Within three years they won the Third Punic War. They burned Carthage and plowed salt in its fields so

THE CAPTURE OF CARTHAGE
Rome won the Third Punic War because it had better resources and more soldiers than Carthage. This painting shows Roman armies destroying the city.
How did Rome's treatment of its conquered people change as a result of the Punic Wars?

that nothing would grow. They killed the Carthaginians or sold them into slavery.

That same year, 146 B.C., the Greek city-state of Corinth and some of its allies refused to obey a Roman order. The Romans attacked Corinth and burned it to the ground. The Romans already controlled Macedonia and Syria. Now they added Greece to the areas under their rule. Rome had become the ruling power of the Mediterranean region.

1. What led to the Third Punic War?
2. What happened to Carthage and its people at the end of the Third Punic War?
3. How did Rome become the leading power of the Mediterranean region?

EFFECTS OF CONQUEST

The conquests and the wealth that came with them had a lasting effect on the Roman economy and government.

AGRICULTURAL CHANGES   Most Romans had been small farmers who believed in hard work and service to Rome. They had few luxuries. As Roman conquests grew, this began to change. The small farms disappeared, to be replaced by huge estates called **latifundias**.

Instead of growing wheat, the main Roman food staple, latifundias produced cash crops for market. Most latifundias were sheep and cattle ranches. Some contained olive groves and vineyards. Thus, the Romans began to import wheat from conquered areas, especially Sicily and North Africa.

A major reason for the change in Roman agriculture was Hannibal's invasion. While his troops were in Italy, they lived off the land. To prevent them from getting enough food, Roman farmers burned their fields and crops. By the time the Second Punic War was over, the land was ruined. Most Roman farmers did not have the money to fix up their farms or restore the land. Only patricians and rich business people had that kind of money. They bought the small farms and combined them to make latifundias. The owners of the latifundias did not need the farmers to work the land because they had slaves to do it instead.

Thus slavery was another major reason for the change in Roman life. When Rome first began expanding, the Romans did not make slaves of the people they conquered. By 146 B.C. that was no longer true. The Romans were impressed by the wealth of Greece, Syria, and Carthage. They liked the way people in those areas lived and decided to imitate them. Since those areas had widespread slavery, the Romans sent thousands of prisoners to Rome as slaves. Most lived and worked on latifundias.

Roman Slave

1. How did latifundias start?
2. How was Roman agriculture influenced by Hannibal?
3. How was Roman agriculture influenced by slavery?

FROM FARM TO CITY   The small farmers who had sold their land had little choice. They could stay and work the land for the new owners or move to the city. Almost all moved to Rome.

ROMAN APARTMENTS
Wealthy Romans built brick and stone apartments. They decorated the floors with mosaics and the walls with paintings. These apartment dwellers owned only a few pieces of furniture, most of which was simple in design.
What was city life like in Rome during the Republic?

There the farmers crowded into wooden apartment buildings six or more stories high. Living conditions were terrible. The aqueducts which brought water to the city were not connected to the apartment buildings. Neither were the sewers that carried away the wastes. The buildings often caught fire or collapsed. Diseases such as typhus were common.

Most farmers could not earn a living in the city. Except for construction, Rome had almost no industry. Most businesses were staffed by Greek slaves, who were better educated and had more skills than Roman farmers. About the only way farmers could get money was by selling their votes to politicians. They sold to the highest bidder.

1. Why did Roman farmers move to the city?
2. What conditions did farmers face in Rome?

DECLINE OF THE ROMAN REPUBLIC   As Rome expanded beyond Italy, the Romans began to demand taxes as well as slaves from the provinces and cities they conquered. Tax **contracts**, or legal agreements, were sold to people called **publicans**. The publicans paid Rome in advance for the contracts. Then they collected taxes from the conquered people. The amount of taxes collected was supposed to be no more than 10 percent above the price paid for the contract. Most publicans, however, tried to make as much profit as they could.

By about 135 B.C. Rome was in serious difficulty. Farmers had lost their land and, as a result, their economic and political independence. Merchants had become poorer because wealthy Romans could get luxury items elsewhere. Craftspeople had lost business because wealthy Romans preferred goods from Greece and Syria. Government officials were too busy getting rich to worry about solving the Republic's problems.

The gap between rich and poor grew greater. The poor hated the rich for what the rich had done to them. The rich hated and feared the poor. Rome was no longer politically stable.

1. What was the job of a publican?
2. What was life like in Rome during the decline of the republic?

ATTEMPTS TO SAVE THE REPUBLIC

Over the next 100 years many different popular leaders tried to improve conditions in Rome. Some were reformers, while others were generals.

Roman Entertainer

REFORMERS   Tiberius Sempronius Gracchus was the first reformer. He thought forcing small farmers off their land had created Rome's problems.

When he became a tribune in 134 B.C., Tiberius Gracchus suggested limiting the amount of land a person could own. He wanted to divide up public lands and give them to the poor. Another tribune vetoed his suggestion. Tiberius Gracchus then convinced the assembly to ignore the veto, to get rid of that tribune, and to put his suggestion into effect. Some senators began to worry that he would go too far regarding reform.

Then Tiberius Gracchus ignored the law and ran for a second term as tribune. The Senate organized a riot and had him and hundreds of his followers killed.

Gaius Marius

In 124 B.C. Tiberius Gracchus' younger brother Gaius Sempronius Gracchus was elected tribune. He thought moving the poor from the city back to the countryside was the answer to Rome's problems.

Gaius revised and extended the reforms of his brother. He also suggested that the government take over the sale of wheat and sell it to the poor below market price. This suggestion became law. Soon wheat was being given away, rather than sold. Nearly one out of every three Romans was receiving free wheat. Meanwhile, the Senate began to feel threatened by some of Gaius' suggestions and in 121 B.C. had him killed.

1. What reforms did Tiberius Gracchus make? Why was he killed?
2. What reforms did Gaius Gracchus make? Who had him killed?

THE GENERALS   After the reformers came the generals. In 107 B.C. General Gaius Marius, a military hero, became consul. The son of a day laborer, Marius was the first lower-class Roman to be elected to such a high office. He was supported by many ex-soldiers who felt the rich and the government had taken advantage of them. Many had been farmers who had lost their farms when they left to serve in the army.

Marius thought he could solve Rome's problems by creating a professional army. Until this time only property owners could become legionaries. Marius opened the army to everyone. He convinced the poor to join by offering them pay, land, pensions, and booty. Marius' plan helped Rome by providing jobs for many out-of-work Romans. At the same time it hurt the Roman Republic. Instead of giving loyalty to the government, the soldiers gave it to the general who hired and paid them.

Marius was opposed by General Lucius Cornelius Sulla. Sulla had been given a military command that Marius wanted. Marius tried to get the assembly to take the command away from Sulla and give it to him. An angry Sulla marched his army on Rome and seized the city. It was the first time a Roman commander had led his troops against the capital.

Civil war, or war between groups within a country, broke out. When it was over, Sulla made himself **dictator**, or absolute ruler, of Rome. Sulla believed the way to solve Rome's problems was by increasing the power of the Senate rather than that of the army. So he doubled the Senate's size. He gave the senators more duties and weakened the power of the tribunes. At the same time he stopped generals from holding the same army command for more than one year at a time.

1. How did Gaius Marius try to solve Rome's problems?
2. What did Marius do to anger Lucius Sulla?
3. What reforms did Sulla make?

JULIUS CAESAR   When Sulla retired in 79 B.C. a new group of generals fought for control of Rome. Two of them—Gnaeus Pompeius, known as Pompey, and Julius Caesar—had different ideas about how Rome should be ruled.

Pompey was supported by Marcus Tullius Cicero. Cicero was an orator, politician, and philosopher, who once served as

THE EXPANSION OF THE ROMAN REPUBLIC

Legend:
- Rome, 500 B.C.
- Start of 1st Punic War, 264 B.C.
- End of 3rd Punic War, 146 B.C.
- Death of Caesar, 44 B.C.
- Hannibal's Route

miles 0 100 200 300
kilometers 0 100 200 300 400

Coin of Julius Caesar

consul. Cicero believed strongly in a republic that was ruled by aristocrat senators. He continued to oppose Caesar up to the time of Caesar's death.

In the struggle for power, Caesar finally gained control after Pompey was murdered in 48 B.C. Caesar was a well-educated politician who had become a soldier. He had both military strength and strong family alliances to back him. He also had the economic support of Marcus Licinius Crassus, the richest man in Rome.

In 58 B.C. Caesar was appointed governor of a Roman province. There he built up a large, strong army that was loyal to him. Within seven years he conquered what is now northern France and Belgium and invaded Britain. The Senate began to fear he was growing too strong. So in 50 B.C. it ordered Caesar to disband his legions and return to Rome. Instead, Caesar entered Rome at the head of his troops. By 46 B.C. he was dictator of Rome.

Caesar brought about many reforms. He helped solve the land problem by redistributing state lands in Italy and by founding new colonies overseas. This gave land to thousands of ex-soldiers who had none. He began such public works projects as building roads and buildings and draining the marshes around Rome. This provided jobs for thousands of Romans who had not been able to find work. He organized and paid for gladiatorial games that were free to the public. This kept the poor and the idle from turning into unhappy and angry mobs. He doubled the size of the Senate. Although this made individual senators less powerful, it gave business people a chance to become senators. He restricted the activities of the publicans. He granted Roman citizenship to Greeks, Spaniards, and Gauls. And he adopted a new calendar based on the Egyptian calendar. Called the Julian calendar, it is still in use today.

Caesar did a great deal for Rome and its people. Still, some Romans were afraid that Caesar planned to make himself king. About 60 men, most of them senators, worked out a plan to kill him. As he entered the Senate on the Ides of March, or March 15, 44 B.C., Caesar was stabbed to death.

1. What helped Julius Caesar become dictator of Rome?
2. What reforms did Caesar make? What effect did they have on Rome?
3. Why was Caesar killed?

END OF THE REPUBLIC   Angered by Caesar's death, the Roman people turned against those who had killed him. Political power passed to a **triumvirate**, or a group of three persons with equal power. Mark Antony, Caesar's closest follower and a popular general, took command of Rome's territories in the east. Octavian, Caesar's grand-nephew and adopted son, took charge of the west. Marcus Aemilius Lepidus, one of Caesar's top officers, took over the rule of Africa. All three shared control of the Italian homeland.

For a while the triumvirate worked. Then fights broke out between the three leaders. When the fighting ended in 31 B.C. Octavian had won. Within four years he became absolute head of the Roman Empire.

1. How was political power divided after Caesar's death?
2. What finally happened to the triumvirate?

CHAPTER REVIEW
SUMMARY

1. In 509 B.C. the Romans overthrew the Etruscans and established a republic.

2. About 450 B.C. the Romans wrote down for the first time the laws which were to be the foundation for all future Roman law.

3. Rome gradually enlarged its boundaries until by 275 B.C. it ruled all of Italy.

4. Roman military power was based on a well-trained and well-organized army that was organized into legions.

5. Between 264 and 146 B.C. Rome and Carthage fought three wars known as the Punic Wars.

6. As a result of its conquests, Rome's small farms were replaced by large estates and most farmers had to leave the land and move to the city.

7. By 135 B.C. Rome was facing serious political and economic problems.

8. The Gracchi brothers tried to improve conditions in Rome by giving land to the poor and by providing free wheat for the hungry.

9. General Marius tried to solve Rome's problems by giving power to the army.

10. General Sulla tried to solve Rome's problems by giving more power to the Senate.

11. In 46 B.C. Julius Caesar became dictator of Rome and brought about many reforms.

12. In 44 B.C. a group of Romans, who were afraid that Caesar was planning to make himself king, killed him.

13. After Caesar's death, political power was divided among Mark Antony, Octavian, and Marcus Lepidus.

14. In 31 B.C. Octavian became the sole ruler of Rome.

BUILDING VOCABULARY

1. *Identify the following:*

Senate	Punic Wars	Gaius Gracchus	Julius Caesar
Twelve Tables	Hannibal Barca	Gaius Marius	Mark Antony
Carthage	Tiberius Gracchus	Lucius Cornelius Sulla	Octavian

2. *Define the following:*

republic	veto	corvus	civil war
patricians	tribunes	latifundias	dictator
plebians	legions	contracts	triumvirate
consuls	legionaries	publicans	

REVIEWING THE FACTS

1. What changes were made in Rome's government as a result of plebian demands?
2. Why was the legion so effective in battle?
3. At first, how did the Romans treat the people they conquered?
4. Why did Rome fight the Punic Wars?
5. How were the Romans able to overcome the Carthaginian navy?
6. What effect did latifundias have on Rome's small farmers?
7. Why were most farmers who moved to Rome unable to earn a living?
8. What effect did Marius' reforms have on the loyalty of legionaries?
9. Why did the Senate order Julius Caesar to disband his legions?
10. Who won the struggle for political power after Caesar's death?

DISCUSSING IMPORTANT IDEAS

1. Do you think the Romans were wise to start making slaves of the people they conquered? Why or why not?
2. Do you think the Romans were wise to start taxing the people they conquered? Why or why not?
3. If you had lived in Rome after 135 B.C., what would you have done to try to solve its problems?
4. If you had lived in Rome when Caesar was killed, how would you have felt about his murder? Explain.

USING MAPS

Refer to the map on page 203, and answer the following questions:

1. When did the Roman Republic reach its greatest expansion?
2. What was the furthest northern expansion? Eastern expansion?
3. During what period did Rome spread mostly into North Africa?
4. During what period did the Roman Republic spread into Spain?

THE ROMAN EMPIRE

15

I n 27 B.C. Octavian announced to the Senate that he had restored the republic. When he offered to resign, the Senate gave him various offices. They named him *princeps*, "first citizen," and *Pater Patriae*, "Father of the Country." He took for himself the title of Augustus, or "revered one." That is what historians usually call him. Octavian thus became the first **emperor**, or absolute ruler, of the Roman Empire.

THE RULE OF AUGUSTUS

Augustus was a clever politician. He held the offices of consul, tribune, high priest, and senator all at the same time. But he refused to be crowned emperor. Augustus knew most Romans would not accept one-person rule unless it was within the framework of a republic. So he restored the republic in form but not in practice.

Augustus kept the assemblies and officials of the republic and was careful to make senators feel respected. He talked of tradition and the need to bring back "old Roman virtues." He made the official religion important once again.

At the same time Augustus strengthened his authority in two ways. First, he had every soldier swear allegiance to him personally. This gave him control of the armies. Secondly, he built up his imperial household to take charge of the daily business of government. He chose people because of their talent rather than their birth. This gave slaves and **freedmen**, or former slaves, a chance to be part of the government.

THE EXPANSION OF THE ROMAN EMPIRE

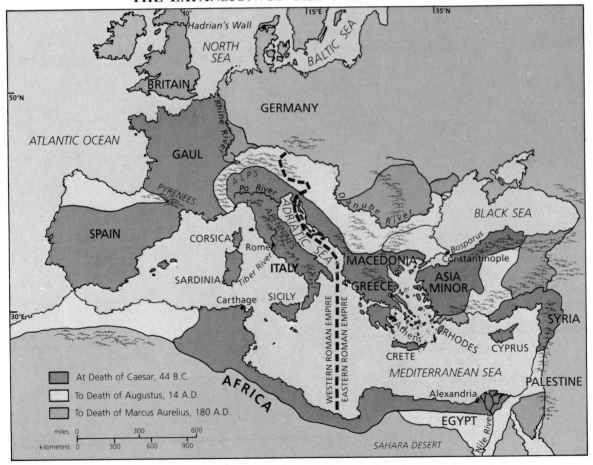

Legend:
- At Death of Caesar, 44 B.C.
- To Death of Augustus, 14 A.D.
- To Death of Marcus Aurelius, 180 A.D.

Augustus wanted boundaries that would be easy to defend. So he rounded out the empire to natural frontiers—the Rhine and Danube Rivers in the north, the Atlantic Ocean in the west, and the Sahara Desert in the south. To keep these boundaries safe from invaders, he stationed legions there.

Augustus was not interested in conquering new territory for Rome. Instead, he concentrated on governing the existing empire. He gave provincial governors long terms of office so they could gain experience in their jobs. He paid them large salaries so they would not feel the need to overtax the people or keep public money for themselves. To make sure that people did not pay too little or too much tax, Augustus ordered that a **census,** or population count, be taken from time to time.

Caesar Augustus

Augustus also made Rome more beautiful. He built marble buildings, many of which were temples and shrines. He wrote strict laws to govern people's behavior in public. He protected the city and the people by creating a fire brigade and a police force. He encouraged learning by building Rome's first library.

Augustus ruled for 41 years. During that time he brought peace and a new sense of patriotism and pride to the people. He made Roman citizenship available to people in the provinces. Most important, however, Augustus reorganized the government of Rome so that it ran well for over 200 years.

1. How did Augustus make the people think Rome was still a republic? Why did he want them to think this?
2. How did Augustus strengthen his authority?

THE PAX ROMANA

The peace which Augustus brought to Rome was called the *Pax Romana*. It lasted for 200 years. Revolts and other internal problems were not unknown during this period. Yet overall the empire and its people prospered. Cities did not need walls for protection. Legionaries served for 20 years without having to fight a single battle. Civilization spread, and cultures mixed.

With peace came increased trade. The same coins were used throughout the empire. There were no **tariffs,** or taxes placed on goods brought into the country. Goods and money moved freely along the trade routes. The Mediterranean was cleared of pirates, making it safe for trade and travel. Shipping became a big business. Every summer hundreds of ships carried grain from

North Africa to Italy. Other ships were loaded with cargoes of brick, marble, granite, and wood to be used for building. Luxury items, such as amber from the north and silk from China, passed overland across Roman roads. The roads also carried imperial mail to and from the provinces.

Increased trade meant increased business for Romans. The city hummed. Shopkeepers grew richer. Wine and oil were the main items bought by other countries. Italy became a manufacturing center for making pottery, bronze, glassware, jewelry, and woolen cloth.

1. Why was the Pax Romana important?
2. What happened to trade during the Pax Romana?

LAW During the Pax Romana Roman law went through major changes. Because conditions were different, the laws originally set down on the 12 bronze tablets were changed. For example, when Rome conquered a new territory, Roman merchants found themselves doing business with non-Romans. In order that both sides be treated fairly, Roman judges had to develop new laws which would be as fair to non-Romans as to Romans. The Roman judges were helped by special lawyers and legal writers called *juris prudentes*.

After a while the judges and their assistants developed certain legal principles that were fair to everyone. A law was

---

CENSUS

For tax purposes, the Roman government kept detailed records on both its people and its land. At regular periods, a census was taken to bring the records up-to-date. Here a group of Romans wait in line to give information to a census-taker. The group consists of patricians and plebeians.

What does the census reveal about the way Roman government was organized?

---

considered just because it was reasonable, not because the government had the power to enforce it. Everyone was considered equal before the law. A person was innocent until proven guilty. The accuser, rather than the person accused, had to prove his or her case. People could not be punished for what they thought.

By about the year 125 A.D., Roman law was **standardized**. This meant that all legal procedures were the same throughout the empire. This helped Rome govern a large area successfully. In later years Roman legal principles formed the basis for the laws of most western nations and of the Christian Church.

Roman Couple

1. What happened to law during the Pax Romana?
2. What were some of the legal principles that developed during the Pax Romana?

DAILY LIFE

In the early years of the empire about 1 million people lived in Rome. Rome suffered from many of the same problems cities do today. There was too little housing and too much traffic. The air was polluted. There was crime in the streets. The cost of living was high. Many Romans could not find jobs. Romans had to pay taxes on almost everything—slaves, estates, roads, crops. There was even a local sales tax.

The rich of Rome lived in a *domus*, or house, with marble walls, colored mosaic floors, and windows made of small panes of glass. A furnace heated the rooms, and pipes brought water even to the upper floors.

Most Romans, however, were not rich. They lived in small, smelly rooms in apartment houses six or more stories high called **islands**. Each island covered an entire block. At one time there were 26 blocks of islands for every private house in Rome. The ground floor of most islands was given over to shops which opened onto the street from large arched doorways.

Rents were high in Rome. They varied according to the apartment floor—the higher up the apartment, the lower the rent. July 1 was **eviction day**, or the day anyone who had not paid the rent was forced to move out.

1. What was living in Rome like during the early years of the empire?
2. Who lived in a domus?
3. What were the homes of most Romans like?

THE FAMILY   In Rome the family was all important. The father was the head of the household. His word was law. He arranged the children's marriages to improve the family's social position or to increase its wealth. Cousins were expected to help one another politically.

Until they were age 12, most Roman boys and girls went to school together. Then the sons of poor families went to work, while the sons of rich families began their formal education. The government usually paid the salaries of the school staff. Each school taught a different subject.

The sons of the wealthy studied reading, grammar, writing, music, geometry, commercial arithmetic, and shorthand. When they were age 15, they entered a school of **rhetoric**, or speech and writing, to prepare for a political career. Some went to schools in Athens or Alexandria for philosophy or medicine.

Girls received a different kind of education. When they reached age 12, their formal education stopped. Instead of going to school, the daughters of the wealthy were given private lessons at home. As a result, many Roman women were as well or better informed than Roman men. Some women worked in or owned small shops. Wealthy women had slaves to do their domestic chores for them. This left them free to study the arts, literature, and fashions, or to ride chariots in the countryside for a day's **pig-sticking**, a type of hunt.

1. How did Romans feel about the family?
2. What kind of schooling did Roman children have?

AT LEISURE   At home the Romans amused themselves by gambling with dice. They socialized at public bathhouses. The bathhouses provided more than baths. Some included gymnasiums, sports stadiums, and libraries. At a bathhouse Romans could take warm, cold, or steam baths. They could watch or play games. They also could listen to lectures, see musical performances, exercise, or just sit and gossip.

The Romans had no team sports to watch. Instead, they flocked to see free public games which often ran from dawn to

---

ROMAN GLADIATOR

On festival days, 50,000 Romans jammed the Colosseum to watch the gladiatorial games. These contests were very violent. Excited spectators often signaled a victorious gladiator to kill his opponent.

What kinds of people became gladiators?

---

dusk. Under the empire, the games were staged by the government. Under the republic, they had usually been staged by politicians who were looking for votes. The games included circuses, chariot races, and gladiatorial games. The most exciting chariot races were held at the Circus Maximus, an oval arena that could seat more than 25,000 people. Every year in September a festival called *Ludi Romani* took place in the Circus.

The men who fought animals and one another in arenas were called **gladiators**. Most were slaves, prisoners of war, criminals, or poor people. They were trained by contractors who hired them out. A few gladiators were upper-class Romans who wanted excitement and public attention.

A ROMAN BANQUET MENU

APPETIZERS AND SOUPS
Snails Fed on Milk
Fried Bulbs
Grilled Truffles in Sausage Skin
Minced Sea-Crayfish-Tail Balls
Barley Soup with Dried Vegetables Topped with Cabbage Leaves
Puree of Lettuce-Leaves with Onions

MAIN COURSES
Boiled Electric Ray with Hot Raisins
Boiled Crane with Turnips
Smoked Pig's Stomach Stuffed with Brains, Pine Kernels, and Peppercorns
Roast Hare in White Sauce
Leg of Boar
Roast Flamingo with Jericho Dates, Dried Onion, Honey, and Wine
Wood-Pigeon Baked in Oil-Flour Pastry

DESSERTS
Sweet Fricassee of Pumpkin
Egg Sponge with Milk in Honey
Stew of Apricots

The night before they were to fight, gladiators would appear at a banquet. There they could be looked over by fans and gamblers who wanted to bet on the outcome of contests. When gladiators entered the arena on the day of the games, they would walk past the emperor's box saying, "Hail Emperor, those who are about to die salute you."

Many gladiators did die. Those whose fighting pleased the crowd became popular idols. A few won their freedom. Those who did not give a good performance had their throats cut.

Gladiator and Animal

All kinds of animals were used in the public games. Some animals pulled chariots or performed tricks. Most, however, fought one another or gladiators. Sometimes as many as 5000 wild animals were killed in a single day. In some cases, such as that of the Mesopotamian lion and the North African elephant, whole species were wiped out.

1. What did the Romans do for entertainment?
2. What were public games?
3. What was the role of the gladiator?

FALL OF THE EMPIRE

The Pax Romana ended after approximately 200 years. From then on, conditions within the Roman Empire grew steadily worse. By 476 A.D. there was no empire left. Instead, much of western Europe was a patchwork of Germanic kingdoms. The eastern portion of the empire, however, lasted about 1000 years longer as part of the Byzantine Empire.

There are many reasons why the Roman Empire fell. Three reasons stand out. The first was political. Neither Augustus nor the emperors who followed him had a formal rule about who was to inherit the throne upon an emperor's death. Sometimes the title was inherited by a son. But usually an emperor's son was too spoiled to be a good ruler. Sometimes an emperor adopted an heir to the throne, choosing the most able and hardest working individual he knew. Between 96 and 180 A.D. all emperors were adopted. The system worked well until after 180 A.D.

Emperor Marcus Aurelius was kind, intelligent, and devoted to duty. His son was just the opposite. He became emperor when Marcus Aurelius died in 180 A.D. But he was so cruel and unpopular that in 192 A.D. he was strangled by the Praetorian Guard, the soldiers on duty at the palace. After killing the

EMPERORS DURING THE PAX ROMANA

Emperor	Reign	Accomplishments
Augustus	27 B.C.–14 A.D.	first emperor of Roman Empire
		reorganized government of Rome; brought peace to Rome
Tiberius	14 A.D.–37 A.D.	reformed taxes and improved financial state of government
Caligula	37 A.D.–41 A.D.	repaired roads and began construction of two aqueducts
Claudius	41 A.D.–54 A.D.	conquered most of England
		extended citizenship to many people outside Rome
		set up ministries to handle government administration
Nero	54 A.D.–68 A.D.	rebuilt Rome after the fire of 64 A.D. and gave it a city plan
Flavian Emperors Vespasian Titus Domitian	69 A.D.–96 A.D.	brought people from the provinces into the Senate
		secured frontier regions
		brought Rome new prosperity
		built the Coliseum
Five Good Emperors Nerva Trajan Hadrian Antoninus Pius Marcus Aurelius	96 A.D.–180 A.D.	built aqueducts, bridges, and harbors
		extended citizenship to more provinces
		cut dishonesty in business and government

emperor, the Praetorian Guard sold the throne to the highest bidder. This set a dreadful example. For nearly 100 years legion fought legion to put the emperor of its choice on the throne. By 284 A.D. Rome had had 37 different emperors. Most were murdered by the army or the Praetorian Guard.

This political problem helped to create the second and third major reasons for Rome's downfall. The second reason was economic. To stay in office, an emperor had to keep the soldiers who supported him happy. He did this by giving them high wages. This meant more and more money was needed for the army payroll. So the people had to pay higher taxes.

In addition to higher taxes, Romans began to suffer from **inflation**, or a period of ever-increasing prices. Since there were no new conquests, gold was no longer coming into Rome. Yet much gold was going out to pay for luxury items. This meant there was less to use in coins. As the amount of gold used in coins decreased, money began to lose its value. Prices went up. Many people stopped using money. Instead, they began to barter to get what they needed.

The third major reason why Rome fell centered on foreign enemies. While Romans argued and fought with each other over politics and money, they left Rome's frontiers open to attack. Gradually Germanic hunters and herders from northern and central Europe began to raid Greece and Gaul. Trade and farming in those areas declined. Cities once again began to surround themselves with walls for protection.

1. What were three major reasons for the fall of the Roman Empire?

THE CITY OF ROME

The city of Rome was located on seven small hills on the Tiber River. Roman emperors sponsored building projects and made Rome a city of monuments, temples, palaces, and stadiums. This map shows the city in 350 A.D.
What problems did Romans face during the last years of the Empire?

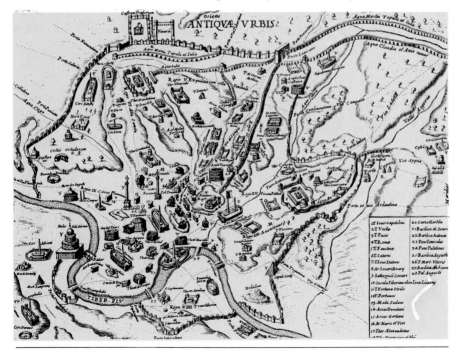

Roman Coins

DIOCLETIAN AND CONSTANTINE I

Two emperors, Diocletian and Constantine I, made strong attempts to save the Roman Empire from collapse.

Diocletian, who was the son of a freedman, ruled from 284 to 305 A.D. He made many changes as emperor. He fortified the frontiers to prevent invasion. He reorganized the state and provincial governments to make them function better. He set maximum prices for wages and goods throughout the empire to stop prices from rising. He ordered workers to stay in the same jobs until they died to make sure goods were produced. He made city officials personally responsible for the taxes their communities had to pay.

One of the most important changes Diocletian made concerned the position of the emperor. Diocletian established the official policy of **rule by divine right**. This meant that the emperor's powers and right to rule came not from the people but from the gods.

Diocletian realized that the Roman Empire covered too much territory for one person to rule well. So he divided it in two. He allowed someone else to govern the western provinces while he kept control of the larger eastern provinces.

In 312 A.D. Constantine I became emperor. He ruled until 337 A.D. Constantine took even firmer control of the empire than Diocletian. To keep people from leaving their jobs when things got bad, he issued several orders. Sons of workers had to follow their fathers' trades. Sons of farmers had to stay and work the same land their fathers worked. Sons of ex-soldiers had to serve in the army.

To escape government pressure and control, wealthy landowners moved to their **villas**, or country estates. Most estates were like small, independent cities or kingdoms. Each produced enough food and goods to supply the needs of everyone who lived on it.

Despite the changes made by Diocletian and Constantine, the Roman Empire continued to decline in the west. In 330 A.D. Constantine moved his capital from a dying Rome eastward to the newly built city of Constantinople in present-day Turkey.

1. What did Diocletian do to try to save the Roman Empire?
2. What did Constantine I do to save the Roman Empire?
3. How did the wealthy landowners react to Constantine's edicts?

END OF THE EMPIRE

Both Diocletian and Constantine I worked hard to save the Roman Empire. However, neither emperor succeeded in the end.

German raids increased, especially in western Europe. There the Germans crossed the Danube River in order to escape from the Huns, nomadic herders who had wandered west from Outer Mongolia in Asia. In 378 A.D., a Germanic tribe defeated Roman legions at the battle of Adrianople.

By around 400 A.D. Rome had grown quite weak. In the winter of 406 A.D. the Rhine River froze. Groups of Germans crossed the frozen river and entered Gaul. The Romans could not force them back across the border.

In 410 A.D. the Germanic chief Alaric and his soldiers invaded Rome. They burned records and looted the treasury. The Roman Senate told the people, "You can no longer rely on Rome for finance or direction. You are on your own."

1. Why did German raids on the empire increase?
2. How did the Germanic tribes gain control of the empire?

CHAPTER REVIEW
SUMMARY

1. Octavian, better known as Augustus, became the first emperor of the Roman Empire in 27 B.C.

2. Augustus reorganized the Roman government so well that a period of peace known as the Pax Romana existed for over 200 years.

3. Trade increased within the empire during the Pax Romana.

4. During the Pax Romana Roman law went through many changes until it was standardized about 125 A.D.

5. During the Pax Romana about 1 million people lived in Rome, which suffered from such problems as overcrowding, fires, unemployment, and pollution.

6. Most Romans were not wealthy and lived in apartment houses called islands.

7. The Roman government staged free public games to entertain the people.

8. The major reasons for the fall of the Roman Empire were the lack of a formal rule about who was to inherit the throne, inflation, and attacks by Germanic tribes.

9. Two emperors, Diocletian and Constantine I, tried to save the Roman Empire from collapse, but neither succeeded in the end.

10. In 410 A.D. Rome itself fell to Germanic invaders.

BUILDING VOCABULARY

1. *Identify the following:*

Augustus	Marcus Aurelius	Diocletian	Adrianople
Pax Romana	Praetorian Guard	Constantine I	Alaric
Circus Maximus			

2. *Define the following:*

emperor	juris prudentes	eviction day	inflation
freedmen	standardized	rhetoric	rule by divine right
census	domus	pig-sticking	villas
tariffs	islands	gladiators	

REVIEWING THE FACTS

1. Why did Augustus give provincial governors long terms of office?
2. How did Augustus make life in Rome safer for its people?
3. How did increased trade during the Pax Romana affect Rome and the Romans?
4. Why did the Romans change the laws set down on the 12 bronze tablets?
5. What was the importance of standardizing Roman law?
6. What did Rome's public bathhouses provide besides baths?
7. What happened to some species of animals as a result of the public games?
8. What did the Praetorian Guard have to do with the fall of the Roman Empire?
9. Why did Diocletian divide the Roman Empire in two?
10. What were the major reasons for the final fall of Rome?

DISCUSSING IMPORTANT IDEAS

1. Do you think Augustus was a good ruler? Why or why not?
2. Why are the principles of Roman law that developed during the Pax Romana important?
3. Do you think you would have enjoyed living in Rome during the Pax Romana? Explain.
4. What happens to a government if there is no rule for passing on its power?

USING MAPS

Refer to the map on page 208, and answer the following questions:

1. Into what areas did the Roman Empire expand between the deaths of Augustus and Marcus Aurelius?
2. What is located at 54° north latitude and approximately 0° longitude?
3. What is located at about 35° north latitude and 8° east longitude?
4. What is the approximate longitude of the division between the western and eastern halves of the Roman Empire?

CHAPTER

CHRISTIANITY

16

Just as the Romans influenced the people they conquered, the conquered people influenced the Romans. Among those who were to have a major influence were the Christians. Their religion, Christianity, started in Palestine among the Jews. Like other religions from the Middle East, it ultimately was brought to Rome.

At first most Romans ignored or ridiculed Christianity. Some emperors treated Christians cruelly. By 400 A.D., however, attitudes had changed. Christianity had become the official religion of the Roman Empire.

BEGINNINGS

Christianity is based on the life and teachings of Jesus, who lived in Palestine during the reign of Augustus. After Jesus died, his teachings were spread by his followers. Christianity survived the fall of Rome and grew to be one of the major influences on western civilization.

1. On what is Christianity based?

THE LIFE OF JESUS   Jesus was born in the town of Bethlehem, but grew up in Nazareth. There he received a Jewish education in the local synagogue. He studied the **scriptures**, or sacred writings, and learned prayers in the Hebrew language. Later he went to work as a carpenter.

When he was about 30 years old, Jesus began to travel throughout Palestine preaching to the people. Men and women came in large numbers from all over the country to see and hear him. Jesus taught that God created all humans and loved them the way a father loved his children. Therefore, people should behave like God's children and love God and one another. Jesus particularly extended God's love to people who had sinned. He told the people that if they were truly sorry and placed their trust in God, they would be forgiven.

Jesus spoke in the everyday language of the people. He presented his teachings in **parables**, or stories, about persons and things that were familiar to his listeners. In this way they could better understand the religious principles he was trying to teach.

In 33 A.D., after about three years of preaching, Jesus and 12 of his **disciples**, or followers, went to Jerusalem to celebrate Passover, the holiday which marks the exodus of the Jews from Egypt. At the time there was much unrest in the city. Many Roman officials believed all Jews were guilty of treason because they refused to worship statues of the Roman emperor. The Jews were tired of the high taxes they had to pay and of the pressure put on them by the Romans. They hoped and waited for a **messiah**, or someone who would save them.

When Jesus arrived in Jerusalem, many Jews greeted him as the messiah. This worried other Jews and Romans alike. Jesus was convicted of treason under Roman law and was **crucified**, or executed on a cross, outside of Jerusalem. Usually only lower-class criminals were executed in this way.

JESUS AND DISCIPLES
Jesus chose 12 disciples to travel with him throughout Palestine. In this thirteenth-century painting, Jesus calls the fishermen-brothers Peter and Andrew to leave their trade and to follow him.
Why were people willing to follow Jesus?

Jesus' disciples were greatly saddened by the loss of their leader. Then they learned that Jesus had risen from the dead. Following the **resurrection**, or rising from the dead, Jesus reportedly remained on earth for 40 days before going directly to heaven. This convinced his disciples that Jesus was the Son of God who had become man. The disciples felt that because Jesus had suffered death and had risen to life, he could forgive the sins of humanity. They thought that anyone who believed in Jesus and lived by his teachings would know eternal life after death. From then on the disciples called him Christ, after the Greek word *Christos*, meaning "messiah."

1. What did Jesus teach? How did he die?
2. How did Jesus' disciples view him after his death?

PAUL   The disciples were among the first people to become Christians. After Jesus died they tried to spread his **gospel**, or teachings, among the Jews in Palestine. They had little success, however. Most Palestinian Jews wanted a political messiah instead of a religious one. The disciples were more successful when they began to preach to Jews who lived outside Palestine. Soon small groups of believers were meeting near the synagogues of Antioch, Corinth, Rome, and other trading cities of the Mediterranean region.

Meanwhile a Jew named Paul decided to preach Christianity to **gentiles**, or non-Jews, as well as to Jews. At one time Paul had been a strict follower of Judaism. He had **persecuted**, or mistreated, Christians since he thought Christianity was a threat to Judaism. However, after reportedly hearing Christ's voice and being blinded by a bright light, Paul became a Christian. He then began to preach Christianity throughout the Roman world.

In each city where Paul preached, new Christian communities formed. Paul wrote letters to guide and advise the members. In his letters he stated that gentiles who became Christians did not have to follow Jewish rituals and laws. All they needed was to have faith in Jesus. This appealed to many people.

Christianity began to grow from the belief of a few into a world religion. Paul was the first Christian **missionary**, or person who spreads religious beliefs to non-believers. After Paul's death, other Christian missionaries continued his work.

1.   Who were the first Christians? How was their message received in Palestine? How was it received in other places?
2.   What change did Paul make in the Christian message?

CHRISTIANITY AND ROME

Paul

The Roman Empire helped Christianity spread. The Pax Romana allowed missionaries to travel all over the empire in safety. The Roman system of roads helped them go from one place to the next quickly. As most of the people spoke either Latin or Greek, the missionaries could talk with them directly.

1.   What helped Christianity spread?

POLITICAL CONDITIONS   Political conditions did not favor the spread of Christianity, however. Although all people in

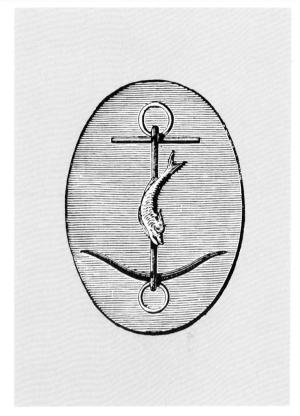

EARLY CHRISTIANITY
Many Christians died during the years of Roman persecution. Christian widows and their children (left) pay their respects at a grave. The anchor and fish (right) are Christian symbols found on many early Christian tombs.
Where did the Christians of Rome bury their dead?

the Roman Empire were allowed to worship freely, Romans expected everyone to honor the emperor as a god. The Christians, like the Jews, refused to do this. They claimed that only God could be worshipped. This greatly annoyed the Romans.

The Romans also did not like some other Christian attitudes. For example, Christians did not want to serve in the army or hold public office. They often criticized Roman festivals and games. They taught that all people would be equal in heaven if they followed Jesus' teachings.

Thus, the Romans blamed and punished the Christians for all kinds of disasters such as plagues and famines. In 64 A.D. they accused the Christians of starting a fire which burned down

much of Rome. Christianity was then made illegal, and many
Christians were killed. Some officials ignored the law which
made Christianity illegal, but Christians still had a difficult time
in most areas of the empire. In Rome they were forbidden to use
regular burial places. They had to bury their dead in crowded
catacombs.

1. Why did most Romans dislike Christianity?
2. How did Roman dislike affect the Christians?

THE SPREAD OF CHRISTIANITY   In spite of the difficulties, however, Christianity continued to spread. At first the rich

THE SPREAD OF CHRISTIANITY

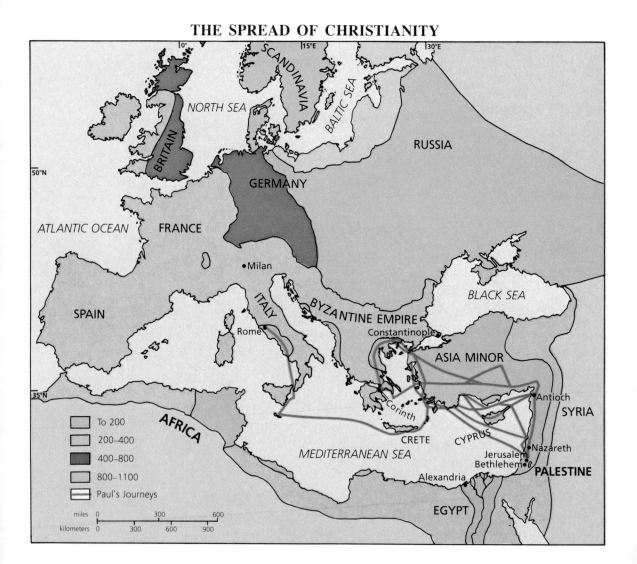

were not interested in it. They did not want anything to do with a religion whose founder had died by crucifixion. Christianity was of more interest to the poor workers and slaves in the cities. They led very hard lives. A religion that promised a happier life after death attracted them.

Silver Cup

Over time Christianity began to draw people from all classes. After 250 A.D. Romans grew tired of war and feared the collapse of the empire. They began to admire the certainty and courage of the Christian missionaries. They wanted the love, kindness, and security that Christianity offered. At the same time, many Christians became less opposed to the empire. Christian writers began to claim that it was possible to be both a good Christian and a good Roman.

1. What groups of people were first attracted to Christianity? Why were they attracted?
2. What factors brought about a change in attitudes between Romans and Christians?

CONSTANTINE I   In 312 A.D. Christianity gained the support of Constantine I, who was a general at the time. Legend says that as he was about to go into battle, Constantine saw a flaming cross in the sky. Written beneath the cross were the Latin words *In hoc signo vinces*, "In this sign thou shalt conquer." Constantine won the battle and with it the throne of the Roman Empire. He believed that God had helped him, so he ordered his soldiers to paint crosses on their shields.

The following year the Edict of Milan was issued. It granted religious freedom to all and made Christianity legal. Constantine I did a great deal to encourage the growth of Christianity. He had churches built in Rome and Jerusalem. He allowed the use of government money to support Christian churches. He permitted church leaders to enter government service and excused them from paying taxes.

The emperor who followed Constantine I continued pro-Christian policies. In 392 A.D. the emperor Theodosius made Christianity the official religion of the Roman Empire and outlawed all other religions.

1. Why did Constantine I support Christianity?
2. How did relations between Christians and the Roman government change during Constantine I's reign?
3. What did Theodosius do to help Christianity?

THE CHURCH

Early Christians thought the end of the world was near. At the time, they believed Jesus would return to set up God's kingdom on earth. While they were waiting for this to happen, they lived together in small groups called **churches**. They shared whatever goods they had and took turns conducting worship services in homes and outdoors. Each group managed its own affairs. **Apostles**, or those followers Jesus chose to preach his gospel, visited the various groups. The apostles taught and gave advice on problems. They also provided a sense of unity.

1. What did early Christians believe?
2. What did the apostles do?

CHURCH STRUCTURE   After the apostles died, Christians realized that Jesus was not going to return to earth as quickly as they had expected. So they looked for ways to hold their churches together. They began to develop a church organization. Since they lived in the Roman Empire, they borrowed its structure of government.

By 300 A.D. each local church was called a **parish** and had a fulltime leader known as a **priest**. Several parishes were grouped together into larger units. Each unit was called a **diocese**, a term that originally meant a Roman military district. A **bishop** headed each Christian diocese. The most important bishops were called **archbishops**. They governed churches in the larger cities of the empire. The five leading archbishops were called **patriarchs**.

As time went on, the archbishop of Rome began to claim authority over the other archbishops. By 600 A.D. he was called **Pope**, a Latin word meaning "father." Latin-speaking Christians regarded him as the head of all of the churches. Greek-speaking Christians, however, would not accept his authority over their churches. They turned instead to the archbishop of Constantinople. In 1054 A.D. the Latin and Greek churches split. The Latin churches as a group became known as the Roman Catholic Church. The Greek churches became known as the Eastern Orthodox Church.

1. Why did Christians develop a church organization?
2. How was the church organized?
3. What caused the split between the Latin and the Greek churches?

Bishop

EARLY CHURCH ORGANIZATION

Patriarchs

Patriarchs were archbishops with the highest standing. They headed churches founded by apostles.

Archbishops

Archbishops were bishops of large cities. They governed an area of several dioceses.

Bishops

Bishops headed a group of parishes called a diocese. They preached, performed important church rituals, collected offerings for the poor, and appointed priests.

Priests

Priests headed the local Christian community, or parish. They advised bishops, preached, led worship services, and carried out missionary work.

Deacons

Deacons assisted bishops and priests in church worship, cared for the poor, and looked after finances.

THE NEW TESTAMENT   At the same time that Christians were developing a church organization, they were deciding what writings to include in the New Testament, or Christian scriptures. Jesus had left no written records. However, after the crucifixion, others wrote about his life and teachings.

Toward the end of the fourth century A.D., four of these accounts were accepted as part of the New Testament. The accounts were believed to have been written by Matthew, Mark, Luke, and John, four of Jesus' early followers. A number of letters written by Paul and other disciples were also accepted as sacred writings.

At about the same time, bishops met in councils to discuss questions about Christian thinking. The decisions they reached at these councils came to be accepted as official **doctrine**, or teachings. The points of view the councils did not accept were considered **heresy**, or false doctrines.

1.   What writings make up the New Testament?
2.   What did the councils of bishops do?

FATHERS OF THE CHURCH   Between 100 and 500 A.D. various scholars wrote works that greatly influenced later Christian thinkers. These scholars were known as "Fathers of the Church." Jerome was one such scholar. He translated the Old and New Testaments into Latin. His work, called the *Vulgate*, became the official Latin bible used by the Roman Catholic Church.

Jerome

Augustine was another important leader of Christian thought. His most famous work was *City of God*. In it he defended Christianity against those who claimed that Rome would not have fallen to Germanic invaders if it had not accepted Christianity. Augustine argued that Rome's fall was a punishment for having become rich and corrupt and for having persecuted Christians. He explained that Rome would have fallen sooner or later because the only eternal city is the city of God.

1.   Who were the Fathers of the Church?
2.   What did Jerome contribute to Christian thought?
3.   What argument did Augustine make in the *City of God*?

MONASTERIES   In the early years of Christianity thousands of Christians often left the cities to live and pray alone in the desert. Such people were called **hermits**. In Egypt and Syria especially, thousands of hermits lived apart from other people. They believed that being a hermit would help them grow closer to Christ.

A hermit was protected from the temptation of daily life. But at the same time, the hermit was not doing anything to improve society. Near the end of the fourth century A.D. a bishop named Basil suggested a different way of life. He said that dedicated Christians should form religious communities near cities. In this way they would be protected from the evils of the world. At the same time they could help others by performing good deeds and by setting an example of Christian living. Many Christians took Basil's advice.

Monastery Bell Tower

The Christian men who did as Basil suggested were called **monks**. Their communities were known as **monasteries**. The Christian women who did the same were called **nuns**. They lived in quarters of their own called **convents**. Basil drew up a list of rules for these communities. This list, which is known as the Basilian Rule, became the model for Eastern Orthodox religious life.

In the West another rule called the Benedictine Rule was followed. It was created in Italy about 529 A.D. by Benedict. The monks who followed Benedict's rule promised to give up all their possessions before entering the monastery. They agreed to wear simple clothes and eat only certain foods. They could not marry. They had to obey without question the orders of the **abbot**, or leader of the monastery. They had to attend services seven times during the day and once at midnight. In addition, they were expected to work six or seven hours a day in the fields surrounding the monastery. When they grew older, the monks did clerical work or worked as carpenters and weavers. In this way, they spent their entire lives serving Christ.

By the seventh century A.D. monks were playing an important role in spreading Christianity throughout Europe. By taking care of old Roman and Greek writings, they helped western civilization survive.

1. What type of life did hermits lead? Why did they live this way?
2. What did Basil suggest? Why did he suggest this?
3. What were some of the rules Benedict expected monks to live by?

CHAPTER REVIEW

SUMMARY

1. Jesus was born in the town of Bethlehem in Palestine.

2. Jesus grew up in Nazareth, where he received a Jewish education, and then went to work as a carpenter.

3. When he was 30, Jesus began to preach about God and His love for all humans.

4. In 33 A.D. Jesus was convicted of treason under Roman law and was crucified.

5. Following his resurrection, Jesus became known as Christ, which means "messiah."

6. Paul preached Christianity to non-Jews as well as to Jews and thus helped make Christianity a world religion.

7. In 313 A.D. Constantine I issued the Edict of Milan making Christianity legal in the Roman Empire.

8. In 392 A.D. Theodosius made Christianity the official religion of the Roman Empire.

9. Christians developed a church organization based on the structure of government of the Roman Empire.

10. By 600 A.D. the archbishop of Rome was called Pope and was regarded by Latin-speaking Christians as head of the Church.

11. In 1054 A.D. Greek-speaking Christians split from the Latin churches.

12. Between 100 and 500 A.D. scholars, such as Jerome and Augustine, wrote works that greatly influenced later Christian thinkers.

13. A bishop named Basil suggested that dedicated Christians become monks and nuns rather than hermits so they could help others by performing good deeds and by setting an example of Christian living.

14. Western monks lived according to a list of rules drawn up by Benedict about 529 A.D.

BUILDING VOCABULARY

1. *Identify the following:*

Jesus	Constantine I	Eastern Orthodox Church	City of God
Bethlehem	Edict of Milan	Jerome	Basil
Nazareth	Theodosius	*Vulgate*	Benedict
Paul	Roman Catholic Church	Augustine	

2. *Define the following:*

scriptures	gentiles	diocese	hermits
parables	persecuted	bishop	monks
disciples	missionary	archbishops	monasteries
messiah	churches	patriarchs	nuns
crucified	apostles	Pope	convents
resurrection	parish	doctrine	abbot
gospel	priest	heresy	

REVIEWING THE FACTS

1. Where did Christianity start?
2. What sort of early education did Jesus receive?
3. Why did Jesus teach in parables?
4. Why were the Jews hoping and waiting for a messiah?
5. What is the legend associated with Constantine I?
6. What did the Edict of Milan do?
7. After 1054 A.D., what name was given to the Latin churches as a group?
8. After 1054 A.D., what name was given to the Greek churches as a group?
9. What kinds of work did monks do?
10. How did monks help western civilization survive?

DISCUSSING IMPORTANT IDEAS

1. Do you think that teaching in parables is effective? Why or why not?
2. If you were an early Christian leader, how would you have organized the church? Why would you have done it this way?
3. Do you think anything could have been done to prevent the split between the Latin and Greek churches? Explain.
4. If you had lived around 600 A.D., would you have become a monk or nun? Why or why not?

USING MAPS

Refer to the map on page 226, and answer the following questions:

1. When did Christianity spread to Antioch?
2. During what time period did Christianity spread the most?
3. Into what areas did Christianity spread between 400 and 800 A.D.?
4. Into what areas did it spread between 800 and 1100?
5. In what area did Paul make most of his journeys?
6. To what cities did Paul travel?

BUDDHISM

Siddhartha Gautama was born in the foothills of the Himalayas about 563 B.C. He was born a Hindu, but he grew up to found a new religion called Buddhism. This much of his life is known to be true. The rest is legend. Yet the story has an important place in Buddhism.

Siddhartha Gautama was the son of a rich noble who wanted to protect his son from human sorrow. The boy grew up shielded from sights that were not pleasant. As a young married man Gautama lived in luxury. His palaces were surround-ed by parks filled with strange birds and rare fish. He was followed wherever he went by servants.

When Gautama was about 30 years old, he made three trips outside his palace grounds. On these trips he met two men, one very old and one quite sick. He also saw a dead man. For the first time Gautama learned about aging, sickness, and death. He was troubled that he and all other humans had to suffer these many tragedies.

On a fourth trip Gautama met a holy man. This man had nothing but a bowl for begging and a single yellow garment. Yet he looked very happy. Gautama realized that there was more to happiness than possessions. He decided to leave his wife and new-born son and to seek truth and wisdom.

For several years Gautama lived as a wandering monk. He starved himself and read the holy books of Hinduism. Still he could not find an answer to freedom from life's suffering.

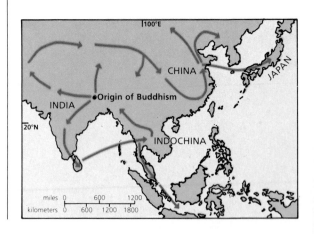

Finally Gautama decided to find life's answers through his own thinking. One day he wandered into a village and sat under a tree. He decided to **meditate**, or think, until he gained **enlightenment**, or understanding. Several hours later enlightenment came.

Gautama learned that people could find freedom from suffering in *nirvana*, or a state of complete happiness and peace. He believed that suffering was caused by human desires. Therefore, by not desiring anything and by living correctly, a person would find peace.

Others learned of Gautama's experience and began to call him Buddha, which means the "Enlightened One." His teachings became a new religion—Buddhism.

One of India's most famous kings, Asoka, was influenced by Buddha's teachings. Asoka ruled India about 260 B.C. He followed Buddha's teachings and became **tolerant**, or respectful, of all living things. Asoka also sent Buddhist teachers to other lands. In later years Buddhism became one of the major religions of Asia.

1. What kind of life did Siddhartha Gautama lead in his youth?
2. What led Gautama to change his way of life?
3. What did Buddha teach? How did his teaching influence others?

UNIT REVIEW

SUMMARY

1. The Etruscans contributed many ideas and customs to Roman civilization.

2. In 509 B.C. the Romans abolished the monarchy and in its place established a republic.

3. Through conquests and alliances, the Romans expanded their territory until eventually they ruled most of the western world.

4. War and conquest changed Roman life and gradually led to the decline of the republic.

5. Augustus, the first Roman emperor, brought to Rome the period of peace and prosperity known as the Pax Romana, during which trade increased, laws were standardized, and Christianity spread.

6. Christianity became the official religion of the Roman Empire and a major influence on western civilization.

7. Political and economic problems which weakened the Roman Empire and made it possible for foreign invaders to defeat Roman armies led to the fall of Rome.

REVIEWING THE MAIN IDEA

1. Explain how the daily life of Romans during the Pax Romana showed the influence of the Etruscans.

2. Explain in what ways the Romans were affected by the religion and the economic life of the different people they conquered over the years.

3. Compare the government of the Roman Republic with the government of the Greek city-states.

DEVELOPING SKILLS

One skill that is needed in order to think clearly is the ability to relate cause and effect. Sometimes one event causes another event. Other times one event follows another in time, but there is no cause-and-effect relationship between the two. That is, the first event does not cause the second event.

This exercise is designed to give you practice in deciding if one event is the cause of another event. Below are five pairs of events. For each pair, tell whether or not the first event was a cause of the second.

1. a. Roman legions conquered what is now the nation of France.
   b. Many French words come from Latin, the language of the Romans.

2. a. Hannibal Barca and his troops roamed the countryside of southern Italy for 15 years.
   b. The Romans began using prisoners of war as slaves.

3. a. Gaius Marius was elected consul of Rome.
   b. Julius Caesar became dictator of Rome.

4. a. Augustus reorganized the government of Rome.
   b. The Pax Romana lasted for 200 years.

5. a. A Jew named Paul decided to preach Christianity to gentiles and to Jews.
   b. Christianity gradually spread throughout the Roman Empire.

SUGGESTED UNIT PROJECTS

1. Find out which words in the preamble to the Constitution of the United States come from Latin.

2. Working in a group, put out a newspaper, complete with headlines, articles, advertisements, and classified ads, that covers events in the Roman Republic or Empire.

3. Prepare a report on the Roman water system. Tell where the water came from, how aqueducts carried it across the valleys, and how it was distributed in the cities.

4. Bring in pictures of buildings or other structures in the United States that resemble those in ancient Rome.

SUGGESTED READING

Cunliffe, Barry. *Rome and the Barbarians*. New York: Henry Z. Walck, Inc., 1975. A description of what archaeologists have learned about the Roman legions and the Gauls, Britons, and Germans against whom they fought.

Dillon, Eilis. *Rome Under the Emperors*. New York: Thomas Nelson, Inc., 1974. A description of the daily life of the families of a senator, a rich businessman, a farmer, and a flower-and-fruit seller in Imperial Rome.

Fagg, Christopher. *Ancient Rome*. New York: Warwick Press, 1978. A description of the civilization of the Romans whose empire dominated the western world for 500 years.

Honness, Elizabeth. *The Etruscans: An Unsolved Mystery*. Philadelphia and New York: J. B. Lippincott Company, 1972. A description of Etruscan civilization.

Liversidge, Joan. *Everyday Life in the Roman Empire*. New York: G. P. Putnams' Sons, 1976. A description of the influence of Rome on the life of people in different parts of the Roman Empire.

Macnamara, Ellen. *Everyday Life of the Etruscans*. New York: G. P. Putnams' Sons, 1973. A description of Etruscan art and artifacts discovered in Etruria.

Stearns, Monroe. *Julius Caesar: Master of Men*. New York: Franklin Watts, Inc., 1971. An account of the life and times of Julius Caesar.

UNIT 6

375 **378** Battle of Adrianople	400	425
	410 Goths attack Rome Angles, Saxons, and Jutes enter Britain	
525	550	575 **597** Christian missiona arrive in Britain
675	700	725
	711 Arab Muslims conquer Spain	**732** Battle of Tours
825	850	875
843 Treaty of Verdun		
975	1000	1035
	c. 1000 Vikings explore North Atlantic	

THE EARLY MIDDLE AGES

0	475	500
455 Vandals sack Rome	**c. 476** Roman Empire ends in West **481** Clovis becomes king of Franks	
0	625	650
0	775	800
		800 Charlemagne crowned emperor **811** Alfred becomes king of Wessex
0	925	950
911 Normans settle in Normandy		

1.   WHY IS THE MIDDLE AGES AN IMPORTANT PERIOD IN HISTORY?

2.   HOW DID EVENTS IN THE MIDDLE AGES INFLUENCE THE GROWTH OF WESTERN EUROPE?

The period from the fall of the Roman Empire to the beginning of modern times is called the Middle Ages. It lasted from about 500 to about 1500 A.D. Historians have looked at the Middle Ages in several different ways.

Some historians see the Middle Ages as a time of darkness. They base their judgment on the fact that during much of the period there was little learning in Europe. Except for religious leaders and some townspeople, few individuals could read or write. Trade and city life declined throughout Europe. Most people lived in the country and knew little about life beyond their villages. There was no central government to keep the peace. Political and military power was mostly in the hands of local nobles.

Other historians consider the Middle Ages as the beginning of present-day western civilization. They point out that western ideas of society, trade, and government began to develop in this period. It was also the time when students and teachers were forming the first universities, and when modern European languages were evolving.

For others, the Middle Ages is the "Age of Faith"— that is, the period in which the Church shaped people's lives. Churches and monasteries were built in every part of Europe. People were willing to serve in armies to fight for the Church.

Most historians agree that the Middle Ages was a time in which western Europe created a new civilization. It was based on Greco-Roman culture, Christian faith, and Germanic practices.

CHAPTER 17

THE GERMANS

During the first 400 years after the birth of Christ, a tall, fair-haired people called Germans left the forests and marshes of northern Europe. Looking for a warmer climate and new grazing land for their cattle, they slowly moved south toward the Roman Empire. They were also attracted to Rome by its wealth and culture. The Germans hoped to live peacefully within the borders of the Roman Empire.

At first the Romans did not want to let the Germans enter their territory. They considered Germans their enemies. But by about 300 A.D. the Romans realized they were not strong enough to keep them out. So they began to let Germans cross the border in small groups.

Many Germans moved into the Danube River valley. There they settled, became farmers, and gradually adopted Roman ways. They traded with Roman merchants and joined the Roman army. Missionaries convinced some Germans to become Christians.

VILLAGE LIFE

Although the Germans took part in Roman life, they also kept much of their own culture. They lived in villages surround-

GERMAN VILLAGE
The Germans built their villages just within the borders of the Roman Empire. They lived together in family groups that included grandparents, aunts, uncles, and cousins. What was German village life like?

ed by farmlands and pastures. Most homes were long thatched-roof huts with an open space around them. The family lived in one end of the hut and divided the other end into animal stalls. The body heat of the animals helped to warm the hut during the cold winters. Wooden tables and benches placed along the walls of the huts were the only furniture. A few wealthier villagers added wall hangings or carpets.

The villagers made their living herding cattle, which provided food and clothing. They also traded cattle for Roman glass vessels, table articles, and jewelry. The Germans farmed, too. They grew barley, rye, wheat, beans, and peas. Most farm work was done by women, children, and slaves. They drew water from wooden wells and stored food in pits lined with basketwork. When the women were not working in the fields or cooking, they spun wool and wove cloth on upright looms.

German dress was simple. Women wore long skirts made of different yarns or one-piece sack-like dresses which extended from the shoulders to the feet. Sometimes they wore scarves or shawls tied with a bone pin. Men wore short woolen tunics and close-fitting trousers. They covered the tunics with cloaks fastened on the right shoulder with a brooch.

The Germans believed in **hospitality**, or welcoming guests and strangers warmly. It was against the law to turn away someone who came to the door. Invited guests and strangers alike were fed and entertained. Feasting, drinking, and dancing were favorite German pastimes. The men also enjoyed gambling with dice. Sometimes they took part in such organized sports as boxing and wrestling. In winter they skated on ice using skates made of flat bone.

The Germans spoke a language that later became modern German. At first the people could not read or write because their language had no alphabet. However, some learned to speak and write Latin. Gradually they began to use Roman letters to write their own language.

1. Where did the Germans live? How did they earn their living?
2. What did the Germans do for entertainment?
3. How was the German language influenced by the Romans?

WARRIORS　　German men were warriors. They spent most of their time fighting, hunting, or making weapons. They began training for war when they were young boys. When a male

German Helmet

GERMAN WARRIORS
Some German families claimed descent from the gods, had wealth, and supplied leaders in time of war. A German warrior and his family (left) are dressed in their finest clothing. A warrior band and its chieftain (right) celebrate a victory over the Romans.
How did German warriors dress for battle?

reached manhood, he was brought before a special gathering held in a sacred grove under a full moon. He received a shield and a spear, which he had to carry with him at all times. The loss of the shield and spear meant the loss of honor.

The Germans were divided into **clans**, or groups based on family ties. At first the Germans gave their greatest loyalty to their clan. But after a while they developed a strong feeling of loyalty toward a military leader called a **chieftain**. A warrior had to be a good fighter to be a chieftain. In the beginning the chieftain was elected by a band of warriors. Later the office of chieftain became hereditary.

Chieftains provided warriors with leadership, weapons, and a chance for wealth and adventure. They also settled disputes among warriors. In some cases the chieftains gave warriors food and shelter. In return, warriors gave their chieftains total loyalty. Warriors took an oath to defend and protect their chieftains.

Individual warriors even gave chieftains credit for brave deeds they themselves performed. In battle, chieftains fought for victory, and warriors fought for their chieftains.

Chieftains and their bands did not have fixed plans of fighting. Each warrior band was small. It usually fought on its own, apart from other bands. The bands made surprise raids against their enemies. Warriors on foot and on horseback would charge wildly, yelling in loud voices to frighten their foes. They fought with daggers, short swords, and heavy axes made of metal and stone. They carried light wooden shields and wore suits of leather. A successful attack provided warriors with human captives, cattle, and other treasures.

The Germans' love of battle was closely linked to their religion. They had many gods who liked to fight and to hunt. The chief god, Woden, was the god of war, learning, poetry, and magic. Another god of war was Woden's son Thor, who was also the god of thunder. The Germans believed that the sound of thunder came from Thor's chariot wheels rolling across the heavens.

The Germans admired bravery. Like the Spartans, they expected their warriors to win in battle or to die fighting. The only German shields left on the battlefield were those of dead warriors. The Germans believed that goddesses carried the spirits of warriors who died in battle into the afterlife. There, in a place called Valhalla, the warriors would feast and fight forever.

German Sword

1. What kind of training did a German boy receive?
2. How were chieftains chosen?
3. How did Germans fight?
4. What were some features of the German religion?

THE LAW Romans believed that law came from the emperor. The Germans believed it came from the people. German rulers could not change the law unless the people approved.

The Germans based their laws on the customs of their ancestors. Instead of writing down the laws, the Germans memorized them and passed them from parent to child.

Reckless fighting, usually caused by too much drinking, created a problem in German villages. The Germans wanted to keep such fights from becoming **blood feuds**, or quarrels in which the families of original fighters seek revenge. Blood feuds could go on for generations. To stop such violence, the Germans set up courts. Judges listened to each side's argument and tried to find a settlement that would bring peace to the community.

The Germans determined who was guilty or innocent in different ways. One way was by oath-taking. People accused of crimes would declare their innocence by oath. Then they would present statements from **oath-helpers**, or people who swore that the accused was telling the truth. The Germans believed that anyone who did not tell the truth when taking an oath would be punished by the gods.

People accused of crimes could not always find oath-helpers to prove their innocence. In such cases, guilt or innocence was decided by **ordeal**. Persons accused of a crime had to walk barefoot over red-hot coals or place an arm into boiling water. The burns of the innocent were supposed to heal within three days. There also was an ordeal by water. A person was bound hand and foot and thrown into a lake or river. The Germans viewed water as a symbol of purity. They believed the water would accept anyone who was pure and reject anyone who was not pure. If the person sank to the bottom, it was a sign of innocence. If the person floated, it was a sign of guilt.

The Germans did not always require a person who was judged guilty to be punished physically. The courts could impose fines called *wergeld*. The exact amount of the wergeld varied. For example, an injury to a chieftain called for a larger payment than one to an ordinary person. The payment for killing a teenage girl was greater than one for killing a woman too old to have children. Though the courts could impose fines, they did not have the power to collect them. They had to rely on public opinion to force a guilty person to pay the fine.

The German legal system kept the peace, but it did not treat all people fairly. A person's wealth and importance, instead of the crime, determined the penalty. Still, the Germans believed that laws came from the people rather than the ruler. And no ruler could change the laws without the people's approval. Ideas such as these are still in practice in many societies in the world today.

1. What led Germans to set up courts?
2. How did Germans determine a person's guilt or innocence?
3. What were some strengths of German law? What were some weaknesses?

German Chieftain

GERMAN LAW

The Germans believed that the gods revealed a person's guilt or innocence through ordeals. Here a German leader performs a ritual over boiling water. He asks the gods to decide the outcome of a trial.

What were ordeals like?

THE GOTHS AND THE VANDALS

The Goths were a Germanic people who lived in the Balkan peninsula of southeastern Europe. They were divided into two smaller groups called East Goths and West Goths.

In the latter part of the fourth century both groups of Goths were attacked by the Huns. The Huns swept into Europe from central Asia under a leader named Attila, or "Little Daddy." Attila and the Huns conquered the East Goths. The West Goths were afraid they, too, would be conquered. So they asked the Roman emperor for protection. The emperor allowed them to settle just inside the frontier of the Roman Empire. In return, they had to give up their weapons and promise to be loyal to Rome.

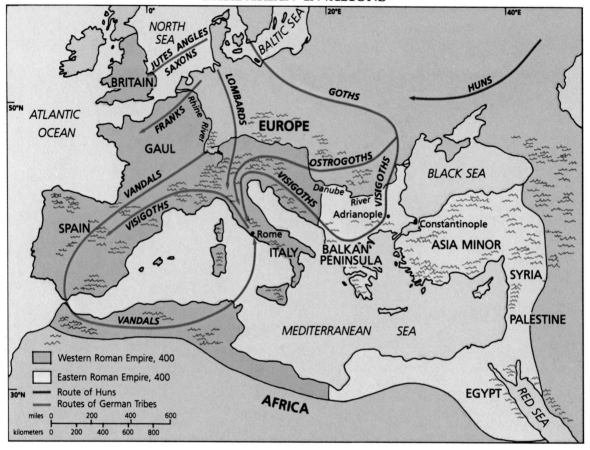

Before long, trouble broke out between the West Goths and Roman officials. The Romans were supposed to supply the West Goths with food and clothing. Instead the West Goths had to buy food at very high prices. The Romans kidnapped many young West Goths and sold them as slaves.

Finally the West Goths rebelled against the Romans and defeated them at the battle of Adrianople in 378. But the West Goths did not stop there. In 410, led by the chieftain Alaric, they captured and robbed Rome. This astonished and horrified many people throughout the empire. For the first time in 800 years, Rome had fallen to a foreign enemy.

After the capture of Rome, the West Goths continued on to Gaul. Then they moved into Spain, which was occupied by Romans and another Germanic group called Vandals. The West

Goths ended Roman rule in Spain, drove out the Vandals, and set up their own kingdom.

The Vandals in turn crossed the Mediterranean to North Africa. They became pirates and raided cities along the Mediterranean coast. From these raids came the English word "**vandalism**," meaning the willful destruction of property.

In 455, led by their king, Gaiseric, the Vandals attacked and burned Rome. They did, however, spare the lives of the Romans. After the attack the Vandals returned to North Africa.

1. What happened to the East Goths? What effect did this have on the West Goths?
2. Why did the West Goths come to dislike Roman officials? What did they do to show their dislike?
3. What did the Vandals do to Rome?

THE GERMANIC KINGDOMS

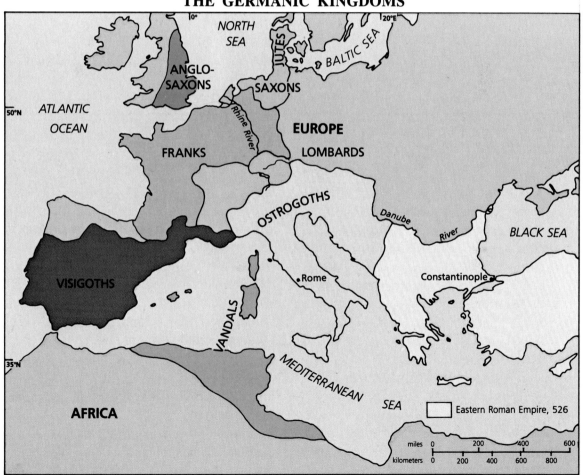

THE END OF THE EMPIRE

As a result of Germanic invasions, the Roman Empire in the West began to fall apart. Generals fought each other for control of Rome and Italy. Many of these generals were Germans who, when victorious, usually chose Roman citizens to serve as emperor. These emperors had little power of their own and followed the advice of the general in control.

In 476 a general named Odoacer took control of the government. He did not bother to appoint an emperor. Instead he ruled the western part of the empire for almost 15 years. After his death a group of East Goths invaded Italy and set up a kingdom under their leader, Theodoric.

By 550 the Roman Empire in the West had faded away. In its place were six major and a great many minor Germanic kingdoms. Although Roman rule was no more, many Roman beliefs and practices remained to shape the civilization of the early Middle Ages.

1. What happened to the office of emperor after the Germanic invasions?
2. What replaced the Roman Empire in the West?

CHAPTER REVIEW
SUMMARY

1. About 300 A.D. groups of Germans began settling in the Roman Empire.

2. German men were warriors, while German women did the farm work.

3. German warriors were organized into bands headed by chieftains, to whom the warriors gave complete loyalty.

4. The Germans' love of battle was closely linked to their religion.

5. The Germans determined a person's guilt or innocence through oath-taking or ordeal.

6. German courts often imposed fines rather than physical punishment.

7. The penalty for a crime depended on a person's wealth or importance.

8. The Germans believed that law came from the people and that a ruler could not change the law without the people's approval.

9. In 378 the West Goths defeated the Romans at the battle of Adrianople.

10. In 410 the West Goths captured and robbed Rome before setting up their own kingdom in Spain.

11. The Vandals, who had lived in Spain, moved to North Africa and began to raid cities along the Mediterranean coast.

12. By 550 the Roman Empire in the West had been replaced by six major and a great many minor Germanic kingdoms.

BUILDING VOCABULARY

1. *Identify the following:*

Germans	Goths	Adrianople	Gaiseric
Woden	Huns	Alaric	Odoacer
Thor	Attila	Vandals	Theodoric
Valhalla			

2. *Define the following:*

hospitality	chieftains	oath-helpers	wergeld
clans	blood feuds	ordeal	vandalism

REVIEWING THE FACTS

1. Why did the Germans begin to move south toward the Roman Empire?
2. Why did the Romans start allowing Germans to cross the borders of the Roman Empire?
3. Who did the farm work in German villages?
4. What did the loss of his shield and spear mean to a German warrior?
5. What did a German chieftain do for the members of his band?
6. How did warriors show their loyalty to their chieftain?
7. What did the Germans believe the afterlife would be like?
8. According to the Germans, where did law come from?
9. Why did the Germans use an ordeal by water?
10. Why did the West Goths want to enter the Roman Empire, and how did they come to do so?

DISCUSSING IMPORTANT IDEAS

1. Do you think you would have liked living in a German village? Why or why not?
2. Was religion important to the Germans?
3. Do you believe that the penalty for a crime should depend on a person's wealth or importance? If not, on what do you think it should depend? Explain.
4. What do you think might have happened if Roman officials had treated the West Goths fairly? Explain.

USING MAPS

Compare the maps on pages 248 and 249, and answer the following questions:

1. From what area of Europe did the German tribes move?
2. Which German tribe appears to have moved the furthest?
3. Why do you think the German tribes moved west and south?
4. How much of Europe did the tribes occupy in the sixth century?

CHAPTER 18

THE FRANKS

The decline of the Roman Empire led to disorder everywhere in western Europe. Many of the Germanic invaders were too weak to govern well. As a result, towns and villages fell into ruin. Roads and bridges were not repaired. Robbers roamed the countryside, making it unsafe for travelers. Trading and business slowed down, and there were shortages of food and other goods. People were no longer interested in learning, and many books and works of art were damaged or lost.

This period of hardship is called the Early Middle Ages. Some historians have also called it the Dark Ages. It lasted for about 500 years, from about 500 to 1000.

CLOVIS

During this period a Germanic people called Franks became very important. They began to build a new civilization, one that later developed into modern France and Germany. The Franks lived along the Rhine River in the area now known as western Germany. They were more successful in governing than other Germans. One reason for this was that the area in which they lived was close to their homeland, and they felt fairly secure. Also, unlike the Goths and Vandals, the Franks did more than just fight and rule. They became farmers.

At first, the Franks were divided into separate groups without a common ruler. In 481 one of the groups chose a king named Clovis. As a person, Clovis was cruel and greedy. As a leader, he was a good general and an able ruler who brought all of the Franks under one rule. Part of Clovis' kingdom later became the nation of France, which took its name from the Franks.

Clovis was the first Germanic king to accept the Catholic religion. The following story is told about how this happened. Clovis was not happy with the Frankish gods. Even though he prayed to them faithfully, they failed to help him win battles. His Christian wife suggested that he pray to God. Clovis agreed to do so, saying that if he defeated the enemy, he would become a Christian. The Franks won their next battle. Clovis and some 3000 of his soldiers, still in full battle dress, immediately **converted**, or changed religion, to Christianity. It was not long before all the Franks followed their king's example.

When Clovis became a Christian, he gained the support of the Romans in his kingdom. They had lived in Gaul before the Franks arrived, and most of them already were Christians. Before long the Franks began speaking a form of Latin that later became the modern French language. Now all the people of Clovis' kingdom practiced the same religion and spoke the same language. This helped them feel more united.

The Church taught that God gave the king the right to rule. Therefore, in order to govern, a king had to have the blessing of

BAPTISM OF CLOVIS

Clovis, the first strong Frankish king, became a Catholic. At his baptism, a bishop pours water over Clovis, making the king a church member.
How did Clovis' becoming a Catholic affect the people of his kingdom?

the Church. Clovis had that blessing. The Pope and other church officials gave him their support. Priests served in Clovis' government and won for it the respect of the people. In return for this help, Clovis was expected to protect the Church against non-believers and heretics.

Clovis extended his rule over what is now France and western Germany and set up his capital in Paris. He admired the Roman Empire and tried to copy its ways. He wore the purple robes of the Roman emperors and used purple ink for his royal decrees. He made Latin the official language of the court.

1. Why were the Franks more successful at governing than other Germanic peoples?
2. Why did Clovis become a Christian?
3. In what ways did Clovis copy the Roman emperors?

CHARLES THE HAMMER

The Frankish kings who followed Clovis were weak rulers. Instead of keeping the kingdom united, they divided it among their sons. The sons often fought over their shares of land. They spent so much time and energy fighting that they lost much of their power to local nobles.

It was not long before the Franks began to accept the leadership of a government official known as the "Mayor of the

BATTLE OF TOURS

Charles Martel (center) leads his armies against the Muslims at the Battle of Tours. The Frankish victory halted the Muslim advance into Western Europe. It also helped the Frankish rulers to build a strong kingdom.

Why was Charles Martel known as "The Hammer"?

Palace." The Mayor was a noble and the most important official in the king's household. As the kings grew weaker, the Mayors took over many of their duties. In time they were conducting wars, giving out land, and settling disputes. Of all the Mayors the most powerful was Charles Martel. He wanted to reunite all the Frankish nobles under his rule. Before long he had gained the support of the Church.

Charles Martel became known as "The Hammer" because of his strength in battle. In 732 he led the Franks in the Battle of Tours, one of the most important battles in European history. The Franks defeated an army of Arabs, a people from Arabia who had conquered Spain in 711. The Arabs were Muslims, or followers of a religion known as Islam. They hoped to spread Islam everywhere.

When Charles Martel died, his son Pepin became Mayor of the Palace. With the help of the Pope and most of the Frankish nobles, Pepin removed the king and started a new dynasty. Pepin was the first Frankish king to be **anointed**, or blessed with holy oil, by the Pope. In return for the Church's support, Pepin helped the Pope when he was threatened by a group of Germans known as Lombards. Pepin led an army into Italy, defeated the Lombards, and gave the land they held in central Italy to the Pope. This gift made the Pope the political ruler of much of the Italian peninsula.

1. What was the role of the Mayor of the Palace?
2. What did Charles Martel want to do?
3. Why was the Battle of Tours important?
4. How did Pepin help the Pope?

CHARLEMAGNE

Pendant

When Pepin died in 768, his kingdom was divided between his two sons. His son Carloman died within a few years. His other son Charles then became king of the Franks. He is best known by his French name Charlemagne, which means "Charles the Great."

Charlemagne wanted to bring all of western Europe under his rule. He also wanted all the Germanic peoples to become Christians. To achieve these goals, he waged a series of wars.

First Charlemagne defeated the Lombards, who had tried to take their land back from the Pope. Next he turned his attention to a Germanic people called Saxons. For years the Saxons had been raiding towns and monasteries inside the Frankish border. Charlemagne killed many of the Saxon leaders and sent thousands of Saxons to Frankish territory. Then he moved his own people onto Saxon lands in what is now northern Germany. Eventually the Saxons accepted Christianity.

Charlemagne also led his armies in several campaigns across the Pyrenees Mountains to fight the Muslims in Spain. A mountain people known as Basques did not want the Frankish armies to cross their territory. When Charlemagne was returning home from one of his Spanish campaigns, Basque warriors attacked the rear guard of his army in a narrow mountain pass. The rear guard was led by Roland, a fine warrior and a close friend of Charlemagne. Since Roland had far fewer soldiers than the Basques, he lost the battle. The fight between Roland and the Basques was remembered, told, and retold throughout Europe. Over time the event became legend and was written down in French as a poem called *The Song of Roland*.

By 800 Charlemagne had created a large empire that included most of the Germanic peoples who had settled in Europe since early 400. Charlemagne also fought against non-Germanic peoples in northern and eastern Europe. These people managed to keep their freedom, but they agreed to respect Charlemagne's power and not fight against his army.

1. Why did Charlemagne go to Italy?
2. How did Saxon lands become part of Charlemagne's empire?

A CHRISTIAN EMPIRE   Charlemagne became the most powerful leader in western Europe. The people considered him as important as any Roman emperor. Charlemagne wanted to keep close ties between the Church and the government. Church officials kept records and helped Charlemagne run the country. Charlemagne appointed the bishops and regarded any act against the Church as a sign of disloyalty to him.

Both Charlemagne and the Pope wanted a new Christian Roman Empire in western Europe. Charlemagne's conquests had brought him closer to their goal. On Christmas day in 800, Charlemagne was worshipping in St. Peter's church in Rome. When the religious ceremony was over, the Pope placed a crown on Charlemagne's head. He then declared that Charlemagne was the new Roman emperor. Although Charlemagne accepted the title, he was not pleased that the Pope had crowned him. Crowning by the Pope made it seem as if the emperor's right to rule came from the Pope rather than directly from God.

Charlemagne was a wise and just ruler who issued a variety of laws. To make sure they were obeyed, he set up law courts throughout the empire. He chose officials called **counts** to run the courts. The counts took care of local problems, stopped feuds, protected the poor and the weak, and raised armies for Charlemagne.

Charlemagne often had trouble keeping the counts under his control because of poor transportation and communication. So he sent special royal messengers throughout the land to check on them. The messengers reported to Charlemagne how well the counts were doing their jobs. Once a year, Charlemagne called the counts and warriors together. They expressed grievances and discussed new laws for the empire. The final decision on what

---

CHARLEMAGNE CROWNED EMPEROR

Many Western Europeans wanted to bring back the glory of ancient Rome. In 800, Charlemagne became emperor of a new Christian Roman Empire. Here Charlemagne kneels in prayer as the Pope crowns him "Emperor of the Romans." The new emperor is surrounded by members of his royal court.

How successful was Charlemagne as emperor?

---

new laws were acceptable was made by Charlemagne. In this way he could keep better control.

Charlemagne ruled his empire from Aachen, known today as Aix-la-Chapelle. He did not always stay in the capital. He traveled throughout the empire accompanied by his advisors and servants. The royal party would stop and rest at different palaces or homes. Wherever the king and his officials went, they were given food and entertained by the people. Such royal visits insured the loyalty of local officials and people to the imperial government.

Students

1. What sort of relation did Charlemagne want between the Church and the government?
2. Why did Charlemagne object to the Pope crowning him emperor?
3. What were some duties of the counts?
4. How did Charlemagne keep control of his empire?

EDUCATION   Most of the people in Charlemagne's empire could neither read nor write. But Charlemagne appreciated learning. Unlike earlier Frankish rulers, he believed in education and was proud of his own ability to read Latin. He kept a slate and copybook next to his bed so that he could practice writing.

Charlemagne wanted his people to be educated. He worked hard to push back the darkness that had followed the decline of the Roman Empire. He encouraged churches and monasteries to found schools. He had a scholar named Alcuin start a school in one of the palaces to train the children of government officials to serve in the Church or in the royal household. The children studied religion, Latin, music, literature, and arithmetic.

Scholars came from all over Europe to teach in Charlemagne's school. One of their tasks was to copy manuscripts. This led to the development of a new form of writing. The Roman writing the scholars used contained only capital letters. These took up a lot of space on a page. So the scholars began to write with small letters instead of capital ones. The new letters not only took up less space but were also easier to read. They became the model for the small letters used today.

Under Charlemagne the arts began to flower again. Painters, sculptors, and metalworkers developed their talents. They built and decorated palaces and churches in the old Roman style of a group of buildings around a large courtyard. Artists covered

CHARLEMAGNE'S SCHOOL
Charlemagne often visited his Palace School, which was attended by children of the court. Directed by the monk Alcuin, the school also provided a place where scholars could gather to share their knowledge and to inspire one another.
Why was Charlemagne interested in learning?

palace and church walls with scenes depicting stories from the Bible. They made book covers and ornamental weapons, and they decorated the manuscripts copied by scholars.

1. How did Charlemagne feel about learning? What did he do to encourage it?
2. What led to the creation of a new form of writing? How was it different from Roman writing?

ESTATE LIFE   **Lords**, or nobles who were the descendents of Frankish warriors and Roman landowners, were the most powerful people in Charlemagne's empire. Most of their wealth came from goods grown or made on their estates. As there was little trade in Charlemagne's empire, each estate took care of its own needs. Craftspeople who lived on the estates made weapons, cooking vessels, and jewelry. Shoemakers, carpenters, and blacksmiths lived and worked on the estates, too.

The nobles lived in stone farmhouses on their estates. Wooden **stockades,** or fences, often surrounded the houses. Each farmhouse had a banqueting hall, sleeping quarters, cellars, stables, storage places, and a small chapel.

Farmers lived in simple wooden houses in small villages on the estates. They worked in the fields, meadows, vineyards, orchards, and forests that surrounded their villages. The fields were owned by the nobles, but the farmers worked them three days a week. The rest of the time they worked small plots of land the nobles had given them as their own.

The farmers divided the land into three sections. They did not use one section at all. On the other two sections, they used heavy metal plows suitable for the hard but fertile soil. In the autumn they planted wheat or rye in one section. In the spring they planted oats or barley in the other section. Each year the farmers **rotated**, or changed by turns, the type of crops they grew in each section. This helped to make better use of the soil.

In addition to working the land, the farmers had to give the nobles food and animals. They had to perform many services for the nobles, too. The men repaired buildings on the estates, cut down trees, carried loads, gathered fruits, and served in the army. The women worked as hard as the men. They looked after the children and the small animals, wove cloth, and sewed clothing copied from earlier Roman styles. The farmers gradually did more and more for the nobles and less for themselves. They were becoming **serfs**, or poor people bound to the land.

FRANKISH VILLAGE
Most Franks lived in villages on the estates of nobles. Around the wooden houses were fields, meadows, and forests.
How did Frankish villagers make a living?

Neither the nobles nor the farmers had much time to learn to read or write or to think about religion. Both groups accepted Christianity, but the new religion had little effect on their daily lives. Both the rich and the poor, however, sang, danced, and feasted on religious holidays. They listened to traveling entertainers called **minstrels**. The minstrels wandered from place to place singing the praises of Charlemagne and his empire.

1. Who were the most powerful people in Charlemagne's empire? Why were they so powerful?
2. What were some of the main features of estates?
3. How did most of the farmers live? In what ways did they serve the nobles?

THE COLLAPSE OF THE EMPIRE The glory of empire did not last long after Charlemagne's death in 814. The empire needed a strong and able ruler. Charlemagne's heirs were neither. The many counts and nobles became increasingly independent. They cared more about their own estates than

THE FRANKISH EMPIRE

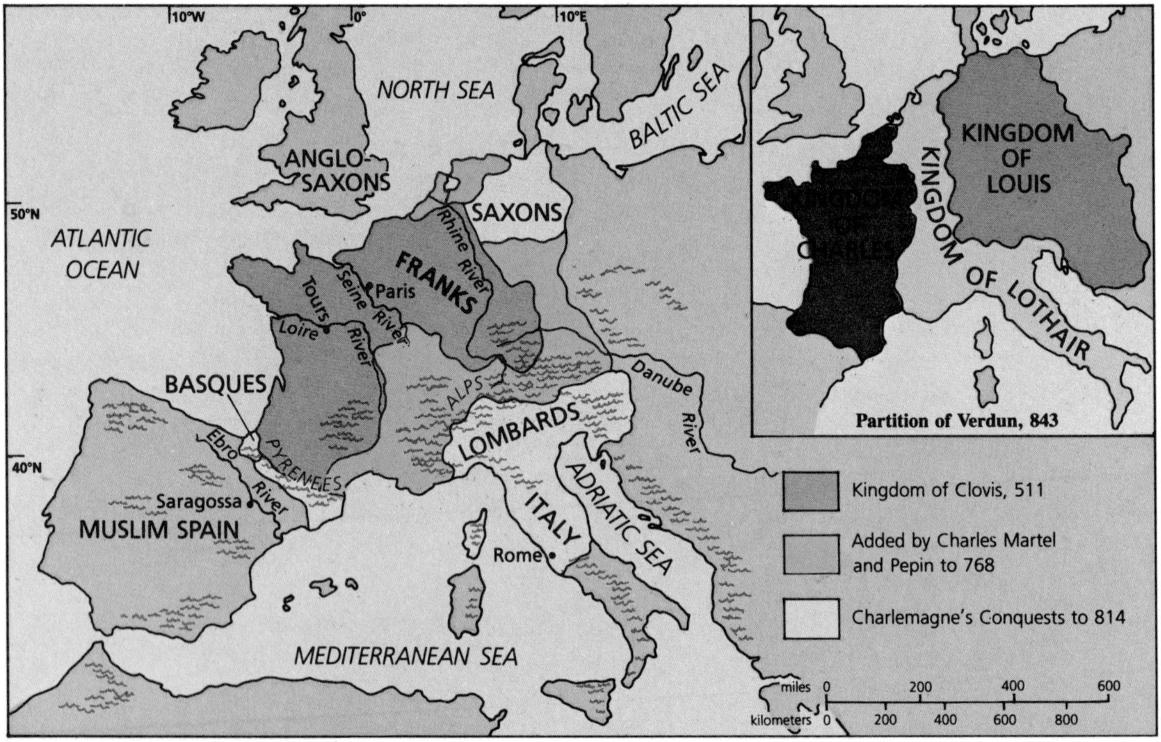

Partition of Verdun, 843

Kingdom of Clovis, 511

Added by Charles Martel and Pepin to 768

Charlemagne's Conquests to 814

about the good of the empire. They refused to obey Louis the Pious, Charlemagne's son and heir.

Louis unknowingly weakened the empire further when he divided it among his three sons. After he died, they began fighting among themselves over their shares. Lothair, Louis' oldest son, had received the title of emperor. His younger brothers Charles and Louis were jealous of Lothair's position.

In 843 the brothers agreed to a new and different division of the empire. Under the Treaty of Verdun, Lothair kept the title of emperor, but he ruled only a narrow strip of the land that stretched from the North Sea to the Italian peninsula. Louis received the area to the east. Called the East Frankish kingdom, it later became the nation of Germany. Charles received the area to the west. Called the Western Frankish kingdom, it later became the nation of France.

The brothers were weak rulers who allowed the counts and nobles to have most of the power. Once again a united western Europe was divided into smaller territories.

1. What happened to Charlemagne's empire after he died? Why did this happen?
2. What were the terms of the Treaty of Verdun?

CHAPTER REVIEW
SUMMARY

1. During the late fifth century the Franks began to build a new civilization which was to develop into modern France and Germany.

2. Clovis united the Franks and set up a capital in Paris.

3. Clovis was the first Germanic king to accept the Catholic religion.

4. The Frankish kings who followed Clovis were weak rulers, so power gradually came into the hands of an official known as the "Mayor of the Palace."

5. In 732 a Mayor called Charles Martel defeated a Muslim army in the Battle of Tours, thus keeping western Europe Christian.

6. Charles Martel's son Pepin, who started a new dynasty, was the first Frankish king to be anointed by the Pope.

7. Pepin's son Charlemagne brought all of western Europe under his rule.

8. In 800 the Pope crowned Charlemagne the new Roman emperor.

9. Charlemagne was very interested in learning and encouraged the founding of schools throughout his empire.

10. Louis the Pious divided the Frankish empire among his three sons.

BUILDING VOCABULARY

1. *Identify the following:*

Early Middle Ages	Arabs	Charlemagne	*The Song of Roland*
Franks	Muslims	Saxons	Aachen
Clovis	Battle of Tours	Basques	Louis the Pious
Mayor of the Palace	Pepin	Roland	Treaty of Verdun
Charles Martel			

2. *Define the following:*

converted	counts	rotated	minstrels
anointed	lords	serfs	stocades

REVIEWING THE FACTS

1. What happened in western Europe after the decline of the Roman Empire?
2. What helped the people of Clovis' empire feel united?
3. Why did the Mayor of the Palace become important?
4. How did Charles Martel gain the nickname "The Hammer?"
5. What were Charlemagne's main goals when he became king of the Franks?
6. How did church officials help Charlemagne?
7. What purpose did Charlemagne's travels throughout the empire serve?
8. What happened to the arts under Charlemagne?
9. What did farmers do to make the best use of the land?
10. How were the nations of France and Germany formed?

DISCUSSING IMPORTANT IDEAS

1. What do you think might have happened to western Europe if the Franks had lost the Battle of Tours?
2. Do you think Charlemagne was wise to travel all over his empire? Explain.
3. Do you think Charlemagne deserved his title of "the Great?" Explain.
4. What do you think Louis the Pious might have done instead of dividing the Frankish empire among his three sons?

USING MAPS

Refer to the map on page 262, and answer the following questions:

1. Under which leader did the Frankish empire begin?
2. Into what areas did Charlemagne extend the Frankish empire?
3. Which city is further east—Paris or Tours? Further west?
4. Who got control of the western section of the Frankish empire in 843?

CHAPTER 19

IRISH AND ANGLO-SAXONS

Off the western coast of Europe lie a group of islands that never became part of Charlemagne's empire. Known today as the British Isles, they consist of Britain, Ireland, and many smaller islands.

Roman legions led by Julius Caesar invaded Britain in 55 B.C. The Romans eventually conquered much of the island and ruled it for almost 400 years. They built cities, country estates, bridges, and roads. They introduced the rose and the beech tree. Missionaries taught Christianity, and they helped spread Roman culture.

Although the Romans brought peace and prosperity, they could not control the entire island. In the northern part of Britain, in the area known today as Scotland, lived peoples called Picts and Scots. They resisted Roman rule and attacked Roman settlements in the south. To keep them out, Roman soldiers built great walls with forts and towers.

The Romans also had difficulties in the area which they did rule. They could not win over a conquered people called Celts. Most Celts lived in their own villages apart from the Roman cities. They grew wheat in small fields and raised animals in pastures they shared with one another. They were not interested in or influenced by Roman culture.

Roman rule in Britain began to crumble during the fourth century. This was because Roman soldiers were called home to defend the empire's borders against invasions by the Germans and the Huns. After the last legions left in 410, the island was gradually overrun by groups from northern Germany and Denmark called Angles, Saxons, and Jutes. All three were seafaring peoples who traveled across the North Sea to Britain in long, open boats. They were strong warriors and controlled most of the island by the seventh century.

The Angles, Saxons, and Jutes united to become the Anglo-Saxons. They built settlements, farmed the land, and set up several small kingdoms. The southern part of Britain soon became known as Angleland, or England. The people became known as English.

CELTIC IRELAND

After the Anglo-Saxons chased the Celts from Britain, Ireland became the major center of Celtic culture. Ireland had no cities. The people were divided into clans, or family groups, that lived in small villages. Most of them farmed and raised cattle. The more cattle a person owned, the wealthier that person was considered to be.

The Irish were a seafaring people, too. They made boats called **coracles** by stretching cow hides over a wooden frame. Some coracles were large enough to hold as many as 30 people. The boats handled well at sea and were used for travel, trade, and fishing.

Irish Bowl

The Irish were able to remain free of Germanic attacks because their island was located further out in the Atlantic Ocean than Britain. The peace and safety of Ireland attracted scholars, artists, merchants, and monks from many parts of Europe.

1. How did the Irish earn a living?
2. Why did Ireland attract people from other parts of Europe?

THE CHRISTIAN INFLUENCE   Irish scholars and artists were strongly influenced by Christianity. The Irish Church was founded by Saint Patrick. Born in Britain in the fifth century, Saint Patrick was kidnapped when a teenager and taken to Ireland by Irish pirates. He escaped to Europe, where he studied to be a priest. After becoming a bishop, he returned to Ireland to win the people to Christianity. He preached throughout the island and set up many churches for the new believers.

Irish Cross

Ireland lost contact with Rome during the Germanic invasions of the Roman Empire. Since it was no longer possible to rely on the Pope for leadership, the Irish Church turned to its abbots. Many of them were related to the heads of the various clans. Each clan sponsored its own monastery.

The monasteries became centers of Irish life even though many were in faraway places on rocky coasts or steep hills. A monastery usually consisted of a group of huts surrounded by a protective wooden stockade. Later, some monasteries were built of stone. Because of poor transportation and communication, church organization was weak. So each monastery controlled its own affairs. Irish monks soon began to follow practices different from those of the Roman Church. They wore their hair in a different style and celebrated Easter on a different day. The rituals they performed were not the same as those in Rome.

Irish monasteries set down few rules. A monk was free to move from one monastery to another. While many monks chose to be hermits, others set up schools to teach Christianity. Still others became missionaries and did a lot of traveling. They sailed the North Atlantic and the Irish Sea seeking new converts and looking for islands on which to build new monasteries.

One of the most famous traveling monks was Saint Columba. He established a monastery on Iona, an island off the west coast of Scotland. From his base on Iona, he did missionary work among the non-Christian Celts along the coast.

Monks from Iona went to northern England to preach to the Anglo-Saxons. Other Irish monks went to northern Europe, where they built monasteries and churches. Many Irish scholars became part of Charlemagne's palace school. They helped spread Christianity and learning throughout his empire.

1. How did Saint Patrick influence Christianity in Ireland?
2. How did the Germanic invasion affect the Irish church?
3. What did Saint Columba do to further Christianity?

ANGLO-SAXONS AND CHRISTIANITY

Ireland was Christian, but the Anglo-Saxon kingdoms of Britain were not. They followed the Germanic religions. Then

IRISH MONASTERY

Irish Christian monks established monasteries throughout the British Isles and Europe. Many of their stone living quarters still stand today along the rocky coast of western Ireland.

What role did monks have in Irish life?

CHRISTIANITY IN ENGLAND

The monk Augustine brought Christianity to the Anglo-Saxons. Augustine preached before the king of Kent and persuaded him to become a Christian. Soon all England accepted Christianity.

Who sent Augustine to England to preach Christianity?

Pope Gregory I decided to convert the Anglo-Saxons to Christianity. Legend states that he saw some Anglo-Saxon boys waiting in the marketplace of Rome to be sold as slaves. Gregory admired their light skin, handsome faces, and yellow hair and asked what their homeland was. When he learned that the boys were Angles, he said they had the face of angels and should be Christians.

In 597 Pope Gregory sent a mission of 41 monks to England under the leadership of the monk Augustine. The missionaries landed in the small kingdom of Kent in southern England. Kent's queen, Bertha, was already a Christian, but its king, Ethelbert, was not. At first Ethelbert was very suspicious of Augustine and the other monks. He even insisted on meeting with them only in the open air where their "magic" could not hurt him. But within a year Ethelbert became a Christian. He allowed Augustine to build a church in the town of Canterbury and to teach the people about Christianity. The Anglo-Saxons

King Alfred

were quick to accept the new religion, and by 700 all England was Christian. They accepted the Pope as head of their church.

Many monasteries were built in England. As in Ireland, they became centers of religion and culture. With the help of the monks, the Irish, Roman, and German cultures blended together to form a new culture.

One of the monks, Bede, was a great scholar. He wrote the first history of the English people. He also introduced the English to the Christian practice of dating events from the year of Jesus' birth.

Even though they accepted Christianity, the Anglo-Saxons kept much of their old culture. They told and retold old legends about brave warriors fighting monsters and dragons. One such legend was about a warrior named Beounif. In the eighth century, it was written down as an epic poem called *Beowulf*. It became known as the most important work of Anglo-Saxon literature.

1. According to legend, why did Pope Gregory I decide to convert the Anglo-Saxons to Christianity?
2. How did Augustine help spread Christianity?
3. What did Bede contribute to English culture?

ALFRED   About 835 bands of Danes began raiding the coast of England. Before long they were making permanent settlements in conquered areas. The English kingdoms decided to resist the invaders. They chose as their leader Alfred, King of Wessex. Alfred later became known as Alfred the Great, one of England's best loved monarchs.

Alfred knew the Anglo-Saxons were not yet strong enough to drive out the Danes. To gain time to build a stronger army, he paid the Danes a sum of money each year to leave England alone. When he felt his army was strong enough, he refused to make any more payments. The Danes invaded the country and defeated the Anglo-Saxons. In the spring Alfred once again gathered his army and met the Danes in battle. This time Alfred and his soldiers defeated the Danes.

Alfred continued to strengthen his army. He built the first English fighting ships and constructed fortresses at regular intervals throughout the country. The entire country rallied behind him. He was no longer just the king of Wessex but the king of all England.

Alfred never became strong enough to drive the Danes completely from England. So he signed a treaty with them. It recognized the right of the Danes to rule the northeast part of the country, an area that became known as the Danelaw. In return, the Danes promised to stay within the Danelaw and not try to conquer more English territory. In later years the English took control of the Danelaw and made it part of their kingdom.

The Danes had destroyed part of the English city of London. Alfred had it rebuilt, and before long it was the country's leading city. To gain the continued loyalty and obedience of the people, Alfred issued new laws based on old Anglo-Saxon customs. The customs protected the weak against the strong and stressed honesty in making agreements.

Alfred was well-educated. He wanted the English people to be well-educated, too. Like Charlemagne, Alfred started a

ENGLAND IN ALFRED'S DAY

Danish Settlements, 9th Century

school in one of his palaces to train nobles' sons for government positions. At that time books were usually written in Latin, a language that most church and government officials did not know. Alfred's scholars translated the books into English. So that the people would become familiar with their history, Alfred had monks begin a record of English history starting with the time of the Romans.

1. How did Alfred defeat the Danes?
2. What did Alfred do to unite the country?
3. What did Alfred do to improve learning among the people?

THE GOVERNMENT   The king was the most important person in Anglo-Saxon England. A council of lords usually elected kings from among members of the royal family. After 700, the Church usually crowned the new rulers. The king directed the central government, which was made up of royal servants and advisors. They handled the king's personal needs and carried out his wishes.

The central government, however, was too weak to govern the entire country. So the king set up a system of local

A NOBLE ESTATE
Nobles were the most powerful group of people in Anglo-Saxon England. Here a noble and his family give out food to hungry peasants on their estate. What were the duties of a noble?

government. England was divided into districts called **shires**. Each shire was run by a sheriff who was a local noble appointed by the king. The sheriff collected money owed to the king, enforced the law, called out soldiers when necessary, and kept the king informed about local affairs.

It was the custom for the king and his household to move from place to place instead of remaining in a capital city. Whatever area the royal household was in was considered to be under the **king's peace**, or royal protection. Fighting and other lawless acts were forbidden. Anyone who committed a crime was punished under the king's laws rather than local laws. In time the king's peace spread to all areas of the kingdom, whether the king was there or not. Thus, everyone could benefit from the king's laws and protection.

Nobles and church officials gave the king advice on how to run the country. They could not, however, order a king to act against his will. A council of nobles and church leaders, known as the **witan**, or "wisemen," met with the king to discuss problems. It approved laws drawn up by the king and his household, and acted as a court of law.

1. What were the duties of a sheriff?
2. How did the king's peace help unite the country?
3. Who helped the king run the country?

THE PEOPLE   An Anglo-Saxon became a noble by birth or as a reward for special service to the king. Nobles had to attend the witan, keep the peace in local areas, and serve the king in war. Noblemen wore pants and knee-length tunics covered by a silk or fur cloak. Noblewomen wore tunics and long cloaks held in place on each shoulder by a brooch.

The king rewarded many nobles with gifts of gold, silver, horses, and weapons. He also gave them estates all over the country. As a result, nobles spent a great deal of time moving from one place to another with their families and servants. A noble's house always had a large hall where family meals were served and guests were entertained. Its walls were covered by **tapestries**, or woven hangings. The only furniture was tables and benches. The bedrooms of the nobles and their families were next to the hall or in a separate building.

Most English people were not nobles. They were peasants who lived in small villages on or near a noble's estate. They

Jewelry

helped each other farm the land by sharing their tools and oxen. Each year the land was redivided, and each peasant received different strips. This practice ensured that each peasant would be treated equally. The peasants produced little more than they needed and did not send much to market.

Peasants lived in one-room wood and plaster huts. Both the family and the animals shared the same room. An open fireside, which provided protection during the cold winter, stood in the center. The smoke from the fire escaped from the hut through a hole in the thatched straw roof.

Peasants led a hard life, constantly faced by famine, disease, and enemy attack. Some of them sought the protection of a nearby noble. The noble often took control of the peasants' land in return. Other peasants rented land from the noble to produce more food. The peasants continued to work the land plus pay the nobles with food from the fields. Many nobles also had the peasants work several days a week in the fields of the estates.

1. What was the life of a noble like?
2. What was the life of a peasant like?

CHAPTER REVIEW

SUMMARY

1. Roman legions led by Julius Caesar invaded Britain in 55 B.C.

2. The Romans ruled most of Britain for about 400 years, but they were unable to win over the conquered Celts.

3. In 410 Britain was overrun by peoples from northern Germany and Denmark who eventually united to become the Anglo-Saxons.

4. After the Anglo-Saxons drove the Celts from Britain, Ireland became the major center of Celtic culture.

5. The Irish Church was founded in the fifth century by Saint Patrick.

6. The monasteries became centers of Irish life.

7. Irish monks gradually began to follow practices different from those of the Roman Church.

8. In 597 Pope Gregory sent a mission of monks led by Augustine to England, and by 700 the entire island had become Christian.

9. Around 835 bands of Danes began raiding England.

10. The Anglo-Saxons united behind Alfred the Great to keep the Danes from spreading their control.

11. Alfred was interested in learning and did much to educate his people, including having books translated from Latin into English.

BUILDING VOCABULARY

1. *Identify the following:*

   Britain   Anglo-Saxons   Augustine   *Beowulf*
   Ireland   Saint Patrick   Ethelbert   Alfred the Great
   Picts   Saint Columba   Canterbury   Danelaw
   Celts   Gregory I   Bede   London

2. *Define the following:*

   coracles   king's peace   witan   tapestries
   shires

REVIEWING THE FACTS

1. Who led Roman legions into Britain?
2. Why did the Romans have difficulty ruling Britain?
3. Why did Roman rule in Britain begin to crumble during the fourth century?
4. What happened to Britain when the Roman legions left?
5. Why did Ireland become the major center of Celtic culture?
6. Why did the Irish Church turn to its abbots for leadership?
7. What were some differences between Irish monks and Roman monks?
8. What was the most important work of Anglo-Saxon literature?
9. Why did the king divide England into shires?
10. What were the duties of the witan?

DISCUSSING IMPORTANT IDEAS

1. What effects did the Roman conquest of Britain have on the development of England?
2. Do you think it is important for people to be familiar with their history? Why or why not?
3. Do you think Alfred deserves to be called "the Great?" Explain.
4. Do you think it was a good idea for a king to move from place to place instead of remaining in a capital city? Why or why not?

USING MAPS

Refer to the map on page 271, and answer the following questions:

1. In what part of England is the kingdom of Wessex?
2. What two groups of people settled in the far northern section of the island of England?
3. In what area of England did the Danes settle?
4. What is the distance across the narrowest part of the English Channel? The Irish Sea?

THE HAN AND THE T'ANG

By the tenth century eight dynasties had ruled China. They were the Hsia, Shang, Chou, Ch'in, Han, Six Dynasties, Sui, and T'ang. Each contributed something different to China's development. The Ch'in, for example, was the first dynasty to unite the Chinese people. From the Ch'in came the name China.

In 206 B.C. the Han Dynasty followed the Ch'in. During Han rule the public granaries were well-stocked, and the government treasuries were full. The arts flowered, and learning and literature flourished. But the Han's greatest contribution to China was a stable form of government that lasted into the twentieth century. It was made up of four main parts—a single ruler; **bureaucrats**, or officials; a system of laws; and an official **ideology**, or philosophy.

The single ruler was the emperor. He made laws, took charge of the bureaucrats, and interpreted the ideology. The bureaucrats were responsible for the proper conduct of China's affairs. There were thousands of bureaucrats organized into six ministries and nine ranks. Each rank wore special clothes and caps with a different color badge. All received their posts on the basis of ability.

The system of laws was strict. There were heavy penalties for those who did not obey the laws. The ideology was Confucianism. All Chinese agreed on the importance of Confucian values. They united the Han and made them strong.

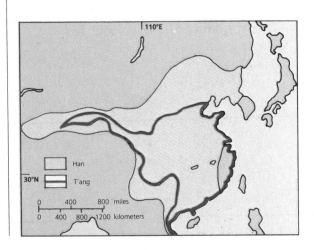

More than 350 years passed before another strong dynasty, the T'ang, came to power. In the nearly three centuries they ruled, the T'ang pushed China's borders outward in all directions and brought China into contact with the outside world.

The T'ang's greatest contribution, however, was cultural. T'ang artisans were the first to add the mineral feldspar to clay before it was molded and fired to produce porcelain. T'ang porcelains have been found as far away as Mesopotamia. The graceful upward curves of the roof edges of Chinese buildings were first seen in T'ang cities. Court **calligraphers**, or artists who write characters, made texts using fine paper tinted in lemon or sulphur yellow or slate blue, which they rolled on ivory or sandalwood cylinders tipped with jade, amber, or rock crystal knobs. T'ang artists were the first to use bright colors in their paintings.

1. What did the Han and the T'ang contribute to China?

CHAPTER 20

THE VIKINGS

During the tenth century Charlemagne's empire and Anglo-Saxon England were attacked by a new group of invaders known as Norsemen, or Vikings. They came from the far northern part of Europe now called Scandinavia. The tall, fair-skinned Vikings became known as brutal fighters and robbers. They spread fear and destruction throughout western Europe for several hundred years. At the same time, however, they opened up new trade routes and brought shipping skills to other Europeans.

The Vikings captured parts of Britain and France. They ruled cities in Russia and set up colonies on islands in the North Atlantic. They even paid a brief visit to North America. Those who went abroad married the people they conquered. They also accepted a new religion and customs. Others stayed in Scandinavia and set up the kingdoms of Norway, Sweden, and Denmark.

THE LAND

The Viking homeland of Scandinavia was an area mostly of forests and long, rugged coastlines. The southern part, known as Jutland, or Denmark, had many natural harbors. It also had large plains where the Vikings grew oats, barley, rye, and wheat and pastured their cattle, sheep, and pigs.

The rest of Scandinavia was not as well suited to farming. Winters were long and cold, summers short and mild, and the soil rocky. The coastline, however, had many **fjords**, or bays. So the people turned to the sea to making a living.

1. Where was Jutland? How was it different from the rest of Scandinavia?

SHIPS AND TRADE The Vikings built ships with timber from the dense forests and sailed out of the fjords onto the sea to make a living. The ships were large and well suited for long voyages. The bodies were long and narrow. The sides, where a single row of 16 oars was placed, were usually decorated with black or yellow painted shields. The tall bows were carved in the shape of a dragon's head. This was supposed to frighten both enemies and the evil spirits of the ocean. The strongly sewn sails were square and often striped red and yellow. The ships bore names like "Snake of the Sea," "Raven of the Wind," and "Lion of the Waves."

An awning in the forepart of the ship protected the sailors from bad weather. They slept in leather sleeping bags and carried bronze pots in which to cook their meals. Whenever possible, they cooked their meals ashore to avoid the danger of a fire on board ship.

The Vikings plotted their courses by the positions of the sun and stars. They sailed far out into the North Sea and the Atlantic Ocean in search of good fishing areas and trade. They did most of their traveling and trading in the spring after their fields were

Dragon Carving

VIKING TRADE AND EXPANSION

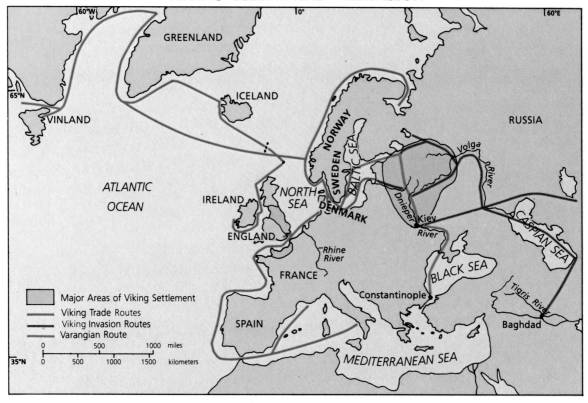

sown, or in the fall after their crops were harvested. They spent the long winters in their villages repairing their boats and weapons.

The Vikings were as successful in trade as the Phoenicians. Viking traders carried furs, hides, fish, and slaves to western Europe and the Mediterranean. They returned from these areas with silk, wine, wheat, and silver.

1. What were some features of Viking ships?
2. Where did the Vikings sail?
3. When did the Vikings sail?

TOWNS, VILLAGES, AND JARLS   Trade led to the growth of market towns in Scandinavia. These towns usually had two main streets that ran along the water's edge. Buyers and sellers set up booths and displayed their wares along the streets. The towns were protected on their land side by mounds of earth surrounded by wooden walls with towers.

Most Vikings lived in villages scattered throughout the country. Their houses were made of logs or boards. The roofs, which were made of sod-covered wood, slanted steeply to shed the heavy winter snows. Carvings of dragons decorated gables at either end. In front of each house was a small porch supported by carved pillars.

Distance and the cold winters isolated the people of one village from those of another. As a result, there was no central government. The people were divided into groups ruled by military chieftains called *jarls*. Jarls either inherited their position or were elected to it. They saw to it that their group's laws were obeyed. Sometimes a jarl became strong enough to take over and unite neighboring territories. When a jarl had enough territory under his rule, he was recognized as a king.

1. What were some features of Viking towns?
2. What kind of government did the Vikings have?

VIKING TRADE

Viking towns and villages were centers of trade. This Viking wall hanging shows traders carrying goods to market.

How was trade carried out in Viking towns and villages?

DAILY LIFE

Family life was important to the Vikings. Most households contained 20 to 30 members including parents, grandparents, married children, and grandchildren. Families often fought bloody feuds to maintain their honor. The payment of fines later put an end to such feuds.

THE PEOPLE   Viking men were warriors called *berserkers*. They believed in a life of action and valued deeds that called for strength and courage. They fought to gain wealth, honor, and fame. They believed that a liking for war brought special honors from the gods.

VIKING CELEBRATION

Viking men enjoyed celebrating special events. Here trader-warriors raise their drinking horns to toast the discovery of new territory.

What were the weapons and clothes of Viking warriors like?

To call their warriors to battle, the Vikings lit bonfires on the tops of mountains. Those who saw a fire would light a new one to spread the message. The warriors fought with battle axes, swords, and spears. Metal helmets decorated with animal figures protected their heads. Shirts made of iron rings and covered by a large cloth protected their bodies. The warriors preferred to die by their own hand rather than give their enemies the satisfaction of capturing or killing them.

A Viking groom bought his wife from her family on their wedding day. If he was not pleased with her, he could sell her. Yet the position of Viking women was quite high. They took complete charge of the home. They could attend public meetings and talk with men other than their husbands. They could own property and get a divorce. Many Viking women grew herbs which were used as medicine. All the women encouraged their men to fight.

Leif Ericson

Both men and women liked fine clothes. The men usually dressed in trousers and woolen shirts covered by knee-length tunics. Broad leather belts held the clothing in place. Sheepskin hoods and caps kept heads warm. For special events the men wore red cloaks with brooches and carried decorated swords and daggers. The women also wore tunics held in place by a belt. They covered their heads with woolen or linen caps, and wore large brooches, pins, and bracelets. Both men and women wore their hair long, and the men took great pride in their mustaches and beards. Calling a Viking man "beardless" was an insult that could be wiped out only by death.

The Vikings had no schools. Parents taught daughters such household skills as spinning, weaving, and sewing. They taught sons to use the bow and arrow and to be good fighters. The boys also memorized tales of heroic warriors and gods, and competed in games that tested their strength and endurance.

1. In what did berserkers believe? How did they dress?
2. How did Vikings call their warriors to battle?
3. What kind of education did Viking children receive?

RELIGION The Vikings worshipped many gods which at first were closely related to Germanic gods. In time they changed the names and activities of their gods to suit the harsh life of Scandinavia. The Vikings believed that the gods were responsible for the weather and for the growth of crops. Since the gods liked to hunt, fish, and play tricks on one another, the Vikings viewed them as extra powerful human beings.

The Vikings bargained with their gods to get what they wanted. Priests offered sacrifices of crops and animals on behalf of the whole community. Most Vikings also had small shrines in their homes where they could pray or offer sacrifices.

The Vikings were proud of their gods and told stories of their great deeds. These stories later became written poems called *eddas*. The Vikings also composed **sagas**, or epic stories. At first skilled storytellers used to recite sagas at special banquets. One such saga took 12 days to recite. After 1100 the Vikings wrote down their sagas. With the coming of Christianity, the people lost interest in these tales. Many were forgotten or were forbidden by the Church. Only the people of Iceland passed on the old tales.

At first the Vikings spoke a language similar to that of the Germans. In time the one language developed into four—Danish, Norwegian, Swedish, and Icelandic. They were written with letters called *runes*, which few people except the priests could understand or use. The Vikings used the runes as magic charms. They wrote the runes in metal and carved them in bone in the hope that they would bring good luck. When the Vikings accepted Christianity, they began to write their language with Roman letters.

Rune Stone

1. How did the Vikings view their gods?
2. How did the coming of Christianity influence the development of Viking languages?

RAIDS AND ADVENTURERS

Scandinavia's population kept increasing. By the end of the ninth century many Viking villages were overcrowded, and there was not enough food for everyone. Since there was no central government, the kings constantly fought one another and made life difficult for their enemies. Before long many Viking warriors began to seek their fortunes elsewhere.

Groups of warriors attacked merchant ships on the open seas. Danish Vikings began raiding the coasts of France, England, and Spain. Swedish Vikings crossed the Baltic Sea and traveled down the rivers toward Russia. They founded settlements and began to trade. They established a water route from

NORSE GODS

Name	Realm
Odin (or Wotan)	king of the gods; sky god; god of war and wisdom; *Wotan's day became Wednesday.*
Baldur	god of light, joy, and spring
Bragi	god of poetry and stories
Freya	goddess of love and beauty
Freyr	god of rain, sunshine, and the harvest
Frigga	goddess of earth, marriages, and motherly love; Odin's wife; *Frigga's day became Friday.*
Hel (or Hela)	goddess of the dead
Idun	goddess of youth
Loki	god of fire; the mischief-maker
Niord	god of the wind
Thor	god of thunder, lightning, and the tides; *Thor's day became Thursday.*
Tyr	god of legal contracts and of truth; *Tyr's day became Tuesday.*

the Baltic to the Black Sea and on to the wealthy city of Byzantium. This water route came to be known as the Varangian Route. In 862 a Swedish chieftain named Rurik founded a Viking state that became the basis of the Russian monarchy. Norwegian Vikings established trading towns in Ireland, explored the North Atlantic, and founded a colony on the island of Iceland.

Led by an adventurer named Eric the Red, the Norwegian Vikings began to move even further west. In 986 they founded a colony on the island of Greenland. Then Eric's son, Leif Ericson, sailed across the Atlantic Ocean and landed on the northeast coast of North America. He and his followers named the spot where they landed Vinland because of the wild grapes they found growing there. Today the area is called New Foundland. The Vikings did not set up a permanent colony in Vinland because it was so far away from home and the winters were so cold.

VIKING CRAFTS
Vikings made metal tools and household articles as well as ships and weapons. Here is a bowl once used at Viking feasts.
What do Viking crafts show about the way Vikings lived?

Most Viking adventurers, however, went to western and southern Europe in search of food and valuables. They disguised their ships to look like wooded islands by covering them with tree branches. Then they traveled far up the rivers to make surprise attacks. They stole goods, destroyed homes, burned churches, and killed or sold as slaves any people they captured. All Europe feared the Vikings. In their churches the people prayed, "From the fury of the Norsemen, Good Lord, deliver us!"

1. Why did many Vikings leave Scandinavia?
2. What discovery did Eric the Red make?
3. What discovery did Leif Ericson make?
4. Why did Europeans fear the Vikings?

THE DANES Some of the Danish Vikings settled in the areas they raided. One group of Danes invaded England and set up settlements there. In 954 an heir of Alfred the Great forced them to leave the Danelaw. In 978 Ethelred, nicknamed the Unready, became king of England. The Danes saw their chance and began raiding England again. At first Ethelred was able to buy them off with silver. But in 1017 a Danish king called Knut, or Canute, took over the country and made it part of his North Sea Empire. Canute was a powerful but just ruler. He converted to Christianity and brought peace and prosperity to England. Soon after his death in 1035, however, Danish control of England came to an end. Some Danes left England. Those who remained became a part of the English people and culture.

VIKING RAIDS

Viking adventurers landed along the coasts of Europe in large "dragon ships." They robbed and burned many towns and villages in search of food and valuables. Many Vikings later settled down in the areas which they had raided. They set up governments in Normandy, Sicily, eastern England, and Russia.
Where were Viking trade routes located?

Another group of Danes tried to take the city of Paris in France, but the French managed to fight them off. In 885 the Danes tried again. The people of Paris held them off for ten months. Finally the French king paid the Danes in gold to abandon their attack.

Led by a warrior named Rollo, the Danes then began settling in large numbers along the French coast opposite England. In 911 the French king signed a treaty with Rollo. He gave the Danes the land on which they had settled. In return the Danes became Christians and promised to be loyal to the French king. The region in which the Danes settled became known first as the Norselaw and then as Normandy. The people became known as Normans.

1. What happened to the Danes who settled in England?
2. What happened to the Danes who settled in France?

CHAPTER REVIEW

SUMMARY

1. The Vikings lived in northern Europe in an area which is today known as Scandinavia.

2. The Vikings were excellent warriors, sailors, and navigators who earned their living mainly by fishing and by trading with other European regions.

3. The Vikings lived in villages that were basically isolated from one another.

4. The Vikings worshipped many gods and often told stories about their great deeds.

5. At first the Vikings spoke one language, but over time it developed into four separate languages.

6. When the Vikings accepted Christianity, they stopped writing their languages in runes and began to write with Roman letters.

7. By the ninth century Scandinavia was over-populated, so many Viking warriors began to seek their fortunes elsewhere.

8. In 862 a Swedish Viking named Rurik established a settlement, and that settlement later developed into the Russian nation.

9. In 986 Norwegian Vikings founded a colony on Greenland, and several years later sailed as far west as the northeast coast of North America.

10. In 1017 a Danish king named Canute conquered England, but after his death Danish control of England came to an end.

11. Other Danish Vikings, after besieging Paris, settled along the French coast in an area known as Normandy.

BUILDING VOCABULARY

1. *Identify the following:*

Vikings	Iceland	Eric the Red	Canute
Scandinavia	Varangian Route	Leif Ericson	Rollo
Jutland	Rurik	Vinland	Normandy

2. *Define the following:*

fjords	berserkers	eddas	sagas
jarls			runes

REVIEWING THE FACTS

1. Why did many Vikings turn to the sea to make a living?
2. How did the Vikings plot their courses?
3. How were Viking houses protected against the winter?
4. Why was there no central government in Scandinavia?
5. How did a jarl become a king?
6. What was the role of Viking women?
7. What did the Vikings tell stories about?
8. In what two ways did the Vikings use runes?
9. What effect did the Vikings have on Russia?
10. Why didn't the Vikings set up a permanent colony in North America?

DISCUSSING IMPORTANT IDEAS

1. Did the Vikings make good use of their natural resources? Explain.
2. What do you think might have happened if many Viking warriors had not left Scandinavia during the ninth century?
3. Do you think you would have liked being a Viking? Why or why not?
4. What effect did the Vikings have on the development of Europe during the early Middle Ages?

USING MAPS

Refer to the map on page 280, and answer the following questions:

1. Where was the largest Viking settlement located?
2. What cities were invaded by Vikings?
3. How far is Kiev from Constantinople?
4. Approximately where was Vinland located?
5. How far south did the Vikings sail? How far west?

UNIT REVIEW

SUMMARY

1. The invasions by Germanic peoples from northern Europe resulted in the fall of the Roman Empire. They also led to the establishment of a number of German kingdoms.

2. The period that began the fall of the Roman Empire and ended with the beginning of modern times is known as the Middle Ages.

3. During the early Middle Ages, the Christian religion continued to spread, and the Church gained widespread power and influence.

4. The Franks set up a German kingdom which became France and Germany.

5. After Roman rule ended in the British Isles, present-day England was taken over by Angles, Saxons, and Jutes. Present-day Ireland became the home of the Celts. Present-day Scotland remained in the hands of Picts and Scots.

6. The Vikings established the kingdoms of Denmark, Norway, and Sweden and captured parts of England and France. They founded colonies in Russia and Greenland; and visited North America.

REVIEWING THE MAIN IDEAS

1. Explain in what ways the Church influenced Charlemagne's empire, England, Ireland, and Scandanavia.

2. Compare the forms of government that developed in western Europe after the fall of the Roman Empire.

DEVELOPING SKILLS

Collecting data is part of being a historian. But unless data are analyzed, they do not help historians learn more about people or events.

One important step in analyzing data is arranging them in order of **significance**, or importance. A person examining several bits of information has to be able to put the most important information first and the least important information last.

This exercise is designed to help you arrange data in order of significance. Read each group of data. Then rank each in order from the most to the least important.

1. The Germans were good fighters because
a. they began training for war when they were young boys.

b. they admired bravery.
c. they were tall and fair-haired.
2. The Frankish civilization developed into the western Europe of today because
a. the Franks became farmers as well as fighters.
b. The Frankish ruler Charlemagne created a large empire that included most of the Germanic peoples who had settled in Europe since the fifth century.
c. the Pope crowned Charlemagne in the year 800.
3. Ireland became the major center of Celtic culture because
a. the island attacted a great many scholars and artists from many different parts of Europe.

b. the Anglo-Saxons chased the Celts from Britain.

c. there were many monasteries in all parts of Ireland.

4. The Vikings were successful traders because

a. most of their homeland was not suited for farming.

b. their ships were large and well-designed for long voyages.

c. they did most of their trading in the spring and fall.

SUGGESTED UNIT PROJECTS

1. Compare the school that was held at the court of Charlemagne with the school you attend.

2. Find out what modern nations are located within the boundaries of Charlemagne's empire.

3. On an outline map of the world, show the routes taken by Danish, Swedish, and Norwegian Vikings during the ninth, tenth, and early eleventh centuries.

4. Working in a group of five, make a chart with five columns, headed Germans, Franks, Irish, Anglo-Saxons, and Vikings. Each person in the group should fill in information about a different people, making sure to include information about where people lived, how most people earned a living, and what people considered important. Then, as a group, compare and contrast the five peoples.

SUGGESTED READING

Carter, Samuel. *Vikings Bold: Their Voyages and Adventures*. New York: Crowell Company, 1972. Traces the history, way of life, trading voyages, and conquests of the Vikings.

Gibson, Michael. *The Vikings*. New York: G. P. Putnams' Sons, 1972. A description based on sagas and other sources of the Vikings as farmers, artisans, traders, storytellers, and warriors.

Knox, Robert. *Ancient China*. New York: Warwick Press, 1979. A history of China from 1500 B.C. to 907 A.D.

Koenig, Alma Johnson. *Gudrun*. New York: Lothrop, Lee & Shepard, 1979. The story of the granddaughter of an Irish king who falls in love with the king of Zealand.

Lester, G. A. *The Anglo-Saxons*. Chaester Springs, Pa.: Dufour Editions, 1976. A description of how Anglo-Saxon society was organized and how the people lived, played, worked, worshipped and fought.

Manton, Jo and Robert Gittings. *The Flying Horses*. New York: Holt, Rinehart and Winston, 1977. A collection of 27 Chinese stories, many of them dating from the Han and T'ang periods.

Munro, Eleanor S. *Through the Vermilion Gates*. New York: Pantheon, 1971. An account of the events and cultural achievements of China's T'ang dynasty.

Treece, Henry. *The Invaders*. New York: Crowell, 1972. Three stories of England's invaders.

UNIT 7

300	350	400
330 Constantinople becomes capital of Roman Empire		

600	650	700
622 *Hegira*		
632 Rule of Rightly Guided Caliphs begins		**726** Emperor Leo III forbids use of icons in worship
633 Muslim conquests begin	**661** Mu'awiyah founds Umayyad dynasty	

900	950	1000
	988 Vladimir I makes Eastern Orthodoxy official religion of Russia	
		1036 Yaroslav becomes grand prince of Kiev

1200	1250	1300
1240 Mongols conquer Russia		
1243 Mongols defeat Seljuk Turks		**1260** Mameluke Baybars takes over throne of Egypt

1500	1550	1600
	1584 Ivan IV dies, and Russia's "Time of Troubles" begins	
1547 Ivan IV crowned tsar of Russia		
1500 Moscow becomes political center of Russia		

FLOWERING OF THE EAST

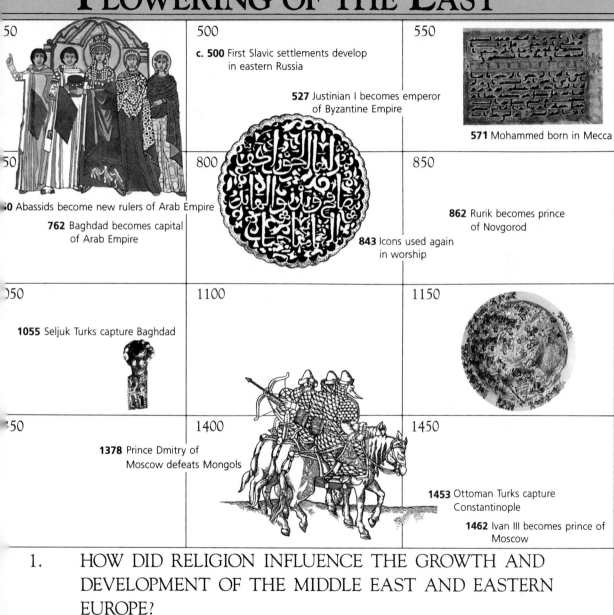

50	500	550
	c. 500 First Slavic settlements develop in eastern Russia	
	527 Justinian I becomes emperor of Byzantine Empire	
		571 Mohammed born in Mecca

50	800	850
		862 Rurik becomes prince of Novgorod
50 Abassids become new rulers of Arab Empire		
762 Baghdad becomes capital of Arab Empire		
	843 Icons used again in worship	

050	1100	1150
1055 Seljuk Turks capture Baghdad		

50	1400	1450
	1378 Prince Dmitry of Moscow defeats Mongols	
		1453 Ottoman Turks capture Constantinople
		1462 Ivan III becomes prince of Moscow

1.   HOW DID RELIGION INFLUENCE THE GROWTH AND DEVELOPMENT OF THE MIDDLE EAST AND EASTERN EUROPE?

2.   IN WHAT WAYS DID THE BYZANTINES, ARABS, AND RUSSIANS INFLUENCE WESTERN EUROPE?

From 500 to 1500 there was a flowering of civilization in what is today Eastern Europe and the Middle East. Two peoples, the Byzantines and the Arabs, built large empires. A third people, the Russians, developed a civilization modeled on that of the Byzantines. Until 1200 the Byzantine and Arab civilizations were more advanced than those of western Europe.

After the fall of Rome in 476, the Byzantines inherited the authority of the Roman emperors and ruled in the eastern half of the Roman Empire. There they preserved classical learning and grew wealthy through trade. Christianity was important to Byzantine life.

The Russians lived to the north of the Byzantine Empire. At the heart of Russian life was the Orthodox Church. Most rulers of Russia were strong leaders who claimed complete control over both the government and the people. They also fought to unite Russia and to extend its boundaries.

The Arabs were traders and warriors from the deserts of the Middle East who were united by a religion called Islam. The desire to spread Islam led Arab armies to conquer lands in Asia, North Africa, and Spain. Arab scholars and scientists studied the classical writings of the West and made many important discoveries. Later, this knowledge led to a new interest in learning.

Other Asiatic peoples besides the Arabs made Islam their religion. When the Arab Empire broke apart, they built new Islamic empires in Asia and North Africa. As a result, Islamic culture continued to develop.

CHAPTER 21
THE BYZANTINE EMPIRE

The emperor Constantine moved the capital of the Roman Empire from Rome to Constantinople about 330. About 100 years later, the Roman Empire in the West fell. The Roman Empire in the East survived and prospered. It became known as the Byzantine Empire. Its people were called Byzantines.

The eastern empire survived for several reasons. One reason was the unity and loyalty of the people. Most were Christians. Their religion united them and taught them to obey and be loyal to their emperor. Another reason was that Constantinople was a mighty fortress which needed few soldiers to defend it. This freed more soldiers to protect other cities and provinces. Still another reason was the empire's wealth, gained through industry, trade, and taxes. There was enough money to support a large army and many officials and to pay invaders to move further west.

The Byzantines developed a civilization based on a blend of Greek, Roman, and Christian ideas. They were eager to spread this civilization to neighboring peoples. In this they were successful. Their ideas and practices later shaped the development of Russia and other Eastern European nations.

THE NEW ROME

When Constantine first chose the old Greek city of Byzantium as the site for his new capital, he was well aware of its advantages. The Roman Empire depended on trade, and the great centers of trade were in the East. Byzantium was on the waterway between the Black and Aegean seas. Its harbor offered a safe haven for fishing boats, merchant ships, and warships. The city sat at the crossroads of the trading routes between Europe and Asia. Its location gave it control of the sea trade between Russia and the Mediterranean area. One of the most important East-West land routes passed through the city, too.

The location also favored the city's defense. The sea protected it on three sides, and a huge wall protected it on the fourth side. Invaders would have a hard time trying to take the new capital.

1. Why did Constantine choose Byzantium as the site for the empire's new capital?

CONSTANTINOPLE   It took more than six years to build the new capital. Constantine modeled it after Rome. The city stood on seven hills. Government buildings and palaces were designed in the Roman style. Streets were narrow and apartment houses crowded. Constantinople even had an oval area much like the Circus Maximus where races and other events were held.

The city's political and social life was patterned on that of Rome, too. The emperor operated under Roman laws and ruled with the help of highly trained officials, who took charge of building roads, bridges, wells, and caravan shelters. The army followed Roman military customs. The poor people received free bread and enjoyed circuses and chariot races put on by the government. The wealthier people lived in town or on large farming estates. Constantine convinced many wealthy Romans to move to Constantinople by offering to build them homes and palaces like the ones they had in Rome.

There was, however, one important difference between Constantinople and Rome. From the beginning Constantinople was a Christian city. It had been dedicated to God by Constantine, who viewed it as the center of a great Christian empire. Instead of temples Constantinople had Christian churches. Constantine saw to it that they were the most magnificent buildings in the city. Government and church leaders gathered **relics**, or valued holy objects from the past, from all over the Christian world and placed them in public monuments, palaces, and churches. The bodies of **saints**, or holy people, rested in richly decorated shrines. Thousands of people came to the shrines seeking cures for their ills.

The city's Christian character could be seen in its attitude toward the needy. The Byzantines believed each Christian was responsible for the well-being of other Christians. Wealthy Byzantines formed organizations to care for the poor, aged, and blind. Even members of the emperor's household took great pride in founding and supporting good causes.

About 600,000 people lived in Constantinople during Constantine's rule. There were Greeks, Turks, Italians, Slavs,

---

CONSTANTINOPLE

Constantinople was protected by its harbor and tall stone walls. Here a celebration takes place at one of the entrances to the city.
Why was Constantinople called "the New Rome"?

Persians, Armenians, and Jews. They spoke Greek among themselves but used Latin, the official language, for government business. Most people became Christians, and all called themselves Romans. Byzantine nobles and rulers continued to boast of their ties to Rome for the next 1100 years.

1. What were some features of Constantinople?
2. In what ways was Constantinople like Rome? In what ways was it different?
3. How did the Byzantines regard themselves?

JUSTINIAN I

After Constantine died his sons ruled the empire. They were followed first by a general named Julian and then by a series of other emperors. Finally, in 527, a Macedonian named

---

JUSTINIAN AND THEODORA

Justinian and Theodora ruled the Byzantine Empire in the early sixth century. In this mosaic, they are dressed in ceremonial robes.

How did Justinian and Theodora govern the empire?

Justinian came to the throne. He was a strong and wise ruler who came to be considered the greatest of all Byzantine emperors.

Byzantine Coins

Justinian had served in the army and was a good commander. He was well trained in law, music, theology, and architecture. He chose the people who served him for their ability rather than their wealth or social position. As a result, many came from common families.

As emperor, Justinian controlled the army and navy, made the laws, headed the Church and government, and was supreme judge. He could declare war or make peace. The Church taught that the emperor's acts were inspired by God. Therefore, what Justinian did could not be questioned. Those who came into contact with him were expected to bow down before him and kiss his feet and hands.

1. What type of person was Justinian?
2. What powers did Justinian have as emperor?

THEODORA   Justinian's wife, the Empress Theodora, often helped him. Theodora's family had been poor, and she had worked as an actress before meeting Justinian. The people of the Empire had a low opinion of actresses. There was even a law forbidding marriages between them and high government officials. But Theodora was pretty, intelligent, and charming; and Justinian fell in love with her. He wanted to marry her. After he became emperor, he abolished the law and made Theodora his empress.

At first Theodora only entertained guests and attended palace ceremonies. Gradually she began to take an interest in politics. Soon she was helping Justinian fill government and church offices. Then she convinced Justinian to allow women more rights. For the first time a wife could own land equal in value to her **dowry**, or the wealth she brought with her when she married. A widow could raise and support her young children without government interference.

In 532 Theodora made her most important contribution. A group of senators had organized a revolt to protest high taxes. They were able to gain much support from the people. The poor were angry because they were receiving less free food and entertainment than before. The wealthy were angry because, for the first time, they had to pay taxes. The leaders of the revolt were prepared to crown a new emperor. Justinian's advisors urged him to leave the city. Theodora, however, urged him to stay and fight. Justinian and his supporters took Theodora's advice. They stayed in Constantinople, trapped those revolting, killed 30,000 of them, and crushed the uprising. As a result, Justinian kept control of the government and became a stronger ruler.

1. How did Theodora help Justinian rule the empire?
2. What was Theodora's most important contribution to the empire?

LAW AND PUBLIC WORKS   Justinian worked to improve the laws of the empire. He was very interested in the law and spent much time reading laws made by other emperors. He decided that the old system of laws was too complicated and disorganized. He appointed a group of ten men headed by a legal scholar named Tribonian to work out a simpler and better system.

Tribonian and the others collected and organized the existing laws. They did away with those that were no longer needed. They arranged in order those that remained and rewrote them. Within six years they had created a legal code that represented the law of the land.

This code came to be known as Justinian's Code. It is considered one of his greatest achievements. It provided a summary of Roman legal thinking and gave future generations insight into the basic ideas of Roman law. The code has had a great influence on the legal systems of almost every western country.

Emperor at Races

Justinian was as interested in public works as he was in law. He was almost always busy with some building program. He built churches, bridges, monasteries, forums, and a system of forts connected by a vast network of roads. When an earthquake destroyed the city of Antioch, he had the entire city rebuilt.

One of Justinian's greatest accomplishments was the church called Hagia Sophia, "Holy Wisdom." Nearly 10,000 workers, watched over by 200 supervisors, labored in shifts to build the church according to Justinian's instructions. The church had a gold altar and walls of polished marble. Gold and silver ornaments, woven textiles, and colorful **mosaics**, or pictures made up of many bits of colored glass or stone, were everywhere. Figures of Justinian and Theodora were among the angels and saints that lined the walls.

Most impressive was the huge dome with its many windows that rose high over the central part of the church. It was the first time such a huge circular dome had been set atop a rectangular opening. During the day sunlight poured through the many windows. At night thousands of oil lamps turned the building into a beacon that could be seen for miles.

Hagia Sophia was later called St. Sophia. For more than 900 years it served as the religious center of the Byzantine Empire. It still stands today.

1. How did Justinian feel about Roman law? What did he do about it?
2. What improvements did Justinian make in the appearance of the Empire?
3. What were some of the features of Hagia Sophia?

CONQUEST   Justinian wanted to reunite the eastern and western parts of the empire and restore the glory and power that was Rome's. To do this, he needed to conquer the German kingdoms in Western Europe and North Africa. He appointed an officer named Belisarius to reorganize and lead the Byzantine army.

The cavalry, which was the most important part of the army, had been divided into groups of private soldiers hired by landowning nobles. Each group had its own commanders who usually did not cooperate with one another. Foot soldiers, who made up the largest part of the army, were called up when needed and then sent back to their homes. As a result they felt little loyalty towards their officers.

When Belisarius took command, he set up a basic group of loyal and heavily armed cavalry soldiers. The group was so strong that the other soldiers willingly obeyed its orders. Then Belisarius developed a series of battle moves that greatly strengthened the army's striking power.

The navy was also improved, and **Greek fire**, the first secret weapon in history, was developed. Greek fire was a chemical mixture that ignited when it came into contact with water. It burned the skin and was not easily put out. The Byzantines guarded their secret so carefully that its exact formula is still unknown.

THE BYZANTINE EMPIRE UNDER JUSTINIAN

With these improvements the Byzantines extended their control in the Mediterranean and won back much of Italy and North Africa. They defeated the Persians, who had again risen to power, and insured the security of the empire's eastern borders. Most of the western provinces Justinian regained were lost again within a generation or so after his death.

1. What was Justinian's goal?
2. What did Justinian do to accomplish his goal? How successful was he?

THE EASTERN ORTHODOX CHURCH

Church and government were closely linked in the Byzantine Empire. Christianity was the official religion; everyone was required to be a Christian. Emperors represented Christ on earth. They were not only the head of the government but of the Church as well.

At the head of the church in Constantinople was the Patriarch, who was appointed by the emperor. Under the

Patriarch were church officials called **metropolitans** and arch-bishops. They took charge of large cities and important provincial centers. Under them were the bishops and local priests. Most of the priests were married. All of the higher officials, however, came from monasteries and were unmarried.

The monasteries played an important role in the empire. They helped the poor, provided hospitals, and ran schools for needy children. They sent missionaries to neighboring lands to help keep the peace. The missionaries translated portions of the Bible into several different eastern European languages. They believed that more people would become Christians if the Bible and church rituals were presented to them in their own language. The missionaries also gave one group of Eastern Europeans called Slavs a new alphabet based on the Greek alphabet. It was called Cyrillic in honor of St. Cyril, the Byzantine Empire's leading missionary.

1. What role did Christianity play in the Byzantine Empire?
2. How was the Church organized?
3. Why were monasteries and missionaries important to the empire?

CONFLICT WITH THE WEST   Religious beliefs and practices were very important to the Byzantines. They often argued about such matters. An argument that divided the empire for more than a hundred years centered around the use of **icons**, or religious images, in worship.

Many Byzantines paid respect to icons. They also kept statues of saints in their homes and covered the walls of their churches with religious paintings and mosaics. Monasteries owned icons believed to work miracles. Some Byzantines, however, demanded an end to the use of icons. They considered devotion to them a form of idol worship, forbidden by God's law.

Painted Clasp

In 726 Emperor Leo III forbid the use of icons in religious worship. He had two reasons for issuing the order. He himself did not approve of images. Beyond that, however, he wanted to keep church officials who favored them from gaining too much political power. The emperor and church leaders argued over the use of icons for many years. Most people sided with the priests, bishops, and monks and refused to give up their icons. In 843 the emperor recognized that the cause was lost and once again permitted their use.

BYZANTINE ICON

The Eastern Orthodox Church was the center of Byzantine life. Byzantines often paid respect to icons in their homes and churches. This mosaic shows Christ and a saint giving a blessing.

Why did Byzantines argue over the use of icons?

The feud over icons damaged the empire's relations with western Europe. Because so few people in the West could read, western bishops and priests used images to explain Christian teachings to the people. When Leo decided to do away with icons, the Pope at Rome called a council of bishops. The council declared that the emperor and his supporters were no longer members of the Church.

An argument also developed between the Pope and the Patriarch of Constantinople. The Patriarch had refused to recognize the Pope as head of the Church. The Pope began to press the Patriarch to accept his authority. When the Patriarch continued to refuse, the Pope broke his ties with the Byzantine emperor and turned to the Frankish kings for military protection. When the Pope crowned Charlemagne "Emperor of the Romans" in 800, the Byzantines were furious. They believed that the title belonged only to their emperors. These disputes helped pave the way for the final split between Western and Eastern Christianity in 1054.

1. Why did Leo III forbid the use of icons? How did the Byzantines react to Leo's order?
2. How did western Europe react to Leo's order about icons?
3. What caused the dispute between the Pope of Rome and the Patriarch of Constantinople?

DECLINE OF THE EMPIRE

The Byzantine Empire lasted for almost 1100 years. Its capital was the largest, richest, and most beautiful city in Europe. Its people were among the most educated and creative of the period. They preserved Greek culture and Roman political techniques for future generations. The empire spread

BYZANTINE HOME

Byzantine nobles lived in richly decorated homes. In this sitting room, a noble-woman prepares to receive guests.

What contributions did the Byzantines make to later civilizations?

Christianity to Eastern peoples. It did much to help the growth of trade. It gave the world new techniques in the fine arts.

In spite of all these achievements, internal problems and outside forces combined to weaken the empire and lead to its downfall. Early Byzantine emperors had relied on the small farmers to make up the army. In return for their services, the emperors gave them land and protected them from the wealthy landlords.

By the 1100's the empire's borders were secure, and not as many soldiers were needed. The emperor decided to cut military costs by changing the policy toward the farmers. Without the emperor's support, the farmers could not stop aristocrats from taking over their property. Once they had lost their land, the farmers found little reason to remain loyal to the empire.

At the same time the empire began to have problems with trade. When the Vikings conquered Byzantine lands in southern Italy in 1080, they threatened to attack Constantinople. The Byzantines no longer had enough soldiers to fight them off. So they turned for help to the Italian city-state of Venice.

The Venetians defeated the Vikings. In return the Byzantine emperor gave them the right to do business tax-free in all of the cities of the empire. Venetian ships and merchants soon

THE END OF THE BYZANTINE EMPIRE

controlled most of the empire's trade. This meant a great loss of income for the Byzantines who had collected taxes on trade goods.

Meanwhile, Christians from the West and Muslims from the East attacked the empire. The empire lost its state of Asia Minor to the invaders. The empire had depended on Asia Minor for food and materials as well as soldiers for the army. This loss greatly weakened the empire. One by one the invaders took over empire lands. Before long its territory was reduced to a small area around Constantinople.

The population dropped to less than 100,000 persons. Docks and market places stood empty. Even the emperors were poor. When Turkish armies with guns and gunpowder attacked Constantinople in 1453, they found it easy to conquer the Byzantines. Before long the Byzantine Empire was just a memory.

1. What factors helped bring about the decline of the Byzantine Empire?

CHAPTER REVIEW
SUMMARY

1. About 330 the Emperor Constantine moved the capital of the Roman Empire from Rome to Constantinople.

2. Constantinople's buildings and political and social life were patterned on those of Rome.

3. Constantinople was a Christian city, filled with churches and shrines, and its people were extremely charitable.

4. After the Roman Empire in the West fell during the fifth century, the Roman Empire in the East became known as the Byzantine Empire.

5. In 527 Justinian became emperor of the Byzantine Empire.

6. One of Justinian's many achievements was a code of law that influenced the legal systems of western countries.

7. Another of Justinian's achievements was Hagia Sophia, which served as the religious center of the Byzantine Empire for more than 900 years.

8. Under Justinian, a general named Belisarius reorganized the Byzantine army and expanded the empire's boundaries.

9. Byzantine missionaries developed the Cyrillic alphabet.

10. Between 726 and 843 the Byzantine emperor and Orthodox church leaders argued over the use of icons.

11. Relations between the Pope and the Patriarch of Constantinople were weakened by the argument over icons and by the Pope's crowning of Charlemagne.

12. In 1054 the Eastern Orthodox Church and the Roman Catholic Church split.

BUILDING VOCABULARY

1. *Identify the following:*

Constantinople	Justinian	Hagia Sophia	Saint Cyril
Byzantine Empire	Theodora	Belisarius	Leo III
Byzantium	Justinian's Code	Cyrillic	

2. *Define the following:*

relics	dowry	Greek fire	icons
saints	mosaics	metropolitan	

REVIEWING THE FACTS

1. Why did the Roman Empire in the East survive?

2. Why was Constantinople a great trading center?

3. How did Constantinople's appearance reflect its Christian character?

4. How did Christianity affect the way Byzantines took care of poor, aged, and blind persons?

5. On what basis did Justinian choose the people who served him?

6. How did Theodora help the role of women in the Byzantine Empire?

7. Why is Justinian's Code important in the world today?

8. Why did Byzantine emperors change the laws and again permit the use of icons?

9. Why did Byzantine farmers gradually lose their loyalty to the emperor?

10. Who conquered the Byzantine Empire in 1453?

DISCUSSING IMPORTANT IDEAS

1. Why were church and government closely linked in the Byzantine Empire?

2. Do you agree with Justinian that ability is more important than wealth or social position when choosing government officials? Why or why not?

3. Do you think images are a good way of teaching people who do not know how to read? Explain.

4. Do you think the Byzantine emperors were wise to ask Venice for help against the Vikings? Why or why not?

USING MAPS

Compare the maps on pages 302 and 306, and answer the following questions:

1. What areas did the Byzantine Empire include before Justinian?

2. Into what areas did the Byzantine Empire spread under Justinian?

3. What areas did the Ottoman Turks control in 1453?

4. What parts of the Empire did not come under Ottoman rule in 1453?

CHAPTER 22
THE SPREAD OF ISLAM

$\mathbf{B}$etween the northeast coast of Africa and central Asia lies the Arabian peninsula. The people who live there are known as Arabs. At one time, most were Bedouins. They were herders who roamed the desert in search of grass and water for their camels, goats, and sheep. They lived in tents woven from camel or goat hair.

Bedouin warriors raided other peoples and fought one another over pastures and springs. They valued their camels and swords above all else. They enjoyed poetry and music. They believed in many gods. They worshipped stones, trees, and pieces of wood that they believed were the homes of spirits with supernatural powers.

In the seventh century a new religion called Islam appeared in the mountainous area of western Arabia known as the Hejaz. Within 100 years, an Arab Empire based on Islamic beliefs had developed. It came to dominate an area larger than that of the Roman Empire.

ISLAM

The word Islam means "the act of **submitting**, or giving oneself over, to God." The followers of Islam are called Muslims, which means "believers." The Islamic religion was founded by an Arab merchant named Mohammed. He came to be known as the prophet of Allah, or God.

Islam shook the foundations of Byzantium and Persia, the two most powerful civilizations of the time. It made Arabic the common language of more than 90 million people. It came to shape a way of life for one out of every seven persons on earth.

1. Why is Islam important?

MECCA   By the middle of the sixth century three major towns had developed in the Hejaz. They were Yathrib, Taif, and Mecca. Of the three, Mecca was the largest and the richest.

Mecca was supported by trade and religion. Traders stopped there for food and water on their way north to Constantinople. Arab **pilgrims**, or travelers to a religious shrine, came there to worship. Arabia's holiest shrine, the *ka'bah*, stood in the center of Mecca. It was a low cube-shaped building surrounded by 360 idols. A black stone was imbedded in one of its walls. The people believed the stone had fallen from Paradise. Nearby was the *zemzen*, or holy well.

According to legend, the original ka'bah had stood in heaven. When Adam was forced to leave the Garden of Eden, he built a structure on earth exactly like the one in heaven. Nearby, Ishmael, the legendary founder of the Arabs, kicked open a well. The town of Mecca grew up around the ka'bah and the well.

Pilgrims came from all over Arabia to worship at the ka'bah. They kissed the black stone and walked around the ka'bah seven times. Some left offerings before the idols.

1. Why was Mecca an important Arabian town?
2. What legend was told about the ka'bah?

MOHAMMED   In 571 a child named Mohammed was born to a poor widow in Mecca. When Mohammed was six, his mother died, and he went to live with a poor uncle. He began working as a camel driver when he reached his teens. At the age of 25, he married a rich 40-year-old widow named Khadijah.

In time, Mohammed was very successful in the caravan business. Then he became troubled by the drinking, gambling, and corruption in Mecca. He began spending a lot of time alone in a cave on a hillside outside the city. There he thought and **fasted**, or went without food and drink. He decided that the Meccans had been led into evil by their belief in false gods. He concluded that there was only one God, Allah, the same god as the God of the Jews and Christians.

MOHAMMED'S BACKGROUND
Mohammed first preached in Mecca, the Arabian city where he was born. An Islamic painting (left) shows the members of Mohammed's family. A European print (right) shows the *ka'bah* in the center of Mecca.
How did the Meccans respond to Mohammed's preaching?

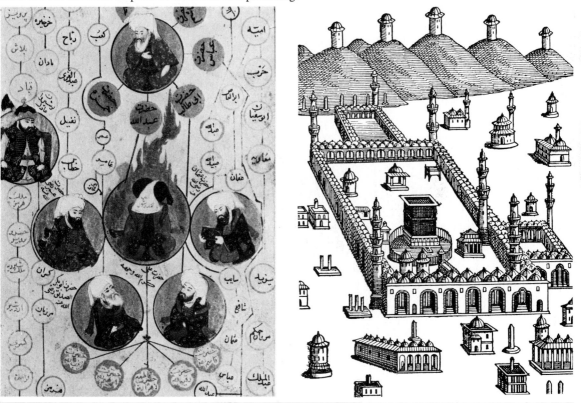

In 610, when he was about 39 years old, Mohammed had a **revelation**, or vision. When he was asleep in a cave, an angel appeared and ordered him to read some writing. He awoke frightened and fled to the top of a mountain. There he heard the voice of the angel Gabriel telling him to be the apostle of God. Mohammed told Khadijah what had happened. She went to see a holy man. He said that the heavenly visitor was the same one who had visited Moses and that Mohammed was to be the prophet of his people. After a while, Mohammed had another revelation in which he was ordered to "rise and warn" the people.

In 613 Mohammed began to preach to the people of Mecca. He told them that the only God was the all-powerful Allah before whom all believers were equal. Allah, therefore, was the only god the people should worship. He explained that nothing happened except by Allah's will. He told the rich to share with

MOHAMMED'S ARABIA

the poor because Allah measured people's worth by their good deeds and devotion to Him. Mohammed saw life as a preparation for the **Day of Judgment**, or the last day on which people would rise from the dead to be judged.

At first the wealthy business and religious leaders of Mecca laughed at Mohammed. But before long they began to feel threatened by him. They were afraid that worshippers of Allah would stop making **pilgrimages**, or religious journeys, to Mecca. And that would ruin the city's economy. So Mecca's leaders started persecuting Mohammed and his followers.

In 620 Mohammed preached to a group of pilgrims from Yathrib. They invited him to come to Yathrib and be their leader. During the summer of 622 several hundred of Mohammed's followers fled from Mecca to Yathrib. The year 622, called *Anno Hegira*, or "Year of the Flight," became the first year of the Muslim calendar. Yathrib became Medina al Munawara, "the enlightened city." Later the name became Medina.

In Medina Mohammed proved that he was a great political leader. He gained more followers and power by giving the people a government that united them and made them proud of their city. He began to lead raids against passing Meccan caravans. In 630 he led 10,000 followers into Mecca. They captured the city, destroyed the idols around the ka'bah, and dedicated the black stone to Allah. Before long Mecca became the center of Islam.

Next Mohammed and his followers conquered Taif. Now they controlled the entire Hejaz. In 631 delegates representing Arabs from all over Arabia came to declare their faith in Allah and offer their allegiance to Mohammed. Mohammed had created an Arab state with a strong army.

The following year Mohammed led the annual pilgrimage to Mecca. Three months after he returned home, he fell sick and died.

1. What were some of Mohammed's teachings?
2. Why did Mohammed go to Yathrib? What did he accomplish?
3. What changes did Mohammed make in Mecca in 630?

THE KORAN   At the heart of Islam is the **Koran**, or Muslim scriptures. Muslims believe it is the direct word of God as revealed to Mohammed. For this reason, they feel they should follow it exactly.

Page from Koran

ISLAMIC FAITH

Muslims learn the teachings of the Koran at an early age. A child (left) studies passages from the Koran. An important teaching of the Koran requires Muslims to pray five times daily. From the prayer towers (right) of each mosque, criers call the people to prayer.

How do Muslims regard the Koran and prayer?

The Koran is written in Arabic. It contains stories, legends, philosophy, and the advice given Mohammed by an angel. The Koran identifies the basic beliefs of Islam and tells how good Muslims should live. According to the Koran, Muslims should not eat pork, drink liquor, or gamble. The Koran also gives advice on marriage, divorce, inheritance, and business practices. It says that thieves should be punished by having their right hand cut off.

The Koran describes the **pillars of faith**, or the five duties all Muslims must fulfill. The first pillar is the confession of faith. All Muslims must recite the Islamic creed that states, "There is no God but Allah, and Mohammed is his prophet."

The second pillar involves prayer. Muslims must pray five times a day—at dawn, noon, late afternoon, sunset, and evening. They pray facing Mecca. Prayers can be offered anywhere. But the Friday noon prayer is usually recited at a **mosque**, or Muslim house of worship. There, believers are led by an *imam* or prayer leader.

The third pillar concerns the giving of **alms**, or charity. There are two kinds of alms. One is the money Muslims donate on their own. The other is the part of a Muslim's income that is collected by the state. It is used for schooling or to help the poor.

The fourth pillar involves fasting. Youngsters, sick people, pregnant women, and travelers do not have to fast. Everyone else must fast each year during the daylight hours of the holy month of Ramadan.

The fifth pillar involves a pilgrimage to Mecca two months after Ramadan. The journey is called the *hajj*. It involves three days of ceremony and sacrifice during which Muslims from all over the world come together.

The Koran promises that believers who have fulfilled their duties will go to Paradise and that everyone else will go to Hell. Paradise is a cool mountaintop with shade, fruit trees, beautiful flower gardens, cold springs, and singing birds. There, the dead find eternal happiness. Hell is a flame-filled pit where drinking water comes from a salty well and where food is a strong-smelling plant that causes hunger. There, the dead are damned forever.

1. What does the Koran contain?
2. What are the five pillars of faith?
3. What does the Koran say will happen after death?

THE ARAB EMPIRE

When Mohammed died in 632, his followers needed a new leader. Without someone to guide them, the community could have broken up, and the faith would be lost. A group of Muslims chose a new leader whom they called *khālifa*, or **caliph**, which means "successor."

THE RIGHTLY GUIDED CALIPHS   The first caliph was Abu Bākr, Mohammed's father-in-law and close friend. Bākr and the next three caliphs were elected for life. These caliphs

THE EXPANSION OF ISLAM

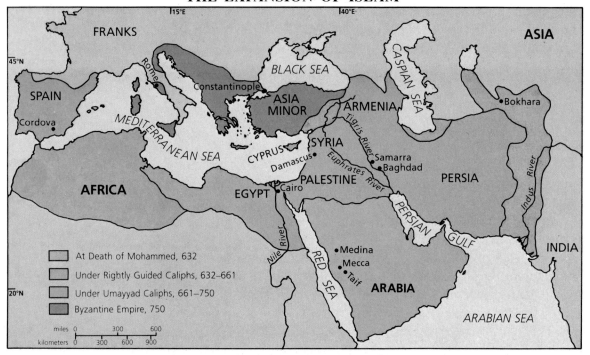

ruled from Medina. They kept in close touch with the people and asked advice of their most trusted friends. For this reason, they were called the Rightly Guided Caliphs.

The Rightly Guided Caliphs honored Mohammed's wish to carry the Word of God to other peoples. They did this by fighting *jihads*, or holy wars, against **infidels**, or nonbelievers. They sent Muslim warriors into Palestine, Syria, Iraq, Persia, Egypt, and North Africa, and conquered them.

The Arabs were successful in their conquests for many reasons. Islam united them. It also taught them that warriors who died fighting infidels went to Paradise. Most of the Arabs had led hard lives that had toughened them mentally and physically. They were willing to take by force what they had not been able to get any other way.

The Arabs were fearless fighters led by strong leaders. The leaders planned and carried out attacks that took the enemy completely by surprise. Then, too, the Arabs handled their camels and horses with great skill.

The Arab way of treating the people they conquered also contributed to their success. Those who gave in without a fight had to pay taxes. In return, the Arabs protected them and allowed them to keep their land. Those who fought and were defeated not only had to pay taxes but also lost their land. In addition, they had to continue farming the land for the Arabs.

1. How did the Rightly Guided Caliphs get their name? How did they expand the empire?
2. Why were the Arabs successful in their conquests?

THE UMAYYADS   Ali, Mohammed's son-in-law and the last of the Rightly Guided Caliphs, was killed in 661. Mu'awiyah, the new caliph, moved the capital from Medina to Damascus and founded the Umayyad dynasty. From that time on, the title of caliph was hereditary.

ISLAMIC SPAIN

Under Islamic rule the Spanish cities of Cordoba and Granada became known for their wealth and learning. The Alhambra, a palace in Granada, is considered the finest example of Islamic architecture in Europe.
How large was the Arab Empire?

Under the Umayyads, the Arabs learned new skills. The empire grew rich from taxes and expanded to include Afghanistan, Turkestan, what is now North Africa, most of Spain, and part of southern France.

The Umayyads ruled more like kings than religious leaders. They reorganized the government and made Arabic the official language. They minted the first Arabic currency. They set up horseback postal routes. They repaired and maintained neglected irrigation canals. They built magnificent mosques and encouraged the arts.

The Umayyads, however, had social and economic problems which led to their downfall. The conquered peoples who had become Muslims complained that they were not treated as equals. They received less money for serving in the army than Arabs did, and they had to pay higher taxes.

The Muslims themselves divided into two groups called Shiites and Sunnites. After a while, civil war broke out between the Umayyads and a group of Shiite Muslims called Abbasids. In 750 the Abbasids defeated the Umayyads and became the new rulers of the Arab Empire.

1. What were some accomplishments of the Umayyads?
2. Who replaced the Umayyads as rulers of the Arab Empire?

THE ABBASIDS   The Abbasids ruled the Arab Empire from 750 to 1258. Their first 100 years in power was known as the Golden Age of Islam.

The Abbasids built a new capital called Baghdad on the west bank of the Tigris River. Designed by a Jewish astronomer and a Persian engineer, it took 100,000 architects and workers four years to build. Baghdad was built in the shape of a circle. It was surrounded by three huge, sloping brick walls and a deep **moat**, or wide ditch filled with water. Each wall had four large gates linked together by two highways which crossed in the center of the city. The highways divided Baghdad into four pie-shaped sections. From the gates, each highway led to a different part of the empire.

The Arab Empire changed again under the Abbasids. All that remained of Arab influence was the Arabic language and the Islamic religion. The name Arab no longer meant only a person from Arabia but any subject of the empire who spoke Arabic.

BAGHDAD
Baghdad, located on the banks of the Tigris River, was a center of trade, government, and religion. During the eighth century it became the world's most important Islamic city.
Who governed in Baghdad from the eighth to the thirteenth centuries?

The Abbasid caliphs ruled and lived like Persian kings. They thought of themselves as God's deputies and took the title of "Shadow of God on Earth." Anyone who approached them had to bow down and kiss the floor. An executioner stood ready to cut off the head of anyone who displeased the caliph.

The Abbasids created the government post of *vizier*, or chief advisor. As the caliph's chief minister, the vizier stood between the throne and the people. The vizier took charge of running the empire and appointed governors of the provinces.

The Abbasids did not try to make new conquests. Instead, they concentrated on trade. Baghdad became the marketplace of the world. The Arabs grew rich. The international trade led to a fresh exchange of ideas. When Syrian Christians and Jews translated Greek writings into Arabic, interest in Greek science and philosophy blossomed again.

Seljuk Turks *c. 900–1258*

Seljuk
c. 900
chief from central Asia; settled with a group of followers near city of Bokhara and became Muslim

Tughril
c. 1055
grandson of Seljuk; conquered Baghdad; took title al-sultan, meaning "he with authority"; set up Muslim kingdom in western Asia

Mongols *c. 1206–1300*

Genghis Khan
c. 1220
united central Asian nomads; conquered Arab territory and created empire that covered most of Asia and eastern Europe

Hulagu
c. 1258
grandson of Genghis Khan; led attack on Baghdad in 1258; became first khan, or overlord, of a Muslim kingdom that stretched from Syria to India

Genghis Khan

Mamelukes *c. 1250–1517*

Shajar
c. 1250
freed slave who became first Mameluke ruler of Egypt; only Muslim woman to rule a country

Baybars
c. 1260
seized throne of Egypt; restored caliphate in Cairo; created Mameluke dynasty until fall of Egypt

Ottoman Turks *c. 1290–1922*

Osman
c. 1290–1326
founded Ottoman dynasty in Asia Minor

Mohammed II
c. 1451–1481
captured Constantinople in 1453; established Ottoman Empire

Mohammed II

Life changed in the empire. The demand for luxury items grew so great that Arab craftspeople began producing some items themselves. As trade increased, more records had to be kept. This led to the opening of banks. People had time to play games like polo, backgammon, and chess. Men stopped wearing the traditional Arab robe and began wearing trousers. Meals were served on tables instead of on the floor.

The empire soon became too large for the caliph to control, and it began to break up into independent dynasties. In 836 the caliph moved to a new capital city called Samarra. In 892 he returned to Baghdad in an attempt to regain power. But by then it was too late. In 945 the Persians took control of Baghdad.

1. What were some features of Baghdad?
2. How did the Arab empire change under the Abbasids?

ISLAMIC LIFE   Islam set the guidelines for the way Muslims lived during the empire. It was a man's world, because the Koran said that "men are in charge of women" and "good women are obedient." Therefore, Muslim women were expected to stay at home and keep out of sight.

Marriage was considered a duty. A Muslim who could afford it could have as many as four wives. Each wife was entitled to her own quarters, cooking and sleeping conveniences, and household slaves. A Muslim usually married for the first time when he was about 20 years old. His bride was usually between the ages of 12 and 20. She had little to say about her marriage, which was arranged by her mother. Her father and the groom-to-be drew up a marriage contract that included the amount the groom-to-be was to pay as a bridal gift.

A Muslim man did not have to give a reason for divorcing his wife. He simply had to repeat the words "I dismiss thee" three times. In three months his divorce was final. A Muslim woman who wanted a divorce had to pay for it by turning her property over to her husband.

Muslims celebrated the birth of a son with a week of feasts and offerings. The Muslim creed was whispered in the baby's ears at birth. Women cared for the boys until they were seven years old. Then they entered mosque schools where they learned to write. After they had learned all they could, wealthy boys went to special classes where they listened to Muslim scholars discuss poetry and the classics.

Seljuk Jug

MARKETPLACE

The bazaar, or marketplace, was an important center of life in an Islamic city. At the bazaar, merchants sold their goods in stalls or shops along roofed streets. Men of the city also met at the bazaar for conversation.

How did trade contribute to the growth of the Arab Empire?

Fathers taught their sons how to be Muslim gentlemen. This meant learning not to eat too much or spit in public. It also meant not saying cruel things about one person to another.

1. How did Muslims view marriage?
2. What kind of schooling did a Muslim boy receive?

ARAB CONTRIBUTIONS

Between the eighth and fourteenth centuries, Arab scholars helped preserve the learning of the ancient world which otherwise might have been lost. They also made many other contributions to modern civilization.

Arab scientists called **alchemists** tried to turn base metals—such as tin, iron, and lead—into gold and silver. Their efforts were not successful. But they led to the practice of making experiments and keeping accurate records of results. Thus, the Arabs are considered the founders of modern chemistry.

Arab astronomers studied the heavens and gave many stars the names they still have today. They accurately described the eclipses of the sun and proved that the moon affects the ocean. The astronomers worked with Arab geographers to determine the size and circumference of the earth. From their studies they concluded that the earth might be round. The astronomer-geographer al-Idrisi created the first accurate map of the world.

Arab mathematicians invented algebra and introduced it to Europeans. The word algebra, in fact, comes from the Arabic word *al-jabr*. It is just one of many Arabic words that have become part of the Spanish and English languages. Arab mathematicians also borrowed the zero and the numerals 1–9 from Hindu mathematicians in India and passed them on to Europeans.

The Arabs excelled in medicine. Unlike doctors in most other countries, Arab doctors had to pass an exam before they could practice medicine. The Arabs established the world's first school of pharmacy and opened the world's first drugstores. They organized medical clinics that traveled through the empire on camel-back providing drugs and care for the sick.

Arab doctors were the first to discover that blood **circulates**, or is carried to and from the heart. They were also the first to diagnose certain diseases. The Persian al-Razi identified the differences between measles and smallpox. Another Persian, Ibn Sina, was the first to recognize that tuberculosis is **contagious**, or can be passed from person to person. He also realized that one way to prevent illness from spreading is to keep sick people apart from those who are well.

Arab doctors advanced medical science by publishing their findings. Ibn Sina's *Canon of Medicine*, an encyclopedia of medicine, was used in European medical schools for 500 years.

Astrolabe

The Arabs also made many contributions in the arts. One of the best known writings is *The Arabian Nights*, a collection of tales put together from Persian stories. The tales paint an exciting picture of Islamic life at the height of the empire. The Persian poet Omar Khayyam's *Rubaiyyat* has been translated into many languages and is considered one of the finest poems ever written.

At first Arab historians wrote about events one year at a time. Then they began to organize events around rulers and peoples, which is what most historians do today. Ibn Khaldun's account of Arabs, Berbers, and Persians was the first to consider the influence of geography and climate on people.

Islamic art was distinct and colorful. It adorned swords, books, rugs, and mosques and other buildings. It differed from most other art because of the Muslim belief that Allah had created all living creatures. Islamic artists considered it a sin to make statues or pictures of Allah's creations. Most of their art consisted of geometric designs entwined with flowers, leaves, and stars.

1. What were some Arab contributions to modern civilization?

CHAPTER REVIEW

SUMMARY

1. Mecca contained a holy shrine to which pilgrims from all over Arabia came to worship.

2. Mohammed was born in Mecca in 571.

3. In 610 Mohammed received a revelation, and in 613 he began to preach that the only God was Allah.

4. In 622 Mohammed and his followers went from Mecca to Yathrib, where Mohammed organized the city's government and formed an army.

5. In 630 Mohammed led his followers into Mecca and dedicated the ka'bah to Allah.

6. In 631 delegates from all over Arabia declared their faith in Allah and their allegiance to Mohammed.

7. Muslim scriptures, which are called the Koran, are written in Arabic.

8. After Mohammed's death in 632, his followers chose a new leader who led them into battle against nonbelievers.

9. The Arabs succeeded in conquering a huge empire.

10. In 661 the capital of the Arab Empire was moved to Damascus by the founder of the Umayyad dynasty.

11. In 750 the Abbasids took over control of the Arab Empire and built a new capital called Baghdad.

12. The Abbasids concentrated on trade rather than warfare.

13. In 945 control of the Arab Empire was taken over by the Persians.

14. The Arabs made many contributions to modern civilization, especially in the fields of chemistry, astronomy, mathematics, and medicine.

BUILDING VOCABULARY

1. *Identify the following:*

Arabs	Mecca	Rightly Guided Caliphs	al-Idrisi
Bedouins	Allah	Damascus	al-Razi
Islam	Khadijah	Umayyad	Ibn Sina
Hejaz	Yathrib	Abbasids	*The Arabian Nights*
Muslims	Medina	Baghdad	*Rubaiyyat*
Mohammed			Ibn Khaldun

2. *Define the following:*

submitting	Day of Judgment	imam	moat
pilgrims	pilgrimages	alms	vizier
ka'bah	Anno Hegira	hajj	alchemists
zemzen	Koran	caliph	circulates
fasted	pillars of faith	jihads	contagious
revelation	mosque	infidels	

REVIEWING THE FACTS

1. How did Bedouins earn a living?
2. How did pilgrims worship at the ka'bah in Mecca?
3. Why did Mohammed begin to spend time alone in a cave on a hillside in Mecca?
4. Why did the leaders of the city of Mecca start persecuting Mohammed and his followers?
5. What is the Islamic creed?
6. In what direction do Muslims face when they pray?
7. What brought about the downfall of the Umayyad dynasty?
8. What did the word "Arab" mean under the Abbasids?
9. What was the role of women in Muslim society?
10. What discoveries did Arab doctors make?

DISCUSSING IMPORTANT IDEAS

1. Why was religion an important part of Arab life?
2. Do you think the numerals 1–9 should be called Arabic or Hindu numerals?
3. What contributions made by the Arabs do you use in your everyday life?
4. In what ways is Islam similar to Judaism or Christianity? How are they different?

USING MAPS

Compare the maps on pages 312 and 316, and answer the following questions:

1. Where was Islam first located?
2. Into what areas did it spread under the Rightly Guided Caliphs? The Umayyad Caliphs?
3. Which city is further north—Mecca or Medina?
4. Is Yathrib the same city as Medina? How can you tell?

THE MIDDLE KINGDOMS OF AFRICA

Long before Westerners came to Africa, black Africans ruled kingdoms larger and wealthier than any European country. The capitals of these kingdoms were busy trade and religious centers. Three of the kingdoms—Ghana, Mali, and Songhai—lay in the center of important trade routes that ran from North Africa to the West African coast. Because of this, they were known as the Middle Kingdoms.

The Middle Kingdoms controlled the rich salt trade. Arab merchants from North Africa crossed the Sahara Desert in camel caravans to exchange their salt for gold mined southwest of the Middle Kingdoms.

The Arab merchants brought the Africans more than salt. They also brought the religion of Islam. The Africans of the Middle Kingdom made Islam their religion and Arabic the language of trade and business. They built schools, libraries, domed white mosques, and square stone houses next to their traditional round dried mud homes. They turned small trading centers into large cities. One of the largest and most important cities was Timbuktu.

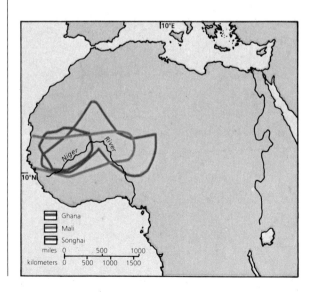

So the gold would keep its value, the kings limited its use. In Ghana, the king alone was allowed to own and use pieces of gold. Everyone else had to use gold dust. Some of the kings gave away gold. In 1324 Mansa Musa of Mali made a trip to Arabia. Each of the 60,000 servants who traveled with him carried a four-pound, or about 1.8 kilogram, gold bar. Mansa Musa gave many of the bars to poor people he met along the way.

The kings wanted to impress the people with their power and to be honored. So whenever they appeared in public, they did so with a lot of ceremony. They surrounded themselves with richly and colorfully dressed officials and military officers. The king of Mali had his arrival and departure announced by trumpeters and drummers. He sat on an ebony throne under an arch formed by large elephant tusks. He never spoke directly to the people. Instead, he had servants standing at the foot of the stairs leading to the throne answer requests.

The Middle Kingdoms ruled in West Africa for almost 1000 years, from about 600 to 1600. At that point in time, Moors from Morocco and explorers from Portugal began to interfere in the trade and government of the area.

Merchants, scholars, artisans, and slaves made their homes in the cities. There merchants sold their wares and argued with each other about prices and artisans made jewelry and metal goods.

Rich kings ruled the Middle Kingdoms and controlled trade. They forced Arab merchants to pay them taxes in gold. They used the gold to build fortress-palaces, set up governments, and raise powerful armies armed with iron weapons.

1. Why were Ghana, Mali, and Songhai known as the Middle Kingdoms?
2. In what ways did the Arabs influence the Africans of the Middle Kingdoms?
3. How did the kings of the Middle Kingdoms use their wealth?

327

THE RUSSIANS

23

North of the Byzantine Empire lived a people called Slavs. All that is known about their origins is that they were Indo-Europeans, like the Aryans who entered the Indus valley and the Dorians who conquered the Myceneans. About 500 B.C. the Slavs began to settle in eastern Europe in the areas now known as eastern Poland and the western Soviet Union.

THE EARLY RUSSIANS

About 500, a group of Slavs began to move eastward. They were hunters and farmers who came to be known as Russians.

They settled in villages made up of about 25 related families. Each family owned a house that was built slightly underground to provide warmth during the cold winter months. The house had low walls and an earth-covered roof. The land, animals, tools, and seed belonged to the village rather than to individuals. Around each village was a wall of earth and a wooden stockade, or protective fence.

The oldest male governed the village with the help of a council. He assigned villagers different farming tasks and judged quarrels. During attacks he acted as military leader.

By the 800's the Russians controlled all of the heavily forested land as far east as the Volga River. To clear the land for farming, farmers used a method called **slash-and-burn**. They cut down trees, which they burnt for fertilizer. On the cleared land they planted such crops as barley, rye, and flax. After a few years, when the wood fertilizer in the soil had been used up, the farmers moved to a new place. There they repeated the process.

RUSSIAN CABIN

Houses in early Russian towns and villages were made of wood. This modern Russian cabin shows the use of decorative styles passed on from early Russian artisans.

How did environment influence the lives of the early Russians?

The forests provided the Russians with furs and timber. The Russians soon became skilled in building with wood. They made musical instruments out of wood and used logs to make boats and *izbas*, or log cabins. The izba was a one-room cabin with a gabled roof and wooden window frames decorated with painted carvings of flowers, fruits, birds, and beasts. The whole family lived, worked, ate, and slept in the single room. Although each izba had a fireplace, some did not have a chimney. Smoke from fires had to escape through shutters that covered the windows.

The villagers worshipped many gods and honored nature spirits and ancestors. The most popular gods were Volos, who protected cattle and sheep; Perun, god of thunder and lightning; and the Great Mother, goddess of the land and harvest. The people built wooden images of their favorite gods on the highest ground outside the villages.

1. Where did the Russians settle?
2. What kind of homes did the early Russians have?

TRADE   There were many slow-moving rivers in the area east of the Volga. At first the Russians used them as roads between their villages. Before long they began using them for trade as well. They set up a trade route that ran from the Baltic Sea in the north to the Black Sea in the south.

By the end of the ninth century, the Russians had built many trading towns along the riverbanks. During the five months of winter, the merchants who lived in the towns gathered furs, honey, and other forest products from the people in neighboring villages. They rode on horseback, pulling **sledges**, or heavy sleds, filled with goods over the deep snow. In the spring, when the ice on the rivers had melted, the merchants loaded their goods on boats and floated south to Byzantium. There the merchants traded their goods for cloth, wine, weapons, and jewelry. Trade helped the Russians to live more comfortably and to develop their civilization.

The Russians had to protect their trade routes. Since they were not fighters, they relied on Viking warriors from Scandinavia. These Vikings, known in Russia as Varangians, eventually became part of the larger Slav population. The name Russia came from the Scandinavian term "Rus," or "warrior band."

1. How and where did the Russians become traders?
2. How did the Varangians help the Russians?

Rurik

KIEVAN RUSSIA

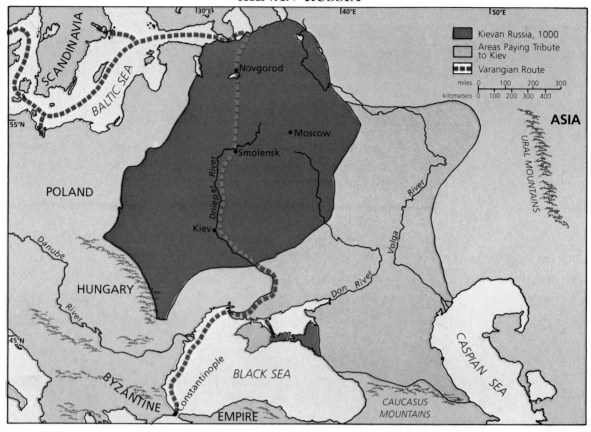

THE EMERGENCE OF RUSSIA

In 862 a Varangian named Rurik became the Prince of Novgorod, a northern town on the Russian trading route. About 20 years later, Rurik's friend Oleg established the first Russian state. He set up his capital at Kiev.

Kiev stood on a hill overlooking the main bend of the Dnieper River. It was the southernmost town on the Russian trading route. Whoever controlled Kiev controlled Russia's trade with Byzantium. Kiev also lay close to where the Russian forest turned into the **steppe**, or grassland. For hundreds of years the steppe had served central Asian warriors as a highway into Europe. Kiev was therefore in a good location to protect merchant ships from outside attackers.

The Russian state that Oleg established was really a collection of small territories. The central ruler was the Grand

Prince of Kiev. He was assisted by local princes, wealthy merchants, and landowning nobles called **boyars**. The Grand Prince collected tribute from the local princes, who in turn collected it from the people in their territory.

A *veche*, or assembly, handled the daily affairs of Russian towns. It did everything from settling business quarrels to accepting or removing a prince. Any free man could call a meeting of the veche by ringing the town bell.

1. What did Rurik do?
2. Where was Kiev?
3. How was the government of early Russian towns organized?

RELIGIOUS LIFE

Eastern Orthodoxy inspired Russian art and architecture. This icon (left) from the city of Novgorod shows a scene from the Bible. Architects, influenced by the new religion, built wooden churches (right) in newly-settled areas.
How did Eastern Orthodoxy become the religion of the Russians?

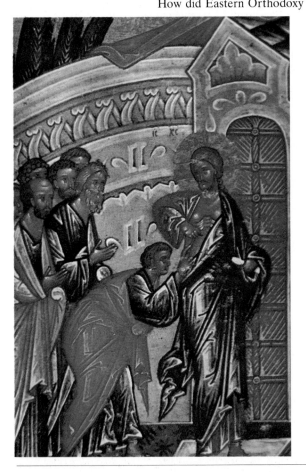 

VLADIMIR I AND THE EASTERN ORTHODOX CHURCH

One of the most important princes of Kiev was Vladimir I. He was a good soldier and a strong ruler who spent the early years of his rule expanding Russian territory. His armies pushed the country's borders west into Poland and north along the Baltic coast.

In 988 Vladimir chose Eastern Orthodox Christianity as the country's official religion. The Russians tell a story about Vladimir's long search for a new faith that would unite the people. Vladimir sent representatives to other countries to observe different religions. The representatives were not impressed by what they saw in Islamic mosques, Jewish synagogues, or Roman Catholic churches. Then, in Byzantium's Hagia Sophia, they observed Eastern Orthodox worship. They were stunned by its beauty. When they returned to Russia, they persuaded Vladimir to choose Eastern Orthodoxy as the official religion.

The Eastern Orthodox Church brought Byzantine culture to Russia. Priests from Byzantium introduced the Russians to colorful religious rituals and taught them the art of painting icons. The Russians learned to write their language in the Cyrillic alphabet. Sons of boyars and priests were sent to newly built schools to learn to read and write. The appearance of Russian towns changed as stone churches with bulb-shaped domes rose among the wooden buildings. Monasteries appeared in the city and in the countryside.

Vladimir's decision to accept Eastern Orthodoxy gave the Russians a sense of belonging to the civilized world. But at the same time it separated Russia from western Europe. Since Russian scholars now had books in their own language, they did not bother to learn Greek or Latin. As a result they did not take advantage of the heritage of the West.

1. What made Vladimir I select Eastern Orthodoxy as Russia's official religion?
2. What effect did Eastern Orthodoxy have on the Russians?

YAROSLAV THE WISE   Another important ruler of early Russia was Yaroslav, son of Vladimir I. Yaroslav became the Grand Prince of Kiev in 1036, after a long struggle with his brothers for the throne. Yaroslav was very interested in learning. He read a lot and gathered a large collection of books. He

Church Vestment

invited scholars from Byzantium to live in Kiev. Because of this interest, he was called "the Wise."

Yaroslav encouraged Russian artisans to practice their skills. He built magnificent brick churches overlaid with white plaster and decorated with gold. The church domes were gilded or tiled in yellow, green, or blue. Russian painters covered the walls of Yaroslav's palace with scenes of music and hunting.

Under Yaroslav's rule, early Russia enjoyed a Golden Age of peace and prosperity. Kiev's population grew until the city became larger than Paris or London. Yaroslav developed closer ties with western Europe by having members of his family marry into other European royal families.

Yaroslav also organized Russian laws. He created a code of law based on old Slavic customs and Byzantine law. Under Yaroslav's code, crimes against property were considered more serious than those against people. There was no death penalty. Instead of being tortured, criminals were fined.

1. What did Yaroslav the Wise do for Russia?

THE DECLINE OF EARLY RUSSIA   Russia began to decline around 1054. There were several reasons for this. After Yaroslav's death, the princes of Kiev began to fight over the throne. They were so busy fighting that they neglected their own territories. This weakened the entire country.

People from the steppe took advantage of the fighting and began to attack Russia's frontiers. The attacks upset the flow of trade along the north-south river route. The loss of trade meant the loss of Kiev's main source of wealth. Also, Russia depended on Byzantium. When it declined, Russia became even weaker and more isolated.

Gradually Russia changed from a trading land of towns and merchants into a farming land of peasants. To escape the invaders from the steppe, many Russians fled to the north and settled in the dense forests along the Upper Volga.

1. What were some reasons for the decline of Kiev?
2. How did the decline of Kiev affect the Russians?

THE MONGOLS

About 1240 a group of people known as Mongols swept out of central Asia and took control of Russia. They destroyed villages and towns and killed many people. They forced the Russians to pay tribute to the **khan**, or Mongol leader. They also forced the Russians to serve in the Mongol armies.

1. What did the Mongols do to the Russians?

THE CHURCH   The Eastern Orthodox Church remained strong despite the Mongol invasion. Eastern Orthodox priests continued to preach and to write manuscripts. The priests encouraged the people to love their land and their religion.

When monks began to found monasteries deep in the northern forests, they were followed by Russian farmers searching for unused land. New towns and villages began to grow up around the monasteries.

PEASANT LIFE

Under the Mongols most Russians were peasants and lived in isolated villages. Here a group of peasants prepare to clear forest land.

How did peasants pass on their heritage to their children?

The Mongol conquest isolated the Russian Church from other Christian churches. As a result, the church developed its own rituals and practices. This united the Russian people and made them proud of their own culture. At the same time, however, it led them to distrust ideas and practices that were not Russian.

1. How did the Eastern Orthodox Church influence the Russians during the Mongol invasion?

DAILY LIFE Most Russians led a simple but harsh life under the Mongols. Wealthy Russians sometimes entertained guests with feasts of deer and wild pig. But the peasants rarely ate meat. They had to make do with dark rye bread, cabbage, salted fish, and mushrooms.

The few pleasures the peasants had were visiting one another, drinking, and singing. They told stories called *byliny* that praised the brave deeds of their warriors and other heroes. The stories were passed from old to young and became part of the Russian heritage.

Peasant men dressed in white tunics, wide linen trousers, and heavy shoes made from tree bark. They tied rags around their legs with pieces of twine to keep out the cold. Rich merchants and boyars were luckier. They had tall fur hats and **caftans**, or long robes usually tied at the waist with a sash, to help keep them warm.

Russian women of all classes wore blouses or smocks, skirts, and long shawls. On holidays they sported headdresses with fancy decorations. The decorations indicated what region a woman came from and whether or not she was married.

1. What was life like for the Russians during the Mongol conquest?
2. What did the Russians do for entertainment?
3. How did the Russians dress?

THE RISE OF MOSCOW

At the time of the Mongol conquest, Moscow was a small trading post on the road from Kiev to the forests in the north. As the Russians moved north to escape the Mongols, many skilled craftspeople settled in or near Moscow's **kremlin**, or fortress.

The princes of Moscow were bold and ambitious. They learned to cooperate with the Mongols and even recruited Russian soldiers for the Mongol army. In return, the Mongols gave the princes of Moscow the power to collect taxes throughout the country. If a Russian territory could not provide soldiers or tax money for the Mongols, Moscow's princes took it over. In this way, Moscow began to expand.

As Moscow grew in size, it became stronger. The princes passed their thrones from father to son. Thus there was no fighting over who the next ruler was to be, and the people remained united.

The metropolitan lived in Moscow. This made it the center of the Russian branch of the Eastern Orthodox Church. The metropolitan blessed the princes for their efforts to make Moscow a great city. The Russian people began to look on the prince as a ruler chosen and protected by God. Encouraged by the Church, they obeyed the prince without question.

Meanwhile, Mongol chieftains began to fight among themselves. As a result, they grew weaker while Moscow grew stronger. In 1378 an army formed by Dmitry, the Prince of Moscow, attacked and defeated the Mongols. Two years later the Russians and Mongols fought again. Once more the Mongols were defeated. They still remained powerful but no longer were feared or obeyed as they had been in the past.

1. Where was Moscow? What helped to make it a power?
2. What did Dmitry do?

IVAN THE GREAT   In 1462 Ivan III, known as Ivan the Great, became Prince of Moscow. In 1478 he ended Mongol control of Russia. He also expanded Russian boundaries to the north and west.

A few years before Mongol control ended, Ivan married Sophia, the niece of the last Byzantine emperor. The Russians felt the marriage gave Ivan all the glory of past Byzantine emperors. The Orthodox Church believed it meant that Moscow had replaced Byzantium as the center of Christianity.

Ivan wanted to show off his power. So he began living in the style of the Byzantine emperors. He used the two-headed eagle of Byzantium on his royal seal. He brought Italian architects to Moscow to build fine palaces and large cathedrals in the kremlin.

Fur-lined Crown

He raised the huge walls that still safeguard the kremlin. He called himself **tsar**, the title given only to the Byzantine emperor and the Mongol khan.

Ivan died in 1505. By then the Russian people were convinced that their ruler should have full power over both Church and state.

1. How did Ivan the Great increase the power of Moscow?
2. What effect did Ivan's marriage have on him and on the Russian people?

IVAN THE TERRIBLE   In 1533 Ivan IV, the three-year-old grandson of Ivan III, became tsar. While he was growing up, a

THE GROWTH OF MOSCOW

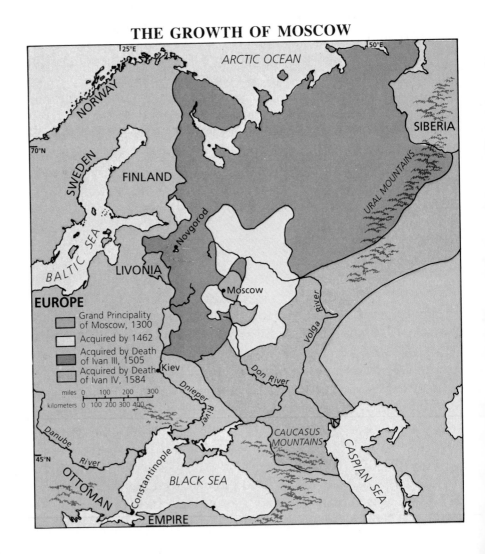

council of boyars governed Russia for him. The boyars, however, wanted more power. To frighten Ivan into obeying them, they began to mistreat him. Ivan came to hate the boyars. At the same time he adopted their cruel habits. By the time he was a teenager, he was killing people for going against his wishes.

When Ivan IV was 16, he was crowned tsar and began to rule in his own right. He ignored the boyars and turned to merchants and personal friends for advice. He gave his advisors gifts of land and jobs as officials. To make sure that the officials' country estates were farmed while they were in Moscow with him, Ivan ordered peasants not to leave their land. Thus, Ivan took the first step in turning free peasants into serfs.

In 1552 Ivan led his armies against Mongol territories on the Volga River. By this time the Russians had learned the use of gunpowder from western Europe. The Mongols, however, still relied on bows and arrows. Within six years Ivan had conquered most of the Mongol territories. Russian settlers began to move east. Some, called Cossacks, began to farm along the Volga.

In 1558 Russian armies attacked Livonia, a land on the Baltic Sea. Livonia's neighbors sent troops to fight the Russians. In 1562 these troops defeated the Russians and took over much of their Baltic territory. Ivan blamed the boyars for his defeat.

In 1564 Ivan suddenly left Moscow and went to a small monastery in the country. A month later he announced that he was giving up the throne because of the boyars. Afraid that without Ivan the empire would fall, the people begged him to change his mind. They told Ivan that if he came back, he could have full authority to punish traitors and to take over their lands.

Ivan returned to Moscow, took over boyar lands, and gave them to 5000 of his most loyal supporters. In return, they formed the *Oprichniki*, or secret police. Members of the Oprichniki dressed in black and rode black horses through the countryside. They attached a dog's head to their saddles to scare the tsar's enemies, and carried a broom to show their desire to sweep treason from the land. They killed thousands of people. When the Oprichniki had defeated the boyars and returned control to Ivan, he broke up the group.

Ivan came to be called Ivan the Terrible. The English translated the Russian word meaning "awesome" as "terrible." But to the Russians, Ivan was a great ruler who protected their country from enemies.

Ivan the Terrible

Ivan encouraged art and learning. He brought artists, scholars, and engineers from western Europe to teach the Russians new skills. He turned Russia into an empire and increased the tsar's power. But when he died in 1584, he left no suitable heir. He had killed his oldest son in a fit of rage. His middle son was feeble-minded, and his youngest son was an infant. As a result, for some 25 years Russia was in a state of confusion and disorder.

1. Why did Ivan the Terrible hate the boyars?
2. How did Ivan get the authority to punish traitors and seize their lands?
3. How did the Oprichniki serve Ivan?
4. What happened to Russia after Ivan's death?

CHAPTER REVIEW

SUMMARY

1. Between the years 500 and 800 a group of Slavs, later known as Russians, settled the forested land west of the Volga River.

2. By the end of the ninth century, the Russians had established a trade route which ran from the Baltic Sea in the north to the Black Sea in the south.

3. Since the Russians were not fighters, they relied on Viking warriors to protect their trade routes.

4. In 882 the Viking warrior Oleg established the first Russian state with its capital at Kiev.

5. Vladimir I chose Eastern Orthodox Christianity as Russia's official religion.

6. The Eastern Orthodox Church brought Byzantine culture, including the Cyrillic alphabet, to Russia.

7. Yaroslav the Wise established a library, organized Russian laws, and encouraged Russian artisans to practice their skills.

8. After 1054 Russia's trade declined and the population shifted from trading to farming.

9. About 1240 Russia was conquered by the Mongols, and many Russians fled north to settle in or near Moscow.

10. Moscow gradually became the center of Russian life.

11. In 1378 and again in 1380 the Russians under Prince Dmitry defeated the Mongols in battle.

12. In 1478 Ivan the Great ended Mongol control of Russia.

13. Beginning in 1552 Ivan the Terrible conquered most of the Mongol territories, and many Russians began moving eastward.

14. Ivan the Terrible used secret police to destroy the power of Russia's land-owning nobles.

15. When Ivan the Terrible died in 1584, he left no suitable heir, so for the next 25 years Russia was in a state of confusion.

BUILDING VOCABULARY

1. *Identify the following:*

Slavs	Varangians	Vladimir I	Dmitry
Russians	Oleg	Yaroslav the Wise	Ivan the Great
Great Mother	Kiev	Mongols	Ivan the Terrible
Volga River	Dnieper River	Moscow	

2. *Define the following:*

slash-and-burn	steppe	khan	kremlin
izbas	boyars	*byliny*	tsar
sledges	*veche*	caftans	*Oprichniki*

REVIEWING THE FACTS

1. To what other Indo-Europeans were the Slavs related?

2. How did Russian houses provide warmth?

3. How did Russian farmers fertilize their land?

4. What did the Russians obtain from the forests?

5. How did Russian traders travel to Byzantium?

6. Why did the Russians invite the Varangians to enter their territory?

7. How was the first Russian state of Kiev organized?

8. How did Yaroslav develop closer ties with western Europe?

9. How did the princes of Moscow become powerful?

10. What did the Russian Church teach the people about the power of a ruler?

DISCUSSING IMPORTANT IDEAS

1. How did Kiev's location affect its rise to power?

2. What were the advantages of Russia'a adoption of Eastern Orthodoxy? What were the disadvantages?

3. Do you think Yaroslav deserved to be called "the Wise"? Explain.

4. Do you think Ivan III deserved to be called "the Great" and Ivan IV "the Terrible"? Why or why not?

USING MAPS

Compare the maps on pages 331 and 338, and answer the following questions:

1. Was Kievan Russia larger than Russia at the time of Ivan IV's death? How can you tell?

2. On what river is Kiev located? Name two other rivers in Russia.

3. What is located at about 54° north latitude and 35° east longitude?

4. Under whom did Moscow show its greatest expansion?

5. Where is Novgorod located?

UNIT REVIEW

SUMMARY

1. After the fall of Rome, civilizations in eastern Europe and the Middle East became more advanced than civilizations in western Europe. Each was united by strong rulers and religion.

2. The Byzantines, ruled the eastern half of the Roman Empire from their capital of Constantinople. They formed a civilization based on Greco-Roman culture and closely tied to the Eastern Orthodox Church.

3. Mohammed, an Arab from Mecca, founded Islam, which became one of the world's major religions.

4. To spread Islam, the Arabs conquered lands in Spain, North Africa, and Asia. They created the Arab Empire.

5. The Russians created a civilization centered first around Kiev and later around Moscow. It was guided and united by the Eastern Orthodox Church and greatly influenced by Byzantine culture.

REVIEWING THE MAIN IDEAS

1. Describe the relationship between religion and government among the Byzantines, Arabs, and Russians. Then compare the three.

2. Explain the relationship that existed between the Byzantines, Arabs, and Russians and the people of western Europe.

DEVELOPING SKILLS

You have probably heard the expression "Do not mix apples with oranges." While both apples and oranges are fruit, you cannot compare one with the other in order to find out which is the riper fruit. You can only compare one apple with another apple or one orange with another orange.

The same is true when examining data. It is important to group similar items together. If data are not correctly grouped, they cannot be properly analyzed.

This exercise is designed to give you practice in **classifying**, or arranging material in groups. Read each group of items below. Eliminate the item that does not belong in the group, and tell what the remaining items have in common.

1. Byzantines, Russians, Arabs, Christians
2. Mecca, Koran, Baghdad, Medina
3. Mecca, Kiev, Constantinople, Moscow
4. Belisarius, Mohammed, Tribonian, Rurik
5. Justinian, Khadijah, Yaroslav, Ivan IV

SUGGESTED UNIT PROJECTS

1. Describe the sights that a Byzantine farmer who is visiting Constantinople for the first time would probably find the most impressive.

2. Check a large dictionary for all the words beginning with "al." Make a poster that shows the English word, its meaning, and the Arabic word from which it came.

3. Working as a class, make an illustrated timeline to highlight life in western and eastern Europe and the Middle East from the fall of Rome.

4. Draw or make an icon.

5. Write five newspaper headlines about major events in the life of Theodora, Mohammed, or Ivan the Great.

SUGGESTED READING

Almedingen, E. M. *Land of Muscovy: The History of Early Russia*. New York: Farrar, Strauss & Giroux, 1971. A detailed account of the life of the Russian people from 1400 to 1600.

Asimov, Isaac. *Constantinople: The Forgotten Empire*. Boston: Houghton Mifflin Company, 1970. Traces the history of Constantinople and the Byzantine Empire and discusses the empire's influence on the civilizations of western and eastern Europe.

Barker, Carol. *A Prince of Islam*. Reading, Mass.: Addison-Wesley, 1976. A description of the childhood and education of the son of a ninth-century caliph.

Brooks, Lester. *Great Civilizations of Ancient Africa*. New York: Four Winds Press, 1971. A discussion of the black civilizations that once flourished in Ghana, Mali, and Songhai, and the economic and political ties between black Africa and ancient Egypt.

Edmonds, I. *Islam*. New York: Franklin Watts, 1977. Recounts the life of Mohammed and discusses the Koran, including the influence of Jewish and Christian beliefs on Islam.

Goldston, Robert. *The Sword of the Prophet*. New York: Dial, 1980. A description of the founding of Islam and its spread through the Arab world.

Townson, Duncan. *Muslim Spain*. Minneapolis: Lerner Publications Company, 1973. A description of Spanish civilization during the centuries of Arab control.

Trupin, James E. *West Africa*. New York: Parents' Magazine Press, 1971. Discusses the political, economic, and cultural history of West Africa from its ancient kingdoms to the present.

725	750	775
732 Charles Martel establishes fief system		

875	900	925
	c. 900 Vikings invade western Europe Feudalism begins	

1025	1050	1075
	1070 Seljuk Turks conquer Palestine	**1077** Pope Gregory VII and Kin Henry IV meet at Canoss **1095** Pope Urban II first crusade **1099** Crusaders Jerusalem

1175	1200	1225
1188 Crusade of Kings	**c. 1200** New farming methods introduced on manors Friars preach reform in cities **1204** Crusaders capture Constantinople **1212** Children's Crusade	

1325	1350	1400

THE AGE OF FEUDALISM

00	825	850
0 Charlemagne crowned emperor **814** Charlemagne's empire begins to decline		
50	975	1000 **c. 1000** First castles built
950 Monks of Cluny support church reform		
00	1125	1150
1122 Concordat of Worms **1123** Roman Inquisition established		**1174** Saladin comes to power in Egypt
50	1275	1300
	c. 1275 Universities develop in western Europe	
	1291 Christian rule ends in Palestine	

1.   HOW WAS WESTERN EUROPE GOVERNED DURING THE MIDDLE AGES?

2.   WHY ARE THE MIDDLE AGES CALLED AN "AGE OF FAITH?"

During the Middle Ages most people of western Europe lived in villages in the countryside. There were only a few towns, and they were far smaller than the busy communities that had once filled the Roman Empire.

Most people lived in the same place all their lives. Travel and communication were difficult, and trade was slow. The people of each community grew their own food and met their other needs with little or no outside help.

Most people who lived in the countryside were poor and enjoyed few pleasures. For comfort and guidance, they turned to the Roman Catholic Church. Religion played an important part in their daily lives. A church stood at the center of every town or village. Not only was the church building a place of worship, but its courtyard was the center of local trade and community activity.

The people constantly faced the dangers of hunger, disease, and outside attack. Nobles, warriors, townspeople, and peasants fought each other over land. Still the people wanted security and protection. But western Europe had no central government to keep the peace. Real power had passed from kings to local nobles. To protect their property, the nobles raised their own armies. They developed what is known as **feudalism**, or government by landowning warrior-nobles.

Feudalism lasted in western Europe until about 1400. It was, however, particularly strong during the eleventh and twelfth centuries, a part of the period known as the Middle Ages.

CHAPTER

24

FEUDAL SOCIETY

Under feudalism the people of western Europe were divided into groups. Each group had duties to perform for the other groups and for society as a whole. The first group was the **clergy**, or religious leaders. Their duty was to teach Christianity and to help the poor and sick. The second group was the nobles. Their duty was to govern, enforce laws, and protect the people. The third group was a small number of townspeople and the **peasants**, or people who farmed the land and provided services for nobles. Their duty was to work for the clergy and nobles.

Although there were more peasants and townspeople, the clergy and nobles had more rights. Almost everyone believed that God wanted it that way. As a result, few people tried to make improvements in society or change their own way of life. Most people remained in the group into which they were born.

THE LAND AND GOVERNMENT

During feudal times power was based on the ownership of land. Before feudalism developed kings owned all the land within their territories. Then in 732 Charles Martel gave his soldiers **fiefs**, or estates, as a reward for their service and loyalty. From their fiefs soldiers got the income they needed to buy horses and battle equipment. From that time on, land ownership was tied to military service.

After 800 the kings of Europe followed Martel's practice. After Charlemagne's death in 814, Europe had no central government. The kings who followed Charlemagne were so weak they could not even rule their own kingdoms well. They ignored their responsibilities and spent most of their time traveling from one royal estate to another. Before long, they began to depend on the nobles for food and horses. Some nobles grew more powerful than the king, and soon they became independent rulers. They gained the right to collect taxes and to enforce the law in their areas. Many nobles raised armies and coined their own money.

Around 900 the nobles took on the duty of protecting their lands and people from the Vikings. They built fortresses on hilltops and fenced in their lands. To support more soldiers, they seized more land. The peasants turned to these powerful nobles for protection. In return they gave the nobles their lands and promised to work for them in the fields. The peasants ended up giving the nobles not only their land but their freedom too.

By 1000 the kingdoms of western Europe were divided into thousands of feudal territories, each of which was about the size of an ancient Greek polis. Unlike the polis, however, a feudal territory had no central city. The noble who owned the land had the political power. Most people were peasants who had no say in the government.

Feudal government was not complicated. It was based largely on the actions of the nobles. The nobles made the laws for their fiefs, and the people obeyed them. The government did, however, provide some protection for the people and for their property.

1. How did land ownership become tied to military service?
2. How did the nobles become so powerful?
3. What were some features of feudal government?

LORD AND VASSAL   Feudalism was based on ties of loyalty and duty among nobles. A **vassal**, or less powerful noble, gave his loyalty to a lord. In return the lord protected the vassal.

The tie between lord and vassal was made official in a special ceremony known as the **act of homage**. The bareheaded vassal knelt on the ground and placed his hands between those of the lord. The vassal promised to serve the lord and to help him in battle. The lord accepted the pledge, helped the vassal to his feet, and kissed him.

In return for loyalty and service, the lord gave the vassal a fief. Since there were few written agreements in the Middle Ages, the lord gave the vassal a glove, a piece of wood, or a lance to show that his word could be trusted. He also gave the vassal the right to govern the people who lived on the fief. The lord promised to protect the vassal from enemy attacks. If he failed to do so, the vassal no longer owed him loyalty. A fief belonged to a vassal for life. When the vassal died, his fief usually passed on to his oldest son, who then performed the act of homage.

KING AND VASSAL

A vassal owed military service to a lord. Kings, as well as nobles, were lords. Here a king receives homage from one of his vassals.
How did feudal government work?

A vassal did not lose his self-respect by seeking the protection of a lord. Many vassals had their own vassals just as some lords owed allegiance to other lords. The ties between lord and vassal could be confusing, because a vassal could owe loyalty to several lords at the same time. In such a case, the vassal chose one lord to whom he was the most loyal. Some vassals just supported the side most likely to win.

Vassals had certain duties to perform. Their most important duty was to help the lord in battle. Vassals had to bring their own

NOBLE FEAST

Nobles celebrated special occasions with elaborate feasts. This manuscript drawing shows a noble and his household at a meal.
What kinds of food were served at a noble's table?

knights with them. They themselves were expected to take part in battle at least 40 days a year.

Vassals had to make payments to their lord. When a lord's son became a knight or his daughter married, his vassals had to give the lord money. If a lord were captured in battle, his vassals had to pay the **ransom**, or sum of money given in exchange for the lord's release. Vassals were also expected to provide food and entertainment when their lord visited them.

Vassals had to attend the lord's court. This was a monthly meeting of the lord's vassals that decided cases involving the vassals. From this feudal court came the modern system of trial by jury.

1. What was the relationship between lord and vassal?
2. What promises were made during the act of homage?
3. What were some duties of a vassal?

Woman and Child

THE NOBILITY

Life was not always comfortable or pleasant for nobles during feudal times. They did, however, enjoy more benefits than the common people.

From the ninth to the eleventh century nobles and their households lived in a **manor house**, or a wooden building constructed to provide protection. A **palisade**, or high wooden fence, surrounded the house. In case of attack, people from the nearby villages sought shelter inside the palisade.

The manor house consisted of one room with a high ceiling and a straw-covered floor. The straw got so dirty with mud, bones, and food that every few months it had to be swept outdoors and burned. All activity took place in the one room. There nobles met with vassals, carried out the laws, and said their prayers. There nobles, their families, servants, and warriors ate and slept. At mealtime wooden tables were set up and piled high with meat, fish, different kinds of vegetables, fruits, and honey. Everybody ate with their fingers and threw scraps of food on the floor for the dogs.

Meals were cooked over fires that were also supposed to heat the manor house. Actually the fires did little to keep out the cold. Smoke from them often stung the eyes and darkened the walls and ceiling.

1. What were some features of a manor house?

CASTLE

A castle was both a noble's home and a military fortress. During enemy attack, people from the surrounding area sought protection within the castle walls. This photo of an English castle shows the moat and castle entrance.
Who was responsible for a castle's care and defense?

THE CASTLE   By the twelfth century manor houses were made of stone and were called **castles.** Because they were designed as fortresses, the castles made the nobles feel secure and independent. The castle had thick stone walls, one within another. Each corner had its own lookout tower with archers in it. Some castles were further protected by a moat whose soft and muddy bottom stopped attackers from using ladders to climb over the walls. To cross the moat, a person had to use a **drawbridge**, or heavy door, that could be raised or lowered. The drawbridge led to the **portcullis**, or heavy oak and iron gate, that served as the entrance to the castle.

Within the castle walls was a large open area. In the middle of this area was a **keep**, or tall tower. It contained a hall, many rooms, and a dungeon. The people of the household lived in the keep. Nearby stood shops, kitchens, stables, and rooms for troops and guests.

Many people lived in the castle. Besides the nobles and their families, there were servants and officials. Since the lord of the castle was away fighting most of the time, the servants and officials were responsible for the castle's care and defense. Most castles had enough space to store a large supply of food and drink. As a result, the people in the castle could hold out against attackers for as long as six months.

1. What were some features of a castle?
2. Who lived in a castle?

CASTLE LIFE   When the nobles were at home, they looked after their estates, went hunting and fishing, and held court. During long winter evenings they played chess. Wandering minstrels sang songs and played stringed instruments to entertain the nobles and their guests.

Noblewomen were called **ladies**. Once they married, their husbands had complete authority over them. Most marriages were planned to unite important families, and a woman had little

---

CHESS PLAYERS

Chess was a favorite game in the Middle Ages. Nobles and their families played chess in their castles during the long winter nights.
What other activities did nobles and their families enjoy?

say about who was chosen for her. The bride's family gave the husband-to-be a dowry. Most nobles looked for wives with large dowries. Women were often married by the time they were 12. Those who were not married by the time they were 21 could expect to stay single for the rest of their lives.

The women helped their husbands run their estates. When the men were away, the women had to defend the castle. The main duty of a wife, however, was to have and raise children and to take care of the household. She was also expected to train young girls from other castles in household duties and supervise

KNIGHTHOOD

For protection, knights wore suits of armor that covered every part of the body. They used different kinds of swords and spears in battle. The responsibility of knights was to defend the land of the nobles.
How did knights train for battle?

the making of cloth and fine embroidery. Another duty was to use her knowledge of plants and herbs to care for the poor and sick on her husband's fiefs.

1. How did a noble spend his time when he was at home?
2. How were marriages arranged among nobles?
3. What was the role of a noblewoman during feudal times?

Knight's Armor

KNIGHTHOOD

Almost all nobles were **knights**, or warriors on horseback. No one was born a knight. Knighthood had to be earned.

Knights were expected to follow certain rules known as the **code of chivalry**. These rules stated that a knight was to obey his lord, to respect women of noble birth, and to help people in time of trouble. A knight was to be honest and to fight fairly against his enemies. Few knights actually lived up to all the rules. The code of chivalry, however, became the guide to behavior from which the western idea of good manners developed.

1. What was expected of a knight?
2. What developed from the code of chivalry?

TRAINING   A noble began training to be a knight when he was seven years old. He was sent to the castle of a great lord where he learned to be a **page**, or a person who helped the knights of the castle care for their horses and armor. He strengthened his arms and wrists by hitting a wooden post with a fake sword. He learned good manners and ran errands for the ladies. As he grew older, he was taught to ride and fight. By the time he was 14, he could handle a lance and sword while on horseback.

When he was 15, the young noble became a **squire** and was put under the care and training of one knight. A squire went into battle with his knight and was expected to rescue the knight if he was wounded or fell off his horse.

If the squire proved to be a good fighter, he was rewarded by being made a knight. This was done in a special ceremony known as **dubbing**. The night before the ceremony the knight-to-be prayed in the chapel. In the morning he knelt before his lord and took an oath to defend the Church against its enemies. He also promised to fight only for his lord and to protect the weak and helpless. Then the lord tapped the squire on the shoulder with the blade of a sword and pronounced him a knight.

1. What were some duties of a page?
2. What were some duties of a squire?
3. How did a noble become a knight?

TOURNAMENTS   Knights trained for war by fighting each other in **tournaments**, or special contests that test strength, skill, and endurance. Tournaments were held outdoors in a large field near a castle. They were festive occasions that attracted lords, ladies, and knights from the surrounding areas. Important guests watched the events from seats in stands covered with colorful cushions, carpets, and tapestries. The most popular event was a **joust**. Two armored knights on horseback and carrying blunt lances galloped headlong towards each other from opposite ends of the field. Each tried with all his strength and skill to knock the other to the ground with his lance.

Tournaments were costly in many ways. Men and horses were killed and injured. Lances, swords, shields, and suits of armor were ruined. The noble who gave the tournament had to feed hundreds of people. In spite of the cost, however,

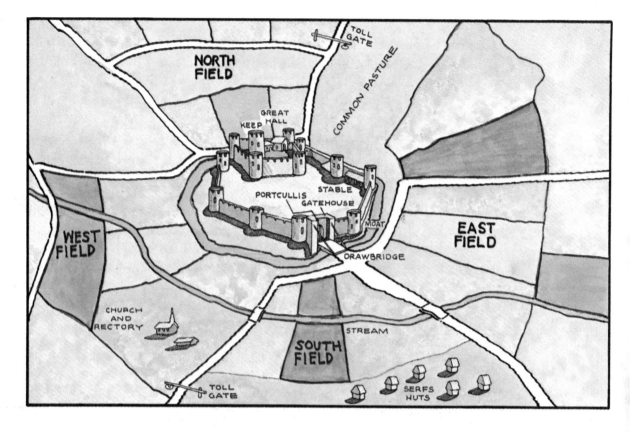

tournaments remained popular. It was believed that a knight who had not learned to fight in a tournament could not fight well in battle.

1. What was the purpose of tournaments?
2. In what ways were tournaments costly?

THE MANOR

Nobles, knights, and peasants depended on the land for food, clothing, and shelter. The land was divided into **manors**, or farming communities. Manors were found on the fiefs of the lords. Some lords owned only one manor; others owned many.

The lord appointed a number of officials to run the manor. They were loyal to the lord and made sure his orders were carried out. One official was the **seneschal**. He looked after all of the lord's fiefs. To do this, he had to visit each fief regularly. Another official was the **bailiff**. He made sure the peasants worked hard in the fields.

Every manor had its own court that dealt out justice. The lord himself sat in on the meetings of the court. The court settled disputes, gave out fines and punishments, and discussed manor business.

Poor transportation and frequent fighting isolated the manors from one another. As a result, the men and women of the manor produced only enough food for themselves and their lord. They raised sheep for wool and cattle for meat and milk. They also grew grain and vegetables, made cloth, built homes, and fashioned tools.

The local lord of each manor lived in a manor house or a castle. Nearby stood a small village of wood and dirt cottages with thatched roofs. The village was surrounded by forests, meadows, pastures, and fields. Most villages had a church, mill, bread oven, and wine press.

The cottages in which the peasants lived were crowded closely together around an open area called the village green. Most cottages had only one room. At night family members slept there on piles of straw or on the dirt floor. Three-legged stools and a table were the only furniture.

1. Who ran the manors?
2. What effect did being isolated have on a manor?
3. What were some features of a village?

FREEMEN AND SERFS Two groups of peasants worked on a manor. One was the **freemen**, or peasants who paid the lord for the right to farm the land. They worked only on their own strips of land and had rights under the law. They moved wherever and whenever they wished. The lord, however, had the right to throw them off the manor without warning.

Harvester

The other group was the serfs. The serfs and their descendants were the lord's property. They could not move to another area, own their own property, or marry without the lord's permission. Serfs, however, could not be driven off the land and did not have to serve in the army. It was not easy for serfs to gain their freedom. One way was to escape to the towns. If they remained in town for more than a year, they were considered free. By the end of the Middle Ages, serfs were allowed to buy their freedom.

As in Charlemagne's time, the serfs worked long hours in the fields and performed many services for the nobles. Serfs

PEASANTS AT WORK

Peasants spent long hours working in the fields of a manor. Here one group of peasants plows the land, while another plants seed. In the distance other groups of peasants farm plots of land.

What type of peasants worked on a manor?

spent three days of the week working the lord's strips of land and the rest of the week caring for their own strips. They gave part of their own crops to the lord. They also paid him for the use of his grain mill, baking oven, and wine press.

In spite of the difficulties, a serf's life had a few bright moments. Sunday was a day of rest from work. At Christmas the lord paid for a great feast and entertainment. Certain holidays were celebrated with singing and dancing on the village green. When they could, the serfs took part in such sports as wrestling, archery, and soccer.

By the thirteenth century changes were taking place. The peasants began to learn better farming methods. They made more widespread and better use of the three-field system of farming. They started to use a heavy iron plow rather than the lightweight wooden plow. The horse collar was invented, and

PEASANTS AT PLAY

Peasants celebrated weddings and holidays with folk dances. Here a group of peasants performs a lively circle dance.

Where in the village did peasants sing and dance?

peasants could use horses instead of slow-moving oxen to plow their fields. All of this allowed the peasants to extend their fields and to grow more food.

1. What rights did freemen have?
2. What did serfs contribute to the manor?
3. What changes took place in farming by the thirteenth century?

CHAPTER REVIEW

SUMMARY

1. In 732 Charles Martel tied land ownership to military service when he gave his soldiers fiefs.

2. After the death of Charlemagne kings began to depend on nobles for food and horses.

3. Some nobles grew more powerful than the king, and they began to collect their own taxes, run their own courts, raise their own armies, and coin their own money.

4. Around 900 the nobles agreed to protect people from Viking attacks in exchange for land and labor.

5. By 1000 the kingdoms of western Europe were divided into thousands of small feudal territories.

6. Lords gave their vassals land in exchange for loyalty and military service.

7. At first nobles lived in wooden manor houses, but by the twelfth century they were living in stone castles.

8. Nobles began training at age seven and spent eight or nine years training to become knights.

9. Knights followed certain rules of behavior which became known as the code of chivalry.

10. Knights trained for war by fighting in tournaments.

11. Land was divided into manors owned by lords and worked by peasants.

12. There were two groups of peasants on a manor—freemen and serfs.

13. Serfs lived hard lives and could not gain their freedom easily.

14. By the thirteenth century changes were taking place in peasant life.

BUILDING VOCABULARY

1. *Define the following:*

feudalism	manor house	ladies	tournaments
clergy	palisade	knights	joust
peasants	castles	code of chivalry	manors
fiefs	drawbridge	page	seneschal
vassal	portcullis	squire	bailiff
act of homage	keep	dubbing	freemen
ransom			

REVIEWING THE FACTS

1. Into what three groups were people divided under feudalism?

2. Who held the political power within a feudal territory?

3. What did a lord give a vassal to show that his word could be trusted?

4. Who usually received a vassal's fief when the vassal died?

5. What did a vassal do when he owed loyalty to several lords at the same time?

6. Why could people in a castle hold out against attackers for a long period of time?

7. What did most nobles look for in a marriage?

8. Why didn't the people on a manor produce a surplus of food?

9. In what two ways could serfs obtain their freedom?

10. What did serfs do for entertainment to brighten their dreary lives?

DISCUSSING IMPORTANT IDEAS

1. Would you have preferred to be a lord or a vassal? Explain.

2. Do you think life in a manor house was healthy? What makes you think so?

3. Do you think you would have enjoyed being a knight? Why or why not?

4. Would you rather have been a freeman or a serf? Explain.

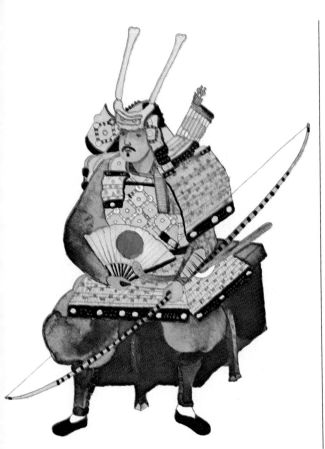

The Japanese Samurai

In the twelfth century large clans fought one another for control of Japan. Japanese royalty was only a symbol of Japanese unity and nationality. It did not control the land or the people. The real rulers were the *shoguns,* or army generals who helped the emperor.

Under the shoguns were *daimyos,* or great lords who lived in outlying provinces. The daimyos ran large estates that were worked by heavily taxed rice farmers. The farmers also served in the army.

The daimyos were supported by armed warriors called *samurai,* meaning "those who serve." They lived on the estates in homes near the daimyo's fortified castle. The samurai were loyal to their family, their clan, and their daimyo. They were proud of their military skills, especially their ability to use a sword. They were good horseback riders and archers.

The samurai had a strict code of honor called *bushido,* meaning "way of the warrior." Unlike European knights, they had no interest in honoring or defending women. The samurai expected their women to be self-disciplined and to fight beside them in times of crisis.

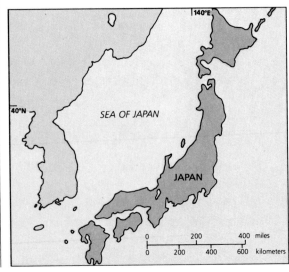

Bushido taught self-discipline. Samurai were expected to endure hardship, pain, and sacrifice. A sense of pride was important. Samurai believed they had to **save face**, or protect their honor. As a result, they took offense at the smallest insult. A samurai who felt greatly shamed saved face by committing *hara kiri*. This was the ritual act of taking one's own life.

Samurai were fearless in battle. They thought it was an honor to die on the battlefield. They compared dying in battle to cherry blossoms falling off a tree.

A samurai dressed for battle was a colorful work of art. Sword and **scabbard**, or sword holder, were finely crafted. Armor was light and flexible, made of hundreds of tiny leather squares. The squares were lacquered to steel hardness and woven into armor with silver thread.

Samurai were as well skilled in the polite arts as they were in battle. They trained themselves to perform the ritual tea ceremony and to write poetry. The samurai also mastered the delicate art of calligraphy.

In Europe the nobles and their traditions were pushed aside to make way for modern ways. This was not the case in Japan. The samurai belief in clan and family loyalty and in ritual and conduct remained and was carried over to business relationships and dealings. Samurai families came to play an important role in helping Japan become a modern industrial state.

1. Who controlled Japan in the twelfth century?
2. What was expected of samurai?
3. How did samurai feel about honor?

THE CHURCH

25

The Roman Catholic Church was the only organization that served to unite western Europeans during the Middle Ages. It took the lead in politics, law, art, and learning for hundreds of years.

By 1000 Catholic missionary monks had brought Catholic teachings to most of Europe. They converted people to the Catholic faith and built new churches and monasteries. Bishops and priests continued the work begun by the monks. They made sure the people gave their loyalty to the Pope in Rome.

Church leaders wanted to develop a civilization in western Europe based on Christian principles. While working toward this goal, the Church helped to preserve and pass on the heritage of the Roman Empire. Latin was made the official language of the Church. Monks copied ancient Greek and Roman manuscripts, thus making sure that the past would not be forgotten.

CATHOLIC INFLUENCE

The Church was the center of daily life in every village and town. On Fridays the people obeyed the Church's rule not to eat meat. On Sundays they went to **mass**, or worship service. Most holidays the people celebrated were in honor of saints or religious events. To become a king, vassal, or knight, a man had to take part in a religious ceremony. Church leaders ran schools and hospitals. Monks provided food and shelter for travelers. Priests alone had the right to record births, marry people, and conduct burials.

The Church taught that all people had sinned and had to rely on God's favor to get to heaven. The only way to receive this favor was by taking part in **sacraments**, or Roman Catholic church rituals.

One of the most important sacraments was **holy communion**, which was celebrated at each mass. A priest blessed wheat wafers and a cup of wine that stood on the altar. He then drank the wine, ate one of the wafers, and gave a wafer to each worshipper. The Church taught that this sacrament was to remind people that Christ had died for them and to help them to be better Christians.

Communion Cup

1. In what ways did the Church influence daily life during the Middle Ages?
2. What was the purpose of the sacraments?

A ROLE IN GOVERNMENT During the Middle Ages, kings, nobles, and church officials worked together to govern western Europe. Only Catholics were considered members of

VILLAGE CHURCH
During the Middle Ages, the church was the religious and social center of the village. Both the local noble and the peasants contributed to the building of the church and its upkeep.
What activities took place at the village church?

society. Those who opposed the Pope on important issues lost their membership in the Church and their political rights.

Most kings could not read and write. So they used bishops and abbots, who could read and write, to carry out such government duties as keeping records.

Bishops and abbots were an important part of the feudal system. Since many of them came from noble families, they received land from kings in return for military service. But as religious leaders they were not supposed to fight. So they gave some of their land to knights to fight in their place. This meant that many bishops and abbots were vassals of lords and lords of vassals with the same duties as any other noble.

Priests in villages and towns conducted worship services and explained Christian teachings to the people. They also took care of the poor and strangers in their parish. Since priests were appointed by local lords, they were expected to tell the people to respect the king, nobles, and other government officials.

1. What part did bishops and abbots play in government?
2. What were priests expected to do in the villages and towns?

THE INQUISITION   The Church wanted to stamp out heresy and strengthen Christian beliefs. At first it tried to stop the spread of heresy by preaching. Then in 1123 a council of bishops set up the **Inquisition,** or a church court, to end heresy by force.

The Church gave the people it suspected of heresy one month to confess. Those who appeared before the Inquisition before the month was up were whipped or sent to prison for a short time. Those who did not appear were seized and brought to trial. The purpose of the trial was to get a confession. Once heretics confessed, they were punished. Then they were forgiven and allowed to become Church members again.

The court called only two witnesses. On the basis of their statements, the court decided whether or not a person was a heretic. Heretics who refused to confess were often tortured. A

CATHEDRAL

Large churches headed by bishops were called cathedrals. Most cathedrals were built in the Gothic style of architecture. Gothic cathedrals were tall and seemed to reach up to heaven. The Cathedral of Notre Dame in Paris, France, was one of the first churches built in the Gothic style.

What groups of people supported the building of large churches?

small number of people believed to be dangerous were turned over to political officials to be burned at the stake.

1. Why did the council of bishops set up the Inquisition?
2. What was the purpose of a trial by the Inquisition?
3. How did the Inquisition decide if a person was a heretic?

A NEED FOR REFORM

The Church became wealthy during the Middle Ages. Church members supported its work by contributing **tithes**, or offerings equal to 10 percent of their income. Rich nobles donated money to build large churches and gave gifts of land to monasteries. The monks worked hard to make the land produce. They became known as the best farmers in western Europe. However, the wealthier the monasteries became, the more careless many monks grew about carrying out their religious duties.

Monks were not the only ones to grow careless about religious duties. When a bishop died, his office and lands were taken over by the local lord. The lord often chose a close relative as the new bishop or sold the office for money or favors. As a result, men who were not very religious often held important church positions. They did not keep church rules or bother with the needs of the poor.

1. How did the Church become wealthy during the Middle Ages?
2. What effect did wealth have on the Church?
3. How did people who were not religious become bishops?

Processional Cross

THE MONKS OF CLUNY   Before long some western Europeans grew concerned about the direction in which the Church was headed. During the late tenth century and early eleventh century they worked to return the Church to its Christian ideals. Devout nobles founded new monasteries that strictly followed the Benedictine Rule.

One of the most important of these monasteries was Cluny in eastern France. The monks of Cluny led simple lives, spending much of their time in prayer. They soon won the respect of the people. The monks insisted that the Church, not lords, should appoint all church officials. To set an example they chose their own abbot, who was totally loyal to the Pope. Gradually a

MONKS

Monks of the Middle Ages had an active role in daily life. This painting shows monks performing a variety of tasks. In addition to prayer and religious worship, they cared for the sick, kept records, and worked in fields and gardens.
How did monks help to promote church reform?

number of new monasteries connected with Cluny spread across Europe. They provided deeply religious and well-educated monks to fill church offices. These monks worked to reform the Church.

1. Why did nobles found new monasteries in the late tenth and early eleventh centuries?
2. What did the monks of Cluny do?

THE AUTHORITY OF THE POPE

The Pope based his right to be called Pope on the traditional belief that Peter the Apostle, the first Bishop of Rome, had been chosen by Christ to be the head of the Church. When Peter died, the authority Christ had given him was passed on to his successors.

The Pope's power had increased gradually over hundreds of years. By the Middle Ages the Pope had become a powerful religious and political leader. He had his own courts of justice and government offices. He ruled from Rome with the help of a group of bishops known as the College of Cardinals.

1. On what did the Bishop of Rome base the claim that he alone had the right to be called Pope?

GREGORY VII   One of the most powerful Popes of the Middle Ages was Gregory VII. He supported the reform movement begun by the monks of Cluny.

HENRY IV AT CANOSSA

King Henry IV of Germany sought the pardon of Pope Gregory VII at the castle of Canossa. Here Henry and his advisors, dressed in black, wait outside the castle for the Pope to admit them.

What powers did Popes have during the Middle Ages?

Gregory had high principles, was a skillful politician, and had a strong will. He wanted to rid the Church of control by kings and feudal lords. He also wanted to increase the Pope's authority over church officials.

Gregory made many changes in his efforts to reform the Church and gain more authority. Church leaders who bought or sold church offices were removed from their posts. Bishops and priests were forbidden to marry.

In 1075 Gregory issued a document stating that the Pope was above all kings and feudal lords. Only the Pope had the power to appoint bishops and other church leaders. The document also stated that government officials who did not obey the Pope could be removed from office. Gregory told the people they did not have to obey officials who disobeyed the Pope.

1. What were Gregory VII's two goals as Pope?
2. What powers did the document that Gregory issued in 1075 give the Pope?

Pope Gregory VII

ROYAL RESISTANCE   King Henry IV of Germany thought Gregory VII's reforms were an attack on his power as king. So he ignored Gregory's decrees and continued to appoint bishops in his kingdom. Gregory condemned Henry for disobeying him. Henry answered by calling a council of his bishops to remove Gregory from the office of Pope. Henry declared that as king he was God's representative on earth and had the right to remove Popes who did not agree with him. Gregory responded by declaring that Henry no longer was a king or a member of the Church.

German nobles who were Henry's enemies asked Gregory to come to Germany and choose a new king. Upon hearing this, Henry decided it was better to make peace with Gregory than to lose his throne. In the cold winter of 1077 he hurried across the Alps to Italy to ask Gregory's forgiveness. Gregory, who was staying at the castle of Canossa in northern Italy, refused to see Henry.

Henry, however, would not give up. For three days he stood in his bare feet outside the castle of Canossa waiting for Gregory to see him. At last Gregory pardoned him, and Henry returned home as king.

1. What did Henry IV do to anger Pope Gregory VII?
2. What made Henry IV decide to seek the Pope's forgiveness?

THE CONCORDAT OF WORMS   Gregory VII won a victory at Canossa. But it did not end the struggle between the Pope and the king of Germany. Not until 1122 was an agreement reached between them. Because the agreement was signed in the German city of Worms, it came to be known as the Concordat of Worms.

The Concordat gave both the Pope and the king a part in the selection of bishops. The king was to give the new bishop a **scepter**, or rod, as a symbol of the bishop's ownership of land and his political duties. The Pope was to give the bishop a staff and a ring as symbols of the bishop's religious authority.

The Concordat of Worms was supposed to be a compromise that would please both the king and the Pope. But it actually increased the Pope's political power. Under feudalism, feudal lords controlled the appointment of church officials. Under the Concordat, no one could hold a church office without final approval from the Pope.

1. What was the purpose of the Concordat of Worms?
2. What did the Concordat actually do?

Saint Francis

FRIARS

During the early thirteenth century preachers called **friars** traveled all over Europe. Since they sold all their possessions before becoming friars, they depended on gifts of food and money from the people. For this reason, they were called **mendicants**, or beggars.

The friars followed many monastic rules, including the one about not marrying. But they did not shut themselves off from the rest of the world. Instead, they lived in towns and worked to bring Christianity directly to the people.

Two well-known **orders**, or groups, of friars were the Franciscans and the Dominicans. The Franciscan order was founded early in 1200 by Francis of Assisi, the son of a wealthy Italian cloth merchant. Franciscans were known for their cheerfulness and for their confidence that God would take care of them. They had a deep love of nature. They believed it was a gift of God and should be respected.

The Dominican order was started in 1220 by a Spanish monk named Dominic. Like the Franciscans, the Dominicans lived a life of poverty. Through their words and deeds, they kept many people loyal to Church teachings.

1. In what way were friars different from other monks?
2. What did the Franciscans believe?
3. How did the Dominicans keep many people loyal to Church teachings?

LEARNING

Stained-glass Window

During the Middle Ages learning was in the hands of the Church. The parish clergy set up schools in **cathedrals**, or churches headed by bishops. The schools were to prepare the sons of nobles for service in the Church. But not every boy who went to school wanted to be a priest or monk. So the schools also trained students to be government officials, lawyers, and teachers. Seven subjects, known as the seven liberal arts, were taught in the cathedral schools. They were grammar, rhetoric, logic, arithmetic, geometry, astronomy, and music.

Students paid a fee to attend classes held in a cold, dark hall rented by the teacher. They sat on a floor covered with straw to keep out the dampness. Books were scarce and costly. So students had to listen carefully to what the teacher read from an ancient text. Then they memorized the teacher's explanation of what was read.

1. Who attended cathedral schools?
2. What was taught at the cathedral schools?
3. What were classes like in the cathedral schools?

UNIVERSITIES   After a while students began to complain that teachers held few classes and did not cover enough material. Teachers began to complain that many untrained people were teaching students. So students and teachers decided to join together and form unions to make some changes in the system. These unions became **universities**, or groups of teachers and students devoted to learning. A church official called a **chancellor** headed each university. No one could teach without the chancellor's permission.

Universities were alike in many ways. They all had well-organized courses of study. Classes were held at set times each day. In class students listened to lectures on a specific subject. All students, whether or not they planned to teach, had to pass

MEDIEVAL UNIVERSITIES

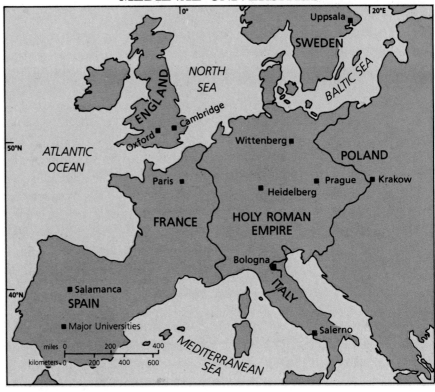

examinations to receive the right to teach. Lecturers had to be at least 21 years old and have studied for at least six years.

By the end of the thirteenth century universities had spread throughout Europe. The university in Paris was known for its training of religious scholars. The one in Bologna, Italy, was noted for the study of law. The one in Salerno, Italy, was famous for its medical training.

Students from all over Europe came to the universities to learn and to hear debates between the great teachers. At first the students lived in boarding houses. Later, wealthy sponsors built special buildings in which the students could live.

Students were often noisy and argued among themselves or with townspeople. To make the students behave, the universities set up rules. Students who missed daily mass, disturbed the peace, or took part in gambling or sword practice were fined.

1. Who started universities? Why were they started?
2. What were four things all universities had in common?
3. Why did universities set up rules?

SCHOLARS AND PHILOSOPHERS   In the Middle Ages the most important areas of learning were philosophy and **theology**, or the study of religious thought. Scholars tried to bring these two together.

One famous medieval scholar was Peter Abelard. He set up his own school in Paris and attracted a large student following. Although the Church forbade scholars to marry, Abelard wed a pupil named Heloise. Heloise's uncle opposed the marriage and separated the couple. In later years Abelard and Heloise wrote love letters to each other. The letters came to be considered among the most beautiful of their kind in world literature.

Like the ancient Greeks, Abelard believed the human mind could discover the truth. He wrote a book called *Sic et Non*, or *Yes and No*, that showed how to use reason and logic in the study of religious ideas. Abelard did this by asking a question and presenting various expert views on the issue. He then asked students to form their own judgments.

Many church leaders opposed Abelard's emphasis on reason. They feared he was giving more importance to reason than to faith. As a result Abelard had to give up teaching and retire to a monastery.

UNIVERSITIES

Universities brought together teachers and students from all parts of Europe. In this print, a teacher at the University of Paris lectures his students on a classical text. What did a scholar have to do in order to become a teacher?

Another famous scholar was Thomas Aquinas, an Italian noble who taught philosophy and theology in Paris and Naples. His lectures and writings impressed many people, and he became known as the "angelic doctor."

Aquinas believed that both faith and reason were gifts of God. He saw no conflict between the two. He thought reason helped people know what the world was really like. It helped people lead a good life. He thought faith revealed religious truths to people. It helped them find life after death with God.

Aquinas wrote a book called *Summa Theologica*, or *A Summary of Religious Thought*. He used Abelard's method of asking questions and presenting different opinions. But unlike Abelard he gave a definite answer to the questions and stated his reasons for the answer. Aquinas' teachings and way of thinking later were accepted and promoted by the Church.

1. What were the most important areas of learning during the Middle Ages?
2. What did Peter Abelard believe?
3. What did Thomas Aquinas believe?

CHAPTER REVIEW
SUMMARY

1. The Roman Catholic Church was the center of daily life during the Middle Ages.

2. Most kings could not read and write, so they used bishops and abbots to carry out many government duties.

3. The Church tried to stamp out heresy, first by preaching and later by the Inquisition.

4. Increased wealth led many clergy members to grow careless about their religious duties.

5. Around 1000 the monks of Cluny began working to reform the Church by giving more attention to Christian ideals.

6. In 1075 Pope Gregory VII issued a document stating that the Pope was above all kings and feudal lords.

7. King Henry IV of Germany disagreed with the Pope and stated that the king was supreme.

8. The struggle between Pope Gregory VII and King Henry IV was ended in 1122 by the signing of the Concordat of Worms.

9. The Concordat of Worms, which gave both Pope and King a part in selecting bishops, increased the Pope's power.

10. During the early thirteenth century preachers called friars tried to bring Christianity directly to the people.

11. By the thirteenth century universities, which grew from cathedral schools, had spread throughout Europe.

12. During the Middle Ages scholars tried to bring faith and reason together.

BUILDING VOCABULARY

1. *Identify the following:*

Cluny	Gregory VII	Concordat of Worms	seven liberal arts
Peter the Apostle	Henry IV	Franciscans	Peter Abelard
College of Cardinals	Canossa	Dominicans	Thomas Aquinas

2. *Define the following:*

mass	tithes	mendicants	universities
sacraments	scepter	orders	chancellor
holy communion	friars	cathedrals	theology
Inquisition			

REVIEWING THE FACTS

1. What was the official language of the Roman Catholic Church?
2. Why did kings use bishops and abbots to carry out many government duties?
3. What happened to heretics who were believed to be dangerous?
4. Why did many monks grow careless about carrying out religious duties?
5. To whom did the abbot of the monastery of Cluny give complete loyalty?
6. Why did Henry IV ignore Gregory VII's decrees at first?
7. Why did some German nobles ask Gregory VII to come to Germany?
8. Why were friars called mendicants or beggars?
9. Who was in charge of education during the Middle Ages?
10. What did medieval scholars try to do with philosophy and theology?

DISCUSSING IMPORTANT IDEAS

1. Do you think it is a good idea for church leaders to help run the government? Why or why not?
2. What kind of civilization did church leaders want to develop in western Europe? Why?
3. If you had been a German noble, would you have supported Henry IV or Gregory VII? Explain.
4. Do you think you would have enjoyed being a student in a medieval university? Why or why not?

USING MAPS

Refer to the map on page 374, and answer the following questions:

1. What is the subject of the map?
2. How many universities are shown?
3. Which university is located about 41° north and 10° east?
4. Which university is northernmost?
5. About how far is Paris from Wittenberg?
6. What territory is located directly north of Italy?

CHAPTER 26

THE CRUSADES

For centuries Christians from western Europe had visited shrines in Jerusalem. Then, in 1070, a people called Seljuk Turks conquered Palestine and took control of the Christian shrines. They began to persecute Christians and kept them from traveling in Palestine.

When news of the events in the Holy Land reached Christians in western Europe, they were shocked and angered. The result was a series of holy wars called **crusades** which went on for about 200 years.

A CALL TO WAR

Even after they had taken Palestine, Turkish armies continued to threaten the Byzantine Empire. The Byzantine emperor turned to Pope Gregory VII for military aid. But the Pope was too involved in church reforms to help. After Gregory VII died, a new Pope named Urban II took his place. Urban II agreed to help the Byzantines. He believed that together the western Europeans and the Byzantines could defeat the Turks and gain control of Palestine. He hoped that in return for his help, the Orthodox Church would again unite with the Roman Catholic Church and accept him as its religious leader.

In 1095 Urban attended a church council in the town of Clermont in eastern France. After the meeting the Pope spoke before a large crowd. He told them that Europe's lords should stop fighting among themselves. Instead, they should fight in a crusade against the Turks.

Urban reminded the people that Europe was not producing enough food to feed its growing population. Palestine, on the other hand, had rich, fertile land on which any knight could live in comfort. The Pope promised that those who went on a crusade would be free of debts and taxes. He also promised that God would pardon the sins of those who died in battle. He encouraged soldiers to go to Palestine wearing a red cross on their tunics as a symbol of obedience to God.

1. Why did Pope Urban II agree to help the Byzantines?
2. How did Urban II encourage people to go on a crusade?

THE PEASANTS' CRUSADE   Urban II spent nine months traveling from one European city to another preaching a crusade. The people of Europe responded eagerly to his appeal. As a sign of their religious devotion, they adopted the war cry *Deus vult*, which means "It is the will of God." The people felt it was their duty as Christians to win back the Holy Land. But they also had other reasons for being willing to fight. Nobles hoped to gain more land for themselves in Palestine. They also wanted the fame a crusade could bring. Peasants wanted to escape from their hard labor on the land.

Urban II wanted the nobles to plan and lead the crusade. But while they were drawing up their plans, the peasants grew impatient and formed their own armies. Even though they lacked training in warfare, they believed God would help them.

In the spring of 1096, about 12,000 French peasants began the long journey to Palestine. They were led by two men, Peter the Hermit and Walter the Penniless. The two leaders rode on donkeys and preached to crowds along the way. The peasants traveled behind them. Two-wheeled carts pulled by oxen carried their belongings. At the same time, two other groups of peasants also set out from Germany and the Rhineland.

As the peasant armies marched through Europe, they did a lot of fighting. They attacked farmers, looted cottages, and burned wheatfields. They **massacred**, or killed, all the Jews they could find. They thought that since Jews were not Christians, they were enemies. Frightened villagers tried to keep the armies away from their homes. At night they often poisoned wells and attacked Crusader camps.

By the time the peasant armies reached Constantinople, they had lost about a third of their number. Their clothes were in rags, and they had no money. They wandered through the streets

PETER THE HERMIT

Peter the Hermit was a powerful preacher-monk, who traveled throughout France by mule. He convinced many European Christians to go on a crusade to regain the Holy Land from the Muslims.

What group of people supported Peter the Hermit's call for a crusade?

CRUSADERS MARCH TO JERUSALEM
After a long and tiring journey, the first Crusaders reached the Holy Land in the summer of 1099. This photo shows a religious procession of Crusaders and other church members carrying a large cross to celebrate their arrival.
Why did the Crusaders want to take Jerusalem?

of the city attacking passersby and stealing from markets and homes. The Byzantine emperor had expected the Pope to send trained warriors, not unskilled peasants. The activities of the western Europeans worried him, and he wanted to get them out of his capital. So he gave them supplies and ships and sent them to fight the Turks in Asia Minor.

In Asia Minor the peasant armies tried to take the Turkish capital of Nicea. They were almost completely wiped out by a force of Turkish bowmen.

1. Why were western Europeans eager to go on a crusade?
2. What did the peasants do on their long journey to Constantinople?
3. What happened to the peasant armies after they reached Constantinople?

Knight Hospitaller

THE NOBLES' CRUSADE   In 1097 the nobles set out on their crusade. Great lords led each army. They brought with them their vassals, wives, children, clerks, cooks, and blacksmiths. The crusade was very costly, as each lord had to provide his own battle equipment, wagons, supplies, and horses. Nobles often had to borrow money or sell their land or jewelry to meet their expenses.

On their way to Palestine the nobles stopped at Constantinople. But they did not get along with the Byzantines any better than the peasants had. The Crusaders' crude manners shocked the cultured Byzantines. The Byzantines' wealth and learning made the Crusaders so jealous that some of them wanted to take Constantinople and its riches. The Byzantine emperor finally convinced the nobles to leave for Asia Minor. The Crusaders took an oath to obey the emperor in return for supplies and military aid.

About 30,000 Crusaders arrived in Asia Minor and defeated the Turks. From there they moved south through the desert to Syria. The Crusaders, however, were not prepared for the heat and did not have enough food or water. As a result, many died of starvation or thirst. Those who survived pushed ahead to Palestine, capturing Syrian cities along the way.

In 1099 the 12,000 surviving Crusaders reached Jerusalem. They captured the holy city, killing Turks, Jews, and Christians alike. They looted the city, taking gold, silver, horses, mules, and houses filled with all kinds of goods.

1. Who went with the nobles on their crusade?
2. What problems did the Crusaders have in Constantinople?
3. Why did so many Crusaders die on the journey between Asia Minor and Palestine?
4. How did the Crusaders treat the people of Jerusalem?

THE KINGDOM BEYOND THE SEA

After the Crusaders captured Jerusalem, they lost much of their religious enthusiasm. Many knights returned to their homes in western Europe. Those who remained in Palestine organized the territories they had won into four feudal kingdoms called **Outremer**, or "the kingdom beyond the sea."

The Crusaders built fortresses to protect the chief towns of their kingdoms. Two **military orders**, or groups of warrior-monks, were formed to take charge of the defense and care of Outremer. They were the Knights Templar and the Knights Hospitaller. The monks took oaths never to marry and to live in poverty. Although they protected Christian visitors and helped the poor and sick, they spent most of their time fighting the Turks.

The warrior-monks were greatly respected for their bravery and way of life. Their military orders were given gifts of land, and soon they became rich. Their influence reached Europe, where they built houses to train new members and to care for elderly knights. Many members of the military orders became bankers and traders.

1. What did the knights who remained in Palestine do with the territories they had won?
2. What was the job of the military orders?
3. How did the military orders grow rich and powerful?

CRUSADER FORTRESS

The Crusaders built fortresses to protect their settlements from Muslim attacks. Warriors and their servants lived in these fortresses. This castle, which stands along the coast of Lebanon, was built by the Knights Hospitallers in the twelfth century. How did the Crusaders govern their territories in the Holy Land?

Bronze Horseman

A NEW WAY OF LIFE   The Crusaders took over estates of rich Turkish and Arab Muslims. The lords divided the properties among themselves and their best knights. Arab peasants worked the land for them and cared for the orchards and vineyards. Other Arabs served as advisors and helped them manage their estates. Friendships developed between the Crusaders and the Muslims. The Muslims admired the Crusaders' bravery. The Crusaders discovered that Arab scholars knew more than they did about medicine, science, and mathematics.

When the lords were not fighting Turks, they ran their estates, went hunting, and attended the local court. Each lord built a castle more magnificent than the one he had in Europe. The castle was more than a fortress. It was a comfortable place in which to live with a large dining room, living room, and bedchambers. The rooms had marble walls and painted ceilings and were decorated with silk hangings, carpets, silver and gold objects, and elegant furnishings.

The Crusaders found that their old style of living did not suit their new surroundings. It was too hot in Palestine to wear fur and woolen clothes. The men began to wear turbans and loose, flowing silk or linen robes. They did, however, continue to fight in armor. The women wore jeweled tunics and magnificent gowns made with gold thread. They adopted the Muslim custom of wearing veils when they were outdoors and learned to use makeup and perfume. The heat also led the Westerners to develop the habit of bathing.

The Crusaders changed their eating habits, too. It was too hot to eat the heavy, solid foods they were used to. They learned to have light meals with less meat and more fruit and vegetables and such new foods as rice, oranges, figs, and melons.

The Crusaders led an easier life in Palestine than they had at home. Still, they had problems adjusting to their new land. Many died in battle against the Turks or in fights among themselves over rights and lands. Others could not survive the hot climate.

1. What kind of relationship developed between the Crusaders and the Muslims?
2. What kind of home did the lords build?
3. What changes did the Westerners who stayed in Palestine make in their way of life?
4. What problems did the Crusaders face in this way of life?

SALADIN AND THE LAST CRUSADES

In 1174 a Muslim military leader named Saladin became the ruler of Egypt. He united Muslims throughout the Near East and started a jihad against the Christians in the East. Saladin's armies were well organized, and his soldiers were devoted to Islam. Groups of warriors headed by leaders called *emirs* made up the armies. Many emirs were known for their honesty and the courteous way they treated their captives. The emirs often were shocked by the cruelty and greed of the Christian warriors.

Saladin's soldiers rode into battle on swift ponies. Their weapons were short bows. Crusaders found it difficult to fight the Muslims. The crusaders' armor was heavy, their swords were too long to handle easily, and their horses were not protected. They had to learn to rely on a new weapon called the **crossbow**, which fired an arrow with great force and speed.

In 1187 Saladin's armies took Jerusalem. Saladin was considerate toward those he had defeated. When he refused to massacre Jerusalem's Christian citizens, he won the respect of many Crusaders.

1. What was Saladin's army like?
2. Why did the Crusaders find it difficult to fight Saladin's armies?
3. How did Saladin win the respect of the Crusaders?

CRUSADE OF KINGS   After Saladin's victory the Church urged another crusade. This time the western armies were led by King Richard the Lionheart of England, Emperor Frederick Barbarossa of Germany, and King Philip Augustus of France. They were the three most powerful rulers in Europe.

Knight's Sword

The Crusade of Kings, however, proved to be a failure. Frederick died in Asia Minor, and many of his troops returned home without ever having fought a battle. Richard and Philip were enemies who were always quarreling. They did take a few coastal cities in Palestine together. Then Philip returned home. Richard and his armies had to continue the crusade alone.

Richard was a brave warrior, but he could not defeat Saladin. In spite of their differences, Richard and Saladin came to respect one another. Years later stories were told in Europe about the kindnesses they showed each other. One story tells how Saladin sent Richard two fresh horses when his horse was killed in battle.

RICHARD THE LIONHEART
King Richard the Lionheart of England was a leader in the Crusade of Kings. Although he won many battles against the Muslims, he failed to capture Jerusalem. Finally he left the Holy Land and returned to England.
Why did the Crusade of Kings fail?

After three years Richard gave up and signed a truce with Saladin. The Crusaders still controlled large areas of Palestine, but Jerusalem remained in Muslim hands.

1. Who led the Crusade of Kings?
2. Why did Richard the Lionheart have to fight the crusade alone?
3. How did Richard and Saladin regard one another?
4. What was the outcome of the Crusade of Kings?

THE LOSS OF AN IDEAL   In 1204 Pope Innocent III called for yet another crusade. Knights from all over Europe answered the call. They decided not to take the land route to Palestine this time. Instead, they chose to go by ship from the Italian port of Venice. Rich merchants there wanted Venice to replace Constantinople as the trading center of the eastern Mediterranean. The Crusaders agreed to pay the merchants a large sum of money and to share half of all their conquests with the Venetians. In return the Venetians agreed to supply the Crusaders with ships and equipment.

When the soldiers found they could not pay all they owed, they agreed to conquer the island of Zara for the Venetians. Then the Venetians convinced them to capture Constantinople. The Crusaders and the Venetians burned and looted Constantinople for three days. They stole valuable articles from palaces, churches, libraries, homes, and shops. Many priceless manuscripts and works of art were either taken to Venice, lost, or destroyed.

The soldiers finally decided not to go to Palestine. Instead, they stayed in Constantinople and divided the city between themselves and the Venetians. The conduct of the soldiers shocked many Western Europeans, who lost respect for the crusader ideal.

CAPTURE OF CONSTANTINOPLE

In 1204, Crusaders fought Byzantines instead of Muslims. They seized Constantinople after a fierce battle and overthrew the Byzantine emperor. The Crusaders ruled Constantinople until 1261.

Why did the Crusaders take Constantinople?

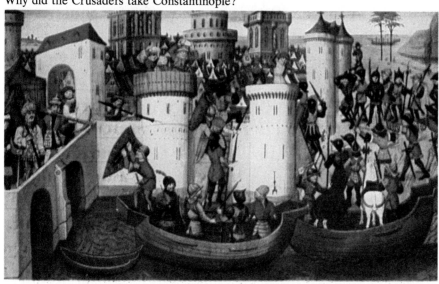

Several other crusades were fought during the thirteenth century, but the Europeans did not win any of them. The saddest of all crusades was the Children's Crusade. A group of French children, led by a peasant boy named Stephen of Cloyes, set sail from Marseilles, France in 1212. Most of the children never reached Palestine. Along the way they were sold into slavery by men from the ships on which they sailed. At the same time, another group of children set forth on foot from Germany, intending to march toward Italy. Most of them, however, died of starvation or disease.

In 1291 the Muslims took over the city of Acre, the last Christian stronghold. The Muslims had won the crusades and now ruled all the territory in Palestine that the Crusaders had fought to control.

1. Why were the Venetians willing to help the Crusaders?
2. What did the Crusaders and Venetians do in Constantinople?
3. How successful were the Crusaders in realizing their goals?

THE CRUSADES

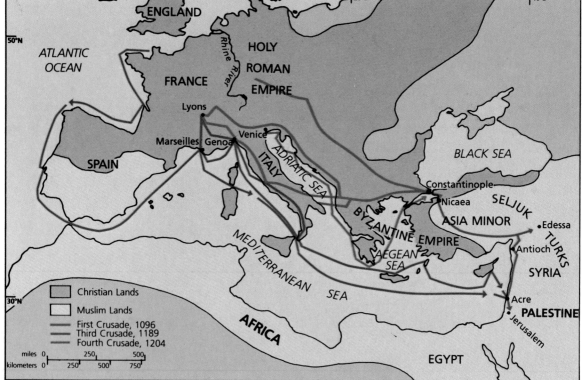

CHILDREN'S CRUSADE

Children throughout Europe decided to go on a crusade to the Holy Land. Here boys and girls from a French village begin their long journey.
What was the result of the Children's Crusade?

EFFECTS OF THE CRUSADES

The Crusades had an important effect on the future of both the East and the West. They brought the East into closer contact with the West. As a result, Europe was no longer cut off from the rest of the world.

The crusades affected the Church in just the opposite way planned by Urban II. The deeds and actions of western Europeans made the Byzantines so angry that the split between eastern and western Christianity became permanent. At the same time, the Byzantine Empire was so weakened by the crusades that it could no longer defend itself. Its decline left Europe open to Turkish attack.

In the West the crusades helped to break down feudalism. While feudal lords were fighting in Palestine, kings at home increased their authority. The desire for wealth, power, and land grew and began to overshadow the religious ideals of many western Europeans.

Jeweled Box

The Crusaders' contact with the cultured Byzantines and Muslims led western Europeans to renew their interest in learning and invention. At the same time, they began to demand some of the luxuries of the East. To meet these demands, the Europeans opened up new trade routes. European merchants brought home spices, sugar, lemons, melons, rugs, tapestries, and richly woven cloth. As trade grew so did the cities of western Europe. As a result, the cities became very important in the life of the late Middle Ages.

1. What were some effects of the crusades?

CHAPTER REVIEW
SUMMARY

1. In 1070 the Seljuk Turks conquered Palestine and began to keep Christians from visiting shrines in Jerusalem.

2. In 1095 Pope Urban II agreed to help the Byzantines against the Turks and called on the people of western Europe to join in a crusade.

3. In 1096 a large group of peasants started a crusade of their own, but they were almost completely wiped out.

4. In 1097 the nobles set out on a well-organized and well-equipped crusade that succeeded in reaching Jerusalem.

5. In 1099 nobles captured Jerusalem from the Turks.

6. Many Crusaders remained in Palestine, where they set up four feudal kingdoms.

7. Military orders made up of warrior-monks were formed to take charge of the defense of the feudal kingdoms established in Palestine.

8. The Crusaders who remained in Palestine developed a new way of life.

9. In 1174 Saladin started a jihad against Christians in the East, which ended in 1187 when he captured Jerusalem.

10. The kings of England, Germany, and France set out on another crusade, but only Richard the Lionheart of England continued to fight for several years.

11. Since Richard was unable to defeat Saladin, the Muslims and Crusaders signed a truce.

12. In 1204 another crusade began, but instead of going by land, the Crusaders decided to go by ship from Venice.

13. Instead of going to Palestine, the Crusaders and the Venetians burned and looted Constantinople.

14. Several other unsuccessful crusades, including the Children's Crusade, took place during the thirteenth century.

15. By 1291 the Muslims had regained all the territory in Palestine that the Crusaders had conquered earlier.

16. The crusades made the split between eastern and western Christianity permanent.

17. The crusades helped to break down the system of feudalism and encouraged the growth of towns and trade in western Europe.

BUILDING VOCABULARY

1. *Identify the following:*

Seljuk Turks	Knights Templar	Richard the Lionheart	Innocent III
Urban II	Knights Hospitaller	Frederick Barbarossa	Venice
Peter the Hermit	Saladin	Philip Augustus	Zara
Walter the Penniless			Acre

2. *Define the following:*

crusades	Outremer	military orders	emirs
massacred			crossbow

REVIEWING THE FACTS

1. What two important events took place in the town of Clermont in 1095?

2. Why did the Crusaders wear a red cross on their tunics?

3. Why did the peasants set off on their own crusade instead of waiting for the nobles to lead them?

4. Why was the Byzantine emperor upset when the peasants' crusade arrived in Constantinople?

5. What effect did the climate in Palestine have on the Crusaders?

6. What happened on the Children's Crusade?

7. Why did the split between eastern and western Christianity become permanent?

8. How did the crusades affect the power of western Europe's kings?

9. What led Europeans to open up new trade routes?

10. Why did western European cities become more important during the late Middle Ages?

DISCUSSING IMPORTANT IDEAS

1. If you had heard Urban II speak, would you have gone on a crusade?

2. Do you approve or disapprove of the way the Crusaders behaved when they captured Jerusalem? Explain.

3. If you had been a Crusader, would you have settled in Palestine or returned home? Explain.

4. Do you think you might have enjoyed knowing Saladin? Why or why not?

USING MAPS

Refer to the map on page 388, and answer the following questions:

1. To what country were the Crusaders traveling?

2. When did the Third Crusade begin?

3. From what city did the Fourth Crusade set out?

4. What is the latitude and longitude of the city of Jerusalem?

5. About how far is the city of Venice from the city of Constantinople?

6. Is Palestine Christian or Muslim?

UNIT REVIEW

SUMMARY

1. During the Middle Ages a system of feudalism developed. It divided western Europe into thousands of territories owned and governed by warrior-nobles.

2. Feudal society was divided into three main groups—clergy, nobles, and peasants and townspeople.

3. During the Middle Ages the Roman Catholic Church united western Europe, influenced almost every part of daily life, and helped to preserve Greco-Roman culture.

4. During the Middle Ages the Pope, who ruled from Rome, became the most powerful political and religious leader in western Europe.

5. To restore Christian control of Palestine after the Muslim conquest in the eleventh century, western Europeans began a series of unsuccessful holy wars called crusades. They lasted 200 years.

6. The crusades brought the East and the West into closer contact, made the split between eastern and western Christianity permanent, and helped to break down feudalism. They also renewed western European interest in learning and led to the opening of new trade routes.

REVIEWING THE MAIN IDEAS

1. Describe the ways in which the Church supported the feudal system.

2. Explain why trade and town life declined during the Middle Ages.

DEVELOPING SKILLS

Artifacts are a very important source of information about the past. So are textbooks. Both artifacts and textbooks provide all sorts of data about people and events.

Yet there is a major difference between these two types of sources. An artifact is considered a **primary source**, or a direct record of what people have done or thought in the past. A textbook is a **secondary source**, or a record based on primary sources or on other second-hand accounts.

Primary sources include such things as buildings, coins, inscriptions, tools, weapons, diaries, letters, and eye-witness accounts. Secondary sources include such things as textbooks, newspaper reports, historical novels, and paintings of past events.

It is important to be able to tell the difference between a primary source and a secondary source. This exercise is designed to give you practice in this skill. Read the following list. Then tell which items are primary sources and which are secondary sources.

1. the ruins of a medieval castle
2. a suit of armor
3. an eighteenth-century painting of a joust
4. a horse collar dating from the Middle Ages
5. a textbook account of the activities of the Inquisition
6. a document issued by Pope Gregory VII

7. the Concordat of Worms
8. a list of courses offered at the University of Bologna in 1250
9. a letter Heloise wrote to Abelard
10. a poem about the romance between Abelard and Heloise
11. *Summa Theologica*
12. a book review of *Summa Theologica*

13. a report of Pope Urban's speech at Clermont
14. a two-wheeled cart used during the Peasants' Crusade
15. a linen robe worn by a Crusader
16. a twelfth-century painting of Saladin and Richard the Lionheart
17. a Venetian coin dated 1204

SUGGESTED UNIT PROJECTS

1. Make a booklet of pictures of medieval castles. Under each picture, write a description of the castle's features.
2. Make a chart comparing the life of a lord, a serf, and a monk. Include information about the home, clothing, food, daily activities, and education of each.
3. Participate in a debate between two groups of students about the quarrel between Pope Gregory VII and King Henry VI of Germany. One group will present and defend Gregory's point of view. The other group will present and defend Henry's point of view.
4. Prepare a poster advertising a medieval university. Include the courses offered and jobs graduates will be able to fill.
5. Write a letter that a Crusader who has helped capture Jerusalem might have sent to his family in England.

SUGGESTED READING

Macaulay, David. *Cathedral*. Boston: Houghton Mifflin, 1973. A description of how nine different craftspeople and their assistants labored 86 years to help build a cathedral.

Namioka, Lensey. *The Samurai and the Long-Nosed Devils*. New York: David McKay, 1976. The story of two unemployed samurai who hire themselves out as bodyguards to a group of foreigners while a lord tries to unify Japan.

Reeves, James. *The Shadow of the Hawk, and Other Stories*. New York: Seabury Press, 1977. A retelling in prose of Marie de France's poems about adventure, love, and the struggle between good and evil during the Middle Ages.

Rosenfield, James. *The Lion and the Lily*. New York: Dodd, Mead, 1972. The story of Philip Augustus, who became king of France at the age of 15, and of Henry II of England, who wanted the French crown for his son.

Unstead, Robert J. *Living In A Castle*. Reading, Mass.: Addison-Wesley, 1973. A description of everyday life in a medieval castle.

Unstead, Robert J. *Living In A Crusader Land*. Reading, Mass.: Addison-Wesley, 1973. A description of everyday life in the four kingdoms established by the Crusaders in Palestine.

UNIT 9

900	925	950 962 Otto I crowned Holy Ro
	936 Otto I becomes king of Germany	

1050	1075	1100
1066 William the Conqueror wins Battle of Hastings	**1086** Domesday Book	**c. 1100** First guilds formed Flanders becomes important trade center
c. 1070 Italian coastal towns control Mediterranean trade		**1108** Louis VI becomes king France

1200	1225	1250
1209 Frederick II becomes Holy Roman Emperor	**1226** Louis IX becomes king of France	
1215 Magna Charta		
1216 Henry III becomes king of England		

1350	1375	1400
		1417 Battle of Agin

1500	1525	1550

THE LATE MIDDLE AGES

~~75~~	1000	1025
	c. 1000 Towns and trade routes begin to develop in Europe	**1042** Edward the Confessor becomes king of England
987 Hugh Capet becomes king of France		

25	1150	1175
	1152 Frederick I becomes Holy Roman Emperor	**1180** Philip Augustus begins rule in France
		1189 Richard the Lionheart becomes king of England
	1166 Henry II becomes king of England	**1199** John becomes king of England

~~75~~	1300	1325
2 Edward I calls meeting of Parliament		
		1339 Hundred Years' War begins
1285 Philip IV begins rule in France		**1347** Battle of Crecy

5	1450	1475
29 Joan of Arc fights for France	**1453** Hundred Years' War ends	**1485** Henry VII establishes Tudor dynasty in England
		1492 Moors surrender Granada to Spain
	1469 Ferdinand II of Aragon and Isabella of Castile marry	**1493** Maximilian I becomes Holy Roman Emperor

1. WHAT LED TO THE GROWTH OF TOWNS AND TRADE IN WESTERN EUROPE DURING THE LATE MIDDLE AGES?

2. WHAT DID KINGS DO TO BUILD STRONG NATIONS IN WESTERN EUROPE?

The period from 1000 to 1500 is called the Late Middle Ages. During this time the people of western Europe became aware of what was taking place outside the manors on which most of them lived. Some even heard about the ways of life in other civilizations.

As outside invasions ended, western European life became more orderly. Farmers learned to grow more food, and the population grew larger. People became more confident about the future. Trade and the exchange of ideas increased.

As trade grew, so did towns. In time they became great trade centers and attracted new residents. The people who lived in the towns were mostly merchants, artisans, and bankers. They formed a new class, higher than peasants but lower than nobles. Many of the townspeople became as wealthy, or wealthier than, the nobles. Their power and influence began to grow, and the power and influence of feudalism began to decline. Over time the towns became independent communities outside the feudal system.

Nations began to replace the many small feudal territories. Kings raised armies and used them to weaken the power of nobles. The kings succeeded in forming strong governments that won the loyalty of the people. Thus, they laid the foundations of the modern nations of western Europe.

CHAPTER

RISE OF TOWNS AND TRADE

27

During the eleventh and twelfth centuries things went well for the people of western Europe. For the first time since the fall of Rome, births outnumbered deaths. Better farming methods helped farmers produce enough food for the growing population. Many peasants left the fields to work in mines or village workshops. They became skilled artisans and began to turn out cloth and metal products.

Western nobles, however, wanted such luxury items as sugar, spices, silks, and dyes. These goods came from the East. So European merchants carried western products to the East to exchange for luxury goods. The increased trade had a major effect on western European life.

TRADING CENTERS

The growth of trade led to the rise of the first large trading centers of the Middle Ages. They were located on the important sea routes that connected western Europe with the Mediterranean Sea, Russia, and Scandinavia. Two of the earliest and most important trading centers were Venice and Flanders.

1. Where were the first large trading centers of the Middle Ages located?

VENICE   Venice was an island port in the Adriatic Sea close to the coast of Italy. It was founded in the sixth century by people fleeing from the Germans.

Since the land was not very fertile, the early Venetians had to depend on the sea for a living. They fished in the Adriatic and produced salt from the seawater. They exchanged their products for wheat from towns on the mainland of Italy. They also traded wheat, wine, and slaves to the Byzantines in return for fabrics and spices.

During the twelfth century Venice became a leading port and the home of Europe's fulltime merchants. Venetian merchants learned to read and write, use money, and keep records. Before long they developed a banking system suited to their needs.

Venice's prosperity soon spread to other parts of Italy. Towns on the Italian mainland began to make cloth, which they sent to Venice to be shipped to other areas. Before long other Italian towns along the seacoast became shipping centers.

The navies of the Italian trading towns drove the Muslims from the Mediterranean, making it safe for Italian seafarers to move into new areas. As a result, the Italians opened the Near East to Europeans.

Before long, however, the Italian trading towns began to quarrel among themselves over profits and trade routes. While they were quarreling, towns along Europe's Atlantic coast began to develop new trade routes. By 1500 these towns had become more powerful than the Italian ones.

1. What led to the development and growth of Venice's trade?
2. What effect did Venice's prosperity have on other Italian cities?
3. What led to the decline of the Italian trading centers?

FLANDERS   Flanders, an area of small towns and villages on the northwest coast of Europe, was the earliest Atlantic trading center. Today it is part of Belgium.

During the Middle Ages the low, marshy land of Flanders was not well suited to farming. So the Flemish people raised sheep and used the wool to develop a weaving industry. The cloth Flemish weavers produced gained fame for its quality and soon was in heavy demand.

MEDIEVAL TOWNS AND TRADE ROUTES

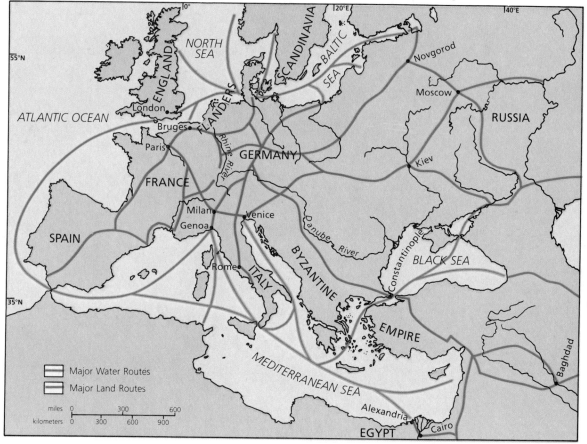

Flanders' many rivers and seacoast helped it become a trading center. The rivers joined together before they emptied into the North Sea. Where the rivers met, the water was deep enough for the Flemish to build harbors. From these harbors they shipped their valuable woolen cloth to other lands.

Flanders soon became an important stopping place for ships traveling along the Atlantic coast from Scandinavia to the Mediterranean Sea. It also became an important link in the trade route that began in Constantinople and continued to the North Sea.

By 1300 Flanders' most important trading partner was England. Flemish traders set up shop in the dockyards of London. They relied on English shepherds to supply them with wool, which they sent to Flanders to be made into cloth. The finished cloth was then shipped back to England.

1. Why did the Flemish raise sheep? What did they do with the wool from the sheep?
2. How did Flanders' location help it become an important trading center?
3. What trade arrangements did Flanders have with England?

WALLED TOWN

Towns in the Middle Ages had high stone walls and lookout towers. As they grew larger, the towns spread outside the walls. This photo shows the French town of Carcassonne, the finest example of a medieval walled town in Europe.
How did towns develop in the Middle Ages?

MERCHANTS

As sea trade grew, so did overland trade. Italian towns began sending goods across the Alps to areas in the north. Soon an overland trade route connected Italy and Flanders. From this route other routes developed and spread across Europe.

As a result of new trade routes and markets, merchants became an important part of European life. The first merchants of the Middle Ages were mostly adventurers who traveled from place to place. As protection against robbers, they traveled in armed groups. They carried their goods in wagons pulled by horses.

1. Who were the first merchants of the Middle Ages?
2. How did the early merchants travel?

Medieval Merchant

FAIRS   Merchants traveling along the main route through eastern France stopped to trade with each other at special gatherings called **fairs**. The fairs were sponsored by feudal lords who collected taxes on sales. Fairs were held for a few weeks once a year at selected places. They eventually attracted merchants from as far away as England and Egypt.

At the fairs merchants could sell and buy goods or settle debts. They set up booths to display such wares as pots, swords, armor, leather goods, and clothing. Before long, instead of bartering, merchants began to pay for goods with money. Italian moneychangers tested and weighed coins from many different lands to determine their value. From the *banc*, or bench, at which the moneychanger sat comes the English word "bank."

1. What did the merchants do at fairs?

THE GROWTH OF TOWNS   Merchants soon tired of traveling from place to place. They began to look for places where they could settle permanently and store their goods.

The merchants usually chose places near waterways or road crossings along a trade route. To protect themselves from robbers and feudal fights, the merchants also tried to settle near the walls of a castle, fortress, or monastery. They would build a marketplace along a nearby stream and enclose it in a palisade surrounded by a moat. Most towns of the Middle Ages developed from these merchant settlements.

The towns came to be called **burgs** because they often overlooked castles, which the Germans called *burgs*. The new towns grew steadily and attracted people from the surrounding countryside. Markets became centers of business and social activity. Once a week lords and peasants sold food for goods they could not make on the manor. Runaway serfs, traders, and wanderers settled in the towns. Artisans came from the villages to find work. Often they brought their families with them.

The towns gradually became more than just centers of trade. They became communities in which people lived.

1. Where did the first towns develop?
2. What contributed to the growth of the towns?

LIVING CONDITIONS By the thirteenth century most towns were wealthy and large enough to have their palisades replaced by walls and towers. Inside the walls, public buildings of stone and houses of wood were jammed close together. To save even more space, the houses had extra stories that extended over crooked narrow alleys.

Most towns grew without planning for future growth and they often spread beyond their walls into the surrounding countryside. New walls were then built around new areas.

The crowded conditions often made towns unhealthy places in which to live. Sewers were open, and there was little concern for cleanliness. People threw garbage out of windows into the streets below. Pigs and rats were everywhere.

Townswoman

During the fourteenth century some diseased rats came in on trading ships from the East. They carried with them a plague called the "Black Death." The disease swept through Europe, killing millions of people. Experts think that one out of three Europeans died in the plague. To escape it, people fled from the towns and settled in the countryside. Trading, farming, and war came to a temporary stop.

1. What were some problems faced by the towns?
2. What led many people to leave the towns and return to the countryside during the fourteenth century?

Burgher Life

Merchants and artisans controlled the town's business and trade. They hired workers from the countryside to make goods

BURGHER'S KITCHEN
The kitchen in a burgher home was managed by the burgher's wife. Here the servants prepare the evening meal under her direction.
What were the responsibilities of a burgher's wife?

for them. At first, the merchants, artisans, and workers who lived in town were all called **burghers**. But after a while the title was used only to mean rich merchants.

The daily life of the burghers and their families followed a set pattern. The day began at dawn with prayers. The burgher drank wine for breakfast and hurried off to work. He went to the docks and market to see how well his products were selling. Then he met with his business partners at the merchants' hall or the tavern.

The burgher's wife stayed at home where she kept house, managed servants, and cared for children. She also wrote music and worked in the garden. The family ate two large meals a day—one at 10 o'clock in the morning and another at 6 o'clock in the evening. A typical meal consisted of eel, roast beef, lark pastry, and larded milk. About 9 o'clock in the evening the family went to bed.

1. Who lived in the towns?
2. Who controlled the town's business and trade?
3. How did a burgher and his family spend their days?

RULE OF THE LORDS

Under the feudal system the land on which towns were built was owned by kings, nobles, and bishops. They taxed people in the towns and charged them fees to use the marketplace. The burghers did not like this. They also did not like some of the other restrictions placed on them. They resented having to get a lord's permission to marry, move around, or own property. And they did not want to serve in the lord's army.

Many lords viewed the rise of towns as a threat to their power. They resented the wealth of the burghers and began to strictly enforce feudal laws to keep burghers in their place. The Church also looked down on the townspeople. Church leaders feared that the making of profit would interfere with religion. They thought it was a sin for townspeople to take money as interest on loans.

The burghers insisted that feudal laws were not suitable for business or trade. They wanted to run their own affairs and to have their own courts and laws to settle legal problems. As city dwellers, they did not fit into the feudal system.

The burghers now had wealth and power. They began to rely less on feudal lords and bishops. Instead, they developed a sense of loyalty toward their town and worked together to build schools, hospitals, and churches. The burghers were not afraid to voice their opinions. Although they still respected the nobles and the clergy, the burghers began to demand changes.

1. Under the feudal system, what rights did nobles and church leaders have in the towns?
2. What changes did the townspeople want to make in the feudal system?

COMMUNES   In the twelfth century townspeople in northern Italy formed political groups called **communes** to oppose the feudal lords and the clergy. The communes fought against the bishops and the emperor who appointed the church officials.

The Italian communes won their battles and eventually became independent city-states. Before long the idea of communes spread to the towns of northern Europe. Some towns there held talks with local lords and gained certain freedoms without violence. The kings and nobles gave the townspeople **charters**. These were documents which allowed towns to control their own affairs.

The charters gave the people the right to elect officials to run the towns. In most towns representatives of the leading business groups made up a council. The council collected taxes and set charges for merchants who bought and sold goods in the town market. It also repaired streets; organized citizen armies; and ran hospitals, orphanages, and special homes for the poor.

Towns enforced their own laws. Special courts were set up to handle cases involving marriages, property inheritances, and business disputes. To cut down on crime, town laws punished lawbreakers severely. Murderers were hanged; robbers lost a hand or an arm. Those who committed such minor crimes as disturbing the peace were whipped or put in the **stocks**, or a wooden frame with holes in which the feet and hands were locked. All punishments were carried out outdoors for the public to watch.

1. When did communes first develop? Why did they develop?
2. What rights did charters give townspeople?

RISE OF GUILDS

Bronze Dragon

Around the twelfth century merchants, artisans, and workers formed **guilds**, or business groups whose purpose was to ensure equal treatment for members. Each craft had its own guild, whose members lived and worked in the same area of town. Guild members were forbidden to compete with one another or to advertise. Each guild member had to work the same number of hours, hire the same number of workers, and pay the same wages.

The guilds controlled all business and trade within a town. Only guild members could buy, sell, or make goods in that town. Outsiders who wanted to sell their goods in the town market had to get permission from the guilds. The guild decided the fair

MERCHANTS

Merchants exchanged their goods at fairs held in towns along the trading routes of Europe. Here a merchant in a German town counts his money after a busy day. How did merchants organize their business activities?

price for a product or service, and all members had to charge that price. Guild members who sold poorly made goods or cheated in business dealings had to pay large fines. They could also be expelled from the guild.

1. What rules did guild members have to obey?
2. What happened to those who did not live up to standards?

GUILD UNITY AND MEMBERSHIP   Guilds were more than business or trade organizations. If guild members became ill, other members provided care and medical aid. If members were out of work, the guild used its profits to provide food and clothing. When members died, the other members prayed for their souls. The guild paid for funerals and supported the dead members' families. Guilds were also centers of social life. Huge banquets were held at the guild hall. Holy day celebrations, processions, and outdoor plays were sponsored by the guild. Close friendships often developed among guild members.

It was not easy to become a member of a guild. A person had to be an **apprentice**, or a trainee, in a trade for ten years. Apprentices were taught their trade by **masters**, or experts. They had to live with and obey the masters until their training was complete.

The next step was becoming a **journeyman**, or a person who worked under a master for a daily wage. After a certain period of time, a journeyman could take an examination to become a master. The examination was given by guild officials. The journeyman had to make and present a "masterpiece" that proved he had learned his craft. A journeyman who passed the examination was considered a master and could make his own goods. Usually he set up a workspace in the back of his house for himself and his apprentices. The products the master and apprentices made usually were sold in a shop in the front of the master's house.

By 1400 many merchants and artisans were challenging the control of the guilds. They felt the guilds prevented them from enlarging their trade and profits. Then, too, apprentices disliked the rigid rules set by the guilds. It was getting harder and harder for apprentices to become masters. Many masters were grouping together and hiring unskilled workers in place of apprentices.

1. How did guilds help members and families of members?
2. How did a person become a master in a trade?
3. Why did people oppose guilds in the fifteenth century?

CULTURAL CHANGES

During the fifteenth century merchants, artisans, and bankers became more important than they had been in the past. Their increasing power led to the decline of feudalism.

Many townspeople were as wealthy as, or wealthier than, the landed nobles. Bankers lent money to kings, lords, and church officials for wars, building repairs, and entertainment. With their new wealth, merchants turned their wooden homes into mansions with carpets and glass windowpanes. Some even bought castles from nobles who had lost all their money.

Worker with Basket

Townspeople began to set fashions. Women wore furs and brocaded gowns. Men dressed in colorful jackets, hose, and feathered caps.

The townspeople had more leisure time and money to spend on their interests. Many of them hired private teachers to educate their sons. The sons later went to universities to study law, religion, and medicine. There was time to enjoy art and books, and soon townspeople began to support the work of painters and writers.

Most of the townspeople had never learned Latin, which was the language of scholars and church leaders. They preferred instead to use languages such as German, French, and English. Now they could read stories and poems in languages they knew. A scholar named Dante wrote the *Divine Comedy* in Italian. It was one of the most famous poems of the period. Geoffrey Chaucer wrote the *Canterbury Tales* in English. The tales are still popular today.

Townspeople thought differently from feudal nobles and peasants. The townspeople came to believe that they should be free to develop their talents and to improve their way of life. They wanted a strong central government that would give them the peace and security they needed to realize their goals. They began to look toward kings to provide leadership.

1. In what ways did the cultural life of townspeople change during the fifteenth century?

CHAPTER REVIEW
SUMMARY

1. During the eleventh and twelfth centuries increased trade between Europe and the East led to the rise of trading centers such as Venice and Flanders.

2. Venetian traders became fulltime merchants who developed an effective banking system.

3. By 1100 the navies of the Italian trading towns had driven the Muslims from the Mediterranean.

4. Flanders was the earliest Atlantic trading center.

5. By 1300 the Flemish had developed an international industry by importing wool from England, turning it into cloth, and then shipping the finished product back to England.

6. Overland trade as well as sea trade developed during the eleventh and twelfth centuries.

7. At first, medieval merchants traveled overland in armed groups and stopped to trade with each other at fairs.

8. After a while, merchants began to settle in permanent places which developed into towns called burgs.

9. Most towns were overcrowded, unhealthy places to live.

10. Artisans and rich merchants called burghers controlled the business and trade of towns.

11. Lords viewed the rise of towns as a threat to their power, and bishops feared that the making of profit would interfere with religion.

12. Burghers resented feudal laws and wanted to run their own affairs.

13. By the 1100's, towns in northern Italy became independent city-states.

14. Guilds set wages, prices, and working conditions and helped members who were sick or out of work.

15. As townspeople grew richer and more powerful, they began turning away from feudalism and looking to kings to provide leadership.

BUILDING VOCABULARY

1. *Identify the following:*

Venice	Flemish	Dante	Geoffrey Chaucer
Flanders	Black Death	*Divine Comedy*	*Canterbury Tales*

2. *Define the following:*

fairs	communes	stocks	apprentice
burgs	charters	guilds	masters
burghers			journeyman

REVIEWING THE FACTS

1. What led to the development of east-west trade during the eleventh and twelfth centuries?
2. What were two important trading centers of the Middle Ages?
3. What did Italian trading towns have to do with driving the Muslims from the Mediterranean?
4. Why were most towns called burgs during the Middle Ages?
5. What groups of people settled in towns?
6. What effects did the Black Death have on Europe?
7. Why were lords opposed to the rise of towns?
8. Why were the clergy opposed to the rise of towns?
9. In what languages were books read by townspeople usually written?
10. How were the ideas of townspeople different from those of feudal nobles and peasants?

DISCUSSING IMPORTANT IDEAS

1. Do you think you would have enjoyed living in a town during the Middle Ages? Why or why not?
2. Would you have supported the position taken by Italian communes during the twelfth century? Explain.
3. Would you have preferred to be a burgher or a feudal lord during the Middle Ages? Explain.
4. Do you approve or disapprove of the rules established by guilds? Give reasons for your opinion.

USING MAPS

Refer to the map on page 399, and answer the following questions:

1. What types of trade routes are shown?
2. What are some Italian trading cities?
3. What city is located about 47° north and 29° east?
4. Which trading city is easternmost?
5. About how far is Bruges from Milan?
6. Into what body of water does the Danube River flow?
7. What body of water is directly east of Scandinavia?

MARCO POLO AND THE MONGOLS

Marco Polo was a thirteenth-century Italian from the city of Venice. He became famous for his travels in Cathay, or China.

Marco's father and uncle were diamond merchants who had traveled to China. There they met the Mongol ruler Kublai Khan, who was Genghis Khan's grandson. He invited the Polos to return to China.

In 1271 the Polos left on another trip to the East. This time they took 17-year-old Marco with them. They sailed to a port in Palestine and then traveled the rest of the way by camel. Three years later, they reached the summer palace of Kublai Khan.

The Polos stayed in China for 17 years. Kublai Khan gave them jewels, silk, and other valuable treasures. Marco became an aide to Kublai Khan and even acted as governor of a Chinese city for three years.

Kublai Khan sent Marco on many tours of the Mongol Empire. Among the places he visited were Burma, Indochina, Malaya, and India. During the tours Marco took detailed notes so he could report to Kublai Khan.

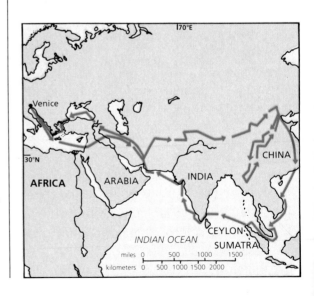

The Polos left China in 1292. When they reached Venice three years later, they found the city at war with Genoa, a rival Italian city.

Marco became the commander of a Venetian **galley**, or ship propelled by oars. He was captured by the Genoese and spent a year in prison. With the help of another prisoner, Marco used his time in jail to write a book called *Description of the World*.

The book told about the Mongol Empire, the largest in the history of the world. It stretched from the Pacific Ocean to the Mediterranean Sea. Within its borders lived hundreds of different peoples.

The book also described Kublai Khan and his court and the cities of China. It told of the great wealth in the Far East and of luxuries far beyond the imaginations of any Westerner. Marco also described the customs, habits, and life styles of the people.

Marco Polo's book gave Europeans some of their first ideas about the Far East. Europeans who read it became interested in trading with China. Mapmakers later made accurate maps based on descriptions in the book. A young captain named Christopher Columbus read the book and later decided to seek a sea route to the Far East.

1. Why did Marco Polo go to China?
2. What did Marco Polo do in China?
3. What influence did Marco Polo's book have on Europeans?

CHAPTER 28

RISE OF THE MONARCHIES

The rise of towns and trade during the Late Middle Ages led to many changes in western Europe. One of these changes was political. Feudalism lost its power, and kings grew stronger. This, in turn, affected the Church and the people. In France, England, Germany, and Spain especially, things would never be the same again.

FRANCE

In 987 Hugh Capet, a French noble, was chosen as the new king of France. At the time, France consisted of many feudal territories. As king, Capet ruled only a small area between the Seine and Loire Rivers.

1. What was France like when Hugh Capet became king?

THE CAPETIANS   Hugh Capet was the first of a line of Capetian kings who ruled France for 300 years. He died in 996. The Capetian kings who followed him for the next 100 years were weak and did little to increase royal power.

In 1108 Louis VI, known as "Louis the Fat," became king. He helped to increase the authority of the monarchy in several ways. He discharged nobles who did not fulfill their feudal duties and replaced them with loyal persons of lower birth. He brought the people security by stopping the raids of lawless vassals. He also granted charters of freedom to many towns, thus winning the loyalty of the townspeople.

The king's authority was further strengthened under Philip Augustus, also known as Philip II. Philip, who ruled from 1180 to 1223, made Paris the center of government. He had churches

---

SAINT LOUIS

King Louis IX of France was known for his honesty and just dealings. After his death, he was made a saint of the Roman Catholic Church. Louis' support of the Church is expressed in this painting of the king feeding a church official. What benefits did Louis IX bring to France?

---

built, streets paved, and a 28-foot, or about 8.5 meter, wall raised around the city. He increased the size of his kingdom through marriage and by winning back French land held by the English. To make sure that nobles did not become too powerful while he was fighting in the Crusades, Philip II appointed royal agents to keep watch on noble fiefs.

In 1226 Philip's grandson became King Louis IX. He ordered the nobles to stop feuding and forbade them to settle disputes by fighting duels. Most nobles **minted**, or coined, their own money. Louis IX made it illegal to use coins made anywhere but the royal mint. He also set up a royal court to which anyone could bring disputes. Under Louis IX there was peace, and the people became more united.

Philip IV, Louis' grandson, ruled from 1285 to 1314. He was known as "Philip the Fair." Philip IV believed that the interests of the state came first. So he seized English fortresses he felt were necessary for the kingdom's security, and he fought the Flemish when they refused to let the French control their cloth trade. Philip IV also believed that a kingdom could not exist without taxes. So he made sure taxes were collected on a regular and permanent basis, and he taxed the clergy. To advise him and help him run the country, "Philip the Fair" formed the Estates-General, an assembly of nobles, clergy, and townspeople. Its formation was the beginning of a national government in France. By the time Philip IV died in 1314, France was united under one supreme ruler.

1. What did Louis VI do to increase the authority of the king?
2. What changes did Philip Augustus bring about in France?
3. What did Louis IX do to help unite the French people?
4. What did Philip IV do to unite and strengthen France?

Golden Bird

ENGLAND

In 1042 the witan made Edward the Confessor, an English prince, king of England. A sincere and religious ruler, Edward gave money to the poor and sponsored the building in London of Westminster Abbey, the church in which later English monarchs were crowned. But he spent so much time in religious work that he failed to carry out his royal duties. As a result, the nobles increased their hold on the country. The most powerful noble

BATTLE OF HASTINGS

William the Conqueror's victory at Hastings made him king of England. This detail from the famous Bayeux tapestry shows Norman troops on horseback. Who fought at the Battle of Hastings?

was Harold Godwinson. When Edward died in 1065 without an heir, Harold became the new king.

1. What happened to the king's authority during the rule of "Edward the Confessor"?
2. Who governed England after Edward's death?

WILLIAM THE CONQUEROR   Harold Godwinson did not remain king for long. William, Duke of Normandy, a cousin of Edward the Confessor, claimed that before Edward died, he had promised him the English throne.

In 1066 William led an army of 5000 Norman archers and knights across the sea to England. They met Harold's army in battle near Hastings, a town just south of London. To stop the Norman charge, English foot soldiers armed with axes formed a wall of shields on the edge of a low hill. William knew he could not break through the wall. So he had his soldiers pretend to retreat. When the English broke formation to follow after them, the Normans turned on the English. By nightfall King Harold was dead, and the English were defeated. On Christmas Day, William, now known as William the Conqueror, was crowned King of England in Westminster Abbey.

At first the English resisted William's rule. To crush English revolts—and to keep his followers in line—William introduced feudalism into England. He seized the lands of English nobles and divided them among Norman nobles. In return for the lands,

MAGNA CHARTA

The Archbishop of Canterbury and the merchants joined the nobles in forcing King John to sign the Magna Charta. Here King John places his seal on the charter. Later, the English people claimed the rights guaranteed to the nobles.

In what ways did the Magna Charta increase the power of the nobles?

the nobles became William's vassals. They promised to be loyal to the king and to provide him with soldiers.

William kept many English laws and government practices. He received advice from the witan, now called the Great Council. He also relied on such local officials as the sheriff. William made many changes. In 1086 he took a census in order to properly tax the people. The census figures were recorded in two huge volumes called the *Domesday Book*.

William also brought **continental**, or European mainland, ways to England. Under his rule, the English learned Norman customs and the French language. The wealthy built castles, cathedrals, and monasteries in the French style. The people learned new skills from Norman weavers and workers.

1. How did the Normans win the Battle of Hastings?
2. Why did William the Conqueror introduce feudalism in England?
3. What changes did William bring to England?

HENRY II   After William died, there was confusion in England until 1154 when William's great-grandson became King Henry II. He ruled England, most of Ireland, Scotland, and Wales. He was also a feudal lord in France, where he owned more land than he did in England. Some of the French lands belonged to his wife, Eleanor of Aquitaine. She lived at her own court in the French town of Poitiers. Knights and minstrels from all over Europe came to see Eleanor and to praise her beauty and intelligence.

Henry II restored order and forced the nobles to give him their loyalty. He also used the law to increase his authority and worked to reform English courts. A central royal court was set up in London with trained lawyers as judges. **Circuit judges**, or judges who travel throughout the country, brought the king's law to all parts of England. They made it the common law of the land, thus helping to unite the country.

In each community judges met with a **grand jury**, or group of people who present to judges the names of people suspected of crimes. Out of the grand juries grew **trial by jury**, a system of justice in which 12 people decide the guilt or innocence of an accused person.

Henry II believed that everyone, including church officials, should be tried in the king's courts. Thomas à Becket, Henry's close friend and the Archbishop of Canterbury, did not agree. Becket wanted church officials free of royal control. The quarrel between the king and the archbishop led four of the king's knights to murder Becket. After the murder, Henry II made peace with the Church by allowing some of the clergy to be tried in church courts.

1. What lands did Henry II rule?
2. How did Henry II improve English law?
3. Why did Henry II and Thomas à Becket quarrel?

THE MAGNA CHARTA AND PARLIAMENT   When Henry II died in 1189, his oldest son Richard became king. Because of his bravery in battle, he was called "the Lion-heart." Richard, however, was more interested in his French lands than in ruling England, and he did little for the English people.

When Richard died in 1199, his brother John became king. John lost most of his lands in France to the French king. When he increased taxes and began to ignore the law, the nobles

Symbol of Royalty

became angry. They refused to obey him unless he agreed to give them certain rights and privileges. In 1215 John met the nobles in the meadow of Runnymede, where they forced him to sign the *Magna Charta*, or Great Charter.

The Magna Charta lessened the king's power and increased that of the nobles. A king could no longer collect taxes without the consent of the Great Council. A freeman accused of a crime had the right to a trial by his peers. The king had to obey laws. Although the Magna Charta was written by nobles for nobles, it came to be viewed as an important step toward democracy. It brought to government the new idea that not even a king is above the law.

John died in 1216, and his son became King Henry III. But Henry was weak and allowed the feudal lords in the Great Council to rule England. In 1264 Simon de Montfort, Henry's brother-in-law, came to power. He gave the people a voice in government by letting them have representatives in the Great Council.

Eight years later, the new king, Edward I, went even further. He called for a meeting of representatives to advise him and to help him make laws. This gathering, known as Parliament, gave the people a greater share in the ruling of their country. Parliament later broke into two separate groups. Nobles and clergy met as the House of Lords, while knights and townspeople met as the House of Commons.

1. Why did the nobles force King John to sign the Magna Charta?
2. What reform did Simon de Montfort make?
3. What was the purpose of Parliament?

THE HUNDRED YEARS' WAR

In the early fourteenth century the English still held a small part of southwest France. The kings of France, who were growing more powerful, wanted to drive the English out. In 1337 the English king, Edward III, declared himself king of France. This angered the French even more. In 1339 the French and English fought the first in a long series of battles known as the Hundred Years' War.

1. Who fought the Hundred Years' War?

ENGLISH VICTORIES   The Hundred Years' War began when the English defeated the French fleet and won control of the sea. The English then invaded France. They defeated the French at the Battle of Crecy in 1347 and again at the Battle of Agincourt in 1417.

The British owed their success on land mostly to a new weapon called the **longbow**, which shot steel-tipped arrows. The French still used the shorter crossbow. The crossbow could not send arrows as far as the longbow, and the French arrows were not as sharp as the steel-tipped English arrows.

1. Why were the English able to defeat the French in the battles of Crecy and Agincourt?

JOAN OF ARC   By 1429 much of France was in English hands. Charles, the French *dauphin*, or prince, was fighting the English for the French throne. Then a 17-year-old French peasant named Jeanne d'Arc, or Joan of Arc, appeared. She said

JOAN OF ARC

Joan of Arc freed the French city of Orleans from English rule and became a national heroine. Here she is greeted by the people of Orleans after the victory. Why did Joan decide to help her people?

that while praying she had heard heavenly voices telling her she must save France. She went to see Charles and told him that God had sent her to help him. She said that if she had an army she would free Orleans, a city the English had been besieging for seven months. Charles gave Joan an army, a suit of armor, and a white linen banner.

Joan led an attack against the English army at Orleans. Within ten days the city was free, and Joan became known as the "Maid of Orleans." Shortly after, with Joan at his side, the dauphin was crowned King Charles VII of France. Joan wanted to return home, but Charles convinced her to stay with the army. A few months later a French traitor captured her and sold her to the English. After spending a year in prison, she was tried as a witch and burned at the stake.

OTTO I

The armies of Otto I put down many rebellions and conquered neighboring peoples. Here Otto and his forces defeat the Hungarians at Lechfeld in 955.
What steps did Otto I take to increase his power?

The French continued fighting after Joan's death. By 1453 the English held only the French seaport at Calais, and the war had come to an end.

1. What did Joan of Arc do for the French?
2. What happened to Joan of Arc after the Battle of Orleans?

RESULTS OF THE WAR   Both France and England were changed by the Hundred Years' War. By 1500 the last French feudal territories were under the king's control, and France was unified. England, too, was unified by the war, but its monarchy was weakened. Not until 1485, when a Welshman named Henry Tudor became king, did the monarchy become strong again.

Playing Card

The Hundred Years' War also increased the importance of the common people both in England and in France. Many peasants had died during the war from disease or fighting. Those who remained were greatly needed as workers. The peasants knew they were needed and began to make demands. They forced the lords to pay them wages and to allow them to move outside the manors. When the lords tried to force them back to the old ways, they revolted. Most became farmers who rented land from the lords.

1. How did the Hundred Years' War affect the monarchies of England and France?
2. How did the Hundred Years' War affect English and French peasants?

GERMANY

During the tenth century Germany was the most important and powerful country in western Europe. Over time German kings lost much of their authority to powerful nobles who wanted to rule their own territories. The king, however, still had the right to remove lords who would not obey him.

1. What right did German kings have regarding their nobles?

OTTO I   In 936 Otto I became king of Germany. He wanted to unite the country and rule without the nobles. He removed disobedient lords and gave their estates to his family. Then he turned to the Church for support. Church officials wanted him to set up a Christian Roman Empire in western Europe. So Otto made many of his loyal followers bishops and abbots and gave them government posts. In return, they supplied him with money and soldiers. Otto then invaded Italy, added the northern Italian trading cities to his kingdom, and freed the Pope from the control of Roman nobles.

In 962 the Pope crowned Otto I emperor of the Holy Roman Empire, a large new state that consisted of Germany and northern Italy. Otto saw himself as the heir of Charlemagne and the Roman emperors and as the leader of the Christian West. He, and the emperors who followed him for the next 90 years, controlled the office of Pope.

1. What were Otto I's goals as king of Germany?
2. How did Otto I's goals change after he became emperor?

FREDERICK I   In 1152 Frederick I became emperor. Because of his full red beard, he was called Barbarossa, or "red beard." Frederick forced the powerful lords to swear loyalty to him and to work for his government.

Frederick's attempts to control the nobles and unify the empire worked against him. The nobles grew wealthy from their government positions. At the same time, the Italian city-states, aided by the Pope, banded together and defeated Frederick's armies. Frederick had to accept a peace that recognized the independence of the city-states.

Frederick died in 1190 while bathing in a river in Asia Minor. Later a legend about him spread among the Germans. It stated that he was not dead but under a magic spell that had put him to sleep somewhere high in the mountains. The people believed that one day he would awake and restore the glory of Germany.

1. What were the results of Frederick I's efforts to unify the empire?
2. What does German legend say about Frederick I?

FREDERICK II   In 1209 Frederick II, Frederick I's grandson, became emperor. He had been born and raised in Palermo, Sicily, which his father had made part of the Holy Roman Empire. So he ignored Germany and concentrated on ruling Sicily.

Frederick was known as the best educated monarch of his time. He founded a university in Palermo so young men could

German Crown

YOUNG MAXIMILIAN

As a young man, Maximilian studied under Renaissance scholars. Later as emperor, he encouraged the development of universities throughout Germany. What other territories in Europe were ruled by Maximilian?

study at home rather than in other countries. He spoke several languages and supported artists and scholars. Although the Church forbade it, he adopted many Muslim customs and conducted scientific experiments.

When Frederick began conquering land in Italy, the Pope became afraid that he would seize church lands around Rome. So in 1227 he **excommunicated**, or expelled, Frederick from the Church and called for a crusade against him. This gave the German princes the chance they had been waiting for. They broke away from the emperor's rule and made Germany a loose collection of states under their control.

1. What kind of ruler was Frederick II?
2. Why did Frederick II and the Pope quarrel?
3. What was the effect of Frederick's excommunication?

THE HAPSBURGS Whenever an emperor of the Holy Roman Empire died, the German princes met in a **diet**, or assembly. There they elected one of themselves as the new emperor.

In 1272 the princes elected as emperor a member of the Hapsburg family named Rudolf. He and members of his family served as Holy Roman emperors for the next 700 years.

One important Hapsburg was Maximilian I, who became emperor in 1493. He worked to gain more land and to extend his power throughout Europe. When he married Mary of Burgundy, he gained control of Flanders and other areas of the Low Countries, or provinces of the Holy Roman Empire in northwestern Europe. By marrying his children into other royal families of Europe, he brought still more countries under Hapsburg influence. The one area over which he could not gain complete control, however, was Germany. There the princes continued to have authority over their own lands.

1. How did Rudolf I become Holy Roman Emperor?
2. How did Maximilian I increase Hapsburg influence?

Spain

While the western European monarchies were increasing their power, Spain was under the control of Muslims called Moors. When the Moors conquered Spain in 711, they brought with them learning and luxury. Most Spaniards, however, were Christians and opposed Muslim rule. They banded together to drive the Moors out of the country. By the thirteenth century the Moors controlled only the small southern kingdom of Granada.

1. How did most Spaniards feel about Muslim rule? Why did they feel this way?

FERDINAND AND ISABELLA   Spain was made up of small kingdoms, the most powerful of which were Castile and Aragon. In 1469 Prince Ferdinand of Aragon married Princess Isabella of Castile. Within ten years they became king and queen and united their kingdoms into one nation. Ferdinand and Isabella worked to drive the Moors out of Spain. In 1492 the Moors at Granada surrendered the last Moorish stronghold. To make their power felt throughout the land, Ferdinand and Isabella took away some of the nobles' privileges. They sent royal officials called *corregidores* to govern the towns and set up special courts in the countryside to punish robbers and other criminals.

Ferdinand and Isabella were known as the "Catholic Monarchs." They believed that to be truly united all Spaniards should be Catholic. In 1492 they ordered Spanish Jews to convert or leave the country. Ten years later, they gave the remaining Moors the same choice.

Ferdinand and Isabella did not trust the Jews and Moors who converted. They believed that the new Christians practiced their old religions in secret. To stop such heresy, they set up a church court called the Inquisition. It tortured, tried, and punished anyone suspected of heresy. Ferdinand and Isabella and later rulers used the Inquisition to force the people to be loyal.

1. What did Ferdinand and Isabella do to make their power felt?
2. Why did they want all Spaniards to be Christians?
3. What did the Spanish Inquisition do?

EUROPE IN THE LATE MIDDLE AGES

CHAPTER REVIEW

SUMMARY

1. The rise of towns and trade in western Europe during the Late Middle Ages resulted in the growth of strong national governments.

2. The Capetian dynasty of France began in 987 and lasted for some 300 years.

3. Capetian kings strengthened the French monarchy by filling government jobs with loyal people, granting many towns charters of freedom, making Paris the center of government, setting up a national court and a national currency, and forming the tax system and the Estates-General.

4. In 1066 William, Duke of Normandy, invaded England and conquered the English at the Battle of Hastings.

5. William the Conqueror continued to accept advice from the witan and to use local English officials, but he also introduced feudalism and the French language into England.

6. Henry II strengthened the English monarchy by making the king's law the law of the land and by developing the system of trial by jury.

7. In 1215 English nobles forced King John to sign the Magna Charta, which established the idea that not even a king is above the law.

8. In 1272 King Edward I set up Parliament to advise him and to help him make laws.

9. Between 1337 and 1453 England and France fought each other in a series of battles known as the Hundred Years' War.

10. The Hundred Years' War unified France and England and increased the importance of the common people.

11. In 1429 a French peasant named Joan of Arc succeeded in driving the English from Orleans and having the dauphin crowned Charles VII.

12. In 962 the Pope crowned the German king Otto I emperor of the Holy Roman Empire.

13. By 1227 Germany was a loose collection of states which were controlled by German princes.

14. The Hapsburg family ruled the Holy Roman Empire from 1272 until the twentieth century.

15. By 1492 Ferdinand and Isabella conquered the Moors and made Spain a Catholic country.

BUILDING VOCABULARY

1. *Identify the following:*

Late Middle Ages	Estates-General	*Domesday Book*	Magna Charta
Hugh Capet	Edward	Henry II	Simon de Montfort
Louis the Fat	the Confessor	Eleanor of Aquitaine	Parliament
Philip Augustus	William	Thomas à Becket	Hundred Years' War
Louis IX	the Conqueror	Richard the Lion-heart	Charles VII
Philip the Fair	Hastings	King John	Joan of Arc

Orleans	Holy Roman Empire	Frederick II	Moors
Otto I	Frederick Barbarossa	Hapsburg	Ferdinand and Isabella

2. *Define the following:*

minted	grand jury	longbow	excommunicated
continental	trial by jury	dauphin	corregidores
circuit judges			

REVIEWING THE FACTS

1. Why did French townspeople become loyal to the king?

2. How did the Estates-General help to strengthen the French monarchy?

3. Why did the Duke of Normandy think he had a right to the English throne?

4. Why did William the Conqueror take a census of the English people?

5. How did Henry II make peace with the Church after the murder of Becket?

6. What changes did the Magna Charta bring about in English government?

7. Why did the position of peasants in England and France improve as a result of the Hundred Years' War?

8. How did Otto I make his empire more Christian?

9. Why did Frederick II ignore Germany and concentrate on ruling Sicily?

10. What did the Moors bring to Spain?

DISCUSSING IMPORTANT IDEAS

1. If you had been King John, would you have signed the Magna Charta? Why or why not?

2. Why do you suppose Joan of Arc was tried as a witch? Give reasons for your opinion.

3. Do you think the Hundred Years' War helped or hurt the development of England and France? Explain.

4. Do you agree with Ferdinand and Isabella that all the people of a nation should follow the same religion? Explain.

USING MAPS

Refer to the map on page 425, and answer the following questions:

1. What is the time period of the map?

2. What territories made up the Holy Roman Empire?

3. What areas did the English control?

4. What French city is nearest England?

5. What is the latitude and longitude of the city of Paris?

6. About how far is Palermo from Rome?

7. What body of water is west of France?

8. What area is directly north of England?

UNIT REVIEW

SUMMARY

1. Increased trade during the eleventh and twelfth centuries led to the growth of large trading centers and the establishment of merchant settlements. They attracted new residents and developed into trading towns.

2. A new class, higher than peasants but lower than nobles, developed in the towns. It consisted of merchants, artisans and bankers.

3. In western Europe the rise of trade and towns and the increased power and wealth of townspeople led to a weakening of the feudal system and to the rise of monarchies.

4. During the late Middle Ages monarchies and strong national governments developed in France, England, Germany, and Spain. They laid the foundations of the modern nations of western Europe.

REVIEWING THE MAIN IDEAS

1. Explain why the growth of towns and trade led to a weakening of the feudal system and the power of the Church.

2. Explain what kings did to form strong governments and win the loyalty of the people.

DEVELOPING SKILLS

Much of the information a person receives is stated directly. But sometimes the meaning of the information is not stated directly. Instead, it is only **implied**, or hinted at. In other words, although the information is there, it is not presented in so many words. It is up to the person who receives the information to determine what is meant. This skill is called **drawing inferences**.

Learning how to draw inferences is a very important skill. It is important to understand what information is presented. It is equally important to understand what information is not presented, so that you will not jump to a wrong conclusion.

This exercise is designed to give you practice in drawing inferences. Following are references to two paragraphs in the textbook. Below each reference are several statements. Reread each paragraph, and use the information in it to decide if you can infer that the statements below the paragraph are true or that they are false. In some cases, you will not be able to infer anything, because there will not be enough information in the paragraph for you to do so.

1. paragraph at the bottom of page 403 and the top of page 404.
   a. A burgher's wife had to be well organized.
   b. Most burghers were fat.
   c. Burghers did not eat many fruits and vegetables.
   d. Most burghers had large families.
   e. A burgher's wife did most of the housework herself.
   f. Music was important in a burgher's household.
   g. Most burgher's wives were good musicians.

h. A burgher family usually slept eight hours a night.

2. first paragraph under "Guild Unity and Membership" on page 406.

a. Guild members were religious.

b. A guild member worried about becoming ill.

c. Belonging to a guild was expensive.

d. Guilds were the only social organization to which workers belonged.

e. Guild halls were large.

f. Running a guild took a great deal of time.

g. Guild members were skilled in nursing.

h. Guild members disliked the theater.

SUGGESTED UNIT ACTIVITIES

1. During the Middle Ages family names came into widespread use in Europe. Find out how each of the following names developed: Bridges, Fletcher, Ford, Masterson, Smith, Taylor.

2. Make a chart comparing the rise of two of the following nations: England, France, Germany, Spain. Include the names, dates, and accomplishments of the rulers who helped strengthen the power of the monarchy.

3. Write an account of the Battle of Hastings as it might have appeared in an English newspaper the day after the battle ended.

4. Working in a small group, prepare a diorama of a medieval trade fair or a burg.

5. Compare a medieval guild with a present-day labor union. Describe the ways in which they are alike and the ways in which they are different.

SUGGESTED READING

Asimov, Isaac. *The Shaping of France*. Boston: Houghton Mifflin Company, 1972. From the death of Louis the Do-Nothing in 987 to the end of the Hundred Years' War in 1453.

Fraser, Antonia, ed. *Kings and Queens of England*. New York: Alfred A. Knopf, 1975. The stories of the men and women who have ruled England for almost 1000 years.

Konigsburg, E. *A Proud Taste for Scarlet and Miniver*. New York: Atheneum, 1973. Recounts the events in the life of Eleanor of Aquitaine as remembered by herself and by three people who knew her well.

Lofts, Norah. *The Maude Reed Tale*. New York: Elsevier, 1972. The story of an English girl who wants to become a wool merchant but is sent instead to a castle to learn to be a lady.

Shuttlesworth, Dorothy. *The Tower of London*. New York: Hastings House, 1970. A description of how and when the stone buildings of the Tower were built.

Sutcliff, Rosemary. *The Shield Ring*. New York: Henry Z. Walck, 1972. The story of a young girl during the time the Normans are fighting for control of England.

Trease, Geoffrey. *The Barons' Hostage*. Nashville: Thomas Nelson, 1975. The story of a teen-age boy who claims a barony during the time of Simon de Montfort.

1270	1285	1300
		c. 1300 Scholars promote classical learning
	c. 1280 Marco Polo travels throughout Asia	

1360	1375	1390

1450	1465	1480 **1485** Henry VII starts Tudor dynasty in England
c. 1450 Merchants challenge power of guilds		**1487** Dias sails around southern tip of Africa
	1469 Lorenzo de Medici rules Florence	**1492** Columbus lands at San Salvador Renaissance comes to France
		1493 Treaty of Tordes

1540	1555	1570
1540 Society of Jesus founded	**1555** Peace of Augsburg	**1576** Frobisher sea for northwes passage
1541 John Calvin brings Reformation to Geneva	**1558** Elizabeth I becomes queen of England	
1543 Council of Trent		
	1562 French religious wars begin	

1630	1645	1660
	1648 Peace of Westphalia	

THE BEGINNING OF MODERN TIMES

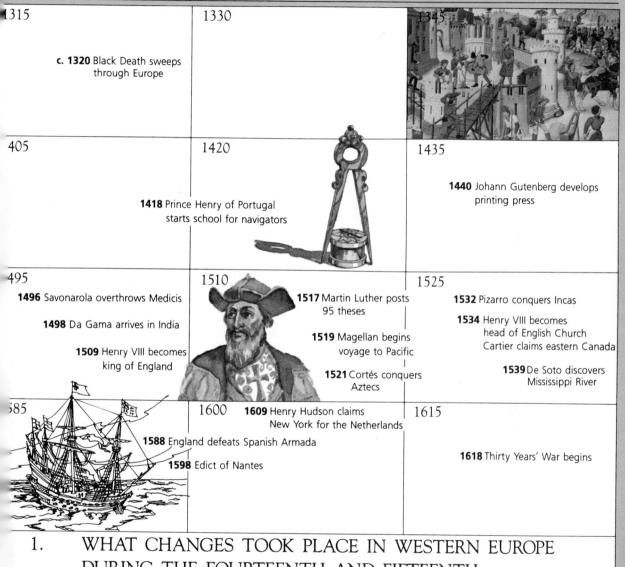

1315	1330	1345
c. 1320 Black Death sweeps through Europe		

1405	1420	1435
	1418 Prince Henry of Portugal starts school for navigators	**1440** Johann Gutenberg develops printing press

1495	1510	1525
1496 Savonarola overthrows Medicis	**1517** Martin Luther posts 95 theses	**1532** Pizarro conquers Incas
1498 Da Gama arrives in India	**1519** Magellan begins voyage to Pacific	**1534** Henry VIII becomes head of English Church Cartier claims eastern Canada
1509 Henry VIII becomes king of England	**1521** Cortés conquers Aztecs	**1539** De Soto discovers Mississippi River

1585	1600	1615
	1609 Henry Hudson claims New York for the Netherlands	
1588 England defeats Spanish Armada		**1618** Thirty Years' War begins
1598 Edict of Nantes		

1. WHAT CHANGES TOOK PLACE IN WESTERN EUROPE DURING THE FOURTEENTH AND FIFTEENTH CENTURIES?

2. WHAT DID WESTERN EUROPEANS LEARN ABOUT THE WORLD DURING THE AGE OF DISCOVERY?

Many changes began to take place in western Europe during the fourteenth and fifteenth centuries. The late Middle Ages came to an end, and western Europe began to enter the modern period. People wanted to learn more about their past. They wanted more freedom to think and act for themselves. Many no longer were willing to accept practices handed down from the Middle Ages. Scholars began to look for new sources of knowledge.

Many western Europeans began to question the Catholic Church and its teachings and to criticize the Church's wealth. They wanted a more personal relationship with God. They called for a **reformation**, or a change in the way the Church taught and practiced Christianity. Many differences of opinion arose about the type of changes needed. Eventually the differences led to a split in the Church which has lasted to the present time.

Western Europeans began to learn more about the world beyond Europe. Merchants discovered that there was a profit in trade with lands in South Asia and the Far East. This led explorers to look for a shorter and less costly route to these far-off lands. While they were searching, they discovered new continents and peoples. As a result, trade grew, and the people became wealthy. At the same time, Europe became the most powerful continent in the world.

CHAPTER 29

THE RENAISSANCE

Around 1300, scholars in western Europe developed a new interest in **classical writings,** or the writings of ancient Greeks and Romans. They improved their knowledge of Greek and Latin, studied old manuscripts, and tried to copy the writers' styles. They also began to accept some Greek and Roman beliefs.

One belief that scholars accepted was the importance of people. Because of this belief, scholars were called **humanists.** Their work led to a break with the thinking of the Middle Ages and to a new age called the Renaissance. During this period people became less concerned with the mysteries of heaven and more interested in the wonders of the world around them.

THE ITALIAN CITY-STATES

The first and leading center of the Renaissance was Italy, which consisted of small, independent city-states. The most important were Florence, Venice, and the Papal States. They had grown wealthy from trade and spent much of their wealth on the arts.

At first, each city-state was ruled by guilds of merchants and artisans. Later, powerful individuals or families took control. They often fought each other for land and wealth. At times they had difficulty gaining the people's loyalty and had to govern by force.

The leaders of the Italian city-states, however, were interested in more than power. They wanted to be remembered as wise, generous rulers. So they spent money on ceremonies and

RENAISSANCE ITALY

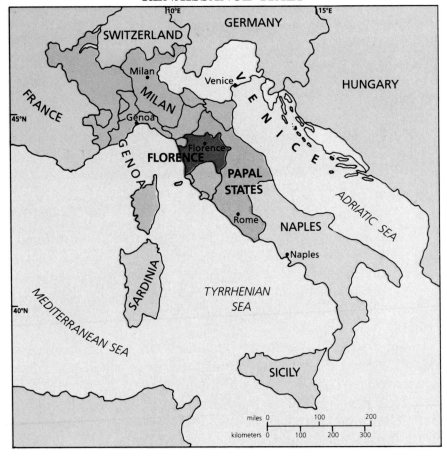

parades to impress and entertain the people. They ordered the building of churches and palaces. They also encouraged scholars, poets, and philosophers to set up palace schools to educate the sons of the wealthy. In these schools pupils learned to develop their minds and their bodies. They spent part of the day studying classical writings and learning good manners, and the rest of the day wrestling, fencing, and swimming.

1. What were the most important Italian city-states?
2. Who governed the Italian city-states at first? Who governed them later?
3. What did the rulers do to show they were wise and generous?

Renaissance Woman

ART   Art was an important part of life in Renaissance Italy. City-states were proud of their artists. They often competed for the services of painters and sculptors. The artists knew they were important and began to seek individual honor and fame. Each artist worked to develop a unique style.

Successful artists were supported by the rulers of the city-states. In return, the artists were expected to provide paintings and sculptures for the rulers' palaces and gardens. Artists often had workshops where they trained apprentices. Apprentices drew in backgrounds, costumes, or hands on paintings.

Renaissance artists developed their style by carefully studying ancient Greek and Roman art, science, mathematics, and the details of nature. They became especially interested in **perspective**, or a way of showing objects as they appear at various distances from the viewer. Above all, the artists studied the structure of the human body to learn how to draw the human form accurately. They began to experiment with light, color, and shade. As a result, they painted and sculpted works that were true to life and full of color and action.

Many artists painted portraits for the wealthy. The artists tried to paint people's facial features so they showed what the people were really like. At first, the portraits were painted only to honor dead or famous people. Later, any merchant with money could have a portrait painted.

One of the greatest Renaissance artists was Leonardo da Vinci. He is known for the "Mona Lisa," a portrait of an Italian noblewoman. He also painted a fresco called "The Last Supper" on the wall of an Italian monastery dining room. It shows Christ

RENAISSANCE ARTISTS

Michelangelo Buonarroti and Leonardo da Vinci were two leading artists of the Italian Renaissance. Michelangelo carved a very large statue of Christ and his mother known as the *Pièta* (left). Da Vinci, on the other hand, tried to capture the personality of an Italian noblewoman in the *Mona Lisa* (right).

What people supported the work of Italian Renaissance artists?

and his disciples at their final meal before Christ's death. In these works Da Vinci tried to reveal people's thoughts and feelings in addition to showing their physical appearance.

Da Vinci was a scientist as well as an artist. He filled notebooks with drawings of inventions far ahead of the times. Da Vinci designed the first parachute and made drawings of flying machines and mechanical diggers.

Another outstanding artist was Michelangelo Buonarroti, who is known for his paintings on the ceiling and altar wall of Rome's Sistine Chapel. He also sculpted the "Pieta," which shows the dead Christ in the arms of His mother. Although Michelangelo studied ancient Greek and Roman sculpture, he went beyond the ancients in the presentation of the human body. His figures are large and muscular and create a sense of motion.

1. How was an artist regarded during the Italian Renaissance?
2. What did Leonardo da Vinci contribute to Renaissance art?
3. What did Michelangelo contribute to Renaissance art?

CITY LIFE Most Italian Renaissance cities had narrow paved streets with sewers in the middle. Merchants and shopkeepers lived on the top floors of buildings that housed their shops. The wealthy built homes in the classical style with large, high-ceilinged rooms. In the center of the homes stood courtyards filled with statues, fountains, and gardens. Most people in the cities, however, were poor. They worked for low wages and lived in rundown areas.

The center of city life was the *piazza*, or central square. There markets were set up, and merchants traded goods. There

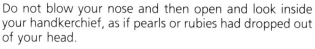

RENAISSANCE MANNERS

Do not blow your nose and then open and look inside your handkerchief, as if pearls or rubies had dropped out of your head.

Do not offer anyone a fruit from which you have already taken a bite.

Do not tell sad stories at parties or mealtimes. If someone starts talking this way, gently and politely change the subject and talk about something more cheerful.

Do not brag about honors, wealth, or intelligence.

Do not speak while yawning.

Do not clean your teeth with your napkin or your finger.

Do not lie all over the dinner table or fill both sides of your mouth with so much food that your cheeks stick out.

Do not undress, comb, or wash your hair in front of others.

Do not stick out your tongue, rub hands together, or groan out loud.

Do not talk too much, especially if your knowledge is small.

people gathered to talk to friends and to carry out business dealings. On holidays the people often watched or took part in parades and ceremonies.

Families were close-knit. Most family members lived and worked together in the same neighborhood. Families arranged marriages as if they were business deals. Women stayed at home, ran the household, and raised children. Men spent long hours at work, talking in the streets, and in taverns.

Most men dressed in tights and simple tunics. Some also wore cloaks and caps. Women dressed in simply cut, flowing dresses with tight bodices and high necklines. The rich usually wore brightly colored clothing made from expensive silks and velvets and trimmed with fur.

1. Who lived in Italian Renaissance cities?
2. What took place in the piazza?
3. How did Renaissance Italians view family life?

FLORENCE   The Italian Renaissance began in Florence, which was ruled by the Medici family. One of its most famous members was Lorenzo de Medici, who became the ruler of Florence in 1469. He made the city a center of art and learning. Artists, poets, painters, and philosophers flocked there to

DAILY LIFE IN FLORENCE
The Medici family sponsored festivals to entertain the people of Florence. This Renaissance painting shows the horse races held every spring.
What was the center of social life in an Italian Renaissance city?

benefit from Lorenzo's generous support. As a result of the city's prosperity and fame, Lorenzo was known as "the Magnificent."

About 1490, Florence's trade started to decline. Merchants began to complain that Lorenzo was too strict and spent too much money. Poor Florentines began to grumble about their poor housing and the shortages of food.

The people looked for an escape from their problems. They thought they found it in religion as preached by a monk named Savonarola. Savonarola accused the Medicis of not ruling justly. He gained the people's support, and he overthrew the Medicis in 1494.

Lorenzo de Medici

Savonarola did not like the gaiety and loose life of the Renaissance. He thought Renaissance attitudes were ruining Florence. On his advice the new government banned parties, gambling, swearing, and horse-racing. Savonarola's supporters also burned paintings, fancy clothes, musical instruments, and classical books.

By 1498, the people of Florence had tired of Savonarola's strict ways, and he was hanged for heresy. After his death, the Medicis returned to power. But Florence's greatness had passed.

1. Who governed Florence during the Renaissance?
2. Why was Lorenzo de Medici called "the Magnificent"?
3. What changes did Savonarola bring to Florence? How did his rule end?

ROME   During the fourteenth and fifteenth centuries, the power of the Popes declined. But they wanted to show Europe's kings that the Church was still powerful. So they began to rebuild Rome, which was one of the cities of the Papal States. They had large churches and palaces built with great gardens and fountains. The buildings were decorated with paintings, tapestries, and sculptures. Piazzas and wide streets were built in areas which until then had been in ruins. Scholars were brought from all over to collect and gather many scripts for the Pope's library.

Most Popes were not very religious. They acted more like political rulers than church leaders. They sent representatives to other states and countries, collected taxes, raised armies, and fought wars.

In 1492 Rodrigo Borgia became Pope Alexander VI. He did this by bribing cardinals to vote for him. Pope Alexander was very ambitious. His goal was to make central Italy a kingdom ruled by the Borgia family. Alexander's children tried to help him achieve his goal. His daughter Lucretia married a noble and became known for her lively parties and her love of music and other arts. She also gained a reputation for poisoning her enemies.

Alexander spent a great deal of money building an army for his favorite son, Cesare. The army marched through Italy and took control of many towns. All of this territory was lost, however, after Alexander's death in 1503. By this time, Rome had regained much of its ancient glory. It soon replaced Florence as the center of the Renaissance.

1. Why was Rome rebuilt?
2. What were most Popes like during the Renaissance?
3. What was Pope Alexander VI's main goal?

VENICE'S GRAND CANAL
The Grand Canal winds through the center of Venice. Palaces and churches built during the years of Venice's prosperity stand along both sides of the canal.
How did Venice's location affect its growth and prosperity?

VENICE The Renaissance did not reach Venice until the late sixteenth century. This was because the Venetians had looked to Constantinople rather than to western Europe for art and literature.

Rabelais

Venice was different from most Italian city-states in other ways too. Its palaces and churches were built on 117 islands linked by nearly 400 bridges. Instead of streets Venice had canals. The largest and busiest was the Grand Canal, which was lined with brightly colored stone and marble palaces. The Rialto, or the business area of Venice, also lay along a stretch of the Grand Canal. There traders from Europe and the East crowded the docks to buy and sell goods.

Venice was ruled by a few merchant aristocrats. They controlled the Senate and the Council of Ten. The Council passed the laws and chose the *doge*, or official ruler. The doge had little power and had to follow the Council of Ten's instructions.

Venetians were expected to place loyalty to their city above concern for their families and themselves. They had to report their neighbors' suspicious actions to the Council of Ten. Citizens who wanted to accuse someone of treason placed a letter stating the charges in special boxes found throughout the city. The accused were immediately arrested and brought before the Council. Council members then met in secret to study the evidence, listen to witnesses, and decide guilt or innocence.

1. Why did the Renaissance come late to Venice?
2. What made Venice different from other Italian cities?
3. How were Venetians expected to behave?

FRANCE

In 1494 the French began invading Italy. French kings became fascinated by Italian architecture, art, and fashions. In the sixteenth century King Francis I arranged for Italian artisans to work for him in France. He became the first monarch outside of Italy to collect Italian paintings and sculpture. He and many of his nobles hired Italian architects to design *chateaux*, or castles, which they had built along the Loire River.

Francis I also encouraged French writers to model their works on those of Italian writers. Every evening Francis and his family listened to readings of the latest books. Many were

RENAISSANCE PEOPLE

Baldassare Castiglione	1478–1529	Italian writer; wrote book on rules of behavior for ladies and gentlemen
Benvenuto Cellini	1500–1571	Italian goldsmith; sculptor; wrote about his life and times
Vittoria Colonna	1492–1547	Italian author; wrote religious and love poems
Nicolaus Copernicus	1473–1543	Polish astronomer; stated that earth moves around sun
Albrecht Durer	1471–1528	German artist; painted and made woodcuts of religious and classical subjects
Beatrice d'Este Isabella d'Este	1475–1497 1474–1539	Italian noblewomen; sisters; honored for their learning; supported writers and artists
Galileo	1564–1642	Italian scientist; did experiments on the motion of objects; used telescope to discover new facts about universe
Niccolo Machiavelli	1469–1527	Italian politician; writer; wrote advice to rulers on how to keep power
Thomas More	1477–1535	English scholar; saint; government official; refused to accept king as church head
Petrarch	1304–1374	Italian poet; scholar; restored study of classics; collected manuscripts; wrote letters and poems
Raphael	1483–1520	Italian religious painter; and architect;
Andreas Vesalius	1514–1564	Italian surgeon; founder of modern medicine; wrote first full description of human body

written by Rabelais, a physician-monk who believed that humans were not tied down by their past and could do whatever they wished. In his most popular book, *The Adventures of Gargantua and Pantagruel*, Rabelais' main characters were two comical giants. He used them to poke fun at outdated customs of the time.

1. What did Francis I do to encourage Renaissance thought in France?
2. What did Rabelais believe?

GERMANY AND THE NETHERLANDS

The Renaissance also spread to the wealthy trading centers of Flanders and Germany. There religious scholars learned Greek and Hebrew so they could understand the earliest versions of the Bible. Their Bible studies helped them appreciate early Christian beliefs and practices. They decided that over the years many church leaders had interpreted the Bible to suit their own beliefs. As a result, the scholars wanted reforms that would simplify Church teachings. One outspoken scholar, a Dutchman named Erasmus, translated the New Testament into Greek. He also wrote *Praise of Folly*, a book that attacked corrupt church leaders and practices.

NORTHERN RENAISSANCE LIFE

The towns of Germany and the Netherlands learned Italian ways and soon made their own contributions to the Renaissance. Northern European painters became known for their detailed scenes of daily life. In this painting wealthy merchants and their wives are playing a card game.

What other contributions did Northern Europe make to the Renaissance?

Typesetter

Northern European artisans made many discoveries during the Renaissance. About 1440 a German named Johann Gutenberg developed a printing press. It used carved letters which could be moved around to form words and then could be reused. Now books could be quickly printed by machine rather than slowly written by hand. This made many more books available and also made them cheaper to buy. Since printing came at a time when many townspeople were learning to read and think for themselves, new ideas spread rapidly.

Northern European artists studied Italian works of art and then developed their own styles. They painted scenes from the Bible and daily life in sharp detail. Hubert and Jan Van Eyck, two brothers from Flanders, discovered how to paint in oils. Soon others began to do the same. The colors of the oil paintings were deep, rich, and glowing with light.

1. What Church reforms did German and Flemish scholars want to make?
2. How did the printing press change European life?
3. What did northern European artists contribute to the art of painting?

SPAIN

The Renaissance took root in Spain in the late fifteenth and early sixteenth centuries. It was influenced by the close ties between the Catholic Church and the government. The leading Church official, Cardinal Jimenez, was a loyal supporter of the monarchy. He was also interested in promoting learning. He founded universities and welcomed students from other countries. He helped scholars produce a new translation of the Bible that had columns of text side-by-side in Greek, Latin, and Hebrew.

In 1555 Philip II became king. He was very religious and did not trust the work of scholars. Many were accused of heresy by the Inquisition and burnt at the stake. Philip had architects build him a new granite palace just outside Madrid. Called El Escorial, it served as a royal court, art gallery, monastery, church, and tomb for Spanish royalty. El Escorial soon became a symbol of the power and religious devotion of Spanish rulers.

Despite strong church and government controls, the arts prospered. The city of Toledo became a center for painters and poets. One artist who settled there was a Greek whom the Spaniards called El Greco. His style was different from that of other artists. He painted figures with very long bodies, parts of which stretched beyond normal size. Some art experts claim that El Greco copied his style from Byzantine artists. Others insist he painted as he did because of an eye problem that distorted his vision.

The theater was also popular in Renaissance Spain. Miguel de Cervantes, a surgeon's son, was one of the most noted writers of the time. He wrote many plays, short stories, and novels. His novel *Don Quixote*, about the adventures of a comical knight and his peasant squire, is still popular today. Cervantes used the characters to poke fun at the code of chivalry and to show the problems people have in trying to reach their ideals in a cruel, uncaring world.

1. What influenced the Renaissance in Spain?
2. How were scholars treated in Spain during the rule of King Philip II?
3. What made El Greco's paintings different from those of other Renaissance painters?
4. What did Cervantes try to show in *Don Quixote*?

ENGLAND

Peace did not come to England after the Hundred Years War. Instead, in 1455 two noble families, York and Lancaster, began a struggle for the throne. The York symbol was a white rose and the Lancaster symbol a red rose. For this reason the struggle was called the Wars of the Roses.

When the wars ended in 1485, a family called the Tudors, who fought on the Lancastrian side, took over the English throne. The first Tudor king, Henry VII, prepared the way for the Renaissance. He strengthened the monarchy and encouraged trade, which made England peaceful and prosperous.

Henry VII's efforts were continued by his son, Henry VIII, who became king in 1509. He enjoyed and encouraged art, literature, music, hunting, and parties. He even composed his own music. Under his rule, English nobles and merchants began to look to Renaissance Italy for guidance in politics, diplomacy, and behavior.

The English Renaissance reached its height, however, during the reign of Henry VIII's daughter, Elizabeth I. She

William Shakespeare

THE TUDORS

King Henry VIII of England (left) and his daughter Queen Elizabeth I (right) were members of the Tudor family, which ruled England from 1485 to 1603. Henry and Elizabeth both were strong and forceful rulers, but they were able to gain the respect and love of their people.

What was life like in England during the rule of the Tudors?

became queen in 1558 when she was 25 years old. Elizabeth often made journeys throughout the kingdom so that the people could see her. During her travels she stayed at the homes of nobles who entertained her with banquets, parades, and dances. Elizabeth was said to dance for hours without getting tired, even when she was well into old age. Poets and writers praised Elizabeth in their writings. Sons of merchants, lawyers, and landowners copied Italian clothes and manners and came to court to capture her attention and favor.

Poetry, music, and drama became a part of daily life. Most nobles wrote poetry. People of all classes enjoyed singing ballads and folksongs. Many played such musical instruments as violins, guitars, and lutes.

The people of Renaissance England were especially fond of plays. Not since ancient Greece had so many plays been written and performed. About 1580, the first theaters were built in

England. Their stages stood in the open air. Most of the audience, however, sat under a roof or some sort of covering. Those who could not afford to pay for seats stood in the **pit**, or open area in front, and on the sides of the stage. Since there were no lights, plays were performed in the afternoon. They attracted large crowds which were sometimes hard to control.

One of the best known English **playwrights**, or authors of a play, was William Shakespeare. He drew ideas for his tragedies and comedies from the history of England and ancient Rome. He often used Italian scenes, characters, and tales in his plays. Many experts consider Shakespeare the greatest writer and the greatest playwright in the English language.

1. What did the Tudors do to encourage the Renaissance in England?
2. What were English theaters like?
3. What did William Shakespeare write about?

ENGLISH MUSIC AND THEATER

The English Renaissance was known for poetry, music, and drama. William Shakespeare presented many of his plays at London's Globe Theater (left). The English also enjoyed cultural events at home. Costumed actors and a musical group perform at a banquet given by a wealthy merchant (right).

What kind of music was popular in Renaissance England?

CHAPTER REVIEW

SUMMARY

1. Around 1300, western European scholars developed a new interest in classical writings and started a new age called the Renaissance.
2. The Renaissance began in the Italian city-states.
3. A great deal of importance was placed on art in Renaissance Italy.
4. Leading Renaissance artists included Michelangelo Buonarroti and Leonardo da Vinci, who was also a scientist.
5. The Italian Renaissance began in Florence, which was ruled by the Medicis.
6. In 1494 a monk named Savonarola gained the Florentines' support and overthrew the Medicis.
7. Savonarola was overthrown in 1498, and the Medicis returned to power.
8. To prove to European kings they were still powerful, Popes rebuilt Rome.
9. By the early sixteenth century Rome replaced Florence as the center of the Italian Renaissance.
10. By the late sixteenth century the Renaissance reached Venice.
11. After 1494 the Renaissance spread to France, where it was encouraged by King Francis I.
12. The Renaissance spread to Flanders and Germany, where religious scholars worked for Church reforms.
13. About 1440 a German named Johann Gutenberg invented a printing press, which helped new ideas spread throughout Europe.
14. In the late fifteenth and early sixteenth centuries the Renaissance spread to Spain, where it was influenced by close ties between the Church and the government.
15. The English Renaissance reached its height during the reign of Elizabeth I, which began in 1558.
16. People of Renaissance England were very fond of plays, especially those written by William Shakespeare.

BUILDING VOCABULARY

1. *Identify the following:*

Renaissance	Venice	Johann Gutenberg	Miguel de Cervantes
Leonardo da Vinci	Grand Canal	Hubert Van Eyck	*Don Quixote*
Michelangelo	Rialto	Jan Van Eyck	Wars of the Roses
Florence	Council of Ten	Cardinal Jimenez	Henry VII
Lorenzo de Medici	Francis I	Philip II	Henry VIII
Savonarola	Rabelais	El Escorial	Elizabeth I
Papal States	Erasmus	El Greco	William Shakespeare
Pope Alexander VI			

2. *Define the following:*

classical writings	perspective	doge	pit
humanists	piazza	chateaux	playwrights

REVIEWING THE FACTS

1. In whose writings were Renaissance scholars interested?
2. Where was the first and leading center of the Renaissance?
3. Why were Renaissance scholars called humanists?
4. What did rulers of Italian city-states do to encourage learning and art?
5. What were some features of Italian Renaissance art?
6. Why did the Florentines turn to Savonarola?
7. Why did Rome replace Florence as the center of the Renaissance?
8. What did Flanders and Germany contribute to the Renaissance?
9. Of what did El Escorial become a symbol?
10. How did the Wars of the Roses get their name?

DISCUSSING IMPORTANT IDEAS

1. Do you think Lorenzo de Medici deserved to be called "the Magnificent"? Explain.
2. Do you approve or disapprove of the Venetian system of justice? Explain the reasons for your answer.
3. Why was the printing press an important invention?
4. If you could go back in time and talk with a Renaissance artist or ruler, whom would you choose? What questions would you ask?

USING MAPS

Refer to the map on page 434, and answer the following questions:

1. What is the subject of the map?
2. What body of water is directly east of Italy?
3. What island is off the southwest tip of Italy?
4. What country was directly north of the city-state of Milan?
5. Which city was located within the Papal States?
6. Which Italian city-state was bordered on the east by Hungary and on the north by Germany?
7. About how far is the city of Florence from the city of Genoa?
8. What Italian city-state also includes an island?
9. What city-state was located about 46° north and 12° east?

CHAPTER 30

THE REFORMATION

The Catholic Church did not adjust to the many changes taking place in western Europe during the fifteenth and sixteenth centuries. Many Europeans began to call for a reformation.

Church leaders, however, were too busy with their own and government affairs to introduce reforms. They did not like the reformers' ideas, especially those that threatened their power. As a result, the Church faced a serious threat to its unity.

MARTIN LUTHER

One reformer who challenged the Church was a German monk named Martin Luther. Luther, born in 1483, was the son of peasants. His family wanted him to be a lawyer, but he was more interested in religion and became a monk instead.

As a monk, Luther faithfully followed Church teachings and practices. Yet he could find no peace of mind. He wondered how God would judge his actions and if he would go to heaven when he died.

While studying the New Testament, Luther found the answer to the questions that had been troubling him. He decided that trusting in Jesus, rather than doing good works, would save people from their sins. Through faith in Jesus, people could be certain that God loved them and that they would go to heaven.

Luther's ideas soon brought him into conflict with the Church. In 1517 Pope Leo X wanted money to rebuild St. Peter's Church in Rome. To obtain the money, he sold **indulgences**, or pardons for sin. Luther felt that by selling indulgences, the Pope was leading people to believe they could buy God's forgiveness for their sins. One night Luther posted a list of 95 **theses**, or statements, to the door of the castle church in Wittenburg, Germany. In the list he stated that only God could forgive sins, and he challenged anyone who disagreed to **debate**, or argue, with him.

The Pope hoped to convince Luther to give up his ideas, but Luther refused. He began to openly attack other Catholic beliefs. He said Popes could make mistakes and the only true guide to religious truth was the Bible, which every Christian had the right to read. He also said that every Christian had the right to pray to God without the aid of a priest.

In 1520 Pope Leo condemned Luther's teachings and excommunicated him. Leo insisted that the German emperor, Charles V, try Luther as an outlaw. Charles was loyal to the Church, but he relied on German princes who supported Luther. To keep the princes' loyalty, Charles agreed to give Luther a fair trial. At the same time, he secretly promised the Pope that Luther would be condemned. In 1521 Luther was tried by the German diet in Worms. When he refused to give up his beliefs, he was condemned for heresy.

1. What did Martin Luther believe could save people from their sins?
2. What did Luther do to protest the sale of indulgences?
3. Why did the Pope excommunicate Luther?
4. What happened to Luther at Worms?

A DIVIDED GERMANY   By 1524 most people in northern Germany supported Luther. They left the Catholic Church and formed the Lutheran Church.

The Lutheran princes of Germany had strong, well-organized armies, which Charles V could not defeat. In 1555, when Charles realized he could not force the princes' territories to become Catholic, he agreed to sign a treaty. Known as the Peace of Augsburg, the treaty said there could be both Catholic and Lutheran churches in Germany. It also allowed the prince of each German state to decide which church would be allowed in his territory. The Peace kept German Lutherans and Catholics from fighting each other for nearly 50 years.

1. What did the people of northern Germany do to show they supported Luther's teachings?
2. What did the Peace of Augsburg allow?

MARTIN LUTHER

In 1521 the Pope decreed that Luther was no longer a Catholic. Luther, however, refused to give up his beliefs, claiming that they were based on the teachings of the Bible. Here he defies the Pope and burns the decree.

How did Luther's teachings influence the future of European Christianity?

GENEVA
Geneva is located at the western end of Lake Geneva in Switzerland. Under John Calvin the city became known as a leading center of Protestantism. This drawing shows Geneva as it appeared shortly after the time of Calvin.
In what ways was Geneva an important center of Protestantism?

A New Religion

Luther's ideas soon spread to other areas of Europe. People in Scandinavia founded Lutheran churches. Preachers and merchants in Switzerland, a small country in central Europe, set up churches known as Reformed.

Because they protested against Catholic teachings, Lutheran and Reformed churches were called Protestant. Instead of priests, Protestant religious leaders were called **ministers**. They did not have the same religious powers as Catholic priests had, and they spent more time preaching from the Bible. They held worship services in the language of the area instead of in Latin. This made rituals easier for people to understand and to share in.

1. To what areas of Europe did Luther's ideas spread?
2. Why were some churches called Protestant?
3. What were some differences between Catholic and Protestant practices?

John Calvin

JOHN CALVIN   The most powerful Reformed group was in the Swiss city of Geneva. There, John Calvin, a French reformer, set up the first Protestant church governed by a council of ministers and elected church members. Calvin also wrote books which became a guide for Protestants throughout Europe.

Calvin believed that God's will was written in the Bible, which ministers had the right to interpret. The ministers also had the right to make sure everyone obeyed God's will. Calvin had the Geneva town council pass laws to force people to follow strict rules of behavior. They could not dance, play cards, go to the theater, or take part in drinking parties. Those who refused to accept Calvin's teachings were put in prison, executed, or sent away.

Calvin was supported by rich merchants whom the new religion taught to work hard and to save money. With their help, he worked to improve Geneva. Streets and buildings became noted for their neatness and cleanliness. New workshops opened, providing more jobs for people. Persecuted Protestants from all over Europe found safety in Geneva. Young men came to study at the school Calvin had founded to train Reformed ministers. Many of the refugees, students, and ministers later returned to their own countries to establish Reformed churches.

1. What did Calvin believe?
2. How did Calvin's beliefs influence Geneva?

CATHOLIC REFORM

While Protestants formed new churches, Catholic reformers worked to improve their Church. Many reformers came from Spain and Italy, the leading countries of the Catholic reform movement.

One of the most famous Catholic reformers was Ignatius of Loyola. In 1521 he gave up his life as a Spanish noble to serve God and the Catholic Church. He later organized a group of followers to spread Catholic teachings. In 1540 the group founded the Society of Jesus, an organization whose members were called Jesuits. Jesuits wore the black robes of monks and lived simply. They set up schools, helped the poor, and preached to the people. They also taught in universities, worked as missionaries, and served as advisors in royal courts.

The Jesuits used reason and good deeds to defend the Catholic Church against Protestant criticisms. They worked hard to strengthen the faith of Catholics and to bring Protestants back to the Church. As a result of their efforts, the Church regained the loyalty of people in such eastern European countries as Poland, Bohemia, and Hungary.

1. What were the leading countries of the Catholic reform movement?
2. Why did Ignatius of Loyola give up his life as a noble?
3. How did Jesuits serve the Catholic Church?

COUNCIL OF TRENT

During the sixteenth century, the Council of Trent helped to renew Catholic life and worship. Bishops and other church leaders from throughout Europe attended the Council. In this painting the delegates debate an issue at a Council meeting held in the cathedral at Trent.

How did the Council respond to Protestant criticisms of the Catholic Church?

THE COUNCIL OF TRENT   At the same time the Jesuits worked for reform, the Pope took steps to strengthen the Church against Protestants. He called a council of bishops to discuss reforms and to defend Catholic teachings. The council met at different times between 1545 and 1563 at Trent, a town in northern Italy. The Council of Trent put an end to many Church practices reformers had criticized for centuries. The selling of indulgences was forbidden. Clergy were ordered to follow strict rules of behavior. Each diocese was told to build a **seminary**, or a school to train priests.

The Council responded to Protestant protests by explaining Catholic doctrine more fully. The bishops said that good works, as well as faith, helped Christians get to heaven. They declared that the Church alone decided how the Bible was to be interpreted and that mass would be said in Latin only.

1. Why did the Pope call the Council of Trent?
2. What did the Council of Trent do?

A Middle Way

The reformation of the Church in England was led by the monarch, not by religious leaders. It started as a political quarrel between the Tudor king, Henry VIII, and the Pope. Religious beliefs did not play a part in the struggle until later.

1. How did the English reformation begin?

Catholic Saints

THE BREAK WITH ROME   The trouble between Henry VIII and the Pope began in 1526. At that time Henry was married to Catherine of Aragon, the daughter of Ferdinand and Isabella of Spain and the aunt of German emperor Charles V. Henry and Catherine had one child, Mary. Now that Catherine was older, Henry feared she could no longer have children. And Henry wanted a son to succeed to the throne.

At the same time, Henry had fallen in love with Anne Boleyn, a young woman of the court. He wanted the Pope to end his marriage to Catherine so that he could marry Anne and hopefully have a son. When the Pope refused, Henry declared that the Pope no longer had power over the Church in England.

In 1534 the English Parliament passed a law stating that the king was head of the English Church. Any English church leader who did not accept the law would stand trial as a traitor. Thomas

HENRY VIII AND ANNE BOLEYN
Henry's determination to marry Anne Boleyn led to a political break with the Pope. This painting shows Henry with Anne at the home of Thomas Wolsey, the king's chief adviser.
How was Henry eventually able to marry Anne Boleyn?

Cranmer, the Archbishop of Canterbury and the most important church leader in England, supported Henry. Cranmer helped Henry end his marriage to Catherine. Henry married Anne Boleyn and made her queen of England. A few years later Henry had Anne executed for treason. He then married Jane Seymour, who died shortly after giving Henry the son he wanted. Anne's only child had been a girl, Elizabeth.

1. Why did Henry VIII want to end his marriage to Catherine of Aragon?
2. What happened when the Pope refused to end the king's marriage?

EDWARD AND MARY When Henry VIII died, his 9-year-old son became King Edward VI. Since Edward was too young and sick to rule, a council of lords governed England for him. Most of the council members were Protestants, and they brought Protestant doctrines into the English Church. Thomas Cranmer supported the lords. He wanted the people to have an orderly

MARY TUDOR

Queen Mary tried to return England to the Roman Catholic Church. She forbade Protestant worship and passed laws against heretics. More than 300 Protestants, among them Thomas Cranmer, were burned at the stake during her short rule. Here Mary meets Protestant leaders kept as prisoners in the Tower of London.
How did the English people view Mary's actions against Protestants?

form of Protestant worship. So he wrote a worship service in English called the *Book of Common Prayer*. It was used in all the churches in England.

When Edward died in 1553, the council tried to name a Protestant noblewoman queen. The attempt failed because the English refused to accept a ruler who was not a Tudor. They wanted Henry's daughter Mary as their monarch.

Mary was Catholic, and, as soon as she became queen, she accepted the Pope as head of the English Church. She insisted that all English men and women return to the Church. When many Protestants refused, she began to persecute them. The people turned against her, calling her "Bloody Mary."

Mary was married to King Philip II of Spain. The English were unhappy about the marriage because Spain was England's enemy and the leading Catholic power in Europe. They feared that the Spanish king and the Pope would become the real rulers of England. The people decided that England would remain free only if it became a Protestant country.

1. What happened to the English Church under Edward VI?
2. Why did Thomas Cranmer write the *Book of Common Prayer*?
3. What did Mary expect the people to do as soon as she became queen? How did the people feel about this?

ELIZABETH'S CHURCH   Mary died in 1558 without a child to succeed her. Her half-sister Elizabeth became queen. Elizabeth I was Protestant and, with the help of Parliament, ended the Pope's authority in the English Church.

Elizabeth was popular with the people. She knew they did not agree about what beliefs the English Church should have. Still, she wanted the country to be united. So she worked to set up a church that would appeal to as many people as possible.

Elizabeth and Parliament decided that the English Church should be Protestant, but with some Catholic features. The monarch would be head of the Church, which would use Cranmer's prayer book and teach Protestant beliefs. At the same time, however, bishops would handle daily affairs as they did in the Catholic Church. Many rituals would also be similar to those of the Catholic Church.

Most English people were pleased with the blend of Protestant belief and Catholic practice. The few groups of Catholics who were not pleased remained outside the English Church. Some groups of Protestants also opposed Elizabeth's Church, but they did not leave it. Because they wanted to purify the Church of Catholic ways, they became known as Puritans.

1. What were the main features of the English Church under Elizabeth I?
2. What groups remained outside of the English Church?

WARS OF RELIGION

By the middle of the sixteenth century, most northern Europeans were Protestants, while most southern Europeans were Catholics. European monarchs had used religion to help unite their peoples and to build powerful nations. The ruler and people of each nation were expected to belong to the same church. Those who refused to be of the same religion as

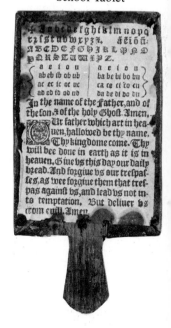

School Tablet

William Tyndale
1492–1536
English Protestant leader;
translated New Testament into
English

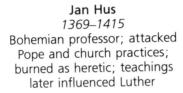

Jan Hus
1369–1415
Bohemian professor; attacked
Pope and church practices;
burned as heretic; teachings
later influenced Luther

John Wycliffe
1320–1384
English priest; declared
that Bible, not Church, was
authority

Ulrich Zwingli
1484–1531
Swiss preacher; ordered
removal of images from
churches; set up new church
ritual; closed monasteries

Charles Borromeo
1538–1584
Archbishop of Milan; saint;
founded order of priests and
wrote on Catholic doctrine

Teresa of Avila
1515–1582
Spanish nun; saint; reformed
convents and wrote on
religious life

John Knox
1515–1572
Scottish religious leader;
set up church based on
Calvin's ideas

everyone else were persecuted. This led to a great deal of bitterness between people of different faiths. Differences in religion also led to wars between nations. Toward the end of the sixteenth century, the people of Europe entered a period of religious wars that lasted until 1648.

1. What led to the wars of religion?

THE ARMADA   Under Elizabeth I, England became the leading Protestant power in Europe. Spain, under Philip II, remained the leading Catholic power. Philip knew that if he could conquer England, Protestant Europe would be open to Catholic control. So he ordered the building of the Spanish Armada, a fleet of 130 ships. The Armada's main strength lay in its large **galleons**, or heavy ships with square-rigged sails and tall decks. In the spring of 1588 the Armada sailed toward England. Its main purpose was to help the Spanish armies on the continent cross over to the English shore.

Elizabeth knew what was coming and prepared England for war. She had naval commander John Hawkins reorganize the English fleet, remodeling old ships and building new ones. He formed a new navy of 134 fighting ships and merchant vessels. Most of the ships were smaller than the Spanish ones, but they had larger guns and more ammunition. Expert sailors handled the English ships with a great deal of skill. One sailor, Sir Francis Drake, was known for his overseas voyages and his capture of Spanish ships.

The English knew they had to make the Spanish ships break formation. Their chance came when the Spanish anchored off the coast of Europe to wait for their armies to meet them. That

---

SPANISH ARMADA

In 1588 the English fleet faced the Spanish Armada in the English Channel. In this painting, English fire ships move toward the Armada. This action broke the curved formation of the Spanish ships and made possible a successful English attack. How did the defeat of the Armada affect Protestantism in Europe?

Catherine de Medici

night the English set fire to eight small ships and sent them into the Spanish fleet. As the fire ships reached the Armada, the Spanish ships broke formation and began to drift. The English were able to successfully fight the Spanish ships one by one.

The Spanish soon realized they were defeated. Short of food and water, they decided to return to Spain. But the voyage was long and difficult. Only one-half of the Armada reached home.

The English celebrated their victory with bonfires and parades. Although Spain was still a powerful enemy, the English had proved they could defend themselves.

The English gained respect throughout Europe as champions of the Protestant cause. The defeat of the Armada brought about many changes. One was that it allowed northern Europe to remain a Protestant stronghold.

1. Why did Philip II of Spain want to conquer England?
2. How did the English defeat the Spanish Armada?

THE HUGUENOTS   While most people in sixteenth-century France were Catholic, many nobles, lawyers, doctors, and merchants were Protestants. These French Protestants, who were called Huguenots, followed Calvin's teachings.

In 1534 King Francis I, who was Catholic, forbade Huguenots to worship freely. He wanted all French people to follow the same religion. Catholics began to persecute Huguenots, and by 1562 a civil war broke out. By then, Henry III had become king. Since he was too young to rule, his mother, Queen Catherine de Medici, ruled for him.

Catherine tried to keep the peace by showing favor first to one group and then to the other. She finally decided to support the Catholics. In 1572 she allowed Catholic nobles to kill the leading Huguenots in Paris. Catholic mobs in other parts of France began to kill Protestants and burn their homes. Many Protestants left the country. The few who remained to carry on the fight were led by Henry of Navarre, a Huguenot prince.

In 1589 King Henry III was killed. Henry of Navarre, who was next in line for the throne, became King Henry IV. He wanted to gain the loyalty of the people. Since most French were still Catholic, he decided to convert. Henry finally ended the fighting between Protestants and Catholics. He made Catholicism the national religion, but at the same time made life easier for Protestants. In 1598 Henry signed the Edict of Nantes, which granted Huguenots freedom of worship. As a result, France became the first European nation to allow two religions to exist within its boundaries.

1. What led to the civil war in France in 1562?
2. How did Catherine de Medici help the Catholic cause?
3. How did Henry IV end the fighting in France?

THE LOW COUNTRIES   The Low Countries were part of the Spanish Empire. The people were divided into Protestants and Catholics. Neither group liked Philip II's harsh rule. They wanted freedom from heavy taxes and Spanish laws. Philip, however, profited from the wealth and trade of the Low Countries. He wanted to keep them under Spanish control.

THE RELIGIONS OF EUROPE

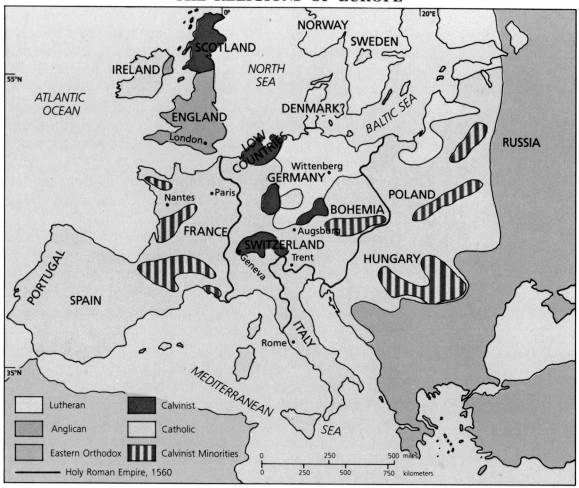

Philip also wanted everyone in his empire to be Catholic. So he set up the Inquisition in the Low Countries to stamp out Protestantism. In 1568 Protestants in the northern provinces revolted. Philip sent troops in to restore order. They were joined by French Catholics from the southern provinces.

The struggle did not come to an end until 1648. At that time, it was decided that the southern provinces, known today as Belgium, were to remain Catholic and loyal to Spain. The northern provinces, known today as the Netherlands, were to be an independent Protestant nation.

1. Why did the Low Countries resent Spanish rule?
2. Why was Philip II determined to keep the Low Countries part of the Spanish Empire?
3. What was the result of the war in the Low Countries?

THE THIRTY YEARS' WAR

During the 1590's and early 1600's, the German states began to quarrel over the terms of the Peace of Augsburg. They formed alliances based on religion. The Catholic alliance was led by the German emperor Ferdinand II.

One Protestant state that resisted Ferdinand was Bohemia. In 1618 the Protestant nobles of Bohemia revolted against Ferdinand, choosing a German Protestant prince as their new king. Ferdinand's armies crushed the Bohemians in a fierce battle, and Ferdinand proclaimed himself king of Bohemia. He forbade Protestant worship and sent Jesuit preachers throughout the country to win the people back to the Catholic Church.

The revolt in Bohemia soon grew into the Thirty Years' War, during which half the armies of Europe fought in Germany. First the king of Denmark and then the king of Sweden invaded Germany. They were Protestants who wanted to stop the spread of Catholicism. They also hoped to conquer territory in northern Germany. When the Swedes were finally defeated in 1634, the French became involved. Although France was Catholic, it entered the war on the Protestant side. France's entry into the war led to a change in the nature of the war. It became less a war over religion and more a fight for land and wealth.

The German people suffered great hardships during the war. Finally, in 1643, after a serious defeat, the German emperor asked for peace. In 1648 representatives of European nations signed the Peace of Westphalia, which ended the war.

As a result of the Thirty Years' War, the German emperor lost much of his power to German princes, while France emerged as a strong nation. After this war, Europeans no longer fought over religion. Instead, nations became interested in gaining power through trade and control of overseas territories.

1. What led to the Thirty Years' War?
2. What change did France's entry into the war bring about?
3. What effect did the Thirty Years' War have on Europe?

CHAPTER REVIEW

SUMMARY

1. In 1517 Pope Leo X sold indulgences to raise money to rebuild St. Peter's Basilica in Rome.

2. A German monk named Martin Luther objected to the sale of indulgences and also attacked other Catholic beliefs.

3. In 1521 Luther was tried by the German diet and condemned for heresy.

4. By 1524 most people in northern Germany had left the Catholic Church and formed the Lutheran Church, which supported Martin Luther's beliefs.

5. The Peace of Augsburg of 1555 allowed the prince of each German state to decide whether the people in his territory were to be Catholic or Lutheran.

6. Luther's ideas spread to parts of Europe and became Protestantism.

7. Protestant religious worship was held in the local language rather than in Latin.

8. The French reformer, John Calvin, established a center of Protestantism in the Swiss city of Geneva.

9. While Protestants formed new churches, Catholic reformers worked to improve their Church.

10. In 1540 Ignatius of Loyola founded the Society of Jesus, whose members became famous teachers and missionaries.

11. Between 1545 and 1563 the Council of Trent reformed many Church practices.

12. In England church reformation started as a political quarrel between Henry VIII and the Pope.

13. Mary Tudor tried to force the English people to return to the Catholic Church.

14. With the help of Parliament, Elizabeth I decided that the English Church would be Protestant but with some Catholic features.

15. In 1588 the English defeated the Spanish Armada, which allowed northern Europe to remain Protestant.

16. In 1562 a civil war broke out in France between Catholics and Protestants called Huguenots.

17. In 1598 the Edict of Nantes made France the first European nation to allow two religions to exist within its borders.

18. Protestants in the northern provinces of the Low Countries revolted against Spanish rule in 1568.

19. The Thirty Years' War, which lasted from 1618 until the Treaty of Westphalia was signed in 1648, was the last religious war fought in Europe.

BUILDING VOCABULARY

1. *Identify the following:*

Martin Luther	John Calvin	Thomas Cranmer	Spanish Armada
Pope Leo X	Ignatius of Loyola	*Book of Common*	Huguenots
Lutheran Church	Society of Jesus	*Prayer*	Francis I
Peace of Augsburg	Council of Trent	Edward VI	Catherine de Medici
Reformed Church	Henry VIII	Mary Tudor	Henry of Navarre
Protestant	Catherine of Aragon	Philip II	Edict of Nantes
Geneva	Anne Boleyn	Elizabeth I	Thirty Years' War

2. *Define the following:*

indulgences	debate	ministers	seminary
theses			galleons

REVIEWING THE FACTS

1. Why did Martin Luther object to the sale of indulgences?
2. What were Protestant churches called?
3. What rules of behavior did Calvin make the people of Geneva follow?
4. What organization did Ignatius of Loyola found?
5. According to the bishops at the Council of Trent, who decided how the Bible was to be interpreted?
6. Why did Henry VIII have his wife Anne Boleyn executed?
7. Why did Mary Tudor become known as "Bloody Mary"?
8. Why did the people of England decide that England had to become a Protestant country?
9. How did the defeat of the Spanish Armada help the Protestant cause?
10. Why is the Edict of Nantes important?

DISCUSSING IMPORTANT IDEAS

1. Do you think you would have liked living in Geneva at the time of John Calvin? Why or why not?
2. Do you agree or disagree that Mary Tudor's marriage to Philip II would have affected the English religion? Explain.
3. Do you approve or disapprove of the way in which Elizabeth I organized the English Church? Give reasons for your opinion.
4. If you had been Henry IV, would you have converted to Catholicism? Explain.

USING MAPS

Refer to the map on page 463, and answer the following questions:

1. What is the time period of the map?
2. What was the main religion of Scotland?
3. What religion was found in Norway?
4. Where were the Calvinist minorities?
5. About how far is Nantes from Augsburg?
6. What areas were Anglican?
7. What city is about 46° north and 6° east?
8. What religions were found in Germany?

CHAPTER   31
AGE OF DISCOVERY

B y the fourteenth century Italy controlled Europe's trade with India and the Far East, including China and the East Indies. Muslim merchants sailed from Africa across the Indian Ocean and brought back spices and fine cloth, which they sold to Italian merchants for a good profit. The Italians sold the goods to other Europeans for an even larger profit.

In time the cost of goods became so high that only the wealthiest people could afford them. The Europeans needed the goods. They needed metal to make coins, and their own supply was running out. They used the spices to make their salted and spoiled food edible. Europeans living in countries that bordered the Atlantic Ocean began to look for a direct sea route to India and the Far East. In addition to their desire for precious metals, spices, and silk, they wanted to spread Christianity to other parts of the world.

MAP-MAKING

Map-makers of the fifteenth century often went on voyages of exploration. They contributed to Europe's knowledge of the world by drawing maps of newly discovered areas. This map, made about 1530, shows the southern tip of South America.
What other developments in the Age of Discovery helped make navigation easier?

By this time, mapmakers, who had been studying the information that came from early explorers like Marco Polo, had begun to make more accurate maps. Meanwhile, the large amount of trade between northern and southern Europe had created a need for bigger and better ships. New ships were built that were faster, less likely to sink, and could carry heavier loads. Navigation was made easier by the improvement of instruments that sailors had used for hundreds of years. One of these was the **compass**, or an instrument with a magnetic needle that always points north. Another was the **astrolabe**, or an instrument that measures the angle of the stars. These developments aided the Europeans in their search for new sea routes.

THE PORTUGUESE

Prince Henry the Navigator, the brother of the king of Portugal, had heard from African merchants about discoveries of gold in Africa. He became eager to explore the western coast of Africa. Henry hoped to find more than gold. He also hoped to find a new route to the Far East. He saw this as a way to extend Portuguese trade and power. It would also increase European knowledge about geography and spread Christianity.

In the early fifteenth century, Henry started the first European school for navigators in Sagres, Portugal. He gathered together Portuguese, Spanish, Jewish, Arab, and Italian mathematicians, chartmakers, astronomers, and sea captains. They came, taught Portuguese sailors all they knew, and left. In the process they helped Henry create better charts, improve naviga-

---

PIONEERS OF EXPLORATION

Prince Henry studied geography and planned explorations at his school in Portugal (left). The Italian explorer Amerigo Vespucci (right) benefited from Henry's efforts. He made three voyages to the New World, which was later named "America" in his honor.

Why did Europeans of the fifteenth century become interested in explorations?

tional instruments, and put together more detailed astronomical tables.

At the same time, Henry worked with others to design and to build better ships. The result was the Portuguese **caravel**. It was a combination of the heavy, square-rigged European ship and the lighter, slimmer Arabian one. The caravel was faster and easier to handle than earlier ships.

Henry sent parties of explorers down Africa's west coast. They discovered the Gold Coast and Cape Verde, as well as the Azore, Madeira, and Canary Islands. They used the islands as supply stations for further explorations.

The explorers found gold dust, ivory, and slaves in Africa. Some explorers began to take more interest in trade than in discovery. The trade brought new wealth to Portugal. Henry watched Portugal grow into a powerful nation. But when he died in 1460, his caravels had gone only a third of the way down the west coast of Africa.

Exploration went on after Henry's death, but more slowly. In 1473 the equator was crossed. Europeans discovered that the sea did not boil and was not the home of great monsters. Gradually and carefully the Portuguese made their way south along the African coast.

In 1487 Bartholomew Dias readied ships for a long, hard voyage. Included for the first time was a supply ship with enough water and food for a long voyage. Dias touched at several points on the African coast before strong winds blew him away from the coast southward. After the storm ended, Dias went on to reach Africa's east coast, without knowing that he had been blown around the tip of the continent. On his return home he knowingly sailed around the southern tip of Africa, which he called the Cape of Storms. The king of Portugal later renamed it the Cape of Good Hope because now the Portuguese knew they could reach the Far East by sailing around Africa.

1. What did Prince Henry do to encourage exploration?
2. Why was Dias' trip important?

VASCO DA GAMA   In the summer of 1497 a Portuguese **cavalier**, or noble, named Vasco da Gama, led a **convoy**, or group, of four ships down the Tagus River from Lisbon, Portugal. His ships were of a type called *naus* that had been designed by Bartholomew Dias. Dias, in fact, accompanied da

Sextant

VASCO DA GAMA

Vasco da Gama opened up India to Portuguese exploration and trade. Here he meets with an Indian ruler at Calicut.

What difficulties did da Gama and his party have in opening up new trade routes?

Gama as far as Cape Verde. Da Gama had orders from the king to "proclaim the Christian faith" and to "wrest kingdoms and new states from the hands of the barbarians."

After three months at sea, da Gama's party rounded the Cape of Good Hope. By then many of the crew were sick. Their water smelled, and their food was spoiling. Still they continued on, sailing north along the east coast of Africa toward the island of Mozambique. The island was a Muslim trading center. There they saw ships loaded with cargoes of cloves and pepper, gold, silver, and pearls and other precious stones. For the first time they saw a coconut, which they described as "fruit as large as a melon, of which the kernel is eaten." When the Muslims found out that da Gama and his party were Christians, they forced the Europeans to leave.

The next stop was Malindi in present-day Kenya. There da Gama's crew took on supplies and learned to make rope from coconut fiber. The king of Malindi sent da Gama a pilot to lead him to his final destination of Calicut, India.

On May 20, 1498, da Gama landed at Calicut. It was a port and trading center on the southwest coast of India. His arrival alarmed Arab and Persian merchants there. They feared that Portugal would take over the trade between Africa and India. There was an attempt made to kill da Gama. In August da Gama decided there was no use staying longer. He and his crew loaded what spices they could and started for home.

COLUMBUS IN AMERICA

Columbus accidentally discovered America while looking for a westward route to India. He and his captains landed on the island of San Salvador and claimed the land for King Ferdinand and Queen Isabella of Spain.

What type of people did Columbus find in the New World?

The trip back took three months. During that time the ships were threatened by storms, and many of the men died of **scurvy**, or a disease caused by the lack of vitamin C. When da Gama finally arrived in Lisbon in 1499, he was greeted with great rejoicing and rewards.

Da Gama's voyage opened the way for later explorations and for a new era of increased trade. Before long Lisbon became one of the major trade centers of Europe.

1. Why did Vasco da Gama go to India?
2. How was da Gama treated in Calicut? Why was he treated that way?
3. What were the results of da Gama's voyage to India?

Spanish Soldier

THE SPANISH

The Spanish were as interested as the Portuguese in the wealth that could be obtained from India and the Far East. But, until the late fifteenth century, they were too busy trying to gain their freedom from the Moors. By 1492 Spain was a Christian country united under King Ferdinand and Queen Isabella. It was ready to enter the race for new trade routes.

1. Why did Spain wait until the late fifteenth century to enter the race to find new trade routes?

CHRISTOPHER COLUMBUS   Christopher Columbus, the son of a weaver, was a skilled navigator from Genoa, Italy. He believed he could reach India by sailing westward. Like most educated people of his time, Columbus believed the world was round, not flat. He had tried for seven years to convince different rulers to allow him to make a voyage to prove his point. He had asked for help from King John II of Portugal but was turned down. Finally, in 1492, Queen Isabella of Spain listened to his plan, the Enterprise of the Indies, and agreed to support him.

Columbus set sail from Palos, Spain in August, 1492, with three small ships—the *Niña*, the *Pinta*, and the *Santa Maria*—and a crew of around 90 sailors. After a stop at the Canary Islands, he set a westward course for Asia.

At first the voyage went well. But the longer they were at sea, the more afraid Columbus' crew became. They urged

Columbus to turn back. When he refused, they began to threaten **mutiny**, or an overthrow of ship officers. Columbus promised to turn back if land was not sighted within three days. The night of the second day a lookout on the *Pinta*, the lead caravel, spotted land. In the morning Columbus landed at San Salvador, an outer island in the Bahamas. Columbus thought he had reached the Indies, so he called the people living on the island Indians. For this reason, Native Americans are still called Indians.

Columbus spent several months traveling around the waters of the Bahamas, Cuba, and Hispaniola, an island which today consists of Haiti and the Dominican Republic. In Cuba he found Indians smoking cigars. Thus, Europeans had their first contact with tobacco.

On Christmas Eve the *Santa Maria* went aground on a reef and was wrecked. Columbus had his crew use the wood from the *Santa Maria* to build a fort. This was the first European settlement in the New World.

In January, 1493, Columbus boarded the *Niña* and headed back to Spain. He brought with him pieces of gold, parrots, cotton, other plants and animals, and a few Indians. In Spain he was received with great honors. Six months later he was leading a fleet of 17 ships and 1500 men on another search for the Asian mainland.

Columbus made four voyages in all. He explored the South American coast and Central America almost as far as present-day Panama. He returned from his last voyage in 1504. Two years later he died still convinced he had found the way to Asia. He never realized he had discovered the New World.

1. How did Columbus believe he could reach India?
2. Where did Columbus actually land on his first voyage?
3. What did Columbus achieve during his four voyages?

THE TREATY OF TORDESILLAS   Columbus had seen some Indians wearing gold jewelry. He wrote to Ferdinand and Isabella and told them that great riches could be found in the islands he had discovered. The Spanish monarchs were worried that Portugal might try to take these riches away from Spain. So they asked Pope Alexander VI to help settle their claims.

In 1493 the Pope drew a **papal line of demarcation**, or an imaginary line from the north to the south pole some 300 miles,

Spanish Explorer

SPANISH TRADE

By 1530, Spain had replaced Portugal as the leader in the race for land and trade routes. Colonies were set up to obtain gold and other products for Spain and its European holdings. Here the first ship loaded with sugar from the Spanish colonies arrives at the port of Antwerp in the Spanish Netherlands.

How did the Treaty of Tordesillas help Spain build an empire?

or about 480 kilometers, west of the Azore Islands. Spain was to have the lands west of the line. Portugal was to have the lands east of the line.

The Portuguese, however, did not like the division and protested. They called for a meeting. As a result, in 1494 the Treaty of Tordesillas was drawn up. It moved the line about 500 miles, or about 800 kilometers, further west. Thus, Portugal was able to claim Brazil. Other nations, like England and the Netherlands, paid no attention to the Pope's rulings. They explored and claimed land where they wished.

1. Why did the Spanish monarchs ask the Pope for help?
2. According to the papal line of demarcation, what lands was Spain to have? What lands was Portugal to have?
3. How did the Treaty of Tordesillas benefit Portugal?

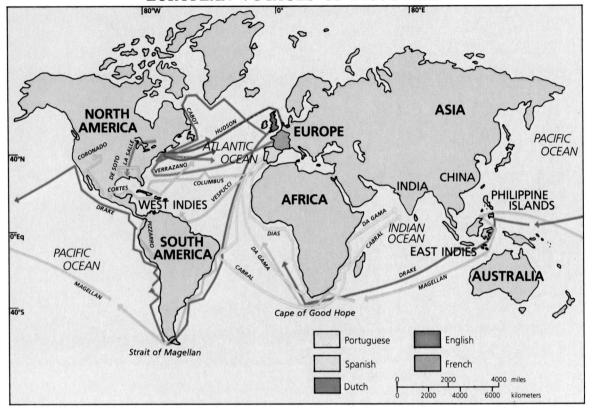

THE CONQUISTADORES   The Spanish were eager to explore their new possessions. Over the next few years a series of Spanish **conquistadores**, or conquerors, set out to find the gold Columbus had talked about and to explore the new lands.

In 1513 Ponce de Leon set sail northward from the island of Puerto Rico and discovered and explored Florida. Between 1519 and 1521 Hernando Cortés invaded Mexico and conquered the Indian empire ruled by the Aztec chief Montezuma. Cortés and his troops took large amounts of gold from the Indians to send back to Spain.

Between 1531 and 1533 Francisco Pizarro invaded Peru and conquered the Inca Empire. Like Cortés, Pizarro took great treasures of gold and silver from the Indians. In 1539 Hernando de Soto sailed from Puerto Rico to Florida and explored westward. He found no gold, but he discovered the Mississippi River. In 1540 Francisco Coronado led an army overland from

Mexico into the present-day United States. He discovered the Grand Canyon, but he returned without finding any treasure. Thus, between 1492 and 1550 Spain explored an area from North America through Central America and the West Indies to South America.

1. What were Spanish conquistadores looking for in the New World?
2. What were some of the discoveries made by the conquistadores between 1513 and 1540?

FERDINAND MAGELLAN   In 1517 Portugal controlled the eastern route to the Indies. As a result, Portugal was growing rich. This angered the Spanish king. So when a Portuguese explorer and sea captain named Ferdinand Magellan offered to find Spain a western route to the Indies, the king accepted the offer. He wanted Spain to become as famous and wealthy as Portugal.

In 1519 Magellan set sail from Spain. He commanded a fleet of five ships and a crew of 270. In October of the following year Magellan sailed through a stormy strait at the tip of South America. Today the strait is named after Magellan. The trip took one month.

From the strait Magellan sailed on into a great body of calm water which was known as the Great South Sea. Magellan renamed it the Pacific Ocean. By this time Magellan had lost two of his ships. He continued, however, until he reached the Marianas Islands. The trip took three months. Conditions were terrible. The drinking water was spoiled and smelled foul. The biscuits were full of worms. The sailors were forced to eat sawdust from the ship boards and leather soaked in the sea and grilled on embers. By the time it reached the Marianas the fleet was almost helpless. The crew was suffering from scurvy and had no food of any kind.

Inca Gold Figure

After they had rested and eaten, Magellan and his crew set a northwest course for the Philippine Islands. There he converted the king and many others to Christianity. Magellan was killed in the Philippines when he tried to force the chief and people of a nearby island to convert to Christianity. Shortly after, several other Europeans were killed, and two more ships were lost.

The one remaining ship continued on into the Indian Ocean and around Africa. It finally arrived in Seville, Spain, in 1522 with 18 men and a load of spices. Theirs was a great accomplishment. They had proved that the world is round. The voyage opened the Pacific Ocean to European ships. More important, it proved beyond a doubt that the lands Columbus discovered were not Asia but a New World.

1. What did Ferdinand Magellan offer to do for Spain?
2. What did Magellan actually do?
3. What did Magellan's voyage prove?

EXPLORERS

Name	Country	Achievements
Amerigo Vespucci	Spain Portugal	explored Atlantic coast of South America, 1497–1503; one of first to believe he had reached a new world
Pedro Álvarez Cabral	Portugal	discovered Brazil and sailed west to India, 1500–1501
Vasco Núñez de Balboa	Spain	first European to sight eastern shore of Pacific Ocean, 1513
Alvar Núñez Cabeza de Vaca	Spain	explored Florida and Gulf plains from Texas to Mexico, 1528–36
Juan Rodríguez Cabrillo	Spain	explored Pacific coast to Drake's Bay near San Francisco, 1542
Richard Chancellor	England	reached Moscow in search of northeast passage to Asia; opened trade with Russia, 1553–54
John Davis	England	explored west coast of Greenland in search of northwest passage to Asia, 1573
Sir Francis Drake	England	first Englishman to sail around the world, 1577–80
Father Jacques Marquette Louis Joliet	France	explored Mississippi Valley to mouth of Arkansas River, 1673
Vitus Bering	Russia	explored coasts of Alaska and northeast Asia; discovered Bering Straight and Bering Sea, 1728–41

SEARCH FOR A NORTHWEST PASSAGE

Even after the New World was discovered, the English, French, and Dutch continued to look for another route to the Far East. Since the Portuguese and the Spanish controlled the southern sea lanes, the others decided to look for a northwest passage.

English merchants persuaded their king to send the Italian navigator John Cabot west by a northern route. In 1497 Cabot set sail with a handful of men. He reached the mouth of the St. Lawrence River and explored the coasts of New England, Newfoundland, and Nova Scotia. His voyage established claims for England in the New World.

In 1524 the French hired Giovanni da Verrazano, an Italian, to find a northwest passage. He sailed along the Atlantic coast from North Carolina to New York harbor. Ten years later Jacques Cartier, a French navigator, sailed up the St. Lawrence River as far as present-day Montreal. This gave the French a claim to eastern Canada.

In 1576, Martin Frobisher, an English **sea dog**, or captain turned pirate, began his search for the northwest passage. He passed through the dangerous icebergs off the coast of Greenland and fought a storm that almost wrecked one of his three ships. Frobisher finally discovered the bay that today is named after him.

In 1609 the Dutch sent Henry Hudson, an English navigator, to locate the passage. He discovered the Hudson River and then sailed up it to present-day Albany. Hudson was never seen again, but his voyage gave the Dutch their claim in the New World.

All of these voyages failed in their search to find the northwest passage to the Far East. They did, however, accomplish something important. They established claims in the New World for England, France, and the Netherlands.

1. Why did the English, French, and Dutch continue to look for another route to the Far East after the discovery of the New World?
2. How did the English, French, and Dutch plan to sail to the Far East?
3. What did these voyages accomplish?
4. What claims did the English, French, and Dutch make?

CHAPTER REVIEW

SUMMARY

1. By the fourteenth century, European nations bordering the Atlantic Ocean began to look for a direct sea route to India and to the Far East.

2. The Europeans were interested in obtaining spices and silk and in spreading Christianity throughout the world.

3. The development of better maps, ships, and instruments for navigation helped the Europeans in their voyages of discovery.

4. In the early fifteenth century, Prince Henry of Portugal started the first school in Europe for navigators.

5. By 1473 Portuguese ships had crossed the equator.

6. In 1487 Bartholomew Dias sailed around the Cape of Good Hope.

7. Between 1497 and 1499 Vasco da Gama sailed from Portugal around Africa to India and back again.

8. Between 1492 and 1504 Christopher Columbus made four voyages westward across the Atlantic to what he thought was Asia but was actually the New World.

9. In 1494 the Treaty of Tordesillas divided newly found lands between Spain and Portugal.

10. In the first half of the sixteenth century, Hernando Cortés and Francisco Pizarro conquered the Aztec and Inca empires of Mexico and Peru and explored much of the New World for Spain.

11. Between 1519 and 1522 Ferdinand Magellan sailed around the world, proving that the lands Columbus discovered were not Asia but the New World.

12. Between 1497 and 1609 the English, French, and Dutch sent many explorers to the New World to search for a northwest passage to the Far East.

BUILDING VOCABULARY

1. *Identify the following:*

Prince Henry	Treaty of Tordesillas	Hernando de Soto	John Cabot
Bartholomew Dias	Ponce de Leon	Francisco Coronado	Jacques Cartier
Cape of Good Hope	Hernando Cortés	Ferdinand Magellan	Martin Frobisher
Vasco da Gama	Francisco Pizarro	Strait of Magellan	Henry Hudson
Christopher Columbus			

2. *Define the following:*

compass	cavalier	scurvy	papal line of
astrolabe	convoy	mutiny	demarcation
caravel	naus	conquistadores	sea dog

REVIEWING THE FACTS

1. Why did the European nations that bordered the Atlantic Ocean begin to look for a new, direct sea route to India and the Far East?

2. What three things helped European explorers in their search for new sea routes?

3. In what ways was the design of the caravel an improvement over earlier ships?

4. What were some of the problems that European explorers had to face on their voyages of discovery?

5. Why did Columbus' crew threaten mutiny against their officers?

6. How did Europeans first learn about tobacco?

7. What was the first European settlement in the New World?

8. How long did it take Magellan's ship to sail around the world?

9. What are three bodies of water named after European explorers?

10. What did the voyages in search of a northwest passage to the Far East accomplish?

DISCUSSING IMPORTANT IDEAS

1. Do you think Prince Henry of Portugal deserved the title "Henry the Navigator"? Explain.

2. Would you have enjoyed being one of the sailors on Magellan's voyage around the world? Why or why not?

3. Why do you think Queen Isabella of Spain agreed to support Columbus after others had turned him down?

4. What do you think competition between nations had to do with the European voyages of discovery?

USING MAPS

Refer to the map on page 476, and answer the following questions:

1. Which countries sent explorers on voyages of discovery?

2. For what country did De Soto sail?

3. Where is the Strait of Magellan?

4. About how far is the Strait of Magellan from the Cape of Good Hope?

5. What body of water is located east of Africa?

6. To what country did Cabral sail?

7. What is the latitude and longitude of the West Indies?

8. What area did Coronado explore?

THE AZTECS

For more than 400 years Mexico was the home of the Aztec Indians. About 1100 the Aztecs were one of several Indian peoples living there. They lived by farming. Their most important crop was corn. But they also grew beans, squash, peppers, and tobacco.

Over time, through trade and military conquest, the Aztecs expanded until they controlled all of central Mexico. They forced the peoples they conquered to pay tribute in the form of gold, precious stones, rubber, and feathers.

The Aztecs built a great capital city called Tenochtitlán on an island in Lake Texcoco. With its gleaming pyramids, huge temples and palaces, gardens, schools, and markets, the city was a place of beauty. About 100,000 people lived there. They dressed with elegance in feathered capes and cloaks of many colors. Women wore flowers and dyed feathers in their hair.

Tenochtitlán was the capital of a military empire. Every young man was expected to go to war. Warriors fought with swords and bows and arrows made of hard wood and volcanic glass. They wore armor made of cane and padded cotton.

War and religion were closely linked. The people worshipped two main gods. One was a rain god that represented the peaceful life of farming. The other was a sun god that represented war and expanding empire. The sun god demanded human sacrifices. The Aztecs believed that

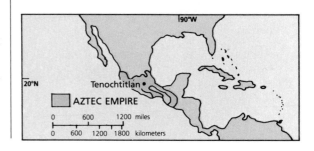

AZTEC EMPIRE

if they did not make the sacrifices, the sun would not rise in the morning. So they had to make war to conquer more people to sacrifice.

The Aztecs also were skilled in arts, crafts, and poetry. They made pottery with a double face that showed the two sides of Aztec life. On one side was a face with full cheeks. On the other was a death skull. They also carved stone images of their gods. One of the most famous is the Sun Stone, a large disk that shows the days of the Aztec week. In the center is the sun god.

In 1521 Spanish soldiers invaded Tenochtitlán. With their guns and horses, they easily defeated the Aztecs. Once they were conquered, the Aztecs lost their empire. Many died of European diseases the Spanish brought with them. Before long, the Aztec Empire completely collapsed. Today Mexico City stands where Tenochtitlán once stood.

1. What were some features of Tenochtitlán?
2. Why did the Aztecs make war?
3. How did the Aztec Empire come to an end?

UNIT REVIEW

SUMMARY

1. A renewed interest in Greek and Roman writings and ideas in the fifteenth and sixteenth centuries led to a new age called the Renaissance. During the Renaissance the arts and the philosophy of humanism flourished.

2. The Renaissance began in Florence, spread to other Italian cities, and then to other parts of Europe.

3. Out of the Renaissance came the Reformation. It was marked by a desire to reform the Roman Catholic Church.

4. In the sixteenth century the first Lutheran and Reformed churches were founded by Protestants. They were followers of a new religion based on the reforms of the German monk Martin Luther.

5. Catholic reformers worked to bring about changes in the Church, but the results did not satisfy many Protestants or Catholics. Soon there was bitterness and war between them.

6. The desire to find new trade routes to the Far East and to spread Christianity led western Europeans to undertake a series of ocean voyages. The voyages resulted in the discovery and exploration of the New World.

REVIEWING THE MAIN IDEAS

1. Describe the cultural, religious, and political changes that took place in western Europe during the Renaissance and the Reformation.

2. Discuss the factors that led to the voyages of discovery and the effect that the discoveries had on the people of western Europe.

DEVELOPING SKILLS

When examining data, historians have to be able to recognize whether or not it will support a **generalization**, or a general statement about the topic. Sometimes an item is factually correct but has nothing to do with a generalization. Other times an item has a direct relationship to a generalization because it helps explain why the generalization is true or provides evidence to support what the generalization says.

This exercise is designed to give you practice in the skill of recognizing whether or not a particular statement supports a generalization. Read the two generalizations below and the five statements that follow each. Tell whether each statement does or does not support the generalization.

1. The Renaissance was a period during which art and literature became very important.
   a. The Renaissance began in city-states.
   b. The printing press was invented during the Renaissance.
   c. A leading figure of the Renaissance was Leonardo da Vinci, who painted the *Mona Lisa* and *The Last Supper*.
   d. Miguel de Cervantes' novel *Don Quixote* was written in Spanish.
   e. The Medici family ruled Florence for many years.

2. The years between 1517 and 1648 were marked by great religious turmoil in western Europe.
   a. In 1517 Martin Luther objected to the sale of indulgences and also attacked other Catholic beliefs.
   b. Martin Luther was a German monk who studied the Bible.
   c. In 1553 the Peace of Augsburg allowed German princes to decide whether the people in their territories were to be Catholic or Lutheran.
   d. Catholic Spain sent a huge Armada against Protestant England in 1588.
   e. Elizabeth I of England was the younger daughter of Henry VIII.

SUGGESTED UNIT ACTIVITIES

1. Plan a trip to a newspaper or printing company to see printing presses in operation. Compare them with Gutenberg's press.

2. Bring in several pictures of Renaissance art to show the class. Provide information about each artist and an explanation of each picture.

3. Act out a scene from one of William Shakespeare's plays. Have a different classmate take each role.

4. Report on the English theater during the Renaissance and Reformation or on the life of Shakespeare, Luther, or Calvin.

5. Working in a group, write a play for class presentation based on the first voyage of Christopher Columbus. You might have three scenes: (1) Columbus at the court of Ferdinand and Isabella; (2) Columbus at sea on October 12, 1492; (3) Columbus landing in the New World.

SUGGESTED READING

Gerez, Toni, comp. *2-rabbit, 7-wind*. New York: Viking Press, 1971. Aztec poems.

Goodenough, Simon. *The Renaissance*. New York: Arco Pub., 1979. An account of life during the Renaissance.

Grant, Matthew G. *Champlain*. Mankato, Minn.: Creative Education, 1974. A biography.

Grant, Neil. *The Renaissance*. New York: Franklin Watts, 1971. A description of events and people in the development of the Renaissance.

Jensen, Malcolm. *Leif Erickson, the Lucky*. New York: Franklin Watts, 1979. A biography.

O'Dell, Scott. *The Hawk That Dare Not Hunt By Day*. Boston: Houghton Mifflin, 1975. A young boy helps smuggle an English translation of the Bible into England.

Syme, Ronald. *John Cabot and His Son Sebastian*. New York: William Morrow, 1972. A biography.

Ventura, Piero. *Christopher Columbus*. New York: Random House, 1978. A biography.

Villiers, Captain Alan. *Men, Ships, and the Sea*. Washington, D.C.: National Geographic Society, 1973. Basic information and not-so-well-known facts about explorers and others.

UNIT 11

1500	1515	1530
1500 Cabral claims Brazil		**1532** Portuguese establish first permanent settlement in Brazil **c. 1535** Spain becomes leading colonial power in Americas **1543**

1590	1605	1620
	**1603** James I becomes king of England **1607** First permanent English settlement at Jamestown **1608** Samuel de Champlain establishes French colony at Quebec **1619** Virginia House of Burgesses meets	**1620** Pilgrims settle at Plymouth Mayflower Compact **1625** Charles I becomes king of England **1628** Petition of Right **1630** Puritans **163**

1680	1695	1710
1682 William Penn founds Pennsylvania La Salle claims Mississippi **1688** Glorious Revolution		**1712** Thomas Newcomen develops first practical steam engine

1770	1785	1800
1770 Boston Massacre **1773** Boston Tea Party **1774** First Continental Congress **1775** Second Continental Congress **1776** Declaration of Independence **1779** James Hargreaves invents spinning jenny	**1789** U.S. Constitution French Revolution begins **1791** First French Republic **1793** Reign of Terror Eli Whitney invents cotton gin **1798** First use of mass production	

1860	1875	1890
1867 English working-class males gain vote		

THE CHANGING WORLD

545	1560	1575
		1580 Portugal claimed by Philip II of Spain
		1585 Sir Walter Raleigh founds English colony in North Carolina
opernicus states that planets evolve around sun		**1588** England defeats Spanish Armada

635	1650	1665
1642 English civil war begins		
1649 Oliver Cromwell rules England		
	1660 Charles II becomes king of England	
tablish Massachusetts Bay Colony		
glish Catholics found Maryland		

725	1740	1755
	1733 John Kay invents flying shuttle	**1763** Treaty of Paris
		1764 Sugar Act
		1765 Stamp Act Congress
		1767 Townshend Acts
		1769 James Watt perfects steam engine

15	1830	1845
	1829 George Stephenson builds locomotive	
	1831 Michael Farraday discovers properties of magnet	**1856** Henry Bessemer makes steel from iron

1. WHAT CHANGES IN GOVERNMENT TOOK PLACE IN THE WEST DURING THE SEVENTEENTH CENTURY?
2. WHAT ECONOMIC CHANGES TOOK PLACE IN THE WEST DURING THE EIGHTEENTH CENTURY?

The discoveries made in the late fifteenth and early sixteenth centuries led to many changes. The known world was suddenly larger. This meant greater opportunity for those willing to take it. For some European nations, the New World was the key to expanding their territory and gaining wealth and power. For some Europeans, it was a place where they could make a new life. As a result trade increased. So did the rivalry between nations.

During the seventeenth and eighteenth centuries, many people in Europe and in the New World felt their governments had too much control. They wanted changes and were willing to fight for them. In England, America, and France this led to **revolution**, or an attempt to overthrow or change the government. The revolutions, however, did not completely change how the people lived. But they did bring about greater political rights for a larger number of people.

In the eighteenth and early nineteenth centuries the western world experienced still another type of revolution—the **Industrial Revolution**. It involved the shift from animal and human power to machine power. It changed manufacturing and industry forever.

By the middle of the nineteenth century, the pattern and quality of life were different from what they had been in the past. There were changes in the way government was run, society was organized, people lived, and goods were produced.

NEW WORLD EXPANSION

The discoveries made in the late fifteenth and early sixteenth centuries expanded the world which Europeans knew to almost twice its size. Europeans willing to cross the ocean could find a new way of life and possibly new wealth.

From the early sixteenth to the eighteenth centuries, several western European countries set out to **colonize**, or build permanent settlements in, the New World. They wanted the riches of the New World. They thought such riches would bring them power. They also wanted the chance to spread Christianity to more people. Soon European nations were competing for land in the New World.

PORTUGAL

By 1510 the Portuguese had claimed all of Brazil. They had also established trading posts in Africa, India, southeast Asia, Malaya, and the Molucca, or Spice, Islands. They took most of the Asian coastal cities by force. Portuguese **men-of-war**, or warships armed with cannons, bombarded the coast. Then trained soldiers went ashore and took over the port. Shortly after, Christian missionaries arrived to convert the conquered people to Christianity. The missionaries passed on the learning of Renaissance Europe. Thus, ideas as well as trade goods were exchanged.

Portugal did not have a large enough population to send settlers to all its territories, some of which already had large populations. In addition, the hot, humid climate of the new trading posts was too uncomfortable for most Europeans. As a result, the Portuguese had to depend on their own sea power and the cooperation of conquered leaders to establish order and protect Portugal's interests.

1. How did the Portuguese acquire most of their trading posts?
2. What did Portuguese missionaries contribute to New World colonization?
3. Why did Portugal not colonize most of its settlements?

BRAZIL   In 1500 the Portuguese explorer Pedro Alváres Cabral claimed the land of Brazil for Portugal. Since no precious metals were found, Portugal did not pay much attention to the discovery.

Other countries, such as France, started raiding the area. They took away **brazilwood**, or a red wood that could be used to make dyes. When the Portuguese realized the value of the wood, they began to take more interest in Brazil. In 1532 they established the first permanent settlement there. The Portuguese king divided Brazil into 15 territorial strips called **captaincies**. Each strip was granted to a different noble Portuguese family.

The owners of the captaincies were called *donatarios*. They had the right to establish towns, distribute land, and organize armies. In return they promised to colonize their captaincies and to protect them from the French, Spanish, Dutch, and English.

Portugal sent large numbers of settlers to Brazil. During the sixteenth and seventeenth centuries, Portuguese sailors landed there and stayed on. Criminals were sent to work off their sentences. Soldiers and officials came to protect royal interests in the colony. Cattleherders arrived with herds and pushed inland looking for new pastures. Missionaries appeared looking for Indians to convert to Christianity. Gradually Brazil was divided into large **plantations**, or farms, most of which raised sugar cane. The plantations were controlled by **patriarchs**, or leading older members of the settlement. The word of the patriarchs was law, and they would put up with no interference.

Workers were needed to clear the forests and labor on the plantations. About 2 million Indians lived in Brazil when the Portuguese claimed the land. The settlers thought the Indians would supply all the labor they needed. So they made slaves of them. But so many of the Indians ran away or died in slavery that the settlers began bringing black slaves from Africa. The number of slaves grew until in some places there were at least 20 black slaves for every European.

By the end of the seventeenth century there was less demand for sugar. *Bandeirantes*, or fortune-hunters looking for runaway slaves and precious stones, began to appear. The Bandeirantes were the frontiersmen of Brazil. They established Portugal's claim to the far western and southern parts of Brazil.

Royal interest in Brazil heightened when gold was discovered there. The king sent workers and government clerks to inspect the mineral resources in the area and to make sure the king received one-fifth of each miner's gold. Gold, and later diamonds, brought still more people to Brazil and more wealth to Portugal. Brazil remained a Portuguese colony until the nineteenth century, when it gained independence.

1. Why did the Portuguese wait so long to colonize Brazil?
2. What did the donatarios promise to do with their land?
3. How did the Bandeirantes help the growth of Brazil?

LOSS OF EMPIRE   Around 1517 the Turks challenged the Portuguese power in the Indian Ocean. Like other Muslim

Inca Weaving

merchants, the Turks resented the Portuguese for taking over their spice trade. They sent two fleets against the Portuguese. Both were destroyed by superior Portuguese warships. As a result, Portugal continued to control much of the trade in the Indian Ocean and South China Sea.

By the middle of the sixteenth century, however, Portugal was losing control of its empire. The government was not well organized, and the conquered people resented the Portuguese for forcing Christianity on them. The Portuguese economy was not in good condition. It had been hurt when other European countries began to expand their trade. By the time the Portuguese king died in 1580 Portugal had little strength left. The king left no heirs, and the throne was claimed by Philip II of Spain.

MONTEZUMA AND CORTES

Montezuma II was the Aztec ruler when Cortés arrived in Mexico. This Spanish painting (left) shows Montezuma in his palace with his council of advisers and workers. Montezuma at first welcomed the Spanish to his capital (right). Later he distrusted them and plotted against Cortés.
What eventually happened to Montezuma and the Aztec empire?

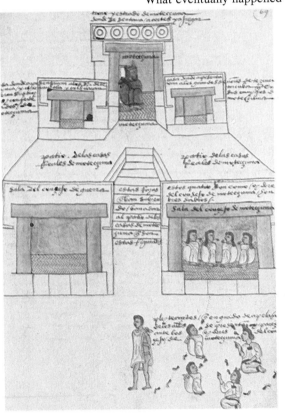 

Spain continued to rule Portugal until 1640, when it regained its independence. During that time the English and Dutch took over most of the Portuguese trading centers in southeast Asia. By the end of the seventeenth century, Brazil was the only important colony the Portuguese possessed.

1. Why did the Turks send two fleets against the Portuguese?
2. Why did the Portuguese begin to lose control of their empire in the sixteenth century?
3. What happened to the Portuguese trading centers and colonies when Spain took control of Portugal?

Spain

By 1535 Spain's colonies reached from southern North America through Central America and the West Indies to South America. Except for Brazil, most of South America was ruled by Spain. The Spanish also had trade interests in the Philippines, a group of islands in the Pacific near the East Indies.

Unlike Portugal, Spain had a strong, centralized colonial government. It also had a fairly large population. Spain sent thousands of settlers to its colonies in the New World.

1. Where in the New World were Spain's colonies located?

MEXICO AND PERU   When Spanish conquistadores led by Hernando Cortés landed in Mexico in 1519, the country was ruled by Aztec Indians. Within two years, Cortés had destroyed the Aztec empire.

Eleven years later the same pattern was followed in Peru. There Francisco Pizarro wrecked the Inca capital at Cuzco. Pizarro's soldiers took all the treasures they could find. Then they headed for the coast, where they built Lima, the "City of Kings."

Mexico and Peru set the style for other Spanish colonies. They were governed by the Council of the Indies, which met at the Spanish court. The Council made laws, acted as a court of final appeal, and chose officials to send to the New World. It even took charge of the Church in the Indies.

The colonies themselves were divided into two **viceroyalties**, or kingdoms—New Spain and Peru. Each viceroyalty was ruled by a **viceroy**, or person who represented the king and acted in his name.

The Spanish settlers mined and sent large amounts of gold and silver back to Spain. They also ran plantations that produced fruits, cocoa, vegetables, coffee, tobacco, tea, and sugar. The settlers forced the Indians to do all of the heavy work. Each Indian chief had to supply the Spanish with men. Groups of 50 to 100 Indians were given to Spanish landholders. Other groups farmed lands for the king or labored in the mines. Most were not treated well. Great numbers died of overwork, disease, and starvation.

By the middle of the sixteenth century, the colonists were divided into definite social groups. At the top were the *peninsulares*, or Spaniards born in Spain. Then came the **Creoles**, or those of Spanish descent born in the New World. Next came the **mestizos**, or people of mixed European and Indian ancestry. They were followed by the Indians. At the lowest level were blacks, **mulattoes**, or people of mixed European and black ancestry, and **zambos**, or people of mixed Indian and black ancestry.

The Catholic Church played a large part in Spanish colonization. It controlled most of the best land in the colonies. Although the Church itself did not pay taxes, it charged the people who rented or farmed its land a 10 percent income tax. Church leaders worked to better conditions for the Indians. The Church built and managed schools, hospitals, and asylums. It established the first two universities in the New World. One was the University of Mexico, which opened in 1551. The other was San Marcos University in Lima, which also opened in 1551. By 1636 there were three more universities in the Spanish colonies.

1. What happened to the Indian empires of Mexico and Peru when the Spaniards came?
2. What did the Council of the Indies do?
3. What role did the Catholic Church play in the Spanish colonies?

Gold Medallion

THE DECLINE OF EMPIRE   Spain received a great deal of wealth from the colonies. But it did not hold on to that wealth. Spain had few industries. The Inquisition had driven out the Jews and Muslims who had been the backbone of Spanish industry. As a result, most of the gold and silver sent to Spain went to northern Europe to pay for manufactured goods.

The Spanish also had trouble transporting gold and silver from their colonies to Spain. Ships loaded with the precious metals were robbed at sea by English, French, and Dutch **privateers**, or pirates. English sea dogs robbed Spanish treasure ships with the blessing of their queen, Elizabeth I. One of the most popular and successful sea dogs was Sir Francis Drake, who later became the first Englishman to sail around the world. When Philip II's Armada was defeated by the English in 1588, Spain lost its power in the Atlantic. This opened the New World to colonization by England, France, and the Netherlands.

1. How did the Spanish spend much of their colonial wealth?
2. Why did the Spanish have trouble transporting gold and silver from the New World to Spain?
3. How did the Spanish lose their power in the Atlantic?

SIR WALTER RALEIGH

Sir Walter Raleigh (left) was a popular nobleman at the palace of Elizabeth I. His efforts led to English attempts to colonize North America. The ornamental globe (right) shows the various groups of stars that were used by the first colonists to find their way on voyages across the Atlantic.

What difficulties did the English face in establishing New World colonies?

ENGLAND

Like Portugal and Spain, England began to look to the New World for gold and silver. English nobles and merchants also saw it as a place to get the raw materials they had to buy from other countries. With enough gold, silver, and raw materials, the English could establish a favorable **balance of trade**. This meant England would be able to sell more products to other countries than it would have to buy from them. The English would no longer have to depend on other countries for their needs.

The English also had other reasons for wanting colonies in the New World. England had such a large population that jobs were becoming scarce. New colonies meant more jobs. Religion was another reason the English wanted colonies. The Anglican faith had become England's state religion, and the English people were expected to follow Anglican beliefs. As a result, Catholics and groups of Protestants called Separatists were looking for a place to live where they could have religious freedom. The Separatists wanted to leave the Church of England. They believed that in the New World they would be able to worship in their own way.

In 1585 Sir Walter Raleigh founded a colony on Roanoke Island off the coast of North Carolina. But after three years the colonists who had settled there disappeared. To this day no one knows for certain what happened to them. For this reason, Roanoke Island became known as the "Lost Colony."

Although the English did not try to found colonies again for over 20 years, in 1600 English merchants formed the East India Company. Its goal was to trade with the East Indies. The company set up trading posts in India, Malaya, some islands of the East Indies, and some of the uninhabited islands of the West Indies.

1. Why did the English want to colonize the New World?
2. What was the first English colony in the New World? What happened to it?
3. Why was the East India Company formed?

JAMESTOWN   In 1606 a group of English nobles and merchants formed the Virginia Company of London. The following year the company sent about 100 settlers to the New World to search for gold and silver. Near the mouth of the

JAMESTOWN

The colonists at Jamestown learned to raise animals and to grow their own food. They built their wooden homes around a village green, where they exchanged goods and met for social activities.

How were the colonists of Jamestown able to make their colony successful?

Chesapeake Bay in Virginia, they founded the first successful permanent English settlement in America. They named it Jamestown after their king, James I.

But the land around Jamestown was swampy and filled with mosquitoes that carried disease. Many of the colonists fell sick and died. When English supply ships arrived a few months after the settlement had been founded, only 38 colonists were still alive.

Captain John Smith kept the settlement from total failure. He made it clear that those who did not work would not eat. He also convinced the Indians who lived nearby to supply the colonists with corn. Life in Jamestown was hard, and the colonists were always sick and discouraged. When Smith had to return to England in 1609, they almost starved to death. Those still alive two years later were all set to return to England. But a British fleet arrived with supplies, and they stayed on.

The settlers worked the land, but they did not own it. It belonged to the Virginia Company. In 1618 the company began granting land to individuals. Once people owned land, they worked harder. Only those willing to work hard had any success. None actually grew rich. The settlers saw the Indians using tobacco and began to use it themselves. Before long they were growing their own tobacco. It became an important crop because people in England were willing to pay a good price for it.

The settlers brought with them English laws and government. But they were far from England, and travel was slow. Soon it became necessary for them to make their own laws. In 1619 they elected 22 **burgesses**, or representatives, from among males over 17 years old. The burgesses met to decide the laws for the colony at Virginia. This House of Burgesses was the first representative government in America. It set an important example of self-government in the New World.

Eventually Jamestown became the capital of Virginia. It remained the capital until 1699, when it was replaced by Williamsburg.

1. Why was Jamestown founded?
2. What was life like in Jamestown?
3. What effects did land grants and tobacco have on the Jamestown colonists?
4. Why did the colonists form the House of Burgesses?

PLYMOUTH   Another company called the Virginia Company of Plymouth, England was also formed in 1606. But it was not successful. In 1620 it was reorganized as the Council for New England. It gained the right to grant land to settlers for colonies in New England.

That same year a group of Separatists called Pilgrims sailed for Virginia on the *Mayflower*. They had received grants of land from the Virginia Company. But strong ocean winds blew the *Mayflower* off course, and the Pilgrims did not land in Virginia. Instead, they landed in New England on the shore just north of Cape Cod, in what is now Massachusetts. The lands in New England belonged to the Council for New England, and the Pilgrims had not been given the right to govern in them. They had been given the right to govern only in Virginia. So they signed an agreement to set up a civil government whose laws they would obey. The agreement, which was called the Mayflower Compact, formed the basis for government in the colony. In it the settlers agreed to govern according to the wishes of the majority.

The Pilgrims named their settlement Plymouth after the English town from which they had sailed. The first winter was hard, and about half of the settlers died. In the spring, those who remained cleared the fields for farming. They planted corn, pumpkins, and beans. The Indians taught them how to use fish as fertilizer for their crops. They also taught them how to hunt and fish for food in the wilderness.

Bridal Chest

The people of Plymouth governed themselves for 70 years with almost no outside control. They elected their own governor and council. In 1691 Plymouth became part of another English settlement called the Massachusetts Bay Colony.

1. Where did the Pilgrims settle?
2. How was Plymouth governed?
3. What did the Pilgrims learn from the Indians?

GROWTH OF EMPIRE   Jamestown and Plymouth were just the beginning. In 1630 a group of Puritans seeking religious freedom sailed to New England. There they formed several settlements in the area around present-day Boston. They called their settlements the Massachusetts Bay Colony. By the end of the seventeenth century the Massachusetts Bay Colony was the largest and most powerful colony in the New World.

In 1634 the English settled what is present-day Maryland. King Charles I had granted the land to his friend Cecilius Calvert, Lord Baltimore. Calvert wanted land in America where English Catholics could live in peace.

In 1682 William Penn, the leader of a religious group called Quakers, founded a colony in what is present-day Pennsylvania. King Charles II had granted Penn the land in payment for a debt he owed Penn's father. Philadelphia became the chief city and port of Penn's colony.

The English continued to settle land in the New World. By 1733 they had established 13 colonies along the Atlantic coast.

1. What group founded the Massachusetts Bay Colony? Why did they found it?
2. Why did Cecilius Calvert want land in America?
3. Who founded Pennsylvania? How did he get the land?

THE NETHERLANDS

In 1602 Dutch merchants founded the Dutch East India Company. The company was to organize Dutch trade in Africa

EUROPEAN COLONIES IN THE NEW WORLD

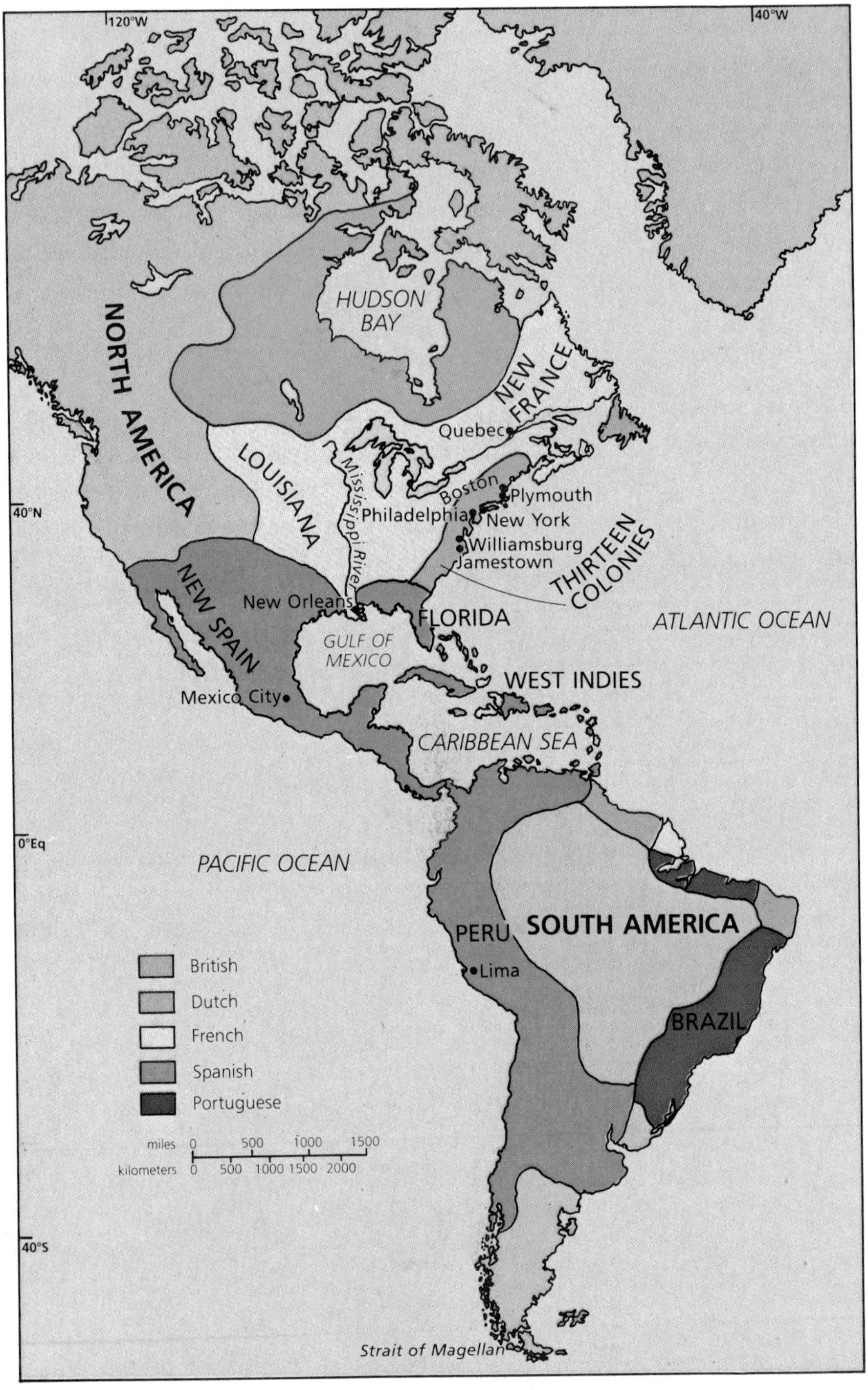

120°W
40°W
40°N
0°Eq
40°S
NORTH AMERICA
HUDSON BAY
NEW FRANCE
Quebec
LOUISIANA
Mississippi River
Boston
Plymouth
Philadelphia
New York
Williamsburg
Jamestown
THIRTEEN COLONIES
New Orleans
FLORIDA
ATLANTIC OCEAN
NEW SPAIN
GULF OF MEXICO
WEST INDIES
Mexico City
CARIBBEAN SEA
PACIFIC OCEAN
PERU
SOUTH AMERICA
Lima
BRAZIL
British
Dutch
French
Spanish
Portuguese
miles 0 500 1000 1500
kilometers 0 500 1000 1500 2000
Strait of Magellan

and the East Indies. The Dutch had a fleet of more than 10,000 merchant ships. They soon became strong competitors of other European countries. One by one they seized Portuguese trading posts in the East Indies. Soon they had control of most of the islands of the East Indies.

In 1621 the Dutch formed another company called the Dutch West India Company. Its goal was to establish colonies in the New World. Colonists were sent to islands in the West Indies and along the coast of South America. In 1625 the Dutch founded the colony of New Amsterdam on the island of Manhattan, which Peter Minuit bought from the Indians for goods worth about $24.00. The Dutch West India Company called the colonies it established the New Netherlands. New Amsterdam became the capital city.

In the seventeenth and eighteenth centuries the rivalry between the Dutch and English led to a series of wars, which the Dutch lost. The English took over most of the Dutch colonies, including New Amsterdam, which they renamed New York.

1. Why was the Dutch East India Company formed?
2. Why was the Dutch West India Company formed?
3. To whom did the Dutch lose most of their colonies?

FRANCE

In 1608 the French explorer and mapmaker Samuel de Champlain founded at Quebec the first permanent French colony in the New World. Soon after, the French established other settlements around the Great Lakes and at the northern end of the Mississippi River and its tributaries. Before long a profitable fur trade developed between the French and the Indians. The French gave the Indians blankets, guns, and wine in exchange for beaver and other animal skins. The French settlements in the New World remained small, however, because few French people wanted to leave France.

In 1682 Robert Cavalier, also called Sieur de La Salle, claimed the Mississippi River valley for France. In honor of the French king, Louis XIV, he named the area Louisiana. The French called Louisiana and their other lands in the New World New France.

The French had also established settlements on islands in the West Indies and in India. In time the French and the English

French Soldier

became great rivals. They clashed in Europe, the New World, and India. The French finally were defeated. In 1763 they signed the Treaty of Paris. They lost their North American colonial empire, their settlements in India, and southern Louisiana.

1. What was the first permanent French colony in America?
2. What area of the New World did Sieur de La Salle claim?
3. What kind of trade did the French develop with the Indians?
4. How did the French lose their lands in the New World?

CHAPTER REVIEW

SUMMARY

1. By 1532 Portugal had a permanent settlement in Brazil and trading posts in Africa, India, and the Far East.

2. Portuguese settlers tried at first to use Indians to work on their plantations and then began bringing in black slaves.

3. Brazil remained Portugal's most important colony until the nineteenth century, when it gained independence.

4. By 1535 Spain had established the largest colonial empire of any western European country in the New World.

5. Spanish conquistadores destroyed the Indian empires of Mexico and Peru and forced the Indians to do the heavy work on the land and in the mines.

6. When the Spanish Armada was defeated in 1588, Spain lost its power in the Atlantic Ocean.

7. The first successful English settlement in the New World was at Jamestown, Virginia, in 1607.

8. In 1619 the Jamestown colonists organized the House of Burgesses, which was the first representative government in the New World.

9. The second permanent English settlement in the New World was at Plymouth, Massachusetts, in 1620.

10. By 1733 the English had established 13 colonies in the New World, all located along the Atlantic coast.

11. The first permanent French settlement in the New World was at Quebec in 1608.

12. In 1763 by the Treaty of Paris, France lost its colonial empire in North America to England and Spain.

BUILDING VOCABULARY

1. *Identify the following:*

Pedro Alváres Cabral	Sir Walter Raleigh	Pilgrims	Cecilius Calvert
Hernando Cortés	Roanoke Island	Mayflower Compact	William Penn
Francisco Pizarro	Jamestown	Plymouth	Samuel de
Council of the Indies	Captain John Smith	Puritans	Champlain
Sir Francis Drake	House of Burgesses	Massachusetts Bay	Sieur de La Salle
Separatists		Colony	Treaty of Paris

2. *Define the following:*

colonize	plantations	viceroy	mulattoes
men-of-war	patriarchs	peninsulares	zambos
brazilwood	Bandeirantes	Creoles	privateers
captaincies	viceroyalties	mestizos	balance of trade
donatarios			burgesses

REVIEWING THE FACTS

1. Why did western European nations want to colonize the New World?
2. Why did the Portuguese settlers in Brazil bring in African slaves?
3. What increased Portuguese interest in Brazil more than 30 years after they had claimed it?
4. On what two things did the Spanish colonies base their social groups?
5. What did the Church contribute to the Spanish colonies?
6. What did the defeat of the Spanish Armada have to do with the colonization of the New World?
7. Why was the colony on Roanoke Island called the "Lost Colony"?
8. What did the Jamestown settlers learn from neighboring Indians?
9. Why did the Pilgrims draw up the Mayflower Compact?
10. What kind of trade did the French establish with the Indians?

DISCUSSING IMPORTANT IDEAS

1. What problems did Europeans face in the New World?
2. What do you think might have happened if Spain had used the gold and silver from its New World colonies to develop its own industries?
3. Would you have liked being one of the Jamestown settlers? Why or why not?
4. What did the establishment of the House of Burgesses have to do with the growth of democracy in the New World? Give reasons for your answer.

USING MAPS

Refer to the map on page 500, and answer the following questions:

1. To what country does the area called Louisiana belong?
2. Into what body of water does the Mississippi River flow?
3. What city in South America is southernmost on the map?
4. About how far is the city of New Orleans from the city of Boston?
5. What city is located about 20° north and 100° west?
6. What British territory is on the east coast of North America?

THE SLAVE TRADE

One of the biggest problems facing European colonists in the New World was finding enough workers. There was always too much work to be done and too few people to do it. At first the Europeans tried to force the Indians to work for them. But the Indians were not used to long hours of heavy labor. Often they died from overwork and disease. So the colonists began to use black slaves from Africa as workers.

The slave trade from Africa to America began in the sixteenth century. As time went by, a system was set up on the coast of Africa to obtain slaves. The British, French, Portuguese, and Dutch set up trading posts called **factories**. European ships brought such goods as cloth and guns to trade to local African rulers. In return the rulers agreed to supply the traders with a certain number of slaves. Once enough slaves were gathered to fill a ship, they were taken to the New World.

The trip to America was terrible and dangerous for the slaves. Ship captains wanted to make as much money as possible. They crammed the slaves aboard and kept them under deck for days and days at a time. Many died from disease and poor food. Often half of the slaves on a ship died before they reached the New World.

Most of the slaves brought to America came from the west coast of Africa. One third were sent to Brazil. Most of the rest were shipped to the Caribbean area. A

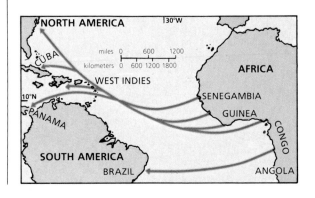

much smaller number went to slave markets in the English colonies of North America. Historians believe that the total number of blacks brought to the New World as slaves was about 10 million.

In the eighteenth century, religious and other leaders in Europe began to call for an end to the slave trade. They believed it was wrong for Christians to make slaves of other people. Gradually the feeling grew.

At the time, the largest shipper of slaves to the New World was England. In 1807 the English government passed a law against the slave trade. The following year the United States did the same. When the Latin American nations gained their independence from Spain in the nineteenth century, they too stopped trading in slaves. Thus, one of the largest movements of people in history came to an end.

1. Why did European colonists begin to use African slaves as workers?
2. How did colonists obtain their slaves?
3. What brought the slave trade to an end?

CHAPTER 33
POLITICAL REVOLUTIONS

$\mathbf{B}$y the eighteenth century, people in the western world had new ideas about government. They were less willing to be ruled without having a voice in government. They wanted more freedom to choose their leaders and to live without fear of rulers. They also wanted equal justice under the law. Educated people began to learn new things and to reason for themselves. They did not believe that monarchs or the Church had to tell them what to do. Thinkers and writers began spreading ideas about freedom, good government, and the right of people to change the government to meet their needs. For these reasons, the eighteenth century came to be known in Europe and the Americas as the Age of Enlightenment, or time of increased knowledge.

ENGLAND

In 1603 the last Tudor, Queen Elizabeth I, died. Since she had never married, the **Crown**, or monarchy, passed to a distant relative. A member of the Stuart family became James I of England.

The Tudors had enjoyed great power. But they were careful to get Parliament's opinion on their actions. James I, however, believed fully in the divine right of kings. He tried to rule without Parliament as much as possible.

Religious differences also came between the Crown and Parliament. James I wanted to force the authority of the Anglican Church, or Church of England, on the people. Many members of Parliament were Puritans. They believed in hard work and somber living. They did not like the free-spending ways of the Crown. They wanted to be able to worship as they pleased. With the support of other groups, they worked against what they felt was the unjust power of the king.

1. How did James I feel about Parliament?
2. Why did the Puritan members of Parliament work against the king?

King Charles I

PETITION OF RIGHT AND THE ENGLISH CIVIL WAR
When James I died in 1625, his son became King Charles I. He held the same beliefs about the monarchy as his father.

In 1628 Charles I was forced to call a meeting of Parliament to approve new taxes to pay debts from wars with France and Spain. Parliament saw a chance to limit the Crown's power and gain more for itself. It drew up the Petition of Right, a document which said that the king could not declare **martial law**, or rule by the army instead of the usual laws. It also said that the Crown could not pass tax laws without Parliament's consent, and that people could not be put in prison just because the king wanted them out of the way. At first Charles I agreed to the petition. But then he realized it would limit his power. In 1629 he broke his word and dismissed Parliament.

In 1640 Charles I needed money to build a larger army to fight the Scots. He had tried to force the Anglican Church on them, and they had revolted, taking over part of northern England. Parliament again saw a chance to limit Charles' power. It passed a law abolishing taxes collected by the Crown without Parliament's consent. It also passed a law to set up regular meetings of Parliament and to do away with the Star Chamber, or the royal court that tried people without a jury.

Once again Charles I accepted the laws at first and then tried to stop them. In 1642 he tried to arrest five leading members of Parliament. When those opposed to him began to form an army, Charles fled.

Civil war broke out between supporters of the Crown and those wanting more power for Parliament. Oliver Cromwell, a Puritan leader who supported Parliament, organized a New

ENGLISH PARLIAMENT

In the seventeenth century, the English Parliament limited the king's powers and made royal officials responsible to the nation. Here Parliament meets to try the Earl of Strafford, one of King Charles I's most hated advisers.

What political reforms did the English Parliament make?

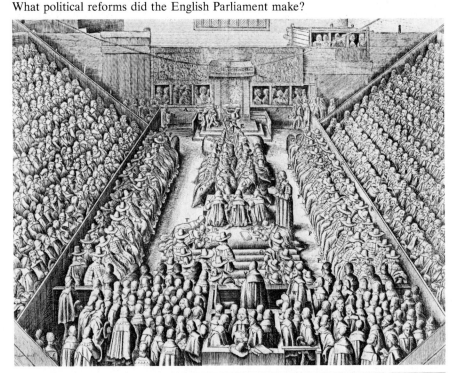

Model Army that drilled hard and followed strict rules. In 1646 it defeated the king's forces and ended the civil war.

Most English leaders still believed that monarchy was the best form of government. But they did not trust Charles I and were afraid to allow him to return to the throne. Cromwell and his supporters had Charles I put on trial, and in 1649 he was put to death. Cromwell took over the rule of England.

1. Why did Parliament draw up the Petition of Right?
2. What three points did the Petition of Right include?
3. Why did Charles I call a meeting of Parliament in 1640?
4. What led to the English Civil War? Who won the war?

Dutch Ship

THE GLORIOUS REVOLUTION   Cromwell ruled England until his death in 1658. Then his son Richard took over. By 1660 Parliament decided that England needed a monarch. It invited Charles II, Charles I's son, who was in France, to become king.

Charles II was very popular with the English people. But he refused to consult with Parliament about **foreign policy**, or relations with other countries. In addition, he was friendly with the Catholic King of France while most English people were Protestant.

When Charles II died in 1685, his brother James II became king. He was Catholic and wanted to allow Catholics into government office. He tried to have the Act of Habeas Corpus **repealed**, or abolished. The act stated that a person could not be put in jail unless charged with a crime. The leaders of Parliament did not like James II and acted to remove him from the throne. They decided to ask his son-in-law and daughter, William of Orange and his wife Mary, to become the new rulers of England. William, who was a Protestant, was ruler of the Dutch. He landed in England in 1688 with a large army, and James II fled to France.

Parliament drew up a Declaration of Rights that established many basic rights of the English people. It stated that the Crown could not repeal laws, keep an army in peace time, or pass tax laws without Parliament's consent. Also, Parliament was allowed to debate freely, meet often, and be freely elected. People could petition the Crown without fear of being punished.

The actions taken by Parliament were seen as a revolution, which came to be known as the "Glorious Revolution." Parliament had won its fight with the Crown. Rule by divine right was gone forever, and the monarch ruled in the name of Parliament and the people of England.

1. Why did Parliament remove James II from the throne? Whom did they choose to replace him?
2. What were three important parts of the Declaration of Rights?

AMERICA

In 1660, when Charles II became king of England, most European leaders believed in an economic system called **mercantilism**. This system included founding colonies that would help the founding country. The English colonies in America were supposed to send to England such goods as tobacco, which could not be grown or made there. They were supposed to buy only items made in England so that English merchants could make money. Trade between England and the colonies had to be carried out in ships built in England or in the colonies and sailed by English crews.

Gradually England brought the governments of the 13 American colonies more and more under its control. By 1760 all but five of the 13 American colonies were **royal colonies**, or colonies belonging to the Crown. The governor and other important officials of royal colonies were chosen by the Crown. Three of the other five colonies were **proprietary colonies**, or colonies belonging to an owner. The governor and other officials of proprietary colonies were chosen by the owner, who also could control laws passed by the legislature. The laws of all of the colonies had to be in line with the laws of England.

1. What were some of the laws concerning trade with English colonies?
2. What did England do to keep control over its colonies?

THE STRUGGLE FOR POWER   The people living in the English colonies in America were proud of being part of England. Still, they felt they had the right to rule themselves as much as possible. They did not believe that Parliament or the Crown could make laws for them. Their legislatures usually controlled the passage of tax laws. Since the governors and other colonial officials were paid out of taxes, they had to do as the colonial legislatures wished. This gave the legislatures a great deal of power.

THE ENGLISH CIVIL WARS

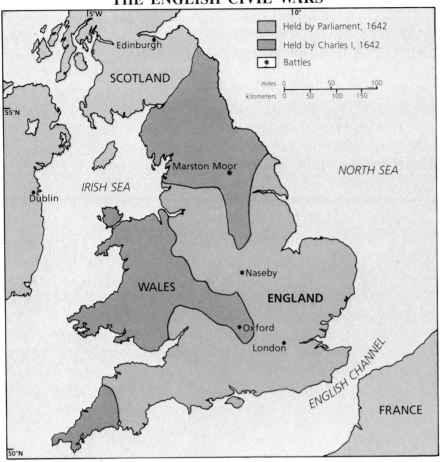

In 1754 the French, who also had colonies in America, built a fort where Pittsburgh, Pennsylvania is today. They and their Indian allies wanted to protect all of western America from the English. But England claimed the area for itself. This led to the French and Indian War. By the time the war ended in 1763, the English had control of nearly all of North America north of Florida.

The French and Indian War had two important effects on the English colonies. The colonists no longer feared that the French would conquer them. As a result, they became more willing to break loose from English control and protection. At the same time, the war left the English government with a large debt, in which it wanted the colonies to share. England moved to raise the money and tighten its control over the colonies.

Colonial Soldier

In 1764 Parliament passed the Sugar Act, which taxed sugar and other goods brought into the colonies. Colonial merchants began to **boycott**, or refuse to buy, the goods. The following year Parliament passed the Stamp Act, which said that all newspapers, legal papers, and many other documents had to have stamps. This was the first tax ever passed on the colonies that was not a tax on trade.

The Stamp Act hurt merchants, lawyers, and people in the newspaper business the most. This group was the most able to lead the people in a fight against British control. Angry mobs formed in many cities. Tax officials were threatened, and stamps were destroyed. In October 1765, delegates from nine colonies met in New York to discuss the Stamp Act. They sent a letter to the British government stating that the colonies had never been taxed by anyone except their own legislatures. Finally Parliament voted to repeal the Stamp Act. But then it passed the Declaratory Act, which restated Parliament's right to make laws on all matters concerning the colonists.

Beginning in 1767 Parliament passed a series of laws called the Townshend Acts, which taxed trade. Many colonial leaders responded with boycotts.

1. How did the English colonists feel about English rule?
2. Why were colonial legislatures powerful?
3. What effects did the French and Indian War have on the English colonies?
4. What did England do to tighten its controls on the colonies?

THE AMERICAN REVOLUTION   In 1768 the English sent soldiers to the colonial city of Boston. They were to make sure the colonists obeyed the new laws. In 1770 an incident occurred that came to be called the Boston Massacre. Colonists began teasing the soldiers and throwing stones at them. Some soldiers fired into the crowd of colonists, killing several of them. The incident probably would have been forgotten. But some colonists used it to stir up feelings against English rule.

Three years later, Parliament gave the East India Company the **monopoly**, or sole right, to bring tea into the colonies. The company decided to sell the tea itself rather than to allow colonial merchants to buy it from them and then sell it in the colonies. This hurt the merchants. It also angered even more those colonists already tired of English policies. In Massachusetts, a mob protested by boarding a ship in Boston harbor and dumping its cargo of tea into the water. This event is known as the Boston Tea Party.

Many English officials felt that if Massachusetts were not punished, England would lose control. So Parliament passed the Coercive Acts which closed Boston harbor and put the government of Massachusetts more firmly under England's control. Next Parliament passed the Quebec Act, which extended the boundaries of Quebec. Quebec now included land the American colonies had claimed as their own. Colonists called all of these laws the Intolerable Acts, or laws which they could not bear.

In September 1774, delegates from 12 of the colonies met in Philadelphia. Called the First Continental Congress, they said

THE AMERICAN REVOLUTION

that the Coercive Acts were against the law and therefore not in force. Colonial leaders, however, were divided among themselves. Some, like George Washington, hoped to settle the differences with England. Others, like Samuel Adams and Patrick Henry, wanted the colonies to become independent. Before any final decision was reached, fighting broke out between the colonies and the English army.

In May 1775, the Second Continental Congress met and named George Washington commander of the colonial armed forces. The colonists tried one more time to settle their differences with England but failed.

On July 4, 1776, the Congress issued the Declaration of Independence. Written mostly by Thomas Jefferson of Virginia, it stated that "all men are created equal." In the Declaration, the colonies broke away from England and became the United States of America.

War between the English and the American colonists dragged on. In 1778 the French, who were old enemies of the English, agreed to help the Americans. In 1781 the Americans and the French forced a large English army to surrender at Yorktown, Virginia, thus winning the most important battle of the war. Two years later, the Treaty of Paris was signed, and the war ended.

1. What did the East India Company do to anger the colonists?
2. What did Parliament do to punish the colonists?
3. What did the Declaration of Independence do?
4. How did the American Revolution come to an end?

THE AMERICAN CONSTITUTION   In 1789 the United States adopted a constitution which created a new form of government. The Constitution of the United States set forth the basic principles of government. One of these was **popular sovereignty**, or the idea that a government receives its powers from the people. It meant that the government could act only if the people agreed to let it do so.

Another principle was that of **limited government**, or the idea that a government may do only certain things and exercise only those powers granted to it by the people.

Later a Bill of Rights was added. It guaranteed all citizens such rights as freedom of worship and speech and the right to fair treatment under the law.

UNITED STATES CONSTITUTION

In 1787, representatives from twelve states met in Philadelphia and drew up a constitution for the United States. In this nineteenth-century painting, George Washington, a prominent figure at the convention, addresses the delegates. In 1789, Washington became the first president of the United States.

What were the principles of the American government?

The making of the new American government inspired people in Europe and in Latin America. The ideas and examples of the American Revolution gave them hope that they, too, could obtain the right to govern themselves.

1. What did the American constitution do?
2. How did the American Revolution affect people in Europe and Latin America?

FRANCE

During the seventeenth and early eighteenth centuries, France was a monarchy. The French rulers believed in the divine right of kings, and ruled with very little help from representatives of the people.

French society was divided into three **estates**, or classes. The first was the clergy. The Catholic Church, France's official church, owned large areas of land. It did not have to pay taxes. Instead, the clergy voted "free gifts" to the government. Higher church officials lived well on the money collected from rents.

PHILOSOPHERS

John Locke
1602–1704
English political thinker; in *Two Treatises of Government,* set forth ideas behind Glorious Revolution of 1688; influenced development of American and French Revolutions

Thomas Paine
1737–1809
international revolutionary and writer; influenced development of American and French Revolutions; wrote *Common Sense* and *The Rights of Man*

Montesquieu
1689–1755
French political thinker; believed in separation of powers of government; wrote *The Spirit of the Laws;* inspired French Declaration of the Rights of Man and Constitution of the United States

Jean-Jacques Rousseau
1712–1778
considered most important writer of eighteenth century; believed that will of the people represents supreme power; wrote *Social Contract;* influenced development of French Revolution and Constitution of the United States

The second class was the nobility. Most nobles held large areas of land but paid little in taxes. The nobles collected rents from the peasants.

At the bottom of the ladder was the Third Estate, or everyone in France except the clergy and nobility. It paid a larger share of taxes than the other two estates together. The largest part of the Third Estate was the peasants. They farmed land owned by the Church or the nobility and did certain kinds of work without pay, including road work. Bankers, merchants, lawyers, and teachers were also part of the Third Estate. Although they controlled much of France's wealth and trade, they had no power in the government.

1. How was France ruled during the seventeenth and early eighteenth centuries?
2. What groups made up the three French Estates?

THE ESTATES-GENERAL By 1787 the French government was in trouble. Educated Frenchmen called *philosophes*, or philosophers, wrote stories and articles pointing out the problems of French society and government. They looked forward to a time when people would be free to think for themselves and to make their own decisions. One of the most widely read philosophes was François Marie Arouet, known as Voltaire. Voltaire favored free speech, a free press, and equal justice for everyone. He did not like organized religion and felt that people were cruel to each other because of their religious beliefs.

Another problem the government had was the lack of money. The Crown had spent a great deal helping the Americans fight for independence. King Louis XVI added to the problem by spending money foolishly. The Crown wanted French nobles and clergy to provide it with money. They, however, had never paid their share of taxes and did not want that to change.

It was decided that, for the first time since 1614, the king should call a meeting of the Estates-General to help decide how best to raise money. In the Estates-General, each estate had always met separately, with each allowed to cast one vote. Since the nobles and clergy together could outvote the Third Estate, they could protect themselves from change. The Third Estate knew this and wanted the Estates-General to meet as a single body with each representative having a vote. It also wanted to have the same number of representatives as the other two estates

Madame Roland

combined. The Third Estate wanted to have more of a voice in the government. It also wanted the tax system changed to make the other two estates share more fairly.

In May 1789 the Estates-General met. The Third Estate had been allowed more representatives, but the other two estates would not meet as one body with them. So the Third Estate and a small number of clergy and nobles met as a separate body. They declared themselves the National Assembly, saying they had the power to represent the French people. When the king ordered the Assembly to break up, the members swore not to do so until they had written a constitution for France. They wanted a set body of laws to limit the monarchy and to give more power to the representatives of the people. The king gave in and ordered the other two estates to sit with the National Assembly.

1. Why was the French government in trouble in the 1780's?
2. Why was the Estates-General called to meet in 1789?
3. Why did the Third Estate want to meet as one body?
4. What did the National Assembly want to do?

THE FRENCH REVOLUTION   When the Estates-General was called to meet, most French people had high hopes for change. But before long they began to fear that nothing would happen to improve things. They were restless. The harvest had been bad, and food was becoming expensive. When the king dismissed a popular advisor, the people grew angry. In Paris, mobs began to form. The people had heard rumors that the Crown had put many people in the Bastille, an old fort used as a prison. On July 14, 1789 a mob attacked and captured the prison and took the weapons stored there. The mob later killed the mayor of Paris and set up a new city government.

News of what happened in Paris spread. In the country, peasants began to arm themselves. They attacked the houses of the rich and destroyed records of rents owed to the nobles.

The National Assembly soon became fearful of what the people were doing. It moved to do away with the privileges of the nobles and clergy. It passed laws to abolish the unpaid work peasants did for the nobles. It made the three estates more equal in tax payment. It made nobles sell off large areas of their land to people who wanted to have small farms of their own.

On August 27, 1789 the Assembly issued the Declaration of the Rights of Man and the Citizen. It said that the government's authority came from the people, not from the Crown. It gave everyone freedom of speech and the right to share in government. Many of the ideas for the Declaration came from the philosophes and from the English and American Revolutions.

1. Why did French mobs attack the Bastille?
2. What did the National Assembly do to try to calm the people?
3. What did the Declaration of the Rights of Man and the Citizen provide?

THE REIGN OF TERROR For the next two years, the National Assembly worked to write a constitution. During this time, people began to disagree over the aims of the Revolution. Some wanted more changes. Others felt that too many changes had already been made. The government took over lands that belonged to the Catholic Church and sold them to pay debts. The clergy had to take an oath to the government.

Many of the very poor had hoped the Revolution would make them equal to everyone else in political rights, in wealth, and in ways of living. The wealthy and the middle class feared this. They felt that the poor and uneducated could not be trusted to help govern.

In 1791 the Assembly completed the constitution. It made France a **constitutional monarchy**, or a monarchy with power limited by written law. The Crown and the legislature together would govern. Only those people who could afford to pay a tax equal to three days wages could vote. Representatives had to have a certain amount of wealth. Still people could not agree over the aims of the Revolution. Once again they began to fight over control of the government. In 1792 they abolished the monarchy. The following year they executed King Louis XVI.

In 1793 a new constitution was written. But it was never used. A special revolutionary **tribunal**, or committee, led by Maximilien de Robespierre took over control of the government. This tribunal began to execute nobles and anyone else suspected of being against the Revolution. The wave of killing came to be known as the "Reign of Terror." Because of it, many people began to oppose Robespierre. In 1794 leaders who hoped to restore order to the government had Robespierre executed.

The following year a third constitution was written. Under it, the government was headed by five directors called the

Directory. The Directory spent much of its time trying to stay in power. The reforms of the Revolution came to a halt.

1. How did the poor and others who were not nobles or clergy disagree over the aims of the French Revolution?
2. Why did people begin to oppose Robespierre?
3. Why did the reforms of the French Revolution come to a halt under the constitution of 1795?

RESULTS OF THE FRENCH REVOLUTION   The French people had started the revolution with a great deal of hope. By 1799 they were ruled by a small group backed by the army. The monarchy was gone. So were the nobles' privileges. A system of public education, which gave greater opportunity to all people in France, had been set up. Although the poorest peasants were

---

REIGN OF TERROR

In July 1793, the French revolutionary leader Jean-Paul Marat was stabbed to death in his home by Charlotte Corday, a young aristocrat who opposed Marat's policies. Another victim of the Terror was the wife of Louis XVI, Queen Marie Antoinette. She was tried and executed for treason in October, 1793.

What was the "Reign of Terror"?

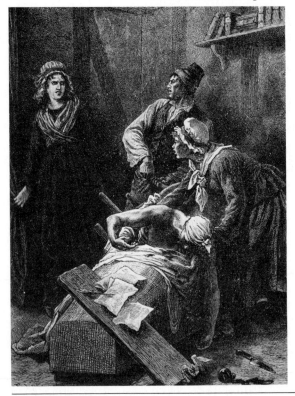

---

still very poor, many people had been able to buy their own land for the first time. Many of the promises of the French Revolution had not come to pass. But the idea remained that all French people had the right to choose their government.

1. What were some results of the French Revolution?

CHAPTER REVIEW
SUMMARY

1. Because of people's new ideas about government, the eighteenth century is known in western civilization as the Age of Enlightenment.

2. England's political revolution began during the seventeenth century when the Crown and Parliament disagreed about religion and the divine right of kings.

3. In 1642 disagreements between Charles I and Parliament led to the English Civil War and the overthrow of Charles I by Puritans led by Oliver Cromwell.

4. In 1660 Parliament restored the monarchy, but 28 years later disagreements between James II and Parliament led to the Glorious Revolution.

5. As a result of the Glorious Revolution, Parliament passed the Declaration of Rights, which established many basic rights of the English people.

6. The French and Indian War made the English colonies feel more secure but left England with a large debt.

7. In 1763 England tried to tighten its control over its 13 American colonies by passing a series of acts that set taxes on the colonies.

8. The colonists objected to paying the taxes because they believed that only their colonial legislatures had the right to make laws for them.

9. In 1776 disagreements between the colonies and England led to the Declaration of Independence and a war that made the colonies an independent nation, the United States of America.

10. In 1789 the United States adopted the Constitution of the United States which created a new form of government in which the people have the right to govern themselves.

11. In 1789, to help decide ways to raise money, the French king called together representatives of the clergy, the nobility, and the Third Estate.

12. Representatives of the Third Estate, who had no power in the government, insisted on writing a constitution.

13. Because the French disagreed over the aims of the French Revolution, three different constitutions were written between 1791 and 1795.

14. By 1799 the monarchy had been abolished, nobles had lost their privileges, and certain economic and educational reforms had been made in France.

15. The French Revolution expressed the idea that people have the right to choose their own government.

BUILDING VOCABULARY

1. *Identify the following:*

Enlightenment	William and Mary	Continental Congress	Voltaire
James I	Declaration of Rights	George Washington	Estates-General
Charles I	French and Indian War	Declaration of	Bastille
Petition of Right	Stamp Act	Independence	Robespierre
Oliver Cromwell	Boston Massacre	Thomas Jefferson	Reign of Terror
Act of Habeas Corpus	Intolerable Acts	Third Estate	Directory

2. *Define the following:*

Crown	mercantilism	monopoly	philosophes
martial law	royal colonies	popular sovereignty	tribunal
foreign policy	proprietary colonies	limited government	constitutional
repealed	boycott	estates	monarchy

REVIEWING THE FACTS

1. Why is the eighteenth century known as the Age of Enlightenment?

2. Why did Charles I dismiss Parliament in 1629?

3. In what did the Puritans believe?

4. Why did the English put Charles I to death in 1649?

5. In whose name does the English monarch rule?

6. Why did England try to tighten its controls over the American colonies?

7. What did the Second Continental Congress do?

8. What does the Bill of Rights do?

9. Before the French Revolution, who had the most power in the government?

10. Why did the French write three different constitutions after the Revolution?

DISCUSSING IMPORTANT IDEAS

1. What economic issues played a part in the Glorious, the American, and the French Revolutions?

2. What political issues played a part in all three revolutions?

3. What changes in government took place as a result of each revolution?

4. Do you agree or disagree with the idea that people have the right to rule themselves? Explain.

USING MAPS

Refer to the map on page 511, and answer the following questions:

1. What is the time period of the map?

2. Who holds London? Wales?

3. How far is Naseby from Marsdon Moor?

4. Where is Oxford located?

Refer to the map on page 513, and answer the following questions:

1. About how far do the Thirteen Colonies extend along the coast?

2. What battles are British victories?

3. What is located about 36° north and 78° west?

4. Where is Boston located?

CHAPTER 34

RISE OF INDUSTRY

In the fifteenth century a system of land division called **enclosure** developed in England. Under this system, landowners combined the many small strips of land worked by tenant farmers into large areas closed in by fences. The tenant farmers had two choices. They could stay on as paid laborers, or they could look elsewhere for jobs. Most became laborers willing to go wherever they could find work. Over time many became industrial workers.

The enclosure system was just part of the agricultural revolution of that period. New methods of growing crops and breeding animals led to greater production of food. More food meant better health and longer lives. It also meant a growing population who wanted to buy products made by industry.

SCIENTISTS

Name	Field	Accomplishments
Johannes Kepler *Germany*	*Astronomy*	announced laws of movement of planets, 1609
William Harvey *England*	*Medicine*	published theory on human blood circulation, 1628
Sir Isaac Newton *England*	*Physics*	stated laws of motion and theory of gravitation, 1687
Antoine Lavoisier *France*	*Chemistry*	discovered nature of combustion, 1777
John Dalton *England*	*Chemistry*	announced atomic theory, 1803
Maria Mitchell *United States*	*Astronomy*	discovered new comet, 1847
Charles Darwin *England*	*Biology*	advanced theory on development of planets and animals, 1858
Gregor Mendel *Austria*	*Botany*	discovered principles of heredity, 1866
Louis Pasteur *France*	*Medicine*	advanced germ theory of disease, 1876; successfully vaccinated against rabies, 1885
Pierre Curie Marie Curie *France*	*Chemistry*	discovered radium and polonium, 1898

About the same time these changes were taking place in agriculture, scientists began to break away from old ideas. They stopped relying on ancient Greek scientists like Aristotle and Ptolemy. Instead, they observed how things happened and formed their own ideas. Then they did experiments to test their ideas. One of the new scientists was Nicolaus Copernicus, a Polish astronomer who observed the motion of the planets. What he saw convinced him that Ptolemy was wrong and that the earth was not the center of the universe. In 1543 Copernicus published a book explaining his theory that planets revolve around the sun.

Copernicus' book began a revolution in scientific thinking. Scientists began to use the methods of observation and experiment, and scientific knowledge grew rapidly. Great advances were made in physics, chemistry, biology, and medicine.

Many more scientific discoveries were made over the next 300 years. A great number of the discoveries found a place in industry. For example, in 1831 Michael Farraday of England discovered that a magnet can produce electricity. His work, along with that of many others, led to electric power, which played an important part in industrial growth and development.

THE INDUSTRIAL REVOLUTION

The Industrial Revolution began in England in the textile industry. In the seventeenth and eighteenth centuries clothmaking was already important. Most of the work was done in the workers' own cottages, where families worked together. Traveling merchants brought the workers raw wool and cotton. Using handpowered, wooden weaving looms, the workers spun the thread and wove it into wool and cotton cloth. The merchants then picked up the finished cloth to sell to a growing population.

As agriculture and medicine improved, the European population grew. This meant there were more people who wanted to buy cloth. There was a market outside of Europe, too. People in English colonies in America, Africa, and India also needed cloth.

1. Where did the Industrial Revolution begin?
2. Where were most textiles made during the seventeenth and eighteenth centuries?

INVENTIONS   Before long, people started looking for ways to make more cloth in less time. The first major breakthrough came in 1733 when a weaver named John Kay invented the **flying shuttle**, or weaving machine. It cut in half the time needed to weave cloth. But the spinners could not keep up with the weavers. Then in 1779 James Hargreaves invented the **spinning jenny**, or spinning machine. It could spin up to 1000 threads in the time it took the spinning wheel to spin one thread.

More progress was made when ways were found to use the power of falling water to run the textile machines. This meant, however, that the machine had to be near a large supply of water. Many workers' cottages were in fields or villages far from water. So **factories**, or buildings in which manufacturing is done, were built next to rivers and streams that could supply the necessary water power. Workers still lived in their cottages, but they no longer worked at home. Instead, they came to the factories to work. In time, towns grew up around the factories.

In 1769 a Scottish engineer named James Watt perfected the steam engine. The first practical steam engine had been developed in 1712 by Thomas Newcomen, an English engineer. But it was used only to pump water from mines. Watt improved Newcomen's engine and used it to replace water power as a major source of power. From then on, one industry after another went through a revolution. Steam-powered machines were used to make shoes, paper, furniture, and machines themselves.

Cotton growers in America and India could not supply enough cotton to meet the needs of English factories. Eli Whitney, an American inventor, found a way to solve the problem. While visiting a cotton plantation in Georgia, he discovered that cleaning the seeds out of cotton by hand took too much time. In 1793 he invented the **cotton gin**, or cotton-cleaning machine. It could clean cotton 50 times faster than a person working by hand.

About five years later, Whitney invented a new way of organizing **mass production**, or the manufacture of goods in large quantities. He first used the new method to manufacture guns. Until then, each worker had made one gun at a time from start to finish. Workers had to be skilled in what they were doing. Under Whitney's system, the work was divided, with each worker making only one part of the gun. Workers no longer had

Cotton Gin

INVENTORS

Name	Country	Inventions
Edmund Cartwright	*England*	power loom, 1785
Alessandro Volta	*Italy*	electric battery, 1800
Robert Fulton	*United States*	first successful steamboat, 1807
Cyrus McCormick	*United States*	mechanical reaper, 1834
Samuel Morse	*United States*	first successful electric telegraph, 1837
Norbert Rillieux	*United States*	evaporator which revolutionized sugar industry, 1843
Alexander Graham Bell	*United States*	telephone, 1876
Thomas Edison	*United States*	phonograph, 1878; electric light, 1879
Gottlieb Daimler	*Germany*	first successful automobile with internal combustion engine, 1887
Guglielmo Marconi	*Italy*	wireless telegraph, 1897

to be skilled. All parts were standardized and interchangeable. Each individual part was the same size and shape, and any set of parts could be used to make or repair any gun. Whitney's system meant that guns could be made much faster and by unskilled workers. Soon other industries began to use Whitney's methods.

As seen in the chart above, one invention followed another. Each brought improvements to industry and advanced the Industrial Revolution.

1. What inventions changed the way cloth was produced?
2. How did new methods of clothmaking change workers' lives?
3. What effect did Whitney's system of mass production have on industry and the work force?

Iron Furnace

MINING To build machine parts, as well as bridges and ships, iron was needed. To fire steam engines, coal was needed. Without iron and coal, the Industrial Revolution could not have continued.

By the early part of the eighteenth century, ironmaking had become expensive. To smelt iron, the English needed **charcoal**, a material made by burning hardwood. The English, however, were running out of forests, which made hardwood scarce and costly. In 1735 a way was found to use coal instead of charcoal for smelting. As a result, iron became cheaper, iron production increased, and coal mining became a major industry.

In 1856 an Englishman named Henry Bessemer found a way to make steel from iron. Called the Bessemer process, it consisted of blasting **compressed air**, or air under great pressure, through **molten**, or melted, iron to burn out the extra carbon and other impurities. Since steel was harder and stronger than iron, it was more useful. For example, more complicated machines could be made with steel. Soon mining towns and steel centers grew up in areas with supplies of iron ore and coal.

1. For what was iron needed? For what was coal needed?
2. What effects did the discovery that coal could be used for smelting have on industry?
3. Why was steel more useful than iron?

TRANSPORTATION Raw materials and finished products had to be moved quickly and cheaply. Before this could happen, transportation had to be improved. Until the eighteenth century the chief means of transportation over land was by horse or horse-pulled cart. English roads were no more than rough, narrow, dirt paths. Travel was slow and uncomfortable, especially when rain made the roads muddy. Late in the 1700's, the English began to improve their roads.

The English also made their rivers wider and deeper and built canals to connect cities and rivers. Horses walked along the side of the canals pulling **barges**, or flat-bottomed boats. The barges moved along the canals a lot faster than carts traveled on roads. By 1830 England had a complete system of inland waterways.

The biggest improvement in transportation was the railroad. For years horses had pulled carts over wooden rails around coal mines. Then the production of iron increased. The wooden rails were replaced by iron ones which could carry much heavier loads. Inventors began to build **locomotives**, or steam engines on wheels, to run along the iron rails. In 1829 George Stephenson, an English mining engineer, won a contest to see who could build the best locomotive. Stephenson's locomotive, called the *Rocket*, could pull a train about 14 miles, or 23.8 kilometers, an hour. The *Rocket* started a railroad-building boom in England.

1. Why did transportation have to be improved during the Industrial Revolution?
2. What did the English do to improve their waterways?
3. What happened to England's transportation system as a result of building the *Rocket*?

RAILROADS

By 1845, British railroads crossed the country and carried freight and passengers. This drawing shows steam-powered trains on the railway connecting the industrial cities of Liverpool and Manchester.
What changes in transportation took place during the Industrial Revolution?

FACTORIES

Factories brought workers together under one roof to work machines and to package goods. Different workers performed each step in the making of a product. Women and children often worked long hours under difficult conditions in the factories. They were paid low wages and lived in poor houses.

Where were the first factories built?

Effects of the Industrial Revolution

The Industrial Revolution produced a new way of life in England. Until the Middle Ages, there had been two main social classes—the aristocracy, who were the upper class, and the peasants, who were the lower class. Then a class of rich merchants developed. These burghers were the beginning of a **middle class**, or a class between the aristocracy and the peasants.

During the Industrial Revolution the middle class increased in numbers and grew richer. Many factory, railroad, and mine owners became as wealthy as the nobles. They began to keep company with the members of the upper class. Some sent their children to upperclass schools. Sometimes the children ended up marrying into the upper class.

Gradually the middle class gained political power. In England its members acquired the right to vote and to be represented in Parliament. Once they had the vote and seats in Parliament, they insisted that the country be governed by Parliament rather than by a monarch or nobles.

The Industrial Revolution also created the **proletariat**, or the industrial working class. Most members of the proletariat were peasants who could no longer support themselves by farming. Since they had no property of their own to sell, they had to sell their labor in order to live. Often they were forced to move to new areas near factories where they could find work.

At first the working class did not benefit from the Industrial Revolution. They worked 12 to 14 hours a day, six or seven days a week, for low wages. They had to work at the pace set by the machines and factory owners. Working conditions were difficult, dirty, and dangerous. Many people were killed or injured by unsafe machinery.

Many children of the working class did not have time to go to school or to play. Instead, they had to work in factories and mines along with the men and women. They were paid even less than the adults. In the mines, they would crawl through narrow tunnels through which adults could not fit. Because their bodies were still growing, children sometimes were crippled by the work they had to do.

1. What happened to the middle class during the Industrial Revolution?
2. What were conditions like for members of the working class during the early part of the Industrial Revolution?

Sewing Machine

GROWTH OF CITIES   Before the Industrial Revolution, less than 10 percent of the people lived in cities. The Industrial Revolution changed that.

Some cities grew up around factories or mines that had been built in **rural**, or country, areas. Most factories, however, were built in cities. Once the factories were built there, the cities grew rapidly. Soon more and more workers were needed in the cities. Fewer and fewer people were needed on farms where machines like the tractor and the McCormick reaper were replacing human and animal power.

So many people moved to the cities to find jobs that the cities became overcrowded. Houses could not be built fast enough. Sometimes a dozen people had to live in one room. Many moved into damp basements and rooms with no windows.

INDUSTRIAL CITIES

The development of industry in Britain led to the growth of large cities. British industrial cities were located near coal or iron deposits. Here is a large nineteenth-century steel factory in the city of Sheffield.

What was the life of workers like in the new industrial cities?

Smoke from the factories darkened the sky and made the air smell bad. Garbage floated in the streets because the sewer had not been built to serve so many people. Water supplies became polluted.

The workers could do nothing about their working or living conditions. They did not have the right to vote. And it was against the law to form **trade unions**, or workers' associations. They saw no choice but to continue as they were.

1. Where did people live before the Industrial Revolution?
2. Why did so many people move to the cities?
3. What problems did the rapid growth of cities cause?

REFORM   The bad condition of the workers in England led some members of the middle and upper classes to work for **reform**, or change. They started schools and hospitals for the poor. More importantly, they worked to change laws.

In 1802 the first laws against child labor were passed. Then the workday was shortened to ten hours. In 1824 trade unions were made legal, which meant that workers could **strike**, or stop work, in order to obtain shorter hours, higher wages, and better working conditions. In 1867 working-class males received the right to vote.

Eventually the working class began to reap benefits from the Industrial Revolution. As more and more goods were produced, prices went down. Clothing, food, and other products became cheap enough for workers to buy.

Reformers also worked to improve workers' living conditions. New laws were passed that required the building of better houses for workers. Every room had to have at least one window, and every house had to have piped-in water. The improvements were slow in coming, but over time life became better for the workers.

1. What did reformers do to improve the living and working conditions of the proletariat?

SPREAD OF THE INDUSTRIAL REVOLUTION

At the beginning of the Industrial Revolution, the English tried to keep their discoveries and inventions secret. Machines or plans for machines were not allowed to be taken out of England. Skilled workers were forbidden to leave the country.

WORLD'S FAIR

In 1851, Britain held a world's fair in London to celebrate its industrial achievements. More than six million visitors viewed exhibits of scientific inventions, industrial products, and art objects in a large "Crystal Palace" built of iron and glass. How did Britain's industrial progress affect other countries?

Early Telephone

By the nineteenth century, however, many workers had ignored the law and left England. These **immigrants**, or people who settle permanently in a different country, brought the English "secrets" to France, Belgium, and the United States.

All of these countries had plenty of iron and coal, which were needed to **industrialize**, or develop industry. France began to industrialize in the eighteenth century, but war and revolution slowed the process. After England, Belgium was the second country to become industrialized. The United States, with its many natural resources, soon followed. By the end of the nineteenth century, it was the largest and most successful industrial country in the world. Although Germany was well supplied with coal and iron, it was divided into more than 30 separate states which were not willing to cooperate in economic matters. Germany, therefore, did not make industrial progress until after the separate states were unified in 1871. By the beginning of the twentieth century, these industrialized countries had become competitors.

1. How did the Industrial Revolution spread?
2. Which were the first countries after England to become industrialized?

CHAPTER REVIEW
SUMMARY

1. Beginning in the fifteenth century, an agricultural revolution took place in England which included a new system of land division and new methods of growing crops and breeding animals.

2. About the same time as the revolution in agriculture, a revolution in scientific thinking began.

3. The scientific revolution was set off in 1543 by a book in which the Polish astronomer Copernicus said that planets revolve around the sun.

4. Many scientific discoveries later found a place in industry.

5. The Industrial Revolution began in England in the textile industry.

6. Many inventions, such as the flying shuttle and the spinning jenny, helped workers produce more in less time.

7. Factories were built near rivers and streams in order to use the power of falling water to run machines.

8. In 1769 James Watt perfected the steam engine, which gradually replaced water power as a major source of power.

9. Eli Whitney invented the cotton gin in 1793 and a new way of organizing mass production in 1798.

10. The use of iron and coal to make steel helped continue the Industrial Revolution and led to major transportation improvements, especially the railroad.

11. The Industrial Revolution increased the size and power of the middle class, and created a new social class called the proletariat.
12. The rapid growth of cities was another result of the Industrial Revolution.
13. The bad living and working conditions of the proletariat led to many reforms.
14. During the nineteenth century the Industrial Revolution spread from England to Belgium, the United States, France, and Germany.

BUILDING VOCABULARY

1. *Identify the following:*

Ptolemy	John Kay	Thomas Newcomen	George Stephenson
Nicolaus Copernicus	James Hargreaves	Eli Whitney	*Rocket*
Michael Farraday	James Watt	Henry Bessemer	

2. *Define the following:*

enclosure	mass production	locomotives	reform
flying shuttle	charcoal	middle class	strike
spinning jenny	compressed air	proletariat	immigrants
factories	molten	rural	industrialize
cotton gin	barges	trade unions	

REVIEWING THE FACTS

1. How did the enclosure system affect tenant farmers?
2. How did Ptolemy view the relation between the sun and the planets?
3. How did Copernicus view the relation between the sun and the planets?
4. How did the Industrial Revolution change textile manufacturing?
5. What was the main source of power during the Industrial Revolution?
6. How did the English try to keep their industrial discoveries and inventions secret?
7. What new social class developed as a result of the Industrial Revolution?
8. Why were many children of the working class unable to attend school during the early years of the Industrial Revolution?
9. What benefits did people of the working class reap from the Industrial Revolution?
10. By the end of the nineteenth century, what nation was the largest and most successful industrial country in the world?

DISCUSSING IMPORTANT IDEAS

1. What did changes in agriculture have to do with the Industrial Revolution?
2. What did the revolution in scientific thinking have to do with the Industrial Revolution?
3. What things do you think are necessary for a nation to industrialize?
4. Do you think that the Industrial Revolution was good or bad for most workers? Explain.

UNIT REVIEW

SUMMARY

1. From the early sixteenth to the eighteenth centuries, Portugal, Spain, England, the Netherlands, and France competed to colonize the New World. They hoped to gain new wealth and power and spread Christianity.

2. Political revolution in England ended the divine right of kings. It also established the basic rights of the people and increased the powers of Parliament.

3. The 13 American colonies rebelled against England and became the United States of America, an independent nation with a representative government based on popular sovereignty.

4. In the eighteenth century the French Revolution established the idea that government authority comes from the people. But the Revolution ended in confusion without fulfilling all its goals.

5. The Industrial Revolution started in England in the eighteenth century and soon spread to other western countries. It completely changed manufacturing and industry by replacing human and animal power with machine power and the factory system. The Revolution led to the creation of a proletariat, the rise of the middle class, the rapid growth of cities, and reform.

REVIEWING THE MAIN IDEAS

1. Compare the governments set up in England, America, and France as a result of political revolution.

2. Explain how the Industrial Revolution affected the economy, social classes, and cities.

DEVELOPING SKILLS

After historians have gathered and studied a body of data, they often make a generalization based on the data. For example, historians discovered that between 3500 and 1500 B.C. the Sumerians developed a civilization in the valley of the Tigris and Euphrates Rivers, the Egyptians developed a civilization in the valley of the Nile River, the Harappans developed a civilization in the valley of the Indus River, and the Chinese developed a civilization in the valley of the Yellow River. From this information they arrived at the generalization that between 3500 and 1500 B.C. early civilizations developed along the banks of rivers.

This exercise is designed to give you practice in generalizing. Read the three groups of statements that follow. Then write a generalization for each based on the statements.

1. *Group A*
a. By 1510 Portugal had claimed all of Brazil.
b. By 1532 Spain had claimed Mexico and Peru.
c. By 1733 English settlers had established 13 colonies along the Atlantic coast of America.
d. In 1682 France claimed the Mississippi River valley.

2. *Group B*

a. One result of the Glorious Revolution was that rule by divine right was gone forever from England.

b. The American Revolution led to a government based on popular sovereignty.

c. In 1792 the French monarchy was abolished by the National Assembly.

3. *Group C*

a. The flying shuttle cut in half the time needed to weave cloth.

b. The spinning jenny could spin up to 1000 threads in the same amount of time the spinning wheel took to spin one thread.

c. The cotton gin could clean cotton 50 times faster than working by hand.

SUGGESTED UNIT ACTIVITIES

1. Stage a debate about the Portuguese and Spanish colonies in Central and South America. One group will present the Indian view; the other will present the European colonists' view.

2. Write a letter that an early Jamestown or Plymouth settler might have sent home to tell about life in America.

3. Make a chart comparing the Glorious, American, and French Revolutions. Include dates the revolutions began and ended, their goals, leaders and results.

4. In a group, prepare a booklet of advertisements that might have been used to sell at least five of the inventions that contributed to the growth of industry.

SUGGESTED READING

Anticaglia, Elizabeth. *Heroines of '76*. New York: Walker and Company, 1976. The lives of 14 women who played important roles in the Revolutionary War.

Boardman, Fon W., Jr. *Around the World in 1776*. New York: Henry Z. Walck Inc., 1975. An account of world-wide events that took place in 1776.

Davis, Burke. *Black Heroes of the American Revolution*. New York: Harcourt Brace Jovanovich, 1976. An account of Blacks in the struggle for American independence.

Forbes, Esther. *Johnny Tremain*. Boston: Houghton-Mifflin, 1971. The story of a 14-year-old boy in Boston in 1773 who becomes involved in the American Revolution.

Holbrook, Sabra. *Lafayette: Man in the Middle*. New York: Atheneum, 1977. A biography illustrated with old prints and photographs.

Holland, Ruth. *Mill Child*. New York: Crowell-Collier Press, 1970. The story of what life was like in America for children forced to work in the mills.

Levitin, Sonia. *Roanoke: A Novel of the Lost Colony*. New York: Atheneum, 1973. The story of a 16-year-old runaway and his sea journey to a new colony in the Americas.

Pratt, N.S. *The French Revolution*. New York: The John Day Company, 1970. Discusses the revolution, its leaders, and the changes it brought about.

UNIT 12

1800

1800 Thomas Jefferson becomes president of United States

1803 Louisiana Purchase

1804 Haiti becomes independent
Napoleon becomes emperor of France

1805

1812 Napoleon invades Russia
1815...

1830

1830 July Revolution in France
Greece becomes independent
French occupy Algeria

1831 Belgium declares independence

1840

1840 American settlers head for Oregon
David Livingstone goes to Africa

1841 Pedro I rules Brazil

1839 Opium War

1860

1860 Lincoln elected president of United States

1861 American Civil War begins
Victor Emmanuel II becomes king of Italy

1862 Bismarck becomes prime minister of Prussia

1865

1867 Austria-Hungary establishes dual monarchy
Benito Juárez becomes president of Mexico

1869 Suez Canal opens

1870

1870 Italy unites

1871 Germany unifies

1874 England takes control of Suez Canal
Henry Stanley explores C...

1890

1894 Sino-Japanese War begins

1895

1895 British establish colony in East Africa
Rhodesia becomes British colony
French set up colony in West Africa

1896 Ethiopia defeats Italy

1898 Open Door Policy
Spanish American War

1899 Boer War begins

1900

1900 Boxer Rebellion breaks out in Ch...

1904 Russo-Japanese War begins

1925

1930

NATIONS AND EMPIRES

1815	1820	1825
Congress of Vienna	**1822** Mexico becomes independent Brazil becomes independent	
1815 Napoleon defeated at Waterloo Louis XVIII becomes king of France	**1823** Monroe Doctrine Uruguay becomes independent	
1816 Argentina becomes independent		
1818 Chile becomes independent		

1845	1850	**1852** Napoleon III rules France	1855
1845 United States annexes Texas California becomes independent			**1858** England takes full control of India
1846 War between Mexico and the United States begins		**1853** Perry goes to Japan Gadsden Purchase	
1847 Republic of Liberia founded			
1848 Second French Republic		**1854** Crimean War begins	

1875	1880	**1882** Britain occupies Egypt	1885
		1884 Berlin Conference	
1877 Queen Victoria becomes empress of India			**1885** Portuguese East Africa established
1878 Henry Stanley serves Leopold II			**1888** William II becomes kaiser of Germany
			1889 Brazil becomes Republic

1905	1910	1915
	1910 French Equatorial Africa set up Union of South Africa formed	**1914** Panama Canal opens
	1912 United States marines land in Nicaragua	
1908 Belgium establishes control over Congo		

1. IN WHAT WAYS DID NATIONALISM AND INDEPENDENCE INFLUENCE THE WESTERN WORLD DURING THE NINETEENTH CENTURY?

2. WHAT CHANGES TOOK PLACE IN AFRICA AND ASIA DURING THE NINETEENTH CENTURY?

During the nineteenth century, the world saw many new nations emerge, grow, and become powerful. It also saw Africa and Asia open their doors to the nations of western Europe.

In the Americas, the people of the United States built a democracy and enlarged the nation. They fought a civil war and then worked to reunite. Industry grew, and with it grew the nation's strength and power.

Spanish and Portuguese colonies in the Americas shed their colonial rulers. But colonial rule had been strict. The people had been given little opportunity to learn how to govern. After independence, landowners and military leaders controlled political life. Most were interested in personal gain. They did little for the people or the economy.

In Europe, the ideals of the French Revolution gained support among the middle and working classes. Monarchs who tried to stamp out democratic and national feelings failed. They were forced to accept constitutions, parliaments, elections, and the creation of new nations.

Toward the end of the century, the European powers and the United States practiced **imperialism**, or the policy of establishing colonies and building empires. In this way, they spread their influence, enlarged their trade, and protected their interests in other parts of the world.

CHAPTER 35

THE AMERICAS

A great many changes took place in the Americas from 1800 to 1870. The United States more than doubled in size, and its government was set on a firm base. This allowed the country to become strong. Latin America, or Central and South America, won independence from European rule. But traditions established under colonial rule remained strong. So despite strong efforts, democracy did not develop. In all, the 70-year period was a time of both great promise and great hardship.

THE UNITED STATES

In the years after independence, the United States grew in population, land area, and wealth. One of the main reasons for

Eagle Drum

this was a **stable government**, or a government that rules from year to year without great changes.

While the people were still under English control, a tradition of representative government had been started. Part of the tradition was that no one small group could hold the power to govern. Instead, a large number of people could take part in electing officials.

At the end of the eighteenth century, two **political parties**, or groups with different ideas about government, developed. One was the Federalist party. It favored a strong **federal**, or national, government. The other was the Republican party. It believed in less power for the federal government and more power for the states.

In 1800 Thomas Jefferson was elected president. He was a Republican. John Adams, who was president before him, was a Federalist. While other countries often fought wars when government power changed hands, the United States proved war was not necessary. Its government changed hands through a peaceful election. People with different ideas about how to run the country were able to get along. This was an important step in giving the country a stable government.

In the election of 1800 mostly men who were wealthy or owned property voted. Around 1830 the number of voters was greatly increased. New states in the western part of the country began to allow all adult white males to vote. They no longer had to own land or have money to vote. Soon other states also began to change their laws so all adult white males could vote.

The southern states, however, did not follow the pattern. There, owners of large plantations still controlled political life. Millions of black slaves in the South still had no political rights. Despite this, the government of the United States was one of the most democratic in the world at the time.

1. What two political parties developed in the United States?
2. What was important about the election of 1800?
3. What was one reason the number of voters increased in the early nineteenth century?

TERRITORIAL EXPANSION   At the end of the Revolutionary War, the United States had claimed all the land east of the Mississippi River. War and disease had broken the power of the Indians in the area. The government created new states there.

Around 1830 it began to move the remaining Indians west of the Mississippi River. There they had to live on **reservations**, or special areas of land. As settlers began moving further west, they took over more and more Indian land.

In 1803 the United States doubled its size by buying the Louisiana Territory from France. The Louisiana Purchase provided an area rich in farmland, minerals, and forests. It also gave the United States control of the Mississippi River and New Orleans, an important seaport.

In 1819 the United States signed a treaty with Spain. The treaty gave the United States Florida and set the boundary between the lands of the Louisiana Purchase and Spanish land to the south and west.

One of the lands belonging to Spain was Mexico. It became independent in 1822. The Mexicans wanted more people to settle in their territory, especially in the northern province of Texas. So they invited people from the United States to live there and become Mexican citizens. About 30,000 settled in Texas.

AMERICAN INDIAN LIFE

The Indians west of the Mississippi River lived in villages along rivers and streams. They farmed the land and hunted buffalo. For recreation, almost all Indians played games. In this nineteenth-century painting, Indian women play *shinty,* a ball game similar to field hockey.

How did the United States government treat the American Indians?

THE GROWTH OF THE UNITED STATES

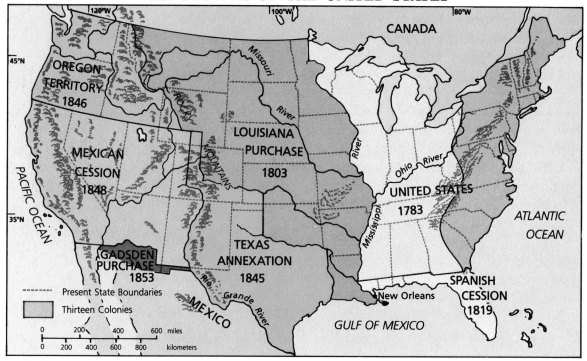

Most of the settlers were from the South, and many owned slaves. When Mexico outlawed slavery in 1829, the Texans quarreled with the Mexican government over slavery and other political issues. In 1835 the Texans revolted. The following year they declared their independence.

Many Americans believed it was the country's destiny to stretch from the Atlantic to the Pacific Ocean. They wanted the federal government to **annex**, or take over and add on, Texas. In 1845 the United States did so. This greatly angered Mexico. The following year the two countries were at war. American troops invaded California, which had been part of Mexico until it declared its independence in 1845. They also captured Mexico City. Mexico was forced to sign the Treaty of Guadalupe Hidalgo which gave the United States almost half of Mexico's land. From this land came the states of California, Nevada, Utah, and parts of Arizona, Colorado, New Mexico, and Wyoming.

Another large area of land added to the United States was the Oregon territory. Around 1840 thousands of settlers made the long, hard trip over the Rocky Mountains to Oregon, which both the United States and England claimed. These settlers assured the United States of control. In 1846 the two countries agreed to divide the territory at the forty-ninth parallel, except for the tip of Vancouver Island. The land below this line later became the states of Oregon and Washington.

In 1853, the United States bought a piece of land from Mexico in hopes of building a railroad to the Pacific. This was called the Gadsden Purchase. The land later became part of Arizona and New Mexico.

In less than a century the United States had grown from 13 colonies to one of the largest countries in the world.

1. How did the United States get the land east of the Mississippi River?
2. How did Texas become part of the United States?
3. How did the United States acquire Arizona, California, Nevada, New Mexico, and Utah?
4. What helped the United States acquire the Oregon territory?

CIVIL WAR AND REUNION As the United States expanded westward, differences arose between the northern and southern states. The northern states contained a growing number of factories. Most of the states supported a strong national government. The southern states depended on such crops as cotton, tobacco, rice, and indigo. They were grown on large plantations that used slave labor. As the country grew, the South wished to expand slavery into new areas. The North wanted the new areas to remain free.

Lincoln and Advisors

In 1860 Abraham Lincoln became president. The South feared he would try to do away with slavery. Seven southern states announced that they were **seceding**, or withdrawing from being part of the nation. The North did not think the states had a right to secede. But the South felt they did, and four more states soon seceded. By 1861 the North and the South were fighting a civil war. In 1865 the North won the war, and once again the country was united.

The Civil War settled the question of whether or not states had the right to secede if the federal government did not want them to do so. It also led to freedom for the nearly 4 million black slaves in the South. The country began to rebuild. By 1870 it was on its way to becoming a strong industrial nation and a growing world power.

1. What way of life developed in the southern states?
2. What way of life developed in the northern states?
3. What action did the South take after the election of 1860?
4. What were two results of the civil war in the United States?

LATIN AMERICA

At the same time the United States was expanding and settling its internal differences, the European-ruled colonies of Latin America were working toward their independence. The revolutions that had taken place in other parts of the world began to affect the thinking of Latin Americans.

HAITI'S LIBERATOR

In 1804 Toussaint L'Ouverture and his troops defeated the French and made Haiti the first free black nation in the Western Hemisphere. Here the Haitian leader meets with French generals to make peace.

What earlier events influenced Latin American independence movements?

In 1791 the people of Haiti, an island ruled by the French, revolted. They were led by Toussaint L'Ouverture, a former slave. The French tried to regain control of Haiti in the next several years, but they were not successful. By 1804 Haiti was a free nation.

Most Latin Americans, however, were ruled by the Spanish, not the French. Many people in the Spanish colonies wanted freedom from Spain. Most who favored independence were creoles. They were well-educated and had enough power and influence to change things. The creoles resented the peninsulares, who controlled the most important government posts. The peninsulares, in turn, thought the creoles were beneath them.

Soon after the French Revolution began, Antonio Nariño of New Granada translated into Spanish the French Declaration of the Rights of Man. Nariño was arrested and put in prison. But that did not stop the spread of the ideas of the French Revolution.

1. What was the first Latin American colony to revolt for independence? Whose colony was it?
2. How did Antonio Nariño help spread the ideas of the French Revolution through the Spanish colonies?

THE INDEPENDENCE MOVEMENT   In 1808 the French invaded Spain. The French ruler, Napoleon Bonaparte, made his brother Joseph the new king of Spain. This led to a struggle for control of the Spanish government that lasted for the next several years.

At first many leading creoles organized to protest against the French. However, the movement quickly changed. The creoles saw their chance to get rid of Spanish control. In 1810 leaders in Caracas, New Granada, organized a **junta**, or committee, to take over the government. Spanish officials soon crushed the movement. But a second movement in the viceroyalty of La Plata was more successful. In 1816 the people there organized several towns and cities into the United Provinces of La Plata.

The independence movement spread quickly to almost all the areas under Spanish control. Latin American leaders of different areas worked to help each other. A soldier named José de San Martín organized an army in La Plata and readied it to help the people of Chile. In Chile another soldier, Bernardo

O'Higgins, led a revolt against Spanish forces. Together San Martín and O'Higgins defeated the Spanish. Chile became independent in 1818.

In 1819, Simón Bolívar, one of the original organizers of the junta, defeated the Spanish in New Granada. Two years later, the last of the Spanish forces were defeated in Venezuela. Bolívar and San Martín planned to attack Peru together. Peru was the strongest of Spain's colonies in the Americas. But San Martín and Bolívar had a falling out, and San Martín left his army in Peru. Bolívar went on to lead the independence movement to victory there. The last Spanish forces in Peru were defeated in 1824. For his efforts, Bolívar gained the title of "The Liberator." The following year Antonio de Sucre, a general under Bolívar, **liberated**, or freed, upper Peru, or Bolivia, from Spanish control.

1. What led the creoles in the Spanish colonies to form juntas?
2. What did José de San Martín and Bernardo O'Higgins do for independence?
3. How did Simón Bolívar earn the title of "The Liberator"?

MEXICO, CENTRAL AMERICA, AND BRAZIL   In 1810 Indians in Mexico revolted. Their leader was Father Miguel Hidalgo, a Catholic priest. He had long been concerned about the poor treatment of the Indians and their loss of land. The revolt failed, and Hidalgo was caught and executed. Father José Morelos, a follower of Hidalgo, led a second revolt. But that one was no more successful than the first one.

In 1820 the creoles revolted. Two years later, Mexico was declared independent. It was ruled by Augustín de Iturbide, who served as emperor. But the Mexicans soon tired of Iturbide's rule. In 1823 they overthrew him and made Mexico a republic.

Brazilian Church

While Iturbide was still in power, Central America became part of Mexico. But the people of Central America did not want to be ruled by Mexico or anyone else. They declared their independence and united to form the United Provinces of Central America. Not long after, the United Provinces split into the nations of Costa Rica, El Salvador, Guatemala, Honduras, and Nicaragua.

While the Mexicans were fighting for independence, the government in Brazil was undergoing changes. When Napoleon invaded Spain and Portugal, the Portuguese royal family left the

INDEPENDENCE IN LATIN AMERICA

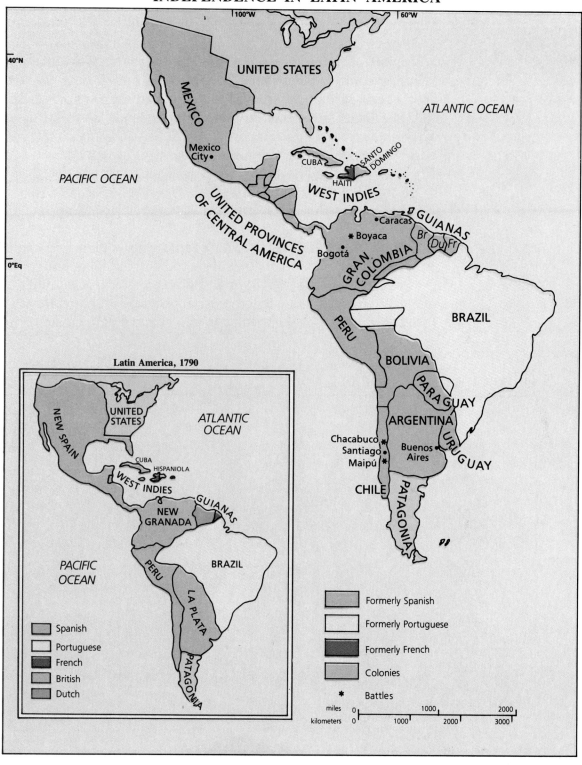

country and went to Brazil. In 1821 King João VI returned to Portugal, leaving his son Pedro to rule Brazil.

Many Brazilians could see no reason to remain a part of the Portuguese Empire. They resented the fact that Portugal was trying to control their trade. They also did not like the way the Portuguese parliament treated the Brazilian representatives. In 1822 the Brazilians declared their independence from Portugal. They made Pedro their emperor. Brazil was the only country in South America to become a monarchy after independence.

1. Why did Father Hidalgo revolt against Spanish rule?
2. Why did Brazil want to be free of Portuguese rule?
3. What was Brazil's government like after independence?

RULE BY CAUDILLOS   The people who helped free Latin America from European control hoped the independent countries would become strong. Simón Bolivár and others wanted the old viceroyalties to stay together and form several large nations. Instead, they began to break up into many smaller countries.

PEOPLE OF THE AMERICAS

Herder
South America
1750

Quicha
South America
1760

Colonists
North America
1770

Wealthy Couple
U.S.A.
1815

Peasant
Costa Rica
1820

Frontie
U.S
18

The old Spanish area of New Granada, renamed Gran Colombia, soon broke up into Venezuela, Colombia, and Ecuador. The viceroyalty of Peru broke up into Peru, Bolivia, and Chile. Paraguay was formed out of the upper part of the old viceroyalty of La Plata. In 1823 Uruguay broke away from both Brazil and the United Provinces of La Plata and became an independent nation.

But Spanish rule had given the people little experience in self-government. Mestizos, blacks, and Indians had received no opportunity for education. Creoles were not willing to share power with other groups. For these reasons, some Latin Americans did not feel that the new countries were ready for democracy.

A new type of leader called a *caudillo*, or military leader, rose to power. Caudillos were supported by the army. Most were backed by large landowners who did not want change that would not benefit them. A certain pattern came into being. A caudillo took over a government by force. That caudillo ruled until he

Wealthy Brazilian 1840

Southern Slave U.S.A. 1850

Politician and Wife U.S.A. 1860

Gaucho Argentina 1860

Chola Bolivia 1870

Western Miner U.S.A. 1870

Native American North America 1870

THE ALAMO

In 1836 Santa Anna and his troops defeated Texas soldiers at the Alamo. Although Santa Anna won this battle, he eventually lost Texas to the United States. What kind of ruler was Santa Anna?

was overthrown by another caudillo. Each change in government was accompanied by a violent revolution and much bloodshed. As a result, most Latin American countries did not have a stable government.

1. What did the Latin Americans who fought for independence expect to happen after independence?
2. Why did democracy fail to develop in Latin America after independence?
3. What effect did caudillos have on the development of stable government?

CORRUPTION AND REFORM Most caudillos ruled as dictators. They did not care about improving the lot of the people or the country. One such caudillo was Juan Manuel de Rosas, who ruled Argentina from 1835 until 1852. He was ruthless and crushed anyone who did not agree with him. During his rule, Argentina was divided into two groups that threatened to split the country. One was the people of the city of Buenos Aires. The other was the ranchers of the *pampas*, or plains. Only the strong control kept by Rosas held the country together.

Another example is Antonio López de Santa Anna. He led his troops into Mexico City in 1833 and had himself elected president. Between 1833 and 1855, he ruled Mexico six times. Under his rule, Mexico lost half of its land to the United States.

A different type of caudillo took Santa Anna's place. He proved that a caudillo could care about other people's needs. His name was Benito Juárez. He was the first Indian to rule Mexico since the fall of the Aztec Empire. Juárez cared deeply about the people of Mexico. He wanted to put an end to the special privileges enjoyed by the rich. He made laws to restrict the power of the Catholic Church. The laws also provided for the sale of church property not used for worship. Juárez also worked to give the poor people of Mexico land of their own. This led to three years of civil war. When it looked like Juárez was gaining ground, his enemies brought in the French. They made a European prince named Maximilian emperor. Juárez and his followers finally won out over the French.

In 1867 Juárez became president of Mexico. He served as president until his death in 1872. During his presidency, Juárez worked to hold free and democratic elections. He started schools to educate Indian children. He reduced the size of the army. In Mexico today, Juárez is still remembered as a great hero.

1. What were most caudillos like?
2. How was Benito Juárez different from most caudillos?
3. What reforms did Juárez make in Mexico?

DEVELOPMENT OF BRAZIL

Brazil's development was different from that of the other Latin American countries. In 1831 Pedro I was forced to step down as emperor. His five-year-old son became the new emperor, Pedro II. Advisors ruled in his place until 1841, when he was old enough to rule on his own. He headed the Brazilian government for the next 48 years.

Pedro II was one of the best-educated rulers of the nineteenth century. More important, he cared for the people of Brazil. He brought the country peace and good government, which allowed it to develop. During his rule, agriculture and industry were encouraged. Large amounts of coffee and rubber were shipped to other countries. Since Brazil's government was stable, England was willing to lend the country money for much-needed construction projects. Railroads, telegraph lines, canals, and factories were built with the borrowed money. This meant not only a better system of communication and more industry. It also meant more jobs and better wages for the people.

1. What did Pedro II do to encourage the development of Brazil?

CHAPTER REVIEW

SUMMARY

1. While under English control, the 13 colonies in the Americas developed a tradition of popular rule.

2. Soon after the United States became an independent nation, two political parties developed.

3. In 1800, political power in the United States passed from one party to the other through a peaceful election rather than through war.

4. By 1830 most adult white males in the United States were able to vote, thus making the government one of the most democratic in the world at the time.

5. By 1853 the United States had added the Louisiana territory, Florida, Texas, almost half of Mexico's land, and the Oregon territory, thus more than doubling its size.

6. Between 1861 and 1865 northern states and southern states fought a civil war.

7. In 1865 the North and the South reunited, and the United States began to develop into a strong industrial nation.

8. In 1804 Haiti was the first Latin American nation to win independence.

9. The Spanish colonies in Latin America and the Portuguese colony of Brazil gained their independence between 1808 and 1825.

10. The newly independent Latin American countries lacked experience in self-government and, as a result, most were ruled by a series of caudillos.

11. Most caudillos were dictators who did not care about the people.

12. One caudillo who cared about the people and worked to give them democracy and education was Benito Juárez.

13. Pedro II, emperor of Brazil from 1841 to 1885, cared for the people and improved agriculture and industry.

BUILDING VOCABULARY

1. *Identify the following:*

Latin America	Treaty of Guadalupe	Bernardo O'Higgins	Juan Manuel
Federalist	Hidalgo	Simón Bolívar	de Rosas
Republican	Abraham Lincoln	Antonio de Sucre	Antonio López
Thomas Jefferson	Toussaint L'Ouverture	Miguel Hidalgo	de Santa Anna
Louisiana Purchase	Antonio Nariño	Augustín de	Benito Juárez
Gadsden Purchase	José de San Martín	Iturbide	Pedro II

2. *Define the following:*

stable government	reservations	seceding	liberated
political parties	annex	junta	caudillo
federal			pampas

REVIEWING THE FACTS

1. What idea did the Federalist party have about government?
2. What idea did the Republican party have about government?
3. What became of the Indians east of the Mississippi River after 1830?
4. What did the United States gain by the Louisiana Purchase?
5. Why did the people of Texas quarrel with the Mexican government?
6. Why did caudillos rise to power in most Latin American countries?
7. What groups supported most caudillos?
8. What happened to Mexico's territory under the rule of Antonio López de Santa Anna?
9. Why is Benito Juárez still remembered as a great hero in Mexico?
10. What did England do to help Brazil develop?

DISCUSSING IMPORTANT IDEAS

1. What is the relationship between a stable government and a nation's development?
2. How did the ideas of the American Revolution and the French Revolution affect the people of Latin America?
3. Do you think Simón Bolívar deserved the title of "Liberator"? Why or why not?
4. Do you think a nation can develop without a democratic government? Explain the reasons for your answer.

USING MAPS

Refer to the map on page 544, and answer the following questions:
1. What is the time period of the map?
2. Where are the Thirteen Colonies?
3. What river forms the western border of the United States in 1783?
4. When was the Louisiana Purchase?
5. Where are the Rocky Mountains?
6. What is the distance across the United States at the widest point?

Refer to the map on page 549, and answer the following questions:
1. To what country does Cuba belong?
2. How far is Caracas from Buenos Aires?
3. What is the southernmost area on the map?
4. How far north does Mexico extend?
5. What is the only French colony?
6. What was Gran Colombia called in 1790?

CULTURAL DEVELOPMENTS

Cultural life flourished in Europe in the eighteenth and nineteenth centuries. Composers performed new types of music on a variety of new instruments. Artists and writers presented the daily life of nobles and common people in their works. By 1850 many artists departed from the traditional rules of painting and developed their own styles. French painters called Impressionists began to use light and bright colors. Their themes were such events as sports and Sunday afternoon

strolls. The new science of photography began to replace art as a detailed recorder of people and events. Opera, with its blend of instrumental music and singing, grew in popularity. The arts also began to serve the Industrial Revolution. To attract buyers, different styles of advertising popularized products. By 1900 the arts belonged to the common people as well as the wealthy.

CHAPTER 36

EUROPE IN FERMENT

By 1799 the French had experienced ten years of revolution and war. They did not like the Directory, their latest revolutionary government. It had not been able to end the fighting or pay the national debt. It could not control inflation. The people longed for a return to peace and order. They were ready for a strong leader to take charge. When that leader came along, he started a chain of events that affected not only France but all of Europe.

THE AGE OF NAPOLEON

When the French Revolution began, a young Corsican named Napoleon Bonaparte was a lieutenant in the French army. By the time he was 28 years old, he had become a general. But Napoleon was an ambitious man and was not satisfied just being a famous general. He wanted all the political power he could get.

In 1799 Napoleon was in Egypt fighting the English. Austria, Russia, and England had united against France. They had defeated the French army in several battles, which caused problems for the French Directory. When he heard that the Directory was in trouble, Napoleon quickly returned to France. There he and two members of the Directory plotted to take over the government. On November 9, 1799, they put their plan in effect and met with success.

Napoleon set up a new government with himself at its head as First Consul. He promised to end the war with Austria, Russia, and England. Since he was a great military leader, the people believed and supported him.

1. Why did Napoleon leave Egypt and return to France in 1799?
2. How did Napoleon become First Consul of France?

THE GOVERNMENT   Napoleon kept his promise of peace. By the time he became First Consul, Russia was no longer at war with France. But Austria and England were. In 1801 Napoleon led his army to victory over Austria. In 1802 he arranged a peace treaty with England.

When Napoleon took over the central government, it was weak, inefficient, and in debt. Once there was peace, he turned his attention to making the government in Paris stronger, more efficient, and richer. He took away the people's right to elect their own local officials. Instead, they were appointed by the central government. He took away the local governments' power to collect taxes and gave it to the central government. Because Napoleon's system was better organized, the government was able to collect more taxes. Within a few years, the government debt was paid, and the economy had improved.

The French Revolution had swept away most laws. And the revolutionary governments had never been able to agree on new ones. As a result, the French legal system was in confusion.

Different laws were followed in different parts of the country. Napoleon appointed a committee of lawyers and told them to write a new code of law as quickly as possible. The code they wrote was called the Napoleonic Law Codes. It established a single set of laws for the entire country. At the same time, it preserved some of the most important values of the Revolution. Serfdom was abolished. People were equal before the law. Freedom of religion was guaranteed. A system of public education was established.

Some rights the people had won in the Revolution were taken away from them. Napoleon did not allow freedom of speech or the press. No one was allowed to criticize the government. A large police force kept watch on anyone suspected of being against Napoleon. Many people were put in jail for political crimes.

Because Napoleon brought the peace and order he had promised, he was very popular. In 1802 he asked the people to vote him First Consul for life, and they did so. Two years later he crowned himself Emperor of France.

1. How did Napoleon strengthen the central government?
2. What rights did the Napoleonic Law Codes give the people? What rights did it take away?

French Soldier

THE GRAND EMPIRE   Being emperor of France was not enough for Napoleon. He wanted a Grand Empire that would take the place of the Holy Roman Empire.

In 1803 Napoleon started another war against England. Before long almost every country in Europe was involved. Napoleon's armies won most of their battles, and in the next few years added several territories to the Grand Empire.

Napoleon had himself crowned king of Italy. In 1806 he created the Confederation of the Rhine, which was a loose union of conquered German states. The following year he invaded Spain and Portugal. In 1809, he put the Pope in prison and made the Papal States part of France. By 1810 Napoleon was the most powerful person in Europe.

The countries in Napoleon's Grand Empire were strongly influenced by French customs and ideals. The French took over the governments in many conquered states. Sometimes Napoleon placed his relatives on the throne of a conquered state. The

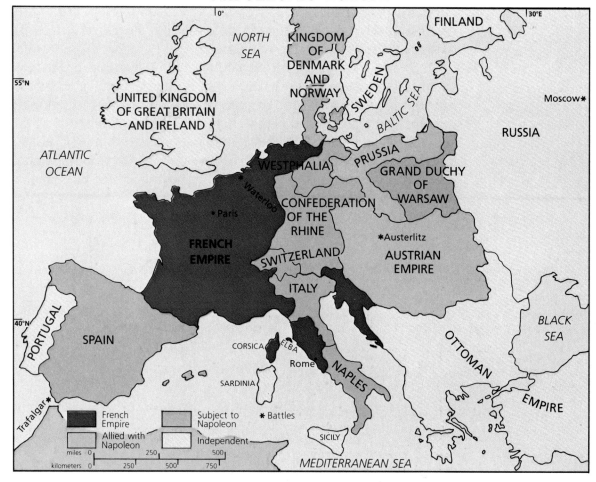

Map legend:
- French Empire
- Allied with Napoleon
- Subject to Napoleon
- Independent
- ★ Battles

Labels on map: NORTH SEA, KINGDOM OF DENMARK AND NORWAY, FINLAND, SWEDEN, BALTIC SEA, Moscow★, RUSSIA, UNITED KINGDOM OF GREAT BRITAIN AND IRELAND, 55°N, ATLANTIC OCEAN, WESTPHALIA, PRUSSIA, GRAND DUCHY OF WARSAW, ★Waterloo, CONFEDERATION OF THE RHINE, Paris, FRENCH EMPIRE, ★Austerlitz, SWITZERLAND, AUSTRIAN EMPIRE, ITALY, BLACK SEA, PORTUGAL, 40°N, SPAIN, CORSICA, ELBA, Rome, NAPLES, OTTOMAN EMPIRE, SARDINIA, Trafalgar★, SICILY, MEDITERRANEAN SEA

miles 0 250 500
kilometers 0 250 500 750

French rulers made the Napoleonic Codes law. Napoleon's conquests helped spread the ideas of the French Revolution throughout Europe.

Only England and Russia remained undefeated by Napoleon. Since the French could not win against the English navy, Napoleon tried a different method. He forbade the countries in his empire to trade with the English. But his order was difficult to enforce, and it soon proved unsuccessful. In 1813 English troops drove the French out of Portugal and Spain.

Meanwhile, Napoleon took on the Russians. In the summer of 1812, he decided to invade Russia. He suffered a serious defeat and lost most of his army. Only about 30,000 of his 500,000 soldiers returned to France. Most had died from disease, lack of food, and the bitterly cold Russian winter. Napoleon quickly raised another army, but the new soldiers were not well-trained. They were soon defeated by the allied forces of Austria, Prussia, Russia, and England.

In 1814 Napoleon was forced to give up his throne. He was sent to live out his days on the small island of Elba off the coast of Italy. But he managed to escape and gather together enough troops to invade France. For a short 100 days, Napoleon again reigned as emperor. The allies finally defeated him in 1815 at the Battle of Waterloo. They gave the French throne to Louis XVIII. They sent Napoleon to the island of St. Helena off the coast of Africa, where he died.

1. Why did Napoleon start a war against England?
2. How was Napoleon defeated?

EUROPE AFTER THE CONGRESS OF VIENNA

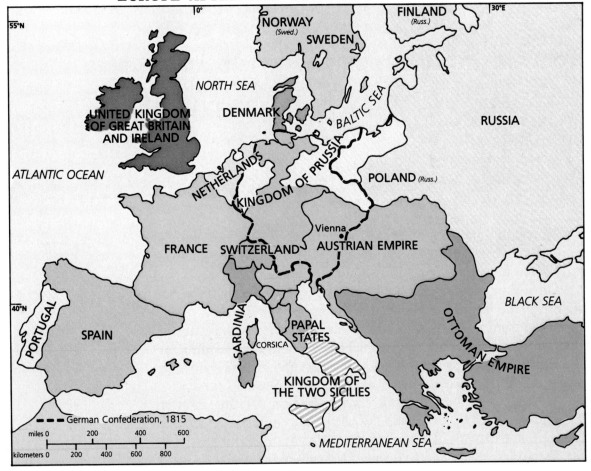

THE CONGRESS OF VIENNA

After Napoleon's defeat in 1814, representatives from Austria, Prussia, Russia, and England met in Vienna to decide France's fate. The meeting was called the Congress of Vienna. The Congress leaders did not want to punish France too harshly and were willing for France to remain a major power. They wanted a **balance of power**, or equal strength among countries. They hoped that in that way no country would be tempted to start another war.

The leaders of the Congress believed that the best way to keep peace and order was to crush revolutionary ideas and bring back divine-right monarchy. Louis XVIII had already been given back the French throne. The Congress also restored the monarchy in Prussia, Austria, and Spain. They made the Pope ruler of the Papal States again.

European Diplomat

Austria, Prussia, Russia, and England divided up Napoleon's Grand Empire. They cut France back to the size it had been before the French Revolution. Russia took Finland and part of Poland. Sweden took Norway. Belgium and Holland were combined. Austria got parts of northern Italy, and England got the islands of Malta and Ceylon. The 39 German states were combined into the German Confederation.

1. Why was the Congress of Vienna held?
2. How was the Grand Empire divided up?

REACTIONS   The balance of power was maintained for many years. But revolutionary ideas never died. Several groups opposed the Congress System, or the political system set up by the Congress of Vienna.

One group was the **liberals**, or those who wanted political reform based on the ideals of the French Revolution. Most liberals were members of the middle class. They wanted reforms that would benefit themselves. They believed in voting rights for property owners, protection of private property, and such individual rights as freedom of speech. Some liberals wanted a **constitutional monarchy**, or a monarch whose power was limited by a constitution. Other liberals wanted a republic. The liberals were strongest in the industrialized countries, especially France and England.

Another group that opposed the Congress System was the **nationalists**, or those who want political independence for national groups who share the same language and customs. The Congress of Vienna had paid no attention to nationalist feelings when it divided the Grand Empire. The Belgians did not want to be part of Holland. The Norwegians did not want to be part of Sweden. The Poles and Finns did not want to be ruled by Russia. Germans, Hungarians, and Italians did not like being dominated by the Austrians.

A third group that opposed the Congress System was the **socialists**, or those who believe that the people as a whole should own all the land, factories, and other means of production. In this way, socialists believe, the workers' poor living conditions will improve, and everyone will be treated fairly. Some socialists tried to set up model communities based on economic cooperation. They thought the communities would show that theirs was a better way of life. Other socialists believed that the only way to get reforms was to have a revolution. One such believer was Karl Marx, a German. He said that a socialist revolution was bound to come. He believed that the working classes would rise up and take control.

1. What did liberals believe?
2. What did nationalists believe?
3. What did socialists believe?

REVOLUTION AND REFORM

In Spain, Portugal, and Russia, liberals, nationalists, and socialists led several revolutions against the Congress System. Most failed. One that did not fail took place in 1821. That year Greek nationalists rebelled against the Ottoman Empire. England, France, and Russia supported the nationalists. As a result, in 1830 Greece became independent.

That same year, there was a revolution in France. King Louis XVIII had been succeeded by his brother, Charles X, who believed in the divine right of rulers. He did not like the liberals. In July, 1830, he issued the July Ordinances. They did away with the newly elected national assembly. They also took the right to vote away from the middle class. Middle-class liberals, helped by students and workers who could not find jobs, overthrew the government. After three days of fighting, Charles X fled.

The July Revolution, as it was called, was a victory for the French middle class. But wealthy property-owners had controlled the rebellion, and they wanted a constitutional monarchy. They gave the throne to Charles X's cousin, Louis Philippe, and gave the right to vote only to the richest members of the middle class. The working-class revolutionaries had wanted a republican government. They also had wanted the right to vote to be given to all males. As a result, they were left disappointed.

Ornamental Egg

The news of the revolution in France touched off rebellions in other countries. In 1831 Belgian nationalists won independence from Holland. The Poles rebelled against Russia, but they were defeated. Uprisings in several German and Italian states were also put down.

In England, however, liberal reforms were made without revolution. In 1832 Parliament passed a bill that lowered the property requirements for voting. This increased by half the number of people who had the right to vote. The bill also gave the new industrial towns more representation in Parliament. These changes gave the English middle class more say in government. Other reforms that helped the working class soon followed. Children no longer were allowed to work in mills and mines. Working hours were limited to ten hours a day.

1. Why was the 1821 Greek nationalist revolution successful?
2. Why did the French rebel in 1830? What reforms did they win?
3. What reforms were made in England?

THE REVOLUTIONS OF 1848   In 1848 there was again revolution throughout Europe. And once again the trouble started in France. Louis Philippe's government did not serve most people's interests. Middle-class liberals and industrial workers became more and more unhappy. At the same time, the economy was bad throughout Europe. Many people did not have jobs. There was not enough food to go around.

Riots broke out in the streets of Paris. Louis Philippe fled, and the revolutionary leaders declared the Second French Republic. They set up a **provisional**, or temporary, government to rule until a new national assembly could be elected. A socialist named Louis Blanc was one of the leaders of the provisional government. He wanted to set up **national workshops**, or factories run by the workers but paid for by the government. He thought the workshops would provide more jobs for the people. The other members of the provisional government did not like the idea. But they needed the support of the workers. So they agreed. The workshops provided jobs for thousands of people. But the numbers of people out of work increased faster than jobs could be created. Before long the government was supporting more than 100,000 people.

When the new national assembly was elected, it abolished the workshops. The workers revolted, fighting violently for three days. They were defeated, but not before thousands of people were killed. The national assembly then drew up a constitution. It provided for a strong president to be elected by all the people. Napoleon's nephew, Louis Napoleon Bonaparte, was elected president. But he believed he had inherited his uncle's destiny, and in 1851 he overthrew the constitution. A year later, the people voted him Emperor Napoleon III.

The revolution in France was again followed by a series of revolutions in other parts of Europe. Hungarians, Italians, and

WORKERS ORGANIZE

During the nineteenth century European workers set up trade unions and political parties to protect and advance their rights. Here German workers gather to protest a government ban on demonstrations. By 1900 most European industrial countries had passed laws that met many of the workers' demands.

What demands did European workers make upon their governments?

Germans each rebelled. But they all failed. Even so, the revolutions of 1848 led to some important changes. The French gained **universal manhood suffrage**, or the right of all males to vote. In the years that followed, this principle became the main goal of revolutionaries in other countries. By the time World War I began in 1914, most northern and western European countries had universal manhood suffrage.

Another result of the 1848 revolutions was increased bad feelings between the working and middle classes. The workers, who felt they had been cheated, began to turn more toward socialism. These feelings led to the First International Working-men's Association. It was organized in 1864 with the help of Karl Marx. The union brought together socialists from all over Europe. It led to the formation of socialist political parties in most European nations.

French Balloon

1. Why did riots break out in France in 1848?
2. How did Louis Napoleon Bonaparte become president?
3. What were some results of the 1848 revolutions?

A New Nationalism

After the revolutions of 1848 failed, the Congress System seemed stronger than ever. However, this was not the case. The system had been meant to keep the peace. But in 1854 the French and English went to war against the Russians. They fought over who would have the most influence in the Middle East. The war was fought mostly on the Crimea, a small Russian peninsula in the Black Sea. For this reason, it was called the Crimean War. It was the first major war since Napoleon's defeat in 1815. Russia was defeated and lost territories that eventually became part of Rumania. As a result, Russia refused to support the Congress System. The balance of power had changed, and Russia could no longer be counted on to defend it.

1. How did the Crimean War show that the Congress System was beginning to break down?

AUSTRIA   Austria became the chief defender of the Congress System after Russia lost the Crimean War. The Hapsburgs ruled Austria as well as much of central Europe. Their empire was made up of many different national groups. During the second half of the nineteenth century, the growth of nationalism led to major losses for the Austrian Empire.

Austria controlled eight of the nine states of Italy. Only the Papal States, which were ruled by the Pope, were free of Austrian control. Over the years Italian nationalism had been growing steadily. The nationalists had tried to unite Italy in the Revolution of 1848 but had failed. They learned, however, that they needed help to defeat Austria.

Count Camillo di Cavour, the prime minister of the Italian state of Sardinia, supported the nationalists. After the Crimean War, he made an agreement with Napoleon III. If the Austrians attacked Sardinia, the French would help Sardinia. When Austria declared war on Sardinia in 1859, Napoleon III kept his word. Austria was defeated, and the Italian state of Lombardy was united with Sardinia.

Although Napoleon III no longer helped, the other Italian states continued to revolt against Austria. By 1860 most of northern Italy was united and at peace with Austria.

A few months later, an Italian nationalist named Giuseppe Garibaldi led another revolution. It added the Kingdom of the Two Sicilies to a growing, united Italy. In 1861 the kingdom of Italy was formed as a constitutional monarchy. Victor Emmanuel II of Sardinia became king. The Pope, however, was against Italian unity. As a result, he lost the Papal States. In 1870 they became a part of the kingdom of Italy. The unification of Italy helped weaken the balance of power.

1. What territory did the Austrians rule?
2. How did Napoleon III help the Italian nationalists?
3. What did Giuseppe Garibaldi contribute to the Italian nationalist movement?

OTTO VON BISMARCK   Nationalist feeling remained strong in Germany. Still the German states were not able to unite. Many of the rulers of the smaller states were not willing to give up their power. Both Austria and Prussia wanted to be the strongest state in the German Confederation.

In 1862 King William I appointed Otto von Bismarck prime minister of Prussia. Bismarck believed that war against a common enemy would bring the German states closer together. He announced that he would unite Germany by "blood and iron." In 1864 Bismarck joined with Austria to defeat Denmark.

EUROPEAN REVOLUTIONARIES
Nineteenth-century revolutionaries worked to change Europe's political and economic life. Karl Marx (left), a German writer, called upon workers to overthrow the factory owners and create a classless society. Guiseppe Garibaldi (right), an Italian soldier, worked to unite Italy as one nation.
How successful were these two revolutionaries in realizing their goals?

He then went to war against Austria. In 1866 a defeated Austria signed a peace treaty that ended the German Confederation. In its place, the treaty set up the North German Confederation, whose leading state was Prussia.

In 1870 Bismarck found an excuse to go to war against the French, the Germans' oldest enemy. As Bismarck had hoped, the southern German states joined the northern states in the struggle. The Germans defeated the French the following year. The victory brought the Germans the territories of Alsace and Lorraine. That same year William I of Prussia was named emperor of the German Empire. A unified Germany meant a further weakening of the balance of power.

1. How did Otto von Bismarck plan to unite Germany?
2. Why was the North German Confederation created?
3. What was the effect of the war between Prussia and France?

THE POSITION OF EUROPE

By the end of the nineteenth century England was at the peak of its power. Its population had greatly increased, and its government was stable. Reforms were being made quietly without fear of revolution.

In 1866 Hungarian nationalists in Austria saw their chance to become independent. They revolted, and in 1867 a weakened Austria agreed to create a **dual**, or double, monarchy. The Hapsburg emperor ruled over two separate kingdoms—Austria and Hungary. Each had its own parliament and laws. However, the Hungarians and other national groups such as the Serbs and the Croats still were not content. They wanted independence.

France was still considered the home of revolutionary ideas. The war with Prussia had cost Napoleon III his throne. By 1871 the country was once again a republic.

THE GERMAN EMPIRE

After Prussia defeated France in 1871, Bismarck (center) proclaimed King William I of Prussia (on platform) the emperor of a new German empire.

What effect did a united Germany have on other European countries?

Italy was united as a country, but the Italians still were not united as a people. The government worked to bring the people closer together. At the same time it tried to establish the country's place in the European family of nations.

In 1888 a new ruler, Kaiser William II, took control of Germany. He did not get along with Bismarck and in 1890 forced the prime minister to resign. The Kaiser had his own plans for the country.

As the nations unified and expanded, they began to grow in strength. This led to the building up of strong armies and navies and the making of alliances. All of this set the stage for what was to be called World War I.

1. By the end of the nineteenth century, what was the condition of England? Of Austria? Of France? Of Italy? Of Germany?

CHAPTER REVIEW

SUMMARY

1. In 1799 Napoleon Bonaparte helped to overthrow the Directory, and by 1804 he had become emperor of France.

2. Napoleon strengthened the central government, established a single code of laws for the entire country, took away certain rights from the people, and conquered most of western Europe.

3. In 1815 Napoleon was defeated and made to leave France.

4. In 1814 representatives from Austria, Prussia, Russia, and England met at the Congress of Vienna to establish a balance of power.

5. The Congress of Vienna brought back divine-right monarchy in many nations and divided up Napoleon's empire.

6. Liberals, nationalists, and socialists opposed the Congress System.

7. In 1821, 1830, and 1848 revolutions broke out in various European nations.

8. After the revolutions, universal manhood suffrage began to spread, and Europe's working class began to turn toward socialism.

9. Liberal reforms were made in England without a revolution.

10. The Crimean War was a sign that the Congress System was breaking down.

11. During the 1860's the Italian states gradually united to form a nation.

12. Between 1862 and 1871 the German states, led by Otto von Bismarck of Prussia, united to form a nation.

BUILDING VOCABULARY

1. *Identify the following:*

Napoleon Bonaparte	Napoleonic Law Codes	Grand Empire	Battle of Waterloo
Louis XVIII	Congress of Vienna	Karl Marx	Congress System

Charles X	Louis Blanc	Count Camillo di Cavour	Otto von Bismarck
July Revolution	Napoleon III	Giuseppe Garibaldi	Kaiser William II
Louis Philippe	Crimean War	Victor Emanuel II	

2. *Define the following:*

balance of power	nationalists	national workshops
liberals	socialists	universal manhood suffrage
constitutional monarchy	provisional	dual

REVIEWING THE FACTS

1. What did Napoleon want after he became a general?

2. How did the Napoleonic Codes change the French legal system?

3. What effects did Napoleon's conquests have on western Europe?

4. Why did the representatives at the Congress of Vienna try to bring back divine-right monarchy?

5. What three groups opposed the Congress System?

6. Why did the French provisional government of 1848 set up national workshops?

7. Why did the Crimean War break out in 1854?

8. Why did the Austrian Empire gradually lose territory during the second half of the nineteenth century?

9. How did the Italian states become a unified nation?

10. Why did Napoleon III lose his throne?

DISCUSSING IMPORTANT IDEAS

1. Do you consider universal manhood suffrage important? Why or why not?

2. Do you think that the conquests made by Napoleon were good or bad for Europe? Explain.

3. How important do you think nationalism was in Europe during the second half of the nineteenth century? Explain.

4. Do you think liberal reforms can be made without a revolution? Explain.

USING MAPS

Compare the maps on pages 561 and 562, and answer the following questions:

1. How far did French territory extend before and after the Congress of Vienna?

2. What is the longitude and latitude of the island that remained French after the Congress of Vienna?

3. What did the Confederation of the Rhine become after 1815?

4. What city is southwest of Austerlitz?

5. Who took control of Napoleon's Grand Duchy of Warsaw?

CHAPTER 37

RISE OF IMPERIALISM

L{.ate} in the nineteenth century an interest in colonization again arose. Many nations rushed to control parts of the world that had not been claimed during the Ages of Discovery and New World Expansion. New colonial powers were added to the old. These included Belgium, Germany, Italy, Japan, Russia, and the United States.

THE MOVE TOWARD IMPERIALISM

There were many reasons why nations decided they had to expand their control. The factories of the industrialized countries needed such raw materials as rubber, cotton, oil, and tin. In addition, there was a growing demand for tea, sugar, and cocoa. Both the raw materials and the food came from Asia and Africa.

Then, too, industries needed new markets for their products. Factories were turning out more goods than people at home could afford to buy. Nations were competing with each other to sell their textiles, machinery, and hardware. To keep another nation's products out, some countries set high tariffs. Many industrial leaders and merchants believed that new markets could be found in Asia, Africa, and Latin America.

Many factory owners had grown rich from profits made during the Industrial Revolution. Wealthy people could not find enough places in their own countries in which to **invest**, or put their money. Even when they did invest, they thought their profits were too small. Investments in undeveloped areas, however, usually gave larger profits. Banks lent money to build roads and railroads, open mines and factories, and start plantations in these areas. But the risks were great. The local people who did the labor were paid low wages. Often they were treated cruelly. To show their feelings, they damaged property owned by outsiders.

Nationalism, or pride in one's country, was another reason for the growing interest in colonies. Many people thought colonies would add to their nation's strength. They did not want unclaimed territory to go to any nation but their own. The newly formed nations of Germany and Italy wanted to catch up with England, France, and other established colonial powers. Just as important as territory to a nation was a strong army and navy. Colonies were a source of soldiers and might provide ports where ships could refuel.

Still another reason for imperialism was the belief that western nations had a duty to "civilize" the "backward" peoples of the world. To many westerners, any people whose way of life and religion were different from their own were "backward." Each industrialized nation thought its culture was the one to carry to these peoples.

1. What were five reasons for the move toward imperialism in the nineteenth century?

AFRICA

The European powers had few holdings in Africa before 1870. Those they did have were seaports and trading stations along the coasts. There were some exceptions. The English, for example, held Africa's southern tip. The Portuguese had colonies on both coasts. And the French held Algeria, which was in the north.

Mungo Park

France and England were rivals for the control of Egypt. Each had made large investments there, which they wanted to protect. By the time the Suez Canal opened in 1869, Egypt became very important to the European powers. The canal connected the Red Sea and the Mediterranean Sea. It made possible the short all-water route to the East that Europeans had sought for hundreds of years. But the Egyptian ruler needed money. So in 1874 he sold his share of the Suez Canal to England. The English and French began to manage Egypt's finances. This made many Egyptians angry. When they rebelled, English troops **occupied**, or moved into, Egypt. At the same time, England took total control of all Egyptian affairs.

The **interior**, or inland areas, of Africa was not yet known to Europeans. They stayed along the coasts where they were safer from tropical diseases and the other dangers of unknown lands. Before long, however, interest in trade and missionary work drew the Europeans inland. In 1770 James Bruce, a Scottish explorer, determined the course of the Blue Nile River. In 1796, and again in 1805, another Scotsman, Mungo Park, explored the course of the Niger River. In 1858 John Hanning Speke, an English explorer, reached Lake Tanganyika and Lake Victoria.

Eighteen years before Speke made his journey, a Scottish missionary named David Livingstone went to Africa to convert the Africans to Christianity. He stayed on there until his death in 1873, returning to England only briefly. During his years in Africa, Livingstone was an explorer as well as a missionary. He crossed the Kalahari Desert from south to north and traced the course of the Zambezi River. When Livingstone disappeared in 1869, Henry Stanley, a New York newspaper reporter, was sent to find him. Stanley found Livingstone two years later and then went on to become an explorer himself. Between 1874 and 1889 Stanley traveled the Nile River and explored the Congo.

The explorers and missionaries brought back stories of the wonders they had seen. Many Europeans were excited by the riches they thought could be gained in Africa.

One of those interested in Africa's interior was King Leopold II of Belgium. In 1878 he hired Henry Stanley to go there to secure lands for him. Between 1879 and 1880 Stanley

THE RHODES COLOSSUS
STRIDING FROM CAPE TOWN TO CAIRO.

BRITISH AFRICA

A late nineteenth-century cartoon (left) shows Cecil Rhodes' dream of spreading British rule in Africa. David Livingstone (right) explored Africa and converted Africans to Christianity.

What obstacles did the British meet in extending their rule in Africa?

signed many treaties with African chiefs in the Congo Basin. Many of the chiefs could not read or write and did not realize what they were signing away. In return for their lands, many of which were rich in minerals and rubber, the chiefs received cloth, beads, and sometimes guns. The signing of such treaties became a common way of getting colonial territory.

The takeover of Egypt and Leopold's acts in the Congo shocked other European leaders into action. The French took territory in the lower Congo. The Germans, then the Portuguese, and finally the English did the same. In 1884 and 1885, the rival nations held a **conference**, or meeting, in Berlin, Germany. They laid down rules for acquiring more African lands. Over the next few years, the European powers divided up the African continent among themselves.

1. Where were most European holdings in Africa before 1870?
2. Why were both England and France eager to control Egypt?
3. How did explorers increase European interest in Africa?
4. What led to the conference in Berlin in 1884 and 1885?

FRANCE   The French also wanted to protect their interests in Africa. In 1880 the lower Congo became a French **protectorate**, or a country under the control and protection of a larger, stronger nation. By 1912 both Tunisia and Morocco were French protectorates, too.

The French also held port cities on the west coast of southern Africa. In 1895 they formed French West Africa. It was a union of several colonies and territories the French had gained earlier. The following year the island of Madagascar became a French colony. In 1910 the lower Congo was joined to three other colonies to form a new, larger colony, called French Equatorial Africa.

By the time the French were finished taking over African lands, theirs was the largest European empire in Africa.

1. Why did the French make African lands protectorates?
2. What areas did the French control in Africa?

ENGLAND   The English, like the French, had interests in Africa they wanted to protect. They already held a group of colonies in western Africa called British West Africa. One of the most important colonies was Nigeria.

While the French pushed from west-to-east, the English moved from north-to-south. The English goal was to control all African land from Cairo, Egypt to the Cape. When the English went south from Egypt into the Sudan, the French opposed them. The rivalry between the two powers continued until 1904 when joint Anglo-Egyptian control of the Sudan was set up.

The English had taken the southern Cape Colony from the Dutch in the early nineteenth century. The Boers, or Dutch people who lived in the Cape Colony, did not want to be ruled by the English. In 1836 many Boers left Cape Colony. They travelled northward across the wilderness in wagons pulled by oxen. They finally settled and founded the independent states known as the Transvaal and the Orange Free State.

When gold and diamonds were discovered in the Boer states in 1885, some English people began to move in. The prime minister of Cape Colony, Cecil Rhodes, decided that some of the wealth from the gold and diamonds should go to England. This led to more bad feelings between the Boers and the English. And in 1899 the Boer War broke out. The English won the war in 1902, and annexed the Boer states. Eight years later, Transvaal and Orange Free State were joined with two other English colonies to form the Union of South Africa.

The English gained other African possessions besides Egypt and South Africa. Between 1890 and 1914, Zanzibar, Uganda, British East Africa, Rhodesia, and Nigeria all came under English control. Except for one German territory, the English had reached their goal.

1. In what direction did the English move to expand their control in Africa?
2. What was the English goal in Africa?
3. How successful were the English in achieving their goal?

OTHER EUROPEAN INTERESTS   Germany and Italy were latecomers to the race for African territory. The Germans set up protectorates over Togo and the Cameroons in 1884. Later they added German Southwest Africa and German East Africa.

Italy did not gain as much territory as the other powers. The Italians added Eritrea, a colony on the eastern coast, and annexed a part of Somaliland. When they tried to take over Ethiopia in 1896, they were defeated. In 1911, however, they won the Turkish province of Tripoli from the Ottomans.

Spain and Portugal, pioneers of colonialism, kept their original possessions. Angola, founded in 1648 by the Portuguese, was the oldest colony in Africa. In 1885 Portugal also made Portuguese East Africa, or Mozambique, a protectorate.

Belgium continued to control the upper Congo, which became the Belgian Congo in 1908. Only two areas remained independent. One was Ethiopia, which had remained free throughout most of its history. The other was Liberia, which had been founded in the 1830s by former slaves from the United States.

1. What areas of Africa were claimed by Germany? By Italy?
2. Which other European countries held possessions in Africa?
3. What two African nations remained independent?

ASIA

The English and the Dutch started trading with Asia in the sixteenth century. But Chinese and Japanese rulers allowed very limited contacts with the West. So Westerners turned their attention to south and southeast Asia.

In the middle of the eighteenth century, the British East India Company, a trading company, got control over much of India. By 1858 the British government had taken control of all the company's land there. Nineteen years later, the English queen, Victoria, was named Empress of India.

Russia also was expanding its territory in Asia. By the middle of the nineteenth century, the Russians had made some advances into central Asia. From 1865 to 1884, most of the central Asian centers of Muslim civilization fell to them. This greatly alarmed the English. They feared the Russians would try to expand into their territory.

INDIAN TEA PLANTATION
In India the British owned large tea plantations, where Indians worked as tea-pickers. This series of drawings shows the steps involved in the growing and preparing of tea for the market in Britain.
How did the British gain control of India?

Both the Russians and the English wanted control of Afghanistan and Persia, or Iran. These countries lay between the Russian possessions in central Asia and the English ones in the Near East. The English also wanted to make sure the Russians did not take land from the weak Ottoman Empire. In 1907 England made Afghanistan a protectorate. Persia was divided up into areas of Russian and English influence.

1. Why did the English and the Dutch turn to south and southeast Asia for trade?
2. Which European nation took control of India?
3. Which nation moved into central Asia?
4. What were the reasons for conflict between Russia and England?

CHINA   From the beginning all trade between the Chinese and Westerners was limited to the city of Canton. The Chinese looked upon Westerners as barbarians, who were beneath them. They expected Westerners to show them respect, follow their rules, and stay away from their people. By the nineteenth century western merchants were no longer satisfied with the limited amount of business the Chinese allowed them. They also wanted the Chinese to consider them as equals.

About this time English traders discovered that the Chinese had a taste for **opium**, or a drug made from the dried juice of poppies. The Chinese government, however, forbade the traders to bring opium into China. When an official in Canton seized and burned a large shipment of opium, English traders became angry. They demanded that the Chinese be punished. Thus, in 1839, the Opium War broke out between the English and the Chinese. In 1842 the Chinese were defeated and forced to sign a treaty that opened more ports to the West. The treaty also gave English citizens in China the **right of extra-territoriality**. This meant that English citizens accused of breaking Chinese laws could not be tried by the Chinese. They could be tried only in English courts.

Before long other western powers demanded and received the same rights as England. The English, French, Germans, Japanese, Russians, and Americans began to influence Chinese affairs. Chinese leaders objected to the foreigners and their interference in Chinese affairs. But the Chinese government did not have the power to keep out the foreign nations.

In 1894 China and Japan went to war over Korea. The Japanese easily won the war. While China was still in a weakened condition, the colonial powers acted. England, France, Germany, and Russia rushed to get **concessions**, or special arrangements and privileges, from the Chinese government. The concessions included rights to develop mineral resources and build railroads and naval bases. Several nations also got leases on Chinese port cities.

The United States did not want to see China divided up among the European powers. But, at the same time, it did not want American merchants to be kept out of trade with China. In 1898 the American government asked the powers interested in China to approve a new policy. It was called the Open Door policy. It gave all nations equal trading rights throughout China.

But the Open Door policy did not please the Chinese. Foreign powers were still trying to control them. So in the spring of 1900 the Chinese began a movement to drive all foreigners from their country. The movement was called the Boxer Rebellion, because it had been started by a Chinese secret society called Boxers. The foreign powers joined forces and rushed an army to China. In 1901 the rebellion was put down. China was made to pay heavy penalties. Now the foreign powers had complete control of China.

Chinese Empress

1. Why did the Chinese want to keep out foreigners?
2. How did the Western powers feel about the Chinese effort to keep them out of China?
3. What did the foreign powers do after China lost a war to Japan in 1895?
4. How did the Chinese react to foreign interference in their country?

JAPAN   Until the middle of the nineteenth century, the Japanese allowed trade only at the port of Nagasaki. The Japanese government even refused to give shelter to shipwrecked sailors. The American government decided to do something about the situation. In 1853 it sent a naval force under Commodore Matthew Perry to Japan. Perry had orders to arrange for a treaty to open up trade and improve the treatment of shipwrecked American sailors. Perry was successful, and Japan signed similar treaties with England, France, Russia, and the Netherlands.

Contact with the West and seeing what happened to China, which did not modernize, convinced Japanese leaders that Japan must become more modern and industrialize. It did so at a rapid rate. By the end of the nineteenth century, Japan was fully industrialized.

Modernization led to problems. Japan was a small country. It did not have enough land to grow what was needed to feed its growing population. It also had to obtain raw materials and markets for its growing industry. To help solve these problems, the Japanese began a program of imperialism. In 1894 the Japanese attacked China. Ten years later the Japanese were fighting the Russians. When the Japanese won the war, the Russians were forced to give Japan territory.

1. Why did Commodore Perry go to Japan in 1853?
2. What was the result of Japan's contact with the West?
3. Why did the Japanese begin a program of imperialism?

SOUTHEAST ASIA AND THE ISLANDS OF PACIFIC

Europeans first entered Southeast Asia in the sixteenth century looking for spices. By the seventeenth century, Portugal, Spain, and the Netherlands all had colonies there. There was an active trade with the islands in the area, but no one paid much attention to lands of the interior.

Hawaiian Queen

In the later part of the nineteenth century, the Europeans once more began to take interest in southeast Asia and other areas nearby. The area was a source of coffee and tea. Later, other resources such as petroleum, rubber, minerals, and precious stones also became important.

Only the Kingdom of Siam, or Thailand, remained independent. England took control of Burma, Singapore, and Malaysia. During this same period, France, Germany, England, and the United States were trying to win control of islands in the Pacific. Some of the islands, such as Hawaii, had rich soil that could be used for plantations. Others had minerals that could be mined. Still others could be used as bases for refueling and repairing ships.

By the end of the nineteenth century, France had claimed the Marquesas, Tahiti, and several other islands. England had taken over, among others, the Fiji, Gilbert, and Cook Islands. The United States controlled Guam, the Philippine Islands,

American Samoa, and the Hawaiian Islands. Western Samoa belonged to Germany.

1. Why did many European nations want to control territory in Southeast Asia?
2. Why did the world powers want to control islands in the Pacific?

LATIN AMERICA

The Latin American nations that gained their independence early in the nineteenth century were faced with many problems. Wealthy landowners with special privileges owned almost all the land. But most Latin Americans were poor and had no land of their own. The new leaders had little government experience. There were many fights in which lives and property were destroyed. These shaky conditions seemed to invite outside interference.

The United States decided to do something to make sure no powerful European nation took over the Latin American countries. In 1823 President James Monroe issued the Monroe Doctrine. It pledged that the United States would not interfere with colonies already in Latin America. The doctrine was also meant to serve as a warning to foreign powers. Any attempt to gain new colonies or to retake independent states in Latin America would be considered an unfriendly act toward the United States. Many Latin Americans, however, saw the doctrine in a different light. They felt the United States was interfering in their affairs. They did not think the United States had any right to do this.

Winning the Spanish-American War of 1898 involved the United States even more in Latin American affairs. The United States won from Spain the Caribbean island of Puerto Rico and the Pacific islands of Guam and the Philippines. All the islands except Cuba became American possessions. Cuba was organized as a protectorate.

Now the North Americans needed a way to protect their new empire. They had to connect their islands in the Caribbean Sea with those in the Pacific Ocean.

In 1903 the United States government supported a revolution by people in Panama against Colombia. At that time, Panama was a province of Colombia. The revolution was a

PANAMA CANAL

The building of the Panama Canal was a major engineering feat. The builders dug a passage through the mountains that linked the Pacific Ocean and the Caribbean Sea. Here workers build the locks which control floodwaters and bring ships through the canal.

How was the United States able to build a canal in Panama?

success. The United States and Panama signed a treaty in which Panama leased land to the United States to build a canal. In 1914 the Panama Canal was opened. The United States now had a way to protect its empire.

The United States' interest in Latin America continued. Some Latin American nations had financial and political troubles that led to riots. The United States wanted to protect its interests and restore order. So between 1912 and 1916, the government sent American marines to Nicaragua, Haiti, and the Dominican Republic. After the marines left, American influence did not always come to an end. The United States government still kept financial control and took charge of elections.

1. Why did the United States issue the Monroe Doctrine?
2. How did many Latin Americans feel about the Monroe Doctrine?
3. What did the United States gain from the Spanish-American war?
4. Why did the United States want a canal in Panama?

EFFECTS OF IMPERIALISM

By 1914 the European powers, Japan, and the United States had achieved their original goals. While doing so, they had brought most of the world under their control. This had some benefits. It set up orderly governments and stopped many local wars. It led to the development of industry and agriculture and the building of roads, bridges, factories, and railroads. New farming methods were put into use. Hospitals and schools were built, and sanitation was improved. Communication was made easier, because French and English was spoken in most parts of the world.

But imperialism also created problems. Contacts between two different cultures often led to conflicts. Many Europeans

IMPERIALISM

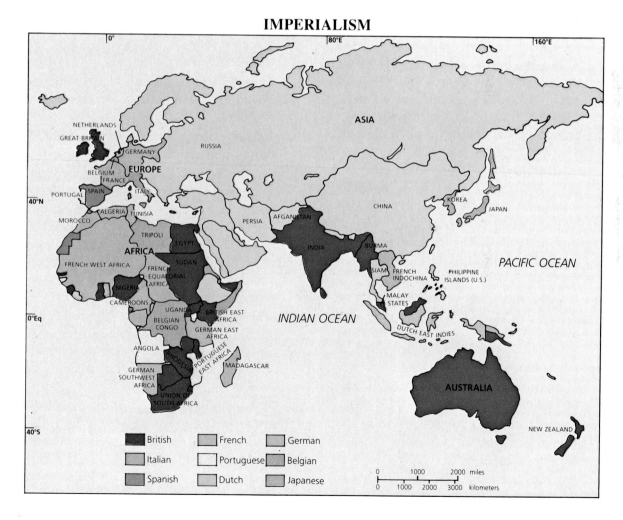

and North Americans thought they were superior to the people in the colonies. The colonists resented this. They blamed the Europeans and North Americans for the loss of their land and for being forced to work on plantations and in factories. These feelings helped nationalism to grow. Many colonial peoples wanted to govern themselves in their own nations. Then, too, the scramble for colonies led to a great deal of competition among the colonial powers. This, in turn, led to disputes that caused future wars.

1. What were some benefits of imperialism?
2. What were some problems of imperialism?

CHAPTER REVIEW

SUMMARY

1. The move toward imperialism in the late nineteenth century came about because of a need for raw materials and new markets for manufactured goods, a desire for investment opportunities, the growth of nationalism, and the belief that western nations had a duty to "civilize backward" peoples.

2. In 1874 England took over the Suez Canal and soon after had full control of Egyptian affairs.

3. European explorers and missionaries gradually opened the African interior to the West.

4. By the early twentieth century the French had the largest European empire in Africa, and the English empire stretched from Cairo to the Cape of Good Hope.

5. Only two African nations retained their independence—Ethiopia and Liberia.

6. By 1858 England controlled India, and Russia was moving into central Asia.

7. Until the Opium War of 1839–1842, Western trade in China was limited to the city of Canton.

8. By 1901 China was completely controlled by foreign powers.

9. Japan did not open up trade with the West until the middle of the nineteenth century.

10. By 1905 Japan was a fully industrialized nation and an imperialist power.

11. By the end of the nineteenth century European nations and the United States controlled most of southeast Asia and many islands in the Pacific.

12. In 1823 the United States issued the Monroe Doctrine to warn European nations not to expand their control in Latin America.

13. The United States won Puerto Rico, Guam, the Philippines and Cuba from Spain in 1898 and leased land from Panama to build the Panama Canal in 1903.

14. While imperialism led to the establishment of orderly governments, the development of industry and agriculture, and social reforms, it also led to bitter feelings, the growth of nationalism, and competition among colonial powers.

BUILDING VOCABULARY

1. *Identify the following:*

Suez Canal	David Livingstone	Cecil Rhodes	Boxer Rebellion
James Bruce	Henry Stanley	British East	Matthew Perry
Mungo Park	Leopold II	India Company	Monroe Doctrine
John Hanning Speke	Boers	Open Door policy	Panama Canal

2. *Define the following:*

invest	conference	opium	right of extra-
occupied	protectorate	concessions	territoriality
interior			

REVIEWING THE FACTS

1. How did the Industrial Revolution influence the move toward imperialism?

2. How did nationalism influence the move toward imperialism?

3. Why was the Suez Canal important?

4. Why did the Egyptian ruler sell his share of the Suez Canal to England?

5. How did some Europeans obtain colonial territory from African chiefs?

6. What caused English settlers to move into the Transvaal after 1885?

7. What two countries were latecomers to the race for African territory?

8. What was the purpose of the Open Door policy proposed in 1898 by the United States?

9. Why did Japan modernize and industrialize so rapidly during the second half of the nineteenth century?

10. How did the United States protect its interests in Latin America during the early years of the twentieth century?

DISCUSSING IMPORTANT IDEAS

1. How were the reasons for imperialism after the Industrial Revolution different from those during the Age of Discovery?

2. Do you think nations would be as interested today in obtaining control of the Suez Canal as they were in the late nineteenth century? Why or why not?

3. What do you think might have happened to Japan if it had not modernized and industrialized?

4. If you had lived in the United States in 1823, how would you have replied to Latin American objections to the Monroe Doctrine?

USING MAPS

Refer to the map on page 585, and answer the following questions:

1. In which continent are most of the European colonies located?

2. What colony belongs to Belgium?

3. Which countries are independent?

4. What is the latitude and longitude of the Malay States?

5. What body of water is directly south of India?

MODERNIZATION OF JAPAN

Shoguns ruled Japan until the middle of the nineteenth century. Many Japanese lords felt the shoguns were keeping Japan from becoming a modern nation. They also resented the government's weakness in dealing with foreigners. The lords overthrew the shogun and restored the power of the emperor.

In 1868 Mutsuhito, a 15-year-old, became emperor of Japan. For the first time in more than 600 years, the emperor was the real ruler of the nation.

Mutsuhito called his reign *Meiji,* which means "enlightened peace." He moved the capital from Kyoto to Tokyo. Then he issued a Charter Oath, in which he promised reforms.

Japanese government leaders were convinced their country had to become more modern. They sent out groups to observe industry and government in the West. After careful study, they adopted that which they felt was good for Japan.

The new government did away with feudalism and gave land to the peasants. It also put an end to the samurai, and in their place set up a modern army and navy.

A new constitution was issued in 1889. A new code of law and system of

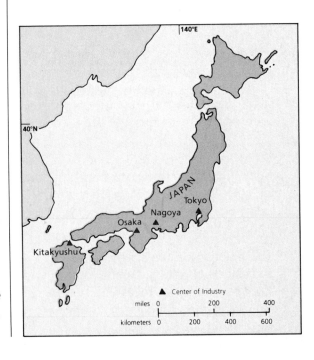

courts were established. The rights of Japanese women were increased. Public schools were opened, and education was required for all Japanese.

Japanese leaders also began a push to develop industry. The government promoted the building of railroads, factories, ports, and telegraph and telephone systems. The Bank of Japan was set up as a central banking office. An official money system was introduced. Thousands of Japanese were urged to start businesses.

The Japanese economy continued to be influenced by the *zaibatsu*. These were the rich and powerful families who controlled many industries. They received special privileges and protection from the government.

The push to modernize led to many changes in Japanese society. The government ordered all Japanese to cut off the topknots worn in their hair. Western-style clothing and a new calendar were introduced.

By the time Emperor Mutsuhito died in 1912, Japan was a modern industrial state. It was the first industrialized nation in Asia. Large cities, such as Tokyo and Osaka, grew up, and the population rapidly increased. Japan had become the strongest nation in Asia.

1. Why was the emperor of Japan returned to power?
2. How was Japan modernized?
3. What were some results of Japan's efforts to become more modern?

UNIT REVIEW

SUMMARY

1. In the nineteenth century the United States expanded its territory and fought a civil war. It became a strong industrial nation that showed that a democratic form of government could be stable.

2. Portuguese and Spanish colonies in the Americas gained independence in the nineteenth century. But they lacked experience in self-government so most remained under the rule of caudillos.

3. In the early nineteenth century, Napoleon Bonaparte made himself Emperor of France and created an empire that included most of Europe.

4. After the allied forces of Austria, Russia, Prussia, and England defeated Napoleon, they divided his Grand Empire among themselves and restored divine-right monarchies. But they could not crush the revolutionary ideas of liberals, nationalists, and socialists.

5. A series of revolutions and strong feelings of nationalism eventually led to universal manhood suffrage, the rise of socialism, the unification of Italy and Germany, and the establishment of a dual monarchy in Austria and Hungary.

6. In the nineteenth century the industrial nations of western Europe, the United States, and Japan undertook a policy of imperialism. They competed with one another to gain control in Africa, Asia, Southeast Asia, the Pacific, and Latin America.

REVIEWING THE MAIN IDEAS

1. Describe the effects of nationalism and revolution on the West in the nineteenth century.

2. Explain what led to the policy of imperialism and the effect it had in different parts of the world.

DEVELOPING SKILLS

It is very important for historians to be able to prove whether or not the data they are using are correct. Sometimes there is a great deal of evidence to support a statement. Other times it is very difficult, if not impossible, to gather enough evidence to support a statement.

This exercise is designed to give you practice in determining whether it would be easy or difficult to prove the truth of a statement. Read the following groups of statements. For each group, tell which statement would be the most difficult to prove.

Group A

1. Thomas Jefferson was elected president of the United States in 1800.
2. Only men voted in the election of 1800.
3. Thomas Jefferson was one of the greatest prsidents of the United States.
4. Most of the people who voted for Thomas Jefferson were property owners.

Group B

1. Napoleon set up a new government in France with himself as First Consul.
2. Napoleon established a single code of law for the entire country.

3. Napoleon did more for France than any leader before or after him.
4. Napoleon escaped from Elba, invaded France, and ruled for 100 days.

Group C

1. Bernardo O'Higgins led a revolt against Spanish forces in Chile.
2. Without Simón Bolívar, Venezuela and Peru would never have gained their independence.
3. Bolivia is named after Simón Bolívar.

4. José de San Martín organized an army in La Plata.

Group D

1. The Boer War could have been avoided.
2. Gold and diamonds were discovered in the Boer states in 1885.
3. Cecil Rhodes was prime minister of Cape Colony during the last part of nineteenth century.
4. The Union of South Africa included Boer states and·English colonies.

SUGGESTED UNIT PROJECTS

1. Write a play based on the last year of Napoleon's reign. Include Napoleon's escape from Elba, the Battle of Waterloo, and Napoleon in exile on St. Helena. Present the play in class.
2. Research the expedition of one of the nineteenth-century missionaries or explorers who entered the African interior. Then write a poem or short story that tells how that person might have reacted to what he encountered.

3. Write an article that might have appeared in a Chinese newspaper of the time about the events of the Opium War or the Boxer Rebellion. Graphically illustrate the main points of your article.
4. Give an oral report on one of the following: (a) the Alamo, (b) Garibaldi, (c) Otto von Bismarck, (d) the founding of Liberia, (e) the building of the Panama Canal, (f) the work of Florence Nightingale in the Crimean War.

SUGGESTED READING

Hall, Marjory. *The Carved Wooden Ring*. Philadelphia, Pa.: Westminster Press, 1972. A story based on the life of Euphremia Goldsborough, a nurse and a spy during the Civil War.

Hays, Wilma P. *For Ma and Pa: On the Oregon Trail, 1844*. New York: Coward, McCann, and Geoghegan, 1972. The adventures of a 13-year-old boy on the Oregon Trail.

Markun, Patricia M. *The Panama Canal*. New York: Franklin Watts, 1979. Traces the Panama Canal from planning through construction to opening.

Roberts, John G. *Black Ships and Rising Sun*. New York: Julian Messner, 1971. The story of how Japan was opened by Commodore Perry and how it industrialized and modernized.

Syme, Ronald. *Juarez, the Founder of Modern Mexico*. New York: William Morrow, 1972. A biography.

Werstein, Irving. *The Boxer Rebellion*. New York: Franklin Watts, 1971. Why and how Chinese revolutionaries tried to drive out the foreigners.

UNIT 13

1903

1906

1905 Revolution of 1905

1909

1911

1921

1922 Mussolini becomes dictator of Italy
Soviet Union formed

1924

1925 Chiang Kai-shek takes
control of Nationalists

1927

1928 Joseph Stalir

192

1939

1939 World War II
begins in
Europe

1942

1941 Japanese attack
Pearl Harbor

1945

1945 United States drops atomic bom
on Japan
United Nations is formed

1947 Marshall Plan
India becomes independen
Nehru becomes prime mini
of India

1957

1957 *Sputnik I*
Vietnam War begins

1958 Nikita Khrushchev becomes leader of Soviet Union
Great Leap Forward announced in China

1960

1960 "Year of Africa"

1961 Berlin Wall built

1963

1964 Leonid Brezhnev and Aleksei Kc
become Soviet leaders

1965 Great Cultur
Revolution

1962 Cuban missile crisis

1975

1976 Chou En-lai and
Mao Tse-Tung die

1978

1978 China begins "four modernisms"

1979 United States
recognizes People's
Republic of China

1981

THE TWENTIETH CENTURY

1912	1915	1918
Chinese Revolution		**1917** Russian Revolution Bolsheviks under Lenin take power United States declares war on Germany
1912 Sun Yat-sen becomes president of China		
1914 World War I begins		
		1919 Treaty of Versailles

1930	1933	1936
becomes leader of Soviet Union	**1933** Hitler becomes leader of Germany	**WORK PROGRAM**
reat Depression begins		**WPA**
	1934 Long March begins	
1931 Japan takes over Manchuria		

1948	1951	1954
1948 Berlin blockade begins Israel becomes Jewish state		**1955** Warsaw Pact
1949 NATO People's Republic of China is proclaimed under Mao Tse-tung Chiang Kai-shek sets up Republic of China on Taiwan		**1956** Suez crisis
1950 Korean War begins		

1966	1969	1972
1967 Arab-Israeli War	**1969** Border clashes between China and Soviet Union	**1972** Americans and Soviets agree to limit weapons
	1968 Americans and Soviets agree to limit weapons	**1973** Arab-Israeli War
	1971 People's Republic of China admitted to United Nations	

1. HOW DID WORLD WARS I AND II CHANGE WESTERN EUROPE'S ROLE IN WORLD AFFAIRS?
2. WHAT ARE SOME OF THE MAJOR PROBLEMS FACING THIRD WORLD COUNTRIES?

By the early twentieth century, the most powerful countries in the world were those of the West. They were industrial countries that controlled world trade. Several also controlled large empires in Africa and Asia. They led the world in education and in new inventions. Their languages were used by many people who had never been in the West. Their scientific and medical ideas were spread all over the world.

In 1914 these countries became involved in a world war, which their leaders said would be the last. They were wrong. By 1945 they had fought another world war. The two wars changed western Europe's role in world affairs. The United States and the Soviet Union became the most important powers in the world. Communism, which had been the politics of a small group, gained strength. It became the guiding philosophy of both the Russians and the Chinese. The Communists made it clear that they wanted to spread their ideas to the entire world. Now there was a First World, which was the West, and a Second World, which was the Communists.

By 1955 there was a Third World. It was made up of the **nonaligned**, or neutral, nations of Asia and Africa. These nations wanted no part in the struggle between the First and Second Worlds. What they did want was independence for European colonies in Asia and Africa. Soon they were joined by nations in Latin America and the Middle East. Together the nations of the Third World are working for **economic development**, or putting resources to use to produce more income and modernize a country. There is no doubt they will have a say in the future of the world.

CHAPTER 38

THE WEST

At the end of the nineteenth century, the most powerful nations in Europe were France, Germany, England, Austria-Hungary, Italy, and Russia. Each nation tried to protect its world trade and its colonies. Each built up its armed forces and tried to make alliances with other nations.

Eventually two alliances developed, one led by Germany and the other by France. The alliance led by Germany included Austria-Hungary and Italy. The alliance led by France included Russia and England. The United States did not get involved in the alliance system. It tried to keep out of Europe's troubles.

Each member of an alliance promised to help other members if they were attacked. Thus, trouble between any two nations of different alliances could draw in other countries. A small war could easily grow into a large one. This was one of the main dangers of the alliance system.

WORLD WAR I

For a long time trouble had been brewing in Europe. It was centered in the Balkans, an area which both Russia and Austria-Hungary wanted to control. A small nation in the Balkans called Serbia hoped to unite the Slavs in the area and expand its territory. Since many Slavs lived in Austria-Hungary, Serbia knew it would have to defeat that country. Serbia hoped to get help from Russia.

On June 28, 1914 Archduke Ferdinand of Austria was shot and killed. Austria-Hungary blamed Serbian leaders for the archduke's death and declared war on Serbia. Russia began to ready its arms to go to Serbia's aid. A few days later, Germany showed its support of Austria-Hungary by declaring war on Russia. German army leaders had long planned for war against their country's enemies. Shortly after, France and England entered the war on the side of Russia.

Italy had been part of the alliance with Germany and Austria-Hungary. In 1915 Italy left the alliance to join France, Russia, and England. In the meantime, Turkey and Bulgaria joined Germany and Austria-Hungary. France, Russia, England, and Italy became known as the Allied Powers. Germany, Austria-Hungary, Turkey, and Bulgaria became known as the Central Powers.

1. What did Serbia hope to do?
2. What led Austria-Hungary to declare war on Serbia?
3. What countries made up the Allied Powers?
4. What countries made up the Central Powers?

FROM 1914 TO 1918   The war that started between Serbia and Austria-Hungary in 1914 grew so large that it came to be called World War I. Although most of the fighting took place in Europe, battles were also fought in the Middle East and Africa. Naval warfare took place all over the world.

At first the Central Powers were more successful than the Allied Powers. The German army captured part of France. But neither side was able to completely defeat the other.

World War I was unlike any other war people had known before. A new weapon called a machine gun fired bullets one after another at a rapid speed. Airplanes carried bombs behind enemy lines and dropped them on enemy cities. Submarines attacked ships at sea. Poison gases were used on a large scale. **Civilians**, or people who are not soldiers, were killed in large numbers.

In 1918 the Germans drove Russia out of the war. The Russians signed a peace treaty in which they gave up huge areas of land in the western part of their country.

In the meantime, German submarines tried to stop ships that were bringing supplies to the Allies. When the submarines sank American ships with civilians on board, it was too much for the United States to bear. Most Americans felt that the Germans had wanted the war. Thus, American sympathies lay with the Allied Powers. In 1917 the United States declared war on Germany.

The United States sent 2 million troops to Europe. The Europeans had been fighting for a long time and were tired. The Americans were just entering the fight and were still fresh. Because of this, they helped to turn the war in favor of the Allied Powers. On November 11, 1918, Germany and its allies agreed to an **armistice**, or a halt to fighting. World War I was over.

1. What made World War I different from earlier wars?
2. What happened to Russia in 1918?
3. Why did the United States join the Allied Powers?
4. Who won World War I?

MAKING THE PEACE   Before the war ended, the president of the United States, Woodrow Wilson, drew up a peace plan called the Fourteen Points. President Wilson believed that punishing the nations that had lost the war would only cause trouble later. The Germans had agreed to the armistice believing Wilson's plan would form the basis of the peace treaties they would have to sign.

But the English, French, and Italians had made secret plans to get what they could from the defeated Central Powers. Each of the Central Powers had to give up land. Germany's African

Woodrow Wilson

colonies were divided between France and England. Japan, which had joined the war on the side of the Allied Powers, took over German colonies in the Pacific. Austria-Hungary was broken up. Four new countries—Austria, Hungary, Czechoslovakia, and Yugoslavia—were created.

The treaty which Germany signed was called the Treaty of Versailles. It put most of the blame for the war on Germany. The treaty stated that Germany had to pay for the damage it had done. Most of the money went to France. Germany also had to limit the size of its army and give up its navy.

For the most part, President Wilson's peace plan was not followed. However, one point was kept. An organization called the League of Nations was established so the countries of the world could come together to talk over their problems. It was hoped that the League could help to prevent future wars. But the League had a serious weakness. It had no army of its own. If a country did not want to obey the League, it could not be forced to do so. The Americans did not join the League. They were

VERSAILLES TREATY

The Versailles treaty was signed in January 1919, at the palace of Versailles outside Paris. Leading the gathering were the four Allied leaders (center, left to right): Orlando of Italy, Wilson of the United States, Clemenceau of France, and Lloyd George of Britain.

How was Germany affected by the Versailles treaty?

angry and bitter about World War I. Like many other nations, the United States was not pleased with the treaties that had been made. Some thought they were too harsh. Others thought they were not harsh enough. After 1918 the United States tried to keep out of European affairs and world problems.

1. What was the purpose of the Fourteen Points?
2. What did Germany have to do under the terms of the Treaty of Versailles?
3. What was the purpose of the League of Nations? Why didn't the United States join it?

EFFECTS OF THE WAR   The problems caused by the war were felt long after the treaties were signed. Large areas of Belgium and northern France had been destroyed in the fighting. Factories and railroads all over France were damaged. Thousands of soldiers were crippled, and others returned home to find no jobs. The countries involved in the war had borrowed money and were heavily in debt.

The Germans replaced the monarchy with a republic, which was faced with many problems. The people were bitter about the terms of the Treaty of Versailles. They felt that they had been blamed unfairly for the war. The German economy was in very bad shape. In addition to its war debt, it had to make payments for war damage. Germany could not provide the jobs or produce the goods needed to improve its economy.

1. What were some effects of World War I?
2. What were some of the problems the new German government faced?

Apple Seller

THE TIME BETWEEN THE WARS

In 1929 a **depression**, or a sudden slow-down in business, set in. Factories closed, and millions of people lost their jobs. World trade was cut by more than half. Since the depression affected business in most of the countries of the world, itis called the Great Depression.

The Great Depression was a terrible shock to most Westerners. As time passed and the depression affected more and more people, many began to question their form of government.

1. How did the depression affect the countries of the West?
2. Why did people question their form of government?

EUROPE AFTER WORLD WAR I

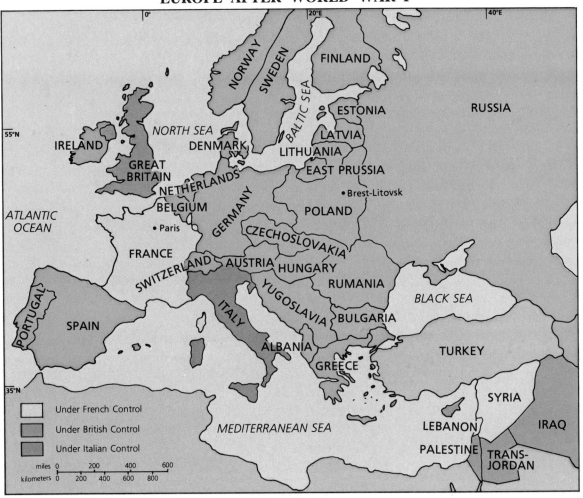

Under French Control
Under British Control
Under Italian Control

THE RISE OF DICTATORSHIPS Most western countries were governed by elected representatives. The people began to feel that a government made up of such a large body of people spent too much time debating issues. They began to wonder if it might not be better to have one strong leader who could make decisions for them. A single leader could act quickly to solve a country's economic problems.

Italy was the first western nation to become a **dictatorship**, or a country ruled by a single person who is not a monarch. In 1922 Benito Mussolini took over the Italian government. He was supported by a political organization known as the Fascists. Mussolini promised to make Italy a world power.

In 1933 Adolf Hitler became **chancellor**, or prime minister, of Germany. Before long he abolished the German republic and set himself up as dictator. He called himself *der Fuhrer*, which means the leader. He called Germany the Third Reich. Hitler was supported by a political party called the National Socialist Party, or Nazis.

Like Mussolini, Hitler promised to make his country strong again and rebuild its armed forces. He said he would change the terms of the Treaty of Versailles. Hitler and the Nazis blamed many of Germany's troubles on the Jews. They took away the Jews' jobs and legal rights and made them wear a yellow star on their clothing. Hitler also fought against the Roman Catholic and other Christian churches, as well as anyone else who disagreed with him or his party.

1. Why did Italy become a dictatorship?
2. What did Benito Mussolini and the Fascists promise the Italians?
3. What promises did Adolf Hitler make to the German people?

WORLD WAR II

Before long Italy and Germany threatened world peace. In 1935 the Italians, still bitter about not getting enough land after World War I, invaded and took control of the African nation of Ethiopia. The League of Nations was powerless to stop the conquest. The following year, the Germans marched into the Rhineland, an area between Germany and France. In 1938, Austria was made a part of Germany.

Other western leaders began to grow uneasy. To calm their fears, Hitler told them that his only goal was to unite all German people into one country. Then Hitler demanded that the Germans living in Czechoslovakia be made part of Germany. The English and the French were afraid of another war. So they remained silent while Czechoslovakia was first divided and then made a part of Germany.

In 1937 the Germans and Italians signed a friendship treaty with the Japanese. Like Italy and Germany, Japan had become a dictatorship. Even though Japan still had an emperor, the military really controlled the country. Japanese army leaders felt that Japan needed more land and natural resources to strengthen

Adolf Hitler

its economy. They built a large army and navy and made plans to take more land in Asia. In 1931 they took Manchuria, the northernmost region of China, away from the Chinese.

Germany, Italy, and Japan became known as the Axis powers. The same year the Japanese signed the friendship treaty, they invaded the main part of China.

Western leaders viewed these events with mixed feelings. The French and English hoped that Hitler would be satisfied with what he had gained and would stop. The Americans were worried about both Japan and Germany, but they made no moves to stop them. The United States still did not want to get involved in Europe's troubles.

Russia, now called the Soviet Union, was most fearful of Germany. The Germans had defeated them in World War I. After the war, the Russian monarchy had been overthrown. The new government was run by **Communists**, or people who believe the government should own all property that is used to produce goods. The Nazis hated communism. But in 1939 Germany and the Soviet Union signed a treaty in which they agreed not to attack each other.

After Hitler signed the treaty, he felt safe to grab more land. On September 1, 1939 the Germans attacked Poland. Soviet troops occupied part of the country while the Germans conquered the rest. The French and English now felt they had made a mistake in allowing Germany to take over other areas. So they promised to support Poland and declared war on Germany.

1. What countries did Italy and Germany take over in 1938 and 1939?
2. What countries united to form the Axis powers?
3. Why did France and England declare war on Germany?

EARLY AXIS VICTORIES   The Axis powers had prepared for war. Early in 1940 German forces overran Denmark and Norway. Next they defeated the French and drove the English army back to England. German and Italian forces overran much of North Africa. The Italians attacked and conquered Albania. In 1941 the Germans and Italians conquered the Balkan countries.

By then Hitler had decided that if the Germans were to control Europe, they would have to defeat the Soviet Union. He decided to forget all about the treaty he had signed in 1939. In June, 1941, German troops attacked the Soviet Union.

While the Germans and Italians pushed through Europe, the Japanese battled in Asia. They took over much of China and the East Indies and all of Indochina. Japanese leaders then turned their attention to the Americans, whose forces in the Philippines could threaten Japanese control of the Pacific. The Japanese decided that the United States had to be defeated. On December 7, 1941, the Japanese navy launched a surprise attack on Pearl Harbor, the American naval base in Hawaii. This dealt a crippling blow to the American navy. The Americans, angered by the Japanese attack, entered the war on the side of England,

WORLD WAR II IN THE WEST

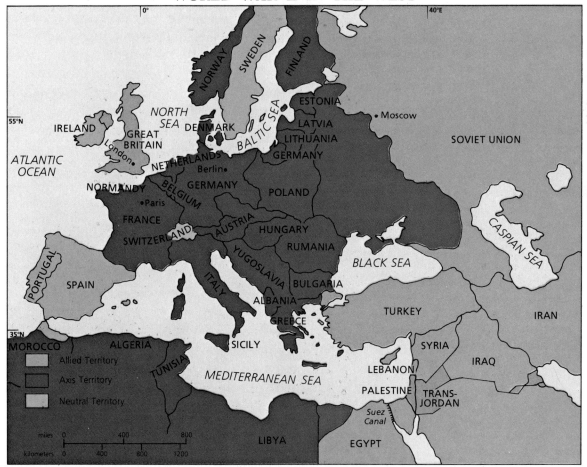

France, and the Soviet Union. They also allied themselves with the Chinese in the war against Japan. Together, these nations came to be known as the Allies.

1. Why did the Germans attack the Soviet Union?
2. What made the United States decide to enter the war?
3. What countries made up the Allies?

THE WAR IN EUROPE   The United States was the greatest industrial power in the world. Soon its factories were turning out thousands of planes and tanks. Ships were built in large numbers. At the same time, the Axis powers were finding it hard to produce enough war materials to keep their forces supplied.

German forces ran into trouble in the Soviet Union. The country proved too large for them to conquer. By 1943 the tables had turned, and Soviet forces were attacking the Germans. That same year Allied armies drove the Axis forces out of North Africa and invaded Italy. The following year Allied forces from England landed in France. The Germans were caught between the Soviets in the east and the American, English, French, and Canadians in the west. In 1945 the Allied forces came together at the Elbe River in Germany. The Germans realized they could not win. Hitler killed himself. Germany was divided into American, French, English, and Soviet zones. The war in Europe was over.

1. How did the United States' industrial power help it in World War II?
2. How did the Germans get caught between Allied forces in the east and the west?
3. What happened in Germany after it was defeated?

The War in Asia

The war in Asia was fought at the same time as the one in Europe. In 1942 American forces struck at the islands the Japanese held in the South Pacific. American naval forces and air power proved too much for the Japanese. Slowly they were driven back. The Americans and Allies hopped from island to island, pushing their way toward Japan. But despite their defeats, the Japanese refused to surrender.

On August 6, 1945, the Americans dropped an **atomic bomb,** or a bomb that gets its power from the release of nuclear

WORLD WAR II IN THE EAST

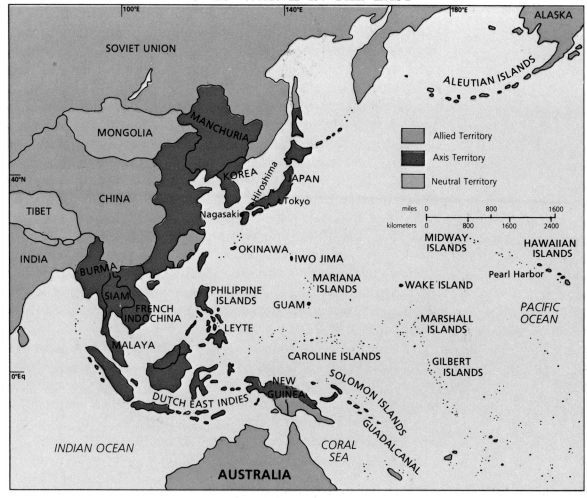

energy. It was the first atomic bomb used in warfare. The bomb destroyed most of the city of Hiroshima and killed tens of thousands of people. When the Japanese still refused to surrender, the Americans dropped a second bomb on the city of Nagasaki. This time the Japanese government agreed to surrender. On September 2, 1945, after six years of fighting, World War II came to an end.

1. What two important advantages did the Americans have in the war against Japan?
2. Why did the Americans drop atomic bombs on the Japanese cities of Hiroshima and Nagasaki?

THE PRICE OF WAR   World War II did even more damage than World War I. More than 15 million soldiers were killed. As many, if not more, civilians were killed. Bombs had heavily damaged or destroyed much of Europe and Asia. Factories, railroads, and highways were in ruins. Millions of people were near starvation.

After the war ended, people learned some shocking facts about Nazi activities during the war. Allied armies in Europe found prison camps where the Nazis had murdered millions of people. The Nazis had rounded up more than 6 million Jews from all over Europe, brought them to the camps, and shot or gassed them to death. The Germans had also used prisoners to do work in factories. These people had been treated like slaves. Many had died from poor treatment and starvation.

In Asia, the Japanese had killed men, women, and children in the countries they conquered. This included any leaders who did not cooperate. At the same time many Allied prisoners of war had died as a result of the poor treatment they received from the Japanese army.

The Allied governments felt that the cruel actions of the Nazis and the Japanese could not be excused as normal events of war. So the Allied governments tried many former German and Japanese leaders for war crimes. Of the 22 top Nazi leaders who were tried, 11 were sentenced to death. Of the 25 top Japanese leaders tried, seven were sentenced to death.

1.   What damage was done during World War II?
2.   After World War II ended, what did the people learn about Nazi and Japanese activities?
3.   What did the Allied governments do to many top Nazi and Japanese leaders?

RESULTS   World War I and World War II helped to lessen the world power of the western European nations. Before 1914 these countries controlled huge empires. They also controlled world trade. The wars wrecked European economies. The nations had to rebuild, and the cost of rebuilding was great.

At the same time, the people in Asian and African colonies controlled by the West worked for their independence. By 1945 many of these colonies had set up their own governments. As a result, the nations of the West lost many of their sources of raw materials and cheap labor. This meant the West had to buy more goods from other areas. The nations of western Europe still remained very important to the world economy. But they lost the role of leadership they had before 1914.

Douglas MacArthur

1. What were some effects World Wars I and II had on powerful western European nations?

THE SHIFT IN POWER

Leaders in the United States and the countries of western Europe wanted to rebuild the war-torn countries of western Europe as fast as possible. The United States started a huge loan program to these countries. The program was called the Marshall Plan. It was named after George Marshall, the Secretary of State of the United States. Under the Marshall Plan, people were given food, factories were rebuilt, and roads were repaired or replaced. Soon the economies of western Europe began to recover and prosper.

There was rebuilding to do in Japan, too. After the war, the United States occupied Japan to supervise its rebuilding. An American general named Douglas MacArthur was put in charge. Many changes took place under his leadership. The military lost its control of the government, and Japan became a democracy. Laws were passed giving the people the right to vote. Loans were made to help rebuild the economy. Before long Japan became a world leader in trade.

1. How did the Marshall Plan help western Europeans?
2. What changes were made in Japan under the leadership of Douglas MacArthur?

THE UNITED NATIONS   Even before World War II was over, the Allied countries had agreed to set up an organization like the League of Nations to prevent war. In 1945 the organization was approved by 51 countries. It was called the United Nations. Today its headquarters is in New York.

The United Nations is made up of six main parts. One of these is the Security Council. The Council has 15 members, five of which are permanent. They are the United States, the Soviet Union, France, China, and England. Each of the countries can veto decisions made by the Security Council.

The main task of the United Nations is to prevent war. But it also performs other services. It lends money to poor countries

GENERAL ASSEMBLY
All members of the United Nations send delegates to the General Assembly. The General Assembly debates important world issues and assists the Security Council in keeping world peace. It also directs the work of other parts of the United Nations. Where are the headquarters of the United Nations located?

and provides them with doctors and medical care. It helps countries to give and receive educational information which will better the lives of the people.

Today most of the countries of the world belong to the United Nations.

1. Why did the Allies decide to establish the United Nations?
2. Who are the five permanent members of the Security Council?
3. What services does the United Nations provide?

THE UNITED STATES AND THE SOVIET UNION   At the end of World War II, two countries became world leaders. They were the United States and the Soviet Union. The United States was the world's leading industrial power. Its factories and farms produced more than any other country. As a result, the Americans lead the world in trade.

The Soviet Union was the largest country on earth, and it had many natural resources. It also had a large population, which meant lots of people to work in factories and on farms.

The war established the two countries as the world's leading military powers. The Soviet Union had gained control of Eastern Europe. It did not take Soviet leaders long to set up Communist governments in the eastern European countries. The countries pledged to support the Soviet Union. The United States became the leader of the western nations. The Americans and the western Europeans wanted to maintain governments elected by the people.

Because of their different goals, the United States and the Soviet Union became rivals. The competition between the two powers led to a **cold war**, or a war without fighting. The cold war, in turn, touched off an arms race between the two countries. Both the Americans and the Soviets have built new weapons that use atomic explosives. Such weapons make it possible to destroy entire countries in a very short time. For this reason, both powers are working, and say they will continue to work, to avoid a third world war.

1. What did the United States and the Soviet Union gain from World War II?
2. To what has the competition between the United States and the Soviet Union led?

CHAPTER REVIEW

SUMMARY

1. At the end of the nineteenth century, two alliances of nations developed in Europe.

2. In 1914 a war started between Serbia and Austria-Hungary that grew so large that it came to be called World War I.

3. World War I was different from earlier wars because of new weapons and the large numbers of civilians killed.

4. The United States entered World War I in 1917 on the side of the Allied Powers, who finally won the war in 1918.

5. The Treaty of Versailles, among other things, created four new countries in Europe and established the League of Nations.

6. The depression of 1929 led many people to question their form of government.

7. In 1922 Benito Mussolini became dictator of Italy, and in 1933 Adolf Hitler became dictator of Germany.

8. Italy and Germany signed a friendship treaty with Japan in 1937.

9. After the German invasion of Poland in 1939, France and England declared war on Germany, and World War II began in Europe.

10. The United States entered World War II in 1941 after Japan attacked the American naval base at Pearl Harbor.

11. World War II ended in 1945, soon after the United States dropped the first atomic bombs on the Japanese cities of Hiroshima and Nagasaki.

12. As a result of World War II, western Europe lost most of its colonies.

13. After World War II, the United States helped rebuild Europe and Japan, the United Nations was established to try to keep world peace, and the United States and the Soviet Union became the most powerful nations in the world.

BUILDING VOCABULARY

1. *Identify the following:*

Archduke Ferdinand of Austria	Treaty of Versailles	Third Reich	Nagasaki
Allied Powers	League of Nations	Nazis	Marshall Plan
Central Powers	Great Depression	Axis Powers	Douglas MacArthur
Woodrow Wilson	Benito Mussolini	Pearl Harbor	United Nations
Fourteen Points	Fascists	Allies	Security Council
	Adolf Hitler	Hiroshima	

2. *Define the following:*

civilians	depression	chancellor	atomic bomb
armistice	dictatorship	Communists	cold war

REVIEWING THE FACTS

1. Why did the United States not get involved in the alliance system at the end of the nineteenth century?

2. What did Serbia want to do?

3. What turned World War I in favor of the Allied Powers?

4. Why did the Treaty of Versailles fail to follow most of Wilson's Fourteen Points?

5. What was the only point of President Woodrow Wilson's peace plan that was kept?

6. What groups within Germany did Adolf Hitler attack?

7. Why did the English and the French remain silent when Hitler took over the central European country of Czechoslovakia?

8. How did Germany and the Soviet Union feel about one another in 1939 when they signed a treaty in which they agreed not to attack each other?

9. What happened to colonies in Asia and Africa as a result of World War II?

10. Why are Americans and Soviets working to avoid a third world war?

DISCUSSING IMPORTANT IDEAS

1. What do you think might have happened if the United States had not entered World War I?

2. What could have been done to prevent Adolf Hitler from threatening world peace?

3. What do you think might have happened if the Japanese had not attacked the American naval base at Pearl Harbor? Give reasons for your answer.

4. Do you think the Marshall Plan was a good idea? Explain.

USING MAPS

Refer to the map on page 600, and answer the following questions:

1. What is the subject of the map?
2. Name two countries which France controlled after World War I.
3. What is the distance from Paris to Brest-Litovsk?
4. What part of Ireland became British after World War I?
5. What country controlled Palestine after World War I?
6. Which countries border the Baltic Sea?

Refer to the map on page 603, and answer the following questions:

1. Which western countries were neutral during World War II?
2. Which neutral countries were surrounded by Axis territory?
3. About how far is the city of London from the city of Berlin?
4. What is the approximate latitude and longitude of Moscow?
5. What city is located about 53° north and 12° east?
6. Was the Soviet Union Allied, Axis, or neutral?

Refer to the map on page 605, and answer the following questions:

1. What countries bordering China were neutral?
2. How far is Pearl Harbor from Tokyo?
3. What island is located about 26° north and 128° east?
4. What southern continent was an Allied power?
5. Was Burma Allied, Axis, or neutral?
6. What island near the Coral Sea was both Axis and neutral?

CULTURAL DEVELOPMENTS

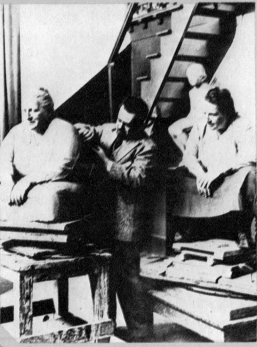

S cientific discoveries shaped the growth of twentieth century cultures. New inventions brought more leisure and a higher standard of living. New kinds of entertainment, such as the movies, became popular attractions. Artists and writers developed new styles and dealt with the problems of modern

life in their works. Women and minority groups demanded equality and gained influence in the arts, sports, business, and politics. Young people developed their own kinds of music and dress. Political changes brought by war and revolution also influenced culture. In dictatorial lands, governments used the arts to glorify the state. In the Third World, artists and writers turned from European and American styles to their own history and culture for inspiration. Television and air travel overcame geographical distances and brought together different cultures.

CHAPTER 39
RISE OF COMMUNISM

Since the early twentieth century communism has greatly influenced the world. Communism can mean many things. It can be a form of government or a system of producing and distributing goods and services. It can be a revolutionary movement or a political party. Communism can also be a set of ideas about history.

Most Communists believe the government should own factories, machines, and other means of production. They also believe the government should make most economic decisions, such as where to build a factory or what price to charge for a product.

Over the years several different kinds of communism have developed, and today there are over 15 countries with Communist governments. The largest are the Soviet Union and China. Like almost all Communist countries, they base their ideas on those developed by Karl Marx.

Marx believed that history is a series of conflicts between the ruling class and the working class. He predicted that the proletariat would overthrow the **bourgeoisie**, or leaders of industry and members of government. He thought that the final result of this revolution would be a society that had no classes. Marx called his system socialism. He viewed it as a step toward communism. His ideas later became known as Marxism.

THE RUSSIAN REVOLUTION

In the late nineteenth and early twentieth centuries, there was a great deal of discontent in Russia. Most of the people were poor peasants bound to the land. The tsar controlled what industry there was. Workers' hours were long, and their pay was low. Students protested, peasants revolted, and workers staged strikes. This unrest had been growing for a long time. Some Russian tsars had ignored their country's problems. Others had tried to bring about reforms, but they usually offered too little.

In 1905 thousands of Russians revolted against the tsar. But their revolt was put down by the army, and the tsar refused to make any reforms. The Russian role in World War I only made matters worse. Russia lost millions of soldiers on the battlefield. There was not enough food or fuel for the soldiers or the civilians.

By 1917 the Russian people could stand no more. In March of that year they reacted. Striking workers demanding bread and freedom jammed the streets of the capital city of Petrograd. Within a few days the demonstration spread to the army. The tsar was forced to give up his throne, and a provisional government was set up.

1. How did the Russian people show their discontent before 1905?
2. How did the tsar react to the revolution in 1905?
3. What problems did World War I cause in Russia?
4. What was the result of the workers' demonstration in 1917?

LENIN   There was much confusion in the months following the overthrow of the tsar. A revolutionary group called Bolsheviks took advantage of this. Led by Vladimir Ilyich Ulyanov, who came to be known as Lenin, they won over the **soviets**, or committees that represent workers and soldiers.

The Bolsheviks were guided by beliefs that came to be known as Marxism-Leninism. They were a mixture of Marx's and Lenin's ideas. Like Marx, Lenin thought the workers would revolt. But he did not think the workers would make a revolution by themselves. He believed they would need a tightly organized group to lead them.

In November, 1917 the Bolsheviks seized power from the provisional government and set up a Communist government.

VLADIMIR LENIN

In 1917 Lenin set up a Communist Party dictatorship in Russia. He ruled the country, now known as the Union of Soviet Socialist Republics, until his death in 1924. Lenin gave powerful speeches, such as this one in Moscow's Red Square, to rally support for the Communist government's policies.

What methods did Lenin and the Communists use to maintain power?

Soon afterward Lenin signed a peace treaty that ended Russia's part in World War I. But the treaty did not end the problems at home. From 1918 to 1920 Russia was divided by a civil war between the Communists and the non-Communists. The Communists were called Reds. The non-Communists were called Whites. Even though the Whites received aid from other countries, including the United States, they could not defeat the Reds.

Lenin used terror and force to keep his power over the people. Workers had to work where and when the government ordered. Peasants had to give up grain to feed people in the cities. By 1921 Lenin realized that his policies must be changed. He introduced a more relaxed policy called the New Economic Policy. It allowed some private industry, trade, and farming. The Russian economy soon began to recover.

In 1922 the Union of Soviet Socialist Republics, or the Soviet Union, was formed. It was made up of four republics, one of which was Russia. By the time Lenin died in 1924, the Soviet Union was completely under the control of the Communist Party.

1. How did the Bolsheviks gain power?
2. What did Vladimir Lenin think the workers needed in order to start a revolution?
3. How did Lenin keep his power over the people?
4. When was the Union of Soviet Socialist Republics formed?

Joseph Stalin

JOSEPH STALIN   After Lenin died, there was a struggle for power. By 1928 the struggle was over, and Joseph Stalin had taken control of the government. He also controlled the Communist Party, the only political party allowed in the country.

That same year Stalin began the first **Five-Year Plan**, or a program to develop the economy over a period of five years. The Plan was a return to earlier Communist policies of total government ownership of production. Its goal was to develop Soviet industry. Factories stopped making clothing and household goods. People were told to sacrifice for the glory of the country. Workers who were absent from their jobs were punished. Factory managers were held responsible for what was done in their factories. If anything went wrong, the managers were put in prison.

The Plan also included **collectivization**, or uniting small farms into large ones controlled by the government. This allowed farmers to share the few tractors and other farm machinery they had. Many peasants did not like this idea. They wanted to keep on working on their individual farms. But those who refused to move were sent to prison, killed, or starved to death. The unrest among the peasants kept them from working the land. The loss of crops led to a famine in which millions of people died.

By about 1935 many people began to oppose Stalin's methods. As a result, Stalin began a program of terror to crush those who did not agree with what he was doing. His secret police arrested millions of people. Some prisoners were shot. Others were sent to labor camps. Stalin controlled everything that was publicly written, said, or heard in the Soviet Union.

1. Who took control of the Soviet Union after Lenin's death?
2. How did Stalin's first Five-Year Plan change Soviet life?
3. How did Stalin treat those who did not agree with his policies?
4. How did Stalin control the Soviet Union?

NIKITA KHRUSHCHEV   Stalin died in 1953, and a power struggle began. By 1958 the First Secretary of the Communist Party, Nikita Khrushchev, had overcome his rivals. He was named premier, or prime minister, of the Soviet Union. Khrushchev began a program of **de-Stalinization**, or an attack on the policies set down by Stalin. Most labor camps were shut down, and the secret police became less violent.

Under Khrushchev, the Soviets had more contacts with the West. For the first time, Soviet writers and artists were allowed a limited amount of freedom. Efforts were made to raise the standard of living.

Nikita Khrushchev

Khrushchev improved relations with the West. But many of his other policies failed. In 1964 he was forced to retire. He was replaced by two other Communist leaders, Leonid Brezhnev and Aleksei Kosygin. Brezhnev soon became the more powerful.

1. What was one of the first things Nikita Khrushchev did after he became premier of the Soviet Union?
2. Why was Khrushchev forced to retire?
3. Who followed Khrushchev as Soviet leader?

MAY DAY

May 1st, the international workers' festival, is a national holiday in the Soviet Union. Here Russians in the city of Leningrad carry balloons, red banners, and a bust of Lenin in a May Day parade.

How has the life of Russians changed since the 1917 Revolution?

PROGRESS AND PROBLEMS   When Brezhnev took over Soviet leadership, life became less free for the people. Once again there was a move toward secrecy.

In the fall of 1967 the Soviets celebrated the fiftieth anniversary of the Russian Revolution. By then most Soviet citizens had come to accept communism as a way of life. Some things had not changed that much since the revolution. Clothing, appliances, and housing were still limited. And often they were of poor quality. Food supplies were sometimes scarce. Often there were few kinds of food from which to choose. The government still controlled the work of artists and writers.

But the Soviets had made many scientific and military advances in the 50 years. In 1957 they launched *Sputnik I*. It was the first spacecraft to circle the earth. This marked the beginning of the Space Age. Four years later a Soviet air force officer named Yuri Gagarin became the first person to circle the earth.

1. What were some changes made in Soviet policy when Leonid Brezhnev came to power?
2. Why was 1967 an important year in the Soviet Union?
3. What were some Soviet achievements in the 1950's and 1960's?

COMMUNIST EXPANSION AND THE FREE WORLD

Toward the end of World War II, Soviet troops helped free many countries in Europe from German control. Before long, the Soviets set up Communist-controlled governments in some of the countries they had freed. Six of the countries became **Soviet satellites**, or countries controlled by the Soviet Union. They were Bulgaria, Czechoslovakia, East Germany, Hungary, Poland, and Romania. Only Yugoslavia, although Communist, refused to be put under Soviet control.

The satellites were cut off from most outside contacts. They had to follow Soviet policies and practices. Winston Churchill, the English prime minister, began to use the phrase "Iron Curtain" to refer to the barriers the Soviets put between the satellites and non-Communist countries.

By the middle of the twentieth century, two great **power blocs**, or groups of nations united by a common interest or belief, came into being. The United States led the Free World bloc. The Soviet Union led the Communist bloc.

1. What happened to six of the countries the Soviets freed from German control?
2. What power bloc was led by the Soviet Union?
3. What power bloc was led by the United States?

BERLIN   At the end of World War II, Germany was divided into **zones**, or areas. Each was occupied by one of the Allies. The German capital of Berlin was also divided into zones. The Soviets occupied the eastern zone and the other Allies occupied the western ones. The English, the French, and the Americans wanted to unify the zones. But the Soviets refused. They wanted to continue to control their zone. In June, 1948 they blocked all land and water traffic into Berlin. They hoped this would force the western nations out of the city.

The United States and England organized an **airlift**, or a system of transporting supplies by airplane. Each day they flew food, fuel, and raw materials into Berlin. In May, 1949 the Soviets finally lifted their **blockade**, or closing off, of the city. That same year two separate governments were set up, one for West Germany and another for East Germany.

Many people who lived in East Germany and the other Soviet satellites were not happy under Communist rule. So they escaped into West Berlin. The East German government wanted to stop the escapes. In 1961 it built a wall along the line that divided East and West Berlin. Some openings were left in the wall so people with special permission could cross from one part of the city to the other. But all of the openings were heavily guarded.

BERLIN WALL

Between 1953 and 1961 three million refugees flocked to West Berlin from East Germany. To block the flow of people, the East German government in 1961 built a 26-mile (46-kilometer) wall through Berlin. The wall has become a symbol of the division of Europe between Communist and western nations.

How did the Soviet Union try to force the western powers from Berlin?

COMMUNIST LEADERS

Salvador Allende
1908–73
president of Chile from
1970 to 1973; first
Marxist freely elected in
Western Hemisphere

Alexander Dubcek
1921–
first secretary of
Communist Party of
Czechoslovakia in 1968
and 1969; introduced
liberal reforms that
threatened Soviet interests

Ché Guevara
1928–67
Latin American guerilla leader;
most powerful member of
government under Fidel Castro;
Cuban minister of industry,
1961-65

Ho Chi Minh   *1890–1969*

revolutionary leader who overthrew French
in Vietnam in 1954; president of North
Vietnam from 1954 to 1969

Kim Il Sung   *1912–*

president of North Korea since 1948; head
of North Korean Communist Party; leader in
efforts toward peaceful reunification of Korea

**Joseph Broz
Tito**   *1892–1980*

founder and ruler of Communist government
in Yugoslavia from 1945 to 1980; first Communist leader to declare independence from
Russia and permit economic and social freedom

Leon Trotsky   *1879–1940*

leader of 1917 Bolshevik Revolution; second
most powerful figure in Russia under Lenin

The spread of communism in Europe and the Berlin blockade convinced the western powers that the Soviets wanted to conquer Europe. Western leaders wanted to guard against this. In 1949 the United States, England, and France joined with nine other nations to form the North Atlantic Treaty Organization, or NATO. They all agreed to help one another if attacked. Six years later the Soviet Union and its eastern European satellites formed their own organization. It is called the Warsaw Pact.

1. Why were separate governments set up in East Germany and West Germany?
2. Why did the Soviets build the Berlin Wall?
3. Why did the western nations form NATO?
4. What organization did the Communist nations form in 1955?

KOREA   In 1950 world attention turned from Europe to Asia. There North Korean troops had invaded South Korea, beginning the Korean War. The war marked the beginning of worldwide competition between Communist and non-Communist nations. The Soviets sent the North Koreans military aid, and Chinese Communists fought on their side. The United Nations sent forces to help South Korea.

The Korean War was called a **limited war**. This means that each side limits its weapons and the territory in which it fights. As a result, it does not lead to all-out fighting among the nations of the world. Still, many people died as a result of the Korean War. And it increased the tension between Communist and non-Communist nations.

In 1953 North Korea and South Korea signed a truce that ended the war. But it did not end the cold war between the Soviet Union and the West.

1. Why did world attention turn from Europe to Asia in 1950?
2. Why was the Korean War called a limited war?

PEACEFUL COEXISTENCE   In 1956 the Soviets announced a policy of **peaceful coexistence**. This meant that they would compete with the West in science and technology, but would avoid war. This was a change from Lenin's belief that war between democracy and communism could not be avoided.

Under the policy of peaceful coexistence, Soviet leaders visited many nations. One of these was the United States.

Relations between the United States and the Soviet Union shifted back and forth between bad and good. Sometimes there was a move toward **detente**, or the relaxation of tensions. Other times there was great strain and disagreement.

In 1962 pressure from the United States forced the Soviets to remove their missiles from Cuba. In a war in Vietnam the United States supported one side while the Soviet Union supported the other. The same was true when the Arabs and Israelis went to war in the Middle East. The United States supported the Israelis while the Soviet Union supported the Arabs. When the Soviets became directly involved in conflicts in Africa, Southeast Asia, and the Middle East, the United States publicly criticized them.

Still, the two nations did agree on some issues. Agreements were reached on limiting weapons and on matters concerning health, trade, and space.

1. How did the policy of peaceful coexistence differ from Lenin's beliefs?
2. What incidents strained relations between the United States and the Soviet Union?

THE CHINESE REVOLUTION

In the second half of the nineteenth century, there were several rebellions in China. Some were started by peasants who wanted land reform and better food supplies. Others were begun by secret societies that opposed the weak government and foreign influence in China. Most of these rebellions failed, and their leaders were severely punished.

In 1911 a rebellion began that did not fail. The government was overthrown, and a constitutional republic was set up. The leader of the revolt was Sun Yat-sen. In 1912 he became president of China. But Sun could not gather enough support, and the army took over the government.

Sun Yat-sen

Sun still went on working to unite the Chinese people. He formed the Nationalist Party. Then he asked for help from the West. When he was refused, he turned to the Soviet Union. When the Soviets gave him help, he encouraged Communists to join the Nationalist Party.

After Sun died in 1925, Chiang Kai-shek became the new leader of the Nationalists. Chiang formed an army and set out to

CHINESE LEADERS

From 1928 to 1949, General Chiang Kai-shek (right) was a powerful leader in China. In 1949, the Communists led by Mao Tse-tung (left) overthrew Chiang's government. Mao proclaimed a people's republic on the Chinese mainland, while Chiang set up a government on the island of Taiwan.

Why were the Communists successful in their struggle against Chiang?

unify China. For a time the Nationalists and Communists fought together against local lords who did not want a unified nation. Then the Communists formed their own army. It was called the People's Liberation Army, or the PLA.

The Communists and Nationalists fought each other for control of China. Each party wanted to set up its own government. In 1934 Chiang forced the Communists to retreat. An army of more than 100,000 Communists marched from southern China to northwestern China. Their journey was called the Long March. It lasted two years and covered more than 6000 miles, or

9700 kilometers. Only a few thousand Communists survived the march. But by its end a major leader named Mao Tse-tung emerged.

1. Why did the Chinese rebel in the nineteenth century?
2. How did Sun Yat-sen become president of China?
3. Why did Sun Yat-sen encourage Communists to join the Nationalist Party?
4. Why did Chiang Kai-shek force the Communists to make the Long March?

CHINA UNDER MAO   The Japanese attacked China in 1937. The Nationalists and Communists joined forces to fight them. After the Japanese were defeated in 1945, the Nationalists and the Communists started fighting each other again. By this time the Chinese Communists had gained a great deal of support, especially from peasants in the countryside. This was because the Communists took land away from rich landlords and gave it to the peasants.

By 1949 the Communists had forced the Nationalists to retreat to the island of Taiwan. There Chiang set up a Nationalist government. He claimed it ruled the Republic of China. The Communists on mainland China set up their own government

RED GUARDS

In the mid-1960's, students known as Red Guards supported Mao Tse-tung. They marched across China to make sure that Mao's teachings were obeyed. Here Red Guards parade through Peking, China's capital city.

headed by Mao Tse-tung. They founded the People's Republic of China. Like the Nationalists, they said that theirs was the true government of China.

Chou En-lai was named premier of the People's Republic of China. He took control of all government departments. He and Mao agreed that the government's first task was to rebuild China. In 1953 the Chinese began a Five-Year Plan. Its goal was to increase production in agriculture and industry. The Chinese government was determined to reach its goal. Thus, it used force to carry out its programs. Anyone who opposed the government or its programs was punished or executed. At the end of five years, many gains had been made. But at the same time, contact with the West was discouraged.

Mao, however, felt that China had to grow still faster. Otherwise it would not catch up with the more advanced countries of the world. So in 1958 the Chinese began a second Five-Year Plan called the Great Leap Forward. It called for China to produce twice as much as it had before. Everyone was urged to join in industrial production. Workers built thousands of small backyard furnaces to produce **pig iron**, or a form of iron cast in blocks. Peasants were grouped into **communes**, or huge farming communities run by the government. Each commune housed thousands of members. Mao believed that everyone should work with their hands to help make China grow. However, despite all efforts, the Great Leap Forward did not reach its goal.

1. What led to the formation of the People's Republic of China?
2. What was the main goal of the Communist government of China?

CHINA, THE SOVIET UNION, AND THE WEST The Chinese Communists and the Soviets did not get along very well. In the 1950's Chinese and Soviet leaders had disagreed over the aims of communism. Over time, the gap between the two continued to widen. In 1969 the Chinese and the Soviets had fights along their borders.

Because of their differences with the Soviets, the Chinese wanted to improve relations with the West. Contacts between China and western nations became more frequent. In 1971 the United Nations voted to admit the People's Republic of China as a member. That same year the United States table tennis team

Under the new government, Chinese relations with the West continued to improve. In January, 1979 the United States officially recognized the government of the People's Republic of China. Since then, visits have been exchanged, and many western tourists have traveled to China. Relations with the Soviet Union, however, continue to be strained.

1. What happened to the Chinese Communist government after the deaths of Mao Tse-tung and Chou En-lai?
2. What are China's goals for the year 2000?
3. How did the change in government affect China's relations with the West? With the Soviet Union?

CHAPTER REVIEW

SUMMARY

1. After an unsuccessful revolt in 1905, the Russian people revolted again and overthrew the tsar.

2. After much confusion, a revolutionary group led by Vladimir Lenin set up a Communist government, which officially formed the Soviet Union in 1922.

3. After Lenin died, Joseph Stalin took control of the government and the Communist Party and tried to modernize and industrialize the nation.

4. After Stalin's death, Nikita Khrushchev took control and removed many government restrictions.

5. In 1964 Khrushchev was replaced by Leonid Brezhnev, who tightened government control.

6. When the Soviets launched the first spacecraft to circle the earth in 1957, the Space Age began.

7. After World War II the Soviet Union set up Communist-controlled governments in six eastern European nations.

8. In 1948 the Soviet Union tried without success to force western nations out of Berlin.

9. In 1961 the Berlin Wall was built to prevent people from fleeing East Germany into West Germany.

10. North Korea, aided by the Soviet Union, and South Korea, aided by the United States, fought a war in 1950.

11. Early rebellions in China were not successful, but in 1911 Sun Yat-sen led a revolt that overthrew the government and set up a constitutional republic.

12. In 1925 Chiang Kai-shek became leader of the Nationalist Party and set out to unify China.

13. In 1934 Chiang forced the Communists to go on a Long March of 6000 miles to the interior of China.

14. The Communists defeated the Nationalists in 1949 and formed the People's Republic of China under Mao Tse-tung, who tried to develop agriculture and industry.

15. China and the Soviet Union did not get along well, so China tried to improve its relations with the West.

16. The Chinese goal is for China to be a modernized socialist country by 2000.

BUILDING VOCABULARY

1. *Identify the following:*

communism	Soviet Union	Iron Curtain	Chiang Kai-shek
Karl Marx	Joseph Stalin	NATO	Mao Tse-tung
Marxism	Nikita Khrushchev	Warsaw Pact	Taiwan
Vladimir Lenin	Leonid Brezhnev	Korean War	Chou En-lai
Bolsheviks	Aleksei Kosygin	Sun Yat-sen	Hua Kuo-feng

2. *Define the following:*

bourgeoisie	de-Stalinization	airlift	detente
soviets	Soviet satellites	blockade	pig iron
Five-Year Plan	power blocs	limited war	communes
collectivization	zones	peaceful coexistence	dissidents

REVIEWING THE FACTS

1. What are the two largest Communist nations in the world?
2. What did Karl Marx believe about history and society?
3. Why did the Russian Revolution break out in 1917?
4. How did Russian peasants react to Stalin's policy of collectivization?
5. In what ways has life for the Russian people changed since 1917?
6. How have things remained more or less the same since the Russian Revolution?
7. Why did the United States and England organize the Berlin airlift?
8. Where did Chiang Kai-shek set up a Nationalist government in 1949?
9. What happened as a result of President Nixon's visit to China in 1972?
10. What do dissidents want to happen in the Soviet Union?

DISCUSSING IMPORTANT IDEAS

1. Do you think the Berlin Wall shows Communist strength or weakness? Explain.
2. How do you think peaceful coexistence has affected the daily life of Americans?
3. Do you think communism has been a success in the Soviet Union? Explain.
4. Do you think communism has been a success in China? Why or why not?

USING MAPS

Refer to the map on page 629, and answer the following questions:

1. What country controls the largest area in the Communist bloc?
2. What island in the Western Hemisphere is Communist?
3. Is China a Communist country?
4. What part of Europe is in the Communist bloc?
5. What part of Europe is in the Communist bloc?
6. What is the latitude and longitude of Cuba?

CASTRO'S CUBA

On July 26, 1953 a young lawyer named Fidel Castro tried to start a revolution on the island of Cuba. He and many of his followers were captured and put in prison. After Castro got out of prison in 1955, he organized a revolutionary group called "The Twenty-sixth of July Movement." The group made surprise attacks against the government of Cuban dictator Fulgencio Batista.

By late 1958 Castro and his followers had the support of most Cubans. Many had lost confidence in Batista and thought Castro would solve the island's problems.

On January 1, 1959, Batista fled the country. The Castro forces took control of the government, and soon Fidel Castro became premier of Cuba.

Castro promised the Cuban people free elections, democratic government, and social and economic reforms. At first, many nations, including the United States, supported Castro. But many of the promises he made were not kept. Cubans who opposed him were jailed or executed. Thousands of Cubans fled to the United States and Latin America. Most did not expect to be in their new homes long. They thought Castro's rule would be a short one, and they soon could return to Cuba.

Before long Castro announced that his government was Communist. He developed close ties with the Soviet Union. The Soviets sent Cuba economic aid and advisors. In 1962 they set up missile bases on the island. But pressure from the United

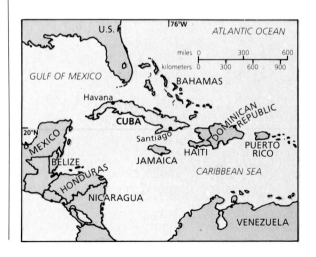

"XX AÑOS DE REVOLUCION
XX AÑOS DE VICTORIAS"

States forced the Soviets to remove the missiles.

Many people consider Castro a modern caudillo. He made many changes on the island. Education is free, and almost everyone can now read and write. All medical care is free. Many large low-rent apartment buildings have been built. Large estates have been turned into **cooperatives**, or farms run by the government for the benefit of the workers. Because of these changes, many Cubans support him even though he rules as a dictator.

Cuba still has serious economic problems. It depends mostly on the sale of sugar for its income. When the price of sugar is low, so is Cuba's income. Then, too, Castro made some costly mistakes. He tried to industrialize Cuba early in 1960.

But Cuba had few mineral resources, no money to buy machinery, and no market for the products. Later he tried to set up a **moneyless economy**, which meant that workers would receive goods instead of wages. This, too, failed.

Under Castro, the poor have a right to a decent job, food, clothing, and cheap housing. But they do not have freedom of speech or of the press. They have to wait in long lines for everything, including food and clothing. The shops are half empty, and everything is in short supply. For these reasons, some Cubans have lost faith in Castro and in his government.

1. How did Fidel Castro come to power?
2. How has Castro's rule affected the Cuban people?

CHAPTER 40

EMERGING THIRD WORLD

Most Third World nations are not as developed as the western and Communist countries that have a lot of industry. Most of the people make their living from the land and usually are poor. The average person earns about $300.00 a year in United States money.

Most developing nations also have rapidly growing populations. Most of the countries cannot grow enough food to feed their people. They must buy food elsewhere. As a result, they do not have enough money to provide housing or decent health care for everyone.

Many Third World countries do not have a **balanced economy**. This means that they depend on trading a single product such as coffee, cocoa, or cotton for more than half of their **national income**, or the amount of money a country as a whole receives. If the crop is poor because of bad weather, there is less national income. If the **market price**, or the price at which goods are sold, is low, there is less national income. Less income means less economic development.

India, Africa, Latin America, and the Middle East are all part of the Third World. All share some of the problems common to developing areas. In addition, each has some problems—and some benefits—that are unique to it alone.

INDIA

India was one of the first colonial nations in which feelings of nationalism began to grow. At first many things seemed to stand in the way of nationalism. There were two major religions—Hinduism and Islam. There were more than 1000 different languages and **dialects**, or regional forms of a language, spoken in the country. This meant that most Indians could not communicate with one another. There were also many regional differences in food, dress, and way of life. But all the problems and differences meant little because the hundreds of millions of Indians had one thing in common—opposition to English rule.

In 1885 a political party called the Indian National Congress was formed. Its members called for changes in the government. By 1919 more Indians were taking part in the government. But the English colonial rulers moved slowly. And by then, allowing a few Indians to have some say in India's affairs was not enough. Most nationalists wanted independence.

Mohandas K. Gandhi

About that time, an Indian leader named Mohandas K. Gandhi began a protest movement against English rule. Gandhi was a member of the upper class, but he identified himself with the common people. They called him "Mahatma," which means "Great Soul." Gandhi did not believe in violence. He believed in a policy of **noncooperation**, or resisting by refusing to perform civil duties. He convinced millions of Indians to show their resistance to the English through peaceful means. They held orderly demonstrations and protest marches. Some went on hunger strikes. Many refused to pay taxes. They even refused to support England during World War II.

The English finally agreed to Indian independence. The country was divided into the two separate nations of Pakistan and India. At midnight the night of August 14, 1947, Pakistan was founded. The following day India became independent. Jawaharlal Nehru, a friend and supporter of Gandhi, became the country's first prime minister. He kept the post until his death in 1964. Two years later his daughter, Indira Gandhi, became prime minister. She held the office until 1977. In January, 1980, she was again elected prime minister.

1. What seemed to stand in the way of Indian nationalism at first?
2. What did the Indian National Congress want when it was first formed? What did it want later?
3. What policy did Mahatma Gandhi urge Indians to follow?
4. When did India become independent?

PLANNED ECONOMIC GROWTH　　The Indian government's main goal since independence has been to raise the people's standard of living. To do this, it set up Five-Year Plans to organize the country's development. India's Five-Year Plans are different from those of the Soviets and the Chinese. In India, people do not have to accept government goals. Also, factories and other means of production are owned by individuals, not by the government.

The first Five-Year Plan began in 1951. Since then, India's economy has improved. In the past, the nation's main industry was textiles. Today it also has such heavy industry as iron, steel, electrical, chemical, and cement manufacturing. There are small factories, too. And India is well-known for goods that artisans make by hand in their homes.

Jawaharlal Nehru

Farm production has also increased over the years. The government has worked very hard to make this happen. Through its efforts, new seeds and farming methods have been introduced. Dams have been built, and agricultural colleges have opened. New kinds of crops, such as soybeans, have been planted. Over 70 percent of the people make their living by farming, which provides about half of India's national income. To feed its growing population and to provide money for more industry, farm production must continue to increase.

The government has also encouraged people to have smaller families. If the population grows faster than industry and farm

INDUSTRIAL INDIA
Industry has grown rapidly in India since the nation became independent in 1947. About five million Indians now work in mills and factories. These workers are employed at a tinplate mill.
How has the Indian government promoted industrial development?

production, the way people live cannot improve. Indian leaders want the population to grow more slowly. That way each person will have more food, decent housing, and better health care.

1.   What is the main goal of the Indian government?
2.   What has the government done to try to meet its goal?

AFRICA

The demand for self-government did not become strong in Africa until after World War II. Many Africans served in the armies of the colonial powers during the war. They were sent to fight in many different places around the world. The soldiers saw new things and learned new ideas and skills. When they returned home, they were not content with the conditions they found there. They began to feel that conditions would be better if they could rule themselves.

The way the European powers ruled their colonies also contributed to nationalism. Each power ruled a little differently. The English allowed some local self-rule. They also provided the Africans in their colonies with a general education. The French and the Portuguese did not allow the Africans in their colonies any self-rule at all. The French educated only a few Africans. And they had to learn French ways and French culture. The Portuguese provided almost no education.

Nationalism grew quickly among educated Africans. They worked for independence in many different ways. They formed political organizations. They refused to buy goods from the colonial powers. They bargained with government leaders. They were not always successful in their efforts. In some cases, violence broke out.

FOOD PRODUCTION

During the 1960's a world-wide effort was started to increase food production in Third World nations. Experts hope that the use of modern farming methods and new crops will provide more food for growing populations. Here a United Nations adviser gives a food demonstration to African women.

What efforts have been made to increase food production in Africa?

In 1960, 17 African nations gained independence. The year became known as "the year of Africa." In the years that followed other African colonies freed themselves from European control. In 1980, Zimbabwe, formerly called Rhodesia, became independent. It was the 51st African nation to be freed from rule by a European power.

1. What effect did World War II have on African nationalism?
2. What did educated Africans do to promote independence?
3. In what year did the newest African nation become independent?

African Student

ECONOMIC DEVELOPMENT   About 70 percent of all African workers make their living from farming. More than half of the continent's national income comes from selling such products as peanuts, cocoa, cotton, and coffee. Still, Africa must buy a great deal of food from other countries. This is partly because most farmland in Africa is used for **subsistence farming**. This means that farmers grow only enough food for their families.

Many African governments want the farmers to change. They want them to raise a greater variety of crops and animals. They also want them to grow more food than they need to feed their families. In other words, the government wants more farmers to raise **cash crops**, or crops and animals to sell to others. If farmers can earn money for their crops and animals, they will then have money to spend for manufactured goods. Government leaders feel this will help the economy to grow. As a result, many African governments are helping farmers to learn new farming methods. They are also building irrigation systems, roads, and storage buildings.

African industry, meanwhile, has been growing at a fast rate. In most countries, however, it only prepares minerals and other raw materials for sale outside Africa. Manufacturing industries produce such basic goods for the home market as clothes, shoes, and soft drinks.

Africa has many energy resources. Coal, natural gas, oil, and hydroelectric power are plentiful. It also is very rich in minerals. There are supplies of copper, tin, iron, manganese, gold, and diamonds. But more money and skilled workers are needed for Africa to make full use of these resources.

By world standards Africa as a whole is still very poor. But it has a good chance to show great economic growth in the future.

1. Why is agriculture important to the economic development of Africa?
2. Why do African governments want farmers to become cash crop farmers? What have they done to promote this?
3. What industries are found in most African countries?

LATIN AMERICA

Most Latin American nations gained their independence in the early part of the nineteenth century. But the first 50 years of freedom were marked by confusion and civil wars. After some law and order returned, many Latin American nations found themselves ruled by caudillos. Even today, many of these nations still do not have stable governments. Revolts and military takeovers are common. Nationalism, however, is strong, and leaders are working to bring about reforms.

1. What happened in many Latin American nations after independence?

FOREIGN DEVELOPMENT   People from other countries have been making investments in Latin America since the early nineteenth century. Industrial nations such as England, France, Germany, and the United States organized businesses in Latin America. They produced mostly bananas, sugar, metals, and oil which were then shipped out of Latin America.

Latin American nations benefited from the foreign investments. National incomes grew. Wages rose, and there were more jobs. Foreign business interests also built roads, railroads, and ports. They set up telephone systems, electric plants, and other public services. Still there were problems.

Most of the countries depended heavily on only one or two products. In addition, most of the goods the countries produced were sold outside Latin America. Food, clothing, household goods, and other such items had to be brought in from other countries.

Since World War II, most Latin American nations have been trying to industrialize. They have greatly increased their production of steel, cars, oil, cement, paper, and similar goods.

THIRD WORLD LEADERS

Kemal Atatürk
1881–1938

founder and first president of Republic of Turkey from 1923 to 1938

Menachem Begin
1913–

prime minister of Israel who signed first formal peace treaty between an Arab country and Israel, 1979

David Ben-Gurion
1886–1973

prime minister of Israel from 1948 to 1953 and from 1955 to 1963; leader of Israeli independence movement

Haile Selassie
1892–1975

emperor of Ethiopia from 1930 to 1936 and from 1941 to 1971; gave Ethiopia first written constitution

Hussein I
1935–

king of Jordan since 1953

Kenneth Kaunda
1924–

president of Republic of Zambia since independence in 1964

Golda Meir
1898–1978

prime minister of Israel from 1969 to 1974

Kwame Nkrumah
1909–72

leader of African independence movement who was first president of Republic of Ghana from 1960 to 1966

Julius Nyerere
1922–

prime minister and first president of Tanganyika in 1961 and 1962; president of Tanzania since 1964

José López Portillo
1920–

president of Mexico since 1976

Anwar al-Sadat
1918–

president of Egypt who signed first formal peace treaty between an Arab country and Israel, 1979

Léopold Senghor
1906–

president of Republic of Senegal since independence in 1960

BRAZILIAN CITIES

Like most Third World nations, Brazil has growing cities with modern apartments, hotels, churches, and office buildings. However, many unskilled city workers live in crowded slums near these new areas of prosperity.

How has foreign investment influenced industrial growth in Latin America?

Yet not enough is produced to meet the needs of the growing population. Latin Americans still have to buy about 70 percent of the manufactured goods they need from other countries.

The Latin American economy still depends on farming. *Campesinos*, or farmers, make up about half of the population. But they have not been able to grow enough food to feed everyone. Most land in Latin America is held in *haciendas*, or large ranches. Most of the work on the haciendas is done by peasants. Most use the same farming methods their parents and grandparents used. They are not encouraged to learn new ways. Peasant labor is cheap, so most hacienda owners have no wish to modernize. The end result often is that the land is poorly managed and crops are small.

The hacienda system holds back economic progress. Peasants get little money for their work. So they have no money to buy manufactured goods. If not enough people buy goods, there is no reason to produce more. Industry does not grow.

In recent years, strong feelings of nationalism have grown among many Latin Americans. They resent such countries as the United States. They accuse the foreign investors of taking all the profits out of Latin America instead of using them to benefit the

Latin American people. The nationalists want to be rid of outside political and economic influences.

1. What did foreign investors do with the goods they produced in Latin America?
2. What did foreign investors do to benefit Latin America?
3. How does the hacienda system hold back progress?
4. Why do Latin American nationalists resent foreign investors?

MIDDLE EAST

During World War I many Arabs fought with the Allied powers against the Turks of the Ottoman Empire. They hoped this would gain them their independence. Turkey was defeated in 1918, but the Arabs did not get their independence. Instead, most Arab lands were put under English or French rule. The disappointed Arabs continued to push for independence and had some success. They won independence for some territories in the 1930's, for Lebanon in 1943, and for Syria in 1946.

One of the territories that was placed under English control was Palestine. Many Jews as well as Arabs lived there. Jews had

---

MIDDLE EAST OIL

Most of the people of the Middle East are poor farmers and live in villages. However, the Middle East is an important oil-producing region that has more than one-half of the world's known oil reserves. The sale of oil to western industrial nations has brought prosperity to some countries of the Middle East.

What political events have taken place in the Middle East since 1945?

also fought on the side of the Allies during World War I. They had made important scientific discoveries that helped the Allied cause. When Jewish leaders pushed to set up a Jewish homeland in Palestine, the English supported the idea. The Arabs did not. Fighting broke out between Arabs and Jews, and the United Nations stepped in to solve the conflict. In 1948 the United Nations gave the land to the Jews, who then established the state of Israel.

Meanwhile, nationalism was growing in Egypt. During the middle of the twentieth century, Gamal Abdel Nasser became the leader of a movement to get the English out of Egypt. By 1956 the last English troops had left the country, and the Egyptians controlled the Suez Canal. The English withdrew from other Arab territories in the 1960's and early 1970's.

1. Why did the Arabs fight with the European powers in World War I?
2. How did Palestine become the Jewish homeland?
3. Who took control of the Suez Canal after England pulled out?

AGRICULTURE AND INDUSTRY   For many years the main source of income in the Middle East has been agriculture. Less than one-tenth of the land can be farmed. Still, more than two-thirds of the people are farmers. Grains are the most important crops, but fruits, nuts, and vegetables also are grown in many cases.

Farm production has increased in the last 30 or so years. This is due to better equipment and seeds, more scientific farming methods, and more irrigation. Yet some Middle Eastern countries still do not grow enough food to feed all their people. So they have to buy more food from other countries.

Manufacturing has also grown. Many Middle Eastern governments do all they can to encourage new industry. The chief products made in the Middle East include building materials, chemicals, processed foods, and textiles. Many new factories have been built in cities in Egypt, Iran, Israel, Kuwait, Saudi Arabia, and Turkey.

Oil has become a very important Middle Eastern product. More than half of the world's oil reserves can be found there. The oil has made some Middle Eastern countries rich. Bahrain, Iraq, Kuwait, and Saudi Arabia, for example, have used their oil profits to build schools, hospitals, airports, factories, and better housing. Countries such as Egypt, which have little or no oil of their own, have developed at a slower rate.

1. Why has agriculture in the Middle East improved in recent years?
2. What products are made in the Middle East?
3. Why is oil important in the Middle East?

THE FUTURE OF THE THIRD WORLD

Most of the people in Third World countries are poor. They do not have the education or skills needed in industry. Most Third World nations are rich in human and natural resources. But they do not have the technology or the money needed to develop the resources.

Many western nations, such as the United States, England, France, and West Germany, have provided developing countries with technology and money. Several Communist countries, including the Soviet Union, have done the same. Both the West and the Communist countries want the loyalty of the Third

DEVELOPING NATIONS

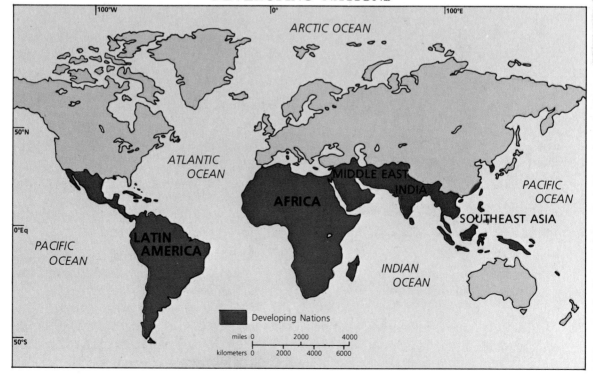

World nations. In some cases, the one willing to provide the most aid receives the most loyalty. Many Third World countries do not want help from either the West or the Communists. They feel that aid brings with it ways of life they do not want.

Most Third World countries now know what their major problems are. Many have begun programs to solve them. Education is now offered free. More doctors, professional people, and skilled workers are being trained. Farmers are being taught to use modern tools and machines and to plant new crops. Married couples are being instructed in family planning. But all of this takes time.

1. What do the Third World nations want?
2. What has the Third World done to solve its problems?

CHAPTER REVIEW

SUMMARY

1. India, Africa, Latin America, and the Middle East are part of the Third World and have common problems.

2. Feelings of nationalism began to grow in India toward the end of the nineteenth century.

3. After World War I Mohandas K. Gandhi began a protest movement against English rule which led to India's independence in 1947.

4. Since independence, the Indian government has tried to raise the people's standard of living.

5. In Africa, the demand for independence was strong after World War II.

6. Many African nations gained their independence in 1960.

7. Africa has many energy and mineral resources but needs to develop its agriculture.

8. Most Latin American countries became independent in the early part of the nineteenth century, and since then industrialized nations have invested large amounts of money there.

9. Economic progress in Latin America is held back by the hacienda system.

10. Strong feelings of nationalism have grown in Latin America in recent years.

11. During World War I many Arabs supported the Allied powers in hopes of gaining their independence.

12. Arab lands put under English or French rule after World War I were independent by the 1970's.

13. In 1948, against the wishes of many Arabs, the United Nations gave the land of Palestine to the Jews, who set up the state of Israel.

14. Oil is the main natural resource in the Middle East, which contains more than half of the world's oil reserves.

15. Third World countries are working hard to solve their economic problems, often with the help of technology and money from western and Communist nations.

BUILDING VOCABULARY

1. *Identify the following:*
   Indian National Congress   Jawaharlal Nehru   Gamal Abdel Nasser
   Mohandas K. Gandhi   Indira Gandhi

2. *Define the following:*

balanced economy	dialects	subsistence farming	campesinos
national income	noncooperation	cash crops	haciendas
market price			

REVIEWING THE FACTS

1. How are most Third World nations different from western and Communist countries?
2. What made the English agree to independence for India?
3. Why is the year 1960 called "the year of Africa"?
4. What kinds of natural resources does Africa have?
5. Why do most Latin American campesinos still use old-fashioned farming methods?
6. Why did the English support the idea of a Jewish homeland in Palestine?
7. How has oil affected the economic development of many Middle Eastern countries?
8. What is the main population problem of Third World countries?
9. What is the main occupation in most Third World countries?
10. Why have western and Communist countries provided developing countries with technology and money?

DISCUSSING IMPORTANT IDEAS

1. What may happen to a nation when it does not have a balanced economy?
2. What usually happens to a nation as it industrializes?
3. How do western and Communist countries compete in the Third World?
4. What do you think developing nations should do to solve their problems?

USING MAPS

Refer to the map on page 645, and answer the following questions:

1. On what large continent in the Western Hemisphere are most of the developing nations located?
2. How far is the southern tip of Latin America from the southern tip of Africa?
3. What country is located about 8° north and 77° east?
4. Through what land areas does the equator pass?
5. Is India a developing nation?

UNIT REVIEW

SUMMARY

1. Nationalism and the alliance system that developed among European nations at the end of the nineteenth century eventually led to World War I. The war damaged the economy of several western European nations. It also resulted in the creation of four new countries and the League of Nations.

2. After World War I a depression set in that contributed to the rise of dictatorships in western Europe.

3. Attempts by Germany, Italy, and Japan to take over areas belonging to other nations resulted in World War II. The war weakened western Europe and Japan and made the United States and the Soviet Union the most powerful nations in the world. It also led to the establishment of the United Nations.

4. The Soviet Union became a Communist country in the early twentieth century. The People's Republic of China was established and became a Communist country in the middle twentieth century. They are the world's leading Communist powers, but they do not agree on the aims of Communism.

5. Most nations of the Third World are not as developed as the industrial nations of the First World and Second World. They are faced with such problems as poverty and overpopulation. Many lack the technology that is needed to take advantage of natural resources.

6. The West and the Communist nations compete for the loyalty of the developing nations. Some developing nations, however, do not want help from either.

REVIEWING THE MAIN IDEAS

1. Discuss the effects World Wars I and II had on the economy, government, and role of western Europe, the United States, the Soviet Union, and China.

2. Compare the problems faced by India, Africa, Latin America, and the Middle East and the steps each has taken to solve them.

DEVELOPING SKILLS

In Unit Review 3 you learned about chronology, which is a time relationship important in the study of history. Another time relationship that is just as important has to do with the length of one historic period as compared to another.

This exercise is designed to give you practice deciding which of two periods in history lasted longer. It also gives you an opportunity to review some of the things you have learned this year about different civilizations. Below are eight groups of historical periods. Tell which period in each group lasted longer than the other.

1. The Paleolithic Age
   The Neolithic Age

2. Ancient History
   The Middle Ages

3. Ancient History
   The United States as an Independent Nation

4. The Renaissance
   The Middle Ages
5. Ancient Greece
   The Age of Discovery
6. The Pax Romana
   Ancient History

7. The Industrial Revolution
   Ancient Egypt
8. Ancient Rome
   The United States as an Independent Nation

SUGGESTED UNIT PROJECTS

1. Report on the life of such former Third World leaders as Kenyatta of Kenya, Nasser of Egypt, and Nehru of India.
2. Working in a small group, research present-day conditions in a Latin American country. Then prepare a detailed plan of how you would go about solving the country's major problems.
3. Make a chart comparing the United States and the Soviet Union. Include information about size, population, government, economic system, income, leaders, strengths, and weaknesses.
4. Draw a poster that might be used in a Third World nation to teach people who cannot read something about health.

SUGGESTED READING

Almedingen, E. M. *Anna*. New York: Farrar, Straus & Giroux, 1972. The story of country life in Russia during the last years of tsarist rule.

Eunson, Roby. *Mao Tse-tung: The Man Who Conquered China*. New York: Franklin Watts, Inc., 1973. A biography.

Gessner, Lynn. *Edge of Darkness*. New York: Walker and Company, 1979. The story of the Soviet takeover of Latvia as experienced by a young Latvian farm boy.

Goldston, Robert C. *Next Year in Jerusalem*. Boston: Little, Brown, 1978. A history of Zionism.

Life: The First Decade. New York: Time Inc., 1979. Two hundred photographs, taken by journalists in different parts of the world from 1936 to 1945.

Reeder, Red. *Bold Leaders of World War I*. Boston: Little, Brown, 1974. Tells about 12 men and women and what they did during World War I.

Scott, John. *Divided They Stand*. New York: Parents' Magazine Press, 1973. A personal account of Germany from before World War II through the division of Germany.

Sidel, Ruth. *Revolutionary China: People, Politics, and Ping-Pong*. New York: Delacorte Press, 1974. A first-hand report on everyday life in China today.

White, Jo Ann (ed.). *African Views of the West*. New York: Julian Messner, 1972. A collection of African writings about the effect Westerners and western civilization have had and are having on Africa.

Glossary

Pronunciations are indicated in parentheses.
Syllables to be stressed are underlined.

A

abbott (ab bit)   Head of a monastery.

acropolis (a crop o liss)   Fortified hill with a temple to the local god at the top.

act of homage   Medieval ceremony in which a vassal promises loyalty to a lord.

agora (a go ra)   Open outdoor market place usually found in a Greek city-state.

alliances (a lion siz)   Agreements between people or countries.

ancestors (an ses ters)   Family members from past generations.

Anno Hegira (on no hi ji rah)   622, the year of Mohammed's journey from Mecca to Medina; beginning date of the Muslim calendar.

anthropologists (an throw pall o jists)   People who study pre-history and early history.

apostles (a pah soles)   The 12 men chosen by Jesus to teach his beliefs to other people.

apprentice (a pren tis)   Person who is learning a craft or trade.

archaeologists (ark e all o jists)   People who study ruins and artifacts.

aristocrats (a rist toe krats)   Members of the upper class.

armistice (arm is tis)   Agreement to stop fighting.

artifacts   Products of human skill.

assembly (a sem blee)   Group of people who give advice to a ruler or government leader; law-making body of government.

B

bailiff (bay lif)   Medieval official whose duty was to see that peasants did their work.

balance of trade   Difference between the amount of goods a country brings in and sends out.

bishop   Roman Catholic religious leader.

blockade (block aid)   Closing of an area by a military force to prevent goods and supplies from getting in or out.

bourgeoisie (boar zwa z)   French term for the middle class.

boyars (bo yars)   Members of the wealthy class in tsarist Russia.

burgesses (bur jis es)   Elected representatives in the English colony of Virginia.

burgs   Towns built during the Middle Ages.

burghers (burg ers)   Freemen or wealthy merchants who lived in towns in the Middle Ages.

C

caliph (kay lif)   Muslim ruler.

campesinos (camp us e nos)   Latin American farmers and peasants.

captaincies (kap tin sees)   Areas of land in Brazil given to Portuguese nobles.

caravans (care a vans)   Groups of traders who traveled together for safety.

caravel (kar a vell)   Small, fast Portuguese sailing ship used in the sixteenth century.

catacombs   Underground cemeteries.

cataracts (kat a raks)   Large waterfalls in the area of the Nile.

cathedrals (kah thee drolls)   Large churches.

caudillo (cow dill yo)   Latin American leader, usually a military dictator.

chancellor (chan sellor)   Head of a medieval English university; leader of a country.

chieftain (chief tin)   Leader of a band or group.

citadel (sit a dell)   Fortress built on high ground.

city-state   City and the farmland around it with its own government and god.

civilians (sive ill e ans)   People who are not soldiers.

civilization (sive a liz a shun)   Society with a developed knowledge of farming, trade, government, art, and science.

clans   Groups of people united by family ties.

code of chivalry (kode of shiv all ree)   Rules knights had to live by.

colonize (call in ize)   To settle an area or land.

comedy (kom ah dee)   Humorous play.

communes   Government-run farming communities in which all work for a common cause.

Communists   People who believe the government should own all property and industry; political group.

conquistadores (kon keys toe doors)   Sixteenth-century Spanish conquerors.

constitution (kon stah <u>to</u> shun) Set of written laws used to govern a country or state.

constitutional monarchy (kon stah <u>to</u> shun el <u>mon</u> ark key) Government headed by a king or queen who must obey a written constitution.

consuls (<u>kon</u> suls) Heads of the ancient Roman Republic.

corregidores (kor <u>reg</u> i doorez) Royal officials chosen by the Spanish ruler to govern colonial towns.

covenant (<u>cov</u> in ent) Promise between God and the Hebrew people.

crossbow Medieval weapon used to shoot arrows.

crown Title given to the head of a kingdom; headpiece worn by a king, queen, emperor, or empress.

crucified (<u>kru</u> sah fied) Put to death by being nailed or tied to a cross.

crusades (<u>kru</u> sayds) Series of wars undertaken by western Europeans to regain the Holy Land from the Muslims.

cuneiform (q <u>nee</u> a form) Sumerian writing made up of wedge-shaped signs.

D

dauphin (doe <u>fan</u>) Title used for the eldest son of the king of France.

decipher (dee <u>si</u> fer) To figure out the meaning.

delta (<u>del</u> tah) Triangular-shaped area of land at the mouth of a river.

depression Time when business is bad and there are not enough jobs for everyone.

detente (day <u>tont</u>) Lessening of tensions or disagreements between nations.

dialects (<u>die</u> a lekts) Forms of a language that are spoken in different parts of a country.

dictator (<u>dick</u> tate tor) Person who takes complete power in running a government.

diocese (<u>die</u> ah sees) Group of local churches.

disciples (diss <u>sigh</u> polls) People who follow and learn from a leader.

dissidents People who are unhappy with and speak out against their way of life.

doctrine (<u>dock</u> trin) Beliefs of a religion or a political party.

domesticated (doe <u>mess</u> teh kated) Tamed.

donatarios (don a <u>tair</u> e ohs) Portuguese owners of land in Brazil during the colonial period.

dynasty (<u>die</u> nas tee) Series of rulers from the same family.

E

eddubas (<u>ed</u> u bus) Sumerian schools.

embalming (em <u>ball</u> ming) Process used to keep dead bodies from decaying.

emirs (e <u>mears</u>) Muslim military leaders.

empire (<u>m</u> pie er) Group of city-states, countries, or territories under one ruler.

enclosure (en <u>klo</u> sure) Method of dividing land in which small areas of land were combined into larger ones and closed in with fences.

exodus (<u>ex</u> o dus) The departure of a large group of people; usually refers to the Hebrews leaving Egypt.

F

fasces (<u>fas</u> eez) Bundle of rods tied around an ax; symbol of Rome and Italian fascism.

federal (<u>fed</u> er el) Relating to central, or national, government.

feudalism (<u>few</u> dull is im) Political and economic system during the Middle Ages based on the relationship of lords and vassals.

fiefs (feefs) Pieces of land given to vassals by their lords.

Five Year Plan Program for a nation's development over a five-year period.

fjord (fee <u>ord</u>) Narrow strip of sea with steep cliffs on either side.

flint Hard stone used by early people to make tools.

freemen Slaves who were set free or who bought their freedom.

frescoes (<u>fress</u> koz) Wall paintings.

friars (<u>fry</u> ers) Traveling priests.

G

galleons (<u>gal</u> lee uns) Spanish ships used in the fifteenth and sixteenth centuries.

gentiles (<u>jen</u> tiles) People who are not Jewish.

geologists (gee all ah jists)   People who study the history of the earth through its rocks and minerals.

gladiator (glad e ate or)   Person who fought men or animals in ancient Roman arenas.

gospel   History of the life and teachings of Jesus.

guilds (gillds)   Organizations for workers of the same craft or trade during the Middle ages.

H

helots (he lets)   Slaves who farmed the land of Sparta.

hereditary (her red it airee)   Passed down from parent to child.

hermits   People who choose to live alone in a lonely place

heresy (hair ah see)   Belief or teaching which is against the popular belief.

hieroglyphics (high roe glif icks)   Ancient Egyptian picture writing.

humanists   Philosophers who believe that people are important.

hypothesis (hi pot the sis)   Possible explanation for a problem.

I

icons (i konz)   Sacred pictures usually used in the Eastern Orthodox Church.

iman (i mam)   Muslim priest.

indulgences (in dull ginz es)   Pardons given by the church that lessen the punishment for wrong doings.

industrialize (in dus tree el lize)   To develop industry.

infantries (in fun trees)   Soldiers who fight on foot.

inflation (in flay shun)   Period when prices go up and the value of money goes down.

inquisition (in qua zish shun)   Court set up by the Church during the thirteenth century to fine and punish non-believers.

J

jarls   Viking military leaders.

junta (june ta)   Committee organized to take over a government; military government.

juris prudentes (jurr is pru denz)   Lawyers.

K

ka'bah (kah bah)   Muslim shrine in Mecca.

keep   Strongest and most important part of a castle, made of stone with thick walls, one entrance, and a narrow stairway for defense.

khan (kon)   Mongol leader.

kitchen midden   Name given to ancient bones and household items.

koran (ko ran)   Muslim bible.

kremlin (krem lin)   Russian fortress; base of the Soviet government.

L

labyrinth (lab ah rinth)   Maze.

latifundias (lat e fun deeaz)   Large Roman estates where crops and animals were raised to sell at market.

legionaries (lee jun aireez)   Roman soldiers.

legions (lee juns)   Divisions of Roman soldiers.

liberals   People who favor political reforms.

logic (lodge ick)   Science of reasoning or thinking things through.

lords   Nobles with great power and authority during the Middle Ages.

M

magistrates (maj is trates)   Judges with the power to enforce laws.

martial law (mar shel law)   Temporary control over a country or state by the military.

mass production   The manufacture of goods in large numbers using machines and an assembly line.

men-of-war   Navy war ships.

mendicants (men dee kents)   Beggars.

mercantilism (mer kant till liz im)   System in which a government controls business while colonies provide wealth to their parent country.

messiah (miss sigh ah)   Savior.

Middle Ages   Period of history that begins with the fall of Rome and ends with the Age of Exploration.

middle class   People who are not very rich or very poor.

minstrels (min strolls) Poets and singers who traveled around entertaining people during the Middle Ages.

monasteries (mon as stare ez) Places where monks live.

monks Men who live in a religious community.

mosque (mossk) Muslim place of worship.

mummy Wrapped body of a preserved dead person.

N

national income Amount of money a nation earns.

nationalists People devoted to their nation.

necropolis (nee crop o less) Cemetery.

nuns Women who live in a Catholic religious community.

O

occupied (ok q pied) Took possession of

olympiads (o limp e ads) Four-year periods between Olympic Games

oprichni ki (o prich ni key) Russian secret police during the rule of Ivan the Terrible.

oracle bones (or a coal bonz) Bones used by Shang Chinese rulers and priests to receive messages from dead ancestors.

oracles (or a coals) Ancient priests who communicated with the gods.

ordeal Ancient method of judging the innocence or guilt of a person.

P

pancratium (pan kray shun) Athletic event of the Greek Olympics that combined boxing and wrestling.

papyrus (pa pie rus) Reed that grows along river banks; writing paper used by the ancient Egyptians, Greeks, and Romans.

parables (pahr ah bulls) Short stories that teach a lesson.

parchment Thin skin of an animal used to write or paint on.

parish (pahr ish) Area assigned to a local church.

patriarchs (pay tree arks) Oldest male members of a group or family.

patricians (pah trish ans) Rich and powerful upper class citizens of ancient Rome.

peaceful co-existence (peas full ko ex is tense) Political policy that avoids war.

peninsula (pen in sue la) Piece of land surrounded by water on three sides.

pentathlon (pen tahth lon) Olympic game made up of five separate athletic events.

phalanx (fay lanks) Ancient Greek battle formation used by foot soldiers.

pharaoh (fair roh) Ancient Egyptian ruler.

philosophers (fill loos o fers) People who study and teach about the meaning of life.

pilgrims People who travel to a holy place to worship.

plebians (plee be ans) Poor and lower class citizens of ancient Rome.

polis (pole is) Ancient Greek city-state.

political parties Groups with set ideas about government and how it should be run.

political science Study of governments and how they work.

Pope Head of the Roman Catholic Church.

prehistoric period Period of time before people began to keep written records.

priest (pree st) Religious leader, usually Roman Catholic or Eastern Orthodox.

priest-king Ancient ruler who was both ruler and religious leader.

proletariat (pro leh ter e et) Working class.

prophets (prah fits) Religious teachers or leaders who tell what will happen.

protectorate (pro teck tur et) Country under the protection and rule of another country.

psalms (sallms) Religious songs or poems.

publicans (pub lee kans) Ancient Roman tax collectors.

pyramids (peer a mids) Large Egyptian tombs.

R

rabbis (rab byez) Jewish teachers and ministers.

reform (ree form) To improve by making changes

resurrection (rez er reck shun) Raising the dead.

rhetoric (ret or ick) Art of writing or speaking.

republic Form of government where citizens choose leaders, usually through an election.

right of extra-territoriality (rite of ex trah tehr rah tore eh tahl it tee) Policy which prevents citizens of one country from being tried by another country for crimes committed within its boundaries.

runes (ruins) Letters of the Viking alphabet.

S

saints People declared holy by the Church.

satrapies (sat trah peas) Ancient Persian provinces.

scepter (sep ter) Rod held by a ruler of a country.

scientific method Three-step method used by scientists to study something.

scribe (skribe) Person who writes; official clerk.

scriptures (skrip chers) Biblical writings.

scrolls (skrolls) Rolls of writing paper; ancient books written on long sheets of paper.

seneschal (sen eh shawl) Official during the Middle Ages.

shadoff (sha doof) Ancient machine used to move water from one place to another.

shires (shy ers) Regions or districts in England.

shrines Sacred or religious places or altars.

social justice Fair treatment of all people.

social order Divisions among people according to their wealth.

socialists (sosh ul lists) People who believe in government ownership of industry.

Socratic method (so krat tick meth od) Method of questioning developed by Socrates.

soothsayers (sue th say ers) People who predict the future by interpreting the will of the gods.

steppe (step) Large plain in southeastern Europe and Asia.

strait (stray t) Narrow body of water between two larger bodies of water.

subsistence farming (sub sis tents far ming) Type of farming in which only enough food to support the farmer's family is grown.

syllogism (sill o jis im) Form of reasoning developed by Aristotle.

synagogue (sin a gahg) Jewish house of worship.

T

tariffs (taar ifs) Taxes placed on goods entering one country from another country.

tells Mounds of earth which contain levels of housing of ancient civilizations.

tenants People who live and work on someone else's land.

textiles (text tiles) Woven cloth.

theology (thee all o gee) Study of God and religion.

tithes (tie thes) Payments people make to the Church.

trade unions Associations of workers in the same job or performing the same craft.

tragedies (traj ed dees) Dramas or plays with a sad or unhappy theme.

treaties Agreements between countries.

tribunes (trib youns) Members of the ancient Roman oovernment elected to protect the rights of the lower class.

triremes (try reems) Ancient Greek or Roman warships with three rows of oars on each side.

triumph Parade to welcome home a Roman hero.

triumvirate (tri um ver it) Group of three people who rule with equal power.

tsar (zar) Russian ruler.

U

universal manhood suffrage Right of all men to vote.

V

vassal (vass ul) Person who served a lord during the Middle Ages.

W

wergeld (wur gild) Fine paid by the family of a person who committed a crime.

witan (wit en) Members of the king's council in Anglo-Saxon England.

Z

ziggurat (zig eh rat) Sumerian or Babylonian temple.

Index